STRATEGIES
OF
Community Intervention
Macro Practice

FIFTH EDITION

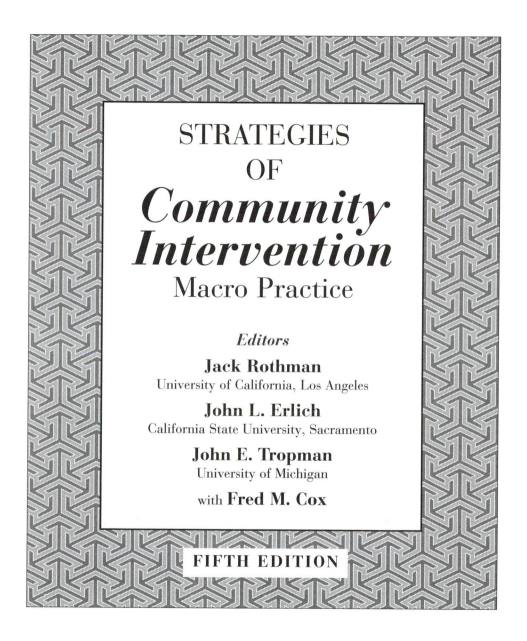

STRATEGIES
OF
Community
Intervention
Macro Practice

Editors

Jack Rothman
University of California, Los Angeles

John L. Erlich
California State University, Sacramento

John E. Tropman
University of Michigan

with **Fred M. Cox**

FIFTH EDITION

F.E. PEACOCK PUBLISHERS, INC.
ITASCA, ILLINOIS

Contents

THANKS TO THE FOLLOWING AUTHORS
AND PUBLISHERS

"Approaches to Community Intervention" by Jack Rothman was written for this volume and is an expanded version of Jack Rothman, "Three Models of Community Organization Practice," from National Conference on Social Welfare, "Social Work Practice 1968" (New York: Columbia University Press, 1968). Copyright © 1968, National Conference on Social Welfare. Revised 1974, 1979, 1987, and 1995.

"A History of Community Organizing Since the Civil War with Special Reference to Oppressed Communities" by Charles D. Garvin and Fred M. Cox was written for the fourth edition of this volume and is used by permission of the authors.

"Cleaning Up in the Nineties" by Kim Bobo, Jackie Kendall, and Steve Max is Chapter 26 from *Organizing for Social Change: A Manual for Activists in the 1990s* (Washington, DC: Seven Locks Press, 1991), and is used by permission of the authors.

"Understanding American Communities" by Phillip Fellin was written for this volume and is used by permission of the author.

"Organizations: Organizations as Polities: An Analysis of Community Organization Agencies" by Mayer N. Zald. Reprinted, with permission, from *Social Work* 11(4) (October 1966), pp. 56-65. Copyright 1966, National Association of Social Workers, Inc.

Community Development Journal 19(1) (1984), pp. 32-39, and is used by permission of the author and Oxford University Press.

"Planning and Policy Practice" by Jack Rothman and Mayer N. Zald is from Chapter 5, "Planning Theory in Social Work Community Practice," in *Theory and Practice of Community Social Work.* © 1985 Columbia University Press, New York. Reprinted with permission of the publisher.

"Being Roughly Right Rather Than Precisely Wrong: Teaching Quick Analysis in Planning Curricula" by Carl V. Patton is from *Journal of Planning Education and Research* 6(1) (Autumn 1986), pp. 22-29. © 1986 Association of Collegiate Schools of Planning and used by permission.

"Planning for Community Health Promotion: A Rural Example" by Janet A. Fuchs is from *Health Values* 12(6) (Nov-Dec 1988), pp. 3-8, and is used by permission.

"Two Types of Planning in Neighborhoods" by Barry Checkoway is from *Journal of Planning Education and Research* 2(1984), pp. 102–109. © 1984 Association of Collegiate Schools of Planning and used by permission.

"Social Action Community Organization: Proliferation, Persistence, Roots, and Prospects" by Robert Fisher was written for this volume and is based, in part, on Robert Fisher, "Community Organizing Worldwide," in R. Fisher and J. Kling, eds., *Mobilizing the Community* (Newbury Park, CA: Sage, 1993). Used by permission of the author and publisher.

"The Tactics of Organization Building" by Warren C. Haggstrom is from "The Organizer," was previously published in the fourth edition of this volume, and is reprinted by permission of the author.

"The Downtown Welfare Advocate Center: A Case Study of a Welfare Rights Organization" by Megan H. Morrissey is from *Social Service Review* (June 1990), pp. 189-190, 193-207. © 1990 by The University of Chicago, All rights reserved. Used by permission of the author and publisher.

"The Revolution of Citizenship" by Dick Flacks is from *Social Policy* (Fall 1990), pp. 37-50, published by Social Policy Corporation, New York, New York 10036. Copyright © 1990 by Social Policy Corporation.

"Managing for Service Effectiveness in Social Welfare Organizations" by Rino J. Patti. Reprinted with permission from *Social Work* 32(5) (Sept-Oct 1987), pp. 377-381. Copyright 1987, National Association of Social Workers, Inc.

"Change Levers for Improving Organizational Performance and Staff Morale" by Jon Sager was written for this volume and is used by permission of the author.

"Shanti: An Alternative Response to the AIDS Crisis by Nancy Hooyman, Karen I. Frederiksen, and Barbara Perlmutter is from *Journal of Administration in Social Work* 12(2) (1988), pp. 17-30. © 1988 by The Haworth Press, Inc. All rights reserved.

"Program Development" by Yeheskel Hasenfeld was adapted from "Guide to Agency Development for Area Planners in Aging," Project T.A. P., funded by the Administration on Aging, Grant SRS-HEW 94-P-76007/5-01 to the Institute of Gerontology, University of Michigan/Wayne State University, and the University of Michigan School of Social Work Continuing Education Program. Reprinted by permission of the author.

Preface to the Fifth Edition

In the book, *Controversial Issues in Communities and Organizations,* McMurtry and Kettner (1994) take the position that the key point of reference in macro practice is not communities but organizations. In their view, practitioners are employed in organizations, carry out their activities through organizational structures, and present themselves as representatives of an organization rather than as community-based change agents. It is not appropriate, therefore, they believe, to convey to students "the image of a social worker acting directly on communities to right wrongs, cure ills, and empower the oppressed" (p.99). Their sponsoring organizations, they tell us, won't tolerate this.

In the same volume, Daley and Netting (1994) mount a counterargument. They agree that community intervention requires a sophisticated understanding of organizational behavior. But they envisage a broader scope, including engaging with informal networks, interest groups, and natural support systems that exist in and comprise the community.

Daley and Netting go on to project a more complex fabric of action: "Community organization is a richly diverse field of practice that includes policy analysts and developers; program planners; administrators and evaluators; resource developers and allocators; and community organizers and developers working with geographically or issue-defined interest groups and communities." This includes work with "oppressed and disenfranchised peoples and for the cause of justice" (p. 105).

Signing on as an employee of a human service organization does not necessarily require giving up a professional concern and personal commitment to promoting social change on behalf of disadvantaged members of society. Indeed, many organizations for which practitioners work, from the American Friends Service Committee to the Children's Defense Fund, are dedicated fundamentally to just such purposes. And professionals have the responsibility to look inward to change their organizations, as well as outward to change community conditions. Often, it is because of, and in collaboration with, citizens and groups in the community that internally directed organizational change ensues.

This volume stands with the broader perspective that was described, and it attempts to articulate this orientation theoretically and in terms of practice strategies and skills. The fifth edition has as its base the intellectual framework that was established previously, but it also departs from it in various ways. The classic introductory "Three Models" article, which has provided the conceptual underpinning for all the previous editions, has been substantially revised and expanded by Jack Rothman. The "models" of action notion has been eased, in order to suggest broader "approaches" or "modes" of intervention. We still view strategies in terms of the community-building emphasis of locality development with its attention to community competency and integration, the data-based problem-solving orientation of social planning/social policy with its reliance on expertise, and the advocacy thrust of social action with its commitment to fundamental change and social justice.

But there is a great deal more consideration given to the overlapping and integration of these general approaches, with particular mixtures now articulated specifically and illustrated through examples taken from the world of contemporary practice. The middle section of the book focuses explicitly on these strategic considerations, as we will discuss shortly.

The book is organized in a different way, and 80 percent of the articles are new, including four original pieces written expressly for this volume. The first of the three parts comprising the book is entirely new. It deals with Parameters of Intervention, setting out a fourfold contextual paradigm for analyzing community intervention. Frameworks, the first of these, includes alternative modes of action, historical trends, and the national political economy. Arenas, the second, encompasses community and organizational systems, which were touched on in beginning these comments. It also includes the task-oriented small group, which is an additional social entity through which much community intervention is carried out.

Core Elements of Practice is the third parameter, covering a cognitive schema for systematic problem solving, the use of persuasive forms of action depending on interpersonal influence, and the employment, contrastingly, of tactics of organized pressure and coercion. The fourth parameter deals with the interplay of micro and macro aspects of practice, including different concepts of integrated or generic practice, and the application of macro methods in micro settings.

The second or middle part of the book can be said to be the centerpiece, in that it concentrates explicitly on strategy issues. For each of the three key intervention approaches there is an introductory conceptual overview, a piece on tactics and roles, one that presents a case illustration of carrying out the strategy in action, and another article that shows how that approach is combined with one or more of the others.

For example, locality development, while rooted in an immediate geographical base, includes linkages to organizations outside the local community setting; social planning and social policy are joined conceptually as a single intervention mode and, while relying on expertise, are shown to often include elements of citizen participation; and social action, while often employing militancy, may involve use of conventional modes of political advocacy and coalitions that include aggrieved or disadvantaged groups acting in concert with others.

The third and concluding part of the book covers the subject of administration and management, which it treats not as a separate mode of community intervention, but as an organizational means for implementing the various forms of community intervention that have been discussed. Administration relates as well to carrying out the varied service and program activities of social agencies. The same intellectual structure is used here: conceptual overview, tactics and roles, case illustration, and mixed forms.

The 90s have not been a reassuring time for those who appreciate the role of the human services, and who are committed to responsibility exercised by the community for its desolate, disabled, and disadvantaged members. Both governmental and voluntary programs of support and aid have been contracted or eliminated. For some of us, hope stirred with the election of a youthful president who seemed to exude intelligence and compassion. But the political and social forces at play have trapped progressive and humane propensities in a morass of gridlock.

Community professionals do not have a great deal of impressive ammunition available to advance their aims. The artifacts of prodigious political and economic power often elude them. But in the complicated game of community change, knowledge of how things work, skill in maneuvering the levers that set new directions, and the ability to make and use a wide range of contacts can have an enormous impact. Those who pursue community intervention need to know how to think, and to put their theoretical and practical savvy on the line in effective ways that advance human values.

It is trite to say that knowledge is power, but it is also profound. We hope that our effort in compiling this book will contribute to the process of progressive social change by intellectually empowering students and professionals—and through them ordinary citizens—to make a difference in a world that often seems foreboding and intractable.

Jack Rothman
John L. Erlich
John E. Tropman

PART ONE
PARAMETERS OF INTERVENTION

Introduction

In Part One we will set out the parameters of community intervention, delineating and illustrating the context within which practice is conducted. A parameter is defined as a "constant" whose properties "determine the operation or characteristics of a system." Assuming that community intervention is a particular and unique system of practice, it is important to know the intellectual boundaries that constrain and shape it.

We begin with **frameworks.** Among these is the area of *strategy,* the fabric of action options that are available for the practitioner's choices in order to achieve change goals. We will spell out a comprehensive action spectrum in cross-sectional fashion. Next we will be informed by *history,* looking at the evolution of different strategies and their fluctuations as seen in longitudinal perspective. History offers a platform from which to make strategic choices as well as to forge new possibilities. There is also the framework of *societal ecology,* with its varied and complex structures, institutions, values, and norms that generate both problems to be confronted and opportunities to be exploited. In this analysis, the political economy of American society will be highlighted, recognizing that fundamental political and economic forces have a decisive impact on the local community situation.

From frameworks we move on to **arenas,** which are the specific social spheres in which the process of community intervention is played out. Three arenas are critical: the *community* itself; *organizations,* both formal and informal, within the community; and *small groups* of various kinds, particularly task-oriented units such as committees, commissions, boards, and the like. These social entities not only comprise the field of action, but also serve both as the vehicles through which community intervention takes place and as targets of change. It is inconceivable to think of engaging in community practice without having both knowledge of these arenas and skills in working with them.

This presentation draws in part on introductory notes by Fred M. Cox in the previous edition.

Community intervention acquires its particular character from certain common or **core elements of practice.** Among these we will examine *problem-solving methodology* to design change and modes of influence to affect change. Professionals typically emphasize a rational, systematic methodology of problem solving. The practitioner has to start with a sophisticated understanding of presenting problems before advancing to a solution stance. A problem has to be identified, bounded, and carefully analyzed so that logically derived initiatives with a high probability of producing effective outcomes are mounted. This kind of disciplined intellectual work distinguishes professional, competency-based practice from intuitive posturing that is well-meaning but often functionally flawed.

Also basic to community intervention are two broad modes of influence that are used to affect community affairs. One involves *interpersonal influence* that is educative, persuasive and consensual in nature. It relies on the practitioner's use of self in personal encounters with others. The other mode involves *organizational pressure* and entails advocacy, political maneuvers, and even coercive measures. It relies on the practitioner's ability to mobilize and orchestrate change forces in the community. The use of a systematic problem-solving schema relates to what has been termed the analytic component of practice; the use of influence as an instrument of change has been termed the interactional component.

The pattern of **macro relationships to micro practice** follows. This final contextual factor relates macro-oriented community intervention, with its emphasis on structural change, prevention, and social reform, to micro-oriented intervention (casework, counseling, clinical treatment), with its emphasis on personal renewal and psychological repair. We know that problems and systems are interconnected: Society and community can cause or exacerbate the troubles of individuals, and distorted values and detrimental behaviors of individuals can undermine the common good. We will show various *generic practice approaches,* wherein the skills of individual and community intervention are combined. We will also note the *use of macro practice to support micro practice*, both by enhancing the agency structure and building a better social policy framework.

FRAMEWORKS

Strategy

Our interest here is community intervention, which has also variously been termed community planning, community relations, planned change, and community work. There are additional preferred terms such as neighborhood work, social action, intergroup work, and community practice. Under whatever label, we will be dealing with intervention at the community level oriented toward improving or changing community institutions and solving community problems. This activity is performed by professionals from many disciplines—social work, public health, adult education, public administration, city planning, and community mental health—as well as by citizen volunteers in civic associations and social action groups. Our own grounding is social work, but the issues and strategies we will cover are rather interdisciplinary in character.

These activities aim at a wide range of purposes. Among them are establishing new community services and programs; facilitating collaboration among them; and building the capacity of grassroots citizens' groups to solve community problems. Also of importance are seeking justice for oppressed minorities, bringing about social reform, and conducting programs of community relations or public education.

The first piece, by Rothman, treats a variety of approaches to community intervention. A set of modes of action are suggested and analyzed in ideal-type form. These are termed locality development (building community competency and integration), social planning (which also includes elements of social policy and focus on rationalistic community problem solving), and social action (organized advocacy). The purposes and the tactical means within each approach differ in emphasis, as the text specifies and illustrates.

Rothman points out that the approaches rarely exist in pure form in practice, and that they tend to overlap, so that bimodal forms exist comprising action/planning, planning/development, and development/action mixes. Each of these has further variations based on the proportionality of the components in the mix. In addition, trimodal combinations of various kinds are common. Thus, a wide scope of strategy options are described, which can be used in a selective manner by the community practitioner. These options can be drawn upon differentially as a project goes through developmental phases or involves different problematic situations over time.

Rothman provides another useful perspective on practice, specifying a set of practice variables that are highly relevant for analyzing community intervention. The practice variables elaborated upon in the article include the following:

- Goal categories of community action
- Assumptions concerning community structure and problem conditions
- Basic change strategy
- Characteristic change tactics and techniques
- Salient practitioner roles
- Medium of change
- Orientation toward power structure(s)
- Boundary definition of the beneficiary system
- Assumptions regarding interests of community subparts
- Conception of beneficiaries
- Conception of the beneficiary role
- Use of empowerment

These practice variables operate differently in each mode of community practice, but in aggregate (the twelve practice variables across the three strategic approaches) generate an array of intervention initiatives that can be used selectively and in combination.

History

Grassroots civic action has been a constant element in community intervention, but to varying degrees and in varying forms over time. Community development and social action at the local neighborhood level reached an apex of sorts in the late 1960s, although certain precursors existed in the preceding decade and other developments have followed into the 1990s. Both social agency programming and independent social forces have contributed to this phenomenon of grassroots citizen involvement. For example, Point 7 of the Urban Renewal Act of 1954 required citizen participation in redevelopment as a condition of federal support. The Housing and Urban Development Act of 1968 reinforced this principle. Urban renewal authorities involved citizens at the grassroots in renewal planning in various degrees and with varying consequences (Wilson, 1963). Programs of the Office of Economic Opportunity around that time gave considerable momentum to the idea of including the poor in policy making and program implementation. Settlement houses have long emphasized organizational efforts in the neighborhoods to enable immigrants and the poor to improve their lot.

Other forces also contributed to the grassroots trend, particularly in the area of social action. The civil rights movement gave great impetus to social action in the black community. Some civil rights groups moved from tactics of protest to neighborhood organization and political action (Rustin, 1965). Growing black nationalism stimulated the beginnings of separatist institutions and programs, with a strong impetus for local control. African-American social action touched off similar activity among other oppressed racial minorities as well as among white ethnics. Student activism on hundreds of campuses underlined the participation concept. The women's movement became a powerful force for mobilizing local participation, as did organizing among gays. Grassroots approaches also developed in fertility control, community mental health, housing, public health, environmental protection, political practices reform, consumerism, and other institutional areas. Also of great significance was the peace movement, aimed at ending the war in Vietnam, with its political ramifications in the McCarthy and McGovern presidential campaigns and related events.

Grassroots civic action is often likened to a falling star—reaching its heights in the 1960s, then plummeting to earth, burned out and dissipated with the transition into the 1970s. A closer look reveals that the legacy of the earlier period has been carried forward, not in as dramatic or comprehensive a way, but nevertheless with vitality and prevalence.

One element of this is the provision for citizen involvement in governmental programs. A kind of participation revolution has been carried out, often somewhat imperceptibly, but usually at least at the level of formal specification or requirements. A broad assessment, which takes into account both governmental and voluntary community factors, has described grassroots activity as follows:

Despite a weakening of citizen input in many programs, new legislation in the mid-1970s strengthened the citizens' role in some instances; therefore, the situation remained mixed. Changes in Title XX of the Social Security Act mandated a period of public review before state plans for a variety of social service programs could be adopted. Some citizens continue to be active in decentralized city halls and neighborhood service centers. Others participate in consumer cooperatives or community development corporations in an attempt to make their neighborhoods more self-sufficient economically. Many citizens have turned to mass consumer education or political activities such as lobbying and legal action (Wireman, 1977).

Some concrete results have come about through these efforts. Wireman lists the following achievements of participation:

1. Bureaucrats are becoming sensitive to the need to take citizen and client opinions into account in planning and delivering services.
2. Improvements have been made in services in accordance with client needs and wishes.
3. Groups are learning how to influence and bypass traditional political and administrative channels.
4. A generation of leaders, especially from minority groups, holds positions of political or administrative authority in federal, state, and local government.

We are warned to learn from history or be victims of its consequences. Charles Garvin and Fred M. Cox provide a broad overview of the broad cultural and social factors that have shaped community intervention, particularly as it has developed in social work. They give particular attention to some of the institutions that emerged in the latter part of the nineteenth century in England and in North America that were the crucible out of which community practice grew. These institutions—charity organization societies, social settlements, councils of social agencies, community chests—gave birth to much of social work and most of what came to be called community organization in social work. The unique role of racial and ethnic groups in the development of community organization is portrayed. Finally, Garvin and Cox discuss the growth of professional community organization practice, as well as some of the main ideas that inform that practice.

Societal Ecology

The disparity between meritorious ideals and practical realities in our society has been termed "The American Dilemma." We espouse equality fervently, however economic and social differences remain sharp and pervasive. Gus Hall (1994) indicates that wealth in the United States is even more concentrated than income. He points out that the richest 1 percent of households held 36 percent of the nation's wealth in 1989, and that this percentage had increased phenomenally by some 70 percent over a six-year period.

Hall feels that this distribution of wealth is detrimental to societal progress and stability for several reasons. An increasing concentration of wealth brings with it an increasing concentration of political power. Further, when much of the population fails to participate in the gains of economic growth, this comes across to many people as politically and morally unjustifiable. Resulting friction can generate social disorder, including crime, conflict, and corruption. It may also result in a depression because of the disparity between the nation's capacity to produce and its ability to consume. In sum: "the growing concentration of wealth in America is politically anti-democratic, morally reprehensible, socially disruptive, and economically perilous" (p. 7).

The Nixon/Reagan/Bush administrations pushed to "get the government off the backs of citizens" and to increase the efficiency of public services through better management. As a means of reducing the scope and costliness of social programs, Nixon and his lieutenants made a deliberate effort to remove as heads of social programs professionals with human-service orientations, and to replace them with business-minded executives who had a predilection for the niceties of accountancy. The Nixon administration's ideological preference for the "hard-nosed" ways of the business world accounted in part for this stance, but there was also an overriding wish to cut back or dismantle many of the programs that had come into being during the Great Society period of the 1960s to aid the poor and reduce economic inequities. The Reagan/Bush administrations accentuated the gap between the wealthy and the impoverished.

Their gambit was given impetus by the overinflated claims of liberal programs, their inadequate funding, the hastily conceived and poorly managed character of many of them, and the political and organizational conflicts that surrounded them. The increasingly bad name of public assistance also served to discredit social programs. Accordingly, when "New Democrat" Clinton replaced conservative Bush, it was on the basis of a platform promising to reinvent government and bring more order and managerial acumen to the federal programs than could the Republicans, and to diminish the scope of income transfer and social amelioration programs.

Disparities in status and wealth exist not only within nations, but also internationally across states. The North/South hemispheric division has both an objective and a psychological dimension, creating a climate of tension and antagonism. Chirot (1994) puts it this way:

The gap between the richest and poorest countries continues to grow. The perception of international unfairness is an important cause of anticapitalist and anti-Western ideological movements in the [less developed] parts of the world. It is clear that Western science and technology are superior and that they must be adopted to some extent. But the feeling that the established industrial powers are simply using their economic and political muscle to keep other societies poor exacerbates jealousy and resentful nationalism. It creates a climate of deep resentment among the proud intellectuals of [developing] countries, and this in turn makes them treat with contempt the ideologies of individualism and democracy practiced by the most successful Western countries (p. 92).

In a close analysis (article 3), Bobo, Kendall, and Max, who are associated with the Midwest Academy, document that over the recent past the wealthiest elements of our society have gained while the poor have become more impoverished. The authors show that, through the Reagan years, public policy served to concentrate wealth at the top. By use of taxation, budget, and spending procedures resources were transferred from the lower economic levels of society to the higher levels. Concurrently, there was a drop in the number of employment situations with high wages and substantial benefits, so that service jobs with low pay scales and few protections have increasingly become the only choice for people with low skill and educational levels. Families have been pushed into having dual wage earners in order to bring in a sufficient income, while many single-parent families have fallen into poverty and have seen their distress intensified.

The global perspective of corporate entities exacerbates these conditions, as the need for corporations to support a healthy and educated workforce within their own national borders has become less relevant. The declining economic strength and political influence of labor unions has further shifted the balance of power toward the haves and away from the have-nots.

These facts of social ecology complicate the operations of locally based community organizations. Forces at the national and international level impinge more on the local situation and, at the same time, are not particularly accessible through local action. The diminishing economic status and political power of low-income people makes it more necessary to organize them to act on their behalf, but at the same time it makes it all the more difficult. There are racial overtones in all of this, inasmuch as those with lower economic means are disproportionately represented by racial and ethnic minorities. The deleterious circumstances and trends that have been described impact these minorities with particular force.

An analysis of the political economy along these lines reveals some unpleasant realities, but it defines the broad context of community intervention pointedly and highlights some important tasks.

ARENAS OF INTERVENTION

A major contribution of the social sciences to the practice of community intervention has been in understanding the context in which change agents work—often called the arenas of community practice. These are the social settings and systems in which practice takes place. These arenas include interpersonal relations, small groups, formal organizations, neighborhoods, communities, and societies. We have chosen three of these arenas—communities, organizations, and small groups—for special attention in this volume. We believe they are particularly salient for community practice.

In the past few years, the social sciences have added a great deal to our understanding of the contextual realities that confront community practitioners. We have been greatly assisted by some of the ways they have conceived of the "booming, buzzing confusion" that confronts us as we go into action in our work.

To view these environmental social units as arenas, instead of as means or ends as others have done, lends a special perspective. As arenas, they are viewed as the boundaries within which action occurs—the conditions of the practitioner's work to be understood and taken as given in doing community work. Time and resources—people, money, influence, and the like—are limited. What is selected for change must be chosen very carefully, calibrated not only to the hopes and aspirations of the clientele and those who assist them but also to available resources. To argue for regarding communities, organizations, and small groups as arenas, then, is to argue for understanding, analysis, and the careful assessment of objectives and possibilities. The impulse to act may prove frustrating and fruitless unless observation, diagnosis, and understanding have come first.

Communities

Community, as conceived here, emphasizes the territorial organization of people, goods, services, and commitments. It is an important subsystem of the society, and one in which many locality-relevant functions are carried on.

Communities are in serious trouble at this point in American history. Pollution; traffic congestion; flight from the cities to the suburbs, exurbs, and rural communities; disinvestment in the central cities; and serious unemployment, crime, racial tensions, drug abuse, and infrastructure deterioration are but some issues that confront citizens and community practitioners alike. If there is to be any hope for the advancement of American society, the problems of the cities surely must be contained.

It is now painfully clear to community practitioners and community residents that the problems of the urban community will not yield quickly to solution. Part of the reason for this intractability lies in the fact that the community is one of the weakest competitors for the time and attention of the contemporary citizen. The family, the workplace, the church, and the school have all been able to attract long-time commitments from citizens. People are fleeing urban places, moving to the suburbs and, if they commute to jobs in the cities, leaving as soon as possible at the end of the workday. Large cities often lack stable populations with whom to plan.

This inability of the community to claim the commitment of its citizens is in itself a serious problem and symptomatic of deeper ills as well. Fundamentally, the modern urban community contains many goods and services, but controls very few of them. Hence, it is increasingly unable to assemble resources to address its important concerns.

A variety of contemporary forces have contributed to the diminishing status of the local community (Warren, 1963). The federal and state levels of government have gained increasingly in authority, size, and importance since the beginning of the New Deal in the early thirties. Tax policies, court decisions, and legislative actions all contributed to the upward migration of governmental power and responsibility. As the upper levels of government in the 1980s began to find themselves pinched by a reduction in tax revenues and economic hardship caused by deindustrialization and an unfavorable balance of trade, they moved to withdraw the economic support they had provided to lower levels, leaving cities in a financial bind and constricting the services and amenities they are able to provide to residents.

The mass media have also played a significant role in this trend. Media enter the individual household directly and operate as a national homogenizing force. Television is privately viewed in one's own living room, enlarging the role of mass culture and reducing the influence of a locally based culture. Therefore, there is less need to go outside of the home into the community for socialization, entertainment, recreation, and other interpersonally shared pursuits. The "couch potato" phenomenon has been detrimental to the vitality of the community. Computer communication networks that are national and international in scope additionally reduce the need for a local community to facilitate human connections. From a social systems standpoint, there is less horizontal interaction among community units and proportionately more interaction with extracommunity entities.

Despite this shift, the local community remains a significant social entity in the lives of most people. In his contribution, "Understanding American Communities," Fellin shows why this is so and provides a broad overview of community functions. He covers this terrain using two broad theoretical categories that encompass ecological and the social system perspectives. In the ecological stance, people are the important unit of analysis and population characteristics are the prime analytical tool. Fellin treats population size, population density, and population heterogeneity. The latter involves social class considerations (an aspect of political economy) and race and ethnic factors.

The discussion of social systems, borrowing from Warren (1963), starts with a delineation of the basic and still-valuable functions of contemporary communities, including economic (production/distribution/consumption), socialization (family, education), political (social control), participation (voluntary associations), and mutual support (health and welfare). Fellin attends to the distinct subsystems within communities that specialize in carrying out each of the functions. The neighborhood is given coverage as a distinct form and level of social system, and one that has particular relevance for community intervention, especially when there are grassroots components.

Clearly, the community is more than a series of problem situations confronted by the practitioner, or a casual backdrop. A major perspective of this book sees the community as the arena in which people still carry out their daily lives and community practitioners do their work. The community and its various elements both limit possible actions and present opportunities for action. The practitioner's task is to acknowledge the former and seize upon the latter. From another perspective, the community and its various elements provide the means for action and are the vehicle through which goals are achieved.

Organizations

Most community practitioners, unlike many other professionals, are salaried employees of organizations, often large and complex ones—schools, community mental health and public health agencies, United Ways, public assistance agencies, hospitals, city planning departments, human relations commissions, and so forth. The major exceptions are university-based consultants and a few organizers who work on a freelance, fee-for-service basis. Even those who work outside of institutional settings—the movement organizers endeavoring to mobilize the latent discontent of oppressed minority groups, exploited workers such as farm laborers and environmental activists, and the like—typically work through some form of organization. Sponsoring organizations, or "change agencies," exert a profound influence on the practitioner's work.

Community organizers of all stripes frequently are engaged in influencing these organizations and others whose activities affect their clientele. Thus formal organizations are often the context within which organizers work, the targets of their efforts to bring about change, and the means used for changing undesirable conditions.

In modern industrial society, complex organizations are essential tools and mediating instrumentalities for achieving collective purposes. They can contribute in significant ways to realizing the kinds of lives people want. However, too often, organizations are neither positive nor benign in their impact upon clients. Practitioners not only need to know how to get organizations to deliver services but often they must have the skills necessary to change the way organizations operate and the kinds of services they deliver to those needing aid or support.

Thus, an understanding of formal organizations is essential for community intervention. Practitioners sometimes become discouraged by the limitations that organizations impose. Although these limitations are often very real, the professional may be able to discover paths around organizational obstacles and find potentialities for action or change. Such discovery may begin with a detailed understanding of the factors affecting organizational behavior. Moreover, at the same time that organizations impose restrictions, they provide resources of various kinds—funds, facilities, contacts, goodwill, and political clout.

Zald, in his perceptive contribution, analyzes the community intervention agency as a sociopolitical entity. He examines its "basic zones of activity, goals, and norms of procedure and relationships." A series of propositions is offered that answer questions of great importance to practioners: Under various conditions, what kinds of goals and activities can one expect of the agencies with which one works? What kinds of roles and what styles of action are likely to be both possible and effective in response to external forces?

Zald treats four dimensions of organizational operation in depth. He is concerned with *constitutions*—the set of procedures or regular patterns that dictate the way the organization works. These patterns establish the boundaries within which community practitioners typically are obliged to function, and they determine whether practitioners can pursue change goals of a social action nature or service goals that have a planning/policy quality.

Next, the *constituency and resource base* are considered. They provide the wherewithal that determines not only what can be accomplished, but how much can be accomplished. These entities are composed of board members, financial contributors, grantors, interested legislators, and other community influentials. Zald goes on to discuss certain external objects of action. Third, in pursuing goals, community intervention agencies delineate a set of *target entities*—populations to be aided, enlisted, or coerced; organizations that can serve as allies or whose resistance needs to be overcome; and decision centers that need to be influenced in various ways.

The fourth dimension is *interorganizational relationships*. Community intervention organizations in the contemporary urban scene cannot function in isolation, but rather are connected to a welter of other organizations and institutions. These can facilitate, hinder, or provide context as an organization pursues its aims.

Small Groups

The group is the smallest and most intimate social unit that is an arena for engaging in community intervention. A variety of different types of task-oriented groups are employed for problem-solving and change purposes—grassroots block clubs, agency boards, municipal commissions, neighborhood committees and councils, staff groups, and others. All community practitioners work with groups of one or another type in the course of their career. It is a generic, ubiquitous element of practice, unlike some other roles that may arise only occasionally or not at all, such as designing a staff-training program, setting up a computerized management information system, or organizing a protest march.

Small groups have certain attributes that distinguish them, particularly the element of face-to-face interaction. Homans (1950) has provided a definition that has stood up over time:

We mean by a group, a number of persons who communicate with one another often over a span of time, and who are few enough so that each person is able to communicate with all the others, not at secondhand, through other people, but face-to-face (p. 1).

A small group is not a population or a mass or an audience, but rather a tangible collection of people who can discuss matters personally and work together in close association. Larger entities sometimes subdivide into small groups in order to get necessary work accomplished.

Bales (1966) found that there are two broad functions involved in the functioning of groups: task functions that have to do with meeting the environmental purposes of the group (solving specific problems that the group was formed to tackle) and socioemotional or expressive functions that relate to keeping the group together and working in relative harmony on its external tasks. Parsons (1955) has referred to these more generally as system functions and uses somewhat different language to connote the same ideas: namely, a division between instrumental and maintenance functions.

Bales indicates that leadership roles in groups involve implementing the two types of functions. Task roles focus on things such as specifying the problem, breaking it into workable parts, deciding on what information is necessary to solve it, determining what kind of pressure needs to be brought to bear on decision makers, and so forth. Socioemotional or maintenance roles involve matters such as notifying people of meetings, keeping a friendly atmosphere, making sure there is enough room available to hold everyone comfortably, giving everyone a chance to speak, for example.

Researchers indicate that there are ordinarily an array of leadership roles that are distributed among members of the group, rather than one all-encompassing leader who alone carries out all of them. Such distribution of roles has also been found to be an effective way for groups to function, in that tasks can be divided efficiently among several members, the skills of the entire collectivity can be brought to play, and new leaders can develop on a continual basis.

The community practitioner needs to be aware of the need for both task and socioemotional functions and leadership roles in any group situation and to cultivate individuals who can perform these. This means encouraging members to take on responsibilities and supporting them as necessary through formal or informal training and psychological reinforcement.

Task-oriented groups typically go through regular stages as they engage in problem solving. It is important for the community practitioner to be aware of these in order to facilitate the process. Bales and Strodtbeck (1968) have charted the stages in the process and indicated some of the prominent member roles during each of them. The stages and related roles are as follows:

Orientation—An exploratory period focusing on determining what information is relevant and useful for dealing with the problem. Members come to understand the problem better and learn in common what is known or should become known by them about it. The key roles during this phase include giving information, asking for information, and clarifying the task.

Evaluation—A more feeling-level interplay during which differences in interests and values are discussed. Judgments now are made about the facts of the situation and about the viability of various courses of action. Key roles include giving opinions, asking for opinions, and expressing feelings about the problem and process.

Control—A coming to grips with the problem by deciding what should be done about it. Decisions made here are binding in that they can be said to be controlling of the actions of the members and potentially of the task environment. Key roles here include asking for suggestions, recommending actions, and giving direction.

The community practitioner can assist in this process by helping people to give the group enough time for orientation before moving into more advanced phases, encouraging appropriate roles at appropriate times, encouraging and protecting people in their expression of affect, and seeing that responsibilities and timing matters are pinned down in the control phase. Group members hopefully will be engaging in such leadership roles themselves; practitioners in general should supplement or fill in when there is a void in such actions by members.

In her contribution to this book, Bakalinsky discusses very broadly the place of small-group activities in community intervention. She considers the question of group size, pointing out that this involves the issues of both numbers of people as well as the scope of representativeness to be included in the group. Representativeness includes the issue of democratic participation by varied interests in the community and also the configuration of skills and competencies that are needed to attack the problem under consideration.

Group composition is also treated, including descriptive criteria such as age, gender, race, and experience, and behavioral characteristics related to group process roles such as conciliator, energizer, analyzer, and the like. The values and effects of emphasizing heterogeneity vs. homogeneity in the make-up of the group come into consideration here. Heterogeneity insures a greater range of views, interests, and resources, but may sometimes inhibit the evolution of collaborative relationships in the group.

This ties into another factor that is covered in the analysis—group cohesiveness. Members ordinarily have in common their concern over a given community issue or problem. That external preoccupation can be a binding element, but in many cases it is not itself enough to sustain continuing action. Members may need to have a sense of belonging to the group itself, to gain gratification in their association with other members, and to be attracted emotionally to the group situation. These elements of group climate and interaction are an additional consideration the community practitioner needs to address.

CORE ELEMENTS OF PRACTICE

Practice in large measure is an art and has many unique, particularistic attributes. Each problem encountered, and its context, has distinct qualities and requirements that cannot be ignored. At the same time, upon more abstract examination, there are basic or common aspects of practice, such as the presence of organizational constraints, the requirements of sufficient resources, and the necessity of leadership of one kind or another. These provide additional parameters within which community practitioners operate. We have chosen two basic practice elements to highlight—the use of a systematic problem-solving methodology to guide interventive behavior, and the exercise of professional influence to advance progress toward intended goals. Two influence modalities will be given attention in separate treatments, one interpersonal in nature (use of persuasion), and the other organizational in character (application of structured pressure tactics). Also, additional modes that are typically employed will be touched upon in this discussion.

Problem-Solving Methodology

Professional intervention as distinct from ordinary engagement in community affairs by volunteer citizens is characterized in part by use of a logical, orderly, and disciplined means of analyzing problems and developing a well-constructed solution strategy based on a solid factual understanding of the circumstances. Pincus and Minahan (1973) refer to this as a "scientific method of investigation and problem-solving" (p. 91), which in this instance means proceeding in a systematic fashion and basing actions on existing theoretical knowledge and situational data.

For many individuals the community system is an amorphous, confusing, and intangible sphere that they do not comprehend or have direct contact with—as they do with a family or a small organization. Faced with the need to affect the community in some way, they do not have a clear sense of how to start or what to take account of. A problem-solving scheme provides a road map of sequential action steps and suggests variables to select out to examine and manipulate. This is analogous to working with individuals in psychotherapy, where a diagnostic framework for assessment and treatment planning is considered a necessary and useful component of practice.

Such an intervention planning framework provides structure and direction; it should optimize the probability of success in achieving intended objectives. In this sense, it injects a measure of control into the difficult and untamed process of steering community change. But we are speaking here of increasing chances of arriving at intended goals, not the certainty of reaching them. Again, turning to clinical practice with individuals, a professionally disciplined somewhat stepwise process is assumed to aid in helping clients reach better mental health, but it does not insure that that end will be attained for each client.

After examining an array of different problem-solving frameworks, Glaser, Abelson and Garrison (1983) indicate that these can be grouped into a half-dozen basic steps.

1. Some problem or need is identified. It can be a concern expressed by an individual or group, an evident discrepancy between what is desired and how things are, or the realization that some new idea or program is not being applied in the local situation. It can be a concrete pressure resulting from defects, hardships, or tensions in the situation. In any case, without the surfacing of an awareness of a problem or need there is little likelihood that ameliorative action will be taken.

2. The problem needs to be defined, delineated, and clarified. Terms such as "assessment" or "diagnosis" are used to convey the notion of comprehending the problem in a realistic and sophisticated way. A faulty definition of the problem can lead to faulty solutions, or to conflicts and holdups resulting in no action at all. Certain involvements should be avoided, such as spending too much time on assessment, responding to demands for a crash program, or the practitioner imposing a favorite diagnosis on the situation. Also, ideological preferences, biases, and blind spots can lead to faulty appraisals that are not in tune with solid progress.

3. Systematic methods have to be employed to obtain accurate information about the problem. Tools of needs assessment, environmental impact study, or historical trend analysis can be employed at this stage. Community people can be drawn in and spoken with informally or through surveys and focus group techniques. Existing information can be gleaned (such as social indicators) or original data can be gathered. Such tools can assist participants in thinking through the issues. But they cannot be used in a mechanical way. In the end, judgment and a reasonable level of consensus among the people who are involved will carry the process forward.

4. From this information pool, alternative courses of action are delineated. These are weighed one against the other, with an examination of specific outcomes, possible side effects, resistances to be encountered, resources necessary and available, popular acceptance within the community, leadership skills that are required, and so forth. A preferred action strategy is chosen, and often contingency actions are identified, should the prime approach run into difficulty. In comparing alternatives, feasibility and promise need to be considered: Can the program be carried out simply and have rapid results? Do participants have high motivation and ample skills to mount it? Is there money to carry the program forward? Is the payoff real and substantial? and so forth.

5. Implementation actions are spelled out. This entails the specific behaviors and responsibilities of the practitioner and others, timelines, tactical techniques, programmatic details, etc. These may have to be framed in general terms, as the situation may not be sufficiently clear until the strategy is set in motion and the reactions of others are evident. The practical aspects of the action become more clear and important at this stage, and can reveal whether the strategy design is realistic at all. Are there enough people who are willing to do the things that are necessary, are they willing to put up with threats or disapproval that might come about, are facilities and equipment at hand to enable movement to take place? If

the plan is not feasible, this suggests moving back in the framework to reassess or choose another among the alternative strategies.

6. Terminal actions are set forth. This typically entails a careful evaluation of effects—what was achieved and what more needs to be done. Evaluation can be formal and use prescribed methods of evaluation research or it can be informal and use thoughtful judgments of those involved in or affected by the change effort. The evaluation may call for a continuation of the process in refined or reconstituted form. In this case the assignment of the practitioner may change or another professional might be assigned to the project. On the other hand, the evaluation may suggest that the practitioner detach from the project as it becomes institutionalized and routinized in the natural flow of the community. Just as there is a logical beginning, there needs to be a logical ending.

The selection by Fred Cox describes a specific problem-solving schema that incorporates these features and expands on them. It was developed initially by the editors of this book and has been used widely over the years. The Cox format includes a number of additional important elements, particularly the identification of the beneficiary system. This has implications for focusing on goals and developing an action system through which the change process is mounted. Cox also distinguishes between strategy and tactics and treats them in separate sections, the latter including such matters as the most effective entry into the change process, the training of participants, and means of dealing with opposition.

While a problem-solving format needs to be logical and orderly, it is not entirely linear. One step can feed back on the other and require a fresh start. As new information is gathered or unexpected results come about, it may be necessary to reassess and reformulate strategy and tactics. The scheme has to be considered suggestive, flexible, and cyclical in character, one that provides structure but is not a rigid blueprint or cognitive straightjacket.

Use of Influence: Interpersonal Interaction and Organized Pressure

The work of community intervention professionals, indeed of any practicing professional, is to produce intended effects. Their mission, sanctioned by society, is to redirect problematic conditions in a beneficial direction (improved health, better educated citizens, reduction of poverty, etc.). This means using the skills and the influence of the professional (in collaboration with others) to bring about these results. In the human services the practitioner ordinarily relies heavily on the use of the self as an instrument of influence and change.

We can conceptualize influence in terms of interpersonal interaction (on a one-on-one basis convincing people, giving them facts, inspiring them, showing them the way) or organized pressure (orchestrating political pressure, legal authority, or protest demonstrations). In the field of community intervention the employment of organizationally based means is recognized and accepted. It is an evident, expected modus operandi and does not have to be justified or explained. What is less clear to many people is that interpersonal influence is also a common and necessary component of community practice. The practitioner is constantly in person-to-person professional contact with individuals of infinite variety, and needs the capacity to comprehend their ways and motives and engage with them in a highly sophisticated way. We will dwell on the interpersonal component in this discussion because it is less well understood.

Specht (1988) highlighted this aspect of influence in his writings. He states that human-service professionals, in addition to dealing with individual clients, have to relate to collaterals of clients (family, friends, and neighbors), colleagues from within their own profession and in other professions, and "sociopolitical others"—who comprise the larger action system of community intervention. These may be local residents, legislative leaders, board members, clergymen, agency directors, PTA presidents, business executives, and many others, cross-cutting class, ethnic, political, and geographic lines. "Sociopolitical interaction can take place in boardrooms, bars . . . at all times of day and night; and in social contexts ranging from office interviews and formal meetings to dinners, parties and 'meeting for a drink'" (p. 61).

In many of these contacts the practitioner is engaged in exchange relationships, purposively seeking some kind of response or resource from others—willingness to participate in a meeting, to support a piece of legislation proposed by an action group, to contribute funds or time to a project, or to stay out of the way and let the action proceed. The interactions should be viewed professionally: They have the purpose of producing benefits for people needing services or who suffer some disadvantage in society.

In return, the practitioner also provides (or exchanges) resources or reacts responsively. This can "involve a range of concrete or symbolic items, including reassuring words, a wink, . . . a food basket . . . "(p. 64). Interpersonal transactions under exchange theory can entail the giving of information, money, goods, status, services, and affective qualities such as attention, approval, and empathy. The professional's organizational base, including the sponsoring agency or a citizen action group, provides many of the resources that can be drawn upon to carry out these exchanges. It is necessary to be able to size up the other person, to individualize sensitively, in order to determine the kind of resource that that person would likely find of value and react to favorably.

According to Specht, interpersonal interactions in the community intervention realm are in some ways more complex and demanding than with clients in clinical work. "The professional exercises less power and authority and maintains less control over the purpose and context of the interaction" (p. 60). The other person may have greater power or status (the mayor or a corporate leader) and there is less prior understanding, and less likelihood of a contract, concerning the rules of the game and expected outcomes than is typical in the clinical situation.

Also, the stakes can be high in a very tangible way—loss of funding for an agency, failure to enact significant legislation, or a decision not to build a low-income housing development or a shelter for the homeless. These results can also be personally embarrassing to the professional because knowledge of them is not confined to the clinical interviewing room; rather they can become public and contentious through reportage in newspapers, television, and community meetings.

These are personal encounters in a macro context, "in which actors share with others their feelings, beliefs, attitudes and fears, entrust others with . . . information about themselves, share secrets and privileged communications and rely upon one another to provide resources and carry out tasks that can affect their welfare [and that of those for whom they carry responsibilities] in significant ways" (p. 71). Interpersonal modes of influence clearly fall in the domain of community practitioner, as a resource to be used and a competency to be mastered.

Recognizing that influence can be either personal or organizational, a variety of different forms of influence can be exerted to obtain desired results. We will review an array of influence modes, five in number, that go from intrusive and forceful to nonintrusive and subtle, namely: coercive, incentive-based, rational, persuasive, and normative. An excellent review of theory and research on influence modes has been provided by Glaser, Abelson, and Garrison (1983), and we will draw on their analysis in this discussion. We have organized their ideas into the five categories mentioned above, which were constructed from their review. (See the Introduction to Part Two for an expanded treatment of influence and strategy.)

Coercive. This approach involves the use of threat, force, fiat, or other means that may lead people to "go along," even against their wishes. Ordinarily, the target feels some degree of tension and stress in these circumstances. The approach may entail legal demands, administrative regulations, political clout, or economic pressure. Typical means applied include marches and other demonstrations, boycotts, legislative campaigns, strikes, and other forms of direct action. There may be the employment or potential employment of violence, civic disruption, or property damage. In other words, the individual experiencing coercive influence is faced with real, material loss or disadvantage in resisting the influence attempt. There is an effort by the change agent to gain compliance on the part of unwilling adversaries, and for this reason there may be a need for follow-up monitoring and recurring sanctions.

Incentive-Based. A frequent mode of influence involves giving benefits or rewards in conjunction with engaging in intended or prescribed behavior. This might involve making a grant, allowing use of facilities, providing staff support, giving a testimonial, or writing off a loan. The entire behavior modification/learning theory school is rooted in this concept, as is exchange theory. The notion is to make it pleasurable and fulfilling for someone to engage in desired behavior. Incentives can be material, as in the examples given above, or they can be socioemotional (clearing the way for the target to belong to a high-status group) or symbolic (bestowing recognition through a medal or certificate).

The first two approaches are often organizational in form, in that they may involve changing structural features of the environment of the persons being influenced—for example their economic situation or political options. However, coercive means and use of incentives can also be applied on the interpersonal level. The approaches that follow are particularly applicable on the interpersonal level.

Rational.   This involves imparting information to individuals with the hope that this will enable the person to make a choice in the right direction. In this formulation, the information is not slanted and is given in an objective or neutral manner. The information may be empirical data, theory, or philosophical frameworks, for example. Some forms of counseling use this approach, as do sensitivity training (T-group) programs. Professionals engage in this form of influence when they indicate to an action group what programs are available to support given purposes, and what the specific consequences might be of choosing each of these. Providing information about health behavior, population trends, and governmental regulations all fit here.

Persuasive.   Here information and argumentation are provided in a proactive fashion. There is a clear message or point of view, using reasoning and rhetoric to convince the targeted individual to believe or act in prescribed ways. Data may be set forth, but they are likely to be selective and slanted in a particular direction. Belief about advisability of a given course is expressed, or proof is given that a particular action will be beneficial or effective. Efforts illustrating this approach include urging people to join an organization, vote for a particular candidate, boycott a product, make a financial contribution to a cause, or exercise daily.

Normative.   Normative influence is more subtle and varied in form. It involves making changes in the perceptions and beliefs of people, so that they internalize norms or values and come to make them their own. Among the different means used to accomplish this is encouraging participation in making decisions so that one is impacted by peer pressures and also becomes a stakeholder in the action plan that is decided upon. Or the change agent can present himself or herself as a friendly and admirable person whom the target individual likes and becomes identified with. The individual then is motivated to act in large measure because of attraction to the professional. When this is coordinated with modeling of the intended behavior by the change agent, the combination is particularly potent.

Two of these influence modes are examined in depth in selections in the text. Simons looks at means of persuasion, pointing out that direct-service professionals as well as macro-level administrators have to use this as a generic skill. He sets forth eight principles of effective persuasion, such as showing the advantages of the position that is advocated, being comprehensible, citing proven results, linking the message to influentials, and minimizing threats to the target. He illustrates with examples of the presentation of a funding proposal to a county board and developing a radio spot to recruit program volunteers.

Zander treats measures that make use of organized pressure. One of these is a coercive approach, including blocking the progress of targets, restricting their freedom of movement, and harming or threatening to harm them. Among the pressuring approaches he also includes are using third parties as a lever, demonstrating successful programs, and engaging in bargaining. Zander observes that pressuring methods cause targets to focus on their environmental circumstances rather than on the quality of the ideas being proposed. Therefore, he suggests, the methods are more effective in changing overt behavior than in modifying internal beliefs and values.

MACRO RELATIONSHIPS TO MICRO PRACTICE

Another contextual factor in community intervention involves the established approaches for achieving human development and social betterment. Typically change efforts along these lines have followed two paths: providing aid directly to individuals experiencing hardships and disabilities, or changing the social environment that may be causing or exacerbating these troubles. The first, a micro perspective, entails casework, counseling, and clinical treatment, with a psychological focus that aims to strengthen the individual. The second, a macro perspective, includes community intervention, policy practice, and administration, with a system focus emphasizing social change or preventive actions.

The approaches should be seen as complementary rather than in basic conflict. Optimal community well-being requires the coexistence of multiple approaches to deal with different problems and populations. The following statement by a long-time social work leader (Schottland, 1962) vividly articulates this orientation:

I view these two aspects of social work—practice and policy, psychological individualization and social reform, improvement of the individualized services and improvement of social conditions, direct rendering of services and broader programs of prevention, personal therapy and social leadership—as a coordinated approach to the solution of these problems, individual and community, with which social work is concerned.

While the casework aspect has tended to dominate, in the recent past opportunities have arisen for social work to strengthen its reform dimension. The social sciences, which had a great spurt following World War II, provide a knowledge base for the planning and social change areas comparable to the base provided earlier by psychoanalysis to the field of treatment.

Furthermore, society's disenfranchised groups have been exerting heavy pressures on the professions to address discrimination, social injustice, and social dysfunction. Contemporary problems such as poverty, blight, racism, delinquency, drug abuse, and educational decline simply do not lend themselves to overall solution through individualized services. While in the past the professions, including social work, have not fully embraced controversial areas involving social conflict, more recently they have begun to respond to such challenges. There is a more balanced micro/macro awareness than in some previous decades.

Generalist Practice—Combining Micro and Macro Methods

The interrelationship of individualized (micro) and community (macro) practice is best reflected in the generalist practice school, also identified by the terms integrated, unitary, generic, holistic, and multirole practice. All of these convey the notion of using both micro and macro practice together in ways that are mutually supplementing and reinforcing. The practitioner starts with a broad assessment of the problem and develops an intervention approach that draws on the full range of practice options, often employing combinations of practice initiatives as appropriate. Teisiger (1983) describes the perspective as follows:

The appropriate starting point for interventions must be determined by examining the entire situation and must not be framed by what is initially presented. The problem . . . selected for intervention will determine the methodology of choice rather than the methodological bias or expertise of the worker... (p. 178).

An excellent overview of approaches to generalist practice is provided by Goldstein (1981), an analysis that indicates variations in emphasis and also suggests components of the approach. Some of the orientations he discusses are presented below.

Combined-Methods Generalist—This conveys the notion of using the discrete disciplines of casework, group work, and community organization in combined fashion, distilling them into a coordinated frame. The practice role that emerges is seen as a hybrid of sorts, comprising a lumped-together composite rather than a smoothly fashioned whole.

Case-Manager Generalist—This concept grows out of the case-manager role and the need to connect highly vulnerable and dependent clients to necessary community supports. This approach highlights integrating the services of fragmented agencies on behalf of clients while working with clients individually.

Generalist as a Role Composite—Here a very wide range of roles are merged to cut across problem and client types. Roles often thought of in clinical terms include supporter, advisor, therapist, and caretaker; then there is the administrator and consultant; further, there is the educator, coordinator, advocate, mediator, broker, and enabler. These roles are visualized as melding to form a coherent and well-articulated intervention package.

Problem-Focused Generalist—The idea here is to break away from specialist roles and agency functions as the determinants of intervention, and rather to build intervention from the requirements of the problem situation. An encompassing problem-solving schema is proposed, allowing the worker to move forward from a multifaceted person-in-environment assessment of client needs. The approach alternatively conceives of the building of practice from broad but common problem clusters, such as aging, physical disabilities, and child welfare.

Systems-Oriented Generalist—This approach starts from systems theory and assumes that human-service professionals relate to a range of different systems that may be dysfunctional, including individuals, families, groups, organizations, and communities. A client's problems may intersect various levels (family tensions, lack of informal social network support, and discriminatory hiring practices in the community) and may require an intervention plan that appropriately cuts across and impacts these levels, simultaneously or in sequence.

An incisive orientation to the generalist approach is provided in the selection on "Integrated Practice" by Parsons, Jorgensen, and Hernandez (1994). They offer a framework for analyzing intervention according to a continuum that ranges from small systems to large systems. Social problems are identified as the fundamental targets of intervention behavior. Further, the authors view education, habitation (growth promotion and inculcating problem-solving skills), and normalization as the guides to role-taking in practice. Empowerment across system levels is seen as central to practice, and a wide array of micro and macro practice roles is required to accomplish the empowering of people.

A different form of mixed practice is suggested in the contribution in this volume by Gutierrez. The starting point is the individual (women of color) and the need to focus on empowerment issues in direct practice with this type of client. Empowerment in this case is not a collective concept, as it is often in community-intervention literature (increasing the ability of a neighborhood to take action on its own behalf). Rather, the objective is to increase the individual's sense of control over her own life and to enhance her feeling of self-worth. This may involve the use of community-intervention perspectives and skills by the practitioner as a supplement to micro methods. Gutierrez suggests practice actions such as engaging in a power analysis of the client's objective situation and fostering within the client relevant skills such as competency in community and organizational change, assertiveness, and advocacy.

Viewing the issue of integrating macro skills into the clinical area more broadly, the whole information and referral aspect of micro practice draws heavily on the techniques and processes of macro practice. This includes helping clients to know how to make use of community resources—the approach to take with different agencies, whom to contact, how to state their case in a way as to gain the best service, how to counter negative responses, and the like. Linking clients with informal social supports such as neighbors, neighborhood organizations such as block clubs and other voluntary associations involves knowledge and skills from the macro area.

Using Macro Practice to Support Micro Practice

We have been describing how macro practice can be used within or generically in combination with micro practice. Macro practice can also be used outside of micro practice to enhance or augment individualized practice. That can occur in two ways. One entails employment of intraorganizational interventions to make the agency setting as understanding and supportive as possible of clinical practice. That will be the emphasis in this discussion. We will also touch on employing policy practice to strengthen the broad policy framework that impinges on the conduct of micro practice.

The human services are basically an organizationally based form of contemporary professional practice, similar to nursing, education, and urban planning. While there are private practice and consulting elements in each of these, the core and most widespread expression or practice takes place in formal organizational settings. As indicated earlier, these organizational structures provide resources but also can constrain the carrying out of clinical and counseling activities. On the positive side, effective staff-development programs can increase the knowledge and skills of clinical workers and result in considerable benefits to clients. Community relations and public relations skills can improve the climate of support in the community for services and expand the agency's resource base for assisting clients. Fund-raising skills, including grant writing, can have a similar and more direct effect on the resource base. Efficient budgeting and accounting methods can preserve that base and make sure that it is used to the best advantage.

Maximal service to clients can also be pursued through recruiting, training, and retaining high-level volunteers. Skills in encouraging community participation can result in the dissemination of appropriate information about agency programs and services, as well as encourage an appropriate level of use of agency programs by residents. Such skills can also garner support from community residents for the agency's objectives and further their involvement in the board, committees, and task forces that promote expanded service to clients. Through improving inter-organizational relationships, there can be better coordination in serving clients, insuring that they obtain an array of necessary services—without the delay, confusion, and struggle they might otherwise have to endure.

One of these organizational means of enhancing micro practice—staff development—is discussed in the selection by Doueck and Austin. These authors see staff development in a broad light and analyze its contribution to upgrading management's decision making and to improving communication within the agency. They also view it as a force for bettering cohesion in agency work groups and for advancing organizational problem solving. All of these factors are meant to improve agency function, but with an eye, ultimately, toward using such organizational progress to make direct work with clients more effective. Indeed, it is suggested that staff development starts, ordinarily, with a broad needs assessment to determine where weaknesses and shortcomings in the agency lie, so that targeted improvements are realistic and responsive to the requirements of quality service to clients.

In her book, *Integrating Social Welfare Policy and Social Work Practice,* McInnis-Dittrich (1994) shows how legislative statutes and policy mandates impinge on the lives of clients and the operations of agencies. The author delineates a number of macro skills that can be employed to modify policies in order to benefit provision of service to clients, including written and verbal communication with legislators, lobbying, public hearings, using the media, supporting a political candidate, and going to court to change policy. The micro practitioner can participate in all of these activities, usually in collaboration with others, and as an adjunct or extension of the work done directly with individual clients.

We have shown ways in which micro and macro practice interconnect, and we have focused on how macro practice can enhance micro practice, but the converse also pertains. Micro methods can facilitate the interpersonal relationships aspect of community intervention and can help planners and organizations understand problems of clients at a very concrete and personal level. This information can contribute positively to the design of plans, the shaping of policy, and the organizing of residents. The complexity and interrelatedness of contemporary community problems invite collaboration and the kinds of cross-method approaches that have been discussed.

The contextual factors that we have presented provide a prism through which to examine community intervention and develop strategies and tactics. The parameters (frameworks, arenas, core areas of practice, and macro/micro relationships) can be seen as a kind of staging area from which informed strategic planning can take place. Part One elaborates on the parameters and Part Two articulates the strategic dimensions.

—Jack Rothman

REFERENCES

Bales, Robert F. "Task Roles and Social Roles in Problem-Solving Groups." In Bruce Biddle and E. J. Thomas, eds., *Role Theory: Concepts and Research* (pp. 254–63). New York: Wiley, 1966.

Bales, R. F., and F. L. Strodtbeck. "Phases in Group Problem-Solving." In Dorwin Cartwright and A. Zander, eds., *Group Dynamics Research and Theory* (3d. ed) (pp. 389–98). New York: Harper & Row, 1968.

Benne, K., and P. Sheats. "Functional Roles of Group Members." In L. P. Bradford, ed., *Group Development* (pp. 51–59). Washington, DC: National Education Association, 1961.

Chirot, Daniel. *How Societies Change.* Thousand Oaks, CA: Pine Forge Press, 1994.

Glaser, Edward M., Harold H. Abelson, and Kathalee N. Garrison. *Putting Knowledge to Use: Facilitating the Diffusion of Knowledge and the Implementation of Planned Change.* San Francisco: Jossey-Bass Publishers, 1983.

Goldstein, Howard. "Generalist Social Work Practice." In Neil Gilbert and Harry Specht, eds., *Handbook of the Social Serviced.* Englewood Cliffs, NJ: Prentice-Hall, 1981.

Hall, Gus. "Who Runs America?" *Forward* (April 1, 1994) p. 7.

Homans, George C. *The Human Group.* New York: Hartcourt, Brace, 1950.

Litwak, Eugene, and Henry J. Meyer. "The School and the Family: Linking Organizations and External Primary Groups." In Paul F. Lazarsfeld et al., eds., *The Uses of Sociology* (pp. 522–43). New York: Basic Books, 1967.

McInnis-Dittrich, Kathleen. *Integrating Social Welfare Policy & Social Work Practice.* Pacific Grove, CA: Brooks/Cole, 1994.

Parsons, Ruth J., James D. Jorgensen, and Santos H. Hernandez. *The Integration of Social Work Practice.* Pacific Grove, CA: Brooks/Cole, 1994.

Parsons, Talcott. "Family Structure and the Socialization of the Child." In T. Parsons and R. F. Bales, eds., *Family, Socialization, and Interaction* (pp. 35–132). New York: Free Press, 1955.

Pincus, Allen, and Ann Minahan. *Social Work Practice: Model and Method.* Itasca, IL: F. E. Peacock, 1973.

Rustin, Bayard. "From Protest to Politics: The Future of the Civil Rights Movement." *Commentary* 39 (February 1965): pp. 25–31.

Schottland, Charles I. "Our Changing Society Challenges Social Work." Keynote Address, University of Pittsburgh School of Social Work Faculty-Alumni Conference, Pittsburgh, PA, March 30, 1962.

Specht, Harry. *New Directions for Social Work Practice.* Englewood Cliffs, NJ: Prentice Hall, 1988.

Teisiger, K. S. "Evaluation of Education for Generalist Practice." *Journal of Education for Social Work* 19(1) (1983), pp. 79–85.

Warren, Roland L. *The Community in America.* Chicago: Rand McNally, 1963.

Wilson, James Q. "Planning and Politics: Citizen Participation in Urban Renewal." *Journal of the American Institute of Planners* 3 (November 1963), pp. 242–9.

Wireman, Peggy. "Citizen Participation." *Encyclopedia of Social Work* (1977), pp. 178–9.

1.

Jack Rothman

APPROACHES TO COMMUNITY INTERVENTION

A PERSONAL PREFACE

This article presents a revision and refinement of the "Three Models" construct, which I introduced originally in 1968 and which has, with minor modifications and updating, provided the organizing framework for this book over its previous four editions. Through that time period, practices and conditions in communities have changed, and certain intellectual loose ends in the formulation have teased at me. My research studies pointed to gaps and uncertainties, and feedback from students and professionals in the field posed dilemmas that were difficult to resolve. It was as though I had packed a large and assorted pile of conceptual clothing into a cognitive suitcase and found there was a sock or the end of a tie sticking out after I had pressed it closed. The publication of this new edition has given me the impetus to try to tidy things up.

The basic ideas, it seems to me, hold up—but there is more complexity and variation than I had perceived. The best way to present the new perspective, I believe, is to do it in two sections. "Core Modes of Community Intervention" lays out the original schema, with some refinements and updating. "The Interweaving of Intervention Approaches" comprises an expansion and reformulation.

My first years of teaching were taken up with grappling to construct some type of unitary approach. But no matter how I labored, there were always contradictions and rough edges (the conceptual suitcase troubles started early). Someone who recently sought to summarize the intellectual contribution of a complex American thinker was led to comment: "At the end of the exercise, worst of all, you may find you are left with a few extra pieces which seem to fit nowhere" (Gellman, 1984, p. xv). That's how I felt about the subject matter I was wrestling.

Meanwhile, as my students presented themselves in class, they also didn't compose a unitary entity. I came to realize that they broke roughly into three types, each of which was looking for different things from the school and from me. There were those who were concerned with the better delivery of services, including coordination among agencies and effectiveness in meeting the needs of various vulnerable populations. They were interested in doing social planning and policy development for organizations such as the United Way or comprehensive health planning councils. Another group had the Peace Corps or VISTA (Volunteers in Service to America) in mind and were focused on working at the grassroots level. They were motivated to bring people together to solve their local problems through discussion on a cooperative, self-help basis. A third group was influenced by the civil rights, antiwar and student movements (such as SNCC, Student Nonviolent Coordinating Committee,

For their cogent comments and suggestions on an early draft of this article, I wish to thank my colleagues Ram Cnaan, Reno Patti, Marc Pilisuk, and Leonard Schneiderman.

and SDA, Students for a Democratic Society) and had a strong social action bent. Their aim was to aid the oppressed, promote social justice, and change society.

It gradually became clear to me that these different interests and motivations could not be encompassed comfortably by one practice orientation, and that it would be useful to think of different approaches that addressed each of the three empirically distinct groupings represented by the students. I began to stake out these three approaches conceptually, delineating a set of practice variables to be used to analyze variations among them. This was, perhaps, a risky departure from the prevailing casework mode, but, in time, clinical practice also broke from its solitary theoretical mold and began to include behavior modification, cognitive therapy, ecological practice, and other frameworks.

Social action presented a special challenge. Professional fields are typically conservative and eschew any taint of militancy—and that was especially true in the wake of the conformity-drenched decade of the 1950s, when any connection with radicalism was viewed with supreme suspicion. I needed to create an intellectual framework that would legitimate social action as an academic activity as well as an area of practice on par with other forms, something that did not exist in professional schools at that time.

I thought of the three approaches, or models, as ideal-types. They did not exist to a large extent in pristine, full-blown form in the real world, but were useful mental tools to help describe and analyze reality. Over time I have come to deemphasize or soften the notion of "models," which gives greater importance and internal validity to the approaches than seems warranted, and to accent the overlap and intermixture among approaches. The next

section of this discussion will sketch out the original approaches as ideal-type constructs, and will also make a cross-comparison of them against a set of twelve practice variables. The last section, which is more practical and the place where the analysis leads, will consider combined and variant patterns that serve to integrate the different modalities.

CORE MODES OF COMMUNITY INTERVENTION

THREE MODES OF INTERVENTION

Planning has been defined as the act of deciding what to do about some community affair while, meanwhile, life is bringing it around to a firm conclusion. And a typical committee assigned to deal with the task is, of course, merely a form of human organization that takes hours to produce minutes. These quips express a widespread popular view of social intervention as it is commonly carried out. Here, we will try to conceive of disciplined human reckoning that plays tricks on the natural course of life and actually begets intended effects, in furtherance of community well-being.

Differing and contrasting formulations of community intervention currently exist, which has been a source of perplexity and discomfort for the struggling practitioner and teacher. Taylor and Roberts (1985) describe the fluid nature of theory development, stating that in this field, "eclecticism, pragmatism and practice wisdom of professionals foster a turbulence and diversity that makes categorization and model-building especially difficult tasks" (pp. 24–25). In the founding issue of the *Journal of Community Practice*, editor Marie Weil states: that in order to "reclaim and strengthen community practice, theoretical approaches, guiding values and practice strategies need to be articulated so that they are both clear and carefully connected . . . a grounding . . . in reality and theory should be part of that movement forward" (Weil, 1994, pp. xxvii).

Three important approaches to purposive community change can be discerned in contemporary American communities, both urban and rural, and internationally. We will refer to them as approaches or Modes A, B, and C, and they can be given the appellations respectively of *locality development, social planning/policy,* and *social action.* Within each mode there are several variations and distinct emphases, but in this initial discussion we will select out and treat one prominent form within the mode for purposes of analysis. The three basic Modes of action do not necessarily exhaust all possibilities, but they offer a serviceable framework for a broad inquiry. These strategies are general in nature and are applicable across professional fields and academic disciplines. However, the author's grounding in social work and sociology will give a particular slant or tinge to the discussion.

In the presentation, community intervention is the general term used to cover the various forms of community level practice. "Community organizing" ordinarily implies social action and sometimes includes neighborhood work involving self-help strategies. But it excludes social planning/policy development approaches. Community organization has traditionally been the inclusive nomenclature, but it often becomes confused with more narrowly focused radical community organizing. Community work is frequently used to convey a locality development outlook. On the other hand, social planning usually fails to embrace grassroots organizing efforts. Recognizing that there is no standard terminology, community intervention seems

to be a convenient and useful overarching term to employ, although "community practice" has similar attributes and will be used occasionally as an alternative.

Administration (or management) is another form of social practice that takes place in the community within organizational settings. It involves developing organizations and keeping them running through obtaining funding and other resources, arranging staffing, establishing and carrying out procedures, maintaining records, and similar activities. Organizations constitute the vehicle through which social goals are pursued and relevant tasks are carried out. Thus, they provide the machinery for steering the endeavors of all three modes of community intervention—in addition to direct-service agencies and a wide spectrum of other programs in the community. Administration practice has a crucial bearing on the performance of all organizations, but it exists in a different dimension than community intervention and will be treated independently and apart from this analysis.

Mode A, Locality Development. This approach presupposes that community change should be pursued through broad participation by a wide spectrum of people at the local community level in determining goals and taking civic action. Its prototypic form will be found in the literature of a segment of the field commonly termed community development. As stated by an early U.N. publication: "Community Development can be tentatively defined as a process designed to create conditions of economic and social progress for the whole community with its active participation and the fullest possible reliance on the community's initiative" (United Nations, 1955).

Locality development is a community-building endeavor with a strong emphasis on what Selznick (1992) terms the "moral commonwealth." He describes this in words such as mutuality, identity, participation, plurality, and autonomy. Locality development fosters community building by promoting process goals: community competency (the ability to solve problems on a self-help basis) and social integration (harmonious interrelationships among different racial, ethnic, and social-class groups—indeed, among all people). Leadership is drawn from within, and direction and control are in the hands of local people. It is a type of activity that has been initiated and sponsored by religious and service groups such as The Catholic Church and The American Friends Service Committee, and it reflects highly idealistic values. The style is humanistic and strongly people-oriented, with the aim of "helping people to help themselves." The process of educating participants and nurturing their personal development has high priority. "Enabling" techniques that are nondirective in character and foster self-direction are emphasized.

Many of the precepts of the feminist perspective on organizing overlap with the locality development approach, including stress on wide participation as well as concern for democratic procedure and educational goals—including consciousness-raising (Hyde, 1989; Halseth, 1993). The approach is also used, some would say misappropriated, by political and business leaders who espouse local initiative and privatization, relying on enterprise zones and like programs that essentially intend to scale back social programs for the poor that are carried out under governmental auspices.

Some examples of locality development as conceived here include neighborhood work programs conducted by settlement houses and other community-based agencies; federal government programs such as Agricultural Extension and The National Service Corps; and village-level work in some overseas community development programs, including the Peace Corps and the Agency for International Development (AID). To these can be added community work in the fields of adult education and public health education, as well as self-help and informal helping network activities conducted through neighborhood councils, block clubs, consumer cooperatives, and civic associations.

Thinkers who contributed intellectual roots for locality development include John Dewey, Mary Follett, Kurt Lewin, and Eduard Lindeman. Among professional writings that express and elaborate this mode are Blakely (1979); Chavis et al. (1993); Cnaan (1991); Henderson and Thomas (1987); Lappin (1985); Mayer (1984); Ross (1955).

The terms "community development" and "locality development" have been used to identify the approach. The locality development nomenclature was employed in the original version of this analysis to convey this perspective on intervention in a precise way. Community development is a more polymorphic term, which sometimes connotes institutional and policy means to strengthen communities from above (Mier, 1993), or suggests industrial expansion through economic development (Bingham and Mier, 1993). Sometimes it has a national or international frame rather than an explicitly local one (Goetz and Clarke, 1993). Locality development will be the terminology of choice here, and when "community development" is used it will connote a Mode A strategy.

While locality development espouses highly respected ideals, it has been criticized for its performance record. Khinduka, in the prior edition of this book, characterizes it as a "soft strategy" for achieving change. He indicates that its pre-occupation with process can lead to endless meetings that are frustrating for participants and conducive to a slow pace of progress. Khinduka further argues that concern with modifying attitudes and values may divert attention from important structural issues that need more direct engagement. Also, many projects draw their participation largely from racial and ethnic minorities and the poor, when it is the attitudes of the affluent and well-placed that need rearranging.

Embracing consensus as a basic modus operandi precludes arbitrary actions from occurring, but it puts those who stand to lose from needed reforms in a position to veto effective action. The heavy emphasis on the local community may be inappropriate at a time when the locality has lost much of its hold over people and patterns of life are influenced significantly by powerful national and regional forces. Khinduka admires locality development for playing a gentleman's game in the often sordid arena of community affairs, but he worries about whether it can win.

Mode B, Social Planning/Policy. This emphasizes a technical process of problem solving regarding substantive social problems, such as delinquency, housing, and mental health. This particular orientation to planning is data-driven and conceives of carefully calibrated change being rooted in social science thinking and empirical objectivity (unlike other existing forms of planning that are more political and emergent). The style is technocratic, and rationality is a dominant ideal. Community participation is not a core ingredient and may vary from much to little, depending on the problem and circumstances. The approach presupposes that change in a complex modern environment requires expert planners who, through the exercise of technical competencies—including the ability to gather and analyze quantitative data and to maneuver large bureaucratic organizations—are needed to improve social conditions. There is heavy reliance on needs assessment, decision analysis, Markov chains, evaluation research, delphi techniques, computer graphics, and a plethora of sophisticated statistical tools.

The design of formal plans and policy frameworks is of central importance, as is their implementation in effective and cost-efficient ways. By and large, the concern here is with task goals: conceptualizing, selecting, establishing, arranging, and delivering goods and services to people who need them. In addition, fostering coordination among agencies, avoiding duplication, and filling gaps in services are important concerns in achieving service ends.

Within the field of social work, educational programs in planning and policy typify the social planning/policy approach. It also finds expression in university departments of public administration, public health, urban affairs, city planning, and policy studies. It is practiced in numerous federal bureaus and departments, in United Ways and community welfare councils, and in city departments and voluntary agencies geared to planning for mental health, health, aging, housing, and child welfare. The National Association of Planning Councils has been formed to strengthen these local community planning efforts.

Intellectual roots for the approach can be found in the thinking of scholars such as Comte, Lasswell, Keynes, Herbert Simon, and Jesse Steiner. Some professional writings that reflect this mode include Gil (1976); Gilbert and Specht (1977); Kahn (1969); Lauffer (1981); Moroney (1991); Morris and Binstock (1966); and Tropman (1984).

While this approach emphasizes rationality in an explicit and formal way, and leans on it to lend legitimation for recommended actions (often by way of voluminous and impressive reports), the other approaches (Modes A and C) also need to be firmly embedded in rationality. Developing a means to successfully achieve broad civic participation or carrying out a protest demonstration to place pressure on public officials each require a high level of strategic calculation, linking chosen means logically to intended ends. The rationality may not be as overt and public, but it is equally related to effective and professionally sound intervention.

Planning and policy are grouped together in this discussion because both involve assembling and analyzing data to prescribe means for solving social problems. They overlap in some measure, but they also probably have distinct features. Frequently, in scholarly and practice writings, the two are treated as though they are mutually exclusive. Policy is often associated with higher social levels—with national and state, governmental structures, and the act of selecting goals and framing legislative or administrative standards rather than actually establishing programs and services.

No clear basis exists for this compartmentalization of policy functions. There is policy development at the local level as well as at higher echelons (Flynn, 1985). It is conducted under private auspices as well as under governmental sponsorship (Pierce, 1984). And it has implementation and monitoring functions in addition to the goal-setting aspect (Pressman and Wildavsky, 1984). Gilbert and Specht (1974) conceive of a "policy planner" and define policy as "a course or plan of action," thereby essentially blending the two.

In this discussion we are addressing policy as professional practice rather than as a method for conducting an analysis to understand social welfare programs (Tropman, 1984; Jansson, 1984). Ironically, many planning and policy scholars write as though the other area does not exist, although upon examination these authors cover a great deal of similar ground. A divergence or different emphasis (areas of less overlap) lies in policy practice's concern with megagoals or quasi-philosophical frameworks that guide legislative enactment and program development, while planning is interested to a greater degree in the details of program construction and service delivery.

In this discussion, "planning" will serve as a shorthand and convenient designation for the planning/policy approach.

The data-driven form of planning and policy practice has a certain currency and appeal, with its coherent intellectual structure and ostensible ease of implementation. Urban planning schools and policy studies programs place a great deal of emphasis on providing students with ever more complex and elegant statistical procedures and computer modeling methods. This may be because these are readily available, can be manipulated easily in a technical sense, and have an aura of mastery and completeness that is missing in more political forms of planning.

Webber and Rittel (1973) state that the data-driven approach is flawed because it is based on the assumption that problems are easily definable, well-bounded, and responsive to professional intervention. Instead, they say, contemporary problems are "wicked" in nature—unique, intractable, intermeshed with others, and situated in a constantly changing and turbulent social environment.

Two important factors place constraints on the prototypical rationalistic mode. The first is the intensification of constituency politics, a contemporary development that makes planning highly contentious and interactive. Interest groups of various kinds feel they should have a say and have acquired a voice, and they place themselves vigorously into the pluralistic process through which decisions are made. Many planners and policy professionals believe that interests of various kinds rightfully should go into the defining of goals and setting the community agenda, because these are socially constructed phenomena and involve value choices that extend far beyond the purview of the expert or bureaucrat.

Another factor confounding prototypical rationalistic intervention is the impact of fiscal constraint. There is public aversion to taxation and to governmental spending for social programs. Concrete economic conditions involving industrial decline and recessionary trends also place objective limits on social program options. These public attitudes and economic strictures have shifted planning from an optimizing stance to what Herbert Simon refers to as "satisficing." The dual effects of contentious community politics and a public leaning toward a "get by" level of social programming place into question the utility of elaborate, data-driven planning modalities.

Mode C, Social Action. This approach presupposes the existence of an aggrieved or disadvantaged segment of the population that needs to be organized in order to make demands on the larger community for increased resources or equal treatment. The particular approach we are describing has a militant orientation to advocacy with respect to goals and tactics (although not all advocacy is militant). It aims at making fundamental changes in the community, including the redistribution of power and resources and gaining access to decision

making for marginal groups. Social action intervention seeks to change legislative mandates of political entities such as a city council, or the policies and practices of institutions such as a welfare department or housing authority. Practitioners in the social action arena generally aim to empower and benefit the poor, the disenfranchised, the oppressed. The style is highly adversarial, and social justice is a dominant ideal.

Classically, stemming from the high point of social action in the 1960s, confrontational tactics have been emphasized, including use of demonstrations, picketing, strikes, marches, boycotts, teach-ins, civil disobedience, and other disruptive or attention-gaining moves. Disadvantaged and aggrieved groups frequently do not have at hand the funds, connections, and expertise available to others, and consequently they rely heavily on the resources of "people power," which has the potential to pressure and disrupt. Training institutes sponsored by the Mid-West Academy and Industrial Areas Foundation have been established to equip low-power constituencies with the skills to impact higher circles of power.

The social action approach has been used widely by AIDS activists, feminist organizing groups, gay and lesbian organizations, consumer and environmental protection organizations, civil rights and black power groups, and La Raza and victim rights groups. It has been embraced by Industrial Areas Foundation and ACORN (Association of Community Organizations for Reform Now) projects, labor unions, including the United Farm workers, and radical political action movements.

Thinkers providing an intellectual foundation for this approach include Marx, Fourier, Bakunin, and Habermas and it was advanced in part by advocacy activities of Jane Addams and her Progressive Era allies. Alinsky's *Reveille for Radicals*

(1946) and *Rules for Radicals* (1972) have typified the orientation of the social action mode. Newer writings also reflect this orientation (Boyte and Riessman, 1986; Burghardt, 1987; Cloward and Piven, 1977; Delgado, 1986; Fisher, 1994; Freire, 1974; Kahn, 1992).

In recent years, social action movements have expanded their strategy bent beyond the confrontational style, and "new wave" organizing now employs a wider range of adversarial tactics. Political and electoral maneuvers that are more fine tuned and diversified are being used in considerable measure. This is because the groups have become more sophisticated over time, there is less public tolerance for disruptive methods, and power elites have become skillful in counteracting confrontations. Organizing has become less stridently ideological, and middle-class groups (and right-wing factions) have been drawn into campaigning on their own behalf or in joint actions.

However, there is a great deal of fragmentation among groups engaged in social action. Advocacy has taken on a particularistic caste, with each aggrieved constituency advancing its own special goals and interests in a "politics of identity." Even among people of color, African-Americans, Hispanics, Asian-Americans, and Native Americans go their own ways, independently and often competitively. Thus, coalition building has become a central concern in social action, since groups are typically not strong enough to achieve significant results on their own. But these coalitions are fluid, shifting, and irregular; new configurations have to be formed for different issues on a continuing basis—thus draining off energy that might be focused on external targets.

Fragmentation is especially handicapping because of the growing concentration of political and economic power locally, nationally, and even globally (see the discussion by Fisher on pages 327–340). Relatively weak local entities that are disunited find themselves contending with powerful extracommunity entities that are functionally consolidated.

Human service professionals have not been prominent in the social action area, but there has been continuing participation on a small-scale basis over the years. Major national organizations such as ACORN and the United Farm Workers Union have been headed by social workers. There are relevant professional groups, such as the Union of Radical Human Service Workers in Boston and the Bertha Capen Reynolds Society nationally, and there is also a specialized periodical, the *Journal of Progressive Human Services.*

Modest salaries and the absence of professional perquisites are a deterrent to long-term involvement. But new graduates with an interest in basic social change are in a position to take this on as a communal responsibility for a limited time at the beginning of their career. The Nader organization's publication *Good Works* (Anzalone, 1985) and the "Community Jobs" newsletter list a multitude of positions and career opportunities. The richness of the experience, the chance to join hands with aspiring members of oppressed and dispossessed groups, and a sense of accomplishment in advancing a valued and meritorious cause can compensate for temporary material loss. Some professionals have and will continue to make this a lifetime commitment.

A PERSPECTIVE ON DISTINCT PRACTICE APPROACHES

Taking an overview, this three-pronged orientation, as a broad cognitive mapping device for community intervention, has a certain intuitive logic. Historically, several schools of social work have developed specialized programs for training according to the three modes. Thus, a community development program that was situated at the University of Missouri epitomized Mode A; the doctoral program in planning at Brandeis University, Mode B; and a social action program based at Syracuse University, Mode C.

Morris and Binstock (1966), based on an empirical examination of community organizations, suggested a similar threefold division. Friedmann (1987) attaches different language to these same approaches— social learning, policy analysis and social mobilization, as does Lyon (1987)—self-help, technical assistance and conflict. The formulation has also provided an effective conceptual framework for a historical volume on community intervention (Betten and Austin, 1990).

Empirical studies of the formulation lend general support. Cnaan and Rothman (1986) found that a sample of community workers in Israel distinguish between these approaches in their perception of their work and in their practice activities. Several studies in progress have replicated the inquiry with apparently similar results in Sweden, Egypt, Japan, Chile, India, and several other countries. (In the original study, social action appeared to be a more complex phenomenon than the other interventions.) In a series of case studies in Canada, Wharf (1979) observed that locality development and social planning were distinctly discernable, but that social action, while evident, again was more diverse. (We will discuss this disparity in the next section, "The Interweaving of Intervention Approaches.") Practitioners in Wharf's project found the framework particularly useful as an assessment tool, as

did those in another Canadian study (Johnson, 1974).

The studies also suggest the existence of variations and mixed configurations, which is the subject of the next section. However, here, for analytical purposes, we view the three approaches as relatively "pure" expressions. The merit in this is suggested by Morris and Binstock (1966) when they refer to their own classification system:

The categories are somewhat arbitrary, for it is sometimes difficult to say that a particular experience fits one category but not another. For these reasons it is particularly important to achieve as narrow a focus as possible in analyzing [intervention]: Otherwise a systematic treatment is virtually impossible (p. 15).

Examining ideal-types, while recognizing they are to some degree artificial, has the particular benefit of allowing us to perceive practice variables and intervention components within the modes in explicit and crystallized form. This generates a wide range of distinct practice options, across intervention orientations, that can be employed selectively and in combination. (This will be expanded upon subsequently.)

PRACTICE VARIABLES AND COMMUNITY INTERVENTION APPROACHES

In order to proceed with the analysis, we will specify a set of practice variables that help describe and compare each of the approaches when seen in ideal-type form. Each of the orientations makes assumptions about the nature of the community situation, goal categories of action, concepts of the general welfare, appropriate tactics, and so on. A set of twelve such variables will be treated in the passages that follow. The variables are based on the writer's long-term experience and review of the analyses of practice by others. They are assumed to be salient but by no means exhaustive. A number of themes from the previous discussion will necessarily be reiterated here, but they will be applied in a different and conceptually systematized way. Table 1.1 (p. 44) provides a summary and substantive overview, and the discussion offers further clarification and interpretation for those who wish to go into the details.

1. Goal Categories

Two main goals that have been discussed recurrently in the community organization and macro practice literature have been referred to as "task" and "process" (Rothman, 1964; Gilbert and Specht, 1977). Task goals entail the completion of a concrete task or the solution of a delimited problem in a community system: establishing new services, improving coordination of existing ones, passing specific social legislation, or changing the behavior or attitudes of residents, say, in regard to health practices. Process goals are oriented to system maintenance and enhancement and local empowerment, with aims such as creating self-maintaining, problem-solving structures, stimulating wide interest and participation in community affairs, fostering collaborative attitudes and practices among people, and enhancing indigenous leadership, all linked to enhancing community integration and local problem-solving capacity. Process goals are concerned with a generalized capacity of the community system to function over time; task goals are concerned with the solution of pinpointed functional problems of the system.

Locality Development. Process goals receive heavy emphasis. The community's growing capacity to become integrated and to engage in cooperative problem solving is of central importance. This view is expressed by Henderson and Thomas (1987) as follows:

The challenge faced by professionals . . . is to realize that they must seek not just to deliver services to meet people's needs but to do so in a way that enhances people's autonomy, self-respect and their ability to work together to solve common problems (p. 7).

Social Planning. There is stress on task goals, focusing on the solution of substantive social problems. Social planning organizations often are mandated specifically to deal with concrete deficiencies, defects, or illnesses, and their official names signify this—mental health departments, municipal housing authorities, legislative committees, The American Cancer Society, commissions on physical rehabilitation or alcoholism, and so on.

These aims of social planning have been described as: the solving of social problems; the satisfying of social needs; . . . coordination of services (including interdisciplinary cooperation), [and] the initiation and development of new services and facilities . . . (Weyers, 1992, p. 133).

It is difficult for many planners to attend to process goals because their organizational assignments often have official mandates, legislative directives, formal time lines, and prescribed procedures.

Social Action. The approach may lean in the direction of either task goals or process goals. Some social action organizations, such as civil rights groups and cause-oriented organizations, emphasize obtaining specific legislative outcomes (higher welfare allotments) or changing specific social practices (discriminatory hiring). Usually these objectives entail changes in policies of government or formal organizations.

Other social action groups lean in the direction of process goals—aiding a constituency to acquire and exercise power—as exemplified by feminist organizing, ACORN, or the early black power movement. This objective of building local-based power and decision-making centers transcends the solution of any given problem situation.

A dual perspective encompassing both goal types has been put forth by Kahn (1982) as follows:

Organizing has both short- and long-range benefits. In the short run it's an effective tool for getting things done: for improving schools, for lowering taxes, for establishing rights on the job, for improving transportation and health care, for protecting and defending neighborhoods and communities . . . . But it is also an end in itself. As we organize, we clarify ourselves as individuals because we learn to speak for ourselves in ways that make us heard (pp. 7–8).

In recent years social action groups have given increasing attention to process goals and capacity building. The feminist movement's theme, "the personal is political," articulates that trend.

2. Assumptions Concerning Problem Conditions

Locality Development. The local community is seen to be overshadowed by the larger society, lacking in fruitful human relationships and problem-solving skills and peopled by isolated individuals suffering from anomie, alienation, disillusionment, and, often, mental illness. Technological change, it is believed, has pressed society toward greater industrialization and urbanization with little consideration of the effects on social relations. Henderson and Thomas (1987) state:

not only are people set apart from each other by conflicts and scapegoating, but we may wonder whether people know *how* to manage their relationships with each other. This state of affairs may have come about partly because social skills involved in neighboring and networking may have atrophied (p. 4).

Alternatively, especially in Third World international projects, the community is often seen as tradition-bound, ruled by a small group of autocratic elite, and composed of an educationally deprived population who lack skills in problem solving or an understanding of democratic methods.

Social Planning. The community is viewed as burdened by concrete social problem conditions. Warren (1972) reflects the outlook of social planners as follows:

It is apparent that certain types of "problems" are broadly characteristic of contemporary American communities. They appear in such forms as the increasing indebtedness of central cities, the spread of urban blight and slums, the lack of adequate housing which people can afford, the economic dependence of large numbers of people in the population, poorly financed and staffed schools, high delinquency and crime rates, inadequate provisions for the mentally ill, the problem of the aged, the need for industrial development, the conflict of local and national agencies for the free donor's dollar, the problem of affording rapid transit for commuters at a reasonable price and at a reasonable profit, and the problem of downtown traffic congestion. This list is almost endless, and each of the problems mentioned could be subdivided into numerous problematic aspects (p. 14).

Social Action. The community comprises a hierarchy of privilege and power in the eyes of those with a militant advocacy stance. There exist islands of oppressed, deprived, ignored, or powerless populations suffering social injustice or exploitation at the hands of oppressors such as the "power structure," big government, corporations, global capitalism, and racist or sexist institutions. This oppression can imply material deprivation or psychological dehumanization. Kahn (1982) states the social action position succinctly:

In the United States today power is concentrated in the hands of a small number of well-organized individuals and corporations. These corporations and the individuals involved in them have extraordinary power to make decisions that affect all our lives . . . regardless of the suffering that it has caused people . . . (p. 14).

Again, we caution that these are dominant motifs rather than discrete categories. Many social actionists are greatly concerned about apathy and substantive problems, even as some social planners are deeply concerned about the quality of social relations. We are defining tendencies in thinking rather than mutually exclusive cognitive compartments.

3. Basic Change Strategy

Locality Development. The basic change strategy may be expressed as "Let's all get together and talk this over." This involves a concerted effort to bring a wide range of community people into determining their "felt" needs and solving their own problems. Local initiative and shared decision making are key.

Social Planning. The basic change strategy in the data-driven modality we are describing is captured by "Let's get the facts and think through the logical next steps." Planners and policy practitioners in this framework focus on gathering pertinent data about the problem and then deciding on an empirically supported and feasible course of action. The practitioner plays a central part in assembling and analyzing facts, establishing goals or policy frameworks, and determining appropriate services, programs, and actions. This may or

may not be done with the participation of others, depending upon the planner's sense of the utility of participation in the given situation and the organizational context within which he or she functions.

Social Action. The change strategy is expressed through "Let's organize to overpower our oppressor and change the system," that is, crystallizing issues so that people know who their legitimate enemy is and mobilizing them to bring pressure on selected targets. Such targets may include an organization, such as the welfare department; a person, such as the mayor; or an aggregate of persons, such as slum landlords.

4. Characteristic Change Tactics and Techniques

Locality Development. Tactics of consensus are stressed, including discussion and communication among a wide range of different individuals, groups, and factions. Blakely (1979) makes a case for cooperative, deliberative techniques in locality development: "Development specialists attempt within the conflict situation to place the stress on problem solving as opposed to win-lose strategies and attitudes" (p. 21).

Social Planning. Fact finding and analytical skills are of central concern. Tactics of conflict or consensus may be employed, depending upon the practitioner's analysis of the situation. For example, writings on managerial planning often emphasize the value of cooperative participation (Peters and Waterman, 1982). At the same time, hostile takeovers are not unheard of in the business world, nor is there a dirth of aggressive moves by planning agencies and their client organizations to win over a larger share of United Way Funding. Policy specialists differentially seek allies from one or another faction to support a preferred legislative initiative as necessary.

Social Action. Conflict tactics are emphasized in the militant advocacy modality, including methods of confrontation and direct action. The ability to mobilize relatively large numbers of people is necessary to carry out rallies, marches, boycotts, and picketing. Success of social action groups is based on: "their ability to embarrass the target or their ability to cause the target political harm if the target is a public official, or financial harm if it is a business" (Bobo, Kendall, & Max, 1991, p. 29).

Alinsky (1962) felt it is important to "rub raw the sores of popular discontent." His strong philosophical/theoretical position was clear:

Issues which are noncontroversial usually mean that people are not particularly concerned about them; in fact, by not being controversial they cease to be issues. Issues involve differences and controversy. History fails to record a single issue of importance which was not controversial. Controversy has always been the seed of creation (p. 7).

5 and 6. Practitioner Roles and Medium of Change

Locality Development. The practitioner's characteristic role is that of an "enabler" or, as suggested by Biddle and Biddle (1965), "encourager." The role has been described in this way by Henderson and Thomas:

At a very basic level, locality development is about putting people in touch with one another, and of promoting their membership in groups and networks. It seeks to develop people's sense of power and significance in acts of association with others that may also achieve an improvement in their social and material well-being (p. 15).

The practitioner employs as a major medium of change the creation and guidance of small task-oriented groups, requiring skill in fostering collaborative problem finding and problem solving.

Social Planning. More technical or "expert" roles are emphasized. Referring to Ross (1955), the expert role contains these components: community diagnosis, research skill, information about other communities, advice on methods of organization and procedure, technical programmatic information, and evaluation. The practitioner employs as a salient medium of change the guiding and maneuvering of agencies, bureaucracies, and legislative bodies in addition to the collection and analysis of data. Weyers (1992) indicates that the role of the planner involves:

correlating identified needs and available resources. The nature and range of these needs are identified primarily with the aid of different forms of research, while the sources, on the other hand, are mainly the concern of formal systems and the structure of authority. To obtain these desired sources, the social worker has to employ available data (for instance in the form of need identification) in order to be able to claim support (p. 132).

Social Action. Roles entail the organization of disadvantaged groups to act on behalf of their interests in a pluralist political culture. The practitioner seeks to create and guide mass organizations and movements and to influence political processes. Mass mobilization is necessary because:

Power generally consists of having a lot of money or a lot of people. Citizen organizations tend to have people, not money. Thus, our ability to win depends on our being able to do with people, what the other side is able to do with money (Bobo, Kendall & Max, 1991, p. 9).

Classic 1960s social action focuses on organizing disadvantaged populations to act on their own in their own behalf, which is seen as true empowerment. We will examine variations from this pattern within the social action mode later.

7. Orientation Toward Power Structure(s)

Locality Development. The power structure is included within an all-encompassing conception of community. All segments of the community are thought of, holistically, as part of the action system. Hence, power elites are considered allies in a common venture embracing the well-being of all. One consequence of this might well be that in this approach only goals that have mutual agreement become legitimate or relevant; goals that involve incompatible interests are ignored or discarded as inappropriate. Hence, aims involving fundamental shifts in the configuration of power and resource control, which can contribute materially to elevating the position of minorities and the poor, are likely to be excluded.

Social Planning. The power structure is usually present as the sponsor or employer of the practitioner. Sponsors may include a voluntary board of directors, an arm of city government, or a legislative unit. Morris and Binstock (1966) state the case this way: "Realistically, it is difficult to distinguish planners from their employing organizations. In some measure, their interests, motivations, and means are those of their employers." Planners are usually highly trained technical specialists whose services require considerable finances for salary as well as support in the form of supplies, equipment, facilities, and auxiliary technical and clerical personnel.

Frequently, planners can only be sustained in their work by those in the society possessing wealth, control of the machinery of government, and high prestige. As Rein (1965) suggests, much planning is by "consensus of elites" who are employers and policy makers in planning organizations. Usually this consensus is reinforced through technical language, selective use of factual data, and an expressed commitment to impartial rationality.

Social Action. The power structure is seen as an external target of action; that is, the power structure lies outside the beneficiary system or constituency itself and is an oppositional or oppressive force.

The person with the power becomes the "target" of an issue campaign. The target (sometimes called the decision maker) is always the person who has the power to give you what you want (If no one has such power, then you haven't cut the issue correctly.) (Bobo, Kendall & Max, 1991, p. 11).

Power elites, then, usually represent a force antithetical to the group whose well-being the practitioner is committed to advance. Those holding power, accordingly, must be coerced or overturned in the interests of equity and social justice.

8. Boundary Definition of the Beneficiary System

Locality Development. The total community, usually a geographic entity such as a city, neighborhood, or village, is the beneficiary system. Accordingly, "Community Development is concerned with the participation of *all* groups in the community—with both sexes, all age groups, all racial, nationality, religious, economic, social and cultural groups" (Dunham, 1963).

Social Planning. The intended beneficiaries may be either a total geographic community or some area or functional sub-part. Community welfare councils and city planning commissions usually conceive of their intended beneficiaries as comprising the widest cross section of community interests. On the other hand, sometimes the service populations of social planners are more segmented aggregates—a given neighborhood, the mentally ill, the aged, youth, juvenile delinquents, or the black community. Policy practitioners work with representatives who may view beneficiaries varyingly in universalistic common-weal terms or in terms of particularistic constituencies.

Social Action. Intended beneficiaries are usually conceived as some community sub-part or segment that suffers at the hands of the broader community and thus merits the special support of the practitioner. According to Kahn (1982):

When people in government, such as community planners and developers, talk about community development, they often mean the development of an entire city. This idea is misleading. You can't develop an entire city. What's good for some people is not good for others. If something is good for one group, another group loses out. There are conflicts within groups. The poverty of one group may be caused by the profits of another (p. 80).

Practitioners are likely to think in terms of constituents, brothers and sisters, or allies rather than in terms of a "client" concept, which is seen as patronizing, detached, or overly clinical.

9. Assumptions Regarding Community Interests or Subsystems

Locality Development. The interests of various groups and factions in the community are viewed as reconcilable and responsive to the influence of reason, persuasion, communication, and mutual goodwill. Hence:

Community developers accept the notion that people, regardless of race, sex, ethnicity or place of birth, can find ways to solve their problems through group efforts. The community development movement is humanistic in orientation. This implies a genuineness or authenticity in relationships that permits open, honest communication and feedback (Blakely, pp. 18, 21).

Social Planning. There is no pervasive assumption about the degree of intractability of conflicting interests; the approach appears to be pragmatic, oriented toward the particular problem and the actors enmeshed in it. Morris and Binstock set out the social planning orientation as follows:

A planner cannot be expected to be attuned to . . . the overriding interests of dominant factions. Considerable study and analysis of factions and interests dominant in various types of organizations will be needed before planners will have sufficient guidance for making reliable predictions as to resistance likely in a variety of situations (p. 112).

Social Action. The approach assumes that interests among community subparts are at variance and not easily reconcilable, that resources are limited or dominated, and that often coercive influence must be applied (boycotts, strikes, political and social upheavals) before meaningful adjustments can be made. Those who gain privileges and profits from the disadvantage of others do not easily give up their edge; the force of self-interest makes it foolish to expect them to do so. Saul Alinsky (1962) states:

All major controlling interests make a virtue of acceptance—acceptance of the ruling group's policies and decisions. Any movement or organization arising in disagreement, or seeking independent changes and defined by the predominating powers as a threat, is promptly subjected by castigation, public and private smears, and attacks on its very existence (p. 6).

10. Conception of Intended Beneficiaries

Beneficiaries are those who are in line to gain from the efforts of the practitioner and the intervention process.

Locality Development. Intended beneficiaries are likely to be viewed as average citizens who possess considerable strengths that are not fully developed and who need the services of a practitioner to help them release and focus these inherent capabilities. The Biddles (1965) express this viewpoint as follows:

1. Each person is valuable, and capable of growth toward greater social sensitivity and responsibility.
   a. Each person has underdeveloped abilities in initiative, originality, and leadership. These qualities can be cultivated and strengthened (p. 60).

Social Planning. The beneficiary group is more likely to be thought of as consumers of services, those who will receive and utilize those programs and services that are the fruits of the social planning process—mental health treatment, public housing, health education, recreation, welfare benefits, and so forth. Weyers (1992) makes this clear in highlighting the provision of social services as a key objective of social planning. "According to this point of view the efficiency of the community's social functioning will depend on the quantity and quality of professional services rendered to the community, as well as the way in which the community's concrete needs are provided for" (p. 132).

In policy settings beneficiaries may be conceived as both consumers and constituents.

Social Action. The intended beneficiaries are seen as aggrieved victims of "the system": of slum landlords, the medical establishment, government bureaucracies, racist institutions, patriarchal entities, and corporate polluters. Those on behalf of whom action is initiated are often characterized in "underdog" terms.

11. Conception of the Role of Intended Beneficiaries

Locality Development. Beneficiaries are viewed as active participants in an interactional process with one another and with the practitioner. Considerable stress is placed on group discussion in the community as the medium through which learning and growth take place. Beneficiaries engage in an intensive group process of exploring their felt needs, determining desired goals, and taking appropriate action.

Social Planning. Beneficiaries are clients, consumers, or recipients of services. They are active in using services, not in the determination of policy or goals.

Opportunities for members and consumers to determine policy are severely limited because they are not usually organized for this purpose . . . the opportunity to control policy is short-lived because the coalition will fall apart, lacking sufficient incentive to bind together the otherwise diverse constituent elements (Morris and Binstock, 1966, pp. 109–110).

Decisions, then, are made through the planner, often in collaboration with some community group—a board or commission, usually composed of business and professional elites, who are presumed to represent either the community-at-large or the best interests of those being served.

The data-driven policy specialist is likely to be looking over his or her back through this process, realizing that constituency interests and pressures could have an impact on policy enactment.

Social Action. The benefiting group is likely to be thought of as an employer of the practitioner or constituents. In unions the membership ideally runs the organization. The Industrial Areas Foundation will usually not enter a target area until the people there have gained a controlling and independent voice in the funding of the organization. The concept of the organizer as an employee and servant of the people is stressed. Kahn (1982) holds that the "staff director of the organization, if there is one, should be directly accountable to the board and should be held accountable by the board" (p. 70). Those not in key decision-making roles may participate more sporadically in mass action and pressure group activities, such as marches or boycotts.

12. Uses of Empowerment

Empowerment is a highly valued concept in contemporary thinking and parlance. However, in some ways it seems to be a buzzword that has to do more with creating a warm feeling than conveying a precise meaning. In the context of our discussion, each intervention approach values empowerment, but uses it in a different, sometimes contradictory, fashion.

Locality Development. Empowerment signifies the gaining of community competence—the skills to make decisions that people can agree on and enact together. It also implies the development of a sense of personal mastery within residents, as individual growth in people is considered a component of community building and a goal of practice.

Social Planning. With its reliance on facts and rationality, this approach tends to associate empowerment with information. Empowerment occurs when residents and consumers are asked to inform planners about their needs and preferences, so that they can be incorporated into plan design. Such information may be obtained through community surveys, including focus group techniques and public hearings, or through analysis of data from agency service records. Through this arrangement, consumers are afforded the right and means to have their views enter into the process by which decisions affecting them are made. Consumers are also empowered when information is provided to them about the various services that are available and particularities about these services, so they become equipped to make the best decisions about what programs and services to use. Information plays an important part in the other approaches also, but is given special emphasis in data-driven planning intervention.

Social Action. Empowerment means to acquire objective, material power—for residents to be an equal party in decision-making bodies such as agency boards or municipal commissions, or to have the political clout to directly affect decisions made by these bodies. Electoral campaigns are mounted to win seats on legislative units by representatives from the group, who will thereby have the authority to vote and engage in tangible trade-offs on the group's behalf. There is also attention to participants' personal sense of empowerment, because those individuals with a feeling of potency are more likely to lend themselves actively to the cause, and to contribute to the number count necessary for "people power" tactics of social action.

There is still another way that empowerment is viewed, emanating primarily from the conservative camp. Empowerment is equated with the elimination of governmental regulations and involvements, so that citizens presumably gain the freedom to conduct their lives without restraint. The popular slogan, "get the government off our backs," characterizes this way of looking at empowerment. It is reflected in the work of neoconservative planners and action groups on the radical right. Getting the government off the backs of some people at the same time removes protections and assistance given to other, disadvantaged, people and simultaneously disempowers them.

USES OF A MULTIMODAL APPROACH

This analysis puts us in a better position now to describe what an ideal-type intervention mode would look like. For an ideal-type mode to be in operation it has to include, in well-developed form, a large proportion of the variables attached to that mode in Table 1.1 (within its column), and to exclude all or nearly all of the components peculiar to any other mode. This is a tough and rare standard to reach in the emergent, disorderly arena of community affairs. Modal *tendencies* are a more realistic prospect.

Still, there are advantages to viewing intervention from the kind of multimodal perspective that has been presented. In the first place, it is important for practitioners who are grounded in a particular organizational situation to be aware of their moorings. This framework provides a means for assessing the strategic leanings in the practice context: What are the basic assumptions and preferred methods of action in the particular setting? In this way, the practitioner is more likely to perform appropriately, consistent with the expectations of supervisors, colleagues, participants, and other relevant actors.

Going beyond conformance to what exists, the practitioner may be in a position to create a form of action to deal with specific problems. Some rough rule-of-thumb guidelines can be posited. When populations are homogeneous or there is a willingness to exchange among various community subparts and interests, it would be useful to employ locality development. When problems are evident and agreed upon in the community and lend themselves to programmed solutions through the application of factual information, social planning/policy approaches would be a viable way to proceed. Finally, when subgroups are hostile and interests are not reconcilable through usual discussion and negotiation methods, it may be functional to engage in social action.

By assessing when one or another form of intervention is or is not appropriate, the practitioner takes an analytical, problem-solving stand and does not become the rigidified captive of a particular ideological or methodological approach to practice. Consequently, practitioners should be attuned to the differential utility of each approach, particularly to the tactics used in each, and should acquire the knowledge and skill that permit them to utilize these in disciplined and flexible fashion. We will be expanding on that theme in the next section.

This discussion has focused on a comparison of practice variables by following Table 1.1 horizontally across the community intervention approaches. For a feel of how each intervention mode would be implemented using its own set of variables interactively in combination, the table should be examined vertically, down the columns. This highlights the particularity and coalescence of each of the approaches, but it also encapsulates them synthetically. The next section demonstrates why that is so.

Before proceeding with the expanded treatment, it is useful to take a moment to clarify the domain of discourse and to

TABLE 1.1
Three Community Intervention Approaches According to Selected Practice Variables

	Mode A (Locality Development)	Mode B (Social Planning/Policy)	Mode C (Social Action)
1. Goal categories of community action	Community capacity and integration; self-help (process goals)	Problem solving with regard to substantive community problems (task goals)	Shifting of power relationships and resources; basic institutional change (task or process goals)
2. Assumptions concerning community structure and problem conditions	Community eclipsed, anomie; lack of relationships and democratic problem-solving capacities; static traditional community	Substantive social problems, mental and physical health, housing, recreation, etc.	Aggrieved populations, social injustice, deprivation, inequality
3. Basic change strategy	Involving a broad cross section of people in determining and solving their own problems	Gathering data about problems and making decisions on the most logical course of action	Crystallizing issues and mobilizing people to take action against enemy targets
4. Characteristic change tactics and techniques	Consensus: communication among community groups and interests; group discussion	Consensus or conflict	Conflict confrontation, direct action, negotiation
5. Salient practitioner roles	Enabler-catalyst, coordinator; teacher of problem-solving skills and ethical values	Fact gatherer and analyst, program implementer, expediter	Activist advocate: agitator, broker, negotiator, partisan
6. Medium of change	Guiding small, task-oriented groups	Guiding formal organizations and treating data	Guiding mass organizations and political processes
7. Orientation toward power structure(s)	Members of power structure as collaborators in a common venture	Power structure as employers and sponsors	Power structure as external target of action: oppressors to be coerced or overturned
8. Boundary definition of the beneficiary system	Total geographic community	Total community or community segment	Community segment
9. Assumptions regarding interests of community subparts	Common interests or reconcilable differences	Interests reconcilable or in conflict	Conflicting interests which are not easily reconcilable, scarce resources
10. Conception of beneficiaries	Citizens	Consumers	Victims
11. Conception of beneficiary role.	Participants in an interactional problem-solving process	Consumers or recipients	Employers, constituents, members

TABLE 1.1 (continued)
Three Community Intervention Approaches According to Selected Practice Variables

	Mode A (Locality Development)	Mode B (Social Planning/Policy)	Mode C (Social Action)
12. Use of empowerment	Building the capacity of a community to make collaborative and informed decisions; promoting feeling of personal mastery by residents	Finding out from consumers about their needs for service; informing consumers of their service choices	Achieving objective power for beneficiary system—the right and means to impact community decisions; promoting a feeling of mastery by participants

indicate what is excluded. Any analysis carves its area of inquiry out of the infinite possibilities in the empirical world. The domain in this instance is the community and, in particular, purposeful community change. This analysis is concerned with how such change is brought about by people at the community level, rather than through societal currents or federal policies. In other words, the community is examined as both the vehicle and the target of change.

Further, the analysis is concerned with the domain of strategy, the broad interventive initiatives employed to create change. These entail general strategic options available to anyone, but the discussion emphasizes actions taken by professional change agents—who may be identified with any professional field or discipline. However, because of the author's background, the discussion is tinged by social work and sociological language and perspectives.

There are other interesting and important areas of community intervention that do not fall within this domain, at least in terms of substantive coverage. Some of these include work with special populations (cultural or ethnic groups, and women), coalition building, interorganizational coordination, metropolitanization, and so forth. Nor does the analysis attempt to provide a ubiquitous theoretical framework for all of macro practice. Any of these areas, and others, are worthy of sustained theoretical development in their own right, and cumulatively will provide a rich, expanding intellectual and conceptual base to inform community intervention.

The approach taken is at the level of middle-range theory. It does not try to develop a grand theory formulation that is highly abstract and comprehensively encompassing. In keeping with a middle-range perspective, there is use of grounded theory, which involves the observing of real-world empirical patterns, identifying them, naming them, and constructing indicative cognitive categories to reflect them. Other approaches to theoretical development could have started more deductively, with concepts such as power structure or exchange theory, and built complex constructs concerning community intervention from these.

Obviously, it would not be realistic to expect middle-range theory to carry the burden of embracing all the dimensions of community intervention, and if it tried to accomplish that it would certainly become

FIGURE 1.1
Intervention Modes as Ideal-Types

FIGURE 1.2
Intervention Modes Shown Overlapping

unwieldy and incoherent. Conversely, hovering at the middle range, this construct does not provide the level of detail desired by some: how community developers should work with task groups, how planners should use data, how social actionists should organize demonstrations or form coalitions. These questions require exercising the art of application of the strategic initiatives, or developing specialized additional constructs.

THE INTERWEAVING OF INTERVENTION APPROACHES

This analysis has attempted to delineate rather distinct and coherent categories of community intervention practice. Alfred North Whitehead offered a rationale for this: "The aim of science is to seek the simplest explanations of complex facts." But while supporting the effort to harness complicated processes, he also alerted us to the underside. We may come to actually believe the original facts are simple because our quest was to arrive at a simplified con-

struction. The French social critic Raymond Aron once spoke of this as *delire logique*—logical delirium. Therefore, Whitehead went on to admonish: "Seek simplicity and distrust it." Following that dictum, we will now reexamine the previous discussion, bringing to it the eye of the skeptic.

Up until now we have treated each community intervention approach as though it were a rather self-contained ideal-type. That conceptualization is depicted visually in Figure 1.1. Actually, intervention approaches overlap and are used in mixed form in practice. Figure 1.2 reflects broadly the movement toward overlapping.

Practice in any mode may require tactics that are salient in another approach. For example, neighborhood social actionists interested in aiding the homeless may find it necessary to draw up a social plan in order to obtain funding for desired service projects from DHHS (Modes C and B). Or social planners may decide that the most effective way of establishing a viable low-income housing project is to engage potential residents in deciding on the geographic layout and common facilities, and to organize a tenant action council to fight drug pushers (Modes B, A, and C).

A more true-to-life depiction of the character of overlapping is in Figure 1.3. Here we see that the ideal-type modes have a limited scope of frequency and that mixtures of various kinds, along the lines just described, predominate.

To clarify the place of the three practice modes in the overall schema of community intervention, it would be useful to turn to the physical world and the phenomenon of color and its properties. We know that there are three basic colors—red, green, and blue. Scrutinizing the properties of these primary colors is valuable because when the properties are mixed they generate an enormous array of hues and shadings. A set of composite secondary colors is yielded when the primary colors are blended in equal proportions. Further mixtures among all of these result in an almost infinite melange of tones.

Realizing that the analogy is not exact, the three intervention modes can be compared to the three primary colors (but they can only roughly approximate perfect composition in the real world). The basic modes are represented by the outer spheres in Figure 1.3. We can visualize them spawning multiple practice combinations. When two combine, the results are composite bimodal interventions, depicted in the figure by the designations Development/Action, Planning/Development, and Action/Planning. These are analogous to secondary colors.

The center of Figure 1.3 depicts mixed interventions that include a cross-section of variables from all three modes. These combinations involving complex balances of variables are difficult to categorize or even visualize in any succinct fasion.

Just as the primary colors make up only

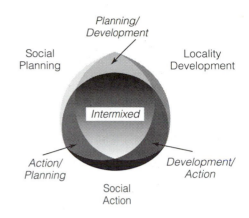

FIGURE 1.3
Overlapping Intervention Modes Showing Estimated Proportional Frequencies of Different Intervention Categories (modal, bimodal, and intermixed)

a very small proportion of the total universe of color, the basic intervention modes comprise only a fraction of the world of practice. Predominately, most practice situations probably entail three-fold mixtures. Bimodal composites, those situations consisting of relatively strong leanings toward two intervention approaches, are probably intermediate in frequency.

These are guesses or loose hypotheses about intricate intervention patterns, rather than verified conclusions. The entire schema is basically a heuristic device that is meant to aid conceptualization. The heuristics, however, have grounded empirical referents and are subject to testing through controlled social research.

COMPOSITE BIMODAL MIXTURES

It would be helpful to further illustrate the overall paradigm in Figure 1.3 and the mixing phenomenon through some examples of the three composite bimodal forms. Note

Locality
Development

Neighborhood
Block Clubs

Feminist/
Organizing

United Farm
Workers

Development/
Action

Social
Action

FIGURE 1.4
Variations Within the Development/Action Mode

that the composite forms are not uniform in character or coloration, as Figure 1.4 depicts. The mid-area in each composite section of the diagram represents an equally balanced mixing of practice variables from the basic modes, but as we move away from the mid-area, toward one or another of the basic modalities, variables from that mode increasingly predominate in the blend. Myriad mixtures are possible. We will discuss each of the bimodal composites in turn below.

Development/Action in balanced form is portrayed in feminist organizing and in the Freire style of grassroots work. Hyde (1989) indicates that feminist organizing comprises a combination of traits that are traditionally considered feminine with those that are often considered masculine. The feminine aspect includes humanistic qualities such as caring and nurturance, coupled with the use of democratic processes and structures (an emphasis on consensus, the rotating of tasks, and respecting and engaging the skills of all participants). These aspects are all associated with the locality development mode.

At the same time, the feminist organizing perspective is concerned with fundamental cultural and political change—the elimination of patriarchal society. Hyde indicates, "feminist practice is revolutionary . . . it provides a vision of a radically different society in which the oppressive means of power and privilege are eradicated" (p. 169). These tougher, more militant elements of the practice in the past often have been associated with a masculine posture and the social action intervention mode. Following Hyde's line of analysis, we can say that the feminist organizing perspective, to a considerable degree, is a balanced composite of practice variables involving assumptions and goals of social action joined with the methods of locality development. (See Figure 1.4 for the location of feminist organizing in the Development/Action composite.)

Pablo Freire's work involves a similar blend, in that he has endeavored through an educational approach to empower impoverished peasants in Brazil and Chile to act against the forces of their oppression. He visualizes "education as the practice of freedom," and through "conscientization" seeks, in a sympathetic and enabling manner, to assist illiterate people to see clearly and realistically their objective state of being (Freire, 1974). Fortified with this information, they presumably will gain the motivation and wherewithal to take the steps necessary to transform the closed, unjust societies that repress them. Again, we see the means of locality development wedded to the goals of social action.

The composites we have illustrated represent a somewhat equal mixing of practice variables from Development and Action. They are akin to what is represented by "pure" secondary colors. But the mix might also involve a disproportionate weighting of variables from one or other of the two

FIGURE 1.5
The Paradigm of Community Intervention
Showing Examples of Organizational Types for Each
Mode of Intervention and Mixed Forms

intervention modes. A composite leaning closer to locality development (see Figure 1.4) is found in Neighborhood Block Clubs. They promote socialization, sharing of information, neighborhood safety watches, mutual aid, and preservation of cherished neighborhood values and landmarks. The overall emphasis is on these Development features. However, when threatened by a porno movie house moving into the area, or the need for a traffic light to protect their children, the organization occasionally swings into a strong and even emotional ad hoc advocacy style.

On the other side of this dual composite stands an organization such as the United Farm Workers, as shown in Figure 1.4. Here the main thrust has been to raise the economic and social well-being of migrant farm workers, using a variety of advocacy measures, such as picketing, marches, and a sustained grape boycott. But there is also a less prominent or visible component that involves mutual aid and community-building among the membership, almost in the form of an extended intraethnic block club. Again, both modes coexist, but in different proportions from the typical block club on the other end of the spectrum.

The Action/Planning composite in balanced form is manifested in the various consumer protection programs of the Ralph Nader organization. This is shown in Figure 1.5, which depicts all the other illustrative organizations mentioned in this presentation. Figure 1.5 will serve as a useful reference guide through the remainder of the discussion. Advocacy in favor of consumer interests is a key thrust with Nader, including tactics that involve media exposure of corporate and governmental abuses, consumer boycotts, legislative campaigns, and the like. At the same time, there is heavy reliance on factual documentation through well-researched and sophisticated reports prepared by expert data analysts and policy specialists. There is also the dissemination of accurate empirical information to consumers so that they can make valid choices. The integration of Action and Planning methods is inseparable. Nader's Public Citizen organization carries out some grassroots programs—particularly on college campuses—which include a locality development component. But locality development is in pale hue, overall. Another prominent example of a close mix of Action and Planning/Policy is The Children's Defense Fund, a high-profile child advocacy organization that uses research data most effectively.

A different type of balanced example is found in municipal-level citizen housing councils. While advocating for more and better housing, consistent with community welfare, these councils have to be prepared to engage in sophisticated interorganizational coordination and negotiation, and to bring to bear the tools and procedures of urban planning professionals, whose analyses and recommendations from within the planning bureaucracy they need to be able to convincingly counter or modify.

Action/Planning with an accent on social action is embodied in organizations on the left that draw up well-formulated policy blueprints for fundamental tax reform, massive low-income housing, and widespread single-payer health services provided under governmental auspices. The groups are essentially geared to social change, but they incorporate data-based reports and policy analyses into their work. The Institute for Democratic Socialism, a "think tank" of the Democratic Socialists of America, is an example. Similar in nature, but pointing to change in another direction (dismantling the welfare state, as an example), are a number of ideologically conservative institutes (the Hoover, for example), commissions, and foundations.

Another example is the area of "advocacy planning" (Davidoff, 1965), whereby grassroots organizations dedicated to change (or blocking intrusive projects) hire a planner or receive pro bono services from a professional, in order to design proposals that can be used with governmental bureaus of planning officials in support of given aims or positions. These planners may serve for only a limited time period or for only one of the many issues being advocated by the organization.

Shifting emphasis toward the planning dimension, Friedmann (1987) suggests a role involving a planner/policy analyst firmly ensconced within a governmental structure, where the professional essentially carries out technical planning functions, but with social reform in mind. Friedmann notes the role of Rexford Tugwell in Roosevelt's New Deal administration as an example. Robert Moses, in his role during the LaGuardia mayoralty in New York City, would be another. The Koerner Commission functioned similarly, transforming an investigation of urban civil unrest from a focus on social control to issues of equal opportunity. The practitioner's position, methods, and tone are fixed within a governmental bureaucracy, but there is a social advocacy dimension. Friedmann conceives of this government-sponsored planned reform as a distinct fourth intervention mode, in addition to the three we have discussed.

Planning/Development mixtures have a different patterning. The United Way, a convenient balanced example, is dedicated to systematic welfare decision making on the community level with regard to fundraising, budgeting, fund allocation, and coordination of services. However, it places a great deal of stress on citizen participation in these processes. Planning *and* volunteerism are the traditional hallmarks of the organization. Planning for the annual campaign and distributing financial resources to agencies are ongoing activities. But a considerable amount of energy is applied to recruiting community participants (who are most often business and professional elites), training leaders, giving workshops, and holding meetings and conferences of various kinds. Planning and Development are intimately intertwined.

Enterprise/empowerment zones also closely blend these modes of intervention, but in a different way. Their aim is to promote community building in inner cities through enhancing the capacity of minority residents to perform in economic and social realms, particularly by starting and running their own businesses. Local initiative and self-reliance are watchwords. But these programs also involve heavy inputs from the outside by corporate and government experts, and the design of elaborate processes to steer a process that is complex and quite technical in nature.

A composite that is weighted toward the planning side is found in citizen advisory committees that are established in the health field by departments of health, community hospitals, and hospital planning councils. These committees have an adjunct role in supporting the basic planning function, which often has a strong technical component. The committees do not ordinarily impact on policy, although they may play some part in policy implementation.

They serve to provide legitimation in the community for decisions of planners and administrators; they also have a public relations element. For this reason, energy is applied by the organization to recruiting members, orienting them, and maintaining their bonds. This locality development component is, generally speaking, token rather than substantive in character.

On the other side of the spectrum, an organization such as the National Center for Neighborhood Enterprise is committed to furthering local initiative in urban neighborhoods, as well as seeking to empower poor and minority communities through self-help (while discouraging the means of political insurgency). The Center reflects the work and views of Robert L. Woodson, Sr., who is perhaps the chief organizer of locality development endeavors within African-American communities. In pursuing its goals, the Center actively compiles relevant data and employs the techniques of policy analysts and social planners. These, however, are subsidiary to and in support of the main development thrust.

Taking a different analytical stance now, the character of composite mixes result from the particular configuration of practice variables from each intervention mode. The exact coloration can be influenced by the sheer *number* or volume of variables from either mode of the *types* of variables from each (goals, assumptions, roles, tactics). The *potency* of different types of variables also may have an effect. For example, in feminist organizing, the goal of fundamentally changing gender roles in society is in ascendancy, sometimes dominating the question of tactics (as indicated by existing tactical variations between the position stated by Hyde and that of the radical lesbian movement).

Trimodal mixtures are even more varied than what we have already discussed. An example should suffice to illustrate the general notion. Community welfare planning councils bring social agencies together to share ideas and information, and to strengthen their bonds, in order to become a more successful and integrated service delivery system. The councils also hammer out specific plans and policy frames, in conjunction with the agencies, that are geared to providing more effective and efficient services to community residents. In addition, these organizations actively engage in advocacy, lobbying the city council and the state legislature for more funds and better mandates to meet client needs and expedite agency operations. Chambers of commerce use the same set of intermingled actions on behalf of the business community.

Illustrating intervention mixtures, with all their gradations, can go on endlessly. Examples given here should suffice to demonstrate the basic concept, to generate useful efforts by others, and to fuel critiques of the general formulation.

DILEMMAS IN EACH INTERVENTION MODE

There are other ways of analyzing the blending of forms of intervention. For each intervention mode we will frame a key issue that confounds the original modal formulation and has implications for expanding and mixing the intervention modes. The dilemmas we will pose spring in part from deliberately positing constructs in ideal or synthetic form, but they arise also from the complex, contentious, constraining, and obdurate social environment in which change agents currently find themselves. In response, practitioners have designed strategies that are more variagated, subtle, flexible, and inventive—and less one-dimensional—than in an earlier time.

Locality Development—External Linkages

We have seen that locality development places heavy emphasis on a self-contained local community context. This circumscribed, while holistic, community system is the arena in which features of grassroots initiative, self-help, intimate relationships, and enhanced competency are played out.

A dilemma is that often locality development programs are sponsored and funded by outside entities: municipal (city department of community development); national (The National Service Corps, Campaign for Human Development of the United States Catholic Conference); or international (The World Bank, The World Health Organization). This poses a threat to the conceptual integrity of the formulation. Jacobsen (1990) observes that "much of the initiative for community development actually originates from outside the community, which is a clear violation of the principles of community development" (p. 395).

Vertically linked organizations provide planning and administrative inputs that are hierarchical in nature. They chose the main goals to be pursued, recruit and select the staff, train them, set the program emphasis, and establish the rules of practice engagement. These planning elements are vividly portrayed in a description of how the New Zealand central government shifted away from a welfare services policy and designed a local community development approach for the native Maori population (Fleras, 1984, see pp. 275–282 of this volume).

Local groups are also often linked horizontally at the city or regional level with other similar local groups. Thus, a block club can affiliate with a council of neighborhood block clubs, or a neighborhood

Local and Community-Bounded	Horizontally Linked	Vertically Linked
Neighborhood Councils Block Clubs Self-Help Projects	Local Block Groups Affiliated with Regional Councils of Block Clubs Coalitions of Local Neighborhood Councils Information Clearing Houses	Peace Corps Projects Church-Sponsored Overseas Development Projects (American Friends Service Committee) United Nations Community Development Projects (World Health Organizations) National Service Corps

FIGURE 1.6
Locality Development Intervention Showing Community-Bounded and Externally Linked Structural Forms
(original construct in shaded area)

citizens association can become part of a citywide council of citizen groups or an interfaith umbrella organization of congregations. Here the coordination and information-sharing aspects of planning play a part, although elements of social action coalition-building may also be involved.

These relationships and entanglements contradict the self-enclosed quality of the original modal formulation. The broader formulation of locality development is shown in Figure 1.6, with the shaded area delineating the original construct.

Social Planning/Policy—Participation

A dilemma in the original social planning concept is that even highly technical planning and policy development that is data-driven and expertise-based often includes elements of participation, in various forms and to varying degrees. The survey by Checkoway (1984) of extant planning endeavors, shown on pages 314–327 of this volume, describes a pattern of extensive

citizen participation in planning endeavors of municipal departments and of private neighborhood planning organizations. This injects an important element of the locality development approach into the picture.

Political analyst Joel Kropkin observed, in the early Riordan mayoralty in Los Angeles, that there was a danger the new civic leader would lean too heavily on his previous corporate experience in his effort to reorganize city government operations and services. In industry, Riordan was able to use soundly conceived technical plans "for brokering deals between well-defined and somewhat logical, shareholders and other constituencies." Planning in a community context is different—more fluid and political—says Kropkin, with no evidence that "once a rational plan is developed, support for it will naturally follow." Instead, he maintains, it is essential that interests of various kinds be drawn into participation in this process, including municipal unions, churches, grassroots groups, city council members, and others (Kropkin, 1993, pp. 1, 6).

Concentrated Decision Making	Dispersed Decision Making			
	Substantive Participation in Decisions		Ancillary Participation in Decisions	
	Policy	Implementation	Facilitative	Symbolic
City and County Departments of Health, Housing, Social Services Boards of Voluntary Social Agencies—Family Service, Citizens' Planning, and Housing Councils	United Way Regional Planning Boards Free Clinics OEO projects—"Maximum Feasible Participation"	Local Branches of National Service or Planning Organizations—NAACP, Cancer Society Federal Program Implementation in the States—Title XX	Regional Meetings on Zoning Changes in City Planning Locally Conducted Congressional Hearings	Planners for Neighborhood Halfway Houses Real Estate Developers of Shopping Malls and Housing Complexes, Environmental Impact Reports

FIGURE 1.7
Social Planning Intervention Showing Concerted Decision Making and Dispersed
Decision Making Involving Various Forms and Degrees of Community Participation
(original construct in shaded area)

A reformulation of planning that includes the participation dimension is in Figure 1.7. We observe that decision making, as proposed in the original modal formulation, is sometimes concerted—in the hands of a small group of elite leaders and professional experts (see the shaded area of the Figure). Often city departments of child welfare, mental health, housing, and health operate in this way, as do the boards of private agencies like family service organizations, Jewish federations, and boys' clubs.

But planning can entail dispersed decision making, where other than elites alone take part in making judgments and choices. This broader form can involve both *substantive* participation in decision making, and *ancillary*, more peripheral involvement.

First, let us consider substantive activity. Residents and citizens can join in *policy decisions* of a basic nature, or they take part in *implementation decisions* that relate to carrying out programs that grow out of policy decisions by others. The OEO "War on Poverty" spawned a multitude of grassroots organizations where "maximum feasible participation" at the highest policy-making levels was emphasized. Free clinics providing health services to low-income ill people have traditionally encouraged such participation. The United Way's Regional Planning Councils attempt to involve local residents in allocation and program decisions affecting the area.

Substantive implementation decisions, within established policy parameters, are frequently given over to members of local branches of national organizations, such as the American Cancer Society, The Urban League, League of Women Voters, and so forth. Federal legislation, such as Title XX, has often left discretion for implementation in the hands of the states, counties, or municipalities.

Second, ancillary participation can be *facilitative* or *symbolic*. The facilitative form draws residents into the decision-making process by seeking their reactions to proposals, or asking for their advice. It may also entail providing information about impending changes in order to prepare people for them, thereby reducing stress or disruption in their lives. Regional meetings called by city planning departments to announce zoning changes or to ask people for their opinions about these changes are an example. Local hearings conducted by Congress or a city council are another, as are hearings related to environmental impact studies.

Symbolic participation serves to provide the appearance or aura of participation, but not its actuality. The aim is cooptation, whereby the opposition is won over or "cooled out." Real estate developers and housing officials often use this approach in trying to influence residents to accept a new project, as do social planners who attempt to establish group living "halfway houses" in urban neighborhoods for the mentally ill, delinquent adolescents, the homeless, and other vulnerable groups.

There is a tendency among human service professionals to instinctively reject the use of symbolic forms of participation, particularly when these are applied to them and their clients. There are, of course, vital ethical objections to the deceptive quality of this tactic but the question is intellectually complex.

Brager, Specht and Torczyner (1987) address this issue in a penetrating discussion, taking the view that "manipulation is an unavoidable component of professional behavior" and that "political maneuvering" is inevitable in community intervention (p. 321). In seeking to advance the interests and well-being of those we seek to benefit, when facing inhospitable or potentially

damaging actions by others, the practitioner is obligated to "employ artfulness in inducing desired attitudinal or behavioral outcome in others" (p. 317). The foes of our allies and constituents use powerful tools of accepted political in-fighting that challenge our capability to provide protection and nurturance. Brager and his associates recognize the importance and delicacy of this issue, and they delineate a set of factors to be weighed carefully in arriving at ethically sound conclusions about tactics. At the same time, they resist discarding the "planned ambiguity" tactic of symbolic participation, which, if it occurred, might mean abandoning to the winds of political fortune in pluralistic American communities the possibility of establishing group homes for the homeless and the mentally ill.

Social Action—Multiple Actors and Conventional Tactics

Social action is more complicated than the original model conveyed, as reflected in studies that found it to have complex qualities. For example, Cnaan and Rothman (1986) in a factor analysis inquiry discovered that planning and development can be explained through a single, consistent factor. However, social action comprised two or more factors, which were difficult to identify with clarity.

There are three dimensions that probably account for this complexity (see Figure 1.8). The original formulation did not take into account, and did not differentiate, the two essentially different types of goals of this intervention mode. These include radical change goals that aim at fundamental alterations in society or at specific policies or institutions within it, and more normative or reformist change goals that aim at incremental alterations. This is a basic

		GOALS	
		Radical Fundamental	Normative Incremental
Radical Disruptive Tactics	Disadvantaged Parties Mainly	American Indian Movement (AIM) ACT-UP	Industrial Areas Foundation Tenant Action Organizations
	Multiple Parties	Greenpeace The 60s Student and Anti-War Movements (SDS)	Ad Hoc Protests by Alliance for the Mentally Ill Animal Rights Groups
Normative Conventional Tactics	Disadvantaged Parties Mainly	Nation of Islam Center for Third World Organizing	La Raza American Association of Retired Persons
	Multiple Parties	Democratic Socialists of America Women's International League for Peace and Freedom	Childrens' Defense Fund Coalition for the Homeless

MEANS (row label at left)

FIGURE 1.8
Social Action Intervention Divided by Type of Goal and Further
Differentiated by Tactical Means and the Composition of the Action Constituency
(original construct in shaded area)

context within which social action needs to be understood.

It is difficult to delineate precisely the division between radical and normative goal changes in social action. Radical change suggests breadth of alteration in the society and culture. Examples of this thrust include organizations that militate to eradicate racism or to transform the relationship between the races (as with the Nation of Islam), or to change the basic economic system of the country (as with the Democratic Socialists of America). However, a change that on the surface seems modest can have a broad impact. As an example, changing regulations about what can appear on TV, or the tone of presentation, can have a rippling effect throughout the entire culture because of the widespread influence of the media.

In addition, fundamental change can be narrow and deep rather than wide in scope. The aim may be to alter a specific law or specific sphere of living in a radical way. As an example, the Pro-Life movement focuses on the single issue of abortion legislation, but is interested in drastically overturning existing legal arrangements rather than adjusting or tampering with them. Because of the saliency of the issue, the change being advocated would be seen by many as fundamental, and a deep threat.

Alternatively, radical change can be accomplished through a particular combination of breadth and depth that in aggregate goes beyond incrementalism. The precise calculus of this combination is elusive, but the possibility of it occurring seems plausible.

In any case, it is difficult to establish a firm dividing line between fundamental and incremental change, partly because incremental change is sometimes carried out as a strategic step leading to fundamental change. The extremes of each are easy enough to discern (the Communist Party as compared to the League of Women Voters); it is pinpointing the middle border that separates the two tendencies that is vexing.

Two other dimensions beside goal categories suggest revisions rather than additions to the original formulation. One of these concerns the constituency action system for the change effort. Going back to the sixties, social action movements focused on the disadvantaged or aggrieved group only as the vehicle of social change, as with the Black Panthers, AIM (American Indian Movement), La Raza, gay and lesbian groups and others, playing out the politics of identity. Going it alone was a way of ensuring that the fundamental interests of the group were safeguarded, that outsiders who might take over were contained, and group self-empowerment was promoted. This was the outlook incorporated within the original modal formulation.

Contemporary "new movement" organizing is seeking to become broader, more ecumenical. Fisher and Kling (1991) speak in support of "a more consciously ideological politics. New formations and groupings will only make community mobilization stronger . . . an explicitly challenging ideology is necessary if community movements are not to remain bound by the limits of personalized and localized consciousness" (p. 81). Advocacy groups across class and ethnic lines are forming, focused on environmental protection, crime prevention, neighborhood preservation, animal rights, and health issues. These new groupings and alliances involve community-building methods for achieving cohesion and continuity. Not only are the economically oppressed organizing to act on their own behalf, but, in addition, middle-class aggrieved persons, including right-wing activists and the Ross Perot movement, are involved in victim rights, tax reduction, Pro-Life, government reorganization, and school reform efforts. The expanded constituencies include linkages and coalitions by grassroots groups that are national in scope (see Flacks, pp. 368–380).

The additional dimension is tactical in nature. Action groups have been characterized by their reliance on aggressive and abrasive advocacy measures, which was reflected in the original formulation. More recently, tactics have been refined and diversified. They are more normative in quality, utilizing conventional political maneuvers.

Many community organizers today cite a trend toward pragmatism that emphasizes electoral politics, consensus building, data collection and research, and the use of political and administrative channels. Confrontational tactics, while sometimes required, are considered ineffective in many cases. Although sit-in and demonstrations have succeeded in creating awareness of problems, administrators and officials also have learned how to defuse them (Hiratsuka, 1990, p. 3).

These new social action elements suggest the inclusion of practice variables from the other intervention modes. For example, conventional advocacy methods, such as factual documentation of environmental despoilment, include data-based techniques from planning and policy practice. Community-building within and among different advocacy constituencies brings to bear locality development practice.

These elements of social action are tied together and systematized in Figure 1.8. The top two shaded cells encompass the original intervention mode, and the additional six are expanded representations of the advocacy strategy. Each cell incorporates a different form of the admixture of: type of goal (radical/normative), type of advocacy (radical/normative), and type of constituency action system (disadvantaged parties mainly/multiple parties). Examples are provided for each of these social action amalgams. The information is essentially self-evident and does not require extended explication.

PHASING, VALUES, AND PRACTICE OPTIONS

The broad approaches, and sets of practice variables within them, offer a range of interrelated possibilities for designing intervention strategies. The point has been stated by Gurin (1966) as follows:

Our field studies have produced voluminous evidence that (various) roles are needed, but not always at the same time and place. The challenging problem, on which we have made a bare beginning, is to define more clearly the specific conditions under which one or another or still other types of practice are appropriate. The skill we shall need in the practitioner of the future is the skill of making a situational diagnosis and analysis that will lead him to a proper choice of the methods most appropriate to the task at hand (p. 30).

In addition to mixing approaches as discussed, there is a phasing relationship among them. A given change project may begin in one mode and then, at a later stage, move into another. For example, as a social action organization achieves success and attains resources, it may find that it can function most efficiently out of a social planning mode. The labor union movement, to a degree, demonstrates this type of phasing. As organizational growth and viability are achieved, headquarters operations (for example, the teamsters or UAW) become larger, more bureaucratized, and more technical, and social policy and administrative factors become more salient. The practitioner needs to be attuned to appropriate transition points in applying alternative modes.

As practitioners phase through their own careers, there will be demands to emphasize one or another modality. Historically, circumstances and preferences change, resulting in shifts in professional fashion and the employment requisites of agencies. For this reason, it is useful for practitioners to be broadly prepared, with the full range of competencies tucked into their professional portfolio.

Locality development was in vogue in the quiescent 1950s, when interactive, enabling practice was considered the quintessence of professionalism (Pray, 1947; Newstetter, 1947). Planning/policy was important during the Charity Organization Society and Community Chest and Council movements of the 1920s, as an aspect of emergent social work institution building. This mode came to the fore again during the New Deal spurt of policy development and program organization intended to cope with the Great Depression. It was called upon again in the Nixon and Reagan-Bush times of policy reversal and program curtailment, where efforts to promote efficiency, scrupulous evaluation, and cost containment were given prominence.

Social action had its heyday during the roiling 1960s, and also in the early years of the century when progressives were advocating for legislation on child labor, workmans' compensation, and housing and municipal reform. Cycles in the relative rise and fall of different intervention modes will doubtless continue in the periods ahead.

In the past, professional actions and conceptualizations were often constrained by particular value orientations to practice—for example, acceptance of only collaborative, nondirective practice (Pray, 1947). Alinsky followers derided all others as "sell-outs," while planners were often disdainful of militants for fomenting disorder and antagonism. The current outlook, however, is more accepting of varying value orientations. An examination of empirical findings on professional values leads to the conclusion that "human service professions do not appear to be highly integrated with regard to the existence of a delimited, uniformly accepted value system" (Rothman, 1974, p. 100). The approaches suggested in this presentation are in the spirit of such a position.

The locality development practitioner will likely cherish values that emphasize harmony and communication in human affairs; the planner/policy specialist will give priority to rationality; the social actionist will build on commitments embracing social justice. Each of these value orientations finds justification in the traditions of the human service professions. It would be difficult to claim monopoly status for any one or other. Indeed, contemporary thinking suggests that values are plural and conflicting, and may well come in pairs of divergent commitments (Tropman, 1984). Mixing occurs on those frequent occasions when more than one value is being pursued at a given time.

The various intervention approaches can all be applied in a way to pursue values conducive to positive social change and human betterment. Our position accepts the validity of each of the stated value postures and encourages their interrelated employment.

Values aside, the intervention modes have to draw from one another because of the inherent functional limitations within each. Planning and policy initiatives have created worthy programs, particularly when pushed by the other two modes, but have accomplished little in redistributing wealth and power or in preventing the victimization of the have-nots. They have typically concealed the vested interests of the professionals and failed to address the widespread alienation of society. Locality development has had its successes in countering isolation and depersonalization in specific places, but not in removing the social conditions that continue to generate anomie and inequality. Social action has confronted power and economic inequities in some measure at the local level, but has not had sufficient potency to cope with larger national power issues or to shape a strategy to rehumanize those it cannot defeat. Each modality alone faces obstacles that the others can contribute to addressing.

Another reason for seeking new configurations of action is that, at the highest societal levels, established institutions and modes of operating are showing grave defects. Eastern European communism, with its outrageous tyrannies and rigidities, has collapsed from within and left a widespread landscape of upheaval and turmoil. But the Western market–dominated countries, who are now the only game in town, are saddled with the cruel by-products of an acquisitive ethic, and they display persistent pathologies of economic and social disparity, industrial decay, recurring joblessness, cultural decline, racism, and anomie—to use the short list.

New social forms are called for that combine the liberal ideal of political democracy and the socialist ideal of economic democracy, ensuring a balance of liberty and equality in both spheres. Barbara Ehrenreich (1993) has stated the challenge aptly:

We must outline how we believe that the community of human beings can live together more equitably and peacefully than it does now. *The vision has to be a vision beyond capitalism, with its inevitable economic injustice. This is a time when people looking for change don't have some kind of precise model to inform that struggle for change.* Everyone has some responsibility to start imagining, dreaming, inventing and visualizing the kind of future we would like.

This discussion prompts us to look back at Table 1.1, the listing of practice variables across intervention modes, and read it in a different light now. The table, in aggregate, provides a repertoire of practice options, for flexible application. Each of the thirty-six cells describes an analytical or behavioral intervention initiative. (This is not a complete enumeration of the possibilities by any means, but it is a suggestive one.) The practice options, when used critically and selectively, can provide vital components to interweave creatively into the design of strategy.

This moves us toward a contingency formulation where practitioners of any stripe have greater range in selecting, then mixing and phasing, components of intervention. An important next step is to identify a set of situational criteria to inform such tactical packaging. A number of social parameters of the situation readily come to mind, among them the type of change goal and its scope, the quality of constituency leadership, availability of knowledge regarding relevant problems and solutions,

the extent and character of resistance, the degree of financial and other resource support at hand, and stage of development of the action system.

There is a need for research concerning which situational criteria, or clusters among them, are most critical for strategy development. Beyond that, it would be useful to study how these criteria specifically inform the selection and meshing of practice options from the repertoire of intervention components, in the interests of designing change strategies with greater impact.

In summary, the goal of this piece has been to lay open and chart a multifaceted change process that plays a large role in inducing the progressive development of society. Historically, what humans have been able to capture cognitively, they often have been able to master behaviorally—which is a reason for persisting in the endeavor. However, there are no panaceas inherent in this text. The world is an unpredictable place, and humans have struggled through time to gain greater control over and better their social environs. One can only believe and hope that a sound, informed analysis coupled with disciplined action will provide some increment of probability beyond intuitive strivings. Through systematic evaluation and other research we can hone our techniques and monitor our results, thereby learning cumulatively from experience and improving our record.

Such efforts are analogous to the realm of interpersonal helping in psychotherapy. It is assumed that use of theory and tested practice will improve on the natural advice and support that neighbors and family provide to one another. Still, despite the best efforts of dedicated therapists some clients remain mired in despair and confusion. Those of us in the human services hold the limited aspiration that, to some unknown degree, what we do will enhance the probability that beneficial results will come to pass.

The sharpening of change methods is an endless and evolving process. The mental skirmishing involved in this revision of an earlier construct is captured in T. S. Eliot's wise and edifying words:

> We shall not cease from exploration.
> And the end of all our exploring will
> be to arrive where we started and know
> the place for the first time.

From that ground, naturally, the exploration begins anew.

BIBLIOGRAPHY

Alinsky, Saul D. "Citizen Participation and Community Organization in Planning and Urban Renewal," p. 7. Chicago: Industrial Areas Foundation, 1962.

Alinsky, Saul D. *Reveille for Radicals.* Chicago: University of Chicago Press, 1946.

Alinsky, Saul D. *Rules for Radicals.* Chicago: University of Chicago Press, 1972.

Anzalone, Joan, ed. *Good Works: A Guide to Careers in Social Change,* 3d ed. New York: Dembner Books, 1985.

Betten, Neil, & Michael J. Austin. *The Roots of Community Organizing, 1917–1939.* Philadelphia: Temple University Press, 1990.

Biddle, William W., & J. Loureide. *The Community Development Process: The Rediscovery of Local Initiative.* New York: Holt, Rinehart & Winston, 1965.

Bingham, R. D., & R. Mier. *Theories of Local Economic Development.* Thousand Oaks, CA: Sage Publications, 1993.

Blakely, Edward J. "Toward a Science of Community Development." In Edward J. Blakely, ed. *Community Development Research: Concepts, Issues and Strategies,* pp. 15–23. New York: Human Sciences Press, 1979.

Bobo, Kim, Jackie Kendall, & Steve Max. *Organizing for Social Change: A Manual for Activists in the 1990s.* Washington, DC: Seven Locks Press, 1991.

Boyte, H., & F. Riessman. *The New Populism.* Philadelphia: Temple University Press, 1986.

Brager, George, Harry Specht, & James L. Torczyner. *Community Organizing,* 2d ed. New York: Columbia University Press, 1987.

Burghardt, S. "Community-Based Social Action." In *Encyclopedia of Social Work,* 18th ed. NASW, 1987.

Burghardt, S. *Organizing for Community Action.* Beverly Hills, CA: Sage Publications, 1982.

Chavis, D. M., P. Florin, & M. R. J. Felix. "Nurturing Grassroots Initiatives for Community Development: The Role of Enabling Systems." In T. Mizrahi and J. Morrison, eds. *Community Organization and Social Administration: Advances, Trends and Emerging Principles,* pp. 41–67. New York: Haworth, 1993.

Cloward, Richard, & Frances Piven. *Poor People's Movements.* New York: Pantheon, 1977.

Cnaan, R. A. "Neighborhood Representing Organizations: How Democratic Are They?" *Social Service Review,* 65 (1991): 614–34.

Cnaan, R. A., & J. Rothman. Conceptualizing Community Intervention: An Empirical Test of "Three Models" of Community Organization. *Administration in Social Work, 10*(3) (1986): 41–55.

Davidoff, P. "Advocacy and Pluralism in Planning." *Journal of the American Institute of Planners, 31*(4) (1965): 331–37.

Delgado, D. *Organizing the Movement: The Roots and Growth of ACORN.* Philadelphia: Temple University Press, 1986.

Dunham, Arthur. "Some Principles of Community Development." *International Review of Community Development,* No. 11 (1963): 141–51.

Ehrenreich, B. From a letter to the membership of Democratic Socialists of America, dated December 1, 1993, New York.

Fisher, R. *Let the People Decide: Neighborhood Organizing in America,* rev. ed. Boston: Twayne, 1994.

Fisher, R., & J. Kling. "Popular Mobilization in the 1990s: Prospects for the New Social Movements." *New Politics* 3 (1991): 71–84.

Flynn, J. *Social Agency Policy: Analysis and Presentation for Community Practice.* Chicago: Nelson Hall, 1985.

Freire, Paolo. *Education: The Practice of Freedom.* London: Writers and Readers Publishing Cooperative, 1974.

Friedmann, John. *Planning in the Public Domain: From Knowledge to Action.* Princeton, NJ: Princeton University Press, 1987.

Gellman, Barton. *Contending with Kennan: Toward a Philosophy of American Power.* New York: Praeger, 1984.

Gil, David. *Unraveling Social Policy.* Cambridge, MA: Schenkman, 1976.

Gilbert, Neil, & Harry Specht. *Dimensions of Social Welfare Policy.* Englewood Cliffs, NJ: Prentice-Hall, 1974.

Gilbert, Neil, & Harry Specht. *Dynamics of Community Planning.* Cambridge, MA: Ballinger, 1977.

Gilbert, Neil, & Harry Specht. "Process Versus Task in Social Planning." *Social Work,* XXII (3) (1977): 178–83.

Goetz, E. G., & S. E. Clarke. *Comparative Urban Politics in a Global Era.* Thousand Oaks, CA: Sage Publications, 1993.

Gurin, Arnold. (1966) "Current Issues in Community Organization Practice and Education," Brandeis University Reprint Series, No. 21, p. 30. Florence Heller Graduate School for Advanced Studies in Social Welfare.

Halseth, Judith H. "Infusing a Feminist Analysis into Education for Policy, Planning, and Administration." In T. Mizrahi, & John Morrison, eds. *Community Organization and Social Administration: Advances, Trends and Emerging Principles.* New York: The Haworth Press, 1993.

Henderson, Paul, & David N. Thomas. *Skills in Neighborhood Work.* London: Allen & Unwin, 1987.

Hiratsuka, Jon. "Community Organization: Assembling Power." NASW News (September, 1990): 3.

Hyde, Cheryl. "A Feminist Model for Macro-Practice: Promises and Problems." In Yeheskel Hasenfeld, ed. *Administrative Leadership in the Social Services: The Next Challenge,* pp. 145–181. New York: The Haworth Press, 1989.

Jacobsen, Michael. "Working with Communities." In H. Wayne Johnson, *The Social Services: An Introduction,* 3d ed., pp. 385–403. Itasca, IL: F. E. Peacock, 1990.

Jansson, B. *Theory and Practice of Social Welfare Policy: Analysis, Processes and Current Issues.* Belmont, CA: Wadsworth, 1984.

Johnson, Marilyn S. *Development of an Action Research Proposal: An Analysis of Practice.* Master of Social Work Thesis. Calgary, Alberta: School of Social Welfare, 1974.

Jones, Wyatt C., & Armand Lauffer. "Implications of the Community Organization Curriculum Project for Practice and Education." Professional Symposium of NASW, National Conference on Social Welfare, 1968.

Kahn, Alfred J. *Theory and Practice of Social Planning.* New York: Russell Sage, 1969.

Kahn, S. *Organizing.* New York: McGraw-Hill, 1982.

Kahn, S. *Organizing: A Guide for Grassroots Leaders.* Silver Spring, MD: National Association of Social Workers, 1992.

Kropkin, Joel. "Riordan's Next Challenge: Become the Political Man." *Los Angeles Times,* December 19, 1993, pp. M1 and M6.

Lappin, Ben. "Community Development: Beginnings in Social Work Enabling." In Samuel H. Taylor & Robert W. Roberts, eds., *Theory and Practice of Community Social Work,* pp. 59–94. New York: Columbia University Press, 1985.

Lauffer, A. "The Practice of Social Planning." In Neil Gilbert & Harry Specht, eds., *Handbook of the Social Services,* pp. 588–97. Englewood Cliffs, NJ: Prentice Hall, 1981.

Lyon, Larry. *The Community in Urban Society.* Philadelphia; Temple University Press, 1987.

Mayer, N. *Neighborhood Organization and Community Development.* Washington, DC: Urban Institute, 1984.

Mier, R. *Social Justice and Local Development Policy.* Thousand Oaks, CA: Sage Publications, 1993.

Moroney, Robert M. *Social Policy and Social Work: Critical Essays on the Welfare State.* New York: Aldine de Gruyter, 1991.

Morris, Robert, & Robert H. Binstock. *Feasible Planning for Social Change.* New York: Columbia University Press, 1966.

Newstetter, Wilber I. "The Social Intergroup Work Process," Proceedings, National Conference of Social Work, pp. 205–17. New York: Columbia University Press, 1947.

Peters, T. J., & R. H. Waterman. *In Search of Excellence.* New York: Harper & Row, 1982.

Pierce, D. *Policy for the Social Work Practitioner.* New York: Longman, 1984.

Pray, K. L. M. "When Is Community Organization Social Work Practice?" *Proceedings, National Conference of Social Work.* New York: Columbia University Press, 1947.

Pressman, J., & A. Wildavsky. *Implementation.* Berkeley, CA: University of California Press, 1984.

Rein, Martin. "Strategies of Planned Change." American Orthopsychiatric Association, 1965.

Ross, Murray G. *Community Organization: Theory and Principles,* pp. 80–83. New York: Harper and Brothers, 1955.

Rothman, Jack. "An Analysis of Goals and Roles in Community Organization Practice." *Social Work* IX (2) (1964): 24–31.

Rothman, Jack. *Planning and Organizing for Social Change: Action Principles from Social Science Research,* p. 100. New York: Columbia University Press, 1974.

Selznick, Philip. *The Moral Commonwealth: Social Theory and the Promise of Community.* Berkeley, CA: University of California Press, 1992.

Taylor, Samuel H., & Robert W. Roberts, eds. *Theory and Practice of Community Social Work.* New York: Columbia University Press, 1985.

Tropman, John E. *Policy Management in the Human Services.* New York: Columbia University Press, 1984.

Tropman, John E. "Value Conflict in Decision-Making." In F. M. Cox et al. *Tactics and Techniques of Community Practice,* 2d ed. Itasca, IL: F. E. Peacock, 1984.

Tropman, John E. "Policy Analysis: Methods and Techniques." In Anne Minahan, ed. *Encyclopedia of Social Work,* 18th ed., pp. 268–83. Silver Spring, MD: National Association of Social Workers, 1987.

United Nations. *Social Progress Through Community Development,* p. 6. New York; United Nations, 1955.

Warren, Roland L. *The Community in America,* rev. ed. Chicago: Rand McNally, 1972.

Webber, M. M., and H. W. J. Rittel. "Dilemmas in a General Theory of Planning." *Policy Sciences* 4 (2) (1973): 155–69.

Weil, Marie. "Editor's Introduction to the Journal." In Marie Weil, ed., "Diversity and Development in Community Practice." Journal of Community Practice 1 (1): xxi–xxxiii. New York: The Haworth Press, 1994.

Weyers, M. L. "Field Practice Models and Strategies in Community Work." In A. Lombard, *Community Work and Community Development: Perspectives on Social Development,* pp. 124–44. Pretoria, South Africa: HAUM-Tertiary, 1992.

Wharf, Briad, ed. *Community Work in Canada.* Toronto: McClelland and Stewart, 1979.

2.

Charles D. Garvin and Fred M. Cox*

A HISTORY OF COMMUNITY ORGANIZING SINCE THE CIVIL WAR WITH SPECIAL REFERENCE TO OPPRESSED COMMUNITIES

This paper traces the development of community organization within American communities since 1865. It is concerned both with community activities in which professionals were engaged and also with indigenous community efforts. Sometimes these two activities are seen as separate. Fisher, for example, identifies three dominant approaches to organizing: social work, political activism, and neighborhood maintenance.[1] He characterizes the social work approach as one that is reformist with a professional at the core; activism as one oriented to a government; and maintenance as a middle-class oriented approach to neighborhood improvement.

In this article, in contrast, we see these three approaches as affecting one another in ways that are determined by historical and contemporary forces. We shall, therefore, present our analysis of interactions among various kinds of organizing activities in the United States, yet pay special attention to indigenous efforts within oppressed groups. This is because of our conviction, somewhat yet not entirely contrary to Fisher's characterization of social workers as organizers, that the most effective kind of organizing is that which complements and supports such indigenous

efforts. We seek to describe, therefore, from a historical view (1) how relevant professional social work efforts were to indigenous ones and (2) how responsive both were to the issues embedded in the larger society.

In order to organize this analysis, we shall emphasize the many important community efforts in which ethnic communities have been engaged. Such organizing has occurred in virtually all ethnic communities. For example, there are many organizations devoted to improved conditions within Jewish, Italian, and Polish enclaves. In this article, however, we focus upon the history of organizing in ethnic communities which are now economically and socially oppressed. These include black, Chicano, Native American, and Asian American ones.

Other ethnic groups also have organized to secure their rights. The same has been true of the elderly, gay persons, and the handicapped. Space limitations, however, make it impossible for us to explore each. We have, however, included the women's movement because of our conviction regarding its broad scope and impact.

For purposes of this analysis, we divide American history since the Civil War into five stages. For each stage we outline the

*The authors are grateful to John Tropman, Barry Checkoway, and Howard Brabson for contributing their views on the most recent developments in community organizations.

[1]Robert Fisher, "Neighborhood Organizing: Lessons from the Past," *Social Policy* (Summer, 1984), pp. 9–10.

social forces and ideologies which affected community organizing; the specific community organization activities; and the institutions that sponsored the organizing efforts. We also describe the types of organizing occurring in oppressed communities. Finally the effects of these social forces, activities, and institutions upon the education of community organization practitioners are described.

1865 TO 1914

During the period between the end of the Civil War and the beginning of World War I, a number of social issues emerged in the United States that had strong impact upon welfare practices. Ideologies developed in response to these social conditions, and solutions were proposed for those defined as problematic. These social issues were the rapid industrialization of the country, the urbanization of its population, problems growing out of immigration, and changes in oppressed populations after the Civil War. These are described and their relevance for the emergence of community organization practice highlighted.

Social Conditions

Industrialization. The growth of technology and the centralization of industry brought with them a wide range of social problems. These included problems of working hours and conditions, safety, and child labor.[2]

Urbanization. A direct consequence of industrialization was the movement of large parts of the population from the country to the city.[3] The many unskilled workers who moved into the city from rural areas, particularly from the South and from Europe, were often forced to take up residence within the oldest and most crowded sections. These districts were inadequate in sanitation, building conditions, and city services. As Jane Addams wrote:

> The streets are inexpressibly dirty, the number of schools inadequate, sanitary legislation unenforced, the street lighting bad, the paving miserable, and altogether lacking in the alleys and smaller streets, and the stables foul beyond description. Hundreds of houses are unconnected with the street sewer.[4]

Immigration. In the early part of the nineteenth century, many immigrants came from northwestern Europe and spread out across the country. By 1890 the frontiers were gone. A large number then came from southern and eastern Europe until the tide of immigration was stemmed by legislation passed shortly after World War I. Asian and Mexican people went to the West and Southwest; small numbers of Puerto Ricans settled in the East.

These people brought with them not only their own social and religious institutions, but a variety of problems. Many came from peasant origins and sought a rural environment. However, most of those who came in the later waves were unable to escape the cities where they landed. Impoverished and often sick from the crossing, they were forced to take whatever work they could find. They clung to their former ways. This later brought them into

---

[2]For a social worker's perception of these conditions, see Jane Addams, *Twenty Years at Hull House* (New York: The Macmillan Co., 1910), pp. 99, 109ff.

[3]For details, see Allan Nevins and Henry Steele Commager, *The Pocket History of the United States* (New York: Pocket Books, 1942), pp. 326–357.

[4]Addams, op. cit., pp. 97–100.

conflict with their children who took on American habits and manners.[5]

Minorities After the Civil War

Blacks. During reconstruction there were many organizations that sought to support and sustain newly won civil rights. After the period of reconstruction there were many efforts on the part of black people to organize themselves "to the point where they could demand those rights which had slipped away since reconstruction."[6] The Supreme Court decision which declared the Civil Rights Act of 1875 unconstitutional was a major source of frustration for it placed the responsibility for protecting the rights of black people largely on the states.

During this period, the Populist Movement in the South was a major political force which attempted to secure black support. Fishel and Quarles quoted the white president of a Populist convention in Texas as saying that the black "is a citizen as much as we are." However, these authors noted that "the elections of 1892 saw their [Populists'] defeat in the South and the end of any political effort to work with the Negro on an equitable basis."[7]

A major concern of the black community was to solve the problem of educational deficits, particularly in vocational and higher education. In this context, an important event was the founding of Tuskegee Institute in 1881. Also, in the fifteen years before 1900 over fifteen hundred black people were lynched, and between 1900 and 1910 another nine hundred black people perished in the same way. "The sickening brutality of the act of lynching was matched only by its lawlessness and, in too many cases, the innocence of its victims."[8] Black support of other oppressed minorities during this period is illustrated by black poet Alberry Whitman's *The Rape of Florida,* an exposition of white degradation of the Seminoles (published in 1884).

Toward the end of this period many industries in the North encouraged black people to migrate from the South. Workers were needed because of the termination of the large European immigrations and the expansion of war industry. As a consequence their urban living conditions were deplorable.

Chicanos.[9] Although we describe community organizing primarily since the Civil War, we must recognize that the history of protest among Chicanos began with the Treaty of Guadalupe Hidalgo, signed on February 2, 1848, which brought a formal end to the Mexican-American War. Under this treaty, Mexico lost 45 percent of its territory including the wealth of the oil fields of Texas and the gold of California. More than a hundred thousand persons who had previously been citizens of Mexico were added to the United States. From this beginning, the rights of these "conquered" people were heavily infringed upon with little legal redress available. Protest took the form of guerrilla activity

---

[8]Ibid., p. 358.

[9]Although the term *Chicano* has not been used throughout all of the historical periods described in this chapter, we use it whenever we refer to those United States residents and citizens who are descended from Mexicans. For details of the evolution of the Chicano movement, see Gilberto Lopez y Rivas, *The Chicanos: Life and Struggles of the Mexican Minority in the United States* (New York and London: Monthly Review Press, 1973), pp. 57–74.

[5]See Oscar Handlin, *The Uprooted* (New York: Grosset and Dunlap, 1951).

[6]Leslie H. Fishel, Jr., and Benjamin Quarles, *The Negro American: A Documentary History* (Glenview, IL: Scott, Foresman & Co., 1967), p. 308.

[7]Ibid., p. 309.

by so-called bandits and armed rebellions that were vigorously repressed by the government. According to one authority, "Organized hunts, murders, robberies, and lynchings of Mexicans were everyday happenings, and cattle rustling and assaults on Mexican merchants were carried out with brutality and savagery."[10]

Native Americans. In the period just before the Civil War, the status of Native Americans was largely determined by the Removal Act of 1830. This act gave the president the right to remove any Indians who lived east of the Mississippi.[11] The Seminoles of Florida and the Sac and Fox of Illinois fought, but most were moved peacefully. A particularly shameful action was that taken against the Cherokees, who were forcibly removed in 1838 from Georgia to what was to become Oklahoma, with a great loss of lives on the way despite their enormous effort to adapt to the new culture forced upon them.

After the Civil War, the removal to reservations continued until the passage of the Dawes Act of 1887 which authorized the president to distribute 160 acres to each Indian adult and 80 acres to each child. This followed a series of major fights with tribes such as the Sioux in 1876, Nez Percé in 1877, Cheyenne in 1878, and Apache a few years later.

The Dawes Act was a failure in that it did not convert the Indians to agriculture as intended. Much of the land given was poor, and funds for its development were unavailable. As a result, between 1887 and 1932, "approximately 90 million acres out of 138 million initially held by Indians passed to white ownership."[12] In view of the exploitation they suffered the survival of many Indian tribes seems miraculous.

Asian Americans. The Chinese, the first immigrants from Asia to come in large numbers, arrived on the west coast in the 1840s. Their labor was sought as the California economy soared with the gold rush. It was in the mining regions that serious hostility to the Chinese first developed. When the Civil War began there were more than fifty thousand Chinese in California, mostly men. By the 1870s violence directed at Chinese was intensified by an economic depression. For example, "some twenty Chinese were killed by gunfire and hanging on October 24, 1871."[13]

Agitation from workers who sought anti-Chinese legislation continued for the rest of the decade. Consequently in 1882, Congress enacted the Chinese Exclusion Act, which was renewed in 1892 and made permanent in 1902.

About two hundred thousand Japanese arrived in America between 1890 and 1924 in an atmosphere hostile to Orientals. The early immigrants were mostly young males from rural backgrounds. Like the Chinese, they were recruited as a source of cheap labor. However, the migration of Japanese women was soon encouraged.

California's Alien Land Bill of 1913 exemplifies general attitudes toward the Japanese. It provided that Japanese aliens could lease agricultural lands for a maximum of three years, and that lands already owned or leased could not be willed to other persons. As the California attorney general indicated in a public speech, the

---

[10]Ibid., p. 33.

[11]John R. Howard, ed., *Awakening Minorities: American Indians, Mexican Americans, Puerto Ricans* (New Brunswick, NJ: Transaction Books, 1970), p. 17.

[12]Ibid., p. 19.

[13]Harry H. L. Kitano, *Race Relations* (Englewood Cliffs, NJ: Prentice-Hall, 1974), p. 196.

intention was to limit the number of Japanese who would come to or stay in California.[14]

Ideological Conditions

These problems were relevant to the emergence of community organization practice as they were affected by ideological currents prevalent during this period. These currents included Social Darwinism, radicalism, pragmatism, and liberalism. These ideologies were, at least in part, a response to problems of industrialization, poverty, urbanization, race relations, and cultural conflicts brought on by immigration.

Social Darwinism. As Max Lerner pointed out:

When the gap between *laissez faire* and social welfare became too obvious after the Civil War, conservative thought called into play the new popular interest in Darwinian theories. The jungle character of the economic struggle was frankly admitted, but it was justified and even glorified by Social Darwinism on the ground that nature had decreed it. The new natural law came to be "natural selection" and the triumph of the "fit" who survived.[15]

This philosophy led to the view that social failure was due to some inherent inferiority in the individual and that assistance to such people was an interference with natural law. This was compatible with the American ideal of "rugged individualism" as well as minimum government. The latter meant that the role of government was to protect property and ensure the enforcement of contracts, but not to interfere in any way with the content of such contracts.

Radical Ideology. While Social Darwinism may have served the interests of the economically secure, other ideologies provided a rationale for the activities of those who sought to change the lot of those who were not. One indigenous American radical, Henry George, "spoke for a 'reforming Darwinism' which saw the social order as the outgrowth of evolution but wanted to use it deliberately in a humanizing effort for the weakest as well as the strong."[16] The radical ideas of this period also stemmed from labor organizers. A Socialist Labor Party (SLP) was organized in the United States in 1876.[17] Within this group were Marxist as well as other ideological influences. Among the demands of the party were that "all industrial enterprises be placed under the control of the government as fast as practicable operated by free cooperative trade unions for the good of the whole people."[18] The Socialist party was founded in 1900 and united several groups, including the SLP.

This discussion cannot deal thoroughly with the history of American labor. However, community organizing aimed at mobilizing the oppressed drew upon this movement.

Pragmatism. This indigenous philosophy, first articulated by Charles S. Peirce and William James and developed by such men as John Dewey and George Herbert Mead, anticipated many efforts at social engineering. As Lerner stated:

Through these variations there ran the common thread of the "revolt against formalism" and

---

[14]Harry H. L. Kitano, *Japanese Americans* (Englewood Cliffs, NJ: Prentice-Hall, 1969), pp. 7, 17.

[15]Max Lerner, *America As a Civilization: Life and Thought in the United States Today* (New York: Simon & Schuster, 1957), p. 722.

[16]Ibid., p. 726.

[17]Called for one year the Workingman's Party of America.

[18]*The Socialist,* July 29, 1876. See also John R. Commons, *History of Labor in the United States,* Vol. II (New York: The Macmillan Co., 1935), p. 270.

against fixed principles or rules—that truth did not lie in absolutes or in mechanical formulas but in the whole operative context of individual growth and social action in which the idea was embedded. This movement of thought was, in a sense, the American counterpart to the Marxist and historical schools of thought in Europe which tried to apply the evolutionary process to social thinking. This intellectual base made possible, as it also expressed, the political reform movement from Theodore Roosevelt to Franklin Roosevelt.[19]

Liberalism. According to Lerner the credo of liberalism "has been progress, its mood optimist, its view of human nature rationalist and plastic; it has used human rights rather than property rights as its ends but has concentrated on social action as its means."[20] Despite its problems, he states, "liberalism has nevertheless emerged as a central expression of the American democratic faith."[21] Liberal ideas have been important in building support among the privileged for the voice of the underclasses to be heard in the councils of government and for them to reap the benefits bestowed by government.

Community Organization Institutions

As we have stated, community organization activities during the period between the Civil War and World War I can be divided into two categories: the first are those which were carried on by individuals or institutions related to present-day social welfare activities. The charity organization societies, settlement houses, and urban leagues are important examples.

A second category of activities are those that were conducted by those with no direct connection to contemporary community organization programs but which have become areas of interest for community practitioners. Examples include the organization of political, racial, and other action groups.

The Charity Organization Society. A number of factors noted above contributed to the emergence of charity organization societies in England in 1869 and, by 1873, in the United States.[22] These societies initially came into existence to coordinate the work of the private agencies which provided for the needs of the poor. Soon, however, these societies began to offer direct relief and other services, as well as to coordinate the work of other agencies.[23] Murphy summarized their program as follows:

They established social service indexes or exchanges listing individuals or "cases" known to cooperating agencies. They evolved the "case conference," in which workers from different agencies interested in the same "case" or the same family—workers from the settlement house, the relief-giving agencies, the child-placing agencies, the agencies established to protect children from cruelty, the visiting nurse association, and others—would meet to plan a constructive course of action in behalf of the "case." In some instances, too, the charity organization societies made broad studies of social and economic problems and recommended specific remedial measures.[24]

These social forces contributed to this development in several ways. The movement of large populations into the cities, as well

---

[19]Lerner, op. cit., pp. 722–723.

[20]Ibid., p. 729.

[21]Ibid., p. 730.

[22]Charles Loch Mowat, *The Charity Organization Society, 1869–1913* (London: Methuen and Co., 1961), pp. 16–21 and 94.

[23]The direct services which had significance for the emergence of social casework will not be pursued in this paper. Only the community organization antecedents will be noted.

[24]Campbell G. Murphy, *Community Organization Practice* (Boston: Houghton Mifflin Co., 1954), p. 35.

as the waves of immigration which met the manpower needs of growing industries, led to many social problems associated with poverty, inadequate housing, illness, and exploitation. Both humanitarian impulses and fear of what these people might do in desperation produced agencies directed to ameliorating conditions. In a sense, this was an effort to counter the more radical ideologies.

Separate efforts also were made by groups associated with different neighborhoods and ethnic and religious groups, and those with different problems. Difficulties which arose repeatedly were: (1) The same people were approached over and over again to provide resources for such agencies, and they began to look for ways to make charitable solicitations more efficient and less demanding on the few. (2) Duplication of aid was apparent, and those who offered it sought ways to avoid this and prevent the pauperization of the recipients which they believed was the inevitable result of indiscriminate relief. (3) Paid functionaries arose who sought to rationalize these activities, drawing their inspiration from the same wellsprings that fed a developing pragmatic philosophy. (4) The resources of some charitable societies were insufficient for the maintenance of required services, prompting an incessant search for new sources of funds.

During this period, leaders of charity organization societies harbored serious reservations about the wisdom of public activity on behalf of the poor. In general, they doubted government's ability to administer aid so that it would be rehabilitative. Darwinian ideology and a hedonistic theory of motivation strongly influenced their views on the matter. The Social Darwinians regarded relief as interference with the operation of natural law, and the hedonists held that the only assurance of hard work

among the poorer classes was the fear of hunger and exposure. This was tempered somewhat by humanitarian impulses. The charity organization societies distinguished between the "worthy" and the "unworthy" poor and chose to aid the former who, for reasons beyond their control, were unable to support themselves and who, through the moral example of the societies' "friendly visitors," could be rescued from pauperization. The rest were relegated to the not-too-tender mercies of the public poor law authorities, never to be supported at a level equal to the lowest wages in the community so that they would constantly be goaded toward self-support.

The functions of the charity organization societies were cooperative planning among charitable institutions for the amelioration or elimination of various social problems and the creation of new social agencies and the reform of old ones. Charity organization leaders were actively engaged in securing reforms in tenement housing codes, developing antituberculosis associations, obtaining legislation in support of juvenile court and probation work, establishing agencies and programs for the care of dependent children, cooperating with the police in programs for dealing with beggars and vagrants, and supporting legislation requiring absent fathers to support their children.[25]

Some of the most significant contributions of the charity organization societies to community organization were the development of community welfare planning organizations and of social survey techniques. One of the earliest and most important examples was that of the Pittsburgh

---

[25]For details on these activities see Frank D. Watson, *The Charity Organization Movement in the United States* (New York: The Macmillan Co., 1922), pp. 288–323.

organization. Writing in 1922, Frank Watson discussed the significance of the Pittsburgh survey:

Few of the offspring of the charity organization movement have had more far-reaching consequences or given greater promise of the future than the Pittsburgh Survey, the pioneer social survey in this country. Interpretation of hours, wages, housing, court procedure and all the rest, in terms of standards of living and the recognition that the basis for judging of social conditions is the measure of life they allow to those affected by them, constitute the very essence of the developments that have since taken place in social work.[26]

Out of the Pittsburgh survey came a council of social agencies which took upon itself the responsibility for acting upon the recommendations of the survey and conducting additional studies and reforms.

The Social Settlements.[27]   Settlements emerged fifteen years after charity organi-

zation societies. Samuel Barnett opened Toynbee Hall, one of the first settlements, in the slums of East London in 1884. Stanton Coit, who visited Toynbee Hall in 1886, established the University Settlement on the Lower East Side of New York later that year. Although charity organization societies and social settlements were prompted by the same social conditions, their analyses of the problems created by industrialization and immigration were quite dissimilar, leading them to different objectives and programs. Barnett, an Anglican clergyman influenced by the Christian Socialists, and John Ruskin sought to bridge the gap between the social classes and restore human values to a society dominated by materialism. Coit, strongly affected by Felix Adler and the Society of Ethical Culture, believed that nothing short of a moral and intellectual renaissance in city life was required. This could best be approached, he believed, by bringing together people of all descriptions into joint efforts, breaking down the barriers of interest, age, social class, political and religious affiliations.[28] Rather than looking to individual character as the root cause of social problems, settlement house leaders typically saw environmental factors as responsible for the conditions they deplored.

Thus, while the charity organization societies seemed more ideologically related to the Darwinian ideology, the settlement appeared to draw more heavily upon the liberal, or even the radical, ideologies of the day. The types of individuals who became involved in these two movements also were different. Charity organization leaders were persons closer to the upper classes in society and epitomized noblesse

---

[26]Ibid., pp. 305–306.

[27]This section rests heavily on the analysis of Allen F. Davis in his *Spearheads for Reform: The Social Settlements and the Progressive Movement 1890–1914* (New York: Oxford University Press, 1967). Although Toynbee Hall is commonly referred to as the first social settlement, it was opened, although only half-completed, on Christmas Eve of 1884 by two Oxford University students (see Davis, p. 3). A. F. Young and E. T. Ashton, in their *British Social Work in the Nineteenth Century* (London: Routledge & Kegan Paul, 1956) claimed that Oxford House was opened in October 1884, while Toynbee Hall was not opened until January 1885 (p. 230). Thus Toynbee Hall was *one* of the first settlements to open its doors. Although Oxford House was technically the first, Samuel Barnett, who fathered the settlement house movement in Great Britain, was associated with Toynbee Hall. This may account for the fact that a number of scholars erroneously regard Toynbee Hall as the first settlement house. See: Frank J. Bruno, *Trends in Social Work* (New York: Columbia University Press, 1948), p. 114; Arthur Hillman, "Settlements and Community Centers," in Harry L. Lurie (ed.), *Encyclopedia of Social Work* (New York: National Association of Social Workers, 1965), p. 690. The authors thank David Gilbert for bringing this to our attention.

[28]Stanton A. Coit, *Neighborhood Guilds: An Instrument of Social Reform,* 2d ed. (London: Swan, Sommerschien and Co., 1892), pp. 7–16, 46–51.

oblige. They favored either reforming the poor or modifying the most adverse of their social circumstances. Although exceptions on both sides can be cited, the settlement house workers were a different breed. Typically well educated and drawn from the middle classes, they were frequently critics of the social order who identified with and shared the lives of the poor in some measure. Their writings usually lack the condescension so often found in those of the charity organization workers.

Perhaps the most striking quality of the settlement program was its pragmatism. Unlike the charity organization societies, settlements had no predetermined scheme for solving the problems of society. In fact, they had no coherent analysis of the problems they confronted. Instead, with a general concern about the impact of such phenomena as industrialization, urbanization, and immigration upon society, they searched for answers that would be both feasible and effective.

Services were a major theme in their activities. They organized kindergartens and clubs for children, recreational programs, evening schools for adults, public baths, and art exhibitions.[29]

Social reform was, perhaps, the most basic and self-conscious thrust of the settlements. Services were often initiated as experiments which, if successful, could serve as models for other institutions. Indeed, many of the programs demonstrated by the settlements were taken over by other agencies.

The settlements' reform efforts went much beyond the organization of new or improved services. They included legislative campaigns at the local, state, and national levels. In the field of education, they worked for the development of vocational education and guidance in the public schools, as well as for the addition of school nurses, hot lunch programs, and education for the retarded and handicapped. They urged the creation of small neighborhood playgrounds, housing code improvements, reduction of congestion through city planning, and the transformation of public schools into neighborhood social centers. Although settlement workers could not agree on the value of immigration restrictions, they organized such groups as the Immigrant Protective League to ease the immigrant's adjustment to the new world. Settlement workers fought for laws to protect employed women and abolish child labor, and they helped organize the National Child Labor Committee and the National Women's Trade Union League. They were often involved in municipal reform activities, both at the ward and the city-wide levels, and many contributed to the platform and organizational work of the Progressive party in 1912.[30]

One theme ran through both the service and reform efforts of the settlements—participation and democracy. Many of their service activities were designed to permit dialogue between working people and settlement residents. The residents involved themselves in the life of the community so that they might know what services were needed. They worked to reduce the barriers that separated them from their neighbors,

---

[29]Contemporary group work also traces its origins to these settlement activities. On the other hand, the major thrust of group work is toward personal and interpersonal problems, and community organization, toward social conditions in a wider context. There is some indication, however, that group work may again be emphasizing its earlier social commitments.

[30]A recent study indicates that, after his defeat in 1912, Roosevelt terminated his relationship with social workers and returned to a more traditional Republicanism. See W. I. Trattner, "Theodore Roosevelt, Social Workers, and the Election of 1912: A Note," *Mid-America* 50, No. 1 (1968), pp. 64–69.

and the neighbors from one another. They invited labor leaders and radicals of their day to use their facilities.

Finally, in everything they undertook, settlements tried to help their neighbors develop their potentialities to the fullest. There was great emphasis on education of all kinds. One of the major reasons for opposing child labor was its negative effects upon the development of children. Municipal reform was viewed, in part, as a process of helping communities gain the capacity to deal with their problems more effectively.

The settlement idea spread rapidly. In 1891 there were six settlements in the United States; by 1910 the number had jumped to over four hundred. Most of them were located in the large industrial cities of the East and Midwest; there were very few in the South or West.

The Organization of Ethnic Minorities and Women. A variety of forms of organization among black Americans was tested during this period as black people coped with their shifting status in American life. One of the earliest of these forms was developed by a group of prominent black people in 1865 and led by Frederick Douglass and George T. Downing who were "charged" with the duty to look after the best interests of the recently emancipated.[31] Almost twenty-five years later, in 1883, a very different kind of step was taken by the Louisville Convention of Colored Men which "concentrated on large issues of political, as distinct from partisan, rights, education, civil rights and economic problems."[32] Five years later, the Colored Farmers Alliance and Cooperative Union came into existence. In 1890, the Afro-American League organized in another direction,

emphasizing legal redress rather than politics.[33] In 1890, blacks from twenty-one states and the District of Columbia organized the Afro-American League of the United States. Issues which concerned this group included school funds, and legal and voting rights. In 1896, the National Association of Colored Women was formed.

Crosscurrents, similar to those which affect the organizations of black people today, were operative between the Civil War and World War I. On the one hand, many efforts were under the influence of Booker T. Washington, who sought an accommodation with white interests in order to maintain their support. In contrast, W. E. B. DuBois epitomized an opposition to this approach in 1905 when he called for "a conference 'to oppose firmly the present methods of strangling honest criticism.'"[34] The Niagara movement grew out of this meeting and by 1909 resulted in the formation of the National Association for the Advancement of Colored People. Such social workers as Jane Addams, Florence Kelly, and Lillian Wald assisted in these organizing efforts.

The Committee on Urban Conditions among Negroes in New York City, later to become the National Urban League, was another organization in which social workers were involved during this period. Its first executive, George Edmund Haynes, "was on the faculty of Fisk University and particularly interested in training black social workers."[35]

As noted earlier, Mexican-Americans, as well as Native Americans, were confronted with efforts that took away their lands. One response to this trend was the development of small groups for protection and support.

---

[31]Fishel and Quarles, op. cit., pp. 259–260.
[32]Ibid., p. 308.
[33]Ibid., p. 312.
[34]Ibid., p. 357.
[35]Ibid., p. 361.

Some, for survival, became bandits. Organized protest, however, for Mexican-Americans began in agriculture or, as Howard states, "The roots of the Chicano movement lie in the fields."[36]

In 1903, for example, Mexican- and Japanese-American sugar beet workers struck in Ventura, California.[37] In addition, throughout this period, but particularly from the 1880s on, many organizations came into existence whose function was, according to Alvarez, to preserve a Mexican-American way of life through "celebrations, social events, provision of facilities, information and communication networks."[38] The function of such organizations was to preserve a bicultural and bilingual existence. Some examples include the Penitente Order in New Mexico in the 1880s and Mano Negra, also in New Mexico, in the 1890s.[39]

The Native Americans during this period continued to have well-developed forms of tribal organization, partly as a heritage of their early struggles for survival against white encroachment. However, the tribes were separated from one another geographically and structurally, thus often rendering them easy prey for governmental manipulation. Nevertheless, the militancy of the period in actual warfare, as well as persistent legal action, represents an impressive, though unsuccessful, effort to secure a greater measure of justice from American society.

The early Chinese immigrants were organized into family or benevolent associations, tongs, or business interests.[40] For the Japanese, the Japanese Association for Issei (first-generation Japanese in the United States) had some similar functions.

Thus, for these Asian groups, a major function of community organizations during this period was mutual benefit and cultural participation. For example,

people from the same *ken,* or Japanese state, often cooperated in various ways, and this was noticeable in particular trades. For example, Miyamoto writes that the first Japanese barber in Seattle was from Yamaguchi-ken. After he became established, he helped his friends from the same ken with training and money, so that, eventually, most of the Japanese barbers in Seattle were from Yamaguchi-ken.[41]

During this era, when associations existed or were created in many ethnic groups, organizations for the benefit of women also emerged. In 1868, Susan B. Anthony was a leading organizer of a working women's association to fight economic discrimination against women. In addition, during the next decade unions of women working in a number of industries such as laundries and shoe factories were organized. By 1886, there were 113 women's assemblies in the Knights of Labor.[42] Other organizations also were concerned about the poor working conditions of women. For example, in 1894, the New York Consumer's League presented

---

[36]Howard, op. cit., p. 95.

[37]Ibid.

[38]Salvador Alvarez, "Mexican-American Community Organizations," in *Voices: Readings from El Grito, A Journal of Contemporary Mexican American Thought, 1967–1973,* ed. Octavio Ignacio Romano-V (Berkeley: Quinto Sol Publications, 1971), pp. 205–214.

[39]Ibid., p. 209.

[40]For a discussion of evolving forms of Chinese-American community organizations, see Melford S. Weiss, "Division and Unity: Social Process in a Chinese-American Community," in *Asian Americans: Psychological Perspectives,* ed. Stanley Sue and Nathaniel N. Wagner (Palo Alto: Science & Behavior Books, 1973), pp. 264–273.

[41]Kitano, *Japanese Americans,* op. cit., p. 19.

[42]For details of these and other endeavors, see "A Century of Struggle: American Women, 1820–1920," in Barbara Deckard, *The Women's Movement: Political, Socioeconomic, and Psychological Issues* (New York: Harper & Row, Publishers, 1975), pp. 243–284. This section draws heavily on that chapter.

information on these conditions. By 1896, this organization had branches in twenty states. In 1900, the International Ladies' Garment Workers' Union was organized and throughout the pre-World I period it continued to organize despite many obstacles.[43]

While working women were organizing themselves in their workplaces, more affluent women organized to secure the vote. The women's suffrage movement and the movement for the abolition of slavery had originally been one. The split came partially because northern business interests stood to gain from the black vote but could see no value in women having the same right.[44] This was symbolized when the American Equal Rights Association, working for black and women's rights, split in May 1869. Later that year moderate women organized the American Woman Suffrage Association while radical women formed the National Women Suffrage Association. These organizations remained separate until 1890 when they merged to form the National American Woman Suffrage Association. Unfortunately, the class bias of these organizations was evident in attacks on blacks as less fit to vote than women and in other statements made to ensure the acceptability of the women suffrage movement in the South.

The women's suffrage movement was able to see to it that the Nineteenth Amendment was proposed every year from 1886 to 1896, although it was defeated each time. The lack of strength to pass the amendment, according to one authority, was due to "their own conservative tactics and racist, elitist positions, which alienated their potential allies."[45] With the emergence of militant supporters, however, such as radical farmers, the Progressive Party, and

the socialists and a shift to more militant leadership, many states did come to adopt woman suffrage. By 1916, both major parties supported suffrage. In 1917, the Women's party turned to more militant tactics and picketed the White House. Partly, also, because of women's activities in the war and the public support of President Wilson, the House of Representatives finally passed the Nineteenth Amendment in January 1918. It took, however, another eighteen months for Senate approval.

Development of the Profession and Professional Education

For this period it is impossible to discuss community organization as a specialization in social work, which had itself not yet emerged as a separate entity. There were individuals concerned with coordinating charity, organizing neighborhood settlements, or mobilizing protest in racial matters, but these people had little common professional identity. Some training activities began to emerge in 1898 when the New York Charity Organization Society started a summer training course. This was expanded to a one-year program a few years later, and by the end of World War I seventeen schools of social work had come into existence in the United States and Canada. The Association of Training Schools for Professional Social Work was formed at that time also. The emphasis, however, was more on what became casework than on methods of community organization.

While the ethnic organizing of the period as well as that among women may have secured the support of social workers as *individuals,* this did not represent activities of the profession or of a social work method called community organization. Nevertheless, many precedents were being created for and lessons learned by those

---

[43]Ibid., p. 270.

[44]Ibid., p. 262.

[45]Ibid., p. 269.

who sought to create a more humane society and this included social workers.

1915 TO 1929

Social Conditions

After World War I, several new conditions emerged that had a significant impact on community organization practice: urbanization increased markedly, industrial potential escalated, and racial conflicts intensified. By 1920 more than half of the population of the United States lived in cities, and industrial innovations were accelerated by the heavy demands on production created by World War I.

The twenties, nevertheless, was a decade of confidence in the economic system. As Lerner stated, "Big business of the 1920s, certain that it had found the secret of perpetual prosperity, claimed the right to the policymaking decisions not only in the economy but in the government."[46]

Ironically, this period also brought some major crises in civil liberties. "After World War I there was a wave of raids and deportations; it arose from the uneasy feeling that the Russian Revolution had caused a shift in the world balance of power and spawned a fanatic faith threatening American survival."[47] The period also witnessed the intensification of activities of groups such as the Ku Klux Klan with antagonism directed against blacks, Jews, and the foreign born.

The Condition of Minorities

Blacks. This was a period during which black Americans made strong attempts to improve their lives and were simultaneously subjected to major efforts at repression. Seventy-six black people were lynched in 1919,[48] and "the white national secretary of the NAACP was badly beaten on the streets of Texas."[49] Chicago experienced a severe "race riot" in 1919 which resulted in the death of 15 white and 23 black persons as well as injury to an additional 537.[50]

However, progress occurred in many spheres of American life. The term *the New Negro* became prevalent in the 1920s, and this was supported by the increased self-respect of many black war veterans. During this period, distinguished people such as Langston Hughes, Countee Cullen, and Paul Robeson began their careers. Black school attendance jumped from 45 to 60 percent of the eligible school population between 1910 and 1930.[51] In fact, in many ways the current emphasis on black power and black identity has ideological antecedents in this period.

Chicanos. These years saw a large immigration of persons from Mexico into what had become the United States. Between 1910 and 1919, almost two hundred and twenty-five thousand persons came, and in the next decade the number was almost double.[52] According to one writer, "that striking increase is directly related to the miserable economic conditions in Mexico after ten years of armed struggle."[53] Specifically, the Mexican economy was in a poor state after the Mexican Revolution while the southwestern United States was experiencing considerable economic growth.

---

[46]Lerner, op. cit., p. 279.

[47]Ibid., p. 455.

[48]Fishel and Quarles, op. cit., 403.

[49]Ibid.

[50]Ibid., p. 405.

[51]Ibid.

[52]Lopez y Rivas, op. cit., p. 85.

[53]Ibid., p. 39.

There was an expansion and development of nonagricultural worker organizations during this period. As Moore notes:

In 1920 Mexican workers struck the Los Angeles urban railway. In later years the strikes in the fields and mines of the Border States were both more numerous and more sophisticated. The earlier ones were significant, however, because Mexicans were generally denied normal channels of political expression in any of the Border States except New Mexico.[54]

Native Americans. During this period, the conditions of Native Americans continued to deteriorate as the government persisted in its policy of implementing the Dawes Act of 1887 which distributed land to individuals. The attempt to undermine the widely practiced custom of holding land in common for the good of all was continued. The act not only created severe economic problems but eroded traditional tribal government.[55] In fact, "The Indian Agent and his staff were 'the government' for most tribes from the cessation of treaty making to the 1930s."[56]

In addition to the effects of the Dawes Act, two other actions also diminished tribal ties. From 1917 to 1921, the trust on land allotments of Indians of less than one-half Indian blood was terminated. Many Indian agents were also eliminated and their wards placed under school superintendents and farmers reporting directly to the Commissioner of Indian Affairs.[57] This focused activities on individuals, not tribes, and presumably moved Indians as individuals into non-Indian education and agriculture.

Asian Americans. The Immigration Act of 1924 epitomized the attitudes of the American government, if not of the society, to the foreign born. No immigration was to be permitted for Asians; low quotas were set for southern Europeans, and high ones for northern Europeans. This made it impossible, particularly for the Chinese who had not come as families, to form or reunite families. In Japanese communities, these years marked the birth and early development of many *Nisei,* or second-generation Japanese-Americans. With great determination, many Nisei moved into middle-class occupations.

Ideological Currents

The ideologies that were prevalent in the earlier period continued to exert a strong influence. The sense of complacency and optimism stemming from economic growth and affluence did find perceptive social critics, however. In addition, the following are ideas which developed during this period and which also molded social work practice.

Psychoanalysis. Some may find it strange to regard psychoanalysis as an ideology; nevertheless, the conditions of the period were conducive to the introduction of psychoanalysis as a major intellectual force in social work. This was a period of affluence, and many believed that the social environment offered so many opportunities and was otherwise so benign that any problems must be the result of individual failure. Psychoanalytic practice was clearly oriented toward changing the individual and not the system. Social workers, as Jesse Taft observed, became preoccupied with the person and all but forgot the situation: "The most daring experimental caseworkers have all but lost connection with

[54]Joan Moore, *Mexican-Americans* (Englewood Cliffs, NJ: Prentice-Hall, 1970), p. 24.

[55]Theodore W. Taylor, *The States and Their Indian Citizens* (Washington, DC: United States Department of the Interior, Bureau of Indian Affairs, 1972), p. 17.

[56]Ibid.

[57]Ibid., pp. 17–18.

social obligation and are quite buried in their scientific interest in the individual as he has evolved through his own unique growth process."[58] The social worker disassociated herself from charity to be reborn a psychotherapist.[59]

Anti-Intellectualism. Despite the increasing popularity of Freud's ideas, this was not a period of intellectual activity in the United States. Vice-President Coolidge attacked the colleges and universities as "hot beds of sedition."[60] Many intellectuals, along with T. S. Eliot, fled to Europe, finding America a "wasteland."[61] American writers such as Sinclair Lewis castigated the American middle class, as F. Scott Fitzgerald did the upper class. It should also be remembered that the Scopes trial, testing the legal right to teach evolution in the schools, took place in 1925. According to one authority "only one event in the 1920s succeeded in arousing intellectuals of every kind of political loyalty: the arrest, trial, and execution of two Italian anarchists, Nicola Sacco and Bartolomeo Vanzetti."[62]

Development of Community Organization Institutions

The Community Chest and United Fund. This period saw a continued increase in the number of welfare institutions. This proliferation of agencies generated insistent demands for coordination. The increase in such institutions was prompted primarily by accelerating urbanization. The war increased the pace as "some three hundred American communities organized war chests to cope with the mounting flood of appeals from national and local agencies."[63] The agencies' increasing needs for financing, despite the affluence of the period, prompted demands from both the philanthropists and the professionals for better fund-raising methods. The interests of these two groups were not identical, and this led to the development of two separate yet interrelated institutions—the community chest or united fund, on the one hand, and the community welfare council on the other. The separation of interests between the suppliers of philanthropic dollars and the dispensers of them had effects which can be seen to this day in community welfare institutions.

Lubove reflected this situation accurately when he declared:

Financial federation captured the imagination of businessmen by promising efficient coordination and organization of the community welfare machinery, immunity from multiple solicitation, economical collection and distribution of funds, and the development of a broad base of support which would relieve the pressure on the small circle of large givers. The corporation, increasingly regarded as a source of gifts, appreciated the conveniences of federated finance.[64]

There was also opposition to this development. National organizations resented the competition for local funds. Of particular importance to the contemporary scene in community organization is resistance to the erosion of "democracy" implicit in the

---

[58]Roy Lubove, *The Professional Altruist: The Emergence of Social Work As a Cause, 1880–1930* (Cambridge, MA: Harvard University Press, 1965), p. 89.

[59]Ibid.

[60]Samuel Eliot Morison, *The Oxford History of the American People* (New York: Oxford University Press, 1965), p. 909.

[61]Ibid., p. 910.

[62]For a brief summary of the case and its effects on opinion, see Frederick J. Hoffman, *The Twenties: American Writing in the Post War Decade* (New York: The Viking Press, 1955), pp. 357–364.

[63]Lubove, op. cit., p. 189.

[64]Ibid., p. 183.

development of a fund-raising bureaucracy. Lubove cited one chest executive who stated, "We are facing here the age-long and inevitable conflict which exists in any society between the urge for individual independence and initiative on the one hand, and the need for social control on the other."[65]

Philanthropists wanted their funds spent efficiently and desired relief from the constant appeals of charitable solicitors. United appeals for financial support were created to serve these objectives, originating with the United Jewish Appeal in Boston in 1895.[66]

Community chests evolved in several ways. First, welfare agencies joined to solicit funds, hoping to raise more money than each could obtain separately. In 1887, the Charity Organization Society in Denver initiated joint fund-raising among fifteen of its twenty-three cooperating agencies, an effort which proved financially successful in its first year of operation.[67] Community chests were also organized by councils of social agencies. In 1915, two years after its organization, Cincinnati's Council of Agencies brought twelve agencies together in a united appeal for funds. Before 1927, councils in St. Louis, Minneapolis, Columbus, New Haven, and Detroit had followed suit.[68]

For the most part, however, community chests were initiated by large contributors. Often their first step was a charity endorse-ment bureau which later reorganized as a community chest. Businessmen and industrialists believed that welfare services, like public utilities, should be held accountable to the public. Because contributors rarely had time to investigate agencies that asked for support, local chambers of commerce organized bureaus to (1) establish standards for welfare agencies; (2) investigate individual agencies and measure their operations against their standards; (3) recommend those agencies that met the test; and (4) encourage members and the public to support organizations that received endorsement.[69]

The endorsement bureau had its critics. Because it mainly represented the large business and industrial contributors, agencies viewed the bureaus as potentially autocratic and a threat to their autonomy. Furthermore, agencies believed that the organization might dampen contributors' interest and enthusiasm.[70] The demands upon a small number of contributors also became very great. The first major effort to remedy these conditions was taken by the Cleveland Chamber of Commerce. After initiating a study of the problem in 1907, the chamber launched the Federation for Charity and Philanthropy in 1913. Cleveland's federation is generally considered to be a major landmark in the history of community chests,[71] a name which was first used in Rochester, New York, in 1919.[72]

Community chests were dominated by three kinds of people: contributors, particularly those who gave large sums; solicitors,

[65]Ibid. p. 196. Lubove, here, was quoting Raymond Clapp, "Who Shall Decide Personnel Policies?" *Survey* 65 (1930), p. 103.

[66]Lyman S. Ford, "Federated Financing," in Harry L. Lurie (ed.), *Encyclopedia of Social Work* (New York: National Association of Social Workers, 1965), p. 331.

[67]William J. Norton, *The Cooperative Movement in Social Work* (New York: The Macmillan Co., 1927), pp. 50–54.

[68]Ibid., pp. 93–99.

[69]Ibid., pp. 24–29.

[70]Ibid., pp. 29–30.

[71]Ibid., pp. 68–71.

[72]Guy Thompson, "Community Chests and United Funds," *Social Work Year Book, 1957,* ed. Russell H. Kurtz (New York: National Association of Social Workers, 1957), p. 176.

the small businessmen, service club members and middle management types who helped to raise the chests' funds; and volunteers representative of the health, welfare, and recreation agencies that were supported by the chests. The membership delegated much of the decision making to a board of directors, which hired an executive. In the beginning, most of the work was done by volunteers. Volunteers still continue to play an important part in community chests.

World War I gave a great impetus to the development of chests. Overseas relief and other war-created welfare needs stimulated the development of nearly four hundred "War Chests." During the 1920s the number of communities with community chests increased from 39 to 353.[73]

The Council of Social Agencies and Community Welfare Council. The first decades of the twentieth century saw the development of an increasing professionalism among those who helped the poor. The friendly visitor was replaced by the paid agent. The charity organization societies founded schools of philanthropy which, beginning around the turn of the century, became graduate schools of social work. The development of the social survey—a disciplined effort to obtain factors necessary for planning—was another manifestation of the growing professionalism. In short, the growing cadre of welfare professionals, with the support of many volunteers who served as board members of charitable societies, was interested in organizing a rational, systematic approach to the welfare needs of communities. Their interest included providing for the gaps in service, detecting problems, and looking to future needs. This combination of professionals and

volunteers formed councils. The first councils were organized in Milwaukee and Pittsburgh in 1909. By 1926 there were councils in Chicago, Boston, St. Louis, Los Angeles, Detroit, Cincinnati, Columbus, and New York.[74]

Because of the potential conflicts noted earlier, one of the problems experienced by councils was their relation to community chests or united funds. Often councils have been regarded as the planning arm of the chest or fund, and this limited their relationship to publicly supported health and welfare agencies. Yet when councils maintained some degree of independence from chests and funds, they seldom could provide the necessary incentives to gain compliance with their plans. Those councils that were heavily influenced by chests or funds were often assigned responsibility for distributing the money raised in the united appeal, a function seldom performed by independent councils.

Another problem of welfare councils was their relation with constituents. In the beginning, most councils were confederations of welfare agencies, largely those supported by chests. Within such a federated structure, councils often found it difficult to take forceful action, not wanting to seriously offend their agency constituents, which had a major stake in welfare plans. With the growing professionalization of councils, they often were reorganized as councils of individual citizens with an interest in welfare problems and services. This shift was indicated in the change in name from "council of agencies" to "community welfare council." Efforts were made to recruit those with a reputation for influence, and decisions have increasingly reflected the views of professional planners and their volunteer constituents rather than

[73]Ford, op. cit., pp. 327–328.

[74]Ibid., p. 37.

welfare agencies. In spite of this, welfare councils have not enjoyed a reputation for effective planning.[75]

The Social Unit Plan. Roy Lubove[76] described a local development which anticipated one trend that later became important in community organization. This plan was launched in 1915 when the National Social Unit Organization was founded. A pilot area was selected in Cincinnati. The sponsors desired to test:

the theory that a democratic and effective form of community organization which stimulated people to define and meet their own needs has to divide the citizens into small, primary units, organize the occupational specialists, and insure an "organic" and coordinate working relationship between the representatives of groups having special knowledge or skill for service to the community and the representatives of the residents.[77]

The social unit plan led to the development of block councils, block workers, and federations of such groups, referred to as the Citizens Council of the Social Unit. Occupational groups also elected a council. This program lasted three years and "concentrated on health services."[78] The movement did not expand in this form, perhaps indicative of the fact that the time for this idea had not yet come.

The Organization of Ethnic Minorities and Women. Particularly in the South, many institutions developed among blacks because of the patterns of discrimination and segregation which existed during this period. Out of school segregation, educational organizations arose. Black newspapers also came into existence because news of the black community was ignored by the white press. The exclusion of blacks from white churches led to a variety of black religious organizations.[79]

Many black soldiers hoped that their return from World War I would see a change in the patterns of racism they had suffered for so long. This was not to occur, as the Klan and other groups intensified their campaigns and "returning Negro soldiers were lynched by hanging and burning, even while still in their military uniforms."[80] One reaction to this was the Universal Negro Improvement Association of Marcus Garvey. This organization rapidly became the largest nonreligious black organization. The purpose of the movement was to send blacks back to Africa, and the attraction of this to many blacks was a clear indication of their disaffection with America.

There was also militancy, and as Franklin stated:

This was the spirit of what Alain Locke called "The New Negro." He fought the Democratic white primary, made war on the whites who consigned him to the ghetto, attacked racial discrimination in employment, and pressed for legislation to protect his rights. If he was seldom successful during the postwar decade and the depression, he made it quite clear that he was unalterably opposed to the un-American character of the two worlds of race.[81]

During this same period, a major thrust of Mexican-American organization was toward integration.[82] This represented the

---

[75]These changes did not occur until the late 1940s and 1950s, but are reported here to complete the discussion of community welfare councils.

[76]Lubove, op. cit., pp. 175–178.

[77]Ibid., p. 176.

[78]Ibid.

[79]Much of the material in this section has been drawn from John Hope Franklin, "The Two Worlds of Race: A Historical View," *Daedalus* 94, No. 4 (Fall 1965), pp. 899–920.

[80]Ibid., p. 912.

[81]Ibid., p. 913.

[82]Lopez y Rivas, op. cit., p. 62.

desires of the growing middle class to se-cure their share of the American wealth. An example was the Order of the Sons of America, founded in San Antonio in 1921. An intent of this organization was to show Anglos that its members were different from Mexicans who cause problems.[83] The League of Latin American Citizens had similar objectives.

Meanwhile, Chicano laborers were wag-ing their own struggle. Lopez y Rivas points out that "all over California, Ari-zona, Texas, New Mexico, and other states they went on strike for better wages and living conditions as well as an end to racist employment practices." These efforts, however, met with "violent repression."[84] Nevertheless, an important development was the founding in 1927 of *La Confedera-cion de Uniones Obreras Mexicanos*. This organization held its first general conven-tion in May 1928. Delegates attended from twenty-one unions as well as mutual aid societies. Farm labor groups also struck the fields throughout California. The *Confed-eracion* itself engaged in major organizing activities throughout the 1920s and 1930s.[85]

The actions of the federal government which had the effect of undermining Na-tive American institutions continued during this period. One piece of legislation, the Snyder Act of 1921, continued to affirm the objective of the Bureau of Indian Af-fairs to provide "for the general support and civilization of Indians."[86] However, the Meriam Report of 1928 recommended "an acculturation program on an understanding of the Indian point of view."[87] Even though these actions may have been inspired by

good intentions, their patronizing nature was unsupportive of indigenous institu-tions.

One author, in an attempt to characterize efforts to organize women after the adop-tion of the Nineteenth Amendment, titles her chapter "Forty Years in the Desert: American Women, 1920–1960."[88] In the first place, there was no indication of a women's bloc vote, which some had feared. This was not to deny the fact, how-ever, that in specific elections in those states that had adopted women's suffrage, the proportions of women voting different-ly than men made a difference in the out-come. An example was the defeat of antisuffrage senator John Weeks in 1918.[89]

The National Women's Party, however, continued to operate. It maintained a plat-form committed to full equality and sup-ported the first introduction of the Equal Rights Amendment into Congress in 1923. However, it was quite small and in 1923 had only eight thousand members as com-pared to fifty thousand three years before.[90]

The League of Women Voters was founded in 1920. This group was much less militant than the National Women's Party and it declared in 1931 that "nearly all dis-criminations have been removed."[91] The League was less concerned about women's issues than child labor laws, pacifism, and other general reforms.

The general conservatism of the 1920s took its toll on the women's movement. The prohibition against child labor, which women's groups favored, was attacked as a subversive plot.[92] It was even charged that all liberal women's groups were part of a

---

[83]Ibid.

[84]Ibid.

[85]Alvarez, op. cit., pp. 211–212.

[86]Taylor, op. cit., p. 19.

[87]Ibid.

[88]Deckard, op. cit., p. 285.

[89]Ibid., p. 286.

[90]Ibid., p. 287.

[91]Ibid.

[92]Ibid., pp. 288–289.

Communist plot.[93] Despite this, women continued to found organizations including the National Federation of Business and Professional Women's Clubs (1919) and the American Association of University Women (1921).

Development of the Profession

Most of those who trained for social work in the first two decades of the twentieth century were studying to become caseworkers. However, by 1920 Joseph K. Hart had written a text entitled *Community Organization,* and between then and 1930 at least five books were written on the subject.[94] It is easy to see why the casework emphasis existed in view of the prevalent ideologies and issues of the period, emphasizing individual conformity to the "system." In fact, community organization practice during this period was aimed largely at enhancing agencies oriented toward personal adjustment. Except, perhaps, for the workers in settlement houses, the "social unit plan," and the organizations developing in the black community, little thought was given to the changing social institutions to meet the needs of individuals. Even in the case of settlements, the workers there often thought of themselves as educators, recreation leaders, or group workers. In the black community, organizers rarely identified with social work.

Nevertheless, some different ideas were beginning to emerge. Mary Follett foresaw the advantages to democracy of the organization of primary groups in the local communities.[95] Eduard Lindeman, who taught for many years at the New York School of Social Work, also spoke of the value of "an attempt on the part of the people who live in a small, compact local group to assume their own responsibilities and to guide their own destinies."[96]

The emphasis of this period, however, was aptly summed up by Lubove when he wrote the following:

Federation employed the rhetoric of the early community organization movement, but its intensive concern with the machinery and financing of social welfare diverted attention from cooperative democracy and the creative group life of the ordinary citizen to problems of agency administration and service. It substituted the bureaucratic goal of efficiency through expert leadership for what had been a quest for democratic self-determination through joint efforts of citizen and specialist. Community organization had barely emerged as a cause before it had become a function absorbed into the administrative structure of social work.[97]

1929 TO 1954

Social work, as well as other institutions in the United States, was deeply affected by the two major cataclysms of this period: the depression and World War II. To regard these years as a single period in American history may seem odd to some readers, but they cover a coherent period in the development of ideas and issues in community organization practice. A departure from this pattern took place in the fifties, marked by the desegregation decision of the Supreme Court and the end of McCarthyism, that period of ideological repression which received its name, as well

---

[93]Ibid.

[94]Meyer Schwartz, "Community Organization," *Encyclopedia of Social Work,* op. cit., 1965, p. 177.

[95]See for example, her book, *The New State: Group Organization, the Solution of Popular Government* (New York: Longmans, Green and Co., 1918), p. 217.

[96]Eduard C. Lindeman, *The Community: An Introduction to the Study of Community Leadership and Organization* (New York: Association Press, 1921), p. 58.

[97]Lubove, op. cit., p. 180.

as much encouragement, from the late Senator Joseph McCarthy of Wisconsin.

Social Conditions

To set the stage for the discussion of the history of community organization during the period, one should call attention to several social forces.

Depression Issues.   The most apparent of the social forces at play was the vast increase in unemployment. The bank and stock market failures also removed whatever reserves people might otherwise have utilized in such a crisis. Mortgage foreclosures deprived many of their homes, farms, and small businesses.

The Growth of Government.   The expansion of government programs was a direct result of the depression. Government expenditures, programs, and controls grew in unprecedented ways. The government became an employer, a producer of goods and services, and a vast resource to restore the industrial processes. The federal government also became the most significant planner and promoter of welfare programs through the enactment, in the mid-thirties, of such legislation as social security and the minimum wage.

The Growth of Unionism.   The depression also stimulated a major upsurge of trade unionism. The founding of the CIO showed that the labor movement was at last free from the limits of a craft basis for organization. The passage of the National Labor Relations Act in 1935 marked the beginning of an era in which government facilitated the development of unions and thereby became less the biased protector of business interests. The development of strong unions in the auto, steel, electrical,

meat-packing, and other industries had a major impact upon the industrial scene. The organization of the Brotherhood of Sleeping Car Porters gave the black community an important labor spokesman, A. Phillip Randolph.

The International Scene.   During this period, it became evident that the Communist party was firmly entrenched in the USSR. In Spain, Italy, and Germany, facist governments seized power. American counterparts of these movements were apparent in the developments within the United States.

On the international level, these developments had consequences of the most serious nature for the United States. Just at the time in the thirties that many programs to solve the social problems of the country were being tested, the need to prepare for and then wage World War II increasingly absorbed the attention and resources of the American people. In fact, only with the war did the country clearly come out of the depression.

The Condition of Minorities

Blacks.   The creation of many New Deal agencies "added credence to the emergent fact that for the first time the federal government had engaged and was grappling with some of the fundamental barriers to race progress."[98] On the other hand, there were many times when Roosevelt, who was highly regarded by many black leaders, failed to deliver on expectations because of political considerations. Where local control was strong, the effect of some of those programs was to continue the exclusion of black people from necessary benefits.

It is undeniable, however, that important strides were made during this period.

---

[98]Fishel and Quarles, op. cit., p. 447.

There was a considerable expansion of opportunities for black people in important governmental positions. Civil service brought many black people into white-collar positions in government. World War II increased this momentum. The Committee on Fair Employment Practice, established by Roosevelt in 1941 to improve employment opportunities in defense industries, was a significant development. In 1948, Truman created the civil rights section of the Justice Department and established the President's Committee on Equality of Treatment and Opportunity in the Armed Services. The courts struck down restrictive housing covenants and outlawed segregation on buses in interstate travel.

Chicanos. During this period, Chicanos began to move beyond the Southwest into many parts of the United States. This was due in part to the processes of acculturation but also to the fact that new Mexican immigrants were willing to work for lower wages than second-generation persons, who then tended to move to new areas. Particularly in the North, jobs were more available and wages better. A pattern of migrant farm labor was also established emanating from the Southwest and spreading to other parts of the country, as Chicanos followed the crops.

Much of the immigration during this period was illegal but responsive to employers seeking cheap labor. Employers aided the smuggling in of such persons.[99] The need for labor was heightened as Asian immigration ended.

In summarizing the period prior to 1940, however, one authority states:

The lot of the Mexican-Americans, except as they were affected by the immigration, changed little during this period prior to 1940. In a real sense, they were forgotten Americans; there was little assimilation to the majority society. They remained a Spanish speaking, largely rural, and generally poor minority. The decline of the small farmer and sheepherder forced many off the land altogether. But even as wage earners, they received no proper return in comparison to their contribution to the building of the economy of the Southwest.[100]

Native Americans. Early in the period being described here, a new approach was adopted to Native Americans: the Indian Reorganization Act of 1934. The intent of this act was to reverse the land policy of the Allotment Act of 1887 and the intent of trying to "stamp out everything that was Indian."[101] The 1934 act specifically provided authorization for the purchase of new land, the initiation of tribal organization, the creation of loan funds for individuals *and tribes,* and extended the trust of Indian lands "until otherwise directed by Congress."[102]

This new policy of a more humane concern for Indians was a part of FDR's New Deal. The Commissioner of Indian Affairs from 1933 to 1944, John Collier, was an anthropologist with a long career of interest in Indian affairs, and this may also have made a difference. Collier was critical of many American values and was identified with the aspirations of many Indian groups, as well as having his own ideas about the potential of Indian society.[103]

Tribal governments, established under this act, were helped to develop constitutions and carry on many operations required of modern governments, economic as well as political. In contradiction to this, however, was

---

[99]Wayne Moquin with Charles Van Doren, *A Documentary History of the Mexican Americans* (New York: Praeger Publishers, 1971), p. 252.

[100]Ibid., p. 253.
[101]Taylor, op. cit., pp. 20–26.
[102]Ibid.
[103]Ibid., p. 22.

the policy of promoting assimilation by urging states to provide the same services for individual Indians as for other citizens.

Asian Americans. This period saw the gradual improvement of the economic status of Chinese-Americans although not necessarily of their social status. As Kitano states:

In the late 1930s and during World War II the Chinese became our friends and allies, although the general tone of the friendship was condescending. . . . Their peace loving nature was emphasized; they had fought valiantly against the "sly, tricky Jap;" they were different from their more aggressive neighbor. . . . In many ways, this praise deflected from the everyday humiliation, harassment, and deprivation faced by many Chinese, even with the relatively favorable attitude toward all Orientals (except the Japanese) at this time.[104]

The most devastating event affecting the Japanese-American community was the wartime evacuation of all persons with as little as one-eighth Japanese blood from the West Coast. By March 1942, one hundred and ten thousand such persons, most citizens of the United States, were in virtual concentration camps in such states as Colorado, Utah, and Arkansas. There was widespread compliance by most Japanese-Americans, even though they had to abandon their homes and possessions. This terrible injustice continued until 1944 when the Supreme Court revoked the policy. Most families who survived the experience had to begin all over again. Little remained of their property or belongings.

Ideological Currents

The most important ideological issues of the period were those stimulated by the conditions of the depression. The emphasis of the twenties upon the individual's responsibility for his or her own destiny could not hold up under the circumstances of the thirties. The literature of this period emphasized the effects of the social order on people and the need to modify that order to solve the spiritual as well as the economic problems which plagued Americans.[105] Many came to regard government, rather than business, as the preferred means for developing a better society. However, except for small minorities, people wanted their government to operate through much the same political processes as it always had, and the economy to remain capitalist, though under strong government controls.

These ideas were not basically shaken by the war. Fascism as an international enemy was further proof that there are forces which transcend the individual and must be controlled by collective action. Although congressional investigations of "un-American activities" received support, the external enemy and wartime prosperity took many people's attention away from problems within the United States. Moreover, Americans' faith in their own political and economic system may have been reinforced by wartime victory. However, the specter of an external enemy acting in concert with internal agents returned with a vengeance with the cold war and the Korean War, dampening criticism of the "American way of life" and making it difficult to gain support for proposals to confront the country's social problems.

Development of Community Organization Institutions

Community organization agencies, like others in social welfare, found themselves

---

[104]Kitano, *Race Relations,* op. cit., p. 200.

[105]It was noted earlier that the ideological antecedents of some Negro militancy were in the twenties. Current white militancy had similar antecedents in the thirties.

unable to cope with the massive needs of the country during the depression. This period marked a shift of emphasis in operations from local and private to regional or national and public. The federal government through its agencies became the main impetus for social planning. At first through the Federal Emergency Relief Administration and later through the Federal Security Agency, standards for welfare activity were set, coordination was promoted, fact finding was conducted, and plans for public education were launched.

World War II advanced the trend toward community planning under national auspices, both public and private. The need for welfare services grew as new and expanding communities of defense workers and soldiers sprang up. The Office of Community War Services in the Federal Security Agency was created to handle some of the planning for recreation and public health needs in affected areas.

Organization of Ethnic Minorities and Women. Organization in the black community remained primarily on a national level, and some authorities have noted a degree of apathy regarding anything beyond that.[106] The NAACP continued to wage campaigns in the courts, the Congress, and the press for the rights of blacks. The Urban League expanded its programs of employment, family welfare, health, and education. The thirties and forties did not foster any prominent new organizational efforts. In addition to the external threats noted earlier, this may have been due to the development of governmental programs, trade union activity, and local activity, which black people believed would provide long-hoped-for access to the "American Dream."

During the 1930s, the organizing activities of the *Confederacion de Uniones Obreras Mexicanas* continued. Efforts to build union organizations also included those of the National Farm Workers' Union. Other organizations emerged, and some examples of these are the League of United Latin American Citizens (Texas, 1929), the *Asociacion de Jornaleros* (Texas, 1933), the *Sociedad Mutualista Mexicana* (Ohio, 1936), the Pan American Student Forum of Texas (1943), and the Community Service Organization (California, 1947).[107] The vitality of Chicano life is apparent in the organizations that were created during these years. These developments may well have provided support for the new programs which emerged in the 1960s.

These years also saw movements within Native American tribes. Through new government policies, many tribal governments were established or strengthened. Tribes assumed authority to:

employ legal counsel; prevent sale or encumbrance of tribal land or other assets without the consent of the tribe; negotiate with federal, state, and local governments; determine tribal membership; assign tribal land to individuals; manage economic affairs; appropriate money for salaries or other public purposes; levy taxes, license fees, or community labor in lieu thereof; control conduct of members of the reservation by enactment of ordinances . . . [108]

As was true of Mexican-Americans, it seems likely that the organizational development of the depression, war, and postwar years was a precursor to militant organizing in the next decade.

A somewhat different type of organizational experience characterizes Chinese-American life. Chinese-Americans had been living within their own communities,

---

[106]Fishel and Quarles, op. cit., p. 450.

[107]Alvarez, op. cit., pp. 209–210.
[108]Taylor, op. cit., pp. 23–24.

but a trend toward some dispersion began at this time. The control exerted by the traditional associations weakened in many Chinese-American communities. Some who had gained status in the broader community did not have it in the ethnic community because of age and cultural difference, including language. Thus, new institutions began to emerge to meet their needs.[109] In many ways, the situation was similar for Japanese-Americans, although recovery from the "relocation" of the war years was a long and hard process.

The period between the depression and the 1950s was not a good one for the women's movement. During the war years many women were employed, and this may have diminished demands for equal employment opportunities for women. However, such issues as adequate child care were central. The conservative swing after the war discouraged militancy among women. Even the League of Women Voters, hardly a radical organization, showed a decline in membership during this time.

Development of the Profession and Professional Education

This, while not a period of innovation in community organization beyond the shift from a local to a national emphasis, was a time of intensive efforts to conceptualize the nature of community organization practice. Writers had three overriding concerns.

The *first* bore upon the relation between community organization and social work. Some contended that community organization was not really a legitimate form of social work practice, and others took pains to establish community organization's

affinity to the basic values and concerns of social work.

The *second* was an interest in the objectives of community organization. On the one hand, practitioners regarded the Industrial Revolution as destructive of personal, face-to-face relations between people and believed that community organization practice should strengthen community cohesion. At the same time, they were disturbed about a number of social problems and thought that community organization practice should prevent or at least ameliorate them.

Third, they struggled with the appropriate role for the practitioner. Neighborhoods and communities needed the help of practitioners if localities were to achieve their objectives. And yet practitioners must not impose their views on those served. One must somehow strike a balance between giving help and fostering self-determination.[110]

1955 TO 1968

The beginning of this period coincides with the end of the McCarthy era and the Supreme Court decision on school desegregation. Whether or not causally related, these events appear to have anticipated a number of other phenomena.

Social Conditions

The Growth of the Civil Rights Movement. Marked by the 1954 Supreme Court decision ending legal school segregation, the rising dissatisfaction of black Americans gave birth or renewed vitality to a number of organizations which have sought to end

---

[109]For a discussion of this development, see Weiss, op. cit., pp. 264–273.

[110]For further details, see Schwartz, op. cit., pp. 177–190.

the inequality of opportunity afforded black people. The Montgomery, Alabama, bus boycott, which began in December of 1955, brought Martin Luther King, Jr., and the Southern Christian Leadership Conference forward as leaders in the civil rights struggle.[111] The Congress of Racial Equality (founded in 1943) sponsored nonviolent resistance in the form of sit-ins, freedom rides, and demonstrations.[112] The Student Non-Violent Coordinating Committee, the Mississippi Freedom Democratic party, the Black Panther party, the Black Muslims, the Republic of New Africa and other black nationalist groups, and the NAACP were among the organizations affected by the rising tide of civil rights activities. The quest for black power grew out of the experiences of the Student Non-Violent Coordinating Committee and other active groups who came to despair of achieving genuine integration. As they began to fight for black pride and capability, they demanded autonomy in black affairs, including neighborhood control of schools and economic institutions.[113]

Subsequently other minority groups asserted themselves, claiming their rights and developing pride in their special identity. The Chicanos of the Southwest made substantial progress in organizing. Stimulated by Cesar Chavez and his success in organizing California farm workers, Chicanos organized groups such as *La Raza Unida* in such places as south Texas, New Mexico, and even where migrant farm workers traveled in search of employment, such as Michigan, where many Chicano farm

workers settled down and sought education and regular jobs. American Indians, whose living conditions are generally worse than those of any other minority in this country, likewise demonstrated solidarity in such ways as occupying Alcatraz Island in San Francisco Bay and obtaining legislative support for expanded fishing rights in Michigan.

As the period continued, one trend was clear: a growing effort to create ethnic minority institutions. Examples include neighborhood control of schools, black-owned business, black professional societies, black-led Model Cities programs, powerful interest groups such as the National Welfare Rights Organization, and black labor unions. Nevertheless, conflicts were evident among the leaders of these groups, often traceable to ideological differences. For example, some black leaders sought parallel black economic organizations, i.e., black capitalism, while others worked for changes in the power bases of all American institutions to include major input from black people and other minorities.

Late in this period, other groups asserted themselves, feeling deprived in comparison with their fellow citizens and encouraged by the achievements of blacks and other minorities. Gay men and lesbians demanded social and economic rights and fought discrimination in jobs and housing. The elderly, sometimes with the support of Grey Panther groups, demanded greater attention to their needs, especially for health care. The handicapped also drew attention to the discrimination they suffer in education, employment, and public facilities. Women, oppressed by the requirements of their traditional roles, demanded liberation and equality. A not fully successful achievement was congressional approval of the Equal Rights Amendment to the federal Constitution and its ratification by many

[111]Martin Luther King, Jr., *Stride Toward Freedom* (New York: Ballantine Books, 1958).

[112]James Peck, *Freedom Ride* (New York: Simon & Schuster, 1962).

[113]Stokely Carmichael and Charles V. Hamilton, *Black Power: The Politics of Liberation in America* (New York: Vintage Books, 1967).

state legislatures. "Middle America" became a potent political force. Disgruntled citizens such as Irene McCabe mobilized large numbers of people who opposed the busing of school children to achieve racial integration. Political candidates (George Wallace, for example) captured the support of large numbers of disenchanted voters who felt strongly about school busing and high taxes and were distrustful of government. An anti-gay movement secured defeat of legislation favoring gay rights in Florida.

The Vietnam War. It is difficult to judge the impact of this war on social work and community organization. Nevertheless, seldom in American history have so many felt so antagonistic to a major involvement of their country. Aside from concerns about the justice of the war, its implications for the allocation of resources to deal with problems on the home front were of grave concern. Some regarded this war and, more generally, what President Eisenhower had referred to as the expanding influence of the "military-industrial complex" and the consequent retreat from dealing effectively with problems of our cities, as the most serious crisis the nation had faced. Certainly, the war led many to doubt the citizen's ability to influence governmental decisions.

The Growth of Student Movements. Stimulated by student involvement in the civil rights movement, student activism among whites as well as blacks and across the whole political spectrum increased phenomenally. Many student activists turned to social work and particularly to community organization in search of a career compatible with their personal commitments. Some students entering school in the mid-1960s were affected by the community

organization projects carried out by the Students for a Democratic Society. Many had experiences relevant to community organization through the Peace Corps or VISTA. Still others were influenced by the dynamic organizing style of Saul Alinsky and many organizations he helped found.

Increasing numbers of black students sought admission to professional schools, including programs offering training in community organization. Puerto Rican and Chicano students did likewise, and there is an indication of similar developments among Japanese- and Chinese-American students, particularly on the West Coast.

Development of Community Organization Institutions

The federal government took increasing responsibility for dealing with a wide range of domestic social problems, primarily through grants-in-aid to state and local governments. This had an important bearing on the growth of community organization practice. For example, early in this period the federal government sharply increased appropriations for mental health, primarily for research, professional training, and mental health clinics. More recently, federal programs encouraged preventive measures and efforts to treat the mentally ill in their local communities, a process requiring community organization skills. Similar developments occurred in programs for the mentally retarded, the physically disabled, and the alcoholic. The construction of hospitals and other health facilities, together with encouragement of health services planning at the state level, also received federal support. Programs of slum clearance, urban renewal, neighborhood development, housing subsidies, and regional planning were created and expanded with federal assistance. Although by no means exhaustive, this list of activities exemplifies the role of the federal government in the fields of health and urban development. Similar changes in related fields such as education and child welfare also occurred, which stimulated additional demand for community organization skills.

The trend toward federal responsibility for welfare problems was escalated by the War on Poverty, a product of the Kennedy and Johnson administrations. This program captured the interest of many community organizers. Among the specific programs were Head Start; VISTA; Neighborhood Youth Corps, Job Corps and other work-training programs; adult basic education; assistance to the rural poor, including migrant farm workers; and a wide variety of locally conceived "community action programs" offering opportunities for local initiative in legal aid, health, housing, consumer education, and so forth. Perhaps the single most important influence these programs had on community practice was the very large number of jobs they offered for people trained as organizers. One much-debated ingredient of these programs was the provision for "maximum feasible participation" of service recipients in program decisions. The how, where, and why of this was often confusing to both professionals and citizens.

Other programs created during this period tried to solve urban problems, which continued to intensify. A major effort was the Model Cities program established in 1966, which provided funds to groups representative of particular neighborhoods within cities. These groups used such funds either to develop new programs within existing civic institutions or to create new institutions where necessary.

In some Model Cities neighborhoods, a vision grew of a "parallel" government manned by the poor within the neighborhoods. This vision was muted, however, by developments which made the existing city governments powerful partners in any operation, under the rationale that coordination and accountability were necessary. This challenged community organizers to help constituents exert influence under these newly instituted rules.

All of these moves to solve urban problems raised the same issues: Which strata of society will have power? How are the poor to be represented? How are priorities to be determined? Community organizers were involved in answering all these questions, offering a variety of answers to each of them.

Ideological Currents

This was a time in which virtually all the previous ideas about community organization practice reappeared. On the one hand this was when American people supported the development of vast new responsibilities for government in solving the problems of welfare. On the other hand, there was a renewed emphasis upon participatory democracy. Local organization, black power, community control, and such concepts as "maximum feasible participation" (which Daniel P. Moynihan has paraphrased "maximum possible misunderstanding") had a wide appeal.

As might be anticipated, those ideological developments were reflected in the political groupings of the period. The Eugene McCarthy campaign for president in 1968 brought together many who saw themselves, at least for the moment, as working within existing institutions. Various groups identified with "the New Politics" continued this effort. On the other hand, as frustration over the lack of federal commitment to civil rights and ending the Vietnam war grew, violent ideologies and solutions also were perpetuated. An alternative "dropout" culture grew as a spin-off of this process. Some community organizers, for example, developed and lived within a growing network of communes.

Alongside interests in added government responsibility and participation of the people has been a strong tide of disengagement from society on the one hand and of violent opposition to those who control society on the other. These currents were reflected in social work, with some students planning government jobs, others looking forward to participation in anti-establishment grassroots organizations, and still others asking if social work and "revolution" are compatible orientations. Moderation and social planning formed the dominant orientation of community organization students, while social work as a whole experienced a marked increase of interest in professionalization, psychotherapy, self-realization and "making a good living."

Development of the Profession and Professional Education

Training for community organization practitioners in social work grew markedly at first. Both the number of programs and the number of students rose sharply. By 1969 the number of schools of social work providing training programs for community organizers increased to forty-eight, from thirty-six in 1965.[114] Community organization was taught in some form in virtually all schools.

Parallel with the increase in numbers were efforts to clarify the nature of community organization, identify what com-

munity organizers need to know to be effective, and give recognition to the development of community organization as a specialized form of practice within social work. In the late 1950s, the Council on Social Work Education embarked upon a wide-ranging study of the curriculum in schools of social work which included separate attention to community organization.[115] The National Association of Social Workers created a Committee on Community Organization which prepared working papers and bibliographies designed to codify practice knowledge and establish the position of the community organization specialty within social work.[116] In 1962 the Council on Social Work Education gave formal recognition to community organization as a method of social work comparable with casework and group work.[117]

An ambitious effort to develop curriculum for training community organizers was initiated in 1963. It, too, was sponsored by the Council on Social Work Education and received financial support from HEW's Office of Juvenile Delinquency and Youth Development.[118] This study culminated in the publication of five book-length reports and numerous journal articles and conference reports.[119] Earlier efforts pointed up the similarities of community organization practice and other forms of social work practice. Perhaps the most significant

---

[114]Arnold Gurin, *Community Organization Curriculum in Graduate Social Work Education: Report and Recommendations* (New York: Council on Social Work Education, 1970), p. 10.

[115]Harry L. Lurie, ed., *The Community Organization Method in Social Work Education,* Vol. IV, Project Report of the Social Work Curriculum Study (New York: Council on Social Work Education, 1959).

[116]See especially National Association of Social Workers, *Defining Community Practice* (New York: NASW, 1962).

[117]Council on Social Work Education, *Curriculum Policy Statement* (New York: CSWE, 1962).

[118]Gurin, op. cit., pp. vii–viii.

[119]For a summary and reference to the various publications of this project, see Gurin, op. cit.

theme of this latest curriculum study was the recognition that community organization practitioners required professional training that is, in many ways, differentiated from training for other social work specializations.

1969 AND AFTER

We have chosen 1969 as the beginning of the current phase of community organization history because of the political events that began that year and the many social changes related to these events. That year was the first one in which Richard Nixon held office as president of the United States. In his, as well as succeeding administrations, many of the programs initiated by Kennedy and Johnson were terminated, particularly those that were associated with the Office of Economic Opportunity and the Department of Health and Human Services (formerly the Department of Health, Education, and Welfare). Nixon's administration did, however, present some alternatives that were intended to link community and social planning more fully to the traditional political structures through such devices as revenue sharing and a community development block grant program.

This trend abated somewhat in the one-term administration of Carter but continued in an even more extensive manner as President Reagan sought to implement his philosophy of reducing the role of government, particularly the national government, in offering programs to solve social problems. This view was closely related to other ideas regarding how to cope with the economic crises brought on by severe unemployment and inflation, namely to reduce government spending while increasing purchasing power through reduction in taxation.

Social Conditions

John Naisbitt in his treatment of trends in society does an excellent job of highlighting the social conditions as well as ideological currents of this period and we draw heavily upon his work in the discussion that follows.[120] We have chosen to emphasize these kinds of trends at this point rather than specific events or programs because of the impact we believe they are having on social work practice at community and societal levels.

The Emergence of an Information Society. This development is associated with a shift in the occupational structure of the United States along with technologies that make this possible. By the 1980s, more than 60 percent of those employed work with information ". . . as programmers, teachers, clerks, secretaries, accountants, stock brokers, managers, insurance people, bureaucrats, lawyers, bankers, and technicians . . . Most Americans spend their time creating, processing, or distributing information."[121]

This trend has had major effects upon people who were already employed but lacked some of the skills now required, upon those seeking employment, and upon the skills people must obtain in order to be employable. This last point has obvious implications for an assessment of the adequacy of educational institutions as well as the educational preparation of the population.

Important technological developments associated with this shift to an information society are those of "high technology." In almost every sphere of life, technological developments have changed the ways we

---

[120]John Naisbitt, *Megatrends: Ten New Directions Transforming Our Lives* (New York: Warner Books, 1982).

[121]Ibid., p. 14.

live. Some examples of this are the utilization of computers for virtually every information processing task; the creation of many devices for monitoring and improving our health; the use of video associated mechanisms for entertainment, education, and marketing; and the employment in the factory of countless new ways of mechanizing production. These changes, in addition to the ways they have altered our lives, have also produced counterforces, according to Naisbitt, in that people have also sought new ways to be together doing simple things with each other.[122]

Growth of a World Economy. The changes that have taken place in the economic status of the United States are that it no longer plays the dominant role in the world economy, its economic growth has stalled, and its domestic market is dominated by foreign products in many sectors. The role of Japan, for example, is well known as a producer of many of the technological products used in the United States. What may not be as well known is the growth of South Korea in steel, of Brazil and Spain in ship building, and of China in textiles. This is leading to vast shifts in investment patterns, interorganizational relationships on a global scale, and the effects that economic developments within the United States have on those in others.

Decentralization. Despite the seeming concentration of power implied by a world economy, the actual trend is toward decentralization. According to Naisbitt, "the decline of American industry and the rise of the new information economy neutralized the pressure to centralize and we began to

decentralize."[123] Some of the examples he cites of this are the proliferation of cable TV stations and lower-powered broadcast TV stations; the increased role that state as opposed to national government is playing in our lives; a vast increase (that we shall discuss later) in neighborhood organizations; the interest in local magazines; and the shift of population to rural areas and small towns.

Ideological Currents

Perhaps the ideological development with the most impact on the current phase of community organizing is the belief in the value of self-help activities—although this might, in a classic social work sense, be thought of as *mutual aid.* In a limited way, this development has been seen by some as an outgrowth of President Reagan's emphasis on reducing people's reliance on government, but we join Naisbitt in seeing this as a culmination of a long historical process in which people reacted to their alienation from their government, their welfare institutions, and their occupations.

Some of the spheres in which we can see the development of self-help are in the ways people are seeking to improve their health through running, eating natural foods, monitoring their weight, and acting to prevent illness. They are also providing each other with mutual support in a manner that often imitates the highly successful program of Alcoholics Anonymous, such as Gamblers Anonymous, Parents Anonymous, Tough Love, Compassionate Friends (for those whose children have died), and groups for those who have had cancer, a mastectomy, a colostomy, Acquired Immune Deficiency Syndrome (AIDS), or

---

[122]Ibid., pp. 39–53.

[123]Ibid., pp. 98–99.

who lost a close friend or relative because of suicide. These are only a few of the hundreds of organizations that have arisen for mutual aid in the last few years and that continue to be created on almost a daily basis somewhere in this country.

As we mentioned earlier in this article the federal programs of the sixties required "maximum feasible participation" of their consumers. While this requirement has abated, in most societal spheres the move toward participation has grown. Naisbitt illustrates this in the creation and development of new political parties, the increase in splits among legislators of the same political party, the rise in the use of initiatives and referenda, and the tax "revolts." He also points to what he refers to as the "participatory corporation" which offers "workers, shareholders, consumers, and community leaders a larger say in determining how corporations will be run."[124] He sees this as occurring through consumerism, the appointment of more outside board members, shareholder activism, and worker participation.

Another trend noted by Naisbitt is toward "networking" in which people seek ways of locating others who can help them achieve desired ends. This has been facilitated by computer utilization in which computer files are maintained that can locate others of similar interests and needs. Examples cited by Naisbitt are the Denver Open Network, the National Women's Health Network in Washington, D.C., and the Newton, Massachusetts WARM LINES.[125]

Finally, we are becoming a society of even more diversity in all of life's spheres. A major example is that of the family in which the traditional notion of a household composed of two adults of different sexes who are married to each other (each for the first time) and who have children is the exception rather than the rule. Blended families, one-parent families, gay male and lesbian couples, and "living together" families are increasingly likely to be found in every community. The options available to women to work in every occupation and to play any and all family roles are accepted and, if not, are fought for. And people living each of these life styles, and many others that exist or are emerging, are developing networks, literature about their aspirations, and unique ways of coping.

Development of Community Organization Institutions

The major shift in community organization practice after 1969 was the withdrawal of federal funding from many community organizations and the termination of many community-oriented federal programs. This trend became most pronounced during the Reagan administration. The casual observer might conclude *incorrectly,* therefore, that there was a decrease in the quantity of community organizations. Nothing could be farther from the truth!

As Perlman states:

The contemporary grassroots movement is new, growing, diverse, and effective. Although its lineage can be traced back to the social movements of the 1960s, the early Alinsky organizations of the 1950s, and the union struggles of the 1930s and 1940s, in its present form it is not yet a decade old. Most of the groups we shall be describing started in the early 1970s, and many are five years old or less. They are growing in numbers and expanding in size so rapidly that any estimates of their size and numbers are outdated as quickly as they are calculated.[126]

---

[124]Ibid., p. 175.

[125]Ibid., p. 193.

[126]Janice E. Perlman, "Grassroots Participation from Neighborhood to Nation," in Stuart Langton, *Citizen Participation in America,* (Lexington, MA: D.C. Heath, 1978), p. 65.

Although, as Perlman states, the number of grassroots organizations is expanding, efforts have frequently been made to assess their quantity. She quotes a figure cited by the National Commission on Neighborhoods of 8,000 groups, and the Department of Housing and Urban Development (HUD) has begun a clearinghouse with 4,000 groups. In addition, the Alliance for Volunteerism estimated there were six million voluntary associations in the United States in 1975. Perlman adds that there are some 10,000 block clubs in New York City alone.[127]

Many local groups are affiliated with regional or national organizations. Among these are Association of Community Organizations for Reform Now (ACORN); National People's Action, and Massachusetts Fair Share. Some organizations also were created to provide support and technical assistance to grassroots groups such as the Center for Community Change, the National Center for Urban Ethnic Affairs, National People's Action, and the National Association of Neighborhoods.[128]

The important difference, however, between this and earlier periods is that these organizations cannot rely on federal financing but, instead, have generated many alternative forms of support. This often comes from state and local governments but also from voluntary donations, fundraising efforts, and support from various constituencies such as labor organizations, churches, and businesses.

The focus of many of these organizations is on specific issues such as housing, the creation of cooperatives, obtaining adequate health care in the community, and a host of consumer related topics. They exist in all ethnic communities and among all socioeconomic groups.

Organization of Ethnic Minorities and Women

The growth of neighborhood organization that we have just described also characterizes some of the major developments within oppressed ethnic communities. A few examples demonstrate the geographical spread as well as breadth of purpose of this. Native American organizations include the Seminole Employment and Economic Development Corporation (Florida); the Menominee Restoration Committee (Wisconsin); and the Zuni Craftsman Cooperative Association and the All Indian Development Association (New Mexico). Hispanic ones include the Mexican American Unity Council (Texas); *Chicanos Por La Causa* (Arizona); and the Council for the Spanish Speaking (California). Asian-American examples are the East Bay Asian Local Development Corporation and the Asian Neighborhood Association (California).

Within the black community, as well as the others we have named, these organizations have been highly issue oriented. The issues in that community have included reducing poverty through neighborhood job creation and training, reversing the trend toward the dismantling of services for children, and reducing illiteracy. Many black organizations have also sought to identify ideologically with peoples of the third world.

An example of these developments is PUSH in Chicago and the activities of its leader Jesse Jackson. That organization has heavily focussed on creating economic opportunities through such campaigns as encouraging black people to spend their money within the black community. Many

---

[127]Ibid., p. 67.

[128]More information on these organizations may be found in Robert A. Rosenbloom, "The Politics of the Neighborhood Movement," *South Atlantic Urban Studies,* Vol. 4 (1979), pp. 103–119.

black churches in keeping with this approach have created credit unions within their communities.

Many developments are continuing to occur within the women's movement and women's organizations. As progress was made in securing women's rights in the workplace, in academic institutions, and in government, this has provided impetus to even stronger commitments of women and women's organizations to refuse to settle for anything less than full opportunity. A recognition that, despite this progress, the "feminization of poverty" continues to be an issue for the entire society has contributed to the specific agendas of women's organizations. The candidacy of Geraldine Ferraro for vice-president has reinforced the conviction that women can and should seek every role available within the political and economic structure of society, and is likely to have effects that have not yet been predicted.

Development of the Profession and Professional Education

We shall not explore this topic at any length here as it is expressed throughout all of the chapters in this book. We believe that an important shift took place during this period, however, that we should draw attention to in this historically oriented analysis. This was the shift to thinking of community organization activities as part of "macro" practice that also includes interventions at organizational and societal levels.

This shift is important because it recognizes that social change takes place through a set of activities that sometimes focuses on a single organization, sometimes on a community, and sometimes on a society as a whole. The skills the practitioner uses when engaged in these activities are sometimes unique to the level (i.e., organization, community, society) but more often are appropriate to several levels. Such skills include needs assessment, group leadership, budgeting, and class advocacy—to name a few. The current edition of this book attests to this evolution.

Students and others learning to practice at these macro levels are likely to be taught this range of skills while being afforded opportunities to practice roles that are defined as management within an organization, organizing within a community, or policy creation and/or implementation within regional and societal institutions.

The tools available to these practitioners have grown over this period and include utilization of computer and other technological resources for communication and data manipulation purposes as well as knowledge regarding organizational, community, and societal phenomena drawn from major advances in the social sciences, particularly sociology, social psychology, anthropology, political science, and economics. Whether this "new world" leads to more successful efforts at social change than those engaged in by previous generations of organizers remains to be seen.

A unity of thinking among all social workers regarding micro and macro practices of change is, at least, encouraged by the spread of systems-oriented and ecologically based thinking throughout the profession. Presumably all social workers are coming to see the necessity for systems changes and the participation of the consumer of social services in these changes. The negative side of the picture is some tendency for social work students and practitioners to be highly concerned about career advancement and to emphasize *therapy* rather than social change in their career goals.

SUMMARY AND CONCLUSIONS

Community organization practice has been examined in its social and ideological context during four periods of its history, separated by events with particular significance for that practice: the First World War and the end of the Progressive Era (1914); the stock market crash (1929) and the Supreme Court decision ending legal racial segregation in the public schools (1954).

It is impossible to understand community organization as an isolated phenomenon or merely as a technique of social engineering, for it is so closely related to what is most important in the lives of those it touches. Industrialization, urbanization, immigration, and minority emancipation created great opportunities and problems. The perspectives of Social Darwinism, socialism, pragmatism, and liberalism through which social conditions were perceived set the stage for many institutional developments important for community organization practice. Among these were charity organization societies designed to coordinate unplanned efforts to rescue the poor, and social settlements intended to help the urban poor get themselves together, unite rich and poor in a common enterprise, and reform the oppressive conditions of life that victimized the poor. Minorities organized, in some cases, to accommodate themselves to the system and, in others, to fight it.

Following World War I, the American people expressed a strong desire to return to "normalcy" and the principles of free enterprise, and they developed a sense of profound optimism toward capitalism. The newly emerging profession of social work withdrew from its prior efforts to change pernicious social conditions. In its place, the profession cultivated a preoccupation with the individual psyche. In this context,

efficiency-oriented community chests were organized by businessmen to spread the cost and reduce the annoyance of charitable solicitations. A growing cadre of welfare professionals promoted councils of agencies to rationalize their efforts, fill the gaps in services, and promote disinterested and effective services supported by dependable and expanding resources. The social unit plan, oriented toward grassroots participation, found little sympathy in the climate of the times.

The depression brought the federal government into welfare planning and strengthened grass-roots activities, particularly through the labor movement. World War II and the government's response to the demands of blacks and others for equality were the beginning of important developments in community organization. Small programs for training community organization practitioners to work with community chests and welfare councils were organized, and their teachers produced the beginnings of a professional literature.

Recent periods are characterized first by the civil rights movements and those of oppressed minorities and by student activism and discontent with the war in Vietnam, generating strong professional interest in grass-roots organizing and planning with local citizens, plus a pervasive sense of anger and alienation.

This was followed by major reverses in the government's commitment to community organizing. Shifts in social attitudes, particularly among young people, were not conducive to organizing. Nevertheless, particularly within ethnic groups and among women, these commitments were kept alive and are now intensifying through the growth of neighborhood organizations.

Where does all this lead? Several major questions dangle precariously overhead like the sword of Damocles: How will impatient underclasses, and particularly large ethnic minorities, respond to current social conditions? Will the necessary wisdom and determination be forthcoming to put our resources to work on the social problems that threaten to divide the nation? What are the most effective ways to accomplish our objectives consistent with our values? The first is a question that only those who are oppressed can answer, and the most persuasive answers are likely to be deeds rather than words. The second is a question for the whole nation, especially the president and Congress, the governors, the state legislatures, the city councils, and the neighborhood groups themselves. The last is a particular responsibility of macro practitioners, including community organizers.

3.

Kim Bobo, Jackie Kendall, and Steve Max

CLEANING UP IN THE NINETIES

The 80s were a capitalist blowout . . . the rich got richer while nearly everyone else paid the price. Cleaning up will be the task of the 90s.

It is astonishing that the author of these words, which appeared in the staid *New York Times Magazine,* was not a writer of the left, but none other than conservative political analyst and former Republican Party strategist Kevin Phillips.[1] "The 1980s were the triumph of upper America," said Phillips, "an ostentatious celebration of wealth, the political ascendancy of the rich and a glorification of capitalism, free markets and finance. But while money, greed, and luxury became the stuff of popular culture," he continued, "few people asked why such great wealth had concentrated at the top and whether this was the result of public policy." In answer to this question, Phillips explained that indeed it was a Reagan Administration policy to enact tax, budget, and spending measures aimed at transferring money from the poor and middle class to the rich.

By now the story of the United States' decline as an economic power is well known. Once the world's largest creditor nation, we are now its largest debtor. Our standard of living has plummeted from first to ninth in the world and is still falling. And we went from being the leader in technology and trade, to desperately playing catch up, and in some industries, giving up altogether.

Accompanying this fall from grace has been a decline in the job market. Jobs with high salaries and good benefits have disappeared from our economy, only to be replaced by lower-paid service jobs, part-time jobs, and temporary jobs. Partly as a consequence of these changes, poverty-wage jobs

---

[1]Kevin Phillips, "Reagan's America: A Capital Offense." *The New York Times Magazine,* June 19, 1990.

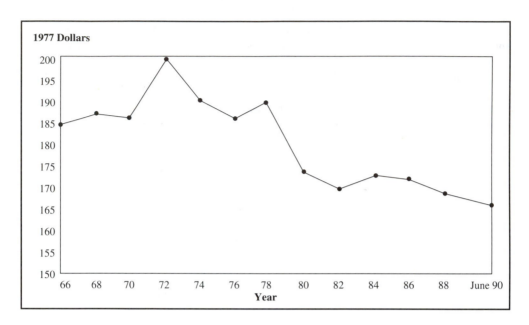

FIGURE 3.1
Average Weekly Pay (Source: "Economic Indicators," Council of Economic Advisors.)

(what a full-time year-round worker would earn without lifting a family of four out of poverty, about $13,104 in 1989) increased from 26 percent of all jobs in 1979 to 31 percent today.[2] A disproportionate percentage of African Americans (40 percent) and Latinos (42 percent) earn poverty wages compared to Whites (29 percent).

Families fared poorly in this environment. Family income after inflation dropped in the first part of the decade but rose in the second half, barely reaching the point it had been in 1973. While some families were able to maintain their economic position by putting both parents on the job, many single-parent families, especially those headed by women, fell into poverty.

Most of the increase in family income went to the rich. In fact, over the last decade, the 40 percent of families with lower incomes actually got poorer. When the changes in family income during the Reagan years are averaged, roughly half the population ended up worse off, while the other half did better financially. Some did very much better, and this encouraged other middle-class people to think that their turn was soon to come.

With these statistics in mind, it seems that many of our perceptions about the prosperity of the Reagan years were illusion. Despite the rise of Yuppies and the glitz of Donald Trump's empire, the real rate of economic growth during the Eighties averaged slightly less than that of the low-growth Seventies, a rate for which President Carter was severely taken to task. What's more, growth was much lower in the Eighties than it had been in the Fifties

[2]Lawrence Mishel and David M. Frankel, *The State of Working America.* Washington, D.C.: Economic Policy Institute, 1990–1991 edition.

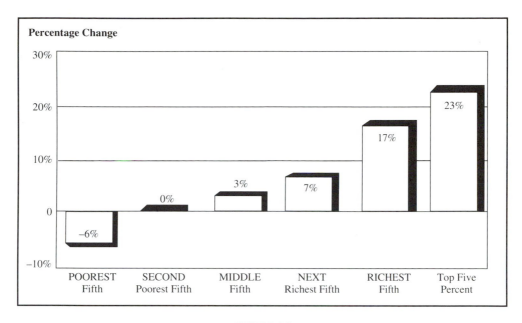

FIGURE 3.2
Average Before-Tax Income Gains and Losses Between 1979 and 1989, By Fifths of All Families
(Source: U.S. Census Bureau, Center on Budget and Policy Priorities.)

or Sixties. In the end, the Reagan economic boom proved to have been living on borrowed time, borrowed money, military spending, and resources stolen from the public. Whether it was through mining and cutting timber on federal land, despoiling the savings and loans, or issuing worthless junk bonds to finance corporate mergers, Republican-sponsored deregulation led to private plundering that greatly enriched a few, but left the nation poorer.

HOW THE POOR GOT POORER WHILE THE RICH GOT RICHER

Throughout most of our history, there have been great differences in income among Americans, but most of us felt that at least we were all moving upward together. Reagan's tax policy did much to change this. The Eighties were characterized by rising inequality,

and as Kevin Phillips has said, this was not an accident. Phillips said, "The reduction or elimination of Federal income taxes was a goal of previous capitalist heydays. But it was a personal preoccupation for Ronald Reagan . . . Under him, the top personal tax bracket would drop from 70 percent to 28 percent in only seven years."[3]

Progressive Robert McIntyre of Citizens For Tax Justice explained the consequences. "The Congressional Budget Office found that nine of ten American families are actually paying a higher share of their incomes in total federal taxes than they did prior to the so-called 'supply-side tax cuts' enacted in 1978 and 1981! Only the richest ten percent of the population has enjoyed a reduction in taxes since 1977, with most of the tax cuts concentrated on the richest one percent." Noting that the super rich have seen their taxes cut by 35 per-

---

[3]Kevin Phillips, op. cit.

cent from the 1977 rate, McIntyre concluded, "If the tax system were made as progressive now as it was prior to the notorious 'supply-side' tax shift . . . then nine out of ten families would pay less in federal taxes, and the government would collect almost $70 billion a year more in revenues."[4] That $70 billion would eliminate about 40 percent of the estimated federal deficit for 1991.

The tax cuts for the rich meant that large amounts of cash were available for the orgy of speculation characterizing the Eighties, which fueled the merger boom and the sale of junk bonds. In the not so long run, this further undermined the position of the middle class by increasing job loss.[5] At the time, apologists for the Administration claimed that merger-mania was a sort of natural broom, sweeping out ineffective management and liquidating unprofitable industries to free up cash for new investment. But many otherwise healthy companies took on such great amounts of debt that they became unstable and collapsed with the economic downturn. Much of the new investment went abroad or into debt payment, not into building healthy American industries.

Failing to heed the consequences of tax breaks to the rich, the Bush Administration has said that it intends to continue its efforts to reduce capital gains taxes. Meanwhile, the share of federal revenue coming from the corporate income tax has been allowed to fall from 30 percent in 1954 to only 11 percent today. This means that individuals pay a much greater share of the federal budget than corporations.

And what exactly are we paying for? One of the largest items in our budget, and one that has enriched many investors, is military spending. During the Reagan years, defense spending rose by over 43 percent as U.S. intelligence warned of a growing Russian menace. That the Soviet Union was in a state of increasing economic and political collapse went oddly undetected by the U.S. spy system, by our extensive diplomatic apparatus, and by hundreds of professional academic "Russia watchers." But our military spending to guard against this menace, much of it borrowed, proved to be a tidy bail-out for investors in the defense industry. Then, just when it appeared that a portion of the vast military cost would at last go to real tax relief and unmet social needs, a new threat appeared in the Persian Gulf. Strangely, U.S. intelligence had also failed to notice the development of this new threat while the Reagan Administration was encouraging the sale of arms to Iraq, some of which were covertly passed through to Iraq by the government of Kuwait.[6]

THE CONSEQUENCES FOR OUR SOCIETY

In contrast to previous decades, the fiscal policy of the Eighties amounted to funding

---

[4]Citizens For Tax Justice, *Inequality and the Federal Budget Deficit.* Washington, D.C.: March 1990.

[5]An analysis of the sources of wealth of the "Forbes 400" richest Americans shows that between 1982 and 1988, the percentage of the "400" whose major source of wealth was real estate and finance rose from 25 to 38 percent. The percentage of those whose wealth came from manufacturing dropped from 26 to 19 percent. Those whose wealth came from high technology, the supposed replacement for basic industry, rose from 3 to 4 percent. James Petras and Christian Bay, "Changing Wealth of the U.S. Ruling Class." *Monthly Review,* December 1990.

[6]According to one analyst: "The Reagan administration, in apparent violation of federal law, engaged in a massive effort to supply arms and military supplies to the regime of Saddam Hussein . . . Today, U.S. troops in the Persian Gulf are facing an enemy equipped with some of the West's most devastating military technologies (Murray Waas, "How The U.S. Secretly Armed Iraq." *The Voice,* December 18, 1989).

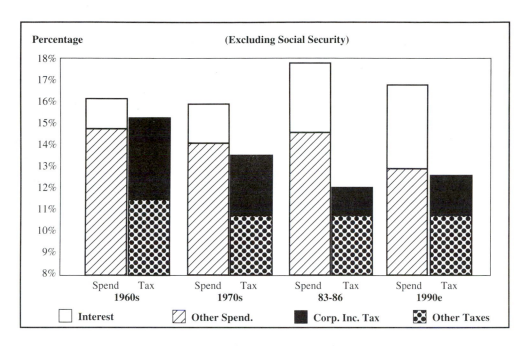

FIGURE 3.3
Federal Spending and Taxes as a Percentage of GNP (Source: Citizens for Tax Justice (CTJ). Washington, DC.)

The set of bars representing the decade of the 1980s is based on the years 1983–1986. This is done to show the effect of the 1981 tax reform that was fully in operation by 1983. The changes brought about by the tax reform of 1986 are reflected in the bars for 1990.

a larger part of the federal budget through borrowing than taxing. Much of the borrowed money was then transferred to the rich as tax cuts, military industry profits, and interest payments on government bonds. It would no doubt have cost less in administrative overhead had the money simply been given away to the rich. One result of this policy was a deliberate underfunding of the national budget and the creation of a permanent fiscal crisis at every level of government. This, in turn, has distorted the debate over social priorities.

The federal budget is most accurately understood by excluding the Social Security Trust Fund. As the Office of Management and Budget puts it, this revenue, coming from a special tax and dedicated to

a single purpose, is ". . . not available for general purposes of government." It should therefore not be thought of as part of the federal budget. The advantage to the administration of including Social Security (and other trust funds) in the budget is that it makes the budget look much larger.

With the budget thus inflated, the deficit and military spending appear smaller in proportion, while social spending, including Social Security, seems larger. It is also helpful to view the budget in relation to the size of the whole economy (GNP). A larger economy provides a larger base to tax, and often a greater need for government spending than does a small economy. [Figure 3.3] shows the budget (excluding Social Security) as a percentage of the whole economy (GNP). The pattern is clear. Non-interest spending has been reduced in the past thirty years, but taxes (also excluding Social Security taxes) were cut even more.[7]

Federal program cuts have left cities and states with financial burdens that they simply cannot carry. While this wasn't obvious everywhere during the boom years, many localities are once again making agonizing choices of whether to lay off police, fire fighters, sanitation workers, or teachers. Middle-class people who moved back to the cities during the boom are starting to flee again. One reason for this phenomenon is the tax crisis at the local level.

In the post-war period, the most dramatic tax increases have been at the local level. In relationship to the size of the whole economy (GNP), federal taxes have risen 6 percent since 1947, while state and local taxes have risen 106 percent.[8] Local taxes, consisting mostly of property and sales taxes, are the least progressive, and the few progressive local income taxes that are in place tend to be even less progressive than those at the federal level. The result is that the rich pay a much smaller percentage of their income for local taxes than does the middle class, while the poor are hit hardest of all. Because local taxes are one of the few areas of life over which everyday people still feel that they have some control, it is no wonder that local taxes have become a major political battleground. The inherent merits of issues like education, housing, law enforcement, or the environment are rarely discussed anymore. Instead, such issues are judged by their impact on local taxes. The deep sense of hopelessness and lack of alternatives that pervades these debates

merely reflects the fact that the cost of doing anything at all has been substantially shifted to people whose income is already declining, and whose livelihoods become more imperiled with each passing year.

Reality is at last intruding on President Bush, forcing him to concede, after nine years of la-la-land Republicanism, that taxes do have to be raised. Before this, the only real-world gesture that the Republicans would make (with much bipartisan support) was to raise Social Security taxes, and then borrow the money for other things. Now, at least, the debate is moving away from "spending versus cuts," an area where progressives, though in the right, have made little headway. The new debate is over who should pay, and that is a very different question, one where majority sentiment can be with us. If the recession deepens and requires large-scale spending to restart the economy, taxing the very rich can have wide appeal. If we organize it right and press for very specific taxes aimed at upper-income individuals, delinquent corporations, and transnationals, we can force conservatives (in both parties) to defend publicly the privileges of the rich at the expense of everyone else, as they did with the capital gains tax cut. This provides a marvelous clarification of why conservatives are unworthy of the support that much of middle America has so generously bestowed on them.

CLEANING UP IN THE NINETIES

The list of unmet social needs and issues on which to organize is always long, even under the best of circumstances, and it is longer than ever today. It isn't our intention here to prioritize the issues, or even catalog them. Instead, we focus on the broader goals of organizing in the Nineties,

[7]Citizens For Tax Justice, *Inequality and the Federal Budget Deficit,* op. cit.

[8]Lawrence Mishel and David M. Frankel, *The State of Working America,* op. cit.

and the role that issues can play in reaching them. Our broader organizing goals in this period should include restoring the vitality of the democratic system by breaking the conservative hold on the whole electoral process. We can do so by creating a vibrant, multicultural progressive populism where people speak out for economic and environmental justice while moving the whole economy forward. Specific shorter-term issues advance these broader goals. Some examples follow.

The Health Care Crisis

Our already inadequate health care system has been further strained by changes in the economy. Poverty-wage and temporary jobs don't bring the same health benefits that a middle-class wage brought. From 1980 to 1989, health insurance benefits fell by 48 percent when adjusted for the health industry inflation rate (which is far higher than general inflation), according to the Economic Policy Institute.[9] At the same time, premiums, deductibles, out-of-pocket ceilings, and co-payments are all increasing.

To make matters worse, the number of workers with health insurance fell over this period by five percentage points, to only 57 percent. Since 1980, the number of people (working and not working) who are without any health insurance grew by 40 percent and has reached 37 million, according to a Citizen Action study.[10] And as many as 70 million Americans who have insurance are vulnerable to catastrophic costs because of the inadequacy of their coverage.

Medicare and Medicaid have failed to meet their mandate of protecting the elderly, disabled, and poor. The elderly are now paying 18 percent of their income for health care. (This will rise with further budget cuts.) Only 40 percent of low-income people are covered by Medicaid, and critical home care and long-term care services remain uncovered.

In short, the U.S. health care system is now both the most expensive and the least accessible in the world, and the worst of any industrial country except South Africa. There is a growing sense that something must be done.

The proposals for cleaning up health care in the United States are wide ranging. They include local measures requiring that the employees of contractors working for county governments be covered with health insurance by their employers, state plans to cover the uninsured, state requirements that all employers provide health insurance, and federal requirements that employers provide health insurance.

All of these are better than what we have now, but all have one major defect: They continue to rely on an endless inefficient web of private profit making insurance companies to finance our health care.

A far better solution is for us to adopt a Canadian-style single-payer health system that eliminates the insurance companies entirely. Instead of paying premiums to insurance companies, Canadians pay them to the government in the form of taxes. The federal and provincial governments then pay health care bills for all Canadians. In that system, doctors remain independent professionals as they are in the U.S. Canadians have the same free choice of doctors and other health care providers that Americans have. Unlike Americans, however, no Canadian has to worry about being able to afford a doctor.

In America, commercial health insurance companies spend 33 cents on admin-

---

[9]Ibid.

[10]Citizen Action and National Health Care Campaign, *National Health Care: An American Priority.* Washington, D.C., 1989.

istration and advertising in order to deliver 1 dollar of health care. That doesn't even count their profits. It costs the Canadians only 3 cents to provide a dollar of benefits, according to a Citizens Fund study.[11] Could that work in America? Yes! Our Medicare system is similar in that it now spends just 2.3 cents in administrative costs for every dollar of benefits. A national health care system could run with that type of low overhead as well. By way of comparison, if commercial insurance companies were as efficient as the Canadian system, they could reduce the premiums for a family policy by almost $600 a year.[12]

Efficiency isn't the only argument for the Canadian system. Because the government pays all the bills, it is better able to contain costs. The same appendectomy that costs $180 in Canada is $797 in America.[13] There are no deductibles, so Canadians tend not to wait until they are really sick before they see the doctor, they get more checkups, there is more preventive medicine, serious diseases are caught sooner, and all this helps to keep costs down.[14] When pollsters asked Canadians if they would prefer the American system, only 3 percent said yes.[15]

National health care is also a way to strengthen America's economy and exports. While not necessarily endorsing the Canadian plan, Chrysler's Lee Iacocca commented,

American industry cannot compete effectively with the rest of the world unless something is done about the great imbalance between health care costs in the U.S. and national health care systems in virtually every other country. That's why a national health insurance program for the U.S. is being discussed widely for the first time since the late '70's.[16]

Conservatives recognize that this is true, but their response is to urge other countries to dismantle health systems that, in the conservative view, are barriers to free trade. According to their logic, national health care unfairly lowers the cost of goods when individual companies are relieved, by a national health plan, of the cost of providing health insurance for their employees. The conservatives are right that costs are lower as a result of national health systems, but wrong that there is something unfair about it.

Discussions of a U.S. national health system began during the Carter Administration and ended with the election of Ronald Reagan. During the Eighties, access to adequate health care moved closer to being the exclusive privilege of the rich, with more and more Americans now just one serious illness away from poverty. The fight for a national health system similar to the Canadian plan is another unifying issue that, when cut sharply, forces conservative elected officials to choose between publicly defending an ideology that just happens to coincide with the interests of the big insurance companies, or supporting the needs of the majority.

---

[11]Citizens Fund, *Premiums Without Benefits: Waste and Inefficiency in the Commercial Health Care Insurance Industry.* Washington, D.C., October 1990.

[12]Ibid.

[13]Ibid.

[14]According to *Statistical Abstracts 1990,* life expectancy in Canada in 1987 was 77.2 years as opposed to 75.4 years in the U.S., while the infant mortality was 7 per 100,000 in Canada against 11 in the U.S. Canadians spend only 8.6 percent of their gross domestic product on health care, in contrast to Americans, who spend 11.2 percent. Last, per-capita health expenditures by Canadians amount to $1,376 per year; in America, this figure is $2,051.

[15]Anthony Schmitz, "Liberty, Justice, and Insurance for All." In *Health,* January/February 1991.

[16]*The New York Times,* May 9, 1989.

Cleaning Up the Economy Through Changing Ownership and Worker Participation

Between 1980 and 1988 . . . , America's trade balance with the rest of the world fell by 402 percent. It seems foolish to place our lives and future prosperity in the hands of corporate management that has lost, or deliberately given up, so vast a share of the market.

Business organizations such as the Business Round Table and the U.S. Chamber of Commerce are already advocating lower American wages and living standards, so that cheap American labor can compete with cheap labor from developing countries. They don't seem to have figured out that this is a sure-fire formula for recession: When every corporation tries to produce as much as possible and pay the lowest possible wages, at some point, the amount of goods produced gets ahead of people's ability to buy it. Then sales fall, followed by lay-offs, and often a recession. Keeping demand high both here and abroad is the key to prosperity. A "consumer economy" won't work unless people can afford to consume (but of course, always with moderation).

During the artificial boom of the Eighties, with so many people making money in the speculative industries such as stock and commodities trading, banking, real estate, arbitrage, and gambling casinos, and with many millions more employed in these industries, consumer demand kept climbing. Once the speculation bubble burst and stock brokers, bank officers, and hundreds of thousands of their supporting staff began to be laid off, consumer demand dropped, and America began to confront the consequences of having become a low-wage nation.

There was a time in the 1940s, 50s, and 60s when U.S. corporations seemed committed to a rising living standard, and they accepted strong labor organizations. Now, in the Nineties, the new direction among large corporations is globalization. Their goal is to free themselves from ties to any one country. Corporations still pretend they are trying to win the trade war for America, particularly when they ask for tax breaks and wage cuts, but there are no more strictly-American corporations. Can we trust corporations that are no longer American to build a strong economy for the American people? In June of 1989, corporate globalization was designated an official economic trend by the people in our society in charge of trends. The Sunday *New York Times* headline said,

U.S. Business to Loosen Links to Mother Country

Globalization is in fact emerging as corporate America's strategy of choice for the 1990s. With a new surge of investment abroad, many American companies are shedding the banner of national identity and proclaiming themselves to be global enterprises whose fortunes are no longer so dependent on the economy of the United States. In a growing number of cases, high paying jobs including those of engineers and other professionals are going abroad instead of being kept at home. Spending . . . on research . . . is rising far more quickly overseas. American companies are increasingly supplying foreign markets from their overseas operations rather than by exporting.[17]

The following quotations from corporate leaders help to explain their new thinking.

The United States does not have an automatic call on our resources. There is no mind-set that puts this country first.
—From the head of Colgate-Palmolive

We try to make balanced decisions that take everyone into consideration, Malaysian and American.
—From the head of Motorola

---

[17]*The New York Times,* May 21, 1989. See also "U.S. Corporations Expand in Europe," *The New York Times,* March 3, 1989.

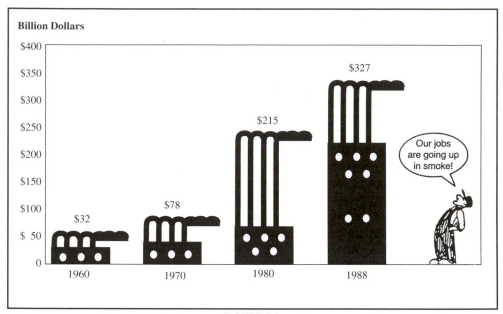

FIGURE 3.4
Billions of American Overseas Investment (Source: "Statistical Abstract of U.S.," Various Years.)

In any country where Ford operates, the amount of manufacturing done in that country should be as great as possible.
—From the director of corporate strategy at Ford

There will be more investment in high tech factories around the world.
—From the head of Stanley Tools

Of course, foreign companies are becoming worldwide operations also, but with a major difference. They are often held to some national identity by their relations to their government and unions. Often, they keep research and skilled work at home. They make foreign plants dependent on home-country machine tools and parts. Not so the American companies. Clyde Prestowitz, a trade negotiator in the Reagan Administration, comments, "Globalization isn't really taking place as a world wide phenomenon. Only American companies are really doing it."[18]

_____
[18]*The New York Times,* May 21, 1989.

Now corporations are switching sides on the trade protection issue. When Goodyear started building a plant in South Korea to produce 10,000 tires a day, it stopped demanding that Korean tires be kept out of America.

The response from Republicans has been to smile on all this and talk about free trade as the cornerstone of prosperity. Among Democrats, the response has been much more varied, with strong language about forcing other countries to buy from "American" corporations.

The conceptual breakthrough that progressives have to make on trade policy in the Nineties is that there is no longer any point in talking about foreign or American corporations. Goodyear and General Motors can act foreign, Honda and Mazda can act American. A key question for us is where the product is made. Every industrial country except America has some form of domestic content legislation. They decide that a certain percentage of the parts in any product sold in their country must be made there. This doesn't necessarily favor home companies, and it doesn't necessarily hurt foreign companies. It does help to keep jobs, and to maintain a better mix of skilled and unskilled jobs. When the United Auto Workers Union tried to win domestic content rules for automobiles, the main opponents were the Big Three auto companies. So heavy were Big Three imports of cars and parts, that they wanted no "protection" from foreign-made goods.

Another alternative to the problem of competing with cheap foreign labor is to help it to become less cheap. An American foreign policy that specifically encouraged union organizing in developing nations instead of discouraging it, would be a big step toward wage equalization.

Even as globalization and disinvestment in America proceed, new forms of management are starting to emerge; with proper encouragement, they could change the corporate culture for the better. Employee Stock Ownership Plans (called ESOPS) are exploding all over the country. A few years ago, employee ownership was an alternative to plant closings. The results were mixed. Recently however, perfectly healthy corporations began using ESOPS to dodge taxes and to protect themselves from hostile take-overs. Suddenly, corporations were selling large blocks of stock to employees. In the final two years of the Eighties, over 200 companies—including Avis, Procter & Gamble, J.C. Penney, Anheuser-Busch, Texaco, Polaroid—sold stock to their nearly 11 million workers in all.[19]

Typically, the employees become the largest single voting block of company stock. Management's motivation is greed as usual. They use ESOPS to tamper with pensions and benefits, as well as to fight off the raiders, but the courts have ruled that workers have the right to choose their own representatives to handle their stock.

It is difficult to guess the impact of the coming recession on the trend toward ESOPS. It seems likely that stock in many corporations may be for sale at bargain prices, but that employees will be more reluctant to buy in. Nonetheless, there may be the opportunity for a historic large-scale transfer of corporate ownership to working people, and even to states and municipalities, as is happening in much of Western Europe. This can happen if federal and state assistance encourages the process by lessening the financial risks, and extending real rights of ownership and management to workers in ESOPS.

Changing ownership can be part of a national strategy to rebuild the economy. Working people are, after all, the only element in the corporate equation with a stake in efficient competitive industries built here in America. It is of little concern to the wealthy where their assets are physically located, so long as the dividends come in. But employee owners, whose incomes depend more on wages than on dividends, would make many decisions differently than present management.

Another road to rebuilding the economy is union participation in management. Working people and their union representatives often know of ways to improve productivity and product quality, and can make wiser decisions at every level of management. While Sweden is the better model, Japanese-owned companies are already implementing their version of worker participation here in America, although sometimes this is used to undermine union

---

[19]"The Rush to ESOPS," *Business Week,* May 16, 1989.

organization. There are places, such as the General Motors–Toyota Saturn plant in California, where the union became involved in management down to the shop floor level.

The Japanese long ago learned that their method of achieving constant innovation and improvement in production on the factory floor required knowledgeable, educated, and motivated workers. The key to this proved to be insuring job security so that workers need not fear that by becoming more efficient, they jeopardize their own jobs. American management, on the other hand, has traditionally sought workers who will shut up and do as they are told, who have only the minimum education needed for the job, and who are motivated mainly by fear of being fired.

One story illustrates the differing attitudes of American and Japanese management. During the 1981–82 recession, American automobile companies cut back production and laid off hundreds of thousands of workers, many of them permanently. In Japan, Nissan Motors also cut back on production, but instead of laying off unneeded factory workers, they retrained the workers as salespeople, and sent them door to door all over Japan selling cars: "I can attest to the quality of this car. I built it." When the economy improved, Nissan called back the "salespeople" to their jobs in the plant, and was able to use the wealth of consumer information gathered at the doors. This was not a marketing gimmick. It was consistent with the large Japanese corporations' policy of shielding their workers from unemployment. The elimination of corporate America's negative and unproductive view of working people, combined with new forms of management and ownership, can play a powerful role in revitalizing the economy.

Union participation in management re-

quires a changed political climate, one that again makes organizing possible. At the high point of union strength in the 1950s, unions represented about 35 percent of the work force. Today, the organized sector is less than 17 percent. In spite of increased conservative efforts to create an antiunion atmosphere, Americans still support unions. In a 1988 Gallup poll, 61 percent said that they approved of unions, and in a 1990 Cable News Network/*Time Magazine* poll, 73 percent said that workers still needed unions.[20] Why then, has private sector unionism declined? (The percentage of public sector union membership remained stable throughout the Eighties.)

The reasons for labor's decline are political as well as ecomomic. One often cited cause is the switch from industrial to service jobs, but a similar thing also happened in Canada with the opposite result. Throughout the Eighties, Canadian union membership grew steadily and is now approaching 40 percent of the work force. The major difference in labor relations between Canada and America is that Canada accepts unions as partners in the Canadian economy, and has a legal framework that reflects the partnership. The same used to be true in America, but since the Seventies, that legal framework has disintegrated, allowing a wholesale corporate attack on unions. A few figures illustrate this point. According to the National Labor Relations Board, in 1960 one worker was illegally fired out of every 100 workers who voted for a union. By 1989, this figure became one out of every five. If voting union means a one-in-five chance of being illegally fired, no wonder union organizing has become much more difficult.[21] The refusal of the

---

[20] Cited in AFL-CIO, Public Employees Department, *Strategies to Help the Working Poor, 1990.*
[21] Ibid.

Republican Administration to enforce the laws protecting workers' rights to organize, or even to adequately staff the National Labor Relations Board, is hastening our descent into a low-wage economy.

The lowest wage is the best wage, according to the conventional corporate wisdom. From the point of view of profits, that may be right, but from the point of view of productivity, it may be wrong. There is good reason to think that high wages lead to more healthy industries. In such countries as Germany and Sweden, where wages are higher than ours, and in Japan, where they are rising rapidly and approaching ours, corporations are forced to find ways to become more innovative, efficient, productive, and competitive, simply in order to survive. In low-wage countries, the temptation is to substitute cheap labor for investment in new technology. Generally speaking, the countries with higher, or faster rising wages than ours, have also become more effective competitors than we.

Cleaning Up the Environment

The last thing that we Progressives really wanted in the Eighties was to be proven right about the environment. If only Ronald Reagan had been correct that there was no such thing as acid rain and that trees caused air pollution. If only it was true that solid waste disposal would be no problem and recycling was unnecessary. If only nuclear energy really was safe, efficient, and cheap, and disposing of the radioactive waste was easy. If only the danger to the ozone layer was fantasy, and global warming unprovable. If only the warnings about toxic dumping actually were a hippie trick to turn people on to LSD, or whatever the administration's excuse was. Unfortunately, we were absolutely right, and a decade was wasted, during which America could

have had the luxury of dealing with these problems in a rapidly expanding economy.

Global warming is potentially the most catastrophic result of the policy of shifting wealth to the rich at the expense of everyone else. While other industrial nations demand that the U.S. join in adopting strong measures to protect the environment, the Conservative Administration has made it clear that corporations are free to use the American environment as an ash tray. Pollution is socialized by giving it away free to all of us, whether we want it or not. This saves corporations money and increases profits (which are not socialized).

Unlike toxic dumping, global warming is experienced less directly by the average citizen. Nevertheless, there has been widespread publicity about the problem, and many citizens have heard of it. They remember and associate summer droughts and other phenomena with global warming, and are increasingly concerned about the health and economic consequences of ozone depletion, smog-ridden cities, and acid rain. All this suggests that people have begun to identify their well-being and the future well-being of their children with efforts to significantly reduce pollution.

In order to mobilize citizens, a sharp focus on those responsible for the problem, coupled with legislative campaigns for stronger regulation, are necessary. We also need to counter the corporate assertion that reducing pollution will cost jobs and undermine competitiveness.

The utility industry provides a good example of our position. The average cost in America of generating one kilowatt hour (kWh) of electricity is six and one-half cents. For only four cents, we can save one kWh of electricity through residential programs, including such measures as adding insulation. In industrial plants, the average cost of saving one kWh is even lower, only one cent. There is great potential to meet future increases in the demand for power by saving electricity already generated, instead of producing more of it. Not only is this better for the environment, but dollar for dollar of investment, electricity saving programs create four times as many jobs as does generating additional electricity.

The primary solutions to global warming will not only expand economic opportunities by creating new jobs, but will allow the U.S. to compete more vigorously in world markets. Consumers will benefit by getting more energy-efficient appliances, lighting, housing, and cars, which are also cheaper to operate. The environment will benefit as well. Many environmentalists argue that Americans can be persuaded to take individual action to reduce their own personal pollution. This is a fine thing, and often the first step in people's awareness of the problem, but to make this issue cut politically, the pressure needs to be solidly on government and corporations.[22]

People's Politics in the Nineties

At the risk of dwelling too much on one moment in time that will be long in the past for many readers . . . , we nonetheless feel compelled to note that on the most recent election day, November 6, 1990, the nation stood on the brink of a war in the Middle East, faced rising inflation, and was at the start of major recession. The next day, another hundred thousand troops were ordered to the Persian Gulf. The price of oil hit $35 a barrel, up from $22 a few months before. New unemployment insurance claims ran 18 percent above the previous year. With so many perils lying ahead and so many vital decisions to be made, one might think that a national election at this crucial moment would be a matter of great interest. The astonishing reality is that only one third of those eligible voted. This, of course, means that candidates might be sent to high office with the support of only 17 percent of the citizens, and in three-way races, as few as 11 percent. Said veteran *New York Times* analyst R.W. Apple Jr.,

The nation's voters didn't much like the choices presented to them . . . Evidently unhappy with politics as usual the voters liked independent candidates beholden to neither party. They liked proposals that would limit the terms of legislators. With one big exception [Jesse Helms], they disliked people they found extreme in style or viewpoint . . .[23]

The falling voter turnout does pose a strategic problem for Progressives: How do we win a game that fewer and fewer people are willing to play? There is always the hope that the last remaining players will be on our side, but long before that, democracy will have ceased to matter. Fortunately, we don't find the dissatisfaction evident at the level of grassroots citizen organizing. Quite the contrary, participation in community activities, student organizations, and citizens' issue campaigns is rising. There are, to be sure, some forms of grassroots activity that we oppose, such as right-wing taxpayer campaigns, but even these indicate that there is not a general retreat from public life, only from the official channels through which people are supposed to participate. There are now two alternatives facing the country. One is a negative race-based politics in which people fight each other for a diminishing share of a shrinking pie. The other is a new progressive populism that not only distributes the pie more fairly but also makes it larger.

---

[22]Ed Rothchild of the Citizen Action staff contributed this view of global warming.

[23]R. W. Apple, Jr., *The New York Times,* November 11, 1990.

In state after state, we get the feeling that a new politics is emerging, but that it has not yet taken shape or direction. There are pieces of it in the Democratic party, some are even in the Republican party, and many pieces are in no party at all. Progressive citizen organizations and community groups are increasingly the institutions to which people turn for solutions, precisely because we are different. We can thus hold the key to the political impasse.

If history is any guide, and it isn't always, the key to a realignment of the political process may well be the development of an overriding issue or set of related issues that both unifies a Progressive constituency and polarizes society. That was the nature of the realignment behind the 1856 candidacy of John C. Fremont, the first candidate of the newly formed Republican party (Lincoln was the second). The issue, of course, was slavery and its related economic questions: the tariff (which northern industry wanted and southerners opposed) and the fate of the western territories (which northerners wanted free of slavery and free of charge for homesteading, and which southerners wanted for the expansion of the plantation system). Both major parties, the Democrats and the Whigs, were divided on these issues, and neither party was capable of giving national leadership on an antislavery platform or even of blocking slavery's expansion.

It had taken several decades for the situation to be sorted out by a combination of the militant organization of the abolitionists and the enlightened self-interest of northern industrialists, but by 1848 the Whig Party had split into "Conscience Whigs" and "Cotton Whigs," and the Democratic Party had split into pro-slavery and Free Soil Democrats. One wing of the abolitionist movement formed the Liberty Party in 1840. Then, in 1848, many of its supporters joined with antislavery forces from the major parties to found the Free Soil Party. Meanwhile, the Whig party, which had in its history elected two presidents, continued to disintegrate. Torn apart over the issue of slavery, it was gone by 1860. The Democrats, minus their Free Soil faction, became the party of slavery. The Liberty and Free Soil parties merged in 1854, and two years later joined with a larger coalition of anti-slavery forces that were leaving both major parties to form the Republican Party.

. . .

The question that this history raises for the Nineties is whether a single issue or a complex of related issues can be developed that is both strong enough to unify a Progressive constituency and polarizing enough to force either major changes within the existing party system, or a fusion of interests into a new political vehicle. It will take a movement of this magnitude to bring energy, enthusiasm, and confidence back to the democratic process and the nation as a whole.

We cannot say exactly what those issues will be—economic justice, health care, and the environment are likely areas, and so are peace, foreign policy, and reducing the military budget. There are others as well. We can and do say that citizen organizing, built on cutting-edge issues, is an absolutely necessary part of cleaning up in the Nineties. We must act as the abolitionists in our own times.

4.

Phillip Fellin

UNDERSTANDING AMERICAN COMMUNITIES

At the macro practice level, social work requires an understanding of communities in American society. Communities constitute an important arena or context for social work at all levels of intervention, but especially with regard to social policy, community organization, and administration and management. In conceptions of social work, communities are viewed not only as arenas for macro practice, but also as targets and vehicles of change (Cox et al. 1987; Kramer and Specht, 1975: Netting, Kettner, and McMurtry, 1993; Rothman and Tropman, 1987). Consequently, conceptual frameworks and empirical findings about communities from the social sciences are useful for human service professionals. This article presents two major theoretical perspectives on communities: human ecology and social systems theory. These perspectives are well developed in the social sciences and are widely used as conceptualizations of the social environment in social work education and practice (Germain, 1979; 1991; Longres, 1990; Chess and Norlin, 1988).

DEFINING COMMUNITIES

There is an emerging consensus in the literature that communities are constituted when a group of people form a social unit based on common location, interest, identification, culture, and/or common activities (Garvin and Tropman, 1992). Following this definition, communities may be classified into two major categories, distinguished by common locality or place, and by interest and identification. These community types often overlap with each other, while displaying significant similarities and differences.

Communities may also be characterized in terms of three dimensions: (1) a functional spacial unit meeting sustenance needs; (2) a unit of patterned social interaction; and (3) a symbolic unit of collective identity (Hunter, 1975, p. 538). Communities of "place" vary along these dimensions, as well as by size, density, and heterogeneity. Locality-based communities are often referred to as neighborhood communities, community areas, local municipal communities, and metropolitan communities. Generally the population size and geographical areas of these communities increase from the neighborhood unit to the metropolitan area. Locality-based communities are usually overlapping, such as neighborhoods within municipalities. Consequently, people generally reside in multiple communities of place—that is, communities within communities.

In addition to membership in locality-based communities, many people have membership in one or more communities of interest and identification (Longres, 1990). These communities are based on some feature of common identity or belief, such as ethnicity, race, religion, lifestyle, ideology, gender, sexual orientation, social class, profession, or workplace. Members of these communities not only have a common identity with their group, but often engage in some level of organizational activity, such as social participation in professional groups, sports clubs, religious groups, and ethnic organizations. Communities of interest and identification often coincide with neighborhood communities. For example, people who identify themselves in terms of common racial, ethnic, religious, or social class membership may live in residential areas that have a high proportion of people with one or more of these characteristics.

The two sets of theory, human ecology and social systems, provide useful perspectives about spacial and geographic communities, as well as communities of identification and interest. This knowledge is directly related to macro social work practice tasks and strategies. For example, knowledge about communities of place forms a basis for social planning, that is, districts for urban planning, service delivery areas for health and social welfare planning, and catchment areas in mental health planning. Understanding of communities of identification, such as racial and ethnic groups, religious groups, social class groups, enhances the practice of organizing for social action. These community groups also become the focus of self-help and mutual aid activities carried out in the practice of locality development (Rothman, 1993).

ECOLOGICAL SYSTEMS

From an ecological standpoint, community may be defined as "a structure of relationships through which a localized population provides its daily requirements" (Hawley, 1950, p. 180). This ecological definition of community focuses on the relationship of populations to their environment, especially in regard to spacial organization—that is, how people and services are distributed. Emphasis is placed on the "division of labor" within a community—types of

occupational groups, and how a structure of occupational stratification emerges through an interdependence within and between communities (Hawley, 1950; 1986).

Theories of human ecology focus on the development of locality-based community structures through several processes, such as competition, centralization, concentration, segregation, integration, and succession (Park, Burgess, and McKenzie, 1925; McKenzie, 1926; Poplin, 1979). A major area of *competition* in communities is over the use of land, as individuals, groups, and social institutions seek an "advantage of place" for commercial, industrial, institutional, and residential purposes. Competition results in dominance when social groups have the power to control the use of the most valued land in a community. Communities are considered dominant when they develop controlling influence over other communities.

Centralization describes a clustering of institutions and services in a central location, such as a business district, a transportation center, or communications center. Decentralization is a process by which organizations move out from a central location. The concept of *concentration* refers to the influx of individuals, especially through migration and immigration, into an urban area. The process of *segregation* describes how individuals, groups, and institutions, distinguished by social characteristics such as race, ethnicity, social class, or religion, become congregated in separate physical locations. *Integration* refers to a situation whereby individuals with a mix of one or more of these characteristics, such as white and minority residents, reside in the same community. *Succession* refers to a process of change, when one social group or set of institutions is replaced by another within a geographic area. These concepts not only denote a processes of change in communities, but are also used to describe end states, such as integrated or segregated neighborhoods.

Application of an Ecological Perspective

An ecological perspective allows us to describe locality-based communities in terms of social geography, that is, the distribution of people, organizations, and resources in space. This perspective calls attention to the physical layout of the community, that is, the location of residences, industry, commercial and business areas, social and health services, churches, recreational areas, and schools. Choldin (1985) refers to these features of the community as the "built environment." Within this environment, one can observe changes over time in the use of space and in the distribution and movements of people. The technique of mapping is used to describe land-use patterns, boundaries of racial, ethnic, religious, and social class groups, rates of crime, rates of poverty, and child maltreatment (Coulton et al., 1990; Green, 1982; Wilson, 1987; Zuravin and Taylor, 1987).

An ecological perspective provides an understanding of the demographic development of communities. Data from the U.S. Bureau of the Census are used to describe a range of characteristics of communities, such as size, density, and heterogeneity. Thus the examination of data about metropolitan areas, urbanized areas, suburban areas, small communities, and rural areas highlights the interrelationships and differences between communities, including exchanges, communications, and interdependencies with one another (Martinez-Brawley, 1990). Analysis of census data leads to an understanding of past as well as ongoing phases of urbanization, including demographic changes in specific communities, such as large, urban, inner city areas.

Population Size

Population size is an important descriptor of locality-based communities. The U.S. Bureau of the Census provides census tract data on the size of population in local neighborhoods, community areas, municipalities, townships, and metropolitan areas. Changes in population size of these communities have accompanied the process of urbanization. Historically, this process has been defined in terms of an increased proportion of the population in urbanized areas in contrast to rural areas. Increasingly, the size of communities has changed due to several patterns, such as technological advancements, changes in transportation and communication, and development of large-scale economic organizations and residential areas away from the central cities. In addition, population changes have occurred due to patterns of fertility of ethnic minority groups, migration within the United States, movement of white and ethnic-minority middle-class populations from central cities to suburbs, and recent immigration of non-European and refugee groups. A major change has been the decline in population size of central cities in major metropolitan areas, especially through "white flight" from cities to suburbs and beyond. These population-size changes have been accompanied by changes in other census demographic characteristics of communities, such as the residential separation of people by race, ethnicity, and social class.

Population Density

Population density is an environmental variable that refers to the number of people within a physical space. Based on the writings of Wirth (1938), density has been thought to lead to a more complex community structure, to a more economically specialized population, to residential overcrowding, and, hence, to "friction and irritation." Density of population is frequently associated with negative factors of city life, such as "too much noise, too much dirt, too much pollution," that is, "an environment that is stress-producing" (Krupat, 1985, p. 95). Krupat has noted that density may lead to crowding, a "psychological or subjective experience that results from a recognition that one has less space than one desires" (p. 100). Crowding occurs in housing arrangements, in transportation, in use of facilities, and in neighborhood communities. Urban inner-city living areas tend to be high in density, in contrast to low density of suburban neighborhoods.

The question of what effects density and crowding have on people and their social relationships has been of particular interest to social workers, social reformers, and urban sociologists, especially from the turn of the century to the present time (Choldin, 1985; Fischer, 1978; Krupat, 1985). Krupat's (1985) review of the research literature on density and social pathology suggests there may be no causal effect of one on the other, but that "high-density living definitely has the capacity to be stressful," especially for people living in poverty (p. 112). Two dimensions of urban life that have attracted special attention for social workers are the adverse living conditions of the poor, and the limits on positive social relationships sometimes imposed upon people in communities of large size and density.

Population Heterogeneity

The composition of the population in a community is often described in terms of its homogeneity or heterogeneity. Such variables as social class, race and ethnicity, religion, age, and gender are used to classify people and describe such groups in relation to their presence in neighborhoods, municipalities, and metropolitan areas. From an ecological point of view, these characteristics are aggregated to indicate the social structure of geographic communities. Groups classified in these terms also represent communities of identification, and in the instance of social class and race/ethnicity there is often an overlap with locational communities. The study of community stratification systems of social class and race/ethnicity has special relevance to the macro practice of social work, inasmuch as membership in these groups affects the quality of life of people in positive and negative ways. People benefit or suffer as a result of their social positions within communities, through differential life chances, employment opportunities, access to social and material resources, and social relationships.

Social Class. Stratification by social class refers to inequalities among people measured in such terms as socioeconomic status and lifestyle. Commonly used indicators of social class include occupation, income, education, and lifestyle. The U.S. Bureau of the Census provides data on these factors, allowing for the development of social profiles of communities. A classic illustration of how census statistics can be used to describe social class differences in communities is provided in the Social Area Analysis framework of Shevky and Bell (1955). This approach involves the use of three major constructs: social rank (education and occupation), urbanization or family status (type of housing, marital status, children, members of household working), and segregation or ethnicity (proportion of minorities in the area compared to the total community population). Of particular concern to human-service professionals is the residential segregation of population groups, by social class and by ethnic minority status, and the impact of residence on community life.

Community profiles of social class illustrate ways of using aggregate data to determine the proportions of people in various social class levels or social ranks. Of course, social class ranking of individuals and households may be influenced by other factors, most notably race, ethnicity, family background, religion, and lifestyle. In fact, individuals in racial and ethnic groups may construct their own rankings within a social stratification system. Factors of occupation, income, and education have in common the fact that they are quantitative indicators that point to inequalities among individuals and among population groups. There is little agreement, however, about where to draw the lines in order to distinguish one class from another, or what to call the various class levels. One commonly used set of names includes the poor, working class, middle class, upper-middle class, and upper class (Jackman and Jackman, 1983).

Social class is often associated with the life chances and lifestyles of community residents. Indicators of lifestyles include such factors as the value and location of homes, clothing styles, consumer spending patterns, travel and vacation styles, and choices of reading. The most prominent of these factors is the value and location of one's residential dwelling. In large urban communities, high value of housing and prestigious location are the signs of upper class membership, just as the Single Room Occupancy housing in a skid row or the low-cost housing in slum areas are signs of underclass membership.

Social class can be a community of identification, based on subjective measures such as class consciousness, class awareness, class identity, and cognitive maps— all images individuals have about their location in the class structure. The concept of social class appears to have considerable meaning in the way community residents view themselves. For example, using residents' reports on their subjective interpretations of social class, Jackman and Jackman (1983) found that social classes, as interest groups, form the basis for the development of social communities.

In recent years, social scientists and human service professionals have given considerable attention to a special group of people within the lower classes (Devine and Wright, 1993; Jencks and Peterson, 1991; Wilson, 1989). Some individuals and families living in poverty appear to fall outside the traditional class hierarchy and are viewed as members of an underclass. These people appear to be restricted by social, economic, and personal barriers from entry into the traditional class structure. As Wilson (1989) has noted, an early and "dominant image of the underclass became one of people with serious character flaws entrenched by a welfare subculture and who have only themselves to blame for their social position in society" (p. 182). More recently, an alternative view based on empirical research has emerged, a view that emphasizes the "severe constraints and limited opportunities that shape their lives," based on "class and racial subjugation in the ghetto" (p. 183).

Wilson's (1987) explanation of the relationship of demographic changes to the social dislocation of African Americans in the inner cities illustrates the use of an ecological perspective to explain the emergence of a ghetto poor minority underclass. Wilson seeks to explain differences in inner-city neighborhood communities prior to 1960 with communities of the 1980s. He notes that "inner-city communities prior to 1960 exhibited the features of social organization . . . including a sense of community, positive neighborhood identification, and explicit norms and sanctions against aberrant behavior" (p. 3). In contrast, these inner cities became the locale for a ghetto underclass associated with problems of social dislocation, such as high rates of "crime, joblessness, out-of-wedlock births, female-headed families, and welfare dependency" (p. 16). These problems are seen as the result of societal, demographic, and neighborhood factors, especially historic and contemporary discrimination, the flow of migrants, changes in the age structure, economic system changes, and concentration effects of living in areas with high rates of poverty (Wilson, 1987, 1989, 1993; Wacquant and Wilson, 1989). Most importantly, Wilson suggests that these concentration effects have led to a lack of social organization in neighborhoods, that is, social isolation and a lack of community resources from social networks, social institutions, and workforce participation.

Given the considerable diversity in the underclass population, social workers participate in a variety of programs directed toward alleviating the problems of these individuals, and in changing the social conditions that retain them in this devastating state of poverty. Social workers may be involved in the development of housing programs and in job training and jobs programs, along with other social welfare programs, in order to help people escape from their underclass conditions. While these programs have helped some individuals move into mainstream society, the presence of a substantial underclass population within urban communities continues to be a major social and community problem, the solution to which requires public policy changes in all community subsystems.

Social workers in policy-making roles can participate in supporting these changes, which, in Wilson's (1993) terms, will enhance social rights for all ethnic and racial groups, that is "the right to employment, economic security, education, and health" (p. 30).

Race and Ethnicity. Race and ethnicity comprise two major concepts used in describing heterogeneity of populations in the United States and within communities (Snipp, 1989). Because of the significance of cultural features that distinguish racial groups from each other, concepts of ethnic group and minority group are often used instead of the concept of race. The term "minority" has come to refer to people of color who are a minority in number within society and have experienced high degrees of discrimination, prejudice, and oppression (Bernal, 1990). The term "ethnic" is combined with "minority group" to refer to people of color—groups identified by the Equal Employment Commission established by the Equal Rights Act of 1964 as African American, Asian American, Native American, and Hispanic (Glazer, 1983). There is considerable diversity within each of these ethnic minority categories, attributable to national origin, social class differences, and state of acculturation and assimilation, as well as to other sociocultural factors.

The Bureau of the Census collects information about the affiliation of individuals with racial and ethnic groups. The population of the United States is classified in terms of racial categories of American Indian or Alaska Native, Asian or Pacific Islander, Black, White, and Other. Hispanic origin is considered as ethnicity, and persons identifying themselves as Mexican, Puerto Rican, Cuban, or Other Spanish/Hispanic origin are classified as of

Hispanic origin. "The concept of race the Bureau of the Census uses reflects self-identification by respondents, that is, the individual's perception of his/her racial identity. The concept is not intended to reflect any biological or anthropological definition" (Statistical Abstracts, 1992, pp. 4–5). One of the consequences of classification is that "nonwhite" status carries with it certain compensations as a result of affirmative action policies, minority contracting set-asides, and anti-discrimination policies (Barringer, 1993). Currently, in the United States, ethnic groups are classified as ethnic minority groups but also in terms of white ethnic groups. These later groups historically have been differentiated in terms of European nationality, for example, white immigrant groups such as Polish, Italian, German, Irish.

A significant dimension of the demographic development of communities in the United States is the diversity of ethnic and racial populations brought about by immigration (Maldonado and Moore, 1985; Tobin, 1987). Census data of 1990 display large changes in the racial and ethnic composition of the United States from 1980 to 1990, with nearly one in four Americans of African, Asian, Hispanic, or American Indian ancestry in 1990 compared to one in five in 1980 (Barringer, 1991). A significant part of this growth came from nearly ten million ethnic minority immigrants, especially in the Hispanic population. Equally dramatic in change is the new diversity of the Asian population due to immigration, with fast growing groups of Vietnamese, Indians, and Koreans.

An important aspect of this growth in ethnic populations from immigration is the distribution of immigrants. An analysis of 1990 census data by Frey (1993) shows that "Most immigrants are flooding into just a handful of states, while the rest of America

is largely untouched by the new immigration" (Tilove and Hallinan, 1993, p. F/1). This change has led some demographers to believe there is a new "white flight" occurring, not just from city and suburban communities, but from states and regions of the United States. In the light of these population changes, Frey (1993) predicts that "What is really developing here is two very separate societies, two separate Americas" (Tilove and Hallinan, 1993, p. F/1).

In summary, ecological perspectives focus on macro-level variables with regard to population, environment, social organization, and technology. Attention is given to "fundamentally important community phenomena such as whether the community is growing or shrinking, whether the population is young or old, whether different segments are integrated or segregated, how densely the population lives, and what sort of transportation and communications systems are used" (Choldin, 1985, p. 59).

SOCIAL SYSTEMS PERSPECTIVES

Social systems theory provides another useful framework for understanding American communities. While this theory is unusually complex, its major concepts provide a guide for examining the structural and functional attributes of locality-based communities. We begin with the idea that a social system involves the interaction of two or more social units, that is, the interactions within and among social groups and social organizations. In order to apply systems concepts to locality-based communities, we are interested in how well the subsystems of a community are functioning, as well as the community as a whole, in meeting the needs of its residents. This involves examination of community subsystems, such as the economic, political, educational, health, and social welfare systems. The major social units within each of these subsystems are formal organizations, such as businesses, governmental offices, churches, schools, health care organizations, and social welfare agencies. Informal groups, including families and social groups, also contribute to the functioning of community subsystems and the total community.

An important feature of social systems theory is the specification of boundaries of the system in relation to its environment. To illustrate, a municipality in a metropolitan area may be defined as a community system, with boundaries that are likely to be both geographical and psychological. The external environment includes other municipalities, as well as state, regional, and national entities with which the municipal community interacts. One of the central functions of such a community system is boundary maintenance. A community engages in activities that will assure its continuance as a separate entity or social organization. Boundary maintenance is exemplified by physical boundaries as well as legal, political boundaries.

Study of the community social system includes attention to the interaction of the system beyond its own boundaries with outside systems, such as other communities and society. This outside system, designated by Chess and Norlin (1988) as the suprasystem, provides inputs into a community system and receives outputs. Thus this interaction provides for inputs into the system, such as culture, money, material resources, and information. Outputs may be thought of as the results of the interactions within a system, such as the goals of a community and/or its subsystems. These goals are related to employment, health, safety and security, social welfare, education, housing, and other indicators of quality of life (Chess and Norlin, 1988).

The concepts of input and output are related to the ways in which interactions of the units within a social system are patterned. Classical social systems theory, particularly as developed by Talcott Parsons (1951), describes these patterns in terms of systems functions. Patterns having to do with the system's external activities serve adaptive and goal-attainment functions, with internal activities serving integrative and pattern-maintenance/tension-management functions. These patterns represent the problems a community must solve in order to maintain itself.

Systems patterns of interaction can be thought of as "task functions" and "maintenance functions." Task functions of adaptation and goal attainment involve relationships with the outside environment through the economy and the polity. Integration functions occur in the juridical system, and pattern-maintenance/tension-management is handled by groups such as the family, education, and cultural units of the community. Communities as systems must relate to changes within and without the system, and maintain themselves through systems functions. From this perspective, a community constantly seeks a level of stability or equilibrium. Thus when the various subsystems of the community change, there is an impact on the total community. When the task or maintenance functions of the subsystems are not carried out successfully, this leads to a lack of goal attainment and may lead to community disorganization.

Application of a Social Systems Perspective

The functions of social systems formulated by Parsons (1951) are applied to locality-based communities by Warren (1963). Community functions include: production/distribution/consumption (economic system), socialization (family, educational system), social control (political system), social participation (voluntary associations), and mutual support (health and welfare agencies, primary groups). These functions are carried out through the subsystems of the community and their various formal organizations, as well as through the actions of primary groups, such as family and other household groups, friendship groups, kinship groups, neighborhood groups, peer groups, self-help groups, and informal social club groups.

Communities interact with other communities, and these external relationships have important implications for the way in which a particular community system maintains its boundaries and its equilibrium. Equally important are the interactions of formal organizations of community systems with similar social units outside the community. These extra-community relationships are identified by Warren (1963) as vertical, in contrast to the horizontal interactions within a community. For example, in regard to mutual support, a typical community unit is a voluntary health association; a unit of horizontal pattern; a community welfare council; a unit of a vertical pattern: a national health association.

Understanding a locality-based community as a social system is enhanced through knowledge about the various community subsystems. The social work professional needs to have a thorough grasp of the health and welfare services subsystem of a community, including knowledge about the organizations that make up various fields of service, and about the horizontal and vertical patterns of organizations of the subsystem. At the same time, such knowledge is also needed about community political, economic, educational, and religious subsystems, since the major community functions identified by Parsons (1951) and

Warren (1963) are carried out through these systems. This knowledge base provides the answers to a number of questions about communities. These include:

1. To what extent and under what conditions do voluntary associations contribute to the healthy functioning of a community, of the various community subsystems, and of individual citizens?
2. To what extent do the formal organizations within a subsystem of the community succeed in carrying out their community functions, through their own performance, and through cooperation with each other and with other subsystems through horizontal interorganizational relationships?
3. In what ways are community actions, as played out in the various subsystems, influenced by vertical relationships with organizations and systems (economic, political, health and welfare, education) outside the community?
4. How do communities and their subsystems handle social conflict among population groups and create and maintain social order?
5. How is the functioning of a community and its subsystems coordinated or influenced by the power and/or decision-making structures of a community? Under what conditions does one or another subsystem become dominant in the community?
6. What mechanisms exist in the community to handle controversies and tensions within and between community subsystems and with other communities?
7. How is social integration created and maintained in communities? How do community systems and their subsystems operate to minimize or eliminate barriers to the full participation of vulnerable populations subjected to discrimination and oppression?

NEIGHBORHOODS

Locality-based communities are made up of neighborhoods, an important context for macro social work practice. Ecological and social systems perspectives can be applied to the understanding of the structure and functioning of neighborhood communities as significant parts of the social environment. Increasingly, neighborhoods provide the location for community-based services for people with special needs, such as people with developmental disabilities, mental illness, and physical illness. Practice activities are often directed toward strengthening of neighborhood social networks, and social controls, including block clubs, church groups, school organizations, and other voluntary associations.

Boundaries need to be established for neighborhoods in order to apply ecological and social systems concepts to these communities. Neighborhoods can be distinguished in terms of geographical area, with immediate neighborhoods referring to areas where a small number of household dwellings are in close proximity to each other. When a household area includes several blocks, it may be referred to as an extended neighborhood. Somewhat larger areas of 30 blocks or more may be designated as community neighborhoods (Litwak, 1985). Boundaries of neighborhoods are established by various groups, including residents, social planners, school boards, political parties, churches, health and welfare service agencies, and the mass media. Once such boundaries are established, census tract data can be used to describe a neighborhood in terms of population size and density, racial, ethnic, and religious composition, education, income, occupational status, level of employment, age structure, and household composition.

Another way of defining neighborhoods is as primary groups. Often, residents define their neighborhood as a small, personal arena that allows for ongoing, personal relationships, neighboring, informal helping, and exchanges of goods and services. The boundaries of a personal neighborhood are likely to cover a small geographical area. These primary-group neighborhoods, as well as extended neighborhoods, provide a number of community functions, such as a sociability arena, an interpersonal influence center, a source of mutual aid, an organizational base, a reference group, and an area signifying status (Warren and Warren, 1977). Consequently, residents of neighborhoods have a potential set of resource and social supports (individuals and organizations) within their local environment.

Social systems perspectives cannot be applied to neighborhood communities in the same ways as are used to understand municipal or metropolitan communities. Neighborhoods do not have similar subsystems that carry out locality-relevant functions in the ways they are performed by larger communities of place. Ecological perspectives more appropriately allow us to examine neighborhoods, especially their demographic characteristics, such as size, density, and heterogeneity. We are also able to examine various types of structures of neighborhoods through attention to community variables such as social class, ethnicity and race, social interaction, identity, and links to the broader community.

MODELS OF NEIGHBORHOOD TYPES

Neighborhood communities have social structures, although social scientists are not consistent in their choices of social dimensions to describe these structures. Several models for analyzing neighborhood structures are available to the macro social practitioner. In a model developed by Warren and Warren (1977), neighborhoods are differentiated in terms of the nature and level of social identity, social interaction, and linkages to the wider community. The six types of neighborhoods—integral, parochial, diffuse, stepping-stone, transitory, and anomic—offer differential benefits as well as social barriers to helping resources for residents (Warren and Warren, 1977). Practice applications of this model are illustrated by Warren and Warren (1977) and Warren (1981) in relation to such questions as when to organize, how to identify leadership resources, how to reach out to a neighborhood, how to assess neighborhood functions, and how to select practice roles and tactics for working in a neighborhood.

A second model for typing neighborhoods, developed by Litwak (1985), emphasizes two dimensions of neighborhood primary groups—the level of membership change or turnover, and the capacity to retain primary group cohesion/social integration. Using these characteristics, three neighborhood types are created: mobile neighborhood (high mobility, capacity to handle change), traditional neighborhood (stability, low capacity for change), and mass neighborhood (high mobility, low capacity for change). The usefulness of this typology for social work practice is illustrated by Litwak (1985) in relation to planning and service needs for older adults. The model can be applied to the various stages of the life cycle. For example, neighborhoods can be assessed in terms of working with young families in need of rapid integration into surburban or inner-city neighborhoods. This typology is useful in selecting interventions that speed up neighborhood social integration, such as creation of voluntary associations.

A third typology focuses on organizational, value, and change dimensions of primary group neighborhoods (Fellin and Litwak, 1963). The organizational base of neighborhoods involves informal contacts and local formal organizations, such as voluntary associations. Neighborhoods can be classified in terms of both their level of organization and their capacity to implement their values, such as orientations toward education, good citizenship, and crime and violence. Recognition of the values of residents in a neighborhood is helpful for both interpersonal and community practice. For example, in areas with high rates of crime and delinquency, the social worker can assess the values of residents toward law and order and toward the tolerance of deviant behavior, and their willingness to organize to implement values to combat violence and crime.

A fourth model, developed by Figueira-McDonough (1991), uses an ecological perspective for classifying communities. Her typology can be applied to neighborhood communities, as it focuses on population and organizational factors. Population factors include poverty and mobility, and organizational factors include informal networks (kin, friends, informal groups), secondary networks (schools, church groups), and external links (external support, resources). These variables are used to create neighborhood types, identified as (1) stepping-stone (nonpoor and mobile, low primary, high secondary networks, high external links); (2) established community (nonpoor, stable; high primary, high-secondary networks, low-external links); (3) disorganized community (poor, mobile; low primary, low secondary networks, low external links); and (4) parochial community (poor, stable; high primary, low secondary networks, low external links). This typology emphasizes sources of resources, by taking into account features of individual households (poverty) and of other members of the community (networks and external links). Hence this typology has particular relevance to social work practice at both the micro and macro levels, since it points to the need for assessment of the level and source of social supports available to community residents.

SOCIAL CLASS AND ETHNIC MINORITY NEIGHBORHOODS

As we have noted, often communities of identification and interest overlap with communities of place. A useful classification of neighborhoods comes from examining the social class characteristics of neighborhoods, as well as the ethnic minority composition. Often these two dimensions of neighborhoods, social class and ethnic minority composition, are combined, since ethnic minority groups are disproportionately represented in the middle-, lower-, and underclass neighborhoods. Attention to the social class level of neighborhoods is important for social workers, since neighborhood location and social class have a powerful effect on the resources and liabilities that affect the quality of life of neighborhood residents.

Ethnic minority neighborhoods are found mainly in the central cities of large urban areas. They are often referred to as "communities," based on a high proportion of residents identified by a single race or nationality group (Rivera and Erlich, 1992). Increasingly, ethnic minority working- and middle-class people, especially African Americans and Hispanics, have moved away from ghetto areas into racially and ethnically integrated communities, as well as to suburban neighborhoods where there is a high concentration of middle-

class minority populations (Nathan, 1991). In the newly emerging middle-class minority neighborhoods, residents have membership in both a spacial community and a sociopsychological community (Taylor, 1979), not unlike many minority residents in inner-city working-class and poverty neighborhoods.

SEGREGATION IN NEIGHBORHOODS

Contrary to the popular image of American society as a "melting pot" of races and ethnic groups, data from the 1990 census indicate that most communities in the United States continue to be highly segregated (Harrison and Weinberg, 1992). The concepts of segregation and integration serve to describe these neighborhood communities, with segregated neighborhoods having a high proportion of ethnic minority and/or cultural group membership (Rusk, 1993). Empirical studies of housing patterns in North American communities continue to leave no doubt that housing segregation is due in large part to discrimination and prejudice based on race and/or ethnicity (Tobin, 1987; *New York Times,* 1991; *Wall Street Journal,* 1992).

Federal legislation, such as the 1968 Fair Housing Act, as well as ongoing court decisions, have brought about some changes in the extent of discrimination in housing. However, the activities of several major groups involved in housing continue to maintain residential segregation, such as real estate brokers, home builders, banks and savings and loan associations, and local, state, and federal governments (Darden, 1987; Karr, 1993). "White flight" of city residents to suburban areas is only one (albeit a major) explanation for the segregation of American communities. Nonracial causes for household moves also contribute to segregated neighborhoods. The ecological concept of succession provides a framework for observing and explaining changes in population composition, especially in changes in population from white to ethnic minority groups.

Programs that seek to intervene in the process of succession and to create and/or maintain residential integration provide opportunities for involvement of professional social workers. Goals for these programs include "achieving a racial balance," "achieving integration," "integration maintenance," and "reduction of segregation." Examples of interventions to reach these goals are related to attempts to attract African Americans into white neighborhoods and whites into areas with high proportions of African Americans (Klibanoff, 1984; Hayes, 1990; Jones, 1990; Pepper, 1990; Dozier, 1993; Hirsch, 1992). In one of the most sophisticated studies of neighborhood integration maintenance efforts, Saltman (1991) identified a number of factors that facilitate the attainment of integration goals and concluded that racially diverse neighborhoods are maintained only with enormous difficulty.

REVIEW

Ecological and social systems perspectives have been presented as approaches to understanding the structure and functioning of the "multiple communities" that make up the social environment. Specific attention has been given to municipal communities (often referred to as "the community"), to neighborhood communities, and to ethnic minority communities of interest and identification. Ecological and social systems perspectives assist in the assessment of the overall functioning of these communities. A useful concept for making this

assessment is community competence, that is, the capacity of a community to engage in problem solving in order to achieve its goals (Cottrell, 1983). In their use of this concept, Barbarin et al. (1981) emphasize that the capacities of social systems, and of the individuals and groups within a community, constitute a dual dimension of competence. In this sense, "Community competence refers both to the ability of social systems to respond to differential needs of the varied populations they serve, and [to] the ability of citizens or groups to use existing resources or develop alternatives for the purpose of solving problems of living" (Barbarin et al., 1981, p. 3). Social systems perspectives provide an understanding of municipal communities that is useful in the assessment of community competence. At the same time, ecological perspectives describe social conditions that may enhance or detract from the competent functioning of locality-based communities, especially municipal and neighborhood communities.

Competent communities are not easy to create or maintain. One of the most significant barriers to community competence involves the values, attitudes, and practices of people toward special population groups. Communities vary in regard to their level of discrimination, prejudice, oppression, acceptance, and tolerance. Many American communities lack an appropriate response to the differential needs of such groups as ethnic minorities, cultural and religious groups, women, physically and mentally disabled persons, gay and lesbian individuals, children, young adults, and older adults. Competent communities make special efforts to create equal opportunity and reduce barriers to the quality of life and full participation in community affairs of people discriminated against and oppressed. Macro-level social workers can contribute to community competence by participating in activities, tactics, and strategies that contribute to improved functioning of communities, especially in their capacity to help vulnerable population groups gain access to and utilize community resources.

REFERENCES

Barbarin, O., P. R. Good, O. M. Pharr, and J. A. Siskind, eds. *Institutional Racism and Community Competence.* U.S. Department of Health and Human Services, Pub. # (ADM) 81-907, 1981.

Barringer, F. "Immigration Brings New Diversity to Asian Population in the U.S." *New York Times,* June 12, 1991.

Barringer, F. "Ethnic Pride Confounds the Census." *New York Times,* May 9, 1993.

Bernal, M. E. "Ethnic minority mental health training trends and issues." In F. C. Serafica, et al., *Mental Health and Ethnic Minorities.* New York: Praeger, 1990.

Chess, W. A., and J. M. Norlin. *Human Behavior and the Social Environment.* Boston: Allyn and Bacon, 1988.

Choldin, H. M. *Cities and Suburbs.* New York: McGraw-Hill, 1985.

Cottrell, L. S., Jr. "The Competent Community. In R. Warren, & L. Lyon, eds. *New Perspectives on the American Community.* Homewood, IL: The Dorsey Press, 1983.

Coulton, C., S. Pandey, and J. Chow. "Concentration of Poverty and the Changing Ecology of Low-Income, Urban Neighborhoods: An Analysis of the Cleveland Area." *Social Work Research and Abstracts,* 26(4) (1990).

Cox, F. M., J. L. Erlich, J. Rothman, and J. E. Tropman. *Strategies of Community Organization.* Itasca, IL: Peacock Publishers, 1987.

Darden, J. T. "Choosing Neighbors and Neighborhoods: The Role of Race in Housing Preference. In G. A. Tobin, ed., "Divided Neighborhoods: Changing Patterns of Racial Segregation." *Urban Affairs Annual Reviews* (32) (1987).

Devine, J. A., and J. D. Wright. *The Greatest of Evils: Urban Poverty and the American Underclass.* New York: Aldine De Gruyter, 1993.

Dozier, M. "Fund to Boost Oakland Integration." *Detroit Free Press,* April 23, 1993.

Fellin, P., and E. Litwak. "Neighborhood Cohesion Under Conditions of Mobility." *American Sociological Review,* 28(3) (1963).

Figueira-McDonough, J. "Community Structure and Delinquency: A Typology." *Social Service Review* (March 1991).

Fischer, C. "Urban to Rural Diffusion of Opinions in Contemporary America." *American Journal of Sociology* 84(1) (1978).

Frey, W. H. *Newhouse Study.* Newhouse News Service, August 23, 1993.

Garvin, C. D., and J. E. Tropman. *Social Work in Contemporary Society.* Englewood Cliffs, NJ: Prentice Hall, 1992.

Germain, C. *Social Work Practice: People and Environments.* New York: Columbia University Press, 1979.

Germain, C. *Human Behavior in the Social Environment.* New York: Columbia University Press, 1991.

Glazer, N. *Ethnic Dilemmas.* Cambridge: Harvard University Press, 1983.

Green, J. W. *Cultural Awareness in the Human Services.* Englewood Cliffs, NJ: Prentice Hall, 1982.

Harrison, R. J., and D. H. Weinberg. *Racial and Ethnic Segregation in 1990.* Washington, DC: U.S. Bureau of the Census, April 1992.

Hawley, A. *Human Ecology: A Theory of Community Structure.* New York: Roland Press, 1950.

Hawley, A. *Urban Ecology.* Chicago: University of Chicago Press, 1986.

Hayes, A. S. "Is Town's Housing Plan the Key to Integration or a Form of Racism?" *Wall Street Journal,* October 4, 1990.

Hirsch, J. S. "Columbia, Md., at 25, Sees Integration Goal Sliding from Its Grasp. *Wall Street Journal,* February 27, 1992.

Hunter, A. "The Loss of Community: An Empirical Test Through Replication. *American Sociological Review* 40 (1975).

Jackman, M., and R. Jackman. *Class Awareness in the United States.* Berkeley: University of California Press, 1983.

Jencks, C., and P. E. Peterson. *The Urban Underclass.* Washington, DC: The Brookings Institution, 1991.

Jones, L. "Balancing Act." *Detroit Free Press,* September 29, 1990.

Karr, A. R. "Consumer Group Finds Marketing Bias in Mortgage Lending in 16 Large

Cities." *Wall Street Journal,* August 13, 1993.

Klibanoff, H. "Chicago Suburb Actively Seeks Racial Diversity." *Detroit Free Press,* October 8, 1984.

Kramer, R. M., and H. Specht, eds. *Readings in Community Organization Practice,* 2nd ed. Englewood Cliffs, NJ: Prentice-Hall, 1975.

Krupat, E. *People in Cities.* New York: Cambridge University Press, 1985.

Litwak, E. *Helping the Elderly.* New York: Guilford Press, 1985.

Longres, J. F. *Human Behavior and the Social Environment.* Itasca, IL: Peacock Publishers, 1990.

Maldonado, L., and J. Moore. *Urban Ethnicity in the United States.* Beverly Hills, CA: Sage Publications, 1985.

Martinez-Brawley, E. E. *Perspectives on the Small Community.* Silver Spring, MD: NASW Press, 1990.

McKenzie, R. D. "The Scope of Human Ecology." *Publication of the American Sociological Society* 20 (1926).

Nathan, R. P. Where the Minority Middle Class Lives. *Wall Street Journal,* May 22, 1991.

Netting, F. E., P. M. Kettner, and S. L. McMurtry. *Social Work Macro Practice.* New York: Free Press, 1993.

New York Times. "Study Finds Bias in House Hunting," September 1, 1991.

Park, R., E. W. Burgess, and R. D. McKenzie, eds. *The City.* Chicago: University of Chicago Press, 1925.

Parsons, T. *The Social System.* Glencoe, IL: Free Press, 1951.

Parsons, T. *Structure and Process in Modern Societies.* New York: The Free Press, 1960.

Pepper, J. "Common Ground: Cleveland Suburbs Work to Achieve a Racial Balance. *Detroit News,* August 19, 1990.

Poplin, D. *Communities: A Survey of Theories and Methods of Research,* 2nd ed. New York: Macmillan, 1979.

Rivera, F. G., and J. L. Erlich. *Community Organizing in a Diverse Society.* Boston: Allyn and Bacon, 1992.

Rothman, J. Personal Correspondence, 1993.

Rothman, J., and J. E. Tropman. "Models of Community Organization and Macro Practice Perspectives: Their Mixing and Phasing." In

F. M. Cox, J. L. Erlich, J. Rothman, and J. E. Tropman, eds., *Strategies of Community Organization,* 4th ed. Itasca, IL: Peacock Publishers, 1987.

Rusk, D. *Cities Without Suburbs.* Baltimore: Johns Hopkins University Press, 1993.

Saltman, J. "Maintaining Racially Diverse Neighborhoods." *Urban Affairs Quarterly* 26(3) (1991).

Shevky, E., and W. Bell. *Social Area Analysis: Theory, Illustrative Application and Computational Procedures.* Stanford, CA: Stanford University Press, 1955.

Snipp, C. M. *American Indians: The First of This Land.* New York: Russell Sage, 1989.

Statistical Abstracts. U.S. Bureau of the Census, 1992.

Taylor, R. "Black Ethnicity and the Persistence of Ethnogenesis. *American Journal of Sociology* 84(6) (1979).

Tilove, J., and J. Hallinan. "A Nation Divided." *Ann Arbor News,* August 22, 1993.

Tobin, G. A., "Divided Neighborhoods: Changing Patterns of Racial Segregation." *Urban Affairs Annual Reviews* (32) (1987).

Wacquant, L. J. D., and W. J. Wilson. "The Cost of Racial and Class Exclusion in the Inner City." *Annals* 501 (1989).

Wall Street Journal. "Mortgage Gap on Racial Basis Persisted in 1991," October 1, 1992.

Warren, R. *The Community in America.* Chicago: Rand McNally, 1963.

Warren D. *Helping Networks.* South Bend, IN: University of Notre Dame Press, 1981.

Warren, R. and D. I. Warren. *The Neighborhood Organizers' Handbook.* South Bend, IN: University of Notre Dame Press, 1977.

Wilson, W. J. *The Truly Disadvantaged.* Chicago: University of Chicago Press, 1987.

Wilson, W. J. "The Underclass: Issues, Perspectives, and Public Policy." *Annals* 501 (1989).

Wilson, W. J. "The New Poverty and the Problem of Race," *O.C. Tanner Lecture.* Ann Arbor: University of Michigan, 1993.

Wirth, L. "Urbanism as a Way of Life. *American Journal of Sociology,* 44(1) (1938).

Zuravin, S. J., and R. Taylor. "The Ecology of Child Maltreatment: Identifying and Characterizing High-Risk Neighborhoods. *Child Welfare,* November/December 1987.

5.

Mayer N. Zald

ORGANIZATIONS: ORGANIZATIONS AS POLITIES: AN
ANALYSIS OF COMMUNITY ORGANIZATION AGENCIES

The interdependence of subject matter in the fields of community organization and sociology has long been recognized by teachers and practitioners. Possibly to a greater extent than with any other segment of social work, the problems of this field of practice are grist for the mill of the student of society and the community. And yet there is no systematic sociology of community organization (hereinafter referred to as "CO"). Such a sociology would include a social history of the emergence and growth of the field of practice, an analysis of its ongoing social system, and diagnostic categories and criteria for investigating community problems and structure.

This paper focuses on one aspect of the social system of the field, presenting, in particular, a set of concepts and propositions about the structure and operation of CO agencies. These concepts and propositions are designed to explain some of the determinants of agency processes and, consequently, the styles and problems of professional practice.

Indeed, much more of the variability of practice in CO is determined by its organizational context, as compared with many professional fields. The needs and problems of the community are not funneled and defined directly between the practitioner and the community segment to which he is related; instead, needs are defined and shaped by the constitution and goals of the employing agency. Furthermore, the means selected to deal with community problems depend on organizational

requirements, stances, and definitions. Whatever the practitioner's activity, he is guided by the structure, aims, and operating procedures of the organization that pays the bills.

Therefore, any useful theory of CO practice must include concepts and propositions about how CO agencies shape practice and how such organizations are themselves constrained. The question then becomes: *How are we to analyze community organization agencies?*

ORGANIZATIONAL ANALYSIS

The general approach used here is that of organizational analysis.[1] It is a form of analysis that takes the total organization,

[1]Organizational analysis has been developed most explicitly by Philip Selznick and his students. For example, see Philip Selznick, *T.V.A. and the Grass Roots* (Berkeley: University of California Press, 1949); Selznick, *Leadership in Administration: A Sociological Interpretation* (Evanston, IL: Row, Peterson & Co., 1957); and Selznick, *The Organizational Weapon* (New York: Rand Corporation, 1952). See also Burton Clark, *The Open Door College* (New York: McGraw-Hill Book Co., 1960); and Charles B. Perrow, "The Analysis of Goals in Complex Organizations," *American Sociological Review,* Vol. 66, No. 6 (March, 1961), pp. 854–866. The following works also are informed by this perspective: David L. Sills, *The Volunteers* (Glencoe, IL: Free Press, 1957); Martin Rein and Robert Morris, "Goals, Structures and Strategies for Community Change," *Social Work Practice, 1962* (New York: Columbia University Press, 1962), pp. 127–145; and Robert D. Vinter and Morris Janowitz, "Effective Institutions for Juvenile Delinquents: A Research Statement," *Social Service Review,* Vol. 33, No. 2 (June, 1959), pp. 118–130.

not some subpart, as its object. Typically, studies using this approach focus on the relation of goals to structure and the pressures to change goals arising from both the environment and the internal arrangements of the organization. A common focus is the allocation of power to different groups and the manner in which subgroup loyalties and power affect the operation of organizations. Furthermore, organizations are seen as developing distinctive characters—styles and strategies of coping with recurring problematic dilemmas of the organization.

Central to organizational analysis, but often only implicitly treated, is an analysis of the polity of organizations—the patterned distribution and utilization of authority and influence. The frame of reference taken in this paper is explicitly quasi-political. CO agencies are among a class of organizations in which goals are often in flux; in which the patterns of power of influence ebb and flow, but are central to understanding the problems of the organization; in which conflict is sometimes subterranean, sometimes overt, but almost always there; and in which organizations are in unstable relations to their environments. Thus, it seems warranted to give explicit attention to problems of power and the modes of binding people together for collective action. CO agencies can be analyzed as miniature polities.

Four interrelated concepts form the core of this analysis:

1. Organizations have *constitutions,* that is, they have basic zones of activity, goals, and norms of procedure and relationships that are more or less institutionalized in the organization and that are changed only with great effort and cost.

2. Constitutions are linked to the *constituency and resource base* of the organ-

ization. The constituency is not the clientele; rather, the term refers to the groups and individuals who control the organization and to whom the agency executive or executive core is most immediately responsible—the board of directors, key legislators, officeholders, major fund-raisers or grantors.

3. CO agencies wish to affect *target populations,* organizations, or decision centers.

4. Finally, CO agencies exist among a welter of other agencies; they have foreign or *external relations* that can facilitate, impede, or be neutral to the accomplishment of their goals.

These concepts are not mutually exclusive, yet each focuses on somewhat different observations. For purposes of exposition they can be treated separately.

ANALYSIS OF CONSTITUTIONS

In a sense, the constitution of an organization represents its social contract—the basic purposes and modes of procedure to which the major supporters and staff of the organization adhere.[2] When attempts are made to change the constitution of an organization, the agency can expect conflict and disaffection, unless clear benefits adhere to the major supporters. The constitution of an organization is made up of the agency's commitments to major programs and modes of proceeding (goals and

---

[2]Not much attention has been paid to organizational constitutions by sociologists because they often work in organizations whose constitutions are not problematic. E. Wright Bakke uses a conception of constitution or "charter" that is even broader than the author's, but has the same intent. See *Bonds of Organization: An Appraisal of Corporate Human Relations* (New York: Harper & Bros. 1950), especially chap. 6, "Organizational Charter," pp. 152–179.

means). This is, of course, more than just the formal or written statement of goals and procedures, for these may have little to do with the organization's actual constitution. On the other hand, many patterned aspects of agency operation may not be part of the constitution, for these patterns may not deal with basic agreements about goals and means.

Analysis of constitution and goals is important for a sociology of CO practice because it clarifies several important aspects of it—the problems agencies confront when they attempt to change goals and structure, the possibilities of effectiveness vis-à-vis specific goals, and the styles of the professional's work. To be fruitful, analysis of constitutions must be broken down into more specific analytic problems. This paper will treat two: analysis of agency goals and constituency and agency autonomy.

Dimensions of Goals

Organizations come into being to pursue collective ends. A central part of the constitution of any organization is the sets of agreements about goals that are understood by major constituents. Not only do goals represent a set of constituting agreements, they focus organizational resources on a problem field. That is, organizational goals along with beliefs about how to attain them set tasks and problems for agency personnel.

Although there are several conceptual and methodological approaches to the study of goals, two aspects are especially crucial here.[3] First, the goals of the organization de-

termine some of the basic types of CO work. Second, attempts to shift the objectives of the organization can threaten its body politic. The goals of CO agencies can be classified along three analytically distinct dimensions: (1) change or service orientation (that is, according to whether the goal is to give the recipient of service essentially what he or his representative wants—information, program, and the like—or whether the community or individual is changed regardless of whether it or he initially wanted to be changed); (2) institution or individual and group orientation; (3) member (internal) or nonmember (external) orientation. The dichotomous cross-classification of these three dimensions yields the typology shown in Figure 5.1.

Of course, it is clear that some of these organizations are more likely to be sites for group work than for CO practice. But community organizers can be found in all of them.

The typology classifies organizations by their target and the ends they wish to achieve with each group. For instance, a community center (Cell D) usually offers services to individuals, rather than attempting to change them; it is oriented to groups and individuals who are members rather than to institutions (other large-scale organizations). On the other hand, in Cell B are agencies that attempt to mobilize people to change the society and its institutions.

The typology brings to the fore regularities of practice problems shared by agencies "located" in the same cell and differences among agencies in different cells. For instance, typically CO organizations aimed externally, at change, and at institutions (e.g., to change the school system) have to be able to mobilize sanctions against the target. On the other hand, those aimed at providing services to individual members (e.g., community centers)

---

[3]See Mayer N. Zald, "Comparative Analysis and Measurement of Organizational Goals: The Case of Correctional Institutions for Delinquents," *Sociological Quarterly,* Vol. 4, No. 3 (Summer 1963), pp. 206–230.

	CHANGE ORIENTED		SERVICE ORIENTED	
	INSTITUTION	INDIVIDUAL AND GROUP	INSTITUTION	INDIVIDUAL AND GROUP
INTERNAL (MEMBER)	**A** Regional planning groups for specific areas New-style welfare councils (planning is change oriented)	**B** Neighborhood block clubs Settlement houses	**C** Old-style welfare council (coordinate, no enforcement power)	**D** Community centers Adult education
EXTERNAL (NONMEMBER)	**E** Lower-class social movements Governmental community projects	**F** Agencies working with street gangs Family service agencies	**G** Regional or community research agency	**H** National health agencies (excluding research)

FIGURE 5.1
Goal Dimensions of Community Organization Agencies

have the problem of finding attractive programs to bring people in the door—no question of conflict or of mobilizing sanctions arises in such cases.

In general, *the more change oriented the goals are, the greater the incentives needed by the practitioner and his agency to accomplish these goals.* (Of course, incentives can come from within the target or client group, e.g., an alcoholic may strongly desire to be cured of his alcoholism.) Furthermore, *the more member oriented an organization is, the greater the likelihood of a consensus on action,* because the act of joining implies some agreement about goals. Member-oriented agencies are more likely to use persuasive techniques than nonmember-oriented organizations (who must use appeals to self-interest or sanctions). Finally, *the more institution oriented the target is, the more likely the bonds of organization are not solidaristic—based on the emotional attachments between agent and client—and the more likely they are based on exchange relations, on criteria of institutional rationality.*

These dimensions also relate to the problems of organizational maintenance in the face of attempts to attain specific goals or to change goals. The constitution of the organization consists of a set of expectations that, if violated, threaten the maintenance and stability of the organization. For example, Peter Clark has discussed the case of a local voluntary organization composed of businessmen interested in taxation and governmental efficiency.[4] The standard activity of the organization was information-gathering and education on different tax and governmental programs. Clark found that when any specific tax legislation or assessment was proposed it was difficult to get the organization to take a definite stand on the proposal. Instead, often a group of businessmen who favored or opposed the tax would form a specific ad hoc committee to lobby for or against the issue. Clark concluded that

---

[4]See "The Chicago Big Businessman as Civic Leader." Unpublished doctoral dissertation, University of Chicago, 1959.

although the organization was concerned with taxation, any specific piece of legislation tended to have differential effects on members and internal conflict would result if any attempt were made to take a definite stand. Instead of fighting an issue through and creating dissension, members took action outside the organization. Clark's case represents a situation in which the constitution did not allow for change attempts. Similar problems occur in other organizations. The general point is that *as an organization begins to change its basic goals, constitutional problems emerge.*[5]

The foregoing discussion of dimensions of goal analysis will also be of relevance in the discussion of constituency and target groups that follows.

Constituency and Agency Autonomy

Some CO agencies have the goals of integrating and coordinating major constituents. However, even when agencies have other goals, the question of constituency-agency relations is a focus of organizational constitutions. A pattern of normative expectations develops about consultation, discretion, and the locus of initiation of agency goals and programs. This pattern is largely a function of the resource dependency of the agency.[6] *To*

the extent that an agency is heavily dependent on its constituency it is likely to develop a constitution giving little room for discretion.[7]

Constituency-agency relations are crucial to understanding executive roles. Professional CO role-taking varies in terms of how much and how often the executive must report to the constituency. Professional roles may vary from a situation in which the executive does little more than facilitate constituency decision making to one in which the constituency is consulted seldom, if at all.[8] What determines these roles?

Three factors (excluding personality style) appear to be important in affecting the level of executive decision making— the fund-raising base, the role of the constituency in accomplishing organizational goals, and the knowledge base differential between constituency and staff.

1. *The more routinized and relatively independent of the constituency the agency's fund-raising base is, the less likely the staff is to consult with and involve the constituency systematically in decision making.* Thus, agencies that have an immediate and vital appeal to the public (such as the national voluntary health organizations) or have legal and routinized access to funds are less likely than others to have broad participation by their constituencies in decision making.

---

[5]On the succession of goals in organizations, see David L. Sills, "The Succession of Goals," in Amitai Etzioni, ed., *Complex Organizations* (New York: Holt, Rinehart & Winston, 1954), pp. 146–158. See also Mayer N. Zald and Patricia Denton, "From Evangelism to General Service: On the Transformation of the Y.M.C.A." *Administrative Science Quarterly,* Vol. 8, No. 2 (September 1963), pp. 214–234.

[6]For one treatment of the problem of organizational autonomy see Charles Perrow, "Organizational Prestige: Some Functions and Dysfunctions," *American Journal of Sociology,* Vol. 66, No. 4 (January 1961), pp. 854–866. See also, Selznick, *Leadership in Administration,* pp. 120–133.

[7]Note that the proposition does not apply to the formal or stated charter of the organization alone, but rather to the expectations that develop out of the actual dependency bases of the organization. The point is important, for many organizations, notably business corporations, formally "decentralize" and on paper sometimes resemble what are called "federated" systems. Yet through the judicious, and sometimes injudicious, use of central power these corporations never really build up a constitution of federalism.

[8]See Rein and Morris, op. cit.; and Sills, op. cit.

2. *When the agency is directly dependent on its constituency for achieving organizational goals, greater attention will be paid to constituency wishes and participation.* An agency is dependent on the constituency for achieving goals when its prestige and influence must be utilized to mobilize other segments of the community. After all, the only moderate prestige and influence of CO professionals is usually insufficient to generate widespread community support. An agency is also dependent on the constituency when it is their change that is sought (when the constituency and the target group are the same).[9] Attention to the constituency may be only formal or surface; nevertheless it affects the conduct of office.

3. *The greater the knowledge differential between staff and constituency, the more likely the staff will be given autonomy in the exercise of their work and the more likely the constituency will be consulted only on "boundary" conditions—changes that affect the relation of the agency to the community.* In general, the more decisions are defined as "professional" problems, the less likely are constituencies to be involved.

It would be wrong, however, to assume that an executive cannot influence agency-constituency relations. Constitutions are not immutable! Furthermore, the executive might not want autonomy; the constituency might represent a resource that can be cultivated usefully.

Constituency Characteristics and Agency Operation

The constitution of an organization emerges and is maintained partly to satisfy the constituency. At the same time that they give the organization its continuing mandate, the characteristics of the constituency may lead to a limit on goals and means.

Class Basis of Constituency. A large body of literature testifies to the greater difficulty of involving working-class individuals in voluntary organizations as compared to middle- or upper-class persons.[10] Extending these findings to CO agencies, the following proposition emerges: *the lower the socioeconomic status of the constituency, the more difficult it is likely to be to maintain their interest and participation.* In other words, the CO practitioner with a lower socioeconomic class constituency will devote more of his energies to motivating the constituency than he would in other organizations.

Not only is level of participation affected by the socioeconomic basis of the constituency, but there is some reason to think that the style of participation is also likely to differ. In general one would expect that *when a CO agency aimed at changing some aspect of the community has a middle- and upper-class constituency it will be more likely to attempt to gain its ends through persuasion, informal negotiation, and long-range harmonizing of interests.* On the other hand, *the more an organization has an essentially lower-class basis, the more it will resort to direct action, open propaganda,*

---

[9]It should be clear, however, that there is an analytic difference between a target group and a constituency. A target group or institution is the change object of the organization. The target group is not directly involved in the choosing of means, the personnel, or the goals of the agency. Target groups become part of the constituency when they become part of the decision-making apparatus of the agency.

[10]For a careful summary of much of this literature and an attempt to understand the dynamics of the phenomenon, see William Erbe, "Social Involvement and Political Activity," *American Sociological Review*, Vol. 29, No. 2 (April 1964), pp. 198–215.

and agitation (when it takes action at all).[11] First, the higher up one goes in the stratification system, the more likely it is that the constituency has easy access to office-holders, can command respect from them, and can threaten use of sanctions that the target person will recognize. Thus, the more élite the constituency the more likely it is that informal negotiations will take place and can be fruitful.

Second, people from higher socioeconomic groups begin having organizational experiences from an earlier age. The higher up in the status system, the more likely the constituency will have had experience in organizational negotiation, the more time they can comfortably spend in organizational participation, and the more rewarding to them is such participation.[12]

Obviously, the CO practitioner must take these factors into account. The attempt to get concrete results, the amount of time spent in agitational versus more neutral activities, and the mechanisms of involving the constituency will each differ depending on the class base of the constituency.

Organizational versus Individual Constituencies. For many CO agencies the crucial characteristic of the constituency is not so much that of its class base but whether its basis is individual or organizational. All else being equal, *the more an agency has a constituency made up of agencies, the harder it is to get commitment to an action program that does not have widespread societal consensus and the more likely the agency is to serve as a clearinghouse for information and co-ordination.*[13]

One of the advantages to a CO agency of having a constituency comprised of organizations is that it then has a built-in multiplier effect. That is, those programs that are agreed to can be disseminated through a wide range of other organizations—the population that can be reached is greater. On the other hand, a constituency made up of organizations requires the agency to work through the problem of new and extreme programs with all constituent agencies. If the new program threatens the autonomy of the organizations or challenges *their* constituencies, there will be little incentive for commitment. Because of the desire to protect organizational autonomy, agencies comprised of organizations are more likely to have a structure similar to a representative assembly, which permits veto powers, while agencies comprised of individuals are more likely to have either straight majority rule or an oligarchic structure.[14]

The "all else being equal" clause in this proposition is especially important. If the organizations have joined the CO agency with

---

[11]See the discussion in Herbert J. Gans, *The Urban Villagers: Group and Class in the Life of Italian-Americans* (New York: Free Press of Glencoe, 1962), especially chap. 5, pp. 104–120. The necessity of active and direct modes of expression in the appeal to lower socioeconomic groups is one of the essential elements in Saul Alinsky's approach to CO.

[12]Catherine V. Richards and Norman A. Polansky have shown that among adult women, those who participated in organizations as adolescents and whose parents also participated were more likely to participate in voluntary associations than those who did not have either of these characteristics in their background. The over-all rate of parent and adolescent participation is, of course, directly related to socioeconomic status. See "Reaching Working-class Youth Leaders," *Social Work*, Vol. 4, No. 4 (October 1959), pp. 31–39).

[13]The author has less confidence in this proposition than in the previous one. For one thing, it may cause comparison of disparate organizations, for instance, neighborhood block clubs with welfare councils. Ideally, to test such a proposition one would take CO agencies in similar types of communities with similar types of goals and see if variation in their constituencies did in fact lead to different types of action programs. Such a design might be difficult to realize.

[14]See Rein and Morris, op. cit., for a discussion of the problems of agencies whose constituencies are made up of organizations.

the expectation that extreme programs would be proposed, then such an agency might be as likely as one comprised of individuals to initiate new and extreme programs rapidly. Thus, some community councils organized for purposes of neighborhood protection and development have been constituted out of organizations and still have initiated "radical" action programs.

TARGET GROUPS AND CO PRACTICE

The purpose of the professional and his agency is to improve the functioning of groups, individuals and communities. To do this he attempts to change individuals and the relationships among individuals and groups. His goal may be reached not only by changing relationships and attitudes, but by changing the facilities—hospitals, schools, trading associations—used by people in carrying out their daily lives. Thus, he may be attempting to mobilize the community for a relatively specific substantive proposal and the target group may only be changed insofar as it has reached a fairly specific decision. Values, norms, and social relations may not be changed; only questions of efficiency may be involved. Differential diagnosis of target problems has important organizational implications. Let us examine two aspects of agency-target relations—the role definitions of line workers and the tactics of institutional penetration.

Role Definitions of Line Workers

The problem can be posed as a question: Should line workers be substantive specialists or should they be "multipurpose" workers coached by substantive specialists? Should the worker be a technical specialist, knowledgeable in the specific problems of the community, or should he be a generalist, knowledgeable about how to relate to communities?

At least partly the answer depends on the extent to which the target group accepts and is committed to the purposes of the agency. *To the extent that an organization's goals are accepted and its functions in a community understood, a specialist organization can most efficiently communicate information and methods that can then be utilized by a target group.* However, *to the extent that members of a target group are suspicious of an agency, communication channels will be blocked.* In such a situation a generalist will be required whose main job is to establish an organization-target group linkage. As that linkage is established, it then becomes possible to reintroduce specialists, now trading on the generalist's relations.[15]

But what of the qualifications of such multipurpose workers? Who should they be? To the extent that the target group is difficult to penetrate because of problems of distrust, and to the extent that major sanctions are not controlled by the organization, the most effective generalist is likely to be one who minimizes social distance at the same time that he represents the "ego ideal" of target group members. "Personalistic" as opposed to "professional" criteria become crucial.

As many field workers have noted in working with lower-income ethnic groups and delinquent gangs, and as Katz and

---

[15]See Albert Mayer and associates in collaboration with McKin Marriott and Richard Park, *Pilot Project India: The Story of Rural Development in Etawah, Uttar Pradesh* (Berkeley: University of California Press, 1958). See also Elihu Katz and S. N. Eisenstadt, "Some Sociological Observations on the Response of Israeli Organizations to New Immigrants," *Administrative Science Quarterly,* Vol. 5, No. 1 (June 1960), pp. 113–133; and Gans, op. cit., chap. 7, pp. 142–162.

Eisenstadt have suggested for Israeli administrative agencies, the overcoming of distrust may require the worker to appear to identify more with the problems and perspective of the target group than with the agency. As the level of distrust decreases, however, the target group becomes amenable to the norms and procedures of the agency and more normal agency-client relations can be established. Thus, in order to be effective, CO agencies must evaluate the extent to which target groups are receptive to their policies. Staff role definitions must be fitted to this diagnosis. Sometimes, however, CO diagnosis involves the question of how one makes specific decisions, not how one reaches a group. When the target question switches to penetrating institutional decision centers, a new set of diagnostic criteria becomes relevant.

Tactics of Institutional Penetration

The legacy of Floyd Hunter and C. Wright Mills to the practice field can be summed up as "to the power structure!" Many CO workers, civil rights workers, and others who are trying to change communities seem to be saying: "If you want something done you must get the power structure behind you." If community organizers followed this dictate, they would find themselves pursuing a chimera. If they tried to mobilize the same élite on every decision, they would fail both to mobilize them and to attain their objectives.

Furthermore, the power structure is often relatively irrelevant to many decisions, for it is often isolated and in an official decision center or is most sharply affected by the sentiments of that most diffuse of all decision centers, the voting populace. Thus, the job of analyzing decision centers requires the most precise diagnosis of the

chain of influence and mechanism of decision making for each specific decision.

If the decision involves a referendum, different kinds of issues appeal to different groups. Machiavellian advice to a community organizer interested in promoting school bonds is to see that the middle class is overrepresented (as it is when the turnout is low), since they tend to vote for school funds. On the other hand, when, as in some states, referenda are held on welfare matters, the lower class should be motivated to vote, for they tend to vote "yes" on these measures.[16]

In mobilizing a target group, the CO practitioner and agency must face squarely the dilemma of their relative commitment to "the democratic process" versus their commitment to specific social values. The advice given above obviously conflicts with faith in the democratic process. This is a dilemma not only for CO practitioners, but for all advocates of social welfare. However, in part the problem of whether to pursue specific goals regardless of an idealized conception of the democratic process resolves itself according to agency goals and mandates. For instance, the more specific and concrete an organization's objectives and the greater the demands on the organization by the constituency, the more likely it is that workers' concerns about "process" will be relegated to the background.

EXTERNAL RELATIONS

In attempting to mobilize a target group, reach a specific objective, or integrate services, CO agencies must deal with other agencies. The

---

[16]For a study that looks at the relation of income and ethnicity to "public" and "self-interest" voting on referenda see James Q. Wilson and Edward C. Banfield, "Public Regardingness as a Value Premise in Voting Behavior," *American Political Science Review*, Vol. 58, No. 4 (December 1964), pp. 876–887.

CO agency may be but one among many and it may be without a mandate to guide, direct, or lead the other agencies. Often a CO agency has as part of its mandate the integration of the disparate institutions, but the mandate may be honored more in the breach.

One of the basic premises of organizational analysis is that only under very special conditions do organizations purposely attempt to decrease their scope, actually admit that they are ineffective, or willingly give up "turf." These special conditions involve low ideological or career commitment to the organization on the part of staff, an increasingly difficult fund-raising problem, and a constituency that increasingly finds better alternative uses of time and money. As a working assumption it is reasonable to assert that most organizations will attempt to maintain autonomy and increase their scope.[17] Even when it is obvious that one agency is more capable of achieving a shared goal than another, it would be rare indeed for the latter to donate its income for the expansion of the former. And it is rarely obvious that one agency has some superiority over another.

Given the assumption that agencies generally wish to increase autonomy and scope, the integration and coordination of agency policy and programs depend on the enlightened self-interest of the treaty signers—the independent agencies. As a general postulate, coordination, sharing of facilities, and proper integration are likely to take place only when both of the autonomous agencies stand to gain. Specific conditions follow.[18]

1. *If two agencies are essentially in a competitive relation to each other for funds, constituency, and staff, full-scale coordination and merger of programs would indeed be unlikely.* (Nor, given the nature of funding processes in which multiple appeals increase the total amount of funds available for the welfare sector, would a merger of identities necessarily lead to a more effective welfare economy.)

2. *The greater the marginal cost of coordination and integration or the lower the marginal profit, the less chance of integration and coordination of programs.* (Cost and profit do not necessarily refer to money; there can be costs of time and energy, for instance.) It follows that coordination will most easily be achieved on problems that are least expensive to both parties. Coordination is more easily achieved on a specific case than on over-all programs.

3. *The greater the organizational commitment to a fixed program or style of operation, the less likely the coordination and integration.* Agencies develop commitment to programs on ideological grounds and, because the programs help the agency to solve problems of identity, they thereby become part of the organizational character.[19] To the extent that a program must be changed by a merger, the costs mount.

---

[17] In addition to Perrow, op. cit., see Norton E. Long, "The Local Community as an Ecology of Games," *American Journal of Sociology,* Vol. 64, No. 3 (November 1958), pp. 251–261.

[18] This discussion draws on the following articles, which have recently discussed problems of coordination and interorganizational relations: William J. Reid, "Interagency Co-ordination in Delinquency Prevention and Control," *Social Service Review,* Vol. 38, No. 4 (December 1964), pp. 418–428; Eugene Litwak and Lydia Hylton, "Inter-Organizational Analysis: A Hypothesis on Coordinating Agencies," *Administrative Science Quarterly,* Vol. 6, No. 4 (March 1962); Sol Levine and Paul E. White, "Exchange as a Conceptual Framework for the Study of Inter-Organizational Relationships," *Administrative Science Quarterly,* Vol. 5, No. 4 (March 1961), pp. 583–601.

[19] On the concept of organizational character see Selznick, *Leadership in Administration.*

These three propositions state the conditions that impede coordination and integration. Stated somewhat differently, they indicate conditions contributing to coordination, cooperation, and integration:

1. *The greater the symbiotic relation between agencies, the more likely the coordination.* For instance, interestingly enough, the police and an agency working with delinquent gangs have more to gain from cooperating than a family service agency and a street work agency. The latter agency can actually contribute only occasionally to aiding the family service agency in its work with its case load and, at best, the family service agency can help "cool out" an offender. On the other hand, the police and the street worker have a strong symbiotic relation. The street worker gains status with the boys with whom he is working by being able to negotiate with the police, while the police have fewer problems with the gang. The same principle applies to the relation of membership groups to the "Ys," of mental hospitals to general hospitals, and so on.

2. *The greater the marginal profits, the more likely the coordination.* Sometimes funds are granted only to cooperating agencies. If the funds are great enough they overcome the costs of integrating or joint planning. Marginal profits of coordination may be seen in the face of a crisis in facilities. When programs become overburdened, when facilities are inadequate and multiple expansion funds are not available, a negotiated settlement may allow specialization between agencies, reducing overall financial needs and making coordination profitable.[20]

There is also some evidence to suggest that overlapping constituencies contribute to such coordination.[21] *The less constituencies overlap, the more likely it is that the constituencies are either neutral to or distrust each other and thus the longer it will take and the more difficult it will be to gain cooperation.*

This last point suggests that external relations may also be related to the concepts discussed earlier; that is, costs and profits are defined in the context of and affected by organizational constitutions and goals, constituency, and target groups.

CONCLUSIONS

In this paper one part of a sociology of CO practice has been developed—the organizational analysis of CO agencies. In each section several testable propositions were presented about the conditions under which different kinds of CO agency problems and processes arise. However, this paper has not presented a complete analysis of CO agencies. First, there are not enough empirical studies of these agencies to permit this. Second, the internal role structure of agencies has not been dealt with. Nevertheless, the writer is convinced that analysis along these lines will be valuable for both sociology and CO practice. For sociology the reward will be rich in that studies of sets of organizations will permit an examination of problems of mobilizing support and community consensus; for community organization the reward will be rich in that an analytic and differential basis will be developed by which to assess CO agencies and evaluate practice roles.

---

[20]See Robert Morris, "New Concepts in Community Organization Practice," *Social Welfare Forum, 1961* (New York: Columbia University Press, 1961), pp. 128–146.

[21]Ibid.

6.

Rosalie Bakalinsky

THE SMALL GROUP IN COMMUNITY ORGANIZATION PRACTICE

Community organization, within social work, has not as yet developed a comprehensive theory of its practice. Part of the problem has been difficulty in defining the essential nature of such practice for it incorporates a wide range of activities with diverse population groups. Rothman (1974) has conceptualized three different approaches or models of community organization, each implying a different set of goals, practitioner roles and strategies of intervention. While a community organizer may tend towards one model over another, an indispensable aspect of his or her practice will be the creation, maintenance and influence of small groups in order to achieve certain objectives. The practitioner may at one or different times be engaged in forming a neighborhood group of low income residents, in staffing an agency board, or in establishing a planning group whose purpose is either the creation of a new service or coordination of existing services. It would seem then, that knowledge and skill in work with small groups would be an important requirement of any type of community organization practice.

While groups in community organization may differ on goals, structure and composition, there are certain characteristics and processes which can be considered generic to all types of groups. This paper will attempt to discuss some of the significant features of groups and their implications for community organization practice. Where implications cannot be readily drawn, questions will be raised which might suggest directions for further exploration and study.

GROUP STRUCTURE AND DYNAMICS: SELECTED FEATURES

The use of groups in any change effort assumes the belief that the group is a more effective or more desirable means of achieving that change than is individual effort. In many organizations, sheer necessity or practicality impels the use of group effort to achieve its goals. Furthermore, democratic values dictate that "rule by the many" is more desirable (even though it may not be more effective or efficient) than "rule by the one."

To create or develop a highly effective group out of an aggregate of individuals is no simple task. Groups, like individuals, have their own unique characteristics and personalities. They can be mature or immature, functional or dysfunctional. As individuals need to be nourished and nurtured to maturity, so do groups. While many factors impact a group's development and functioning, four dimensions will be highlighted for discussion: group size, composition, cohesiveness and leadership. These dimensions can be considered variables which affect or determine the degree to which the group will be functional and effective in attaining its goals.

140

As a frame of reference for the discussion it might be useful to clarify what is meant by a highly functional, mature group. Bradford (1976) has identified the following characteristics:

1. Members are highly involved in the group and share responsibility for its operation.
2. Members assume responsibility for their own behavior and for its effect on both the group task and on the other members.
3. There is an atmosphere of trust and concern which allows members to express ideas, feelings and fears.
4. Conflict is neither suppressed nor repressed. Diversity of opinion is expected and encouraged.
5. Communication is free, open and non-defensive.
6. There is a willingness and capability to examine and evaluate the group's functioning (Bradford, 1976, pp. 29–32).

These criteria are considered essential for maximum group productivity and high member satisfaction.

Group Size

The dimension of size presents a dilemma for the community organizer working with any task or problem-solving group. Research has indicated that the optimum size of a group is from five to seven (Hartford, 1971, pp. 168–169). This range allows for fuller participation and involvement and therefore is more satisfying to all members. As the size increases there is less participation; "the most active participants become more active, while the least active become less active and may even become silent" (Hartford, 1971, p. 165). Larger groups tend to encourage aggression, competition and inconsideration among some members. Furthermore, increase in size requires more formal group structure, greater need for coordination of group tasks and activities, and more time to reach agreement or consensus.

On the other hand, studies have shown that larger groups (that is, of about twelve to fifteen) are more effective in solving complex problems.

Groups may have a greater possibility of accuracy in problem solving because of the greater number of checks and balances. There is the possibility of greater variety of opinion and more ideas if the focus of the group is on some cognitive task (Hartford, 1971, p. 167).

The difficulty is one of assuring a small enough group that will provide the members with a sense of satisfaction and a feeling that their participation is important to the group while at the same time assuring there are sufficient resources within the group to enable task and goal attainment.

In community organization practice, the agency board is one area in which the dilemma of size is most apparent. The number of persons included on a board is determined by many factors: interest in the agency, financial contribution or access to needed funds, representation of significant elements in the agency's constituency, and so on. Frequently members are added because they enhance the prestige and status of the board and agency. These factors, while necessary considerations, can increase the size of the board beyond the optimum. Of perhaps greater significance is the tendency not to remove board members who have proven themselves to be dysfunctional. Rather, the inclination is to add new members. Houle (1960) has written

Sometimes it is necessary to enlarge a board, but the ineffectiveness of the present membership is not very good grounds for doing so. The net result is often a big ineffective board rather than a small ineffective board—and ineffectiveness grows worse as it grows larger (p. 28).

The agency board was used as an illustration; the variable of size has similar implications for other community organization groups. The point at which it is best not to add another member to a group, even though he may contribute a valuable resource, is a question that merits further study.

Group Composition

In selecting members for a group, descriptive and behavioral attributes of potential members are important considerations. Descriptive attributes refer to a position an individual occupies within a classificatory group. Age, sex, ethnicity, education, occupation, etc., are examples of descriptive attributes. Behavioral attributes refer to the way in which an individual behaves in a position. The compromiser, competitor, evaluator, harmonizer, etc., are examples of behavioral attributes (Pincus and Minahan, 1973, pp. 204–205). Homogeneous descriptive attributes facilitate communication, interaction and compatibility among members. Heterogeneous behavioral attributes increase the possibility that members will perform both group task and maintenance roles. The degree of homogeneity and heterogeneity on both descriptive and behavioral characteristics is a key question in group composition. Research has shown that problem-solving groups ". . . with heterogeneous behavioral attributes produce a higher proportion of high quality, acceptable solutions than do homogeneous groups" (Pincus and Minahan, 1973, p. 206).

In community organization, high value is placed on citizen, consumer or client participation in the development and delivery of services that are important to them. A planning, task or advisory group that is comprised of the ethnic minority client or consumer, the professional expert and other important community figures (descriptive heterogeneity) will encounter problems in the group's internal functioning. To the extent that the community organizer will be successful in creating a group climate in which all members respect and trust each other and feel free to express their ideas and opinions, then the diversity in descriptive attributes will not be dysfunctional. If such endeavor fails, then the diversity will handicap the group's functioning even though there may be high agreement on, and interest in, group goals and tasks.

The maxim of homogeneous descriptive attributes has relevance for organizing low-income, ethnically mixed neighborhoods. Brager and Specht (1973), writing about the primary group phase in community organizing have stated

Social bonds are more easily developed among persons who have similar characteristics and beliefs. Groups composed of people of the same ethnicity, color, class, sex, age, and so forth, will be more cohesive than those in which membership characteristics are disparate. . . . Thus, there may be no alternative in ethically mixed communities but to organize ethnically homogeneous groups which later come together to pursue superordinate goals (p. 128).

Organizing separate ethnic groups within a community runs the risk of increasing the competition that may already exist between them. This may handicap later efforts to bring them together on shared concerns and interests.

The trend towards ethnic affirmation, in contrast to "integration" or "assimilation," further complicates the matter. Ethnic affirmation places high value on difference—difference in attitudes, values and lifestyle.

Focus on differences tends to lead to less intimacy, less trust and less cohesion among group members, factors having negative effect on group functioning. Creating ethnically diverse groups, at any stage, may then be most difficult.

At what point in time ethnically mixed groups can be formed for effective problem solving is an important issue warranting further research.

Cohesiveness

Group cohesiveness is reflected by the pride members feel in belonging, by the gratification derived from the group and by coordinated, synergistic group activity or effort. The extent to which members are attracted to the group will determine the extent of its cohesion. A group that fails to coalesce runs the risk of ultimate disintegration and demise.

Hartford (1971), referring to the research reported by Cartwright and Zander has stated that

the individual member's attraction to the group will depend upon four major factors: (1) the incentive nature of the group, its goals, program, size, type of organization, and position in the community; (2) the motivation of the person, his needs for affiliation, recognition, security, and other things he can get from the group; (3) the attractiveness of other persons in the group; and (4) if the group serves as a means for satisfying needs outside of the group (p. 246).

Research has indicated that attraction to a group will increase when a member has prestige, or can potentially obtain it, within the group, and when he or she enjoys acceptance, recognition and a sense of worth by the group. Also, groups in which there are cooperative relationships are more attractive than groups where competitiveness predominates.

The research would indicate that many people volunteer or agree to participate in community organization groups in order to satisfy personal, psychological needs. Even in instances where the primary motivation may be interest in the goals of the group, unless basic psychological needs of acceptance and recognition are satisfied, attraction to the group will decrease. Awareness and assessment of such needs and ability to intervene in the group process to assure their gratification are important prerequisites for the practitioner. Quite often community organizers work with groups as a consultant or on an advisory basis. Freedom to directly intervene in the group process is limited. The equality in relationship power between the members and the practitioner may further limit his or her influence. Thus, the practitioner will have to resort to indirect means through which members' needs can be gratified.

A unique aspect of community organization groups is that in many of them, individuals are members by virtue of the fact that they are representatives of other groups or organizations. In an interagency coordination group, for example, members represent different organizations that frequently are in competition with each other. Competitive relationships could be expected, at least initially, in the coordination group. As was mentioned earlier, competitive relations weaken group cohesion. Creating or developing cooperative relationships would become a critical, albeit difficult, task. An interesting area for further research might be determination of factors or variables that promote cooperative relationships amongst a group of representatives whose surrogate organizations are in competition with each other.

Leadership

One of the most definitive studies on group leadership was conducted by Robert

Bales. In summarizing the findings of his research, Hartford (1971) writes

In any group there emerges task or instrumental leadership and socioemotional or affective leadership. The task leadership facilitates the work. It helps to organize and divide the labor, specify the goals, and move the group toward achieving its goals. The affective leadership. . . . focuses on feelings, mediating differences, soothing ruffled tempers, supporting members, and helping them feel good (p. 212).

An important discovery was that is was rare for one person to fulfill both types of leadership roles, but both are essential for group stability and optimum functioning (Bales, 1966, p. 131).

This conception of leadership implies that at any stage in a group's development both roles need to be performed even though one role may be more needed at a particular point in time than another. It is this point that, I believe, has created some confusion among some community organization writers.

Burghardt (1979) has attempted to relate stages of group development, leadership styles and models or strategies of community organization. He appears to believe that task leaders are not as important or valuable as affective leaders in the locality development model because it is ". . . a method that from the start emphasizes process over task, social interaction over concrete goal directions" (Burghardt, 1979, p. 220). The fact that solution of problems is secondary to development of community capacity and integration does not negate the value of task leadership roles. A group that has been created in order to enhance a sense of community pride in its members, and to increase competence in dealing with community problems, has goals, the goals representing some change in the participants or members of the group. An activity that moves the group closer towards

attainment of that goal can be considered a task leadership activity. An activity that contributes to group solidarity is an affective leadership activity. Conceivably, one can have a group in which members feel very good being and working together but still lacking in competence; indicating a need for task leadership activity. Similarly, I would argue that in social planning groups, where problem solving takes precedence over process, there is just as much need for affective as well as task leadership. For, unless the group achieves integration and a sense of well-being, it will not be effective as a problem-solving medium.

The confusion might be semantic. Rothman distinguishes locality development and social planning by defining the former as involving process goals and the latter task goals. Process goals refer to the development of community self-help and integration; actual solution of problems is a lesser priority. Task goals refer to actual solution of community problems (Rothman, 1974, p. 26). "Task" and "process" as related to group leadership have a different connotation though there is a conceptual similarity. As has already been noted, task leadership refers to activities that move the group towards goal attainment; affective leadership, towards group integration and maintenance. All groups, whether formed for purposes of changing attitudes or feelings in the participants, or for achieving some change external to the group members, require both types of leadership. Thus, in locality development and social planning groups, both task and process are dimensions of *equal* importance.

Given the validity of this argument, then it is essential that a community organizer maintain an appropriate balance between the two forms of leadership in the groups with which he or she is engaged; and if one or both are lacking, he or she may need to perform the necessary role. Brager and Specht (1973) support this position. In analyzing the instrumental and expressive roles of the community worker they state

Paradoxically, the community worker must attempt to fill either role—or however inconsistent it may seem, both at once—depending on the state of equilibrium (or lack of it) which exists within his group at a particular time (p. 85).

The research on leadership vitiates the concept of the leader as a person with unique or superior qualities or attributes. There is wide acceptance of the idea that leadership is not vested in one person but is shared by all members in the group (Bradford, 1976, pp. 10–14). Many groups in community organization have formal, designated leaders. The committee chairperson, elected or appointed, is frequently referred to as the leader of the group. If the chairperson is perceived by self and others as carrying major responsibility for task and/or affective functions, the risk of a passive, apathetic, ineffective group with disgruntled members is greatly increased. A crucial responsibility of the chairperson then, is to help group members perform the necessary leadership functions. In other words, the chairperson's role is that of facilitator, not leader.

This raises a dilemma for the chairperson because it implies relinquishment of certain prerogatives as a group member. As a facilitator, the chairperson cannot forcibly advocate one position over another. His or her responsibility is one of encouraging expression of all positions and assuring that all receive equal hearing. Jay (1979), writing on committee meetings, addresses this dilemma and offers a questionable solution. He states

Regardless of whether leadership is in fact a single or a dual function, for our purposes it is enough to say that the chairman's best role is that of social leader. If he wants a particular point to be strongly advocated, he ensures that it is someone else who leads off the task discussion, and he holds back until much later in the argument (p. 264).

Jay suggests that the chairperson can always find opportunity to express his or her preference when summarizing the meeting. Though his point seems to be that it is more important for the chairperson to maintain affective rather than task leadership, the rationale for his position is not clear. Jay's solution to the dilemma is open to question for it assumes that the chairperson ought to adopt one of the two types of leadership roles; an assumption negated by the studies on effective group leadership.

Suffice it to say, however one may conceive of the chairperson's role, it demands much skill in and knowledge of group dynamics. The fact that many chairpersons of community organization groups are not professionally trained or skilled in this area raises the question of their capability to develop a highly productive, effective group.

CONCLUSION

Small groups constitute an ubiquitous element in community organization. Yet, very little of group theory is reflected in both its theory and its practice. One wonders if many committees and other groups flounder because insufficient consideration is given to important aspects of group structure and process. In this paper, only a few components have been discussed. There are others, such as group conflict and its resolution, norm development, decision making, and so on, that are of equal relevance. Given the different nature of client groups, goals and strategies of intervention in community organization, there is need for more rigorous study and research on the application of small group theory within this area of social work practice.

REFERENCES

Bales, R. F. "The Committee Meeting." In William A. Glasser and David L. Sills, eds. *The Government of Associations.* Totowa, New Jersey: The Bedminster Press, Inc., 1966.

Bradford, L. P. *Making Meetings Work.* La Jolla, California: University Associates, 1976.

Brager, G. and H. Specht. *Community Organizing.* New York: Columbia University Press, 1973.

Burghardt, S. "The Tactical Use of Group Structure and Process in Community Organization." In Fred M. Cox, John L. Erlich, Jack Rothman and John E. Tropman, eds. *Strategies of Community Organization,* 3rd ed. Itasca, Illinois: F.E. Peacock Publishers, Inc., 1979.

Hartford, M. E. *Groups in Social Work.* New York and London: Columbia University Press, 1971.

Houle, C. O. *The Effective Board.* New York: Association Press, 1960.

Jay, A. "How to Run a Meeting." In Fred M. Cox, John L. Erlich, Jack Rothman and John E. Tropman, eds. *Tactics and Techniques of Community Practice.* Itasca, Illinois: F. E. Peacock Publishers, Inc., 1977.

Pincus, A. and A. Minahan. *Social Work Practice: Model and Method.* Itasca, Illinois: F. E. Peacock Publishers, Inc., 1973.

Rothman, J. "Three Models of Community Organization Practice." In Fred M. Cox, John L. Erlich, Jack Rothman and John E. Tropman, eds. *Strategies of Community Organization,* 2nd ed. Itasca, Illinois: F. E. Peacock Publishers, Inc., 1974.

CORE ELEMENTS OF PRACTICE

7.

Fred M. Cox

COMMUNITY PROBLEM SOLVING: A GUIDE TO PRACTICE WITH COMMENTS

This problem-solving guide was developed by the editors and their students. Community practitioners will find that the guide directs their attention to a number of factors central to assessing community problems and developing a course of action for attacking them.

There have been a number of efforts to provide a model to guide community organization practice. Murray G. Ross developed a set of principles to guide community organization and a discussion of the roles of the organizer (16, pp. 155–228; 17, pp. 157–231). Ronald Lippitt and his collabora-tors studied a wide range of planned change efforts, which include efforts at the community level. From this study, they formulated a discussion of the phases of planned change, the role of the change agent, an approach to diagnosis in planned change, and an analysis of the forces operating for and against changes (9). Roland Warren provides a five-stage model of the "development and change of community action systems" (25, p. 315 and pp. 303–39). Robert Perlman and Arnold Gurin offer a "problem solving model" in their study of community organization, prepared under the auspices of the Council of Social Work Education (12, pp. 61–75). This list is by no means comprehensive (19, pp. 504ff.), but it includes those that have been most influential in shaping the present effort.

The guide is ordered sequentially as the factors considered are likely to be encountered in practice. The guide should be used flexibly. The experienced practitioner may not need to explore each point as carefully as one new to a situation. Few will have the opportunity to employ it systematically in every practice context. Nevertheless, we believe the practitioner will find it useful as a reminder of issues that may otherwise be overlooked or questions that provoke thought that may have an important bearing on practice decisions and outcomes. Some practitioners will be confronted with more "givens" and fewer choices than others. A clear understanding of the "givens" as well as the options is crucial for effective practice.

Like most general models, this one may fail to call attention to certain questions of importance in specific situations. Many practitioners will want to refine and elaborate the guide to suit the particulars of the practice situation in which they are involved. In general, however, we believe that the guide can contribute to a more logical and coherent approach to confronting problems in the multiple pressures and confusions of community practice.

THE GUIDE

This section briefly outlines the main categories comprising the guide to community problem solving. It will be followed by a more elaborate commentary that provides further detail about each of the steps in the process. In preparing a problem-solving statement at the outset of a project, the practitioner uses this commentary as a basis for deciding about what to include in the initial analysis.

I. Preliminary Considerations

A practitioner starts out by spelling out certain givens in the intervention situation that serve to structure and shape further actions. Intervention is typically carried out within an agency or organization that establishes the ground rules and gives the worker an assignment (whether specific or broadly conceived) to implement. The sponsoring agency has a preexisting mission and formulates the broad goals that are to be aimed for. It also typically has evolved preferences about strategies and tactics, which the practitioner has to take into account. Within the agency, factors of various kinds color the work: specific decision makers who create policy, lines of authority, norms of operation, and programmatic structures. The practitioner, as an employee of the agency, brings to bear on the assignment personal motivations and capacities, which intersect with the opportunities that are provided in the organizational environment and form a unique meld. Such factors should be made explicit at the outset as part of designing a plan of action.

II. Problems

An early step in all practice entails a problem analysis and needs assessment in order to provide a firm basis for action steps. It is important to identify the type of problem, its location geographically and socially in the system, and its scope, and to determine those who are affected by it. Past change efforts should be clarified so that they can be built upon in an effective way. The practitioner brings to the situation only one perspective among others; therefore it is useful to discern the perceptions of those who are participants in the action or who will be affected by it in one way or another.

III. Social Context of the Problem

To gain a meaningful understanding, the problem has to be examined in a sophisticated way. What was the origin of the problem? Can it be explained through some theoretical perspective such as communication blocks, institutional racism, or interorganizational conflict? What structures and factions either maintain or can potentially alleviate it? What are the consequences of taking action or failing to do so for different elements in the community: Who gains and who loses?

IV. Intended Beneficiaries

Who are the people or groups that stand to gain from the intervention? These can be identified with respect to demographics, spacial location, ethnic identity, economic and political standing, and so forth. Cleavages within the beneficiary group should be described, as well as their relationships with various parts of the community system.

V. Goals

The goals of various parties in the situation should be clarified, including the beneficiary system, the agency, and significant others. Based on the overall analysis, the practitioner needs to delineate a set of professional preferred goals, with an order of priority. These should include task goals related to concrete problems and process goals related to community competency and system maintenance.

VI. Strategy

The practitioner needs to go on to design potential strategies to address problem situations. A set of relevant tasks have to be laid out and an action system conceived that is made up of participants and allies. In addition, it is important to identify people and forces who will interfere with or resist the action plan. Needed resources and their availability have to be assayed. In light of this examination a preferred strategy should be outlined.

VII. Tactics

Tactics comprise the mechanics of carrying out a strategy. First there is the question of entry—where to start and with whom? The beginning phase also entails the notion of leverage—what initial actions give the best chance of sustaining the strategy? There exists the important matter of determining how to work interactively with the action system. Specific expectations have to be formulated, including an informal "contract" between the practitioner and those making up the action system. Some implementation steps include training and supporting participants, scheduling actions over time, using resources effectively, and dealing with the opposition in appropriate ways.

VIII. Evaluation

Action in itself is not the essence of intervention. Actions are calculated to bring about beneficial outcomes. It is important in thinking ahead to consider means whereby to examine results in order to determine objectively and empirically whether goals were achieved and to what extent. The practitioner should indicate how the effectiveness of the strategy will be measured, as well as the effectiveness of the tactics.

Only in this way will learning be derived concerning the viability of various practice options, thereby improving practice.

IX. Modification, Termination, or Transfer of Action

As an intervention experience nears resolution (as indicated through evaluation), it may be necessary to formulate new goals and strategies in order to move into a next phase. On the other hand, it may be time for the practitioner and agency to withdraw. In that case certain termination actions are necessary, including preparing the action system for the change. Concluding steps may involve transferring responsibility to a new agency, or institutionalizing the results within the community to insure the stability of the change. It might be useful in doing a problem-solving analysis to look ahead and devise a scenario that predicts potential results and suggests terminal actions.

ELABORATIONS[1]

As part of the effort to increase the professional character of community organization practice, we need to develop guidelines for decision making that are grounded upon tested generalities. As our knowledge base expands, it should be possible to rely more heavily on insights drawn from the social and behavioral sciences. The problem in basing decisions on tested knowledge is to find a way to join the hodgepodge which is the reality of community practice and the generalizations derived from research,

which necessarily oversimplify, and select a few factors believed to be of overriding importance.

This problem is a difficult one for at least two reasons. First, our knowledge of what factors are most influential and their effects upon matters of importance to the practitioner, together with the various conditions that affect such cause and effect relationships, is very limited. Typically, we must be content with a combination of practice wisdom and partially tested theory validated under conditions quite different than those faced by each practitioner. For example, conclusions about group behavior are often based on laboratory data rather than field studies.

Second, even when knowledge is very full and based on rigorous study, there are serious problems in applying it. Scientific knowledge is the knowledge of probabilities, of the chances that certain actions or events are likely to be followed by particular consequences. But even a high probability of B being followed by A leaves room for the possibility, in some minority of instances, that A will not produce B. And there are always newly emerging contingencies, the effects of which are unknown, and relatively unique configurations of events and conditions that were not anticipated in the research studies. Thus, even under the best conditions, we must guard against expecting too much from scientific knowledge in guiding practice decisions.

What does the problem-solving guide contribute to this process? First, it suggests the major types of information that must be obtained by the practitioner if he or she is to reach informed decisions. Second, it offers the outline of an interconnected set of frameworks within which to collect this information. It does not, however, provide propositions or generalizations to which decisions must be referred; these comments

[1] The author acknowledges the contributions made by his colleagues John L. Erlich and Jack Rothman, whose critical comments and suggestions were used extensively in preparing this supplement to the preceding guide.

will suggest some additional sources we have found useful for this purpose. The comments are organized in the same order and under the same headings as the guide above. Wherever possible we relate these comments to the three modes of community organization around which this book is organized.

I. PRELIMINARY CONSIDERATIONS

A. Summary of Assignment

The practitioner provides a brief orientation to the nature of the assignment. If the guide is used for training purposes, the instructor may find this summary particularly useful.

B. Agency

The organization that sponsors the practitioner's work is the agency referred to. Its primary significance is in the possibilities it opens and the constraints it places upon practice.

Social action is typically sponsored by groups of like-minded people who feel generally oppressed by the wider society, are offended by particular governmental decisions or social norms, or share common interests they believe can be achieved more effectively through collective action. The group is held together by some common identity (ethnic or racial characteristics, ideological or cultural similarities, goals, a piece of turf, a shared sense of being oppressed by the larger society). While the sponsor is likely to be homogeneous in some respects, necessary funds may be generated by the group itself or may come from outside sources which may not fully identify with the sponsor, its goals, or, particularly, its methods. This constitutes a problem for some social action groups because, as they engage in controversial activities, they may jeopardize their financial support. On the other hand, to the extent they are homogeneous they are able to pursue their objectives single-mindedly, without undue debate over ends and means.

Locality development may be sponsored by a national government, as in the case of many community development programs in developing countries or in industrialized countries with groups of people isolated from modernization. In such cases there may be conflict between the aims and values of the national government and the people toward whom locality development is directed. Governmental sponsorship, however, may bring otherwise unavailable resources to bear upon problems of underdevelopment. In other cases, locality development is sponsored by groups who seek self-development, often at the initiative and with the continued assistance of some outside group (American Friends Service Committee, a community development program in a land-grant college). Under these conditions, considerable emphasis is placed upon representing various segments of local people and upon their voluntary choice of aims and activities. Given the diversity of people within a locality, problems often arise in finding consensus and in sustaining motivation to work on common problems, but, because these are necessary, the programs chosen represent what local people really want and may be more permanent than those imposed from outside.

Social planning may be sponsored by government at various levels or by private organizations. Backed by constituted authorities or the socially or politically elite, these agencies tend to view their mandate as deriving from the established political process or from democratic procedures in which all citizens are at least nominally free to participate. They typically focus on bringing technical skills to bear upon social problems and are dependent upon the sources of legitimacy, so that they often overlook the views of those who are the presumed beneficiaries or targets of their planning efforts. Insistent demands for wider participation may create operating problems for social planning agencies. If the agencies can secure substantial support, both financial and political, and highly qualified specialists, however, they may be able to resolve social problems to a greater degree than if support from those affected by the plans were required or fewer resources were available.

The extent to which organizations are bureaucratized has a major impact upon the kinds of tasks they can undertake and the strategies and tactics available to the practitioner. Organizations vary not only in internal structure but in relations with the social environment. They emerge out of the needs of particular constituents, with whom they have a variety of understandings about goals and methods. As noted in the text above, social action agencies are oriented toward their members, while social planning agencies are created by elites to control social problems experienced by nonelites. Zald discusses this with special reference to factors affecting the autonomy of the strategies available to the community organization agency (Article #5). Rein and Morris discuss the effects of the planning organization's goals and structure upon the strategies it employs (13, pp. 127–45).

Parenthetically, it should be noted that formal organizations may be important to the practitioner not only as sponsors of action but as allies in a joint effort or as targets of strategy.

C. Practitioner

The practitioner's activities can be analyzed from two perspectives. The first, which examines the practitioner's motivation, capacity, and opportunity, was developed by faculty members at the University of Chicago's School of Social Service Administration (14). This perspective raises three general questions: (1) To what extent do the personal and professional goals of practitioners coincide, reinforce, compete, or conflict with the goals of those they are trying to help and with those of the sponsoring agency? (2) Does the practitioner have the basic qualities of intelligence, ability to empathize with others, a sense of personal identity, and the special skills and knowledge necessary to operate effectively in a particular community organization assignment? (3) Does the practitioner have the support of the agency, the human and financial resources that are necessary to do the job with a reasonable expectation of effective performance? If there are impediments in the situation, what, if anything, can be done to correct them? Ronald Lippitt and his collaborators give attention to some of these questions (9, pp. 92–99).

The motivation, capacity, and opportunity required will vary with the type of practice and the nature of the sponsoring agency. For example, the practitioner's ideological predilections and world view will affect the motivation to work for various types of agencies and the willingness to use different strategies and tactics. Skills in working with different kinds of people (poor people, local elite) and in using various techniques (making population projections, teaching people how to handle unfamiliar situations) affect the capacity to work in different settings. The types and amounts of resources needed for effective practice vary for agencies with various scopes, goals, and strategies.

Role theory provides perhaps an even more useful perspective for analyzing the practitioner's work. The ambiguity and conflict in role definitions by various persons with whom the practitioner interacts, the discontinuity between the various roles one plays currently and between past and present roles, and the personal strain involved in learning a new role and coping with the problems inherent in role ambiguity, conflict, and discontinuity must be taken into account in understanding the practitioner's behavior and decisions (22, pp. 17–50; 9, pp. 91–126).

II. PROBLEMS

This section of the guide directs the community organization practitioner's attention to an analysis of the difficulties he or she is trying to remedy. The problems of concern are usually social rather than personal, affecting a substantial portion of the people served and out of harmony with their preferences. They may be substantive in character, i.e., problems such as mental illness, insufficient housing, or delinquency, or they may involve process, affecting the way the society, the community, and its institutions are organized, formally or informally, for dealing with social problems. Often the two are closely connected as, for example, when it is assumed that the negative reaction to the mentally ill stems from the lack of community-based institutions for dealing with them—well-organized family care homes, recreation programs, emergency services for coping with personal life crises, etc. Community practitioners are typically concerned with problems of both substance and process.

At this point the guide calls for careful observation and description. Explaining the problem is reserved for the next section.

The practitioner describes the kind of problem dealt with as clearly as possible, where it is located, how widely it is distributed among different kinds of people, and the degree to which one group is affected in comparison to another. The practitioner looks at past efforts to improve conditions, who made them, the extent of their successes or failures, and the probable reasons for these outcomes. He or she gives particular attention to differences in perceptions of the problem among the affected groups.

The varying ways in which the problem is perceived will be of particular importance. The agency, various subgroups of the client, and the practitioner may all see the problem a little differently and thus favor different solutions.

In the context of social action, the problem will be viewed as one of social injustice—an oppressed minority not receiving its fair share of political, economic, and educational resources, a group that has been deprived of some benefit or has had some social cost inflicted upon it, or a group seeking some benefit for itself at the expense of others for reasons it considers justified. Of increasing importance recently, many negatively regarded groups seek improved status and respect.

In a locality development context, the problem will often be defined as a failure to modernize, to develop the necessary capital and skills to facilitate industrialization at an appropriate rate or to build the necessary services ("infrastructure") needed to support an urbanizing population. The problem may be regarded as opposition to change (strong traditional or new but counterproductive forms of social organization), anomie (languishing social organization), or loss of local autonomy (an organized community losing control to national business, philanthropic, and governmental institutions). A normative view held by some community developers is that the problem stems from the failure of local democracy, the lack of concern about and a sense of responsibility for local problems.

Social planning agencies tend to define the problem as one or more fairly discrete social problems (mental illness, crime and delinquency, poverty, poorly organized services) for which they seek various technical solutions. The problems with which social planners deal are seen as forms of deviant behavior or social disorganization. Deviant behavior, such as mental illness, delinquency, or child abuse, is at variance with prescriptions for particular social roles. Merton makes a useful distinction between two types of deviant behavior, nonconformist and aberrant, which is particularly appropriate in the light of unrest among women minority groups, gays and students (10, pp. 808–11). The nonconformist announces his or her deviant behavior, challenges the legitimacy of rejected social norms, tries to change norms regarded as illegitimate, and calls upon higher social values as justification for actions. Conventional members of society recognize that the nonconformist is dissenting for disinterested reasons. In contrast, the aberrant individual hides his or her acts from public view, does not challenge the legitimacy of broken norms, tries to escape detection and punishment, and serves personal interests through aberrant behavior.

Social action groups of oppressed people may define their behavior as nonconformist and seek responses from the rest of society that first confirm this definition and ultimately redefine the behavior, prompting the nonconformity as acceptable rather than deviant. For example, those seeking abortion law reform, acceptance of homosexual preferences, or equality in job opportunities may use nonconformist means to secure redefinitions of abortion, homosexual behavior, and equal employment opportunities as nondeviant. Social planners may assist them through legitimate ("conformist") means that are possible within the context of their work—drafting legislation, taking matters to court, enlisting the support of community leaders, and so forth. Social planners may also participate in efforts to redefine the behavior of some deviants who, by this definition, are aberrant but whose crimes are trivial and are not regarded as morally reprehensible, or as victimless. The smoking of marijuana in moderation may increasingly be regarded as a trivial offense at best or a victimless crime at worse. Those who engage in drug abuse, prostitution, gambling, and homosexuality are often hurting no one but themselves. Even where behavior cannot be redefined as acceptable, social planners may assist in relieving exacerbating responses, through plans for bail reform and community care for the mentally ill, for example. Finally, planning services to modify the behavior of deviants, using new techniques such as behavioral modification, will continue to be useful for a number of forms of deviant behavior.

Other social problems are regarded as symptoms of social disorganization, not necessarily involving deviations from prescribed norms but rather reflecting incompatibilities between various parts of a social system, such as different rates of change (for example, technology changes more rapidly than social values). Poverty, housing shortages, water pollution, unemployment, and racial discrimination are often regarded as examples of social disorganization that constitute social problems social planners seek to solve.

Locality development practitioners typically view social problems from this standpoint, focussing on those that retard the maintenance or enhancement of a society or community (sharply increasing birth rates, general apathy, lack of entrepreneurial skills, or a failure of leadership). They are also concerned with the inability of a locality to obtain resources or achieve results from self-help efforts.

Another way of looking at social problems is offered by Arnold Rose (15, pp. 189–99), who defines two perspectives. One, which we will call "disjunctive theory," regards social problems as arising from different meanings being attached to objects that form the context of social interaction or from different values being assigned to the behaviors displayed in relation to those objects. Marijuana (an object) is regarded by some as a potentially dangerous mind-altering drug and by others as a means to a pleasant "high." The smoking of marijuana (behavior in relation to the object) is disvalued by some and enjoyed by others. Poverty in the United States today (a set of objects or conditions) is regarded by some as an unfortunate but inevitable by-product of the free enterprise system and by others as a needless hardship inflicted upon substantial (though decreasing) numbers of people by the economic system. Living in poverty (behavior in relation to that condition) is regarded as avoidable and remediable by individual effort or as essentially irremediable "tough luck" by some and as unnecessary deprivation remediable by collective effort by others. In each case, the problem is regarded as arising from lack of agreement on meanings, values, or both.

The disjunctive theory is often held, at least implicitly, by those practicing locality development and leads to emphasis upon the socialization process, education, and communication. If meanings attached to the same objects differ, efforts can be made to give people "the facts" so that increas-

ingly meanings can be shared. If values associated with particular behaviors conflict, communication between those who disagree may ultimately lead to a greater degree of consensus.

The other perspective Rose calls "conflict theory." From this point of view, social problems are the product of competition for scarce resources (wealth, prestige, power) which results in painful struggles over their distribution, with some being dissatisfied at the outcome.

Conflict theory assumes that values are held in common, that is, most people want the same things and will fight over their distribution, while disjunctive theory assumes that social problems arise from wanting different things or defining the same things in different ways. Those engaged in social action tend to regard social problems from the perspective of conflict theory. Although these practitioners may agree that some secondary grounds for conflict may arise from different meanings being attached to the same events (for example, the lack of a common understanding about the "facts" of poverty), they argue that the basic problem is one of maldistribution (of jobs or income). Social action practitioners try to solve social problems by mobilizing power to induce a redistribution of the valued objects in favor of their constituents or intended beneficiaries.

III. SOCIAL CONTEXT OF THE PROBLEM

A. Origins

The practitioner must take care to interpret the origins of a problem. He or she may understand how a problem came to be by examining its origins, but cannot thereby explain its persistence. Conditions that brought about a problem originally often fade, so that present conditions can only be explained by reference to factors currently operating. The practitioner must search for contemporary conditions that are causally connected with the problem and try to change them.

An effort should be made to understand the historical roots of the problem, particularly if there is a long or significant history affecting the present state of affairs. Coleman discusses what he calls residues of organization and sentiment that build up as people interact in community life and may take the form of collaborative patterns, expressed in latent or manifest forms of social organization or in organized cleavages such as those between rival political parties or ethnic groups. They may also be expressed in sentiments of liking and respect or of hostility (4, pp. 670–95).

B. Theory of the Problem

It is at this point in the analysis that attention is directed toward a search for controlling factors. Assuming that most problems are sustained by a wide variety of factors and that some are more influential than others, the practitioner's task is twofold: First, one must locate factors that have a major effect on the problem to be corrected. Second, one must choose problems one can reasonably expect to influence, given the time, money, personnel and other resources at one's disposal.

In many social action contexts, the problem will be understood as some form of conflict between "haves" and "have-nots." But greater specificity is required. Which particular interests are pitted against one another? What are the dynamics of the conflict? Are there any aspects of the problem or any facts that do not seem to fit into a conflict perspective? What are the implica-

tions for intervention? In many cases of locality development, the problem will be regarded as arising from barriers to communication or different rates of change, i.e., some form of disjunction or social disorganization. But it is important which specific theory or set of theories is selected, for this will exercise an important influence on strategies and tactics chosen. Most practitioners engaged in social planning will consider alternative theories explaining various social problems they are charged with ameliorating. But, again, the specific theory chosen is of great importance in shaping the action taken. If, for example, lower-class male delinquency is conceived of as arising from a lack of legitimate opportunities for success in American society, efforts will be made to expand those opportunities. If, on the other hand, delinquency is thought to arise from psychological problems or parental rejection, efforts will be directed toward various forms of counseling or the strengthening or substitution of parental relations. Or, if the labeling of youngsters as delinquent and the consequent processing through the criminal justice system are thought to be responsible for the perpetuation of delinquent behavior, efforts will be made to decriminalize certain behavior and handle young people who transgress social norms outside the criminal justice system.

Unfortunately, the explanation of the problem chosen by (or more typically implicit in the behavior of) the practitioner is usually limited by the ideology and values of the employing organization or the practitioner. The practitioner should explore his or her own preconceptions and those of the employer to determine what limits such preconceptions place on the choice of an explanation for the problem. However the theory of the problem arises, whether it is implicit in various predisposing values or is more rationally developed, it will have a major influence on the goals and strategies chosen for dealing with the problem.

C. Structural-Functional Analysis of the Problem

The practitioner begins with an assessment of available "theories of the problem." One selects the most reliable theories, and within them the factors that are both potent and potentially controllable. The next step is careful observation of the particular social problem in its context, collecting information within the framework of the theories and hypotheses selected earlier. The outline suggests that both the impact of various factors on the social problem in question and the effect of the problem on these factors be assessed. For example, we might identify particular social structures (schools, employers) that systematically deny opportunities to persons of lower socioeconomic or ethnic minority status, thus creating discontent, delinquent behavior, and so forth. We might then show the impact of such behavior on schools, ethnic minorities, and so forth, emphasizing the differential effects on various groups. This, of course, has implications for which groups, individuals, or organizations may be recruited into organized efforts to alleviate the problems.

Two useful terms in this section of the commentary are *functional* and *dysfunctional*: The functional consequences of action strengthen and unify social systems; dysfunctional consequences produce conflict or threaten disruption of existing social patterns. However, these terms should not be confused with "good" and "bad." Functional consequences can perpetuate what is, from the practitioner's perspective, an undesirable system, such as patterns of racial discrimination in housing and employment. Likewise, dysfunctional consequences may be exactly what the practitioner desires. For example, the early sit-ins, in addition to disrupting preexisting patterns of race relations, tended to enhance the self-esteem of black people and provide experience in contentious organized action.

IV. INTENDED BENEFICIARIES

The "client" is defined as the intended beneficiary of the practitioner's activities. It may be a group of people, a formal organization, or a population category. Clients can be analyzed in terms similar to other forms of social organization. Some of the factors that may be most important are outlined in the guide. The major implication of this section is that the beneficiaries must be identified and understood both in their context, i.e., their relations to other social phenomena, and in their internal structure. We must also be sensitive to changes that have taken place in the group and the reasons for them.

The definition of intended beneficiaries forces the practitioner to be clear about whom he or she is trying to help and to differentiate them from others who are regarded in more instrumental terms. There was a time when it was conventional for the community organizer to say that the client is the community. This rhetoric tends to hide the fact that particular actions may benefit some, harm others, and have little effect on still others. The suggested definition makes the practitioner consider whose interests will be sacrificed last if decisions must be made requiring that someone pay a price. It also demands that the practitioner consider how much to expect others to "pay" for the sake of the intended beneficiaries and decide whether the price is justifiable.

Who is client system in your group pros?

If they are a group of individuals with strongly held common interests that can be rather precisely defined, the practitioner will have little difficulty in knowing what benefits to work for on their behalf. On the other hand, one is likely to have difficulty in gaining allies and support for the group. If they are a heterogeneous group with common interests that can be defined only at the most general level, the practitioner probably will have trouble in defining precisely what to aim for. The chances of alienating some faction of the clientele are increased, but the group is likely to be much more inclusive, and thus the practitioner will have less difficulty in gaining needed outside support.

As Rothman notes (Article #1), the beneficiary group is viewed differently in the several contexts of practice. In locality development, they are citizens and participants in local problem solving. In social planning, they are consumers and recipients of services. In social action they are victims of oppression and employers or constituents of the practitioner.

The kind of beneficiaries one is able to serve is limited, in important ways, by the type of organization that employs one. That is, it is most difficult for a practitioner to give primacy to the interests of a group that is not the primary beneficiary of his or her employer. Blau and Scott have developed a typology of organizations based on the identity of the groups that are the primary beneficiaries of organizations (2, pp. 42–57). The main implication for practice is that the practitioner experiences grave difficulties in making clients out of groups other than those that are naturally the primary beneficiaries of the type of organization employing him. For example, the primary beneficiary of a mutual benefit association is its members. If practitioners employed by, say, a labor union define some nonmembers as the client—perhaps the people living in an impoverished neighborhood—they are likely to run into difficulties with members who resent the diversion of their dues for purposes not directly related to their welfare. Community practitioners employed by such agencies as public assistance bureaus sometimes experience difficulties when they select goals with which the public is out of sympathy. Part of the reason for these difficulties is a failure to recognize the true character of such social service agencies as commonweal organizations whose prime beneficiary is the general citizen instead of, as commonly believed, service organizations whose primary beneficiary is the clientele.

V. GOALS

At some point in his or her work, the practitioner must define as clearly as possible the particular goals to be achieved with the beneficiary. Lack of clarity may lead to goal displacement, i.e., the unintended replacement of goals by new, often unrecognized objectives. Under some conditions—when the situation is very unstable, when there is little experience to guide action, or when knowledge of aims would help those opposed to them—it may be necessary to be vague in public statements or to move toward goal definition through a process of successive approximation. Many other factors also lead to goal displacement—insufficient resources to pursue multiple goals, factional differences in interests, procedures which come to be valued by those who benefit from them, and so forth. Precise goal definition is one defense against goal displacement, however, and provides some criteria against which results can be measured. Resistance to goal displacement should not be used as an excuse to avoid adopting new goals when old ones have been achieved or are no longer appropriate, or new resources make it possible to add goals.

The practitioner must take into account not only his or her personal objective but also the views of the sponsoring organization, the participants, and other groups whose support is needed or whose resistance or objections must be anticipated. It is not necessary to accommodate the interests of the opposition or of those who are largely indifferent to or unaffected by the action, but one must do so for those whose cooperation, whether as active collaboration or passive awareness and the absence of hindering responses, one must have. Those whose interests must be taken into account if the practitioner is to achieve his or her objectives are called the "action system." (This term is used in the guide under the heading "Strategy.")

As suggested above, various groups have different *goals*, attach varying *importance* to particular goals, and have contrasting sets of *priorities*. Factions within groups may also differ in these ways. In taking these differences into account, the practitioner may decide on a strategy of "something for everyone," or may begin with one easily achieved goal of fairly high importance to all elements in order to build confidence in the organization's capability. One may develop some other rationale for selecting goals, but information about the relative priorities and salience of the goals of different factions is essential to a reasoned decision (11, pp. 25–31).

Social problems may reside in a group's relations with its environment (inadequate police protection or unresponsive public officials) or among its members (uncoordinated activities, low morale, lack of commitment). Goals are of two parallel kinds.

For example, a welfare council may appeal for additional public funds for a child care center or try to develop support for a human relations commission. These are commonly referred to in the literature as "task goals." Other goals affect the maintenance and enhancement of the organization (resolving destructive factional rivalry or transforming member apathy into involvement and commitment). These are called "process goals." In general, both types of goals must be served, but at particular times one type may be more important than another. At one time it was generally believed that the community practitioner should pursue only process goals, that is, be concerned exclusively with facilitating or "enabling" clients to achieve self-defined goals. Rothman argues persuasively that the practitioner need not be limited in this manner (18, pp. 24–31).

VI. STRATEGY

Perfect rationality (or anything approaching it) is unattainable in most practice situations. Computer technology may enable some to come a bit closer. But most of us must, as Herbert Simon puts it, "satisfice" rather than "maximize" the efficiency and effectiveness of our decisions (20, p. xxv).

However, some practitioners approach questions of strategy with predetermined formulas, agency traditions, and little imagination. While it is not feasible to consider every possibility and identify the single best way to achieve objectives, it does not follow that one strategy is as good as the next. We ask the practitioner to consider at least two good possibilities and exercise judgment in choosing the best one.

Perhaps more than any other activity, strategy development offers the practitioner an opportunity for creativity. In applying the guide, he or she sketches each strategy, outlining the minimum tasks required to achieve success; the necessary elements of the action system; the resistance (opposition), interdependence (entanglements), and interference (competition and indifference) forces that may be encountered; and the plans to handle them (9, pp. 71–89). Finally, the practitioner evaluates his or her ability to carry them out and develops a rationale for choosing between the various strategies being considered. As a general approach to decision making this applies to all types of practice. However, the relative emphasis given to various tactics (research, client participation, confrontation with organizations and their leaders) will vary with the model of practice used.

To the extent that success depends upon a correct theory of the problem and an effective strategy, success may be limited by the choices permitted by the elites or the political process. Because social planning strategies normally depend upon the effective manipulation of large-scale bureaucracies, success may also depend heavily on whether the strategy chosen can be effectively administered. And finally, because those whose actions are required for success—the functionaries and the targets—are not ciphers but people with interests and values that guide what they will respond to and what they will do, strategies that assume values about which there is little consensus or which assume a nonexistent community of interests are likely to enjoy limited success.

Some recent analyses suggest that strategies that operate as much as possible in a way analogous to a competitive market situation are most likely to succeed. They maximize individual choices and allow for individual differences. They require a minimum of bureaucratic complexity, especially detailed rules and numerous functionaries

to enforce or monitor compliance. It has been suggested that this is the reason for the failure of such programs as the War on Poverty, the success of Social Security, and the potential of income maintenance programs based on negative income tax principles (7).

VII. TACTICS

Strategy shades imperceptibly into tactics. The inspiration for much of this part of the guide comes from Lippitt and his colleagues (9). Among the questions the practitioner is asked to consider are: Where is it possible to gain a foothold in the targets? At what point are efforts likely to be most effective? For example, the practitioner may have access to other practitioners working in low- or middle-echelon positions in a target organization. His or her analysis, however, may lead to the conclusion that, to achieve the objective, the practitioner must gain access to the top executive. One may, therefore, bypass colleagues in the target organization and approach a member of one's board with the necessary social and political contacts to gain the ear of the target agency executive.

In order to avoid misunderstandings, it is important for the practitioner to communicate with key people in the action system (those whose cooperation is needed to carry out the strategy) so that they may develop common ideas about such things as definition of the problem, objectives, approaches, roles each participant will perform, and amount of time each participant will commit to the endeavor. The resulting set of agreements is referred to as the contract. Although the concept is borrowed from the law, it does not imply legal or even written form. The expectations must be as clear and unambiguous as possible, and all necessary participants must understand and commit themselves to the terms of the contract.

In carrying the plan into action, it may be necessary to train and support participants who feel more or less uncertain about what they are doing. This is particularly relevant for those who are inexperienced in the sort of activities required by the contract. The timing of various actions must be carefully planned. Resources of several kinds may require difficult coordination—it may be necessary to induce competing professionals to work together or to provide the press with newsworthy events involving large numbers of people so that politicians will take the action system's demands seriously.

It is desirable to consider an "action-reaction-action pattern" borrowed from Alinsky (1). We refer to these patterns when one group makes a move, intended to elicit a response from an adversary, that makes possible further action to achieve objectives that could not have been otherwise undertaken. For example, a group might leak information to an adversary that it plans a massive disruption of the adversary's business. The expected response is an offer to negotiate which, in turn, makes it possible to obtain concessions favorable to the group that would not have been secured by an initial request for negotiations. Such tactics depend on credibility; if the adversary does not believe that there is a genuine threat, it is not likely to negotiate.

The practitioner should anticipate that some form of opposition to the program undertaken by the action system may emerge and make plans to handle it. Under some circumstances, no such opposition will develop—organizing a council on aging or applying for funds from the federal government to mount programs for the aging should arouse no controversy or

opposition. If insurmountable opposition can be expected, however, plans should be changed unless the practitioner is deliberately trying to heighten awareness of impotence and stimulate anger as a prelude to other, perhaps stronger forms of action. If opposition is inevitable, a variety of approaches is available to cope with it in ways that may further the action system's objectives.

VIII. EVALUATION (3, 5, 6, 21, 24)

Evaluation should be an ongoing process. Plans must be worked out for the collection of information from participants in the action system regarding effectiveness with respect to both task and process goals. This may be quite informal (setting aside a portion of a meeting to discuss "how we're doing") or much more rigorous (standardized data collection, written reports) depending upon the size, complexity, and other requirements of the effort in which the practitioner is engaged. The important thing is that assessment not be overlooked, for the process allows the practitioner and the organization to revise their program if activities are found to be less than satisfactory.

Practitioners often find annual or semi-annual meetings good opportunities for taking stock. The results may be set forth in a periodic report. There is a tendency at such meetings to "put the best foot forward" and overlook difficulties in order to maintain or enhance morale, build financial resources, and avoid offending those who have been active in the organization. Ordinarily it is best to find ways to say what may be the unpleasant truth in a manner that minimizes problems. For example, it is possible to express gratitude for individual contributions while calling attention to persistent difficulties that exist "in spite of the best efforts of everyone involved."

IX. MODIFICATION, TERMINATION, OR TRANSFER OF ACTION

Evaluation of program and organizational effectiveness may lead to any one of several conclusions. First, the practitioner may conclude that the program is operating much as expected, is achieving its intended purposes, and should be continued. Second, he or she may find that some aspects are faulty, because of an erroneous analysis of the situation, a poor strategy, or particular actions that were inappropriate or poorly carried out. This conclusion should lead to necessary revisions. Third, the practitioner and those he or she is working with may conclude that the program has served its purpose or, alternatively, is hopelessly inept. In either case, the conclusion should be to discontinue operations and the practitioner must plan carefully for this. Finally, for a variety of reasons the practitioner may be leaving the job. Under these conditions, it is necessary to arrange either the transfer of professional responsibilities to another practitioner or the termination of the program.

CONCLUSION

These comments suggest how the guide may be used and offer some additional references which are intended to give it a broader scope and greater utility. We hope that practitioners will use the guide to remind themselves of some of the more important factors they need to take into account in planning their work.

Obviously the busy community practitioner will be unable to utilize fully the analysis suggested here in daily work. However, many of the steps in the problem-solving process will become part of the professional "equipment" he or she may apply, perhaps less formally and less rigorously but nonetheless effectively, in making day-to-day practice decisions. This is the hope we have had in preparing the guide and using it in teaching community practice.

BIBLIOGRAPHY

1. Alinsky, Saul D. *Reveille for Radicals.* Chicago: University of Chicago Press, 1946; and *Rules for Radicals.* New York: Random House, 1971.
2. Blau, Peter, M., and Richard W. Scott. *Formal Organizations.* San Francisco: Chandler Publishing Co., 1962.
3. Campbell, Donald T. "Reforms as Experiments." *American Psychologist* 24 (April 1969): 409–29.
4. Coleman, James S. "Community Disorganization," in Merton and Nisbet, op, cit., pp. 670–95.
5. Herzog, Elizabeth. *Some Guidelines for Evaluative Research.* Children's Bureau Publication No. 375. Washington, DC: U.S. Dept. of Health, Education, and Welfare, 1959.
6. Hyman, Herbert H., and Charles R. Wright. "Evaluating Social Action Programs," in *The Uses of Sociology*, edited by Paul F. Lazarfeld, William H. Sewell, and Harold Wilensky. New York: Basic Books, 1967. pp. 741–82.
7. Levine, Robert A. *Public Planning: Failure and Redirection.* New York: Basic Books, 1972.
8. Levine, Sol, Paul E. White, and Benjamin D. Paul. "Community Interorganizational Problems in Providing Medical Care and Social Services," *American Journal of Public Health* 53 (August 1963): 1183–95.
9. Lippitt, Ronald, Jeanne Watson, and Bruce Westley. *The Dynamics of Planned Change: A Comparative Study of Principles and Techniques.* New York: Harcourt, Brace and World, 1958.

10. Merton, Robert K. "Epilogue: Social Problems and Sociological Theory," in *Contemporary Social Problems*, 2d ed., edited by Robert K. Merton and Robert A. Nisbet. New York: Harcourt, Brace and World, 1966.

11. Morris, Robert, and Robert H. Binstock. *Feasible Planning for Social Change*. New York: Columbia University Press, 1966.

12. Perlman, Robert, and Arnold Gurin. *Community Organization and Social Planning*. New York: John Wiley and Council on Social Work Education, 1972.

13. Rein, Martin, and Robert Morris. "Goals, Structures and Strategies for Community Change." In *Social Work Practice 1962*. New York: Columbia University Press, 1962.

14. Ripple, Lillian. "Motivation, Capacity and Opportunity as Related to the Use of Casework Services: Theoretical Base and Plan of Study," *Social Service Review* 29 (June 1955): 172–93.

15. Rose, Arnold. "Theory for the Study of Social Problems," *Social Problems* 4 (January 1957): 189–99.

16. Ross, Murray G. *Community Organization: Theory, Principles and Practice*. New York: Harper & Bros., 1955.

17. Ross, Murray G., with B.W. Lappin. *Community Organization: Theory, Principles and Practice*. 2d ed. New York: Harper & Row, 1967.

18. Rothman, Jack. "An Analysis of Goals and Roles in Community Organization Practice," *Social Work* 9 (April 1964): 24–31.

19. Sanders, Irwin T. *The Community: An Introduction to a Social System*. 2d ed. New York: The Roland Press, 1966.

20. Simon, Herbert A. *Administrative Behavior,* 2d ed. New York: The Macmillan Co., 1957.

21. Suchman, Edward A. *Evaluative Research: Principles and Practice in Public Service and Social Action Programs*. New York: Russell Sage Foundation, 1967.

22. Thomas, Edwin J., and Ronald A. Feldman, with Jane Kamm. "Concepts of Role Theory," in *Behavioral Science for Social Workers*, edited by Edwin J. Thomas. New York: The Free Press, 1967.

23. Thompson, James D., and Arthur Tuden. "Strategies, Structures and Processes of Organizational Decision," *Comparative Studies in Administration*, edited by J. D. Thompson et al., pp. 195–216. Pittsburgh: Pittsburgh University Press, 1959.

24. Tripodi, Tony, Phillip Fellin, and Irwin Epstein. *Social Program Evaluation: Guidelines for Health, Education and Welfare Administrators*. Itasca, Ill.: F. E. Peacock Publishers, 1971.

25. Warren, Roland L. *The Community in America*. Chicago: Rand McNally, 1963.

8.

Ronald L. Simons

GENERIC SOCIAL WORK SKILLS IN SOCIAL ADMINISTRATION: THE EXAMPLE OF PERSUASION

Increasingly there is consensus in the literature on social welfare management that social service administration differs in significant ways from general administration and hence requires a particular type of educational preparation (Hasenfeld & English, 1974; Patti, 1983; Steiner, 1977). Having agreed that social service administrators need to be educated in a fashion that differs from that of the general administrator, there is much disagreement concerning the form that education for social welfare management should take (Perlmutter, 1984). Even if a consensus could be reached concerning the ideal curriculum for students interested in social administration, it is not clear that this would have a significant impact upon the way programs are managed as the administrators of most human service organizations are direct service workers who have been promoted into supervisory positions (Patti, 1983).

This paper takes the position that both social welfare administration and direct service social workers require a common set of skills. Of course, both the administrator and direct-service worker must also know the proven theories and techniques associated with his or her level of practice. However, these specialized procedures only serve to compliment or build upon generic skills that characterize all social work practice. Hence, the social worker who receives a rigorous education in the generic skills of social work practice would be prepared, with little additional training,

to practice as a direct service worker or social administrator.

In an effort to develop this contention, the next section of this paper defines and discusses the concept of generic skills as it relates to the service effectiveness of human service administration. A set of persuasive strategies is then developed as an example of empirically based generic procedures appropriate to the demands of both administration and direct service work.

GENERIC SKILLS AND SOCIAL ADMINISTRATION

As noted above, most experts in the area recognize social welfare administration to be different from administration in general. One of the major differences is that human service organizations assume a commitment to client welfare or service effectiveness rather than profit or some other outcome (Patti, 1985). In the course of pursuing this performance objective, the social administrator must also be concerned with efficiency, productivity, resource acquisition, and staff morale (Rapp & Poertner, 1985). All of this requires the execution of tasks such as obtaining funds and clients, supervising and motivating personnel, juggling the conflicting demands of multiple constituents, managing information on program performance, and the like. At first glance, this diverse set of activities seems to demand a set of competencies quite different from those assumed in direct service work. However, a closer examination shows that to a large degree these administrative tasks rest upon the ability to carry out the general skills of the problem-solving process. Importantly, these problem-solving skills are the same ones employed by direct service workers.

As Perlman (1957) noted some years ago, social work is a problem-solving activity. This is true whether one is employed as an administrator or a direct-service worker. The steps and skills associated with problem solving remain the same regardless of level of practice (Simons & Aigner, 1985). To see how this is so, consider the problem-solving process:

First, data must be collected in order to assess the problem. The principles of interviewing, observation, questionnaire construction, and sampling are the same whether one is collecting data on clients, employee morale, or the impact of a management information system. Next, based upon the assessment of the problem, specific goals must be established and a sequence of tasks identified for reaching the goals. The skills associated with goal setting and task planning are the same for direct service and administrative problems. Action systems must often be formulated to carry out the tasks that have been identified, and a common set of skills are required in order to pull together and run a group whether it be a committee or treatment group. Usually some individual or group must be influenced to change if the problem of concern is to be resolved. The target may be a client, a board member, or a funding agency, but the principles for effective persuasion, inducement, or constraint remain the same.

An important component of the problem-solving process is the evaluation of the attempted solution. This involves collecting data concerning the impact of the problem-solving effort. Thus one schooled in the general skills of problem solving must know quasi-experimental research procedures required for evaluation.

The canons of quasi-experimental design remain the same whether one is evaluating a direct-service intervention or some component of organizational performance.

All this suggests that the human service administrator and the direct-service worker employ a similar set of skills. These problem-solving skills, which are relevant to any setting or level of practice, should be considered the generic skills of social work. Unfortunately, the term "generic skills" does not have a common meaning among social work educators. Often times it is used to refer to processes such as facilitating, mediating, relationship enhancement, and the like. When defined in this fashion, the skills suggest little in terms of specific practice guidelines and have limited utility for social workers employed in the areas of policy and administration. Stated differently, such formulations are not really informative or generic.

To be generic, a set of skills must be organized around the activities that characterize social work in various settings and level. Thus the skills should relate to the problem-solving process endemic to all social work practice (Simons & Aigner, 1985). To be useful, to facilitate effective practice, the skills must indicate specific, empirically based tasks and activities. The skills should involve clearly identified practice principles based upon empirically proven theories and techniques (Simons & Aigner, 1985).

As an example of a set of principles which meet these criteria, the following section develops a list of practice guidelines with regard to the skill of persuasion. The ability to exercise influence through persuasion is important in human service administration as funding bodies must be persuaded to invest in the program, legislative and policy-making groups need to be persuaded to establish priorities and guidelines which facilitate quality programming, community agencies must be persuaded to refer clients, community residents may need to be persuaded to serve as board members or as volunteers, and so on. The social administrator is constantly attempting to persuade some person or group to contribute the time, energy, or other resources required for effective service delivery. Hence, the ability to exert influence through persuasion, like the other generic skills, is an essential component of successful human service administration.

Given how often program viability and success hinges upon the manager's ability to influence certain individuals and groups, it is essential that social administrators be schooled in techniques for maximizing the efficacy of the persuasive communications. Recently, the author employed theory and research from the literature on attitude formation and change to deduce various strategies for exercising influence (Simons, 1982; Simons & Aigner, 1985). These strategies were presented as generic approaches, i.e., as procedures that might be employed to enhance the effectiveness of social workers practicing in any role or setting. Since the publication of these articles, the author has decided that the principles regarding persuasion should be reformulated so as to increase their utility to macro practitioners. It is not that the principles as originally stated are now viewed as incorrect; rather it is a matter of recasting them in a fashion that allows for greater flexibility and ease of use.

The previous statements emphasized the way that role reversal, giving both sides of an issue, stressing consistency, and identifying self-defeating behavior might be utilized to persuade a target system to change. The principles were presented as alternative approaches to constructing a persuasive appeal, or as strategies which might be employed in a serial fashion in the course of dialogue with the target. Although well suited to the needs of the direct-service worker, a good bit of ingenuity was required in order to combine the principles into a single persuasive appeal as macro practitioners must do in funding proposals, presentations before boards, media campaigns, etc. In the section to follow, the principles of persuasion are reformulated and integrated with research and theory regarding the adoption and diffusion of new ideas.

PRINCIPLES FOR EFFECTIVE PERSUASION

As noted above, persuasion involves producing change through the provision of new information—that is, the target receives information that influences him or her to think, feel, or act in a new way (Gamson, 1968; Pincus & Minahan, 1973). Or, as Larson (1983) states, "the process of persuasion involves your presenting good reasons to people for a specific choice among probable alternatives" (p. 281). Theory and research on persuasion are concerned with identifying the characteristics of messages which persons find appealing, with discovering the nature of communications which are perceived to contain "good reasons" for adopting the position being advocated. Based upon the findings of several decades of research, the following factors appear to be important components in effective persuasion appeals.

Emphasize Advantages or Rewards

People are constantly processing the information available to them and making decisions as to how they might best satisfy their needs and achieve their goals. Hence, the probability that individuals will change their behavior in response to a communication is increased when the message provides information indicating that the change will enable them to more effectively satisfy their needs and desires.

Several studies show that a target audience is more apt to adopt a favorable attitude toward a behavior or procedure when they perceive it to have a relative advantage over existing or alternative practices (Coleman, Katz & Menzel, 1966; Rothman, 1974). Rogers (1968) notes that the advantages or rewards associated with an action may not be economic or material. The benefits of adopting the line of action being advocated may be largely psychological, leading to an increase in prestige, status, or satisfaction. People must have sufficient reason for modifying their behavior or for adopting a new procedure. One good reason for doing so is because the new approach yields rewards at a level unavailable through existing practices or alternative actions.

Be Comprehensible

The action being advocated must be presented in a language that is readily understood by the target audience. Technical jargon should be avoided if possible. People will not adopt a line of action which they do not fully comprehend. Simple, easily understood ideas are more likely to be accepted than arguments which are complex and hard to follow (Glaser, Abelson & Garrison, 1983; Rogers, 1983; Zaltman, 1973).

Show Compatibility of Values

There is substantial evidence that people are more apt to accept an idea if it is perceived as consistent with their present beliefs, values, and ways of doing things (Rogers, 1983; Rothman, 1974; Zaltman, 1973). For instance, Woolfolk, Woolfolk and Wilson (1977) found that students who were shown identical videotapes of a teacher using reinforcement procedures evaluated the teacher and the technique more favorably when the videotape was described as an illustration of "humanistic education" than when it was labeled behavior modification. And Saunders and Reppucci (1977) reported that the reaction of school principals and superintendents to a program proposal varied according to whether or not the program was identified as employing a behavior modification approach. Such studies are a clear demonstration of the way that one can destroy an audience's receptivity to an idea by using words or phrases which the group perceives as representing beliefs or practices contrary to their value commitments. Indeed, the label or name selected for a program or activity should be chosen with great care (Rogers, 1983).

Various groups, whether human service agencies, funding bodies, or civic organizations, are often committed to a particular sociopolitical, treatment, or practice ideology (Rappoport, 1960; Hasenfeld, 1983). An idea is more apt to be accepted or assimilated by a group if it is perceived to be compatible with the assumptions, principles, and procedures that make up the group's ideological orientation (Glaser, Abelson & Garrison, 1983). Compatibility promises greater security and less risk to the receiver while making the new idea appear more meaningful (Rogers, 1983).

Cite Proven Results

An audience is more apt to accept an idea if its consequences have already been observed. When people can see the positive results of an action or procedure they are more likely to adopt it (Glaser, Abelson & Garrison, 1983; Rogers, 1983). Given this finding, a stepping-stone approach is often the most effective way of selling an idea. First, a small group is persuaded to test the procedure. The positive results obtained in this demonstration project or pilot program are then cited in persuasive communications designed to promote the idea across a broader population (Rothman, 1974; Rothman, Erlich & Teresa, 1981).

Allow for Trialability

The target group will perceive less risk if the new idea can be tried on a piecemeal basis prior to wholesale adoption of the procedure (Rogers, 1983; Rogers & Svenning, 1969). As Glaser, Abelson, and Garrison (1983) observe:

The extent to which a proposed change is known to be reversible if it does not prove desirable may affect its adoption. Not all innovations can be discarded later with impunity; the bridges back to the status quo ante may have been burned. Situations in which the user need not "play for keeps" provide more opportunity for innovation (p. 61).

People are reluctant to commit themselves to a line of action which does not allow for a later change of mind. An idea is more apt to be adopted if it can be broken into parts which can be tried one step at a time, with the group having the option of discontinuing the new procedure at any time in the process should they decide that it is not producing the anticipated results (Rogers, 1983; Rothman, Erlich & Teresa, 1981).

Link Message to Influential Others

Consistent with the predictions of Balance Theory (Heider, 1958), several studies indicated that people tend to adopt the same attitude toward an object or idea as

that held by someone they like, and that they tend to adopt the opposite attitude toward an object or idea as that held by someone they dislike (Tedeschi & Lindskold, 1976). In this way, individuals maintain cognitive balance.

These findings suggest that an idea is more likely to be accepted if it is linked to persons that the target likes. The most direct method for doing this is to have someone the target likes or respects deliver the persuasive appeal. When this is not feasible, reference might be made to influential others as part of the communicated message. For instance, if a city council member is known to be a firm supporter of the state governor, and the governor is known to have the same views on an issue as the social worker who is trying to influence the council member, this information could be presented to the council member. This general tactic can be used whether the favored person is the president, a movie star, a well-known expert on some topic, or the target's colleague, friend, or spouse.

The social worker might cite individuals similar to the target when information about whom the target likes or respects is lacking. This strategy is based on the extensive body of research indicating that people tend to be attracted to people they perceive as similar to themselves. Thus, when attempting to persuade a landlord to make repairs, the worker might name other landlords who have made such repairs; when attempting to persuade a principal to institute a drug education program, the worker might cite principals from other schools in the city who have begun such programs, and so forth.

Avoid High-Pressure Tactics

Research based upon Reactance Theory shows that when individuals feel pressured to select a particular course of action, whether through the promise of rewards, the threat of punishment, or intense appeals, they tend to increase their valuation of alternatives to the position being advocated (Brehm, 1966; Wicklund, 1974). High-pressure tactics create a boomerang effect. The use of pressure to persuade people to adopt an idea frquently creates resistance and a determination to act in a manner which is contrary to the proposed action. Human beings value their freedom and will resist attempts to circumscribe their choice of self-determination. Therefore, messages should be presented in a manner that minimizes any threat to the target's feeling of freedom. Phrases such as "It's your decision," "But, of course, it's up to you," and "Think about it and see what you want to do," serve this function; whereas words such as "must," "should," and "have to" are likely to arouse resistance (Brehm, 1976).

In addition to using phrases such as those just cited, reactance can be lowered through the use of two-sided messages (Secord & Backman, 1974). Two-sided communications acknowledge the limitations of one's own position and grant some merit to alternative points of view. A two-sided argument is more effective when the opposing view is presented first and the view preferred by the communicator is presented last (Johnson & Matross, 1975). Thus, when attempting to persuade an audience who is committed to another point of view, the social worker should begin by acknowledging the perspective to the group. The worker should assure them that he or she understands and appreciates their point of view. Such a beginning lowers audience defensiveness and makes the worker appear less one-sided and more objective.

Minimize Threats to Security, Status, or Esteem

Change agents often commit the "rationalistic bias" of assuming that people are reasonable beings who, when presented with the logic of a new and better approach, will recognize its merits and embrace it without hesitation (Zaltman & Duncan, 1977). However, events frequently fail to unfold in this fashion. People's logic and reason are often distorted by less rational processes. Sound judgment may be clouded by a defensive emotional response. Emotional defensiveness may be produced because a group fears the new procedure will signal a diminution in their prestige or power (Bright, 1964; Berlin, 1969). Those persons who have benefited the most from existing practices are likely to be threatened by a change in procedures. Other individuals may fear that the new approach will devalue their knowledge and skills and that they will have a difficult time learning the new procedures (Bright, 1964; Glaser, Abelson & Garrison, 1983). In still other instances, persons may be reluctant to adopt a course of action because they feel they will lose face with their friends or some constituency.

The wise change agent will construct his or her communications in a manner that alleviates such threats. Whenever an idea might be interpreted as threatening to the target group's security, esteem, or sense of competence, these fears should be discussed and objectively examined as part of the communication process. By acknowledging and evaluating these concerns through the two-sided approach discussed above, defensiveness may be reduced and reason allowed to prevail.

We began this section by noting that people are persuaded by a message when it provides them with "good reasons" for selecting the advocated course of action over alternatives. Based upon attitude change research and studies of the adoption and diffusion of innovations, eight principles for enhancing the persuasiveness of a communication have been identified. These principles of communication are listed in Table 8.1. The principles might be summarized as suggesting that people are most apt to perceive that they have good reason to adopt the position being advocated when it has advantages over alternatives, is easily understood, is compatible with existing values and practices, has been shown to have positive results, can be adopted on a trial basis, is endorsed by admired others, may be accepted or rejected, and contains no threats to security or esteem.

EXAMPLES OF THE PRINCIPLES IN USE

As observed earlier, social administrators frequently employ persuasion in an effort to obtain the resources necessary for a viable program, such as funding, clients, personnel, and community goodwill. In this section, two illustrations are provided of the way in which the principles identified above might be combined to maximize an administrator's persuasiveness. The first considers the situation of presenting a

funding proposal to a county board while the second concerns the formation of a radio spot designed to solicit local citizens to serve as program volunteers.

Assume that a social worker is interested in persuading the board of supervisors in his or her county to provide funding for a new community corrections halfway house. After reviewing the eight principles of persuasion, the individual might construct a presentation which contains the following: First, the advantages of the program must be noted. Community correctional programs are cheaper and often produce lower recidivism rates than alternative facilities (Advantages Principle). Since the residents of the halfway house would be working during the day and living in the house at night, attention might be drawn to the way in which the program is consistent with community values of work and supporting oneself (Compatibility Principle). Concerns about the dangers posed by convicted criminals living in the community would need to be acknowledged and addressed through a description of the screening procedures to be employed in selecting residents for the house (Threats Principle). The positive results obtained by similar programs in other communities should be cited (Proven Results Principle). Mention might be made of any influential politicians or organizations who support the correctional halfway house concept (In-

TABLE 8.1
Principles for Constructing Persuasive Communications

1. Emphasize Advantages.
2. Be Comprehensive.
3. Show Compatability of Values.
4. Cite Proven Results.
5. Allow for Trialability.
6. Refer to Influential Others.
7. Avoid High-Pressure Tactics.
8. Minimize Threats to Security, Status, or Esteem.

fluential Others Principle). The idea could be presented as reversible. At the end of a certain period an evaluation might be planned and a decision made as to whether the results obtained warrant continued support (Trialability Principle). Finally, an effort would be made throughout the presentation to be clear and understandable (Comprehensibility Principle) and to emphasize that it is the board's decision, that they should only adopt the proposal if they perceive that it is a good idea (Minimal Pressure Principle).

Of course, the presentation would need to contain information in addition to the material just mentioned. The board would probably want details regarding where the facility would be located, how it would be staffed, the costs to be incurred, and the like. However, many proposals are largely limited to a consideration of such items. If a proposal is to be persuasive it should also address the issues identified in the eight principles discussed above.

As a second example, assume that a radio spot is to be constructed in an effort to solicit volunteers to work in a psychiatric halfway house. The announcement might begin by describing the problems in living faced by the residents of the facility and the way that volunteers can help solve such difficulties (Advantages Principle). Attention might be drawn to the way in which volunteering is consistent with the American tradition of helping one's neighbor to get back on his feet during hard times (Compatibility Principle). The valuable consequences that have been obtained through the use of volunteers, either in this program or in similar others, could be noted (proven Results Principle). In citing these consequences, the rewards for both the resident and the volunteer should be described (Advantages Principle). The announcement might acknowledge listener concerns regarding the time that may be involved and doubts about being able to function as an effective volunteer (Threat Principle). These issues could be addressed by briefly noting how many hours a week are required and by assuring the listener that volunteer training and supervision are provided. The listener might be informed that the commitment is time limited, say six months or a year, with the option of volunteering again at the end of the period (Trialability Principle). An influential community person might be recruited to read the announcement (Influential Others Principle). Everyday language, rather than psychiatric argot, would need to be used to describe the program and the services provided by the volunteers (Comprehensibility Principle). The appeal should be made in a warm, factual fashion which avoids the appearance of a hard-sell campaign (Minimum Pressure Principle).

As these two examples demonstrate, the eight principles of persuasion, so long as they are employed in an honest and forthright manner, do not violate the values of the social work profession. None of the principles involve the use of trickery or hidden agendas. Rather, they merely suggest the types of information that the target will desire prior to committing to the idea being presented. Of course, the principles might be used in an unethical fashion. For instance, a person might claim that a program has been shown to produce certain results when it has not, or that a procedure can be tried on a trial basis when in reality it can only be discontinued through great expense and inconvenience. The principles imply no value dilemmas, however, so long as an individual utilizes them with sincerity and honesty.

CONCLUSIONS AND RECOMMENDATIONS

This paper has exemplified the generic skills approach to social work practice as it relates to the need for administrators to manage their influence with an array of internal and external constituents in order to enhance service effectiveness. The eight principles of Persuasion articulated here may be used by social workers in a variety of administrative and direct-service settings. Given the fact that often conflicting demands are placed upon administrators from the political environment in which human service organizations operate, the ability for administrators to use persuasion in their efforts toward improving service effectiveness for clients is a critical skill.

To be truly generic, skill training for administrators and students must be organized around the components of the problem-solving process. It is problem solving that characterizes all levels of social work practice. And, if it is to be really useful, this training must focus upon specific techniques and activities which have some empirical basis. In the present paper, several principles concerning the skill of persuasion were presented as an example of a set of practice principles meeting these criteria. Elsewhere an effort has been made to identify such practice guidelines with regard to other steps in the problem-solving process (Simons & Aigner, 1985).

Given the fundamental nature of generic, problem-solving skills for the profession, there is a critical need for more social workers to become involved in research concerned with the design and development of such procedures. However, we already know a lot that can be passed along to administrators and students. This material should be taught in a rigorous fashion with a profusion of role plays and exercises directed toward various direct-service, planning, and administrative problems.

To ensure that students appreciate the general applicability of the skills, instructors in clinical, community, and planning and administration classes should underscore the way in which the material in their courses builds upon and serves to compliment the basic social work skills. Educating students in this fashion would begin to address the problem of most social administrators being promoted to direct-service workers with little administrative training.

REFERENCES

Berlin, I. N. "Resistance to Change in Mental Health Professionals." *American Journal of Orthopsychiatry,* 1969, *39,* 109–115.

Brehm, J. W. *A Theory of Psychological Reactance.* New York: Academic, 1966.

Brehm, S. S. *The Application of Social Psychology to Clinical Practice.* New York: Halsted, 1976.

Bright, J. R. *Research, Development, and Technological Innovation: An Introduction.* Homewood, IL: Irwin, 1964.

Coleman, J. S., E. Katz, & H. Menzel. *Medical Innovation: A Diffusion Study.* New York: Bobbs-Merrill, 1966.

Gamson, W. A. *Power and Discontent.* Homewood, IL: Dorsey, 1968.

Glaser, E. M., H. H. Abelson, & K. N. Garrison. *Putting Knowledge to Use.* San Francisco: Jossey-Bass, 1983.

Hasenfeld, Y. *Human Service Organizations.* Englewood Cliffs, NJ: Prentice-Hall, Inc., 1983.

Hasenfeld, Y., & R. A. English, eds. *Human Service Organizations.* Ann Arbor, MI: University of Michigan Press, 1974.

Johnson, D. W., & R. P. Matross. "Attitude Modification Methods." In F. H. Kanfer & A. P. Goldstein, eds. *Helping People Change.* New York: Pergammon, 1975.

Larson, C. U. *Persuasion: Reception and Responsibility,* 3rd ed. Belmont, CA: Wadsworth, 1983.

Patti, R. J. *Social Welfare Administration: Managing Social Programs in a Developmental Context.* Englewood Cliffs, NJ: Prentice-Hall, Inc., 1983.

Patti, R. J. "In Search of Purpose for Social Welfare Administration. *Administration in Social Work,* 1985, *9,* 1–14.

Perlman, H. H. *Social Casework: A Problem-Solving Process.* Chicago: University of Chicago Press, 1957.

Perlmutter, F. D. "Social Administration and Social Work Education: A Contradiction in Terms?" *Administration in Social Work,* 1984, *8,* 61–69.

Pincus, A., & A. Minahan. *Social Work Practice: Model and Method.* Itasca, IL: F. E. Peacock, 1973.

Rappoport, R. *Community as Doctor.* London: Tavistock Publications, 1960.

Rapp, C. A., & J. Poertner. *A Performance Model for Human Service Management.* Manuscript, University of Kansas, 1985.

Rogers, E. M. The Communication of Innovations in a Complex Institution. *Educational Record,* 1968, *48,* 67–77.

Rogers, E. M. *Diffusion of Innovations.* 3rd ed. New York: Free Press, 1983.

Rogers, E. M., & L. Svenning. *Managing Change.* Washington, DC: U.S. Office of Education, 1969.

Rothman, J. *Planning and Organizing for Social Change.* New York: Columbia University Press, 1974.

Rothman, J., J. L. Erlich, & J. G. Teresa. *Changing Organizations and Community Programs.* Beverly Hills: Sage, 1981.

Saunders, J. T., & N. D. Reppucci. "Learning Networks Among Administrators of Human Service Institutions." *American Journal of Community Psychology,* 1977, *5,* 269–276.

Secord, P. F., & C. W. Backman. *Social Psychology.* New York: McGraw-Hill, 1974.

Simons, R. L. "Strategies for Exercising Influence." *Social Work,* 1982, *27,* 268–274.

Simons, R. L., & S. M. Aigner. *Practice Principles: A Problem-Solving Approach to Social Work.* New York: Macmillan, 1985.

Steiner, R. *Managing the Human Service Organization.* Beverly Hills: Sage, 1977.

Tedeschi, J. T., & S. Linskold. *Social Psychology: Interdependence, Interaction and Influence.* New York: Wiley, 1976.

Wicklund, R. A. *Freedom and Reactance.* Hillsdale, NJ: Lawrence Erlbaum and Associates, 1974.

Woolfolk, A. E., R. L. Woolfolk, & G. T. Wilson. "A Rose by Any Other Name. . . . Labeling Bias and Attitudes Toward Behavior Modification. *Journal of Consulting and Clinical Psychology,* 1977, *45,* 184–191.

Zaltman, G. *Processes and Phenomena of Social Change.* New York: Wiley, 1973.

Zaltman, G., & R. Duncan. *Strategies for Planned Change.* New York: Wiley, 1977.

9.

Alvin Zander

PRESSURING METHODS USED BY GROUPS

We turn now to methods which agents of change are likely to use when they are sure of the ends they seek and wish to induce target persons to accept and work toward those goals. In the sequence of procedures we examine here, the activists increasingly employ incentives that are desirable (or repulsive) to the target persons in order to get them to change things.

CHANGE AGENTS SEEK THE HELP OF LEGITIMATE THIRD PARTIES

Persons who wish to develop acceptance for an idea may realize that they are being ignored by those they hope to influence. The advocates, because they feel that their goal is just, turn to a method that will earn their cause due attention. They employ one of the procedures available in every community to help persons with grievances confront those whom they want to reach. These are *legitimate* methods in the sense that residents of the area have established and approved of them, often by passing laws. The common denominator among these approaches is that a third party (or its stand-in) is asked for judicious help through the use of formal rules, the presence of mediators, or both.

Consider examples in which the third party is represented by, let us say, a set of rules. Take the guidelines prepared by a city planning commission, which citizens in the community are to follow if they wish to bring business before the board. These regulations require that would-be speakers request permission in writing to take the floor, describe the topic of their comments, and promise to talk no longer than five minutes. They are not allowed to speak at a meeting of the board unless they adhere to these rules. Persons who wish to prove that there is a need in the town for a new bus line may circulate a petition among neighbors, asking them to sign it if they approve of the idea. To make these petitions valid, the individuals circulating them have to follow requirements concerning signers' age, place of residence, and length of residence. Likewise, if reformers want to apply pressure on state legislators to pass a law on conservation of water, they must obtain the required number of signatures and present these to the legislators. Comparable procedures are to be used if they wish to place the name of a candidate on the ballot.

At other times, reformers may try to bolster their case by getting target persons to agree that they will accept the help of a mediator. This official is to keep the discussion between presenters and listeners flowing smoothly. He or she may function in accord with rules that discussants develop ahead of time or in line with rules that have the weight of state or local law. Management and labor, for instance, can create their own procedural plans before a bargaining session begins and pledge to abide by the outcome of this process. In so doing, they also must conform to general laws governing mediation of labor-management disputes. An arbitrator provides the same help as a mediator but also has the right to reach a decision, hand it down, and require that it be obeyed by all concerned. This process is called *binding arbitration.* Members of elected boards in public agencies are usually prohibited from submitting to binding arbitration, since they are legally beholden to the people who elected them, not to an arbitrator.

Another kind of third party is a judge in a court of law. Agents of change may request an injunction from the court to stop a practice that they think should be restricted, such as dumping toxic waste in a river, running machinery before it has been inspected for safety, or harassing homeless people who try to get a hearing before the social services commission. An increasingly common technique used by groups that have been created to complain about the negligence of companies is to sue a firm, provided that the plaintiffs can show they have been hurt by the actions of those they bring to court. For example, Meier (1987) reports that over six hundred suits were filed against businesses by citizens before 1987 in matters of environmental control. Although companies that have been sued have protested these suits, saying they were frivolous, were in support of the plaintiffs' pet projects, or were forms of extortion, the number of suits is expected to continue rising, along with the stakes involved. The Clean Water Act, passed . . . by Congress, provides for daily fines of $10,000 to $25,000 for each violation. Before this legislation existed, similar complaints were directed to local, state, or federal government in an effort to make officials enforce laws already on the books. More recently, the emphasis has shifted to the polluters themselves, usually manufacturers, because the new law now allows that shift. Sometimes a company forestalls a lawsuit by promising to clean up its act and making a contribution to the organization that brings the complaint. This practice keeps the firm out of court, saves the expense of hiring lawyers, costs less than what a jury might award the plaintiffs, and allows the firm to claim that it has made a tax-deductible contribution to a nonprofit agency. Other companies have reached agreements whereby they put sums of money aside that must be handed over if they break the law again. Such suits and agreements provide a way for citizens to have a useful part in ensuring that laws are well enforced.

The use of a legitimate method by agents of change requires that certain general conditions be present. Clearly, rules must exist before the process begins, whether these are created by officials of the larger community and have a regular place in a legal code or are developed by activists themselves. These regulations, by solemn pledge on both sides, are to be obeyed in implementing both the discussion and the content of the final agreement. The legitimacy of the rules may also derive from contracts, tradition, or custom. The important point is that all participants promise to abide by the regulations. Legitimate methods, to be used well, ordinarily require knowledge and skill. People must understand them and be able to follow where they lead. In many instances, complainants hire a person trained in the law who puts their case forward, for a fee, in court. Such

moves require money, patience, and plenty of time, since the wheels of justice grind slowly. Above all, complainants must have a good case: Otherwise, it is a waste of resources to appeal to a third party for help.

Why are legitimate procedures used? They are usually employed because other methods have failed, and the innovators are not able to get a reasonable hearing from target persons about changes they wish to propose. The innovators may also have been heard by target persons, who then keep the complainants waiting too long. A request by change agents is considerably more potent if they ask that an accepted rule be obeyed than if they press for a change on the grounds of logic or preference (Frank, 1944). A legitimate method is also useful if agents of change do not trust the target persons and want a disinterested entity involved in the discussion, to keep the talks fair and aboveboard. The reason labor-management bargaining sessions use a mediator or an arbitrator, for example, is that neither side is confident that its counterpart is telling the truth. Many formal organizations are governed by laws that state whether and how changes can be made in the way they operate. Funk (1982) describes a number of these regulations and their effects.

The main reason for using a legitimate approach is that (in principle, at least) the issue is settled once and for all. After an agreement is reached, there should be no more pressuring, on the one hand, and no more opposing or resisting, on the other (unless the verdict is appealed). Participants must obey the decision. There is also a reasonable chance that justice will prevail. The method offers an opportunity for change agents to have an impact that they might otherwise never achieve, provided that they have a good case.

The effects of using such processes are

noteworthy. As mentioned, participants come away feeling that the matter is settled. Everyone must abide by the outcome, whether it is palatable or not. Furthermore, the decision provides criteria for determining what is proper behavior, and these criteria can be used later to assess how closely participants are sticking to the rules. The use of a mediator or a referee may have other good consequences (Deutsch, 1973). A mediator can help participants face up to the issue and understand it, including some aspects of it that are hidden or embarrassing to reveal. He or she can help bargaining move along by providing favorable circumstances, devices, tools, or tricks that allow participants to reach a full understanding of the issue. In so doing, he or she can assist all parties by correcting misperceptions that they develop about one another's statements. A mediator can establish rules for courteous interaction, so that discussants show respect for one another. He or she can help determine which ideas are worthy of consideration as possible solutions and which ones are unlikely to lead anywhere. A mediator can press leaders to promise that they will abide by the decision, whatever it is. He or she makes the final agreement palatable to all, so that no one will regret the outcome, and helps make the decision acceptable to bystanders who have a vested interest in this discussion. Although the issue is settled, there may be a residue of hard feelings among those who lose. Persons recall things said during the process that were derogatory or unfair. The winners, for their part, may feel that they have not gained everything they wanted.

How is a third party used most effectively? The agents of change should have a good case and be able to demonstrate that the matter under discussion is a source of a serious deprivation for them and others or that it offers an opportunity for improving a current state of affairs. When taking a suit to court, moreover, they hire a lawyer to guide them through the legal system, and they furnish that person with effective witnesses, data, money, and encouragement. Finally, agents of change who use a third party need to be persistent and patient. A third party (or strict rules) can slow progress. Target persons may also stall or employ tactics that embarrass agents of change, so that the latter give up the fight.

To sum up, a number of issue-settling procedures are legitimate because they have been approved by citizens in the community as ways to judge the validity of complaints and to get relief from these. Such methods ordinarily require participants to abide by the outcome. They are unlike some other methods often used by agents of change who are trying to influence target persons. They are based on strict regulations, and participants must abide by these rules. They require knowledge of the process before they can be used wisely. They demand that participants have a good case, and they require time, patience, money, and expert help. The value of these procedures is that they usually solve the problem once and for all, unless the decision fosters anger and a desire for retribution among those who did not get their way.

REFORMERS NURTURE PERSONS IN NEED

Some groups are created to improve conditions for persons outside the unit. They may describe to officials the situation facing disadvantaged individuals and tell these listeners what ought to be done for the needy ones, or they may develop a demonstration of a helpful service, with a view toward inspiring decision makers to support a similar program in the future. We are interested here in the altruistic acts of change agents and how these can influence target persons. This display of nurturance is, in a way, another example of modeling. We are taking it up here as a separate method, however, because reformers who demonstrate how to care for needy persons may plan to improve things for others with no help from neighbors, or they may wish to show decision makers how to be caring persons. The deprived individuals may become target persons themselves if they are urged to help in plans and actions for the nurturance of their disadvantaged colleagues, or citizens at large may become target persons if they are pressed for money and labor to support the helping program. Finally, a model activity to care for the deprived takes much energy, time, and compassion. Persons who create a model must feel deeply that what they are doing is important: It is not simply a temporary, interest-arousing process.

The kinds of demonstrations that helping persons develop are well known. They provide resources to persons who need them, such as food, clothing, shelter, or money. They care for personal needs of individuals through educating, healing, reforming, or saving their souls. They provide emergency assistance in case of a fire, flood, storm, or accident. To provide such nurturance quickly or frequently, they may form enduring organizations whose members are trained to do what is needed.

The motivation of members in these groups is to benefit disadvantaged persons, without receiving any payment themselves other than the satisfaction of helping deprived ones. This help is provided either by the innovators or by the target persons who agree to furnish care for those in need of it (Bar-Tal, 1976; Macaulay and Berkowitz,

1970). The reformers also help decision makers by showing them how they can better provide a particular kind of nurturance. It is not always easy for reformers to interest officials in offering a new service. If the officials agree to a change, they are admitting, in effect, that they have not been operating as wisely or compassionately as they should, and the implementation of a new plan reveals this. The target persons also may believe that individuals who require help are lazy, greedy, or unwilling to take care of themselves and therefore do not deserve to be nurtured. Caring programs, moreover, cost money and have a way of becoming more expensive once they are under way.

Activities to help others are complicated and require their initiators to have sufficient good will, patience, know-how, and resources to accomplish what they set out to do. Why do agents of change choose to provide nurturing? The most obvious reason is that deprived persons appear unable to improve their situation on their own. They do not have the knowledge, tools, or money to get the kinds of services they need. What is more, the deprived often do not ask for help because they do not want to be obligated to benefactors, are embarrassed to admit that they cannot help themselves, or do not think that they can get the kind of aid they need. The helpers, for their part, prefer to be kindly volunteers in these efforts because they prize the satisfaction they derive from helping. Their cause is also more convincing to target persons if they do not accept payment for the services they provide.

What are the consequences of such an approach? If the disadvantaged persons value the help given to them, they will be grateful but at the same time will feel obligated to those who provide it. Because of this, they may refuse further assistance or accept as little as possible, for fear that they will be expected to reciprocate but will be unable to. Sometimes the help of reformers is not welcomed by those to whom it is offered because it creates a burden for the receivers, who must agree to be saved, give up past beliefs, or take care of a "gift horse." Not uncommonly, the effort of do-gooders is more bother than it seems to be worth, yet those who provide assistance feel good about themselves. They are proud of their efforts, even when the outcome is not all they had hoped for.

Several conditions cause such a demonstration to be more effective in the sense that the disadvantaged are actually assisted or the target persons agree to sponsor further assistance. Helping behavior is more likely to succeed if the innovators derive satisfaction from aiding disadvantaged persons. Thus, they examine what deprived persons need and plan what they should do to meet those needs. In a successful nurturing group, members provide help in ways that do not make the assisted persons feel incompetent or dependent on their helpers. If the initiators intend to rescue people who are in an emergency, they practice how to perform this mission speedily and work to improve their operation. The reformers make sure that official persons know about the demonstration, learn what favorable outcomes it provides, and recognize that such services need wider and continuing support from the community.

To summarize, agents of change may influence decision makers by providing or demonstrating services that help individuals who cannot help themselves. Initiators of nurturing expect no reward other than the satisfaction they derive from knowing that deprived persons have been assisted. They intend their appeal or demonstration to persuade target persons to provide continuing support for such a program.

. . .

AGENTS OF CHANGE BARGAIN WITH TARGET PERSONS

Suppose that individuals advocating a change tell listeners that they are willing to eliminate some parts of their request if the listeners will drop their objections to other parts. The approached persons, in turn, offer to adopt some of the suggestions made by the agents of change, if the latter will alter some of the ideas they have brought to the conference. This process, in which persons on each side give some things and gain others, is called *bargaining.* Members of a new neighborhood association, for instance, say they will stop making a plea for new sidewalks if the city will promise to pave their streets. Participants ostensibly work toward a solution that is equally valuable to persons in both parties. Often, however, one side gains more and yields less than the other; it obtains a better bargain. As another instance, members of both parties refuse to change their initial stand, so that the bargaining stalls and becomes an empty exercise.

Why do agents of change try to bargain with target persons? In most cases, they do so because they believe that the others are willing to think about modifying their practices in some way, may give up something during a bargaining discussion, or may make a deal with the innovators. Bargaining often develops after other methods fail. Those on each side feel that they can have some control over their rivals by making attractive offers and counteroffers. Reformers are also likely to try bargaining if they believe that they have enough power to influence the acts of target persons and are not merely weak pleaders. They may have this power because there are many members in their group of change agents, they represent an official body that is known to be powerful, they have sponsored frequent and influential media campaigns urging the decision makers to introduce changes, or they have been coercive toward target persons to make them willing to bargain.

Change seekers may also want to bargain because they recognize that they have something the target persons covet, such as votes, funds, expertise, community support, or labor; therefore, bargaining is sensible for all concerned. The proposers may perceive that their ideas can be improved through the discussion involved in bargaining because the process gets target persons thinking about changes they may be willing to make, or agents of change may bargain because they believe that they can get their own way, without giving up much.

The consequences of bargaining depend in good part on the content of the bargain. Participants may hit on a mutually agreeable plan that satisfies those on both sides, or those in one party may be pleased because they have won what they wanted, while members of the other party are dissatisfied because they have lost on a point they value. If this loss is great enough, the losers may become angry and force the winners to defend themselves against their wrath. It is not uncommon for bargaining to deteriorate into conflict, in which persons on each side try to coerce the other side, rather than make concessions. After a bargaining session, the winners feel satisfied with themselves and rest contented, but the losers examine, evaluate, and improve on their argument, so that they can bargain better in the future. In the long run, losers are indirectly helped because they must overhaul their case and their strategy. Winners, however, may not see the need to engage in such self-appraisal and passively rest on their laurels (Zander, 1982).

When is bargaining most effective? Consider the circumstances needed if the outcome is to be equally satisfying to change agents and target persons alike. Both sides must be fairly equal in their ability to influence the other; otherwise, those with the greater influence will listen little, talk a lot, and push the matter in ways that suit themselves. Effective two-way bargaining also requires members on one side to make an offer to compromise—to give in on some matter, in the hope that those on the other side will do likewise. The initial offer is something that the providers know or hope the others want. A responding offer will likewise be on a matter that is probably desirable to the others. Ideally, then, the sacrifice and the satisfaction should be equal on both sides. There is a danger in making the first offer, however, because persons on the other side may see this as a sign of weakness and believe that those making the first offer are giving in. The ones who receive the original compromise may accept it but make no counterproposal, since they are now ahead of the game.

It helps for people on both sides to have a clear understanding of what people on the other side want and to be able to satisfy this desire amply during the bargaining session. Neither side should offer anything that is considerably more valuable than what the other side can give, since doing so makes it appear that the offer is a bribe.

Pruitt (1972) describes several ways for bargainers to be sure that concessions are equal. One is to make a small unilateral concession, with the statement that no further offer will be made until the target individuals advance something in return. Another is to propose an exchange of concessions; persons on one side say that they are ready to concede on a given point, if those on the other side will also make a concession. It helps to make this proposition through an intermediary, whose offer can be disowned if the other side is not interested, or to call in a mediator who talks with those on both

sides and thus opens communication on issues that have been avoided.

If bargainers approach a session as
though it were a contest that they intend to
win, their tactics are different. To come out
ahead, they must gain more and give up
less than the others do. Accordingly, the
would-be winners make sure that they
know the preferences of the persons with
whom they are bargaining, know what the
others are offering, top that offer, and emphasize that this will be the last chance for
a settlement. Initial stakes of a truly competitive bargainer are set high, so that the
respondents will feel compelled to bargain,
for fear of losing if they do not. Demands
stated in strong terms at the outset lead
those on the other side to recognize that
they cannot hope to get all they want from
such hard bargainers, and so they keep
their own aspirations low.

Strong bargainers tend to become assertive, in order to bolster their stand. Assertive tactics are described by Bailey
(1983):

1. Make a frontal attack on the premises
   and values of those on the other side.
   Urge them to abandon their views, on
   the grounds that they are not convincing. Display raw emotion, to create fear
   or shame in the others, or to play upon
   their pity and compassion. Ask the listeners if they can bear the consequences
   that will follow from an unfair bargain.
2. Argue on grounds that are prized by all
   concerned, such as democratic values,
   the need for equality, or the golden rule.
3. Appeal to the importance of using reason and logic, and to the value of an
   open mind that considers both sides of
   an issue.
4. Remind listeners that they have a duty
   toward others who will be affected by
   the agreement being formed.

5. Appeal to the other side's cunning self-
   interest. Be smart; look after yourself
   first. This is especially useful when past
   obligations can be invoked, and when
   others can be pressed to undertake new
   obligations or can be invited to enter
   into a special deal.
6. Appeal to the mutual interdependence
   among the persons involved, and stress
   that each side needs the other.

If people on one side hope to benefit
more as a result of bargaining, they cannot
let themselves give in to threats, pressure,
or other forms of coercion, and they cannot
let differences escalate in such a way that
those on both sides will not listen to the
give-and-take while a conflict grows. The
winner in a bargaining session wants to
prevail without generating resistance that
may interfere with easy access to the gains.

In summary, while bargaining over a
proposed change, members of two units
holding incompatible views try through
discussion to reach a mutually agreeable
decision by giving up some things in order
to gain others. Agents of change usually
are not able to get target persons into a bargaining relationship unless they have
power fairly equal to that of the persons
they hope to influence. To reach an agreement that pleases both sides, participants
must be ready to compromise. To win,
those on one side make the other side see
that it cannot get what it wants while ignoring their desires. In the long run, it is better
if each side wins equally.

AGENTS OF CHANGE REWARD
TARGET PERSONS

People working for reform may try to make
their proposals acceptable to target persons
by offering to reward them if they do as

they are asked. Such rewards include having their pictures in the newspaper; receiving public praise, medals, plaques, statues, or banquets in their honor; having streets named after them; or receiving a day of celebration for the new development. Target persons will reject such benefits, however, if they see them as bribes, payoffs, inadequate prizes, or illegitimate offers. Sometimes rewards are given to target persons after they have behaved in an admirable fashion, with an eye toward teaching them to continue their good efforts.

Apparently, a reward promised in order to induce a particular action is not always taken to be a bribe, if the offer is made for a good cause. For example, when staff members of a government agency and a private foundation told townsfolk that they would be given a grant if they planned ways to improve social services in their community and followed procedures prescribed by the granters, the offer was accepted without guilt (Marris and Rein, 1967). It is not unusual for an official body in a community to offer rewards to groups of citizens. For instance, police patrols are often increased if neighbors requesting such protection help by monitoring their own streets.

The reasons behind the use of rewards are well known. Persons who want to influence specific others sense that those others are uninterested, and so they offer a reward to arouse their enthusiasm (Gamson, 1975). The offer may be made as part of a proposal for change, in which case it will be provided only if the decision makers actually do introduce the innovation; or the reward may be used as a reinforcement for approved past behavior, and the recipients are led to understand that they will be rewarded again if they repeat their good actions. One advantage of publicly rewarding target persons is that bystanders see certain actions rewarded and assume that anyone else (themselves, for instance) who behaves in the same fashion will also be rewarded.

What are the consequences of receiving a reward? We know from research that a person who gets a reward is grateful toward those who provide it, but not if the reward is seen to be payment for services agreed on and rendered or deserved for some other reason. In such a case, the gain is not a reward; it is a payment ("I had it coming"). A reward will not be effective if it is not valued by the receiver. Moreover, if the same reward is offered repeatedly, its value falls, and it is no longer satisfying. Those who are rewarded many times eventually raise their price and want more for the same amount of service.

Persons who move into action solely because of an offered reward are ordinarily motivated only to earn the reward, not to carry out an action that is valuable or sensible in its own right. The reward, not the change, is the incentive. When this is the case, people do only what is necessary to get the reward. They behave in the ways requested by the reward giver. They make these actions visible, so that the agent of change knows that their behavior deserves to be rewarded. The agent of change keeps an eye on the target persons, to be sure that they do the things that warrant the prize. Because target persons' overt acts can be observed, rewards are useful ways to encourage behavioral innovations. If a reformer seeks transformation of the beliefs or attitudes of the target persons, however, it is difficult to determine whether they have in fact made such changes. People can say that they have revised their thinking in order to win a reward when actually they have not. The point is that rewards are more effective in changing target persons' overt actions than in changing their covert beliefs.

Agents of change can be expected to use rewards in several ways to enhance their influence over target persons. They make sure that the object or event they offer as a reward is valued by target persons, since a reward is not a reward unless the receivers believe it is. They make sure that the persons being rewarded know why they have won approval, so that the awarded behavior will be repeated. They make sure that bestowal of the reward is made public, so that it will provide a lesson to bystanders. They make sure that the reward is not offered in such a way that it is taken as a bribe, since such offers are demeaning, unethical, and often ineffective. They take care to have plenty of rewards available, so that their supply does not run out. They do not offer the same reward repeatedly. They recognize that by using rewards they can influence overt behavior better than hidden feelings, ideas, or beliefs.

In summary, change agents try to influence the behavior of target persons by providing events or objects that the latter value, on the assumption that rewards will stimulate target persons' interest in creating a change. The persons who benefit feel grateful toward the providers of the reward, unless the receivers do not place much value on the reward or feel that they have earned it as payment for their efforts.

AGENTS OF CHANGE COERCE TARGET PERSONS

Activists become coercive when they intend to constrain freedom of choice among persons they wish to influence. In using coercion, change agents threaten to punish target persons if they do not do what they are asked to do or do not stop behaving in undesirable ways. The coercers inflict a penalty or punishment on the ones being coerced, until the latter change their behavior. There is no limit to the ways in which reformers can be coercive. For example, citizens interfere with a session of the city council by interrupting unwanted speakers. Workers employed downtown block access to the city's parking structure after the city raises rates on streetside parking meters. Homeless squatters build shacks on university property, to make their deprivation visible. Parents threaten the school board with recall if the board does not fire the football coach. Students raid a building where animals are housed for use in medical research. A neighborhood organization stops making contributions to the town's United Fund because the local athletic club was not given a grant that it requested. A nuclear power plant is set on fire by activists opposed to such sources of electricity. Bus drivers run late because of alleged discrimination by the traffic commission in the hiring of homosexual women.

We shall consider three types of coercive action here. First, activists interfere with efforts of target persons, so that the latter cannot do their regular work. Second, they physically limit the freedom of target persons or hostages. Third, they threaten harm or inflict it on target persons, other individuals, or things of value. But first, a few comments on the nature of coercion.

Any coercive act places constraints on the behavior of those toward whom it is directed. The threatened penalty is repulsive, and in order to avoid this punishment, the persons being coerced do what is asked of them. The driver obeys a traffic cop. A university's board of regents stops talking when students crowd its meeting room to shout insults. Constraints are stronger as the proffered punishments are more undesirable. If the target persons see the penalty as not repellent (or not likely to occur), they will pay little attention to coercive demands. Like rewarding, coercion changes overt behavior more effectively than it changes covert beliefs, since visible actions can be monitored by the coercer, but ideas and attitudes cannot. Therefore, those who use coercion typically spy on persons they put under pressure, to make sure that punishment is promptly delivered when it is deserved. . . . [T]he threat of coercion, its actual use, and the subsequent surveillance put on persons who have been pressed to change generate poor interpersonal relations between the agents of change and the target persons. These in themselves become a separate cause for concern.

We get an insight into how often activists use coercion from the study done by Gamson (1975). Gamson examined the strategies employed by a number of protest movements. Most of these bodies had hundreds or thousands of members, and so they are not replicas of the units we have been considering. Nevertheless, much of what they did took place in community settings, and so Gamson's findings are not wholly irrelevant to our purpose. Gamson looked for two kinds of success in the work of these groups. One kind is the community's *acceptance of the change agents' group* (that is, the unit was seen as a set of spokespersons who represented legitimate interests). The activists were therefore respected and given attention. The other kind of success is that Gamson calls *attainment of new advantages* (that is, the group achieved its objectives to some degree or won other valued outcomes). Thus, the unit won respect as a group, accomplished something worthwhile, or both. The organizations in Gamson's sample had similar rates of success in winning acceptance (47 percent) and in achieving new advantages (49 percent). Gamson was interested in two ways of protesting. One way limited the

freedom of target persons and included instances of strikes, boycotts, vituperation, discrediting of antagonists, or restricting the moves of those being pressed. The other way was more violent and included harmful attacks or threats to persons or property. The freedom-limiting behavior was used by 42 percent of the groups, and violence was used by 25 percent. The larger the organization, the more its members were likely to engage in violence; the smaller the group, the more likely it was to be the recipient of violence. We shall review more of Gamson's results later.

Blocking the Progress of Target Persons Toward Their Goals. In some methods of coercion, activists set out to make it difficult for target persons to conduct their regular business or achieve their normal objectives. The blockers say (or shout) that they will continue their obstruction until they get their way. I can think of five different blocking maneuvers.

In one form, called a *sit-in,* participants seek services in a place where they have been forbidden to enter. They remain until they are forced to leave. For example, black students walk into restaurants, libraries, or bus stations that they are not supposed to use. Workers slow their actions to a snail's pace, so that production is reduced to a trickle. Dissidents stand or sit on a highway, so that trucks and cars cannot move into a nuclear power plant or remove weapons from a munitions depot.

In a second way of creating a barrier, agents of change interfere with the business of target persons. They strike, walk out, sabotage machinery, or take over a meeting and allow only their own members to talk.

In a third type of blocking maneuver, reformers interfere with the work of persons in an organization whose practices they wish to change. They attend the meetings of a decision-making body, such as a city council or a board of education, and prevent business as usual by making loud comments (from the audience), seizing the microphone, occupying all the seats in the hall, refusing to be quiet, making it impossible for speakers (on the wrong side of the issue) to be heard, or bringing along a brass band.

Alinsky (1971) urges members of inner-city neighborhood community councils to make their grievances known to governmental officials in no uncertain terms. He says, "Our concern is with the tactic of taking; how the have-nots can take power from the haves" (Alinsky, 1971, p. 126). He provides a set of rules (actually, they are maxims) for what he calls *power tactics.* He means, in our terms, successful coercion of decision makers through interference with their meetings. Alinsky's list of rules includes the following: "Power is not only what you have but what the enemy thinks you have" (p. 127); "Make the enemy live up to their own book of rules" (p. 128); "Ridicule is man's most potent weapon" (p. 128); "Keep the pressure on" (p. 128); "The threat is usually more terrifying than the thing itself" (p. 128); and "The price of a successful attack is a constructive alternative" (p. 130).

The leaders of an organization of tenants in a housing project created a rent strike, refusing to pay what they owed until their apartments were rehabilitated. Brill (1971), in a book-length description of this strike, says that central members prevented the eviction of tenants for nonpayment of their rent by threatening to create a riot if nonpayers were forced to move out of the housing project. This threat worked so well that they used it repeatedly thereafter.

A fourth form of blockage is a *boycott,* in which dissatisfied persons agree to buy nothing from or provide no services to individuals who are responsible for an unpleasant state of affairs. Familiar examples are refusals to shop in certain stores, ride local buses, or work for particular bosses.

A fifth form of blocking maneuver is a hostile demonstration, in which disadvantaged persons reveal the depth of their displeasure by breaking windows, vandalizing furniture, or destroying equipment used by target persons.

The common feature of these five blocking moves is that reformers willfully create barriers that interfere with the productivity of those they want to influence. Why do activists use such approaches? They use them mostly because these are ways of getting attention from individuals who are ignoring the demands made by the change agents. Blocking actions force the affected people to pay attention to ideas that they prefer to ignore (Carter, 1973). These methods also allow activists to indicate clearly that they are angry and dissatisfied and want a change. Change agents use barrier-producing procedures if they know how target persons work and can therefore see how to block their work. They also hope to create confusion, which arises out of the obstructed persons' uncertainty about how to respond to the interventions. The target persons want to prevent interference with their work, but they also feel guilty if they do not provide a fair hearing to the reformers, and they become anxious if they provoke criticisms among bystanders who feel that the complainers have had too little (or too much) sympathetic attention.

The members of a group devoted to social action will be more ready to interrupt the work of target persons, according to Levitt (1973), if they feel and are willing to express moral outrage at the behavior of these decision makers. The change seekers are sure that their view is superior in its virtue to all others, and yet it is being ignored. They also are more inclined to intervene in the work of target persons if they want a solution to their troubles very soon but the officials are dragging their feet or are only pretending to give the matter consideration. The change seekers therefore feel that they can open the issue only by confronting the officials. They do not mind having their tactics or themselves disparaged, disapproved, criticized, or resented, and their courage to act is based on their faith in the cause they represent. Although their actions are a form of blackmail, they are prepared to use this method to get their way.

Robertson (1988) believes that protests are frequent in and around San Francisco because there are many universities in the area that create a ferment of ideas. There is a tradition of strong unions, with an emphasis on group discipline and a "them against us" attitude. There is a variety of races, politics, ethnic bodies, and sexual preferences, which make conflict a regular part of life. Moreover, the climate allows year-round outdoor gatherings and demonstrations. Robertson remarks that many San Franciscans ally themselves to causes because they get a sense of identity from doing so and they enjoy rebelling against authority in outrageous ways. It is fun and provides excitement.

What effects do methods like these have on persons at the receiving end? Of course, they are seldom welcomed. To limit the length of the following discussion, I shall concentrate on procedures used in interrupting a meeting, since the psychology of such an action is typical of what happens in other ways and places. Furthermore, any blockage of work eventually must be settled at a conference table, where changers and target persons meet face to face. As we have remarked, blocking behavior is hard

for recipients to handle. The aggressive recklessness that characterizes such behavior generates anger or defensiveness among target persons, as well as a temptation to respond in kind. The inclination to imitate the style of the interrupters is exacerbated if the ideas that the reformers propose are not useful. Indeed, it often happens that activists have no innovations at all to offer; they simply want to stop what is going on, to counter an operation that is responsible for their dissatisfaction. They block a meeting and demand that the program they dislike be cancelled, but they have no suggestions for a better way of doing things when they are asked what improvements they recommend. For example, college students want "irrelevant" teaching stopped, but they cannot say what ought to be taught or how, or interrupters make proposals, based on misinformation, about the organization they are attacking, and the target persons are embarrassed by trying to respond soberly to these far-out ideas.

A group of target persons whose members are prevented from working is faced with several alternatives: giving in to the interrupters and acceding to their demands, trying to reason with them, sitting and being reviled, or clearing the room. Any effort to suppress noisy confronters can backfire if bystanders are drawn into helping the suppressed persons and if these newcomers sharpen the aggressiveness of the activists. Then each side becomes increasingly hostile in response to the actions of the other. Under laws requiring that public organizations hold open meetings, it is not permissible to meet secretly and thereby dodge such interference. A likely resolution of this intervention is for the target persons to propose a meeting with the protesters, in order to engage in constructive problem solving. The target persons may be uneasy about proposing to do this, since past actions of the disrupters do not suggest that they will behave in ways necessary for a sensible session. Nevertheless, I believe that assertive interventionists can become calmly objective once they have an opportunity to present their case to target persons and can evaluate it against other proposals (see Lancourt, 1979).

How can barriers be used effectively? Consider two broadly different types of action: those in which change agents are disobedient (but their behavior is civil), and those in which the success of their intervention depends on a discourteous style. In civil disobedience, activists visibly violate customs or laws governing behavior, continue to do so when asked to desist, and respond to aggression against them with no hostility, since angry behavior could make them guilty of assault and battery or generate public reaction against them. For example, a number of citizens occupied a mayor's office, refused to leave when asked, and went limp when dragged from the building. At the first opportunity, they reentered the office and began their vigil once more, singing, chanting, and smiling to those whose work was interrupted. Such group action requires members who have strong faith in their convictions, so that they can withstand criticism and attempts to repress them. They are civilly passive in order to demonstrate their moral strength and the faith they have in the rightness of their cause, not because they are weak and hesitant. Civil disobedience is more effective, as we noted earlier, if it generates feelings of guilt in target groups who ignore requests for relief. Reformers induce guilt by emphasizing the unfairness of the situation they wish to change. Their perseverance in the face of demands that they stop protesting increases guilt among target persons, and the reformers generate even more shame among target persons if they

are forced to cease and desist. A demonstration of civil disobedience requires participants to engage in shared planning and to agree to stick to their plan. Passive resistance, as we saw earlier, may cause low morale among the resisters because their progress is bound to be slow. Therefore, managers of such a procedure repeatedly reassure members that their plan is a wise one, that their unit's success will be all they have hoped for, and that they are gradually winning their way, even though this may not yet appear to be the case. How to maintain morale among the courteously disobedient should be given more study.

Levitt (1973, p. 77) believes that the success of face-to-face confrontation depends on the use of "pushiness, jarring rhetoric, and sometimes outright violence." The actions are carefully staged, to get wide publicity at the expense of adversaries. This style of influence goes beyond mere persuasion because those who use it anticipate open disapproval of their methods and intend to ride roughshod over such criticism. The appearance of resistance among target persons is taken by the activists as evidence of the effect they desire to have. Levitt (1973) states that interrupters depend on exaggeration in word or deed. They overstate their case, sharpen the issue and force listeners to respond. The confronters hammer away at only one or two issues and refuse to be drawn into discussing other topics. They express righteous anger and say repeatedly that the target persons are at fault. If and when members of the audience change their minds, they do so in order to stop this harassment.

Restricting Target Persons' Freedom of Movement. In this approach, change agents seize one or more persons and keep them isolated or under guard. They often take persons other than decision makers and declare that they will not set these victims free, or will harm them, if stated demands are not met by officials within a given period of time. The incentive presented to decision makers in order to make them act on these threats is to stop the suffering of the captured persons. In a related approach, activists may conduct a coup d'état, in which a band of militant persons captures key leaders in the governmental bureaucracy and forces them to do as they are told or replaces them with individuals who will act as ordered. Because this instructed subset occupies a central place in the organization, the remaining members follow the instructions issued by their usual superiors, and the administrative machinery continues to run as it always has (Luttwak, 1968).

Other examples of the use of physical restraint to force a change are noteworthy. The regents of a university are locked in their meeting room by students who are demanding that the school recruit a larger proportion of black, Asian, and Chicano students. Individuals whose behavior in the community does not suit self-appointed reformers are seized as a way of making them obey rules laid down by the vigilantes. Managers of a company are barred from their offices until they develop new methods for protecting workers from accidents. A well-known individual is taken as a hostage, so that the complaints of the kidnapers will be given wide notice. Trains, planes, or ships are hijacked, and passengers are kept under armed surveillance until the grievances of their kidnapers are resolved (or the aggressors themselves are apprehended).

Why do change agents adopt such methods? A major reason is that a small band can accomplish much in this way. It gains immediate attention from the news media, which make a wide audience available at no cost and describe the unsatisfactory state of affairs about which the hijackers are complaining. The hijackers thereby get a hearing from persons they otherwise could not reach, and sometimes they win sympathy from observers who have never heard of them or their cause. The act itself is a form of propaganda by deed, since it implies that the perpetrators have a good reason for taking such measures; they are asking for help in eliminating an entrenched deprivation.

Because hostage taking is illegal in most places, officials concerned with protecting public safety soon become involved. They must choose among stalling and saying nothing to the kidnapers, in the hope that the latter will decide that their attempt has failed; talking with the captors in ways that keep them calm; bargaining, in order to see what freedom for the hostages would cost; and attacking the place where the hostages are kept, in order to rescue them and arrest the criminals.

What conditions cause such hostile behavior to be successful? Gamson (1975) reports that the social movements he studied were more likely to attain at least some of their objectives through blocking, vituperation, or violence if they had strongly centralized (formal) supervision of their organizations, aimed to displace the leaders among target persons, and were not disposed to altruism. The writings of Hyams (1975), Laqueur (1979), and Luttwak (1968) suggest what takers of hostages usually have going for them. The actions are mounted by a small, well-drilled, closely directed group whose members have rehearsed their operations well. The small size of the unit makes it inconspicuous, hard to find, and not easy to identify. The squad works quickly and carries out actions that the actors know will stimulate outrage and repugnance among hostages and observers. Each member of the unit knows exactly what he or she is to do. Leadership is strong because the uncertain situation may make it necessary to revise the initially planned procedure after the operation begins. The squad's members are obedient and willing to do what they are told, no matter how repulsive these actions may be. They feel deeply about the importance of the group's objectives and are therefore willing to be fanatics.

Because publicity is necessary for the success of such an activity, participants are schooled in how to talk to reporters and how to state their demands clearly. The kidnapers are also trained in bargaining because a hostage-taking event involves oral give-and-take (at a distance) with police or other officials. Success often depends on the ability to drive a hard bargain, and so the kidnapers must be articulate, unflappable, aware of what they can and cannot concede, and apparently fearless. They learn the tricks of haggling, such as offering concessions at one time and cancelling them later, showing an iron fist at one moment and a velvet glove at another, changing their minds whenever an agreement is near, setting a deadline for action by target persons, and stalling for time when stalling is useful. Above all, they attempt to encourage sympathy among bystanders by making it appear they have been and are being treated unfairly. One problem for persons who use these methods is that there is no clear point at which to stop or give up. They are breaking the law, and so part or all of their energies are engaged in avoiding penalties.

A coup d'état (a type of activity not often used in democratic society) demands a precise set of circumstances if it is to be used effectively, according to Luttwak (1968). First, "The social and economic conditions of the target [organization] must be such as to confine political participation to a small fraction of the population" (p. 32). Second, "The influence of foreign powers in its life must be relatively limited" (p. 32). Third, "The target state must have a political center. If there are several centers these must be identifiable and must be politically, rather than ethnically, structured. If the state is controlled by a nonpolitically organized unit, the coup can only be made with its consent or neutrality" (p. 45). The strategy of a coup is controlled by two considerations: the need for speed, and the need to neutralize any opposing forces. Care is taken to avoid bloodshed (which can arouse resistance) during the coup. If there is a delay, the intentions of the rebels will become visible, and there may be enough time for opposition to be organized. If things move swiftly, however, enemies and friends alike will hold their fire, to see what leaders of the coup intend to do. (They learn this too late, after the new regime is already in command.)

Harming or Threatening to Harm. In the most extreme form of constraint, initiators inflict pain or damage on persons and objects, or they warn that they will do such things if their wishes are not met. Bombs are exploded in public places, citizens who have no relevance to the activists' grievance are injured, community leaders are harmed, informants are grilled or tortured, undesirable people are lynched, and prominent figures are assassinated or replaced by members of the opposition as part of a coup d'état. Threats are delivered through anonymous telephone calls, unsigned letters, burning crosses, or hostile graffiti. For example, a leader of organized crime and politics in China warns dissidents by depositing a black coffin in the living room of a misbehaver, or members of the Mafia deliver a dead fish to convey the same kind of message.

Brill (1971) tells how leaders of a rent strike at a city-owned housing project tried to frighten city officials into meeting the strike group's demands. They used planned behavior to show that they were powerful and angry. They all stared stonily at the mayor while refusing to answer questions (silent stubbornness was perceived to be a way of displaying strength), exaggerated the number of persons taking part in the strike, used military terms when addressing one another in a public meeting, boasted publicly about the effectiveness of their hostile acts, and showed up at bargaining sessions wearing African tribal costumes.

Actions like these are often said to be forms of terrorism because they terrify those who are harmed, are threatened with harm, or observe such events. The term *terrorism*, however, has different meanings among students of such behavior. Here are a few typical definitions; all describe terrorism as a *political* act. Terrorism is the "use of terror by political militants as a means of overthrowing a government in power, or of forcing that government to change its policies" (Hyams, 1975, p. 46). It is "the use of covert violence by a group for political ends and [it] is usually directed against a government, less often against another group, class, or party" (Laqueur, 1979, p. 79). It is "the use or threatened use of violence in behalf of a political or ideological cause" (Newhouse, 1985, p. 46). "Terrorism is the deliberate and systematic murder, maiming and menacing of the innocent to inspire fear for political ends" (Netanyahu, 1978, p. 48). Hitchens (1986) remarks that it is difficult to find a definition of terrorism that is not tautological or vacuous (the use of violence for political ends), a cliché (an attack on innocent men, women, and children), or a synonym for the actions of swarthy opponents of United States foreign policy. He reviews five re-

cent books on terrorism and concludes that the term is essentially a cliché in search of a meaning. It is a handy label that obliterates the need for making distinctions among various kinds of violent acts employed to encourage social change. (A synonym in the urban drug culture of today is simply "criminal gang behavior.") This vague and emotionally loaded notion of terrorism has generated numerous misconceptions. Laqueur (1979, p. 219) lists several such beliefs: "Terrorism is a new and unprecedented phenomenon." (In fact, it has a long history in many parts of the world.) "Terrorism is used only by persons at the left end of the political spectrum." (In fact, dictatorships of the right always depend on it to ensure their power, and so do criminal leaders.) "Terrorism is employed by persons who have a legitimate grievance; removing the cause for the complaint will therefore eliminate the terrorism." (In fact, the complaints of terrorists are often hard to understand, impossible to remedy, or exceedingly self-centered.) "Terrorism is always effective." (In fact, it is useful only in limited circumstances, when a mass movement makes it part of a grand strategy or when it follows a political assassination.) "Terrorists are really human idealists and more intelligent than ordinary criminals who perform terrorist acts." (In fact, some of the worst horrors in history have been carried out by persons with strong ideals, and most of the successful terrorists of our time have the overt and full support of a specific religious group.) "Terrorism is used as a weapon only by the poor and weak." (In fact, many ardent terrorists are wealthy and powerful leaders.)

All in all, the term *terrorism* is too obscure and sweeping for our purposes. Its frequent use in daily discourse indicates that some agents of change choose to inflict deliberate harm on those they intend to influence. Fortunately, we seldom see such violent acts in American community groups engaged in social action except among (or between) criminal gangs, which use many of the methods that political terrorists use.

Why do activists plan to do harm to persons or objects? This question has many answers because reasons differ in different settings. One explanation points to the personal characteristics of those who use violent behavior or threats. Attempts to learn whether violence-prone people are similar in their personalities and different from the nonviolent have yielded few reliable or useful findings. It is evident, however, that harmdoers are most often young middle-class males (Laqueur, 1979). They frequently begin their careers by pressing for social change in legitimate ways, but because they are not successful with that approach, they turn to more extreme methods, assuming that doing damage to people or property will work. They know that hostile behavior will win the attention of the persons they hope to influence. Hyams (1975) asserts that agents of change use violence in order to weaken the status of local officials. Citizens observe that their leaders have not protected them from danger, and so they doubt the ability of the office holders and no longer want them in office.

Users of violence give other reasons for choosing an aggressive style. They think it will overcome the inertia of target persons and force them to attend to issues they have been avoiding. The aggressors also believe that this style will earn them the support of observers if their hostile actions are met with force. They assume that the products of modern technology make it easier to do harm without being caught. Examples of such products are plastic explosives, bombs that can be triggered at a distance, devices

to interrupt or tap into enemy computers, poison darts, mind-altering drugs, and instruments that allow eavesdropping on private conversations over radio waves or telephone lines. In several parts of the world, and in some ethnic neighborhoods of the United States, a man who is wronged is disapproved of by his peers until he has had his revenge on the ones who offended him.

Doers of harm are skilled in rationalizing their behavior to themselves and to critics. Their usual argument is that the ends they seek are so valuable (fair, beneficial, overdue, correct) that they may properly use any method that will work (Pfaff, 1986). Any harm this procedure causes to target persons is a fair price, they think, for getting rid of a deplorable situation. The ends justify the means. As a variation on this theme, hostile change agents believe that the persons they are treating violently are so evil, wrong, and despicable that they have no rights. Such views have been expressed over the years by writers who support the infliction of pain as a method of introducing change.

Hyams (1975) reviews arguments expressed by philosophers of violence around the turn of the century, including Max Stirner. Writing in 1906, Stirner based his ideas on the necessity for ultraindividualistic behavior. Each person, he said, is alone against all others. A state or a government is not needed to provide for or protect a citizen. If an individual cannot get others to provide what he demands of them, he should take it by force. Faults in society are not due to the strength of the masters but to the weakness of the underlings. Each person must make his own way, depending on nobody else. (Where have we heard such ideas more recently?)

Nechayev (also cited by Hyams) advised individuals to transform themselves into ruthless egos dedicated to creating a revolution by creating fear in any who resist. First, revolutionaries are to assassinate all intelligent and important persons. They also must get rid of the would-be reformers because such persons may be successful in introducing desirable modifications and may thereby weaken people's interest in rebelling. Stupid and unimportant citizens should be left alone because their behavior warrants revolution and should visibly illustrate the need for reform. A more recent writer who offers comparable rationalizations is Fanon (1966), who declares that violence is "a cleansing force" that "frees the black from an inferiority complex, restores his self-respect, and invests his character with positive and creative qualities" (p. 73).

What effects do harmful actions have? They often intimidate target persons or cause them confusion about how to deal with such acts. Weak and hesitant responses occur if the persons under attack are not prepared to handle hostility or if they are not able to resist the change agents. They may unwillingly do what is asked, in order to keep the peace or avoid harm. They will not let themselves be so influenced, however, if they can deviate from the wishes of change agents without this deviance being detected. If the target persons are strong enough to ignore the activists' threats, they will meet aggression with their own aggression, which often encourages further and hotter hostility from the agents of change, and a cycle of escalation begins. The issue at hand is ignored because of anger and the desire on both sides to meet fire with fire.

Gamson (1975) found that participants in 25 percent of the protesting social movements he examined used violence against people. Movements that used violent behavior won about as much acceptance and respect as those that did not employ it, but violent actions allowed activists to accomplish more. Among groups that threatened to harm people, 75 percent gained their objectives and 25 percent did not. Among those that used civil methods, 53 percent reached their objectives and 47 percent did not. In Gamson's groups, violence paid off; it helped groups get the changes they sought.

We see, then, that violence can be successful as a stimulator of change. What may account for this success? Perhaps harmdoers prevent escalation of anger by indicating after an aggressive act that they are willing to negotiate or bargain with the target persons. Coercive activists often get their way simply because they have the power to use hostility in a telling fashion. They employ force to win and have enough control over future events to maintain the victory thereafter. The social changes introduced by criminal gangs or dictators are examples.

The most effective groups that use violent behavior are able to suppress quarrels among their own members. They avoid tiffs caused by anxiety over the commitment of their members to group values and objectives. Such conflict is kept under control because the members need one another for protection from the external threats that their groups face and that enhance group cohesion. Even so, several writers believe that most members of a violent team drop out sooner or later, unless they can keep up their enthusiasm for their cause. Leaders of violent gangs try to avoid having their units fall apart by assuring colleagues that they all have the same objectives and by preventing quarrels among participants over who is most faithful to group goals. One wonders how the dynamics of a ruthless, coercive group differ from those of an altruistic body. Do the two have similar problems in keeping the unit effective?

In summary, agents of change may threaten harm or do actual harm to individuals they want to influence, to observers, or to objects of value. They do these things in order to get the attention of target persons and the support, perhaps, of bystanders, and to create an incentive—a negative one—for change. These efforts may generate timid acceptance of their demands or aggressive counteractions. Even though most officials do not like to bargain with users of violence, they usually do. Activists who employ violent methods probably get their way as often as they fail.

SUMMARY

When activists use constraining methods to try to influence target persons, target persons pay less attention to the quality of the ideas proposed by the initiators than to the incentives (to win a reward, or to avoid a penalty or punishment) that accompany the proposals. The receivers agree to introduce changes, in order to attain effects that they value or to avoid ones they dislike.

When they employ pressuring methods, activists realize that target persons may acquiesce in order to win a favorable response or avoid an unfavorable reaction. Thus, they try to determine whether target persons have really changed or are only pretending to have done so. The use of constraining methods requires close monitoring of target persons' behavior. If they do not want to change in the ways proposed by activists but do wish to win favorable reactions or avoid unfavorable responses, then they will pretend to have changed. Activists can monitor overt actions by target persons more reliably than covert shifts in target persons' beliefs, attitudes, or values. Therefore, activists who use constraining methods are often more effective in influencing the overt behavior of target persons than in changing their covert beliefs or feelings.

REFERENCES

Alinsky, S. *Rules for Radicals.* New York: Random House, 1971.

Bailey, F. *The Tactical Uses of Passion.* Ithaca, NY: Cornell University Press, 1983.

Barbrook, A., and C. Bolt. *Power and Protest in American Life.* Oxford, England: Martin Robertson, 1980.

Bar-Tal, D. *Prosocial Behavior: Theory and Research.* New York: Wiley, 1976.

Bellah, R., and others. *Habits of the Heart.* New York: Harper & Row, 1985.

Berry, J. "Beyond Citizen Participation: Effective Advocacy Before Administrative Agencies." *Journal of Applied Behavioral Science,* 1981, *17,* 463–477.

Berscheid, E., and E. Walster. *Interpersonal Attraction.* Reading, MA: Addison-Wesley, 1978.

Bollinger, L. *The Tolerant Society: Freedom of Speech and Extremist Speech in America.* New York: Oxford University Press, 1987.

Boulding, E. "Image and Action in Peace Building." *Journal of Social Issues,* 1988, *44,* 17–38.

Brehm, S., and J. Brehm. *Psychological Reactance: A Theory of Freedom and Controls.* Orlando, FL: Academic Press, 1981.

Brill, H. *Why Organizations Fail.* Berkeley: University of California Press, 1971.

Caldwell, L., L. Hayes and I. MacWhirter. *Citizens and the Environment.* Bloomington: Indiana University Press, 1976.

Capraro, J. "The Revitalization of Chicago Lawn: A Private Sector Response to Local Decline." *Commentary,* 1979, *3,* 11–14.

Carter, A. *Direct Action and Liberal Democracy.* New York: Harper & Row, 1973.

Cartwright, D., ed. *Studies in Social Power.* Ann Arbor: Institute for Social Research, University of Michigan, 1959.

Cartwright, D. "Influence, Leadership, and Control." In J. March ed., *Handbook of Organization.* Skokie, IL: Rand McNally, 1965.

Cartwright, D., and A. Zander. *Group Dynamics: Research and Theory.* New York: Harper & Row, 1968.

Chamberlain, D. "Town Without Pity." *Image,* Aug. 2, 1987, pp. 23–28.

Commager, H. *The Era of Reform, 1830–1860.* New York: Van Nostrand Reinhold, 1960.

Cordes, C. "Responding to Terrorism." *The Monitor,* 1986. *17,* 12–13.

Crowfoot, J., M. Chesler, and J. Boulet. "Organizing for Social Justice." In E. Seidman, ed., *Handbook of Social Intervention.* Newbury Park, CA: Sage, 1983.

Deci, E. *Intrinsic Motivation.* New York: Plenum, 1975.

Delbecq, A., and A. Van de Ven. *Group Techniques for Program Planning.* Glenview, IL: Scott, Foresman, 1975.

Delgado, G. *Organizing the Movement: The Roots and Growth of ACORN.* Philadelphia: Temple University Press, 1986.

Deutsch, M. *The Resolution of Conflict.* New Haven: Yale University Press, 1973.

Diringer, E. "Earth Lovers Tell Why They Turned Tough." *San Francisco Chronicle,* Dec. 7, 1987, p. A-8.

Douglas, M., and A. Wildavsky. *Risk and Culture.* Berkeley: University of California Press, 1982.

Fanon, F. *The Wretched of the Earth.* New York: Grove Press, 1966.

Flinn, J. "Playing Mental Games." *San Francisco Examiner,* Jan. 21, 1988, p. B-8.

Frank, D. "Experimental Studies of Personal Pressure and Resistance." *Journal of General Psychology,* 1944, *30,* 23–41.

Fraser, J. *The Chinese: Portrait of a People.* New York: Summit Books, 1980.

French, J., and B. Raven. "The Bases of Social Power." In D. Cartwright, ed., *Studies in Social Power.* Ann Arbor: Institute for Social Research, University of Michigan, 1959.

Fuchs, L. "The Role and Communication Task of the Change-Agent Experience of the Peace Corps Volunteers in the Philippines." In D. Lerner and W. Schramm, eds., *Communication and Change in the Developing Countries.* Honolulu: East-West Center, 1967.

Funk, D. *Group Dynamics Law: Integrating Constitutive Contract Institutions.* New York: Philosophical Library, 1982.

Gamson, W. *Power and Discontent.* Homewood, IL: Dorsey Press, 1968.

Gamson, W. *The Strategy of Social Protest.* Homewood, IL: Dorsey Press, 1975.

Gerlach, L., and V. Hine. *People, Power, and Change: Movements of Social Transformation.* Indianapolis: Bobbs-Merrill, 1970.

Goodenough, W. *Cooperation in Change.* New York: Russell Sage Foundation, 1963.

Gotshalk, D. *Human Aims in Modern Perspective.* Yellow Springs, OH: Antioch Press, 1966.

Gusfield, J. "The Study of Social Movements." In D. Silk, ed., *International Encyclopedia of Social Sciences,* Vol. 14. New York: Macmillan, 1968.

Hammond, K., and L. Adelman. "Science, Values, and Human Judgment." *Science,* 1976, *194,* 389–396.

Hanley, R. "The Hot Dirt Rebellion." *San Francisco Chronicle and Examiner,* Sept. 14, 1986, p. A-5.

Hine, R. *California's Utopian Colonies.* New Haven: Yale University Press, 1953.

Hirschman, A. "Reactionary Rhetoric." *Atlantic Monthly,* May 1989, pp. 63–70.

Hitchens, C. "Wanton Acts of Usage." *Harper's,* Sept. 1986, pp. 66–76.

Holsti, E. "Crisis, Stress, and Decision Making." *International Social Science Journal,* 1971, *23,* 53–67.

Hornblower, M. "Not in My Backyard, You Don't." *Time,* June 27, 1988, pp. 44–46.

Hyams, E. *Terrorism and Terrorists.* New York: St. Martin's Press, 1975.

Janis, I. *Victims of Groupthink.* Boston: Houghton Mifflin, 1972.

Janis, I., and L. Mann. *Decision Making.* New York: Free Press, 1977.

Kahneman, D., and A. Tversky. "Prospect Theory: An Analysis of Decision Under Risk." *Econometrica,* 1979, *47,* 239–291.

Kanter, R. *Commitment and Community.* Cambridge, MA: Harvard University Press, 1972.

Kiesler, C. *The Psychology of Commitment.* Orlando, FL: Academic Press, 1971.

Knoke, D., and J. Wood. *Organized for Action: Commitment in Voluntary Associations.* New Brunswick, NJ: Rutgers University Press, 1981.

Kweit, M., and R. Kweit. *Implementing Citizen Participation in a Bureaucratic Society.* New York: Praeger, 1971.

Lancourt, J. *Confront or Concede.* Lexington, MA: Heath, 1979.

Langton, S. "Current Reflections on the State of the Art." In S. Langton, ed., *Citizen Participation in America.* Lexington, MA: Heath, 1978.

Lanternari, V. *The Religions of the Oppressed.* New York: Knopf, 1963.

Laqueur, W. *Terrorism.* Boston: Little, Brown, 1979.

Lebow, R., and J. Stein. "Beyond Deterrence." *Journal of Social Issues,* 1987, *43,* 5–71.

Levitt, T. *The Third Sector: New Tactics for a Responsive Society.* New York: American Management Association, 1973.

Lindgren, H. "The Informal-Intermittent Organization: A Vehicle for Successful Citizen Protest." *Journal of Applied Behavioral Science,* 1987, *23,* 397–412.

Lippitt, R., J. Watson, and B. Westley. *The Dynamics of Planned Change.* San Diego, CA: Harcourt Brace Jovanovich, 1958.

Lipset, S., and E. Raab. *The Politics of Unreason.* New York: Harper & Row, 1970.

Liversidge, D. *The Luddites: Machine Breakers of the Early Nineteenth Century.* New York: Watts, 1972.

Luttwak, E. *Coup d'état: A Practical Handbook.* New York: Knopf, 1968.

Macaulay, J., and L. Berkowitz. *Altruism and Helping Behavior.* Orlando, FL: Academic Press, 1970.

Madison, A. *Vigilantism in America.* New York: Seaburg Press, 1973.

Marris, P., and M. Rein. *Dilemmas of Social Reform.* New York: Lieber-Atherton, 1967.

Mayer, A. "The Significance of Quasi-Groups in the Study of Complex Societies." In M. Banton, ed., *The Social Anthropology of Complex Societies.* London: Tavistock, 1966.

Meier, B. "Citizen Suits Become a Popular Weapon in the Fight Against Industrial Polluters." *Wall Street Journal,* Apr. 17, 1987, p. 17.

Moreland, R., and J. Levine. "Socialization in Small Groups: Temporal Changes in Individual-Group Relations." In L. Berkowitz, ed., *Advances in Experimental Social Psychology,* Vol. 15. Orlando, FL: Academic Press, 1980.

Morgan, G. *Images of Organization.* Newbury Park, CA: Sage, 1986.

Moscovici, S. *Social Influence and Social Change.* Orlando, FL: Academic Press, 1976.

Moynihan, D. *Maximum Feasible Misunderstanding.* New York: Free Press, 1970.

Netanyahu, B. *Terrorism: How the West Can Win.* New York: Farrar, Straus & Giroux, 1987.

Newcomb, T. *The Acquaintance Process.* New York: Holt, Rinehart & Winston, 1961.

Newhouse, J. "The Diplomatic Round: A Freemasonry of Terrorism." *The New Yorker,* July 8, 1985, pp. 46–63.

Nisbet, R. *The Quest for Community.* New York: Oxford University Press, 1953.

Nisbett, R., and L. Ross. *Human Inference: Strategies and Shortcomings of Social Judgment.* Englewood-Cliffs, NJ: Prentice-Hall, 1980.

Olsen, M. *Participatory Pluralism.* Chicago: Nelson-Hall, 1982.

Osborn, A. *Applied Imagination.* New York: Scribner's, 1957.

Perlman, J. "Grassroots Participation from Neighborhoods to Nations." In S. Langton, ed., *Citizen Participation in America.* Lexington, MA: Heath, 1978.

Pfaff, E. "Reflections: The Dimensions of Terror." *The New Yorker,* Nov. 10, 1986, pp. 122–131.

Piven, F., and R. Cloward. *Poor People's Movements: Why They Succeed and How They Fail.* New York: Pantheon, 1977.

Prestby, J., and A. Wandersman. "An Empirical Exploration of a Framework of Organizational Viability: Maintaining Block Organizations." *Journal of Applied Behavioral Science,* 1985, *21,* 287–305.

Priscoli, J. "Implementing Public Involvement Programs in Federal Agencies." In S. Langton, ed., *Citizen Participation in America.* Lexington, MA: Heath, 1978.

Pruitt, D. "Methods for Resolving Differences of Interest: A Theoretical Analysis." *Journal of Social Issues,* 1972, *28,* 133–154.

Pruitt, D., and J. Rubin. *Social Conflict: Escalation, Stalemate, and Settlement.* New York: Random House, 1986.

Robertson, M. "A Penchant for Protest: Why the Bay Area Likes to Demonstrate." *San Francisco Chronicle,* Mar. 25, 1988, pp. B-3–B-4.

Rogers, E. "Social Structure and Social Change." In G. Zaltman, ed., *Process and Phenomena of Social Change.* New York: Wiley, 1973.

Rogers, E. *Diffusion of Innovations.* New York: Free Press, 1983.

Rosenblatt, R. "The Demogogue in the Crowd." *Time,* Oct. 21, 1985, p. 102.

Rosener, J. "Matching Method to Purpose: The Challenge of Planning Citizen Activities." In S. Langton, ed., *Citizen Participation in America.* Lexington, MA: Heath, 1978.

Rothman, J., J. Erlich, and J. Teresa. *Promoting Innovation and Change in Organizations and Communities.* New York: Wiley, 1976.

Rude, G. *The Crowd in History: A Study of Popular Disturbances in France and England, 1730–1848.* New York: Wiley, 1964.

Ruffner, F., ed. *Encyclopedia of Associations,* 5th ed. Detroit: Gale Research Co., 1968.

Schachter, S. *The Psychology of Affiliation.* Palo Alto, CA: Stanford University Press, 1959.

Seligman, M. *Helplessness: On Depression, Development, and Death.* New York: W. H. Freeman, 1975.

Sieber, S. *Fatal Remedies: The Ironies of Social Intervention.* New York: Plenum, 1981.

Stone, C. *Should Trees Have Standing? Toward Legal Rights for Natural Objects.* Los Altos, CA: Kaufmann, 1974.

Thum, G., and M. Thum. *The Persuaders: Propaganda in War and Peace.* New York: Atheneum, 1972.

Toch, H. *The Social Psychology of Social Movements.* Indianapolis: Bobbs-Merrill, 1965.

Trotter, R. "Stop Blaming Yourself." *Psychology Today,* 1987, *21,* 31–39.

Tversky, A., and D. Kahneman. "Causal Schemata in Judgments Under Uncertainty." In M. Fishbein, ed., *Progress in Social Psychology.* Hillsdale, NJ: Erlbaum, 1978.

Unger, D., and A. Wandersman. "The Importance of Neighbors." *American Journal of Community Psychology,* 1985, *13,* 139–169.

Vander Werf, M. "Sign Man Calls 'Em, Wears 'Em." *Arizona Republican,* Oct. 4, 1987, p. B-1.

Vogel, E. *Modern Japanese Organization and Decision Making.* Berkeley: University of California Press, 1975.

Walton, E. "Establishing and Maintaining High Commitment in Work Systems." In J. R. Kimberly, R. H. Miles, and Associates, eds., *The Organizational Life Cycle: Issues in the Creation, Transformation, and Decline of Organizations.* San Francisco: Jossey-Bass, 1980.

Wandersman, A. "A Framework of Participation in Community Organizations." *Journal of Applied Behavioral Science,* 1981, *17,* 27–58.

Wandersman, A. "Citizen Participation." In K. Heller, R. Price, S. Rienharz, and A. Wandersman, eds., *Psychology and Community Change: Challenges of the Future.* Homewood, IL: Dorsey Press, 1984.

Wandersman, A., and others. "Getting Together and Getting Things Done." *Psychology Today,* Nov. 1985, 64–71.

Wandersman, A., and others. "Who Participates, Who Does Not, and Why? An Analysis of Voluntary Neighborhood Organizations in the United States and Israel." *Sociological Forum,* 1987, *2,* 534–555.

Warren, R. *Social Change and Human Purpose: Toward Understanding and Action.* Skokie, IL: Rand-McNally, 1971.

Warren, R., S. Rose, and A. Bergunder. *The Structure of Urban Reform.* Lexington, MA: Heath, 1974.

Weick, K. *The Social Psychology of Organizing.* Reading, MA: Addison-Wesley, 1979.

Wicker, A. "Behavior Settings Reconsidered: Temporal Stages, Resources, Internal Dynamics, Context." In D. Stokols and E. Altman, eds., *Handbook of Environmental Psychology.* New York: Wiley, 1987.

Wilson, J. *Introduction to Social Movements.* New York: Basic Books, 1973.

Woito, M. *To End War: A New Approach to International Conflict.* New York: Pilgrim Press, 1982.

Wood, J., and M. Jackson. *Social Movements: Development, Participation, and Dynamics.* Belmont, CA: Wadsworth, 1982.

Zander, A. *Motives and Goals in Groups.* Orlando, FL: Academic Press, 1971.

Zander, A. *Groups at Work: Unresolved Issues in the Study of Organizations.* San Francisco: Jossey-Bass, 1977.

Zander, A. *Making Groups Effective.* San Francisco: Jossey-Bass, 1982.

Zander, A. "The Value of Belonging to a Group in Japan." *Small-Group Behavior,* 1983, *14,* 3–14.

Zander, A. *The Purposes of Groups and Organizations.* San Francisco: Jossey-Bass, 1985.

Zander, A., J. Forward. and R. Albert. "Adaptation of Board Members to Repeated Success or Failure by Their Organizations." *Organizational Behavior and Human Performance,* 1969, *4,* 56–76.

Zander, A., and T. Newcomb, Jr. "Group Levels of Aspiration in United Fund Campaigns." *Journal of Personality and Social Psychology,* 1967, *6,* 157–162.

10.

Ruth J. Parsons, Santos H. Hernandez, and James D. Jorgensen

INTEGRATED PRACTICE: A FRAMEWORK FOR PROBLEM SOLVING

Social workers in the year 2000 will practice in a postindustrial era. As Bell (1973) and Naisbitt (1982) pointed out, the late 1900s are a new societal era characterized by different problems and needs than those to which social work has responded in the past. Naisbitt characterized this era as the information society in which adaptive generalists instead of potentially obsolete specialists will be needed. The complexity of technological advancement has the potential to increase alienation by decreasing connectedness between people and their communities. These views of the emerging society challenge the basis of social work practice and call for a new look at social work intervention. The authors submit that social workers in the new era must be generalists prepared to design interventions for solving social problems, not indepth specialists within a limited dimension of a particular social problem. As Walz and Hoffman (1982) suggested, a society in transition must rebuild and redesign the social institutional base. Thus social workers must grasp a broader domain in which human problems and solutions require the investments of many institutions and professions, only a small portion of which will be social workers. Generalists will need to guide and engineer the problem definition and means of solution, as well as the development and management of community resources for mutual problem solving. Such a view describes social work generalists as creative problem solvers in a specific practice arena (Heus & Pincus, 1986).

Integrated practice, a practice model organized around this view of social work, focuses on a social problem as a target, and uses differential role taking in intervention (Hernandez, Jorgensen, Judd, Gould, & Parsons, 1985). The model suggests that both prevention and habilation are optional intervention points. Professional social workers are educators and mobilizers of resources, not specialized therapists. Practice principles are guided by a habilation model that includes promotion of competency, normalization, and empowerment. Integrated practice builds and expands on contemporary social work practice models including Anderson's (1981) micro and macro frameworks, Germain and Gitterman's (1980) life model, and Maluccio's (1981) competency-oriented practice. Practice strategies include differential role taking, teaching problem-solving models, networking, team building, and mutual aid and self-help.

SOCIAL PROBLEMS AS TARGETS

In integrated practice, the target of social work intervention is the whole of social problems, rather than the rehabilitation of victims of social problems alone. Traditionally, social work has defined itself as promoting the interaction between individuals and their environment for the betterment of both (Bartlett, 1970) and has distinguished itself from other related professions by that attribute. This definition implies that the question of location of the problem is open. Rather than assuming that the problem is within an individual, the problem also may be defined as located in the interaction between the individual and the environment or within the environment. Moreover, the question of where to intervene is open. The location of the problem and the focus of intervention need not always be the same.

Using systems concepts as a theory base, social work practice is framed as boundary work (Gordon, 1970). Intervention in either macrosystems (the broader society and communities), mesosystems (neighborhoods, organizations, and groups), or microsystems (individuals and families) can effect results at other levels. A social problem calls for multilevel systems intervention that links systems for a synthesis of energy aimed at problem resolution or reduction. However, in actuality, current social work intervention tends to follow the methodological expertise of the practitioner. This is the "law of the instrument" principle, which uses the expertise of the practitioner to define the area in need of intervention (Kaplan, 1964, p. 23). Described as "specialization by solution," this tendency has guided social workers to work only with the victims of social problems (Heus & Pincus, 1986, p. 15). Victims of social problems are those targeted as the "deviants" in U.S. society. They are the drinkers in the social problem of alcoholism. They are the abusers in the social problem of child abuse. They are depressed or angry women and minorities in the social problems of sexism and racism. They are the most accessible and easily labeled participants in social problems, and society is more willing for social workers to work with these victims than with other components of social problems. Using the medical model as a theoretical screen, "curing" of the sick is more politically acceptable than targeting either the cause or the major contributing factors to social problems. This social pathology view of social problems blames the victims of social problems for their own role in the dynamics of the problem (Rubington & Weinberg, 1981).

Integrated practice, by contrast, views social problems from the labeling perspective suggested by Becker (1963, p. 19). This perspective defines social problems as reactions to an alleged violation of rules or expectations and focuses on the conditions under which behaviors or situations come to be defined as problematic or deviant. A problem is a situation evaluated as undesirable by someone, and may be an unsuccessful solution to another problem. Problems and solutions become different dynamics of the same set of variables. The discrepancy between the expected norm and the labeled behavior can be viewed as the interaction between an individual and the environment, which is the traditional arena of social work practice.

Viewing social work practice in this context opens up the option of prevention as a viable practice arena. Prevention has been dismissed too often as an intervention point in social work because of lack of knowledge regarding causality. Pinpointing the cause of social problems is viewed as a political and theoretical enigma. In fact, it is not necessary to know the cause of social problems to create prevention intervention. It is, however, necessary to target certain contributing factors related to the problem that may be ameliorated, even though these factors may not be readily identified as causal.

Support for this approach can be found in the mental health prevention literature.

Albee (1982) proposed that determining intervention points in prevention can be facilitated by viewing mental dysfunction as a product of several factors (Table 10.1).

Individual differences and environmental stress are relatively difficult to affect. Situational factors, coping skills, self-esteem, and support systems are more likely to be amenable to change. Change in any of these factors affects the incidence though not necessarily the cause. Using this formula, the incidence of concern can be reduced by compensating for organic factors. Compensation can be achieved by reducing environmental stress and/or increasing coping skills, self-esteem, or support systems.

Bloom (1979) suggested that a new paradigm for prevention in mental health should abandon the search for cause and pay closer attention to precipitating factors. The paradigm assumes that people are variously vulnerable to stressful life events and that people may all respond differently to the same event. Therefore prevention programs can aim to facilitate mastery or reduce the incidence of particular stressful life events without focusing on understanding their origins. Linking preventive services with stressful life events such as

TABLE 10.1
Mental Dysfunction

$$\text{Incidence of mental dysfunction} = \frac{\text{organic factors} + \text{stress}}{\text{coping skills} + \text{self esteem} + \text{support system}}$$

school entrance, parenting, divorce, and widowhood, Bloom argued that competence building may be the single most effective preventive strategy for dealing with individual and social issues in most communities. He proposed that availability of community resources, and knowledge and skills for accessing those, are keys to building power, self-esteem, and competence of individuals.

Integrated practice, then, is constructed on the assumption that problems are interactional between an individual and the environment. Intervention takes on dimensions of choice and decision making, and raises a question about where intervention should occur. Intervention is not viewed as directed toward either small or large systems. Instead, intervention is viewed on a continuum (Table 10.2). At one end, intervention engages victims of social problems for habilitative purposes. On the other end, intervention engages both victims and non-

TABLE 10.2
Integrated Practice Intervention Continuum

Small Systems ⟵			⟶ Large Systems
Work with:			
Individuals or groups of victims	Groups of victims	Victims and nonvictims	Victims and non-victims or nonvictims only
For what purpose:			
Habilitation, educations, and sensitization	Enabling victims to create support systems	Creation of and access to needed services structures	Social problem reduction, alleviation, and prevention

victims in action-directed environmental changes that mitigate against the contributing factors in the problem.

An illustration of this practice model can be found in viewing the problem of single room occupant (SRO) elderly in inner-city neighborhoods. A traditional view of the problem views the SRO elder as the problem, and therapeutic interventions are created to bring them in line with society's expected norms for behavior. The labeling perspective opens up the definition of the problem and arenas for solution. From an integrated practice perspective, the problem is defined as the elderly's isolation and lack of access to services. SRO elders are seen to be potentially competent persons who are caught in an interactive dynamic of lack of economic resources, preferred autonomous life-styles, chronic illnesses, powerlessness, and learned helplessness. Intervention then would be targeted toward all points along the intervention continuum. The elderly themselves should be offered programs designed to build trust, assess need, educate, and raise awareness about their situation. Support groups can be created in the hotels and apartments to raise awareness and decrease isolation. The service sector should be educated about the population and its isolation. Creative ways to deliver services can be created and taught to the service sector. Finally, advocacy for creation of housing facilities should be conducted.

EDUCATION AS A GUIDE IN ROLE TAKING

An important theoretical assumption in this model is the function of the social worker as educator-generalist. Generalist skills are required; the specialized area of knowledge of practitioners lies in the dynamics of the social problem as a whole and in problem solving. Moreover, as social workers assume different roles along the intervention continuum, an educational emphasis shapes each role or point of intervention.

Rationale for this assumption can be found in the critical consciousness concept of Friere (1972), which suggested that oppressed persons often live in a "culture of silence" and do not possess the capacity for critical awareness and response. They do not see that their situation can be different from what it is, nor do they perceive themselves as having potential power to intervene in the social world and change it. To raise a critical consciousness, education of oppressed people, Friere suggested, should begin with development of self-concept in which they become subjects able to determine their situation, not mere objects at the mercy of whatever happens to them. Education can be an antidote for learned helplessness.

McKnight (1977) strongly critiqued traditional professionalized service. He questioned the service culture that translates need into deficiency, places that deficiency in the client, and then separates that deficiency into components requiring specialties for intervention. Specialization of problems in the minds of professionals provides rationale for their specializing in minute arenas. They develop expert tools, instruments, and a complex language that is not understood outside of their arena. McKnight criticized such professional help for its disabling effects. His views caution social work as a profession not to emulate related specializations and reinforce the role of social workers as generalists who seek to understand social problems from a complex perspective of individual dynamics interacting with sociopolitical forces. In addition, McKnight suggested that if victims and nonvictims are to participate in problem resolution, social workers will have to educate both groups all along the breadth of the intervention continuum, rather than withhold information in the role of expert diagnostician and solution specialist. Social workers' expertise is in the defined problem and the ability to mobilize victims and nonvictims for problem reduction.

HABILITATION VERSUS REHABILITATION

Practice principles for the integrated practice model are based on habilitation. Habilitation implies growth promotion or provision of means for problem solving. Rehabilitation, by contrast, implies rebuilding or restoration. Habilitation does not deny the existence of impairment resulting from victimization, but it changes the focus of intervention from the impairment to the competency of the impaired individual (Table 10.3).

Habilitation builds on three conceptual components: (1) a view of human behavior in a normalized political and socioeconomic context (as opposed to a view of behavior through a labeled deviancy screen); (2) an assumption of competency on the part of victims of social problems; and (3) empowerment as a goal of intervention.

TABLE 10.3
Habilitation and Rehabilitation Principles

	Habilitation	Rehabilitation
View of client	Problems between person and environment	Problem in the person
	Victim of social problem	Devalued deviant with dysfunctional condition
	Expectation of fundamental competence and learning of coping skills	Expectation of helplessness
View of client behavior	Behavior on a normative continuum	Behavior as dichotomous; abnormal or normal
	Behavior viewed in environmental context, code of cultural conventions	Behavior attributed to need, deficiency, or pathology
	Current events cause current behavior	Past events cause current behavior
	Behavior as troubling to society	Behavior as the client's problem
Relationship between social worker and client	Coequal problem solvers, each with unique expertise	Dysfunctional client and the social worker as healer
	Treatment expertise not needed, but instead education and mobilization	Expert therapist; client a recipient of service
	Risk and responsibility expected from client	Fostering of dependency of client
	Client expected to learn new coping skills and resources	Client expected to be dysfunctional due to pathology
Intervention	Intervention independent of etiology	Cause necessary for determination of cure
	Education and acquisition of new skill	Treatment and cure implied

Normalization

The view of behavior from a normative environmental context, instead of a normal/abnormal dichotomy, attempts to decrease labeled deviancy. Positivistic thinking views dysfunctional behavior as caused by either individual factors or environmental factors. A normalized approach suggests that behavior cannot be viewed objectively, but must be viewed in terms of a person's intentions, motives, and reasons. Three factors must be considered in this view of behavior (Ingleby, 1980). First, behavior viewed in its environmental context becomes understandable in its specific circumstances and, given that set of circumstances, most people would respond similarly. Second, behavior is purposive. It is intended to convey a message about the specific situation. Behavior can be viewed as a form of protest against environmental pressure or as a way of coping with the environment. Third, behavior is understandable when viewed in its cultural code of conventions. These factors invite the examination of behavior in its political and socioeconomic context, which is important for social work because a large number of social work clients are women and racial minorities, and thus are economically and socially discriminated against.

Competence

According to the integrated practice perspective, victims of social problems are fundamentally competent persons who are participants in an interaction in a problem, a condition broader than their behavioral reactions. The principle of competency in assessment suggests that client systems have the capacity for learning, understanding, and solving problems. It assumes that clients' coping skills can be increased and that they have a right to risk and fail. They are viewed as the best experts on and resources for their problems. In what Maluccio (1981) referred to as a new/old approach to social work practice, competence-oriented social work is based on an ecological transaction that contains three components: (1) clients' capacities and skills, (2) clients' motivation, and (3) the environmental qualities that impinge on clients' functioning. He suggested that client and social worker roles must be redefined as persons who share a task. Power invested in the social worker must be decreased; social distance reduced; and clients' identity, autonomy, and reciprocity in the relationship promoted.

Empowerment

Empowerment is the major principle guiding work with client systems. According to Solomon (1976), empowerment is a

process whereby the social worker engages in a set of activities with the client or client system that aims to reduce the powerlessness that has been created by negative valuations based on membership in a stigmatized group (p. 19).

Solomon (1976, p. 19) further described powerlessness as the inability to manage emotions, skills, knowledge, or material resources in a way that effective performance in valued social roles will lead to personal gratification. Therefore, powerlessness can be viewed as one's inability to obtain and use resources to achieve personal goals, and powerlessness in groups and communities can be viewed as the inability to use resources to achieve collective goals. Empowerment then is "the process of development of an effective support system for those who have been blocked from achieving individual or collective goals" (p. 19).

Power is central to a helping process that enables clients to solve their own problems. If clients lack power, then social workers must enable them to achieve it in relationship to themselves and to oppressive systems. Ryan (1971) proposed that power is a central component in the helping process when he suggested that self-esteem is to some extent an essential to the human survival; [self-esteem] depends partially on the inclusion of a sense of power within self-concept; and mentally healthy persons must be able to perceive themselves as at least minimally powerful and capable of influencing their environment to their benefit. Furthermore, a sense of power must be based on the actual experience and exercise of power. Competence, power, and self-esteem are linked inextricably and their loss may be a powerful stress.

Empowerment as the primary principle of intervention carries two key assumptions. As was suggested earlier, it makes the job of the social worker one of power broker. It suggests that it is the job of social workers to provide supports so that clients may have access to the benefits and prerequisites accorded to the mainstream of society.

If client problems are viewed as a disparity between coping skills and environmental pressures, social work intervention may be at either end of that relationship (Maluccio, 1981). Empowerment intervention, however, must go beyond simply a choice of intervention points: Social workers must leave capacity to solve problems in place when they leave. An evaluation of empowerment asks the question "Did the client system retain increased capacity for solving problems when the social worker no longer was present?" "Was expertise given to the client?" The belief that client systems have capacity for problem solving is based on the use of self-fulfilling prophecy as a positive expectation. Learned helplessness must not be reinforced, but must be decreased. To empow-

er SRO clients, it is necessary to educate them about their situation and teach them new skills to access resources and act on their own behalf.

INTEGRATED PRACTICE AND CONTEMPORARY STRATEGIES

Several social work practice theories have emerged during the late 1970s and early 1980s that provide appropriate bases for this practice model. Germain and Gitterman's life model (1980) is based on the interaction between individuals and their environments, and suggests that coping skills of individuals and environmental resources can be enhanced to empower clients' process through life transitions. Pincus and Minahan's (1973) framing of the target system as different from the client and change systems supports the idea of choice of intervention across a continuum. Middleman and Goldberg's role quadrant (1974, pp. 15–31), further elaborated upon by Anderson (1981), provides a practice framework for intervention across a continuum of decision points. The view of a social worker as a generalist problem solver is supported by Heus and Pincus (1986).

These theories contribute to the view that problem-solving approaches not only must involve all five client systems (communities, organizations, groups, individuals, and families), but that social workers also must assume a variety of roles with client systems. Reduction of powerlessness must be approached from a variety of roles. Effective problem solvers cannot afford to rely on one role as the means to solution.

Roles are those behaviors through which social workers empower clients. They include conferee, enabler, mediator, broker, advocate, and guardian. Roles are assumed to be appropriate interventive behaviors across the five client systems depending on the chosen points of intervention. Roles can be clustered into four groups. The conferee/enabler role includes consultation with the client system regarding a problem and decisions about strategies for solutions. This role includes education of the client system about resources and information regarding others with similar problems, and enabling support and encouragement of clients to seek out solutions. The mediator role includes facilitating conflict resolution and enabling clients to negotiate solutions to problems. The broker/advocate role includes the brokering and creation of services and advocacy for individual clients or groups of clients toward problem-solving resources. Guardianship is a necessary role social workers assume in the absence of other guardians when a client's level of functioning is so low that competency is destroyed. All of these roles are assumed to be applicable to all five client systems on the intervention continuum.

The breadth of knowledge and skill suggested here may appear too broad for one social worker's expertise. The authors are not proposing a practice model that requires social workers to know everything, but, instead, a narrowing focus to select strategies used within the roles along the continuum of intervention. In this way, this practice model goes beyond the social worker's position as an advanced generalist. The model calls for strategy selection within role taking with the five client systems to be problem solving in nature, and employs a principle of education. Strategies are selected that educate clients and can be shared with clients.

Solomon's (1976) critique of traditional social work roles as not empowering clients adds an important dimension to this model. She argued that work with op-

pressed populations must be educational. Linking clients to resources is not empowering, but education about resource access is. The failure of an individual to learn cognitive, interpersonal, and technical skills in the ordinary course of events increases dramatically the probability that that individual will need professional help. The capacity of individuals, groups, and larger institutions to cope with problems can be increased substantially by providing needed information, knowledge, and skill to both victims and nonvictims of social problems.

A problem-solving framework similar to Compton and Galaway's (1984) problem-solving process is a guiding framework for social workers and provides a basis for deciding how to intervene. Such a framework includes exploration, assessment, goal formulation, planning, implementation, and evaluation. Specific strategies that follow this problem-solving model are selected for intervention. For example, in the conferee/enabler role, the task-centered system of Reid and Epstein (1978) is used to confer with client systems regarding problems. This model is selected because it is problem solving in nature and can be taught to clients. Self-help, mutual aid, education, and skill development groups are significant strategies because they also are educational. In the mediator role, the focus is on educating client systems about alternative means for negotiating and resolving conflicts. In organizational and community intervention, strategies that educate are team-building, conflict resolution, networking, self-help groups, and process organizational development. Role-taking strategies share education as a goal. By teaching problem-solving strategies, social workers empower clients and themselves to cope with social problems and reduce their impact on clients and society.

REFERENCES

Albee, G. (1982). "Preventing Psycho-Pathology and Promoting Human Potential." *American Psychologist, 37,* 1043–1050.

Anderson, J. (1981). *Social Work Methods and Processes.* Belmont, CA: Wadsworth.

Bartlett, H. (1970). *The Common Base of Social Work Practice.* New York: National Association of Social Workers.

Becker, H. S. (1963). *Outsiders: Studies in the Sociology of Deviance.* New York: Free Press.

Bell, D. (1973). *The Coming of a Post-Industrial Society: A Venture in Social Forecasting.* New York: Basic.

Bloom, B. (1979). "Prevention of Mental Disorders: Recent Advances in Theory and Practice." *Community Mental Health Journal, 15,* 179–191.

Compton, B., & Galaway, B. (1984). *Social Work Processes.* Homewood, IL: Dorsey.

Friere, P. (1972). *Pedagogy of the Oppressed.* New York: Herder & Herder.

Germain, C. B., & Gitterman, A. (1980). *The Life Model of Social Work Practice.* New York: Columbia University.

Gordon, W. (1970, April). *Social Work as Boundary Work.* Paper presented at the Third Annual Institute on Services to Families and Children, School of Social Work, University of Iowa, Iowa City.

Heus, M., & Pincus, A. (1986). *The Creative Generalist.* Barneveld, WI: Micamar.

Hernandez, S. H., Jorgensen, J. D., Judd, P., Gould, M., & Parsons, R. J. (1985). "Integrated Practice: Preparing the Social Problem Specialist Through an Advanced Generalist Curriculum." *Journal for Social Work Education, 21,* 28–35.

Ingleby, D. (Ed.). (1980). *Critical Psychiatry.* New York: Pantheon.

Kaplan, A. (1964). *The Conduct of Inquiry: Methodology for Behavioral Science.* San Francisco: Chandler.

Maluccio, A. N. (Ed.). (1981). *Promoting Competence in Clients.* New York: Free Press.

McKnight, J. (1977). Professionalized Service and Disabling Help. In I. Illich, ed., *Disabling Professions* (pp. 69–91). London: M. Boyars.

Middleman, R., & Goldberg, G. (1974). *Social Service Delivery: A Structural Approach to Social Work Practice.* New York: Columbia University.

Naisbitt, J. (1982). *Megatrends.* New York: Warner.

Pincus, A., & Minahan, A. (1973). *Social Work Practice: Model and Method.* Itasca, IL: F. E. Peacock.

Reid, W. (1978). *The Task-Centered System.* New York: Columbia University.

Rubington, E., & Weinburg, M. (1981). *The Study of Social Problems,* 3rd ed. New York: Oxford University Press.

Ryan, W. (1971). *Blaming the Victim.* New York: Random House.

Solomon, B. (1976). *Black Empowerment: Social Work in Oppressed Communities.* New York: Columbia University.

Walz, T., & Hoffman, F. (1982). "The Professional Social Worker and the Year 2000." In D. Saunders, O. Kurren, & J. Fischer, eds., *Fundamentals of Social Work Practice* (pp. 236–245). Belmont, CA: Wadsworth.

11.

Lorraine M. Gutiérrez

WORKING WITH WOMEN OF COLOR: AN EMPOWERMENT PERSPECTIVE

Women of Color—black, Latina, Asian American, and Native American—make up 20 percent of the total female population of the United States (Lin-Fu, 1987). Although the populations encompassed by this umbrella term differ in many respects, they have similarities in status and power. Women of color experience the "double jeopardy" of racism and sexism in U.S. society. They are hampered by average earnings that are lower than those of white women, by overrepresentation in low-status occupations, and by an average low level of education (Gordon-Bradshaw, 1987: Kopasci & Faulkner, 1988; Lin-Fu, 1987). Correspondingly, women of color are underrepresented in positions of power in government, corporations, and nonprofit institutions (Gordon-Bradshaw, 1987; Zambrana, 1987). These facts suggest that if social workers are to work effectively with women of color, they need to address how the powerless position of these women in society contributes to individual client problems.

Powerlessness has direct and concrete effects on the experiences of women of color. Lack of access to many social resources is both a cause and an effect of the powerlessness of this population. The poverty rate of women of color is more than double that of white women: 32.3 percent of all black women and 26.4 percent of all Latinas live below the poverty line (Wilson, 1987). Therefore, women of color are more likely than white women to suffer

from poor or no housing, insufficient food and clothing, and inadequate access to health services (Gordon-Bradshaw, 1987).

Even for women who are not poor, powerlessness contributes to poor mental health outcomes. Women, the poor, and members of ethnic and racial minority groups have much higher rates of mental illness than do men, whites, and the more affluent (Pearlin & Schooler, 1978; Thoits, 1983). Most studies of the connection between membership in these groups and mental health have focused on the stressful life circumstances of these groups and the strain that these circumstances put on their capacity to cope (Pearlin & Schooler, 1978: Silver & Wortman, 1980). However, this link may be analyzed from the perspective of power and the effect that powerlessness has on reducing the ability to exercise personal control, on the development of negative stereotypes of women and minorities, and on gaining necessary social and material resources.

Within existing models of social work practice, especially those focused on the individual, the problems of women of color are couched in individual terms and analyzed in relation to a specific client situation; the role of objective powerlessness often is overlooked. Intervention often focuses on assisting women to cope with or accept a difficult situation rather than on working to change the situation (Gould, 1987a, 1987b; Morell, 1987). A social worker may be aware that a client's problem is rooted in the lack of actual power, but increasing the client's actual power is rarely the goal of an intervention. Social work education is partially responsible for this oversight: methods for increasing the power of individual clients are not taught in most programs.

An empowerment perspective, which assumes that issues of power and powerlessness are integral to the experience of women of color, can address this oversight. It proposes concrete and specific ways in which practice can help resolve the personal problems of women of color by increasing their power on a number of different levels. The author outlines the assumptions of the empowerment perspecitve, the internal processes that it involves, and specific techniques for empowering women of color. Because women of color make up one of the fastest-growing segments of the American population (Lin-Fu, 1987), skills to work with this group will be of increasing importance for social workers.

DEFINING EMPOWERMENT

Empowerment is a process of increasing personal, interpersonal, or political power so that individuals can take action to improve their life situations. Empowerment theory and practice have roots in community organization methods, adult education techniques, feminist theory, and political psychology. Therefore, use of the term empowerment is often vague and can mean different things. Authors on the macro level often define *empowerment* literally and depict it as the process of increasing collective political power (Fagan, 1979; O'Connell, 1978). Conversely, on the micro level, *empowerment* often is described as the development of a personal

feeling of increased power or control without an actual change in structural arrangements (Pernell, 1985; Pinderhughes, 1983; Sherman & Wenocur, 1983; Simmons & Parsons, 1983a, 1983b). A third group of authors has begun to grapple with the interface of these two approaches: how individual empowerment can contribute to group empowerment and how the increase in a group's power can enhance the functioning of its individual members (Bock, 1980; Gould, 1987a, 1987b; Kieffer, 1984; Longres & McLeod, 1980; Morell, 1987; Schechter, Szymanski, & Cahill, 1985).

This article is written from the third perspective on empowerment, which, according to Rappaport (1985),

suggests a sense of control over one's life in personality, cognition, and motivation. It expresses itself at the level of feelings, at the level of ideas about self worth, at the level of being able to make a difference in the world around us. . . . We all have it as a potential. It does not need to be purchased, nor is it a scarce commodity (p. 17).

This definition of empowerment includes combining a sense of personal control with the ability to affect the behavior of others, a focus on enhancing existing strengths in individuals or communities, a goal of establishing equity in the distribution of resources, an ecological (rather than individual) form of analysis for understanding individual and community phenomena, and a belief that power is not a scarce commodity but rather one that can be generated in the process of empowerment (Biegel & Naperste, 1982; Kieffer, 1984; Rappaport, 1981).

Empowerment theory is based on a conflict model that assumes that a society consists of separate groups possessing different levels of power and control over resources (Fay, 1987; Gould, 1987a,

1987b). Social problems stem not from individual deficits, but rather from the failure of the society to meet the needs of all its members. The potential for positive change exists in every person, and many of the negative symptoms of the powerless emerge from their strategies to cope with a hostile world (Pinderhughes, 1983). Although individual clients can be helped to develop less destructive strategies, changes in the social order must occur if these problems ultimately are to be prevented (Rappaport, 1981; Solomon, 1982).

The process of empowerment occurs on the individual, interpersonal, and institutional levels, where the person develops a sense of personal power, an ability to affect others, and an ability to work with others to change social institutions. The literature describes four associated psychological changes that seem crucial for moving individuals from apathy and despair to action:

1. Increasing self-efficacy. Bandura (1982, p. 122) defined *self-efficacy* as a belief in one's ability "to produce and to regulate events in one's life." Although this term was not used in some of the empowerment literature, all authors described a similar phenomenon, using such concepts as strengthening ego functioning, developing a sense of personal power or strength, developing a sense of mastery, developing client initiative, or increasing the client's ability to act (Fagan, 1979; Garvin, 1985; Hirayama & Hirayama, 1985; Mathis & Richan, 1986; Pernell, 1985; Pinderhughes, 1983; Shapiro, 1984; Solomon, 1976).

2. Developing group consciousness. Developing group consciousness involves the development of an awareness of how political structures affect individual and group experiences. The development of group consciousness in a powerless person results in a critical perspective on society that redefines individual, group, or community problems as emerging from a lack of power. The development of group consciousness creates within the individual, or among members of a group or community, a sense of shared fate. This consciousness allows them to focus their energies on the causes of their problems, rather than on changing their internal subjective states (Burghardt, 1982; Friere, 1973; Gould, 1987a, 1987b; Keefe, 1980; Longres & McLeod, 1980; Mathis & Richan, 1986; Solomon, 1976; Van DenBergh & Cooper, 1986).

3. Reducing self-blame. Reduction of self-blame is tied closely to the process of consciousness raising. By attributing their problems to the existing power arrangements in society, clients are freed from feeling responsible for their negative situation. Because self-blame has been associated with feelings of depression and immobilization, this shift in focus allows clients to feel less defective or deficient and more capable of changing their situation (Garvin, 1985; Hirayama & Hirayama, 1985; Janoff-Bulman, 1979; Keefe, 1980; Longres & McLeod, 1980; Pernell, 1985; Solomon, 1976).

4. Assuming personal responsibility for change. The assumption of personal responsibility for change counteracts some of the potentially negative results of reducing self-blame. Clients who do not feel responsible for their problems may not invest their efforts in developing solutions unless they assume some personal responsibility for future change. This process is similar to Friere's notion of becoming a subject, or an active participant, in society rather than remaining a powerless object (Bock, 1980; Friere, 1973). By taking personal responsibility for the resolution of problems, clients are more apt to make an active effort to improve their lives.

Although these changes have been described in a specific order, the empowerment process does not occur in a series of stages. Instead, the changes often occur simultaneously and enhance one another. For example, as individuals develop self-efficacy, they may be more likely to assume personal responsibility for change. Researchers who have studied the process also suggest that one does not necessarily "achieve empowerment" but rather that it is a continual process of growth and change that can occur throughout the life cycle (Friere, 1973; Kieffer, 1984). Rather than a specific state, it is a way of interacting with the world.

EMPOWERING TECHNIQUES

As stated above, social work practitioners may be aware of how a lack of power affects clients, but they may lack knowledge of how individuals can gain power, especially in the context of individual practice. When social workers attempt to help women of color who may be overwhelmed by their particular situation, this lack of knowledge can lead to frustration and can disempower the social worker. Fortunately, the literature suggests specific techniques and forms of intervention that can lead to empowerment.

The Helping Relationship

The basis of empowering practice is a helping relationship based on collaboration, trust, and the sharing of power. To avoid replicating the powerlessness that the client experiences with other helpers or professionals, it is critical that the worker perceive himself or herself as an enabler, an organizer, a consultant, or a compatriot with the client. The interaction between worker and client should be characterized by genuineness, mutual respect, open communication, and informality. It presumes that the worker does not hold the answers to the client's problems, but rather that in the context of collaboration, the client will develop the insights, skills, and capacity to resolve the situation (Bock, 1980; Fagan, 1979; Keefe, 1980; Pinderhughes, 1983; Schecter et al., 1985; Solomon, 1976).

Along the same lines, the worker also can facilitate empowerment by helping the client to experience a sense of personal power within the helping relationship. This technique is based on the assumption that from the experience of power within the intervention the client can generalize to feelings of power in the larger social environment. Workers can facilitate this experience by having clients role play and practice powerful behaviors, by engaging clients in roles in which they help others, and by having clients take control of the helping relationship by setting the agenda, sharing the leadership of groups or meetings, and researching resources (Pernell, 1985; Pinderhughes, 1983; Schechter et al., 1985; Shapiro, 1984; Simmons & Parsons, 1983a, 1983b).

Actively involving the clients in the process of change is another aspect of the helping relationship that encourages empowerment. According to Solomon (1976), empowerment is a

> process whereby the social worker engages in a set of activities with the client or client system that aim to reduce the powerlessness that has been created by the negative valuations based on membership in a stigmatized group (p. 19).

Like other authors, Solomon describes empowering interventions as those that are focused on activities ranging from the exploration of a problem to the development of alternative structures in a community (Beck, 1983; Checkoway & Norsman, 1986; Fagan, 1979; Garvin, 1985; Hirayama & Hirayama, 1985; Mathis & Richan, 1986; Pinderhughes, 1983; Solomon, 1976). What is common to this range of activities is praxis, the blending of reflection and action. Because clients are actively involved in change, they also are reflecting on and analyzing their experience, and the results of their analyses are then integrated into the development of future efforts (Bock, 1980; Burghardt, 1982; Friere, 1973; Keefe, 1980; Longres & McLeod, 1980; Resnick, 1976; Rose & Black, 1985).

Suggested Modalities

The literature on empowerment suggests interventions on the individual, group, family, and community levels. Practitioners are advised to develop intervention skills on all these levels and to feel comfortable moving from one modality to another. However, small-group work is presented as the ideal modality for empowering interventions, because it is an effective means for integrating the other techniques. It can be the perfect environment for raising consciousness, engaging in mutual aid, developing skills, and solving problems and an ideal way for clients to experience individual effectiveness in influencing others (Coppola & Rivas, 1985; Garvin, 1985; Hirayama & Hirayama, 1985; Pernell, 1985; Sarri & du Rivage, 1985). The emphasis on small-group work holds true in the literature across all levels of intervention, whether the goal is empowering individuals or changing institutions.

In the same spirit, the literature recommends involvement of clients in mutual aid, self-help, or support groups. In the context of empowerment, mutual aid, self-help, and support groups are formed by people experiencing similar problems, who then focus on providing emotional and concrete support (Garvin, 1985; Sherman & Wenocur, 1983). The groups facilitate empowerment by creating a basis of social support through the change process, a format for providing concrete assistance, an opportunity to learn new skills through role playing and observing others, and a potential power base for future action (Hirayama & Hirayama, 1985; Keefe, 1980; Pinderhughes, 1983; Solomon, 1982). They also can provide the context for developing group consciousness, by involving clients in dialogue with others who share their problems.

Techniques

Within the context of a collaborative helping relationship and a small-group work modality, the specific techniques described below have been suggested for empowering clients.

Accepting the Client's Definition of the Problem. Accepting the client's definition of the problem is an important element of an empowering intervention. By accepting the client's definition, the worker is communicating that the client is capable of identifying and understanding the situation. This technique also places the client in a position of power and control over the helping relationship, and it does not preclude bringing up new issues for exploration, such as the connection between personal and community problems (Beck, 1983; Fagan, 1979; Garvin, 1985; Shapiro, 1984).

Identifying and Building upon Existing Strengths. By identifying and building upon existing strengths, the empowering practitioner gets in touch with the client's current level of functioning and current sources of functioning and current sources of individual or interpersonal power (Mathis & Richan, 1986; Pinderhughes, 1983; Shapiro, 1984; Sherman & Wenocur, 1983; Solomon, 1976). This technique is most effective if the worker can recognize that the client has been involved in a process of struggle against oppressive structures and that this struggle has required considerable strength. By analyzing elements of the struggle, client strengths can be more easily identified, communicated to the client, and then used as a basis for future work.

Engaging in a Power Analysis of the Client's Situation. Engaging in a power analysis of the client's situation is a critical technique for empowering practice. It first involves analyzing how conditions of powerlessness are affecting the client's situation. A second crucial step is to identify sources of potential power in the client's situation. An indirect technique is dialogue between the worker and the client that is aimed at exploring and identifying the social structural origins of the client's current situation (Keefe, 1980; Longres & McLeod, 1980; Resnick, 1976; Solomon, 1976). Another, more direct, technique involves focusing the client's analysis on a specific situation—either the client's own situation or a vignette developed for the intervention (Bock, 1980; Pinderhughes, 1983; Schechter et al., 1985; Solomon, 1976). Clients and workers should be encouraged to think creatively about sources of potential power, such as forgotten skills, personal qualities that could increase social influence, members of past social support networks, and organizations in their communities.

An effective power analysis requires that social workers fully comprehend the connection between the immediate situation and the distribution of power in society as a whole (Garvin, 1985; Keefe, 1980; Mathis & Richan, 1986; Pernell 1985). The process may require consciousness-raising exercises to look beyond the specific situation to problems shared by other clients in similar situations. Also, it is crucial that workers not adopt feelings of powerlessness from clients, but rather that they learn to see the potential for power and influence in every situation.

Teaching Specific Skills. Teaching specific skills is one means of helping the client to develop the resources to be more powerful (Mathis & Richan, 1986; Pernell, 1985; Shapiro, 1984). The skill areas most often identified in working with women of color include problem solving; skills for community or organizational change; "life skills," such as parenting, job seeking, and self-defense; and interpersonal skills, such as assertiveness, social competency, and self-advocacy (Checkoway & Norsman, 1986; Fagan, 1979; Garvin, 1985; Hirayama & Hirayama, 1985; Keefe, 1980; Schechter et al., 1985; Sherman & Wenocur, 1983; Simmons & Parsons 1983a, 1983b; Solomon, 1976). When teaching these skills the worker should adopt the role of a consultant or facilitator rather than an instructor, so as not to replicate the power relationships that the worker and client are attempting to overcome (Schechter et al., 1985; Sherman & Wenocur, 1983; Solomon, 1976).

Mobilizing Resources and Advocating for Clients. Mobilizing resources and advocating for clients also are useful strategies if the worker and the client together lack adequate resources for empowerment. Mobilizing involves the worker in gathering concrete resources or information for clients, as well as in advocating on their behalf when necessary. Although some have argued that advocacy can be in conflict with the goal of empowerment because it can reinforce feelings of powerlessness (Rappaport, 1981; Solomon, 1976), it may be carried out in a collaborative way that includes the client and that involves learning new skills. Through advocacy and resource mobilization, the worker and client together ensure that the larger social structure provides what is necessary to empower the larger client group (Checkoway & Norsman, 1986; Mathis & Richan, 1986; Pinderhughes, 1983; Sherman & Wenocur, 1983; Solomon, 1982).

CONCLUSION

The techniques described above form the basis for empowering practice with women of color on the personal, interpersonal, or political level. For social workers to have an impact on conditions of powerlessness, they need to rethink both the mode and the focus of practice. These techniques would require practitioners to move beyond work with individual clients and problems, to thinking of ways to engage women of color in group efforts toward both individual and community change.

If empowering practice is to be effective, it calls for some changes in the current structure and content of social work practice and education (Gould, 1987a; Hasenfeld, 1987; Morell, 1987). Social workers must pay attention to the effects of powerlessness and oppression on clients' lives and to techniques for overcoming them. Social workers also need to develop skills in the area of small-group work and community practice if they are to work in empowering ways, and the organizations that

employ them must support their efforts to engage themselves in the social contexts of their clients and to move among levels of intervention. These changes, and others, are critical for the implementation of empowering practice.

Working with women of color can be challenging and gratifying. The literature on empowerment suggests specific ways in which social workers can move individual women from feelings of hopelessness and apathy to active change. When these techniques are applied effectively, they can contribute to the empowerment of individual women and to their involvement in solving the problems of all women of color.

REFERENCES

Bandura, A. (1982). "Self-Efficacy Mechanism in Human Agency." *American Psychologist, 37,* 122–147.

Beck, B. (1983). *Empowerment: A Future Goal of Social Work.* New York: CSS Working Papers in Social Policy.

Biegel, D., & Naperste, A. (1982). "The Neighborhood and Family Services Project: An Empowerment Model Linking Clergy, Agency, Professionals and Community Residents." In A. Jeger & R. Slotnick, eds., *Community Mental Health and Behavioral Ecology* (pp. 303–318). New York: Plenum.

Bock, S. (1980). "Conscientization: Paolo Friere and Class-Based Practice." *Catalyst, 2,* 5–25.

Burghardt, S. (1982). *The Other Side of Organizing.* Cambridge, MA: Schenkman.

Checkoway, B., & Norsman, A. (1986). "Empowering Citizens with Disabilities." *Community Development Journal, 21,* 270–277.

Coppola, M., & Rivas, R. (1985). "The Task-Action Group Technique: A Case Study of Empowering the Elderly." In M. Parenes, ed., *Innovations in Social Group Work: Feedback from Practice to Theory* (pp. 133–147). New York: Haworth.

Fagan, H. (1979). *Empowerment: Skills for Parish Social Action.* New York: Paulist Press.

Fay, B. (1987). *Critical Social Science.* Ithaca, NY: Cornell University Press.

Friere, P. (1973), *Education for Critical Consciousness.* New York: Seabury.

Garvin, C. (1985). "Work with Disadvantaged and Oppressed Groups." In M. Sundel, P. Glasser, R. Sarri, & R. Vinter, eds., *Individual Change Through Small Groups*, 2nd ed. (pp. 461–472). New York: The Free Press.

Gordon-Bradshaw, R. (1987). "A Social Essay on Special Issues Facing Poor Women of Color." *Women and Health, 12,* 243–259.

Gould, K. (1987a). "Feminist Principles and Minority Concerns: Contributions, Problems, and Solutions." *Affilia: Journal of Women and Social Work, 3,* 6–19.

Gould, K. (1987b). "Life Model vs. Conflict Model: A Feminist Perspective." *Social Work, 32,* 246–351.

Hasenfeld, Y. (1987). "Power in Social Work Practice." *Social Service Review, 61,* 469–483.

Hirayama, H., & Hirayama, K. (1985). "Empowerment Through Group Participation: Process and Goal." In M. Parenes, ed., *Innovations in Social Group Work: Feedback from Practice to Theory* (pp. 119–131). New York: Haworth.

Janoff-Bulman, R. (1979). "Characterological Versus Behavioral Self-Blame: Inquiries into Depression and Rape." *Journal of Personality and Social Psychology, 37,* 1798–1810.

Keefe, T. (1980). "Empathy Skill and Critical Consciousness." *Social Casework, 61,* 387–393.

Kieffer, C. (1984). "Citizen Empowerment: A Developmental Perspective." In J. Rappaport, C. Swift, & R. Hess, eds., *Studies in Empowerment: Toward Understanding and Action* (pp. 9–36). New York: Haworth.

Kopasci, R., & Faulkner, A. (1988). "The Powers that Might Be: The Unity of White and Black Feminists." *Affilia: Journal of Women and Social Work, 3,* 33–50.

Lin-Fu, J. (1987). "Special Health Concerns of Ethnic Minority Women." *Public Health Reports, 102,* 12–14.

Longres, J., & McLeod, E. (1980). "Consciousness Raising and Social Work Practice." *Social Casework, 61,* 227–267.

Mathis, T., & Richan, D. (1986, March). *Empowerment: Practice in Search of a Theory.* Paper presented at the Annual Program Meeting of the Council on Social Work Education, Miami, FL.

Morell, C. (1987). "Cause Is Function: Toward a Feminist Model of Integration for Social Work." *Social Service Review, 61,* 144–155.

O'Connell, B. (1978). "From Service Delivery to Advocacy to Empowerment." *Social Casework, 59.* 195–202.

Pearlin, L., & Schooler, C. (1978). "The Structure of Coping." *Journal of Health and Social Behavior, 19,* 2–21.

Pernell, R. (1985). "Empowerment and Social Group Work." In M. Parenes, ed., *Innovations in Social Group Work: Feedback from Practice to Theory* (pp. 107–117). New York: Haworth.

Pinderhughes, E. (1983) "Empowerment for Our Clients and for Ourselves." *Social Casework, 64,* 331–338.

Rappaport, J. (1982). "In Praise of Paradox: A Social Policy of Empowerment Over Prevention." *American Journal of Community Psychology, 9,* 1–25.

Rappaport, J. (1985). "The Power of Empowerment Language." *Social Policy, 17*(2), 15–21.

Resnick, R. (1976). "Conscientization: An Indigenous Approach to International Social Work." *International Social Work, 19,* 21–29.

Rose, S., & Black, B. (1985) *Advocacy and Empowerment: Mental Health Care in the Community.* Boston: Routledge & Kegan Paul.

Sarri, R., & du Rivage, V. (1985). *Strategies for Self Help and Empowerment of Working Low-Income Women Who Are Heads of Families.* Unpublished manuscript, University of Michigan, School of Social Work, Ann Arbor.

Schechter, S., Szymanski, S., & Cahill, M. (1985). *Violence Against Women: A Curriculum for Empowerment* (facilitator's manual). New York: Women's Education Institute.

Shapiro, J. (1984). "Commitment to Disenfranchised Clients." In A. Rosenblatt & D. Waldfogel, eds., *Handbook of Clinical Social Work* (pp. 888–903). San Francisco: Jossey-Bass.

Sherman, W., & Wenocur, S. (1983). "Empowering Public Welfare Workers Through Mutual Support." *Social Work, 28,* 375–379.

Silver, R., & Wortman, C. (1980). "Coping with Undesirable Life Events." In J. Garber & M. Seligman, eds., *Human Helplessness: Theory and Application* (pp. 279–375). New York: Academic Press.

Simmons, C., & Parsons, R. (1983a). "Developing Internality and Perceived Competence: The Empowerment of Adolescent Girls." *Adolescence*, 18, 917–922.

Simmons, C., & Parsons, R. (1983b). "Empowerment for Role Alternatives in Adolescence." *Adolescence*, 18, 193–200.

Solomon, B. (1976) *Black Empowerment*. New York: Columbia University Press.

Solomon, B. (1982). "Empowering Women: A Matter of Values." In A. Weick, & S. Vandiver, eds., *Women, Power, and Change* (pp. 206–214). Silver Spring, MD: National Association of Social Workers.

Thoits, P. (1983). "Dimensions of Life Events that Influence Psychological Distress: An Evaluation and Synthesis of the Literature." In H. Kaplan, ed. *Psychosocial Stress: Trends in Theory and Research*. New York: Academic Press.

Van DenBergh, N., & Cooper, L., Eds. (1986). *Feminist Visions for Social Work*. Silver Spring, MD: National Association of Social Workers.

Wilson, J. (1987). "Women and Poverty: A Demographic Overview." *Women and Health*, 12, 21-40.

Zambrana, R. (1987). "A Research Agenda on Issues Affecting Poor and Minority Women: A Model for Understanding Their Health Needs." *Women and Health*, 12, 137–160.

12.

Howard J. Doueck and Michael J. Austin

IMPROVING AGENCY FUNCTIONING THROUGH STAFF DEVELOPMENT

INTRODUCTION

In an era of accountability and limited resources, it becomes important for human service agencies to have ongoing assessments of their staff functioning. There are numerous indicators that an agency can use for such an assessment. Patti (1983) describes four criteria for gauging performance in organizations: productivity or output, efficiency, quality of services, and service effectiveness. One could also add client satisfaction, worker satisfaction, resource acquisition, or organizational growth to name a few others. Since some of these criteria have different meanings depending on your role in an agency, a problem can arise when staff and management are gauging their agency's performance.

For example, in the field of child protective services, workers gauge their performance by whether they have been effective in limiting the risk of abuse to the child. They worry about the quality of service that their clients are receiving and whether they will be able to provide the unique array of services required to meet a family's need. A successful case outcome might be to lessen the risk of abuse to a single child. Managers, on the other hand, are not only concerned about worker effectiveness, but also are concerned about how productive and efficient their workers have been. They are interested in aggregate case data for all families and children seen in the system. Productivity is measured by the amount of case movement and effective service is sometimes interpreted as efficient service. The result is increased tension between management and staff caused by their somewhat different views of what constitutes effective service and successful client outcomes. While staff development personnel have been concerned about organizational functioning in the past (Lauffer, 1978; Lippit, 1979), they tended to distinguish staff development roles that focus on improving organizations from those roles that focus on enhancing the capacities of staff (Lauffer, 1978). We believe that the agency's staff development personnel are capable of doing both, improving individual worker skills and knowledge as well as improving agency functioning simultaneously, and that there needs to be a blending of roles if this is to take place effectively.

The work of staff development personnel has been defined many different ways. One definition distinguishes between training, which involves enhancing the job skills and knowledge-base needed to perform agency-related tasks, and development, which seeks to promote professional growth and career enhancement. A second definition distinguishes between in-house staff development and courses or educational programs offered by a college or university known as continuing education. A third definition of staff development encompasses all the scheduled work activities planned to enhance a worker's ability to do their job, e.g., peer review, case conferences, guest speakers at staff meetings, and supervisory conferences. All of these definitions reflect the common goals of empowering staff to implement agency policies and/or to expand their own capacities.

In accordance with our belief about the dual purpose of staff development, we pro-pose an alternate definition which addresses both staff training and organizational functioning. In our definition, staff development includes those activities related to planning and/or providing training to enhance staff functioning as well as to improving the decision-making/problem-solving processes of management in order to enhance agency functioning by bridging the gap between managements' and staffs' perceptions of organizational performance.

We begin by exploring a framework for viewing staff development practice within a human services agency. Using examples from child protective services throughout our analysis, we explore four roles for staff development personnel that we believe are fundamental for effective organizational intervention. These four roles are policy analyst, interpreter, organizational change facilitator, and staff advocate. These roles relate to improving management decision making, enhancing organizational communications, facilitating work group cohesiveness, and improving organizational problem solving. We distinguish these roles from others that are more closely related to staff enhancement, namely assessor of training needs, planner of staff development activities, adult educator/teacher, and researcher/evaluator. We conclude the paper by discussing the balancing of the staff enhancement and the organizational functioning roles.

A FRAMEWORK FOR ANALYSIS

The focus on the needs of workers and the needs of administrators requires a different framework for promoting dialogue and understanding within the organization. If staff development personnel are to play a significant role in bridging the gap between the workers' perspective and the administrators' perspective, then a systems view of the agency is needed and new roles need to be developed.

A systems view is critical for another reason. Since each level of an organization speaks its own unique language (Austin, 1979), part of a proactive approach is for staff development personnel to understand those languages and to be multi-lingual. For example, executive level management speak the language of resource allocation, budgets, and strategic planning. Program level management, on the other hand, talk about staff efficiency and productivity, while supervisory management discuss the day-to-day concerns of unit level operations. Line staff talk the language of counseling and direct service provider, including client self-determination, behavioral contracting, and individualized service plans. Finally, trainers speak of adult education, learning goals and behavioral objectives. The differences in language are, in part, a consequence of the responsibilities and location that each staff occupies within the organization. Figure 12.1 provides a preliminary framework for viewing an agency from a systems perspective.

At the top of Figure 12.1, executive level management reflects a primary concern with interpreting social policy mandates and specifying the agency's philosophy and its goals. Of necessity, much of their focus is external to the agency in an effort to understand and influence the agency's environment upon which it depends for resources (Hasenfeld, 1983).

Program level management are responsible for transforming the agency's general goals into specific program policies and procedures. As can be seen in Figure 12.1, the input they receive during their efforts is generally from other managers, i.e., executive level and supervisory, and not directly

from staff. Program level managers are also responsible for identifying the program conditions that staff work under, including staffing patterns and workload assignments.

Supervisors are responsible for linking the day-to-day operations of front-line staff with the program procedures and expectations of management. As middle managers, they have the potential for significant impact on the decision-making and problem-solving processes of their agency. However, they frequently experience "the middle management bind," caught between the demands of administration for accountability and the desires of staff for more autonomy (Austin, 1981). For example, in protective services, supervisors may be accountable to the community regarding concerns about an intervention with a particular family, while at the same time need to allow their staff the independence necessary to deal with highly emotional and volatile family situations.

Staff are responsible for the actual delivery of service to clients. They interface with other professionals within the community as well as with other individuals in the client's environment, e.g., friends, family, relatives, neighbors, and are constrained by the limits of their own capacities as well as the current level of technology (skills, research, and knowledge) available to them. Their major link to the decision-making processes of upper level management is through their supervisor who is expected to be supportive of their desires and to protect them from what they perceive as the unreasonable demands of administration (Crowell, 1982).

While the roles and functions of supervisors and program managers overlap, each group tends to have its own, somewhat limited, perspective of the agency's functioning that is based upon their position

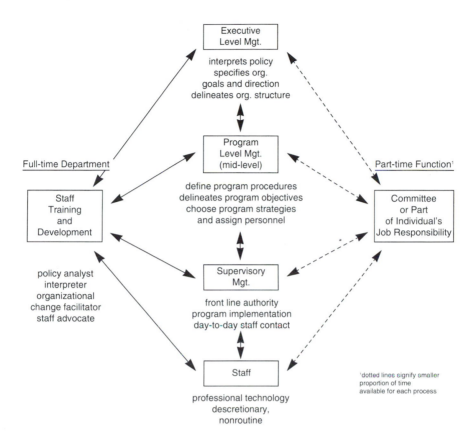

FIGURE 12.1
A Systems Framework for Staff Development in Human Services Agencies

within its hierarchy. Most managers interact primarily with other managers, while most staff relate exclusively with other staff or front line supervisors. In contrast, staff development personnel need to interact with all levels in the organization in order to carry out their responsibilities and to link the social policy expectations of management with the intervention technology utilized by staff. As a result, staff development personnel are in a position to bridge the gaps between the multiple perspectives of how well the agency is performing.

Staff development within an agency can be a full-time or part-time job responsibility. It can also be carried out through the use of a committee of staff members representing all levels of the organization. The amount of time devoted to staff development activities, the resources available, and the interest of top management will vary. Regardless of how many staff members are involved, an overall agency systems perspective is needed in order to manage an agency's staff development program (Austin, Brannon, & Pecora, 1984).

NEW ROLES FOR STAFF DEVELOPMENT PERSONNEL

Based upon the different levels of responsibility for promoting organizational effectiveness noted in the framework, it is now possible to identify specific staff development roles which relate to agency functioning. We view these roles within the context of analytic and interactional functions on a continuum as noted below. On the analytic side, we include the policy analyst and the interpreter roles. On the interactional side is the staff advocate and the organizational change facilitator roles. The use of the continuum is to show that the roles are not mutually exclusive and that they tend to overlap.

```
            policy        organizational
            analyst       change facilitator
analytic ─────────────────────────────── interactional
            interpreter   staff advocate
```

These new roles allow staff development personnel the flexibility to perform the following task sequences:

1. to identify changes in focus, philosophy, strategy, or perceptions of policy planners and/or upper level management;
2. to assess new environmental demands on the agency which impact the knowledge and skills needed by staff for effective service provision;
3. to analyze inter-agency structures, formal, or informal relations which enhance or impede effective service provision;
4. to strengthen those structures and linkages which will enhance effective service provision; and
5. to institute a systematic problem solving process which includes assessment, planning, implementation, evaluation, and feedback to allow for a process of ongoing agency change.

Analytic Functions

Policy Analyst—Enhancing Management's Decision Making. Training serves as a crucial link in the social policy formulation and implementation chain. Changes in policy have an impact on the way workers perceive their job and how they interact with clients on a day-to-day basis. In the policy analyst role, staff development personnel can help management analyze the unstated assumptions, values, and intentions of social policy changes as well as their impact on both workers and agency training efforts. To do this, the staff developer needs to be familiar with the language of social policy, understand its training implications, and be able to interpret these implications to others.

For example, in 1974, Congress passed the Child Abuse Prevention and Treatment Act which required states which were receiving federal funds to implement a reporting law, to investigate reports of suspected abuse or neglect, and to have procedures to deal with the problem of abuse or neglect. In essence, a state agency that provided services to victims of abuse or neglect and their families might need to change its goals, focus, and philosophy to be in compliance with the above Act. The agency would need to set up procedures for investigating and documenting incidents of abuse and neglect. Workers would also be expected to investigate referrals as well as to substantiate the report's accuracy. The staff development implications of major policy changes included the need to train staff in assessing the indicators of abuse and neglect, expanding staff's investigation skills, enhancing their capacity to work with angry/hostile clients, and increasing their knowledge of parents' rights. These new directions might require changes in the staff's own concept of professional practice. Supervisors would need to develop new procedures to monitor new staff functions. In the role of policy analyst, the staff developer could help management interpret the impact of a social policy on organization performance, and design a plan to minimize the disruption for clients and staff that might be caused by the changes.

Interpreter—Enhancing Organizational Communication. As interpreters of organizational communications, staff development personnel are in a position to facilitate understanding between management and staff by serving as third party mediators between the two groups. To do this effectively, they need to be able to understand the language of both direct service practitioners and managers, to interpret what is being said, and to translate for both parties. Analysis skills are needed to identify the unstated assumptions and values that are being expressed and to find commonalities that can serve as a foundation for planning. In part, staff development personnel need to have negotiation skills, skills in establishing trust between themselves and others in the hierarchy, and the ability to design processes to facilitate communication flow.

The interpreter role can be identified within the context of a training session where information about the agency is freely exchanged. During a training session, child protective services workers might inform the trainer that, due to the high volume of intakes, they are only able to do one home visit for each case situation. They consider this a disaster, since last year they were able to conduct at least two home visits per case. They feel that clients are receiving inadequate services to address the seriousness of their situations. Staff are concerned that the agency is unable to meet its goals of adequate investigation and service provision to children and families at risk.

Analysis of this communication might lead to the following scenario. Staff

development personnel could interpret the communication and ask management representatives to participate in training sessions in order to deal with such issues as "staff performance," "organizational effectiveness," "productivity," "agency structure," and "goal attainment." The training session might then be used to formulate recommendations for procedural changes designed to restructure the intake function so that more families get referred to other appropriate resources prior to investigations being implemented. If such recommendations appear to be unrealistic, staff and administration could be assisted in designing goals and objectives that would be more congruent with staff capabilities. In essence, staff development serves as a critical link in the communication chain, as a mediator between staff and management, and as a facilitator of communications within the agency.

Interactional Functions

We have explored the two analytic roles of policy analyst and interpreter. Now we turn to the two interactional roles of organizational change facilitator and staff advocate.

Organizational Change Facilitator— Enhancing Work Group Cohesion. The changes that occur in an organization's environment can have a major impact on its functioning (Hasenfeld, 1983). These changes, which cause disruption in the day-to-day operations of both managers and staff, can have a negative impact on client outcomes if they are not anticipated and handled properly. It is not surprising, therefore, that staff can be resistant to change. The use of planned change techniques can help minimize, if not eliminate, some of the major negative consequences of organizational change (French, Bell, & Zawacki, 1983).

Human services agencies are constantly changing and staff development personnel are in a good position to serve as change facilitators in their organizations. To begin with, the basic beliefs of staff developers coincide with the philosophies that underlie organization development. Organization developers believe in humanism, democracy (Freidlander & Brown, 1983), and the ability of individuals to be masters of their own fate (French, Bell, & Zawacki, 1983). These same values are espoused by the adult education literature which serves as a foundation for staff development. Organization development goals include improving organizational effectiveness, enhancing communications within organizations, and improving management decision-making process (DeSanctis & Courtney, 1983). These are quite consistent with the goals of training and development (Fine, 1980).

The structure of the organization generally lends itself to utilizing staff development personnel as organizational change facilitators. Staff development personnel generally do not have line authority which may be an important attribute when working on team issues with managers and staff. They also tend to provide continuity, [tend] to have detailed knowledge of what is going on in the organization, and can make interventions that might be seen as more credible as it is based upon this knowledge (Blake & Mouton, 1983). In the role of organizational change facilitator, staff develop personnel need to have the support and participation of both management and staff.

There are several issues faced by human services organizations that might benefit from planned change. Agency goals are sometimes very vague, not well understood, and frequently contradictory. Staff development personnel can work with staff and management in the ongoing planning process to articulate the differences that exist in expecta-

tions, identify specific goals attainment. Similarly, when an organization undergoes structural changes, e.g., decentralization, perhaps causing problems with authority, decision making, and communications, staff development personnel can help staff and management identify problems and can assist in facilitating the design of plans to address these problems. In short, the change facilitator role is based on a long-term process of enhancing managerial decision making and improving organization effectiveness, and ultimately, enhancing work group cohesion.

Staff Advocate—Enhancing Organizational Problem Solving. Line staff in agencies tend to view themselves as having little power within the organization's structure. As a result, they sometimes feel disenfranchised, overburdened by an unresponsive administrative structure, or alienated from the agency's mission. These symptoms, if allowed to persist, can lead to excessive job stress, low morale, and high staff turnover. Efforts have been made recently to empower staff to effect change within the organization (Resnick & Patti, 1980). Staff development personnel are in an excellent position to facilitate this process by modeling a proactive stance of staff advocacy. This includes working with staff to identify organization constraints to effective service delivery, to decide on possible alternatives to address these constraints, and to share this information with management to aid in problem solving. For example, if CPS staff are feeling excessive stress due to high caseloads and an inability to follow families through to termination, this stress will come out during training sessions. Along with staff, staff development personnel might identify a need to restructure the CPS job function, e.g., have one worker doing intakes/investigation while other workers provide ongoing services instead of everyone doing everything. The staff developer could advocate for position or job rotation in order to give staff a chance to follow some cases through to conclusion and to provide them with a broader perspective of the agency. During the process of advocacy, staff input into the problem-solving process not only helps management gain additional information about the functioning of the agency, but it also serves to improve staff morale regardless of whether or not their suggestions are adopted (Resnick & Patti, 1980).

STAFF DEVELOPMENT—A BLENDED APPROACH

We have explored the four highly interrelated roles of functioning: policy analyst, interpreter, organizational change facilitator, and staff advocate. These roles are really part of a management "mind set" (Austin, Brannon, & Pecora, 1984; Lauffer, 1978) needed by staff development personnel to maximize agency functioning and to meet the needs of staff throughout the agency. We began by stating that there needed to be a blend between the staff enhancement approach to staff development (providing training in skills and knowledge) and the managerial approach to staff development which seems to have a greater impact on the organization's functioning. How can these roles be integrated?

The skills needed to accomplish each of the four managerial roles described in this paper are similar to the staff enhancement roles noted in the introduction. Briefly, the training needs assessment role involves working with individuals and groups, gathering and analyzing data, and assessing the meaning and impact of this information on the training program as well as the agency. This staff enhancement role is similar to the organizational functioning role of policy analyst.

Second, the adult educator/teacher role encompasses the same skills as the interpreter role, namely the ability to hear, understand, translate, and interpret information from one individual or group to another individual or group. Third, we have seen the similarities between organization development (the basic foundation for the organizational change facilitator role) and staff development in general. The staff development planner role can be viewed as counterpart to the change facilitator role. Finally, the researcher/evaluator role encompasses similar skills as the staff advocate role, helping management look at options and assessing their feasibility and success potential. Clearly, the skills needed to perform the agency functioning roles need to be balanced with the roles of staff enhancement.

If resources for a staff development committee or a staff development unit are limited, it is important to start small and informal with one or two of the roles. A part-time staff development person or committee might stick with the policy analyst or interpreter roles in the beginning in order to assess current policies or issues for their staff development implications.

Some of the potential challenges to the blended approach are that staff development might be perceived as a handmaiden of management, an advocate of unpopular changes, or as usurping the prerogatives of staff. With each challenge, however, is the chance to mediate between the varous groups in the organization and to have the opportunity to assist the organization in fulfilling its mission and accomplishing its goals.

The blended approach seeks to assure workers that their concerns and dilemmas will be shared with other levels of the agency's hierarchy. While changes might not always be forthcoming, at least the worker will have a sense that they have had some input into the problem-solving and decision-making processes of the organization. It can be seen as a process of staff suggesting directions for possible change and management designing procedures to accomplish these changes. Further, managers are assisted in communicating their philosophy, policies, and procedures for organizational functioning and in facilitating planned organizational change that minimizes agency disruption.

This paper has left several questions unanswered concerning the efficacy of the balanced approach. For example, what would it take for top management to adopt the balanced approach to staff development? Would the balanced approach reduce turnover costs and promote higher staff morale? What is the best approach to evaluate staff development's role in improving communications and problem solving within the agency? And, finally, how can we determine if the balanced approach to staff development contributes in any way to the improvement of services received by clients? Answers to these questions can be sought through the application of the following staff development principles for improving agency effectiveness: (1) social policies at the federal, state, and local levels have training implications for both management and line staff which must be identified before policies are implemented; (2) the agency's response to increased demand for services have staff training implications which need to be identified in conjunction with identifying new and creative organization and workload processes; and (3) irrespective of external forces impacting an agency, all of its members possess differences of opinion, work styles, and values which require new learning and the continuous attention of staff development personnel. From this perspective, staff development activities may prove to be an essential ingredient of agency survival in the decades ahead. A balanced approach to carrying out staff development roles may prove to be the agency challenge of the 1990s.

REFERENCES

Austin, M. J. "Designing Human Services Training Based on Worker Task Analysis." In F. W. Clark et al., eds., *The Pursuit of Competence in Social Work.* San Francisco: Jossey-Bass, 1979

Austin, M. J. *Supervisory Management in the Human Services.* Englewood Cliffs, NJ: Prentice-Hall, Inc., 1981.

Austin, M. J. et al. *Managing Staff Development Programs in Human Service Agencies.* Chicago: Nelson-Hall, 1984.

Blake, R. R., & Mouton, J. S. *Consultation: A Handbook for Individual and Organizational Development.* 2nd ed. Reading, MA: Addison-Wesley, 1983.

Crowell, J. "Understanding Clinical Staff's View of Administration." In M. J. Austin & W. E. Hershey, eds., *Handbook on Mental Health Administration.* San Francisco: Jossey-Bass, 1982.

DeSanctis, G., & Courtney, J. F. "Toward Friendly User Misimplementation." *Communications of the A C M,* 1983, *26,* 732–738.

Fine, J. *Planning and Assessing Agency Training.* Washington, DC: U.S. Government Printing Office, 1980.

French, W. L., et al., eds. *Organization Development: Theory, Practice, and Research.* Rev. ed., Plano, TX: Business Publications, 1983.

Friedlander, F., & Brown. L. D. "Organization Development." In W. L. French et al., eds., *Organization Development: Theory, Practice, and Research.* Plano, TX: Business Publications, 1983.

Hasenfeld, Y. *Human Service Organizations.* Englewood Cliffs, NJ: Prentice-Hall, Inc., 1983.

Lauffer, A. *Doing Continuing Education and Staff Development.* New York: McGraw-Hill, 1978.

Lippitt, G. L. "The Trainer's Role as an Internal Consultant." In C. R. Bell & L. Nadler, *The Client-Consultant Handbook.* Houston: Gulf Publishing, 1979.

Patti, R. J. *Social Welfare Administration: Managing Social Programs in a Developmental Context.* Englewood Cliffs, NJ: Prentice-Hall, Inc., 1983.

Resnick, H., & Patti, R. J., eds., *Changing from Within: Humanizing Social Welfare Organizations.* Philadelphia: Temple University Press, 1980.

PART TWO
STRATEGIES

Introduction

In the black winter of 1909
When we froze and bled on the picket line
We showed the world that women could fight
And we rose and won with women's might.
— From the poem, "The Uprising of the 20,000,"
honoring the waistmakers' strike of 1909

Whether we are moving face first or the other end first toward the twenty-first century is a matter of some contention. Indeed, in trying to confront the critical problems of our era we might be well advised to keep in mind the admonition of Pogo (and his cartoonist Walt Kelly): "We have met the enemy and he is us." The unfortunate (and sometimes very counterproductive) tendency to either promise much more than we can deliver or attempt to avoid all major controversial issues is still very much a part of macro-level social work. One important reason for this is that our idealism (and often our ideology) goes far beyond our change technology. If we are to join the struggles by which we are confronted in any significant way, the question of strategy must not be neglected.

A fundamental problem for nations, for organizations, and for individuals is that of getting from where they are now to where they would like to go. The action-idea or process-idea by which nations and individuals (and everything in between) guide the actions they take in order to drive toward chosen objectives may be referred to as strategy. Because strategy involves an action-idea, it is dynamic, and depends upon assessments of the actions of others involved in the situation. These assessments are both anticipations (judgments about what others will do, and what you will then do, made in advance) and on-the-spot action/reaction sequences. This sense of the word "strategy" is derived from game theory, which distinguishes games of individual skill, games of chance, and games of strategy—the last being those in which the most effective course of action for each player depends upon the actions of other players and the initial players' anticipation and assessment of those moves. As such, the term emphasizes the interdependence of allies' and adversaries' decisions and their various expectations about each others' behavior.

The centrality of strategy for the community practitioner is undeniable. Without it, ideology and commitment are reduced to empty rhetoric. On the other hand, actions without strategies are not helpful either. Used by themselves, interventive actions tend to become merely forays against *ad hoc* "targets of opportunity" without any sense of how they may fit into some larger plan. The vigor with which problems of strategy are endlessly debated is but one example of their critical importance to community practice. Only through a consideration of alternatives that is both thoughtful and pragmatic can a reasonable evaluation of various plans of action and their respective strengths and weaknesses be made.

Just what is strategy? How may it be distinguished from tactics? When and how should one change strategies? What tools, what action "rules of thumb" are available to guide practitioner actions? Each community intervention mode can be thought of as a strategic approach to the problems of social injustice, uncoordinated services, and lack of community. But when should one be used and others set aside? When should one be an initial strategy, to be followed by others at a later time?

These are the questions faced by community practitioners every day. However, efforts to pose these issues sharply, or explicate them fully, are few and far between in the literature. Part Two is an attempt to accomplish just this task.

In keeping with the construct presented in Part One, we will view strategy in terms of three basic intervention approaches and combined forms among them. Separate chapters are devoted to each of these modes—development, planning and policy, and action—with examples of mixing given for each. Our discussion highlights means of influence as a core element of strategy, and we will show that different means of influence are associated with different strategic modes of intervention.

However, before undertaking this core analysis, we will examine some underlying elements of strategy that contribute to our understanding of the concept. Among these elements are strategy as a goal, as orchestration, as an amalgam of conflict and consensus tactics, as a task and process phenomenon, and as a means-ends spiral. We will also consider contextual variables that influence the exercise of strategy. With these ideas in place, we will be in a position to elaborate on social influence—modes of intervention, which provide the organizing framework for the readings in Part Two.

UNDERLYING ELEMENTS OF STRATEGY

Strategy As a Goal

Basically, we regard strategy as an orchestrated attempt to influence a person or a system in relation to some goal which an actor desires. It is "orchestrated" in the sense that an effort is made to take into account the actions and the reactions of key allies and adversaries as they bear upon the achievement of the proposed goal. That goal tends to be general, such as a particular "state of the system" desired by the change agent. It is sometimes called "strategic intent" (Hamel and Prahalad, 1989). For example, exorcising white racism from a big city educational bureaucracy may be a state-of-the-system goal.

Articulating a strategic intent, however, is not an easy task. While it is beset by numbers of difficulties, four deserve special mention—the articulation of goals, the substitution of ideology for goals, the trivialization of goals, and the measurement of goals.

The Articulation of Goals.   Practitioners should select and articulate goals at a level of public understanding such that they have a possibility of being achieved, and so that the public will know (and the worker will know) when they *have been achieved*. For example, a worker who sets as a goal the global aim of eliminating racism in a particular community is bound to be disappointed. This is not to say that the elimination of racism should not be a goal, but rather that it should not be *the* goal. On the other hand, if the goal is one of bringing integration to a suburban housing area, or providing new job or educational opportunities for African-Americans, then the results can be monitored more effectively. Without intermediate and feasible proximate goals, the worker's interventions cannot be evaluated to any significant degree and progress cannot be assessed. Specifying general strategic purposes, and more concrete strategic goals, is an important part of the community intervention process.

Ideological Substitution.   Because goals are hard to articulate and specify ideological commitment to some general value is substituted for the actual goal. Practitioners become "true believers" in the sense in which Eric Hoffer (1958) has suggested. Progress toward the desired goal becomes transformed into an assessment of the "purity" or motivation of the practitioner. While not more typical of community organizers than any other group of change agents, this solution tends to move the goal out of the realm of the "practical" or empirically concrete and to develop a series of personalistic assessments. From this perspective, "commitment" becomes a culmination for the believer; without it, progress becomes impossible. However, all too often, this commitment concern becomes ideological enmeshment, and is associated with a lack of real progress toward visible accomplishments (for example, full employment).

Goal Trivialization.   With goals hard to specify, the substitution of means for goals is not that uncommon. It is sometimes called "means ritualism." Here we find, for example, the agency that relies heavily on a continuing series of community meetings from which nothing ever seems to emerge.

Measurement.   Part of the problem, of course, is that achievement and accomplishment are hard to measure. Goals must have measures, milestones, and benchmarks that can be used to assess progress. Without such measurement, goals become hollow.

Strategy As Orchestration

While most practitioners are well acquainted with thinking about strategy as goal setting, the notion of orchestration probably bears further attention. In a sense, it is intended to convey a dramatic "arrangement"—with different performers, each with various skills and roles, each of whom may enter and leave the scene according to some action plan. Solos articulate with the movement of the whole piece. The change agent's roles include prompter and producer-conductor. He or she lays out a "score" for the performance and attempts to integrate its diverse elements as the performance goes forward. In all likelihood the score itself will have to be changed—in response to shifting conditions—one or more times during any given performance.

But more is implied here than the interplay of many persons, or persons and institutions, at any given movement. There is a progression over time—as each phase of the action scheme is completed. Indeed, it suggests the notion of a "means-end chain," where all of the simultaneous performances are at once ends in themselves, and means to a more general end. A familiar example to practitioners is the community clean-up or safe neighborhood campaign. The project is an end in itself, as well as a means to the more general goal of community cohesion and pride. Thus community strategy often involves a complex and dynamic pattern of performances within performances. However, in this general framework there are several critical issues that need to be explored in more detail.

Strategic Focus: Conflict Versus Consensus Approaches

The problem of strategy is often dichotomized into a choice between conflict and consensus approaches. This trend toward polarization invites many of us to think in terms of "choice" between "brave" and "cowardly" strategies, or "radical" versus "establishment" modes. The tension between conflictual approaches and consensus-seeking ones is real. As Weber points out, "Conflict cannot be excluded from social life . . . 'peace' is nothing more than a change in the form of conflict or in the antagonists or in the objects of the conflict, or finally in the chances of selection" (Coser, 1956, p. 21).

Yet consensus is, paradoxically, a part of conflict, as much as the converse is true. Without subsequent negotiation, agreement, and some form of reconciliation, the fruits of conflict are likely to be meager indeed. Even when total revolution or the transfer of substantial power is effected (or attempted), the "outs" who are now "in" must move to consolidate their gains through at least a modicum of consensus and reconciliation. (The situation in the former Soviet Union provides an excellent example.) At the same time, the current powerful thrust toward "conflict management" is also to be closely scrutinized. Any attempt to move everything by consensus and agreement, to keep everything "nice," may be used to mask significant problems and avoid the possibility of arriving at decisions on critical issues. It has been previously pointed out that the use of conflict or consensus may be predominant in a given mode of practice—such as conflict in social action or consensus in community development. Seen more broadly, conflict and consensus are viewed as the Siamese twins of social progress. If both these task and maintenance functions are not attended to, progress toward social goals may be sharply truncated, if not halted, as William Gamson points out in his article on "Rancorous Conflict in Community Politics" (Gamson, 1966). Clearly both are needed. To assume a battle-ready posture, where there is (or may be) no conflict, is often to create a hostile environment in which movement by consensus cannot take place.

Strategic Focus: Task Versus Process Approaches

In working with collectivities and groups, as planners and organizers almost always are doing, tension rises between focus on the "task" (paint, fix up, for example), and the "process" (building communities and networks through common activities). In a task emphasis, community building and bonding take a second seat; in process orientations, task accomplishment is in second place. Task goals refer to "hard" production-oriented functions in which decisions are made, individual interests neglected, and feelings disregarded. Process goals involve the repair of ruptures caused by task activities and an attempt to create a higher level of group solidarity through which task business can proceed more effectively. Clearly it is here, also, that a mix of strategic approaches is needed. An outline of some possibilities is suggested in Figure 1. This grid outlines some of the choices of emphasis that the practioner can make. "Locality development" typically occupies the bottom half of the grid, with a focus on the right-hand corner. Sometimes, though, group bonding is developed through opposition to other groups. "Policy and planning" occupy the upper part of the grid, with policy tending to center in the upper-left quadrant (because policy requires decisions, and decisions often involve conflict), and planning occupying the right half (because planning requires cooperation to get the program together and running.) "Social action" tends to occupy the left two quadrants, focusing on both task accomplishment and the challenge of getting specific improvements, and on process activities that include conflict, involving challenging power holders and beneficiaries on socially unjust practices and processes.

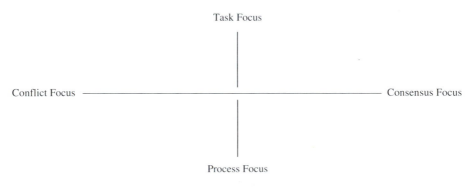

FIGURE 1
A Strategic Grid of Conflict/Consensus and Task/Process Foci

However, it is also important to note that the whole system tends to turn (or rotate) and turn again in a spiral fashion. For example, dramatic social action efforts to draw attention to hate crimes may give way to more consensus-oriented policy and planning decisions to combat it. Moreover, ongoing programs to support and welcome diversity may need to move back and forth between modes embracing both conflict and consensus, and modes emphasizing either task or process—or both from one issue to the next.

The Means-Ends Spiral

Most practitioners recognize the operation of means-ends chains as common practice experiences. Putting the two notions together, strategy can be redefined as an outward means-ends spiral, alternatively emphasizing task and process, conflict and consensus modes.

The concept of strategy as an orchestrated means-ends spiral has a number of important consequences for community intervention. For one thing, it suggests that total reliance on a strategy of either consensus or conflict will in most circumstances be unsuccessful. It anticipates the skill of the organizer in moving with the community or group between task and process phases. And it offers the idea of progression toward concrete intermediate objectives as a measure of strategic success. Now let us turn to an examination of the contexts in which strategic successes must be achieved.

Contextual Variables in Strategic Assessment

Strategy is not devised in a vacuum. The strategic thinker works in some specific community, with specific groups and probably for some organization. As a plan is developed, there are a number of factors that should be taken into account.

Strategic thinking and development must begin with a consideration of the agency resources in people, money, and equipment which the agents have at their disposal. Often there are inter-agency fights over the allocation of these resources. And, whatever the level, we know that in community practice there are rarely sufficient amounts of any one of the resources to meet the demand. Since they are scarce, competition for them becomes intense. The more scarce the resources (and thus, the more intense the competition), the more a strategy of power-building self-help is indicated.

The resources of the broader system in which the organizer must act are another consideration. Such resources may be the availability of money, on the one hand, and that amorphous but all-important resource, public support and understanding on the other. Sometimes the agency and the system have resources differentially available to them. In some developing countries, community agents have access to expensive and sophisticated equipment which the indigenous population does not know how to use. Thus, even the presence of resources does the worker no good if they cannot be used. More frequent, and characteristic of many urban change programs in America, is the target system that has more resources than the change agency.

Hence, from a strategic point of view, the system (or particular elements within that system) can "hold out" much longer than any agency-backed client organization and win most struggles. In general, when the target has more resources than those available to the change agent or agency, a social action strategy is indicated.

The amount of resistance to change objectives is a third factor of critical importance. Generally, we assume some resistance to change proposals as a matter of course. Sometimes, however, the complexity of the problem itself gives the appearance of resistance. We must be careful to distinguish between a situation where a social problem is complex, but there is no substantial resistance (for example, many public health problems fall into this category) and one where many solutions are known but there is strong resistance (for example, income maintenance). Then, too, areas where important gains can be made, and where the system is neutral to mildly opposed (for example, tutorial enrichment programs), a social planning strategy should be considered.

In modern urban America, class variables are a very strong predictor of behavior and institutional preferences, from sex habits to styles of child rearing, from religion to responses to pain (Bendix and Lipset, 1966). It is thus with some concern that we note the absence of literature which substantially attempts to exploit these differences in the conceptualization of strategic alternatives.

Generally speaking, the change agent can represent a constituency which is of higher, equal, or lower social class than the change target. For the community practitioner this situation offers certain strategic "hints." They devolve upon the fact that change strategies are "handicapped" by their class of origin—particularly as viewed by the recipient of the change proposal. For example, a change proposal coming from a high-status change agency (or agent) to a low-status community has a good likelihood of "success," particularly if the agency is willing to utilize its prestige in achieving the desired goal over the objections of community residents. On the other hand, a change proposal coming from a lower-class constituency directed toward a middle-class formal organization is likely to be stalled, sidetracked, and indefinitely tabled or ultimately defeated. It is all too easy for the class "handicap" (either positive or negative) to obfuscate the merits of any given change proposal. Many of the demands for "power" of various sorts—as enunciated by the poor, gays and lesbians, racial and ethnic minorities, and women—can be understood as a demand for a new set of handicapping arrangements in the system. Welfare mothers, for example, suffer from the stigma of poverty and recipient status. Welfare rights organizations attempt to redress this balance and place recipient mothers on a more equal basis for negotiation with middle-class welfare bureaucrats. Problems of lower-class constituencies may be handled by developing social action strategies to build a new handicapping system (that is, causing shifts in power and/or resource allocations), followed by appropriate strategies of development and planning.

Variability in problem complexity is a relevant issue and poses questions of problem "tractability." Community problems are comprised of many unique and interrelated elements. Sometimes even the simplest technical problems—garbage collection, for example—are confounded by political complexities of great magnitude. On the other hand, problems which have substantial support across a wide range of publics—job-training projects—may falter on technical insufficiencies. Other complexities—from agency staff changes to national upheavals—also may enter the picture. Fundamentally, the change agent, taking the problem in all its ramifications, must be able to assess the degree of complexity involved, and how amenable to solution it may be. Different degrees of complexity require different kinds, timing, and sequencing of strategies.

Legitimacy—of either a target of change or a change agent—is a key variable for the community practitioner. Indeed, a change target of dubious legitimacy has a built-in vulnerability that may be exploited. On the other hand, a target with broad legitimacy in the community may be especially difficult to attack. Change agents need to make a realistic assessment of their own legitimacy and act accordingly. That is, an inadequate legitimacy must often be strengthened for effective action to take place; a charismatic legitimacy can carry the change agent a long way before an action begins.

In our modern bureaucratized society, organizational strength of either change target or change agent is often a vital contextual problem. As a change target, weaker organizations are more vulnerable to a variety of change efforts. Strong organizations, however, typically present special difficulties even for the most enterprising of change agents. Since organizations are many times vehicles through which change is carried out, their strength must be carefully appraised as part of the planning for change efforts. Six substantive problems—resources, resistance, class, complexity, legitimacy, and organizational strength—in the development of a successful community intervention strategy have been discussed.[1] There is no implication that these six are the only important factors; nevertheless they seem significant in that they cut across any functional area of community action and are common to most social-change situations. Clearly, it also seems important to note that race and/or gender issues must often be taken into account as well. At times, they are neglected at great peril to both the change effort and the practitioner. Still, a key question remains. How can all these "problem" factors be dealt with in a conceptually interrelated way? One source of help is in emerging social science theories and approaches.

MEANS OF INFLUENCE AND MODES OF INTERVENTION

Strategy and Means of Influence

Often we become confounded by the variety of styles of influence (as well as current vogues) and fail to recognize that there are fundamentally three, and only three, core modes of influence. To get another person, group, or organization to do what is desired, force, inducement, and agreement (or "hit, buy, and woo") may be used.[2]

---

[1] For a useful consideration of some others, see Neil Gilbert and Harry Specht, eds., *Planning for Social Welfare* (Englewood Cliffs, NJ: Prentice-Hall, 1977), and Thomas Meenaghan et al., *Macro Practice in the Human Services* (New York: Free Press, 1982).

[2] These dimensions are similar to the modes of compliance used by Etzioni. See Amitai Etzioni, *A Comparative Analysis of Complex Organizations* (New York: The Free Press, 1961), and the approaches explored in Robert Fisher, *Let the People Decide: Neighborhood Organizing in America* (Boston: Twayne Publishers, 1984).

These three modes occur not only on the individual level as strategies of influence, but they are main change initiators at the societal level as well. Let us consider each in some detail.

Force, or coercive power, has been a vital concept in the analysis of human events. The possession of force, or control over the means of force, gives the change agent an important weapon. Often it is not necessary to actually use available force, but simply to make a *credible threat*. At other times, the actual application of force is necessary (for example, to establish credibility through a "show of strength"). Modes of force may range from physical violence and war, on one end of a continuum, to sit-ins, confrontations, and personal harassment at the other end. Drawing on our previous distinction, force constitutes a conflict strategy, and its use typically creates resentment. The use of force also suggests the existence of resistance. Indeed, there are strong moral sanctions against using force when resistance is absent, as in the case of "shooting an unarmed man" or attacking a "defenseless" nation. In all well-integrated social systems, the subsystem which has primary responsibility for control over the use of force is the polity, or governmental structure. Agents of force, such as the police and the army, for example, are under this kind of political control. Access to certain positions in the polity are sought because of the relationship they have to the potential mobilization of force, even though the notion of force may be obscured or veiled.

The second means by which social goals may be achieved is inducement. Often, goals can be purchased or traded. Force need not be used, although value consensus may not be present. For example, people who argue that integrated housing is a "good investment" are using an inducement strategy. On a more fundamental level, the entire economic system is an inducement system. People contribute to the system and receive differential payments in return. This pay can be traded for many other goods in the system. The purchase of goods is, in turn, an inducement to the manufacturer to create new and more profitable goods. Inducement frequently involves the use of facts and information to persuade people to lend themselves to certain programmatic approaches. The factual information sets forth convincingly the benefits to be gained through accepting a particular plan or course of action.

In using coercive power, one has to control the means of force. To use an inducement strategy, one needs to manipulate the goods by which people may be induced. Money is one such "good." Interestingly, power is another. (This suggests an interaction between the three main modes, which we shall discuss momentarily). Status positions, prestigeful associations, jobs, symbols of recognition and access to personnel and equipment are also among the most desired goods. In earlier times, salvation and indulgences were coin of the realm. Increasingly, control over information (and the emerging information highway) is coming to be an important and negotiable commodity. As society comes to be more and more complex, more and more specialized, more and more technological, detailed information is required to solve even apparently simple problems. Hence, it becomes a desired good, and a most significant one.

Perhaps the most subtle and sophisticated method for achieving social goals is through value consensus or agreement. A consensus mode proceeds through the development of an agreement between the actors that a course of action should be followed. Typically, the consensus is based upon fundamental agreements on underlying values in the social system. Then the parties attempt to demonstrate that the position they wish to take is closely attuned with the value or operates according to it. One simple example deals with the vote. In the United States, it is common and widely accepted practice to settle matters in dispute with a vote of those present. This procedure requires a plurality achieved through the rule of one-person-one-vote. However, the strong biases inherent in this procedure are often ignored. The intensity of preference on an issue—the fact that some people may feel very strongly while others take the matter rather lightly—is simply neglected in this procedure. Similarly, with each member having a single vote, differences in knowledge, experience, and analytical ability are not accorded any special weight. The presumption is made that somehow the most desirable alternatives possible will receive a full hearing.

Value consensus usually emerges through some kind of socialization process. In the most obvious case, of course, it is the socialization of infants and children to the norms and mores of the dominant culture or their own ethnic group. Less explicit, but socialization nonetheless, is a host of processes that go on in adult life—the peer group of friends, the informal "clique" at the workplace or factory. Then too, many of us have a broader and more undefined group which we use as a reference point to assess our own attitudes and progress (political parties, a profession, the church, etc.).

Relating Influence and Modes of Intervention

These three types of influence have some very interesting additional properties. For one thing, each may be a goal as well as a means to the others. Thus, inducements can be used to secure power and the control over force. Force can be used to secure agreement, although in perhaps a more limited fashion. Inducements, when applied over time, tend to produce value agreement. This is the time-honored process of "cooptation."

Second, each is the basis for an important part of the stratification system in society. Certainly people possess different amounts of power and can be located somewhere on a power continuum ranging from most to least. People also have differential control over various inducements, such as money and information. A rank ordering can be done of those "commanding" salient inducements. Finally, people are closer to, or farther from, valued positions in society. This is often referred to as "status." For this reason, each of these means of influence is an important "good" in the system. One might conceptualize the task of the community worker in terms of equalizing the distribution of these "goods," or improving the position of his or her constituency on one or more ranking scales. Often the worker will attempt to capitalize on the properties of one system to produce increments in another.

Third, none of these influence means can exist without the others. Not only do they interpenetrate on a goals-means basis, but they also are mutually supportive. Hence, the use of force generally exists within some context of agreement about the conditions under which force may be used and the amount of force necessary to produce certain results, etc. On the other hand, the amount of force often produces a new situation with which the existing web of value agreements must cope. Both are supported by a framework of inducements. Without inducements, the potential user of force cannot often muster the necessary elements of force.

Finally, force, inducements, and value agreement are the means by which society at large insures order and stability in the social system, and the means by which the society is changed. Force, for example, can be a means by which order is maintained, or disrupted. Inducements are used to develop commitments to the system, or to lure people to other competing systems. Values are at once sources of common bonds and of great divisiveness in the society.

It might be useful at this time to relate these three means of influence to the earlier discussion of the three models of community intervention (Article 1). On the intervention level, social action is most closely related to the force variable. Police, courts, and the military are typical examples of force used to maintain the system. As a change variable, civil disobedience and other forms of disruptive militancy are typical. Social action usually attempts to build up the pressure of cumulative force through massing large numbers of people in united and often dramatic activity. Although in a quite different fashion, policy is also related to the force variable. That is, legal and legislative machinery are often the impelling force behind the use of policy as an intervention system maintenance mode. As a change mode, the courts can be used, in this case, to support such efforts as class action suits.

Planning as an intervention technique articulates best with the inducement means of influence. Planning involves a complex of processes (which may include, as elements, development, action, policy, and administration). Fundamentally, the planner attempts to induce the system to adopt a proposed plan through a variety of techniques. Typically the situation is one of high complexity, and the planner brings to bear significant expertise on the location and extent of the problem, past attempts to deal with it, and the most desirable alternatives in view of current circumstances (especially resource availability).

The value means of influence best articulates with the locality development mode of intervention. In both cases, the achievement of value agreement and common orientations is a central focus of either change or system-maintenance objectives.

The development of these two sets of terms—one pertaining to means of influence and the other to modes of intervention—permits us to develop a framework for considering the types of styles and strategies available to the change agent. This framework is displayed in Figure 2.

Figure 2 suggests that there are at least nine basic strategic themes that may be employed. While as we pointed out, each mode of intervention is characterized by a particular means of influence (as indicated by its location on the diagonal in Figure 2), in actuality other means of influence are also typically utilized. Thus, while militancy often is expressed in social action, inducements through negotiation take place, as well as value consensus through moral exhortation.

In addition, each mode of intervention offers special leverage on a key contextual variable or general problem situation. Thus social action is concerned especially

MODES OF INTERVENTION

Basic Means of Influence	Action	Planning/Policy	Development
Force (power)	*Militancy* Disruption, sit-in, "liberation" of institutions, para-military activities	*Power Elite* Involve influential elites	*Reconciliation* (Client system with power groups)
Inducement	*Negotiation* Bargain, confrontation with "facts"		*Pilot Projects* (Illustrative of potential gains, build to larger tasks)
Value Consensus	*Moral Exhortation* Expose, "Radical thought"	*Representation* "Federation" of interests	*Group Development*

CRITICAL CONTEXTUAL PROBLEMS

	Action	Planning/Policy	Development
	Low social class High resistance	High complexity	Low resources

FIGURE 2

A Matrix of Intervention Strategies, Means of Influence, and Contextual Variables

with unequal distribution of goods and resources in the society as reflected in class stratification; planning deals with matters of high complexity; policy may be especially important in either augmenting or undermining the legitimacy of the political system and its institutions; and locality development is particularly useful with a situation of limited communal resources.[3]

THE MIXING AND PHASING OF STRATEGIES

Strategy Confrontation: The Mixing and Phasing of Strategies

It is often the case, as we have suggested in the means-ends spiral notion, as well as in the Introduction to the entire volume, that the practitioner must move from one strategy to another as shifts occur in the conditions affecting his overall objectives.

---

[3] Furthermore, each intervention mode is often associated with particular patterns of linkage. Thus, social action typically involves local primary groups banding together to make demands upon (or link up with) formal organizations. Planning often includes a number of cross-linkages to improve, for example, service delivery. Policy usually involves the linkage between some larger aggregate (like a legislative body) that takes action for change and formal organizations through which the new mandate is carried out. Locality development usually requires the establishment of good working relationships among primary groups and, at a later stage, cooperative arrangements with appropriate formal organizations.

Figure 2 suggests a possible scheme for mixing and phasing the strategies under two fundamental problem conditions.

The first set of problematic situations requires moving horizontally across the chart. It assumes that society or some target system is using one of the means of influence to maintain a problem condition. If the change agency, for example, is dealing with a problem defined by the system as one of force and power, one begins with a militant action strategy to build power and influence, and then moves to a planning strategy to consolidate the acquired influence and build a power block, to a development strategy for building value consensus and establishing channels for negotiating the allocation of scarce resources.

In contrast, where inducement is the main mode of maintaining the status quo, one begins with a planning strategy, bringing expertise to bear on a detailed analysis of the problem. One might then seek to build consensus through a development strategy, backed up with the potential of action, if needed.

In the case where values form the main vehicle of conservative influence, value "liberation" needs to take place (often in small groups) followed by a more action-oriented strategy of moral confrontations and radicalization, to a planning framework in which a number of interests are represented as negotiations take place.

The second problem orientation begins not with the mode through which society maintains the status quo, but rather with the mode of intervention to which some change agent or agency is committed. This orientation helps to illustrate the type of strategic configuration which remains within one intervention mode. If an agency is committed to a social action mode, its scenario begins with militancy. After a militant demonstration, one moves to a position of bringing values in line with action, and then to a negotiating position. On the other hand, a development-oriented agency, because of its limited resources, usually begins in a group organization phase and moves through an inducement phase before coming to an action phase. Planning starts with the calling together of experts, moves to building a power block, and concludes with some representation of all significant interests.

The main point is that one can use either the characteristics of the problem or the type of change agency (action, planning and policy, or development) as a point of departure. In either case, to achieve closure on particular problems, a differential set of strategies needs to be used, perhaps relying on different agencies and different persons at different phases of action. Two elements remain constant in either perspective: One is the notion of the means-ends spiral, and the other is that the *beginning* strategy should be articulated with the primary maintenance means (and this initial target of change) in the system.

All of these change processes (or change attempts) may be seen in struggles surrounding such current issues as managed care, case management, violence containment, health care reform, and welfare reform. In the final analysis, what is being contested is, "Who will pay for what services to be offered to whom?"

ANALYSIS OF MODES OF INTERVENTION IN PART TWO

Three means of influence and modes of intervention are described and illustrated in the articles in Part Two. In addition, variations in the modes of influence are discussed, which suggests mixtures among them, either cross-sectionally at a given juncture or longitudinally over a period of time.

Locality Development

Locality development is characterized by Cnaan and Rothman as an intervention approach that emphasizes community building and social integration. Arriving at widely agreed upon goals and forms of action through broad citizen participation is central to this approach, including a process wherein value consensus plays a prominent part. These authors draw on Durkheim's concept of organic community to encapsulate the goals of locality development. The organic notion signifies solidarity among residents, including interdependence, mutual responsibility, and interpersonal exchange, with noncoercive norms guiding social interaction.

The discussion goes on to point to two core features of locality development: Local residents rather than professional change agents decide on the ends to be pursued, and collaborative tactics predominate in moving toward change. The practitioner seeks to establish local representative groups to deliberate and act, thus group development and interactional skills are highly important.

An example of locality development tactics is given in the article by Martí-Costa and Serrano-García. They place needs assessment in an ideological context, showing that in locality development this technique is used both to engage citizens actively in determining what problems are of importance to them, and to help make them conscious of the impact of these problems on their lives.

Rather than being only an objective research tool, needs assessment is simultaneously an action instrumentality. Needs assessment provides a basis for going through four intervention phases: (1) increased familiarization by residents with the community, (2) creation of a core group of community people and professional interveners to manage the assessment, (3) formation of grassroots task groups to analyze findings and devise relevant goals and action plans, and (4) involvement of new and expanding groups in a cyclical manner as action proceeds and new circumstances evolve.

A vivid illustration of locality development is presented in the article by Kaul. He describes efforts to organize an oppressed minority community in the East Akron area through a neighborhood settlement house. Kaul provides step-by-step information about the process he went through to encourage self-help efforts by residents, employing the means of forming block clubs throughout the area. These were later incorporated into a block club council having greater scope and containing greater human resources than the single units. Through their own efforts, residents carried out a wide range of beneficial actions that involved recreational and cultural programs, health and sanitation, neighborhood beautification, safety, and housing. Local leadership was nourished and developed in the process.

A variation in the locality development approach is described in the article by Fleras. Here, a national governmental program in New Zealand, involving social welfare planning and policy development, is integrated with local development efforts. The analysis shows how the Department of Maori Affairs shifted from a traditional social welfare program that engendered dependency on the part of native populations, to a program of community development that relies on self-determination and self-help by local peoples. A national bureaucratic structure continues to exist, but through the "Tu Tangata" philosophy, Maori initiatives and Maori ways play a major part in the character of the services and in the procedures that are employed. In this way, social policy approaches and locality development approaches are blended in a combined formulation.

Planning/Policy

The planning/policy intervention mode is depicted in the article by Rothman and Zald, in which they discuss a data-driven, rationalistic approach to promoting change. Planning/policy in this context relies on facts and logic to persuade individuals to take certain actions—the inducement being alleviation of difficult and vexing problems that affect them directly or indirectly, such as crime, urban blight, homelessness, and child abuse. These authors indicate that comprehensive societal planning has not been characteristic of the American experience, but that it has been attempted in sectoral areas, such as state prison systems, social security, and corporate planning. At the community level, The United Way, welfare councils, and hospital planning councils have injected a rationalistic dynamic into the process of community problem solving.

These authors indicate that the rationalistic approach has received criticism in recent years because it wrongly assumes that sufficient information can be assembled to resolve highly complex problems. Also, communities are in a state of flux and turbulence, thus the orderly and painstaking accumulation of data that planners bring to bear on problems contains a time lag. Finally, this approach fails to take into account sufficiently the input of citizens who are in constant touch with and affected by problems—hence, it is in conflict with basic democratic values. While planning and policy development serve to bring evidence and objectivity into the realm of decision making, a rigid and stereotypic adherence to rationalistic means is described by these authors as self-limiting.

The gathering and use of data in planning and policy practice is examined from another perspective by Patton. He feels that elaborate measuring instruments and complex data analysis methods are more appropriate for formal research purposes than for designing plans and policies. Policy makers need ballpark answers in a timely manner. Thus, Patton suggests the technique of "quick analysis" for a planning setting. This means such things as focusing sharply on the central decision issues, using available data sources whenever possible, and avoiding the "tool-box approach," whereby standard textbook techniques are employed rather than the simplest method relevant to the particular problem.

Patton specifies the steps involved in the policy analysis process, from defining the problem, through developing alternative actions, to monitoring and evaluating outcomes. For each step, he specifies the quick-analysis techniques that are most appropriate at that stage, including back-of-the-envelope calculations, feasibility manipulations, and sensitivity analysis. Patton views his approach not as an alternative to the rational model, but as one that makes the rational model practical and feasible in the face of the criticisms to which it has been subjected.

An example of rationalistic community planning is provided by Fuchs in her description of a health promotion initiative in rural areas of Ohio. The PATCH program (Planned Approach to Community Health) is sponsored by the Centers for Disease Control, and attempts to encourage collaboration by local communities with federal and state health agencies. The author shows how the project communities moved through all the basic phases of planned change: data collection and analysis, problem identification and prioritizing, intervention planning and implementation, and program evaluation. Fuchs indicates that greater community coordination resulted from this activity, and she also identifies substantive outcomes, such as a youth smoking-curtailment program, infusion of monies from a variety of funding sources, and the development of a public school health-education curriculum. The project included citizen participation as an aspect of the work.

Citizen participation is the focus of a concluding planning article by Checkoway. When participation is emphasized in the planning mode, that brings into play a variation from the rationalistic theme, and involves the blending of planning with aspects of locality development and social action. Checkoway delineates two forms of local community planning: subarea planning and neighborhood planning. In subarea planning, citywide agencies and institutions decentralize services and facilities, diffusing them into grassroots locales. Neighborhood planning, on the other hand, involves local citizens taking the initiative and developing plans and programs for their own benefit. Both of these approaches to planning include local citizen involvement, but it is more prominent and organic in the latter.

Checkoway describes the historic development of each of these forms of planning, and gives examples of a range of relevant organizations across the country. In his view, both of these forms are legitimate and useful; the professional task is to determine the appropriate agenda for each and to clarify under what conditions one or another form might be most effective.

Social Action

Fisher, in his overview article, describes the classic conception of social action, and shows how it has evolved and changed in recent decades. Early notions of social action viewed it as "grassroots-based, conflict-oriented, with a focus on direct action, and geared to organizing the disadvantaged or aggrieved to take action on their own behalf." It relies on the means of force or pressure to obtain concessions from individuals having a great deal of power and prestige in society. Examples are given from the Alinsky school of organizing, liberation struggles of people of color, urban decentralization actions, and the New Left.

Fisher goes on to describe "new social movements," which embrace efforts in feminist, ecological, gay and lesbian, and oppressed minority organizations. Developments in recent organizing efforts include national and global elements, a longer time frame for organizational activity, and a changing context within which to function. Democracy and diversity are central themes in this trend, however culturally oriented, identity-based actions result in fragmentation and stalemate. Fisher believes there has been a concomitant reduction in emphasis on meeting the material needs of the poor. He advocates practice initiatives directed at building coalitions, entering into electoral politics, and reinvigorating an ideological commitment to social justice and community solidarity.

Some tactics and techniques of organization building in this mode are detailed by Haggstrom. He indicates that the process begins with the organizer bringing people together at a meeting. Individuals are encouraged to express their acute concerns, admitting them openly to themselves and others, and to engage in responsible planning to seek relief. The organizer highlights the conflicts in the situation, because the problems of low-income, low-power people cannot be resolved without threat to the self-interests of those in advantaged positions.

Haggstrom warns about symbolic concessions that are made tacitly by elites when faced with organized pressure. The organizer has to help the group at that time to move to a new line of action focused on forcing the opponent to follow through on these agreements. Haggstrom views social action as a morality drama wherein the organizer strives to see that the action episode is projected publicly as a struggle between the forces of good and the forces of evil. The script is written in such a way that the action group controls the conflict, and the other parties are put in the position of responding to and containing it. Haggstrom addresses the ethical and moral dimensions of everyday organizing head-on and in a philosophical key. He also deals with hard political and personal tactical choices that confront the social action practitioner.

Many of these same issues are demonstrated in the case study presented by Morrissey. The Downtown Welfare Advocate Center (DWAC) in Manhattan is a second-generation welfare action group. Early welfare rights activity originated in the civil rights era and sought to build a poor people's movement. The later welfare rights effort, of which DWAC was a part, emphasized that welfare is more a concern of poor women than poor people in general, and was animated in large part by feminist perspectives.

DWAC emphasized public actions and demonstrations to dramatize their plight and highlight their demands. Some of these demonstrations drew public attention to welfare received by the rich through governmental subsidies and tax benefits. Demonstrations also were aimed at obtaining immediate, particular benefits for AFDC recipients through such actions as a Clothe Our Children Campaign. Overall AFDC grant increases were also pursued, in part through mass gatherings at the state capitol in Albany.

The case study, which records the rise and demise of the organization, illustrates some problems of leadership, staffing, and tactics in social action movements. Sometimes charismatic leaders take on a dominant role, and when they move on a vacuum is left. Other leaders become burned out because of continual stress and overwork. Also, success in achieving short-term objectives can create enthusiasm in members but, at the same time, result in defection by those who feel their immediate needs have been fulfilled.

Some further complexities and opportunities in social movements are described in the article by Flacks. He feels that left-leaning activists have relied too heavily on the concept of a powerful party and that the most meaningful progressive change comes about through mass-based movements. However, Flacks criticizes preponderant reliance on a local base, a single, bounded constituency, and direct-action protest tactics by organizations wedded to the classic social action modality.

Flacks calls for breaking out of a single-issue focus that often employs the politics of single-group identity, and he encourages greater effort to forge coalitions of various kinds. He sees the need for national-level strategies and organizational forms that are tied in with local organizing efforts. This entails a bimodel social policy/social action intervention formulation.

This link of community organizing to the national level, to electoral politics, and to governmental structures leads Flacks to recommend a number of future initiatives. Among these are federal subsidies for community organization, a revitalization of federal "block" grants to support progressive decentralized community-building endeavors, and the use of social and economic impact reviews of public programs in parallel with environmental impact reviews.

SOME TASKS AHEAD

As always, times of great unrest and turmoil, such as those in which we live, may be regarded primarily as periods of either great danger or enormous opportunity for change. To personally and professionally maximize the possibilities for positive change in the late 1990s, there are certain steps we can take as part of our strategic efforts. One is to help in the translation of private (individual, small-group, community) troubles into public issues where they can be seriously addressed (community care for AIDS patients, for example). A second is to resist the pressure to cannibalize each other in response to the demands for downsizing and cost containment. A third is to seek ways of bringing to reality—when and where we are able—the promise of a multicultural society. The last step is to remember that, if we use well the tools at our command, we can play a vital roll in determining the shape of human services for the first quarter of the twenty-first century.

—John E. Tropman
John L. Erlich

REFERENCES

Bendix, Reinhard, and Seymour M. Lipset, eds. *Class, Status and Power*. New York: The Free Press, 1966.

Coser, Lewis. *Functions of Social Conflict*. New York: The Free Press, 1956.

Etzioni, Amitai. *A Comparative Analysis of Complex Organizations*. New York: The Free Press, 1961.

Fisher, Robert. *Let the People Decide: Neighborhood Organizing in America*. Boston: Twayne Publishers, 1984.

Garrison, William. "Rancorous Conflict in Community Politics." *American Sociological Review* 31 (1) (February 1966): 71–81.

Gilbert, Neil, and Harry Specht, eds. *Planning for Social Welfare*. Englewood Cliffs, NJ: Prentice-Hall, 1977.

Hamel, Gary, and C. K. Prahalad. "Strategic Intent." *Harvard Business Review*, 67 (3) (May-June 1989): 63–76.

Hofer, Eric. *The True Believer*. New York: The New American Library, 1958.

Meenaghan, Thomas, et al. *Macro Practice in the Human Services*. New York: The Free Press, 1982.

13.

Ram A. Cnaan and Jack Rothman

LOCALITY DEVELOPMENT AND THE BUILDING OF COMMUNITY

THE FUTURE OF COMMUNITY

Social critics and moral philosophers have lamented detrimental contemporary trends, including ever-encroaching technology, disintegration of the family, ecological destruction, and widening economic and social disparities. They cite among these the erosion of community life, indeed, the "eclipse" of community as a viable social institution. Locality development is a community intervention modality that specifically aims to address that concern.

Before dealing with locality development as an intervention mode, it would be useful to define the term "community" and establish the need for efforts aimed at the enhancement of communities. One source is Warren's (1978) classical work, *The Community in America*, which defines community broadly as "that combination of systems and units that perform the major functions having locality relevance," namely, "production-distribution-consumption, socialization, social control, social participation, and mutual support" (p. 170).

Cox (1987) states that "the community may be perceived of as a place where a group of people live and conduct various activities of daily living: earn a living, buy goods and services they are unable to produce for themselves, school their children, transact their civic and governmental affairs, etc." (p. 133). Clearly such a holistic, self-contained community is a rarity in our time.

One hears it widely lamented that modern communities do not offer what, in some past golden days, "gemeinschaft" had presumably provided, namely, an environment characterized by intimate, spontaneous, inclusive, and enduring personal relationships. In this type of community people knew each other well, their fates were intertwined, and there was a great deal of solidarity, mutual concern, and social responsibility. Tonnies (1957) distinguished between this harmonious "gemeinschaft" and the alienated and transitory "gesellschaft."

The decline in the importance of local communities manifests itself not only in waning interpersonal relationships, but also in the weakening of the local community as a force that bears on the destiny of its members. In modern societies, local institutions are significantly impacted by wider social, economic, and political systems— urban, regional, national, and international. Culture no longer evolves locally, but is a product of powerful vertical, extracommunity influences such as the mass media.

Two key questions arise from this. First, if the community is declining as an institution, why be concerned with community practice? Second, if the local community is still a relevant institution, how can it be enhanced? The remainder of this section will answer the first question, while the rest of the chapter will answer the latter.

An old Jewish parable, attributed to Rabbi Menachem Mendel of Kotzeck

(Sade, 1993), uses an allegory that conceives of a person as a spiritual tree. When asked about moving to another location, Rabbi Menachem Mendel responded that moving from one city to another is a major event involving not only one's body and personal belongings that are on the ground but also one's more celestial spirit. People are planted in their community, and being forced to move entails cutting both their earthly and their psychic roots.

One may be able to grow new roots in another community, but frequent relocation results in weaker roots, and each move may be painful, especially at a later stage of life. It takes years to develop a network of meaningful social ties, and although modern means of transportation and communication allow us to keep in touch with people who are afar, most of our meaningful social contacts are with those we can meet on a frequent basis within a circumscribed geographic space. Informal mutual aid, such as baby-sitting in case of emergency, is provided locally by people who know and care for each other. Newcomers find it difficult to blend into such informal systems.

In some instances, people can easily define their community; in others they find it difficult. When asked to identify their community, most people mention its boundaries. Milton Kotler notes, "The most sensible way to locate the neighborhood is to ask people where it is, for people spend much time fixing its boundaries. Gangs mark its turf. Old people watch for new faces. Children figure out safe routes between home and school. People walk their dogs through their neighborhood, but rarely beyond it. Above all, the neighborhood has a name" (cited in Morris and Hess, 1975, p. 40).

The issue of a geographically defined area with discernable boundaries raises distinct possibilities for community practice. We know that boundaries and borders are commonly used in distinguishing among nations, but they are important at the community level as well. A border between countries serves three key functions: (1) to assure physical safety (this denotes what is defensible and where to position security forces in advantageous posts); (2) to secure natural resources (such as fishing territories or national ownership over mines); and (3) to protect national heritage and solidarity (including language, norms of behavior, and citizenship-membership).

We suggest that borders of local communities serve the same functions in a less pronounced way. Historically, the borders of local communities (which often included walled defenses) were designed to assist in assuring security, and they still do. Local watch groups and police departments in American cities and universities reflect this.

Communities attempt to give preference to locals in enjoyment of facilities and amenities. In rural communities, the use of open spaces is a guarded privilege of local people, and in many urban congested neighborhoods parking spaces are reserved for area residents. Further, many studies have found that people who own living units or work in a certain community are more invested and willing to volunteer to uphold the local community for the benefit of its residents (Freidmann, Florin, Wandersman, & Meier, 1988). Accordingly, Morris and Hess (1975) observed that the first stage of community identity often begins with residents organizing to maintain the integrity of their area against intrusive outside interests and to preserve its resources for themselves and their neighbors.

Some local communities seek to maintain their heritage through historical societies, museums, monuments, and celebrations. Local parks, coffee houses, bars, and barber shops become part of the community's collective identity and sense of distinctiveness. People identify themselves (proudly or otherwise) by the community to which they belong, usually the one in which they live. One's identity, especially during childhood, is established by the community of residence. However, people today often were not born into the community in which they live as adults, but rather they settle there by choice. This choice is not always purely a matter of personal preference, but rather a compromise between aspirations and financial ability. Thus, people end up in localities (an affluent suburb, the countryside, downtown) that serve to define their social and economic status and to reflect their self-image.

Before concluding this section, it is important to note that some contemporary definitions view the community somewhat more abstractly in terms of common activities and purposes. Using this orientation allows one to conceptualize a community not only as a geographical entity with physical boundaries but also as a community of interest or affinity, such as people with a similar political ideology (liberals), social-class position (workers) or a physical or mental disability (cancer patients). Murray Ross (1967) has referred to these as functional communities, which though intangible have psychological boundaries and group identities that separate insiders and outsiders. The focus of this chapter is on geographical communities, but the discussion can be readily applied to functional and affinity communities.

Communities of today are not what they used to be; one may ask if they ever were what some people idealistically think they "were in the past." While people are more mobile and share their energies and invest-

ments among various separate social entities (residential, work, recreational), communities still hold importance for many people.

Even if people are unaware of it, they share many needs and problems by the mere fact of geographical proximity or common fate. If the water system breaks down in a certain area and becomes polluted, all residents of the area have the same need for fresh water, and their lives are intermingled regardless of whether they acknowledge it or wish it to be so. Frequently the needs and problems shared by people do not necessarily unite them to take corrective steps. Often, a concerted effort by a professional is required to mobilize people into problem-solving action, which is the rationale for locality development practice.

CONCEPTUALIZING LOCALITY DEVELOPMENT

Locality development is a method used as part of community organization intervention. It gives high priority to building community solidarity and competence. It seeks

to educate and motivate people for self-help; to develop responsible local leadership, to inculcate among the members of rural communities a sense of citizenship and among the residents of urban areas a spirit of civic consciousness; to introduce and strengthen democracy at the grassroots level through the creation and/or revitalization of institutions designed to serve as instruments of local participation; to initiate a self-generating, self-sustaining, and enduring process of growth; to enable people to establish and maintain cooperative and harmonious relationships; and to bring about gradual and self-chosen changes in the community's life with a minimum of stress and disruption (Khinduka, 1987, p. 353).

Rothman in Article 1 of this book notes that locality development involves "broad participation by a wide spectrum of people at the local community level in determining goals and taking civic action" (p. 28). The most common interventions are increasing communication among residents, educating, forming groups, seeking consensus, encouraging group discussion, and focusing on common concerns and problems. The individual who engages in locality development practice has to be a good group facilitator, coordinator, teacher, and conciliator and has to have patience with a slow pace of change, as the process of community building is more important than any single given problem. Locality development brings to mind the metaphor of teaching a hungry person the skill of fishing as opposed to occasionally plying the poor soul with a fish for dinner.

Practice aimed at these objectives has been identified by the terms "community development" and "locality development." The locality development nomenclature was employed originally by Rothman in the first edition of this book to clearly designate this process-oriented approach to practice. Community development is a more eclectic or amorphous term, which sometimes connotes institutional and policy means to strengthen communities from above (Mier, 1993), or implies the promotion of industrial expansion through economic development (Bingham & Mier, 1993). Sometimes it incorporates a national or international perspective rather than a strong local emphasis (Goetz & Clarke, 1993). For this reason, we will favor the locality development terminology, and when we alternatively use "community development" it will be in this more delimited sense.

Locality development has been practiced in both rural, less developed areas of the world and urban settings. In developing countries, locality development often was related to economic development, while in urban areas it contained an element of political empowerment. Yet, in cities, economic issues such as rent control or unemployment are important matters, just as in rural areas the political process and control by traditional elites can be a critical factor. Rubin and Rubin (1992) observe that in urban centers, recently, "local groups . . . have started Community Development Corporations (CDCs) to run or finance local businesses and housing. Among many other projects, CDCs have built or rehabilitated housing for poor and moderate-income families, established and managed neighborhood shopping centers, and worked to establish local businesses" (p. 27). Thus, currently we consider both settings (urban-rural) and both areas of concentration (politicial-economic) as integral to locality development.

An important set of assumptions or values drives locality development. First, people who suffer from a common problem often may be unaware of it, attempt to ignore its existence, or even believe there is nothing they can do about it. Locality development is thus a purposive process by which awareness emerges along with a desire to act in order to resolve problems.

Second, community workers engage a very broad cross-section of community members and do not lean in the direction of elite, influential members. In this respect, they apply the principle of the "more the merrier" and believe that the more extensive the representation the better.

Third, practitioners start "where the people are" and gradually move to where they come to want to go—not necessarily to where the practitioner would like them to be. Local self-determination is strongly valued.

Fourth, locality development eschews exclusionary or discriminatory approaches; minorities of all sorts are welcomed and their unique perspectives and needs are acknowledged and incorporated into the general agenda. Multiethnic and cross-cultural perspectives are highlighted.

Fifth, locality development seeks to empower local residents to gain the capacity to solve problems and successfully cope with powerful authorities and institutions that affect their lives. Self-help is a core concept.

Sixth, the prime constituents of the locality development practitioner are the local residents and not established organizations and authorities in the community who may pay the salary of the community developer. Keeping this type of arrangement operative requires a high degree of sophistication, involving both interpersonal and political skills on the part of the practitioner, as well as a clear sense of direction.

Seventh, locality development assumes that planned intervention in the community is better than allowing a flawed status quo to prevail. This assumption is sometimes questioned, especially in developing countries, by those who claim that often the results of locality development practice are iatrogenic and involve breaking down an existing indigenous system and replacing it with an inferior one (Goulet, 1989). The critique needs to be recognized and attended to, within a framework that is explicitly change-oriented and optimistic about human potential. Also, promoting genuine active involvement of local participants helps to insure that changes are in keeping with indigenous culture and aspirations.

THEORETICAL GROUNDING FOR LOCALITY DEVELOPMENT

Community organization in general and locality development in particular are often criticized for lacking a theoretical or conceptual base. In this section we draw upon Durkheim's (1933) categorization of organic and mechanistic communities as an element in constructing a theoretical underpinning for locality development. Durkheim's most famous works involve the study of the etiology of suicide and the phenomenon of anomie (the breakdown in guiding norms and mores resulting from the combination of urbanization, secularization, and industrialization, combined with the decline of the extended family and the rise of new forms of social problems). These works led Durkheim to study ways by which people in the emerging industrial society could function advantageously and live a good life.

Durkheim suggested that people in a centrifugal type of situation need some form of social glue to hold them together: This he called solidarity. Solidarity is the means by which people feel shared commitments and willingly join together to improve their common quality of life. Solidarity can be achieved in two ways, organic and mechanistic. It is the role of community development to sustain organic solidarity and minimize mechanistic solidarity.

Locality development is consistent with Durkheim's (1933) concept of an organic community, a community manifesting high degrees of interdependence among individuals—with exchanges, legal contracts, and norms guiding these interrelations. Legal codes in an organic community are comparatively less punitive and more "restitutive," specifying noncoercive ways to redress violations of normative expectations and reintegrate violators back into the network of interdependencies that typify organic communities. Individual freedom in such a community is highly valued and, in fact, norms stressing respect for the personal dignity of the individual dominate the highly abstract collective conscience. In such a community, contracts (such as the norms of disposing of garbage) are not only a means of communication and bargaining; they also serve to foster a cohesive outlook reinforcing the mutual responsibility and commitments of members of the same community.

In an organic community residents know each other and, if a common problem emerges, they discuss it and attempt jointly to cope with it. The ongoing interaction assists in facilitating communitywide involvement and concern so that the power of the community to cope with threats is the power of the collective, and is often stronger than the simple sum of individual members. This type of community was beginning to disappear in Durkheim's time, and he feared that anomie would result in a new kind of social order, the mechanistic community.

A mechanistic community bases the essence of solidarity upon a repressive collective conscience that regulates the thoughts and actions of individuals located in the structure. A mechanistic community utilizes repressive legal codes and punitive sanctions, thereby limiting individual freedom, choice, and autonomy. The collective conscience dominates people and their actions, and needs are constrained by its dictates and those of cohesive subunits. Durkheim seems to have been anticipating elements of German National Socialism and the Russian Leninist scenario.

Tonnies (1957) had a related formulation in his distinction between Gemeinschaft and Gesellschaft. The Gemeinschaft (the organic community) allows the individual to experiment and decide internally whether to conform. The Gesellschaft (the mechanistic community) keeps the individual in line by exerting external pressure that is internalized involuntarily or obeyed in an uncritical way.

According to Durkheim, a community with a low degree of organic solidarity is bound in the long run to generate many social problems and be detrimental to its residents. He predicted that mechanistic communities will show higher rates of anomie and, consequently, experience more social problems. He looked for means to increase organic solidarity, and one of his ideas was a single-industry town, in which all residents are bound by the common interest of their source of employment.

Using this scheme, we can see that locality development practitioners attempt to shift the balance from a mechanistic-type community toward an organic-type community. This is accomplished by helping to make people jointly aware and responsible for their quality of life, thereby increasing residents' solidarity. By fostering widespread participation among residents and building a consensus among them, norms are self-generated and the need to use coercive measures is mitigated.

This theoretical formulation, of necessity, has been presented in brief, contracted form. It should, however, suggest in a general way how the framework can be applied to locality development issues. It also illustrates the manner in which other sociological constructs can be drawn upon to contribute to theory building in this area of practice.

RESIDENT INITIATIVE AND COLLABORATIVE TACTICS: THEMES AND VARIATIONS

In this section we will treat two important aspects of locality development: the source for determining the program and the preferred tactical approach. Locality development favors working with clients to decide what they need and not deciding for clients what is good for them. The emphasis is on direct initiation of goals by local people rather than the more indirect or circumlocutious shaping of goals by the practitioner or other external parties. The preferred mode of problem solving and program implementation is consensual, not conflictual.

Garkovich (1989) states, "if community development as a discipline and a practice is to be relevant to the needs of the communities of tomorrow, the challenge is to shift the focus of training and activities to the more difficult and time-consuming, yet eminently more effective, strategy of local capacity building" (p. 215). This requires that local people take the initiative and be allowed the time required to plan their own destiny.

Khinduka (1987), on the other hand, is critical of what he perceives to be an overemphasis on process in community development and the lack of focus on task goal attainment. In his words, "the community development approach to social change, by and large, is still dominated by a process orientation which evaluates the actual outcome of a community project primarily in terms of what happens in the minds of men rather than in terms of its impact on the social structure" (p. 354).

However, it is clear that modifications in people's behaviors and attitudes can be correlated with successful changes in their environment. These two outcomes are not necessarily antithetical. Also, encouraging self-help does not blindly preclude other options regardless of the circumstance.

Sometimes local residents in complex situations or at an early stage of development are not in a position to move forward, and a practitioner will take the lead. For example, active negotiating by a community developer with a landlord on behalf of residents to supply heat during the winter

months may be preferable to waiting until tenants become miserable and ill enough in the bitter cold to decide to petition the landlord. Thus, occasionally and as a variant, the community development practitioner acts assertively on the behalf of residents (Batten, 1967; York, 1984).

Collaboration has long been a watchword in this area of practice. Kettner, Daley, and Nichols (1985) suggest that collaborative and educational tactics have the advantage of minimizing potentially negative side effects. These approaches build and strengthen communities by cementing relationships among people and increasing their knowledge about the problems they face. Collaborative tactics engender attitudes of good will and mutual support, and foster creative and democratic decision making. But, as in the previous discussion, the approach cannot be applied in a single-minded and uncritical manner. Occasionally pressure tactics may be called for.

The reader of this volume is already aware that social action, the primary arena for conflictual methods, is discussed in the next section of this book. Yet, conflict as a practice method may overlap with locality development and cannot be ignored in that context. Sometimes intractable problems do not yield to tactics having a high degree of civility, and participants tire and become impatient with drawn-out processes of accommodation and compromise (Bryant, 1979; Epstein, 1970).

Coleman (1957) notes that conflict is one of the most powerful tools available to powerless segments of society when dealing with societal problems. It is understood, however, that conflict should be reserved for infrequent application in locality development practice, and used as an option of last resort. Conflict is very difficult to retreat from and, once begun, difficult to set aside in order to resume a collaborative mode (Kettner, Daley, & Nichols, 1985). Furthermore, there is a risk that changes brought about by conflict may be reversed by those on whom they were applied (Marris & Rein, 1973).

There is another way of looking at this issue. Conflict is associated with an *advocacy* role for the practitioner, while collaboration is associated with an *enabling* role. Enabling and facilitating constitute the prime thrust in locality development, but, as we have seen, advocacy with its conflictual *modus operandi* cannot be dismissed. While for many years locality development literature viewed enabling and advocacy as distinct and competing approaches, today it is commonly accepted that the two can be used jointly in keeping with the principle of mixing and phasing various models and strategies.

The term "enabler," advanced in 1947 by K.L.M. Pray from the functional school of social work at the University of Pennsylvania, distinguishes the community social worker from the community organization agitator such as a union organizer (Dunham, 1959; Lappin, 1985; Pray, 1948). The enabler, using a direct mode with residents, applies an objective approach and helps awaken and focus discontent about existing conditions that are harmful to the community, attempts to assist local residents in getting organized by providing them with information and technical skills, and supports their struggle to improve existing conditions or combat oppressive policies.

The term "advocate" is associated with the social movements of the 1960s. In that period, simply enabling local residents to cope with the paternalism of formal and private agencies was viewed as no longer enough to evoke the cooperation or sympathy of neighborhood people. Residents, radicals, and local professionals looked for committed people who would not question the need to act on behalf of clients—to remedy injustices stemming from previous actions taken by government authorities, businesses, voluntary organizations, and powerful individuals (Perlman & Gurin, 1972). This approach also assumes it legitimate for locality developers to act as "political tacticians." That is, they are expected to seize opportunities and apply pressure, when possible, to guarantee maximum benefits to the residents of the neighborhood (Brager, 1968).

A traditional enabler might face a credibility problem, as residents come to doubt the practitioner's motives because of not taking a militant or partisan posture when problems are serious and unyielding. A committed advocate might face problems in making necessary linkages with significant agencies, systems, and individuals that had been attacked and offended through previous actions. Henderson and Thomas (1980) aptly note that, "the worker often has to handle such [. . . unpredicted and contrasting . . .] situations within a short span of time, and he or she is therefore always working with different audiences and constituencies from varied role positions" (p. 3). The dominant themes of locality development have to leave room for necessary variations.

PROBLEM-SOLVING ROLES IN LOCALITY DEVELOPMENT

It is said that community intervention entails analytical and interactional roles. The analytical ones concern the issues, needs, and objectives being addressed and encompass problem-solving activities. The emphasis is on task goals. Interactional roles concern human and process-oriented aspects of the work, including promoting good working relationships, and encouraging group development. The emphasis is on process goals.

In locality development, even analytical, problem-solving elements have strong interactional aspects, in that problem solving typically is done with the participation of residents rather than independently on their behalf. Community building, the major aim, is by definition permeated with process goals. In this section we will discuss problem-solving elements, and in the next one we will examine interactional and group development factors.

Authors have approached the analytical aspect in different but overlapping ways. Lindeman (1921) introduced an early model that had a balanced treatment of analytical and interactional features. He employed 10 stages to describe the steps in community development: developing a firm consciousness of need, spreading this consciousness of need, projecting this consciousness, stimulating an emotional impulse to meet the need expeditiously, presenting alternative solutions, allowing for dispute on solutions, engaging in fact gathering, holding an open discussion of issues and strategies, bringing about an integration of solutions, and working out compromises on the basis of tentative progress. Lindeman concentrated on problem identification and decision making around solution overtures but did not continue into the phases of implementation and evaluation of outcomes.

Dunham (1958) later proposed a nine-step model that focuses on solving the problem through logical planning, with less attention to participant involvement. The stages include: recognition of a need or problem, analysis of the need or problem, fact-finding, planning, gaining official approval, action, recording and reporting, making adjustments, and evaluation.

Batten (1967), in his formulation, highlights interactional matters, particularly the stages through which group members typically move, from passive residents to committed citizens aware of their situation. Batten proposed that, in order to go from one stage to the other, the worker must stimulate the process by raising the right questions. His list of stages follows with examples of the worker role in parentheses: (1) People are vaguely dissatisfied but passive (worker stimulates people to understand why they are dissatisfied); (2) People become aware of the need (worker encourages people to think about desirable changes); (3) People become aware of what type of change they are looking for (worker stimulates people to consider what actions they can themselves take to bring about the change); (4) People decide whether or not they want to act (worker aids people to examine optional means of getting organized); (5) People plan what to do and whether they are able to do it (worker helps them think of obstacles, crises, the need to shift direction, and so forth); and (6) There is an assessment of satisfaction with the results (worker encourages people to examine how far they have come and what else they want to accomplish).

Ross (1967) has formulated a set of practice areas providing an aggregate picture (analytical and interactional) of problem-solving activities, but not in sequential order. His six proposed areas, with some illustrative roles, include: system maintenance (organizing and organizational archive), planning (priority rating of community needs), facilitating relationships (mediation), mobilizing initiatives (fund raising), fostering innovation (leadership development), and interpretation and education (publications).

Henderson and Thomas (1980) more recently have taken the practitioner as the point of departure, examining the detailed steps required by the professional from beginning to end. The nine stages in this model are planning and negotiating entry into the community, getting to know the community, determining a general approach, making contacts and bringing people together, forming and building organizations, helping to clarify goals and priorities, keeping the organization going, dealing with friends and enemies, and separating and terminating.

Brager, Specht, and Torczyner (1987) offer a more general perspective. The worker's "first task in working with the community is to map out the intricate patterns of economic and social relationships by which the community carries out its purposes and functions." They suggest further that "organizers seek to work with and to change some of these patterns by developing an organization to promote effective relationships, maximize assets, generate power, and increase the emotional, social, and material resources of its members" (p. 51).

Locality development is not a linear, mechanical process that can be articulated in tightly compartmentalized stages; even experts do not agree upon specific stages. The processes described above do have similarities and reflect some key dimensions. A practitioner's day, nevertheless, may be composed of numerous meetings with people and activities that may seem on the surface irrelevant to the implementation of locality development.

Yet the activities serve to establish contacts, make both the worker and the cause visible, help set the agenda, and stir "the pot" in the community. Biddle and Biddle (1965, p. 224) observe that community developers have "a habit of being around and accessible in a community meeting place— a coffee shop, a bench under some trees in the market square or wherever people gather to gossip, to watch the passerby and enjoy their company, until such time as both curiosity and familiarity prompt the first exchange of greeting and inquiry." This illustrates that the role of a community developer is in many respects informal, complex, and emergent.

Problem solving in locality development is based on the logic of identifying and delineating the causes of the problem, making the problem visible and widely agreed upon, devising intervention, and implementing the planned intervention. In itself this is not at all unique, but it does contain special features. What is distinctive is the multiplicity of individuals and groups that are intimately and integrally brought into all aspects. Locally based groups are the core medium that locality development practitioners rely on to solve problems and foster community capacity.

INTERACTIONAL AND GROUP DEVELOPMENT ROLES

A key task of locality development practitioners is establishing self-sustaining representative organizations. Mondros and Wilson (1993) noted that "involving, engaging, and sustaining a large and strongly identified group of participants is important to achieving organizational goals" (pp. 69–70). Yet we know that 50 percent of voluntary neighborhood organizations may become inactive after their first year of existence (Prestby & Wandersman, 1985; Yates, 1973). Furthermore, many of the surviving organizations develop oligarchic structures that separate out active leaders, who by default become the experts, from the rest of the local citizens (Cnaan, 1991). Thus, maintenance of a genuine ongoing neighborhood organization represents a greater challenge in many ways than its formation.

Mondros and Wilson (1993) suggest that voluntary community organizations should be highly accessible. That is, they should encourage as many people as possible to join while losing as few as possible. These organizations make themselves accessible for new people, accept them willingly, avoid insider jargon, and hold open meetings at convenient locations and times. They accept members' suggestions and willingly discuss them, do not rely heavily on a small and traditional cadre of leaders, and maintain amicable and frequent contacts with many other organizations. Mondros and Wilson also discuss recruitment and engagement techniques such as focusing on those people who are likely to join with fellow residents, forming cogent messages that communicate, using multiple recruitment methods, providing orientation for new members, and facilitating easy access to committees.

Brager and Specht (1973) propose a model of community organization built on four stages of group development and two types of tasks—technical (or analytical) and interactional—to be carried out within each stage. The four stages include socialization of groups, primary group formation (developing affective relations), forming an organization, and mediating the relations between individuals and institutions. This model has the virtue of emphasizing more than one dimension at any stage. On the negative side, however, it seems to present all tasks as the purview of the practitioner, who then becomes more a leader than an enabler.

Cnaan and Adar (1987) have proposed a detailed model for fostering and nurturing what they define as instrumental groups. While group work is a key practice tool in social work, it is used in this context not to deal with members' psychological or adjustment problems, but as a means of

purposively creating a unit of people willing to work collaboratively on solving tangible problems. The Cnaan and Adar model is based on tasks to be carried out in order to enhance the likelihood that a group of people will function conjointly with effectiveness. The tasks and the emphasis placed on them varies, according to the life cycle (stage of development) of the group and its circumstances. Based on work with many practitioners, Cnaan and Adar note that groups do not necessarily progress linearly through stages but often regress to an earlier stage.

These authors use a five-stage process that may loop back: (1) preliminary development work; (2) creating the initial group; (3) establishing internal mechanisms and operative planning; (4) execution of the plan and goal attainment; and (5) summing-up and reevaluation. Within each of these five stages Cnaan and Adar have identified four specific interactional dimensions: (1) ideological–value dimension; (2) organizational–administrative dimension; (3) activity–professional dimension; and (4) interpersonal–social dimension. The model, then, entails a variety of activities that should be performed by group members and/or professionals to assure that the four interactional dimensions are covered in each of the five stages.

Kahn (1991) focuses on organizing techniques at the local level. He spells out a large number of scenarios for use in mobilizing groups of people: leadership, forming an organization, membership, constituencies, meetings, communication, and practical operation of the organization. Kahn's approach is a more comprehensive and updated version of an earlier work by Huenefeld (1970). In a similar vein, Rubin and Rubin (1992) have provided a rich account of how to run three types of meetings (the membership meeting, decision-making meeting, and training session), which are the backbone of locality development.

It is important that the process of bringing grassroots people together to form an organization takes profoundly into account the varied cultural patterns, values, and aims of local racial and ethnic groups. The poverty and discrimination experienced by minorities make them a prime constituency for efforts directed at improving their life circumstances, either by developing their own services or by applying pressure to external institutions for the transfer of resources. Indeed, Hutcheson and Dominguez (1986) found that in Atlanta 40 percent of the Latino population participated in an activity of a Latino voluntary association at least once in the past 12-month period.

In addition, as Kahn indicates (1991), there is a strong need to organize cross-racial and intercultural coalitions in order to create broad-based community instrumentalities. This requires particular alertness to group differences (for example, the disinclination of Korean communities to form formal representative organizations as compared to those put together along family lines or through churches).

There are some guides to this kind of culturally informed interactional process. Rivera and Erlich (1992) have compiled a volume of illustrative case studies of work with diverse populations, such as Native Americans, Chicanos, African-Americans, Puerto-Rican and Chinese Americans. This book enables the reader to look at cultural differences across a multiplicity of groups and situations. Burghardt's (1982) *The Other Side of Organizing* also examines cultural diversity and the relevance of culture in various community organizing roles. Several of the selections in the locality development and other sections of the book in hand also deal with the subject.

The formation and maintenance of community-based groups is a highly engaging and complex process, in which unexperienced practitioners can easily fail. The practitioner has to be able to attend to personal needs, interpersonal issues, educational factors, cultural variations, external pressures and so forth—without losing sight of the overall task goal and without taking control of the group away from the local leaders. Such a process requires patience, willingness to accept and work with others, sensitivity, and readiness to respond to the changing needs of the group, without becoming lost in the process. Not every person can do this work. In the next section we address the issue of who are employed as community developers and the settings in which they work.

EMPLOYMENT OF LOCALITY DEVELOPMENT PRACTITIONERS

Community developers can be employed by a variety of organizations, including local government, private social-welfare organizations, churches, and local initiative entities. We will describe these settings briefly.

In quite a few countries in the world, locality development is an official function of the local government, sometimes through programs and policies of the national government. In Hong Kong, India, Israel, Sweden, and the U.K., by law or through formal regulations, each local authority employs community developers and, in some cases, will even have a designated department for this purpose. Such workers and units are sometimes considered part of the social welfare department or alternatively as part of an adult education and/or recreation department. It is interesting to note that in some of these countries a key role of such practitioners is to form neighborhood-based representative organizations and citizen boards with a chief aim of enhancing democratic processes.

These workers may be assigned to planning tasks but rarely to social action. In Israel, when the community workers of the City of Jerusalem engaged in social action, they were moved from one department to another, sanctions were applied, and their activities were curtailed. Similarly in Great Britain. In Kuwait, where community organizers are also employed by local authorities, they are prohibited from engaging in either social action or group formation and are restricted to rather conventional roles. Locality development also takes place through several arms of the United Nations, including the World Health Organization, the World Bank, and others. In the United States, the Peace Corps, A.I.D. (Agency for International Development), and Agricultural Extension have conducted governmentally sponsored programs.

However, generally in the United States locality development has been carried out through private/voluntary sources. Historically, the settlement house movement involved itself in neighborhood work and social reform efforts needed to improve neighborhood conditions, symbolized by the endeavors of Jane Addams, Lillian Wald, and Robert Woods, among others. Religious organizations, such as the Friends Service Committee have sponsored programs in this country and overseas, providing a model for the establishment of the Peace Corps.

Churches and synagogues have taken an active role in locality development in a variety of ways. Saul Alinsky's well-known social action projects were financed by the Catholic Church through the Industrial Areas Foundation, but congregations have been much more involved in locality development than in social action. Currently, in emerging ethnic neighborhoods containing new immigrants from Southeast Asia, Latin America, and the Caribbean, churches are often the first community institution to take steps to unite these people and work with them to obtain the resources needed to improve their life conditions.

In many communities, an umbrella organization of interfaith congregations is one of the key sources of employment of community developers in the United States. The Campaign for Human Development that operates under the United States Catholic Conference employs community developers in areas where local organizations ask for this assistance. These practitioners help form local citizens groups to promote social change and self-reliance and, after a few years, are assigned to a new location.

While social workers are familiar with the locality development area of practice and have been active in it, they are sometimes not aware of other auspices and patterns for the conduct of locality development. Union organizers use the skills of locality development in building solidarity within the organization, relating the membership to community institutions, and assisting them to address community problems that affect them. In rural development, people with agricultural and technological expertise are the leading professionals. In some instances individuals with business education are the main organizers, especially when economic development is the focus of change. Health educators engage citizens around wellness and disease-prevention concerns. Urban planners comprise another group of professionals often involved in community development, especially when the issues at hand involve housing, transportation, parks, or zoning.

Lay people who gain firsthand experience in organizing and are then solicited by local agencies to come on board as paraprofessionals make up another group of community developers. The paraprofessional designation refers to individuals with relevant life experience and skills, who lack formal training. In communities where the process of development extends over years, some residents acquire the capabilities necessary to do the work.

These individuals perform effectively in building a bridge between local citizens and agencies or authorities. Locality development provides a means for upward mobility for some. Local residents have been identified as an enormous source for spearheading locality development (Huenefeld, 1970). Kahn (1991) asserts that change is most frequently the result of local initiatives carried forward by residents, often out of frustration, who bring neighbors together to create organizations and seek change.

Chavis, Florin, and Felix (1993) have proposed ways of establishing entirely self-run local bodies through empowering activities instigated by an external support organization. These authors have developed what they call "enabling systems," that is, "a coordinated network of organizations that nurtures the creation and maintenance of a grassroots community development process through the provision of resources, incentives and education" (p. 48). These organizations enact the professional function of providing a foundation to spur local self-help activity. In this approach, instead of hiring individual community developers to enter the local community, a system of experts is brought in for a limited period to train and support self-sustaining grassroots leaders.

Chavis, Florin, and Felix describe a variety of enabling systems: some train potential leaders, others provide seed money for local grassroots activity, while still others provide data and information relevant to community needs. The authors also list various types of organizations that serve as enabling systems. For example, local chapters of the United Way of America provide training, prepackaged materials or tools for fundraising, community planning guides, conferences, and publications. The Citizens Committee for New York City annually supports 3,000 volunteer neighborhood organizations with small grants and printed materials. The federal government allocates 44 million dollars to the Community Partnership Demonstration Program to support programs in 150 communities, and the Henry Kaiser Family Foundation has launched community health promotion programs and a corresponding enabling system in seven southern states and the District of Columbia.

As financing for community development and other human services dwindles, professionals can anticipate that these enabling system activities will become more significant. For a foreseeable period of time, professionals may increasingly serve in supportive roles with indigenous leaders and staff, rather than as primary practitioners.

THE OUTLOOK FOR LOCALITY DEVELOPMENT

A few studies have been carried out to determine which models of community organization are typically applied by practitioners. In one of the first studies of its kind, Cnaan and Rothman (1986) found that Israeli community organizers, both in their perception and in actual activities, distinguish between locality development, social planning, and social action in their professional work. Furthermore, the authors discovered that locality development was both perceived as the most relevant model of community organization and the one most practiced. This study discovered that the gap between perceived importance of a practice mode and the one actually used in practice was the smallest for locality development. Thus, community organizers in Israel identified locality development as a distinct model, perceived it as most important, and practice it to a substantial extent.

In a more recent study that is ongoing, the Cnaan and Rothman results are being examined from a cross-cultural perspective. Using the same study instrument originally employed (a 30-item questionnaire), and also focus groups and in-depth interviews, Matts Mattsson in Sweden (1992), Carmen Diaz and Nilsa Burgos in Puerto Rico, Mohammed M. Eweiss in Egypt, Marta Jara-Jubilar in Chile, Rama Pandy in India and the United States, Masaaki Yoshihara in Japan, and Ram Cnaan in the United States have tentatively arrived at findings similar to the earlier study. Locality development, apparently, has a high degree of use by professionals on a cross-national basis.

As noted above, locality development is a means to energize people and to teach them through experiential means to act on their own behalf in order to improve their quality of life. There is, and likely always will be, a need to aid local citizens to find their collective voice and participate in decision making and policy making around matters that impact on their well-being. Unfortunately, these actions are often not self-generated, and professional intervention of a nonintrusive nature is required to motivate people and inculcate effective skills of self-help. The analogy of teaching the skills of fishing rather than providing a fish for one meal bears reiteration. It brings home the notion of fostering personal com-petency in the same way that locality development conveys the notion of promoting community competency and social cohesion. In the face of potent contemporary trends engendering community disintegration, locality development stands as a countervailing community building force.

REFERENCES

Batten, T. R. *The Non-directive Approach in Group and Community Work*. Oxford, U.K.: Oxford University Press, 1967.

Biddle, W. W., and L. J. Biddle. *The Community Development Process: The Rediscovery of Local Initiatives*. New York: Holt, Rinehart, & Winston, 1965.

Biklen, D. P. *Community Organizing: Theory and Practice*. Englewood Cliffs, NJ: Prentice-Hall, 1983.

Bingham, R. D., and R. Mier. *Theories of Local Economic Development*. Thousand Oaks, CA: Sage, 1993.

Brager, G.A. "Advocacy and Political Behavior." *Social Work*, 13(2) (1968): 5–15.

Brager, G., and H. Specht. *Community Organizing*. New York: Columbia University Press, 1973.

Brager, G., H. Specht, and J. Torczyner. *Community Organizing*, 2nd ed. New York: Columbia University Press, 1987.

Bryant, R. "Conflict and Community Work: A Case Study." *Community Development Journal* 14(2) (1979): 1–7.

Burghardt, S. *The Other Side of Organizing*. Cambridge, MA: Schenkman, 1982.

Chavis, D. M., P. Florin, and M. R. J. Felix. "Nurturing Grassroots Initiatives for Community Development: The Role of Enabling Systems." In T. Mizrahi and J. Morrison, eds., *Community Organization and Social Administration: Advances, Trends, and Emerging Principles*, pp. 41–67. New York: Haworth, 1993.

Cnaan, R. A. "Neighborhood Representing Organizations: How Democratic Are They?" *Social Service Review* 65 (1991): 614–634.

Cnaan, R.A., and H. Adar. "An Integrative Model For Group Work in Community Organization Practice." *Social Work with Groups, 1987* 10(3) (1987): 5–24.

Cnaan, R. A., and J. Rothman. "Conceptualizing Community Intervention: An Empirical Test of 'Three Models' of Community Organization." *Administration in Social Work* 10(3) (1986): 41–55.

Coleman, J. S. *Community Conflict*. New York: Free Press, 1957.

Cox, F. M. "Communities: Alternative Conceptions of Community: Implications for Community Organization Practice." In F. M. Cox, J. L. Erlich, J. Rothman, and J. E. Tropman, eds., *Strategies of Community Organization: Macro Practice*, pp. 232–243. Itasca, IL: Peacock, 1987.

Dunham, A. *Community Welfare Organization: Principles and Practice*. New York: Crowell, 1958.

Dunham, A. "What Is the Job of the Community Organization Worker?" In E. B. Harper and A. Dunham, eds., *Community Organization in Action*, pp. 463–471. New York: Association Press, 1959.

Durkheim, E. *The Division of Labor in Modern Society*, G. Simpson, trans. New York: Free Press (original work published in 1893), 1933.

Epstein, I. "Professional Role Orientations and Conflict Strategies." *Social Work* 15(4) (1970): 87–92.

Friedmann, R. R., P. Florin, A. Wandersman, and R. Meier. "Local Action on Behalf of Local Collectives in the U.S. and Israel: How Different Are Leaders from Members in Voluntary Associations?" *Journal of Voluntary Action Research* 17(3&4) (1988): 36–54.

Garkovich, L. E. "Local Organizations and Leadership in Community Development." In J. A. Christenson and J. E. Robinson, eds., *Community Development in America*, pp. 196–218. Ames, IA: Iowa State University Press, 1989.

Goetz, E. G., and S. E. Clarke. *Comparative Urban Policies in a Global Era*. Thousand Oaks, CA: Sage, 1993.

Goulet, D. "Ethics in Development Theory and Practice." In D. S. Sanders and J. K. Matsuoka, eds., *Peace and Development*. Honolulu, HI: University of Hawaii School of Social Work, 1989.

Henderson, P., and D. N. Thomas. *Skills in Neighbourhood Work*. London: George Allen & Unwin, 1980.

Huenefeld, J. *The Community Activist's Handbook*. Boston: Beacon, 1970.

Hutcheson, J. D., and L. H. Dominguez. "Ethnic Self-help Organizations in Non-barrio Settings: Community Identity and Voluntary Action." *Journal of Voluntary Action Research* 15(4) (1986): 13–22.

Kahn, S. *Organizing: A Guide for Grassroots Leaders*. Silver Spring, MD: National Association of Social Workers, 1991.

Kettner, P. M., J. M. Daley, and A. W. Nichols. *Initiating Change in Organizations and Communities*. Monterey, CA: Brooks/Cole, 1985.

Khinduka, S.K. "Community Development: Potentials and Limitations." In F. M. Cox, J. L. Erlich, J. Rothman, and J. E. Tropman, eds., *Strategies of Community Organization: Macro practice*, pp. 353–362. Itasca, IL: Peacock, 1987.

Lappin, B. "Community Development: Beginnings in Social Work Enabling." In S. H. Taylor and R.W. Roberts, eds., *Theory and Practice of Community Social Work*, pp. 59–93. New York: Columbia University Press, 1985.

Lindeman, E. C. *The Community: An Introduction to the Study of Community Leadership and Organization*. New York: Association Press, 1921.

Marris, R., and M. Rein. *Dilemmas of Social Reform*, 2nd ed. Chicago: Aldine-Atherton, 1973.

Mattsson, M. *Community Work in a Political Framework: An International Research Project*. A paper presented at Inter-University Consortium on International Social development, Washington, DC, July 1992.

Mier, R. *Social Justice and Local Development Theory*. Thousand Oaks, CA: Sage, 1993.

Mondros, J. B., and S. M. Wilson. "Building High Access Community Organizations: Structures as Strategy." In T. Mizrahi and J. Morrison, eds., *Community Organization and Social Administration: Advances, Trends, and Emerging Principles*, pp. 69–85. New York: Haworth, 1993.

Morris, D., and K. Hess. *Neighborhood Power: The New Localism*. Boston: Beacon Press, 1975.

Perlman, R., and A. Gurin. *Community Organization and Social Planning*. New York: John Wiley, 1972.

Pray, K. L. M. "When Is Community Organization Social Work Practice?" *Proceedings, National Conference of Social Work*, 1947. New York: Columbia University Press, 1948.

Prestby, J., and A. Wandersman. "An Empirical Exploration of a Framework of Organizational Viability: Maintaining Block Associations." *Journal of Applied Behavioral Science* 21 (1985): 287–305.

Rivera, F. G., and J. L. Erlich. *Community Organizing in a Diverse Society.* Boston: Allyn and Beacon, 1992.

Ross, M. G. *Community Organization; Theory, Principles and Practice.* New York: Harper & Row, 1967.

Rothman, J., and J. E. Tropman. "Models of Community Organization and Macro Practice Perspectives: Their Mixing and Phases." In F. M. Cox, J. L. Erlich, J. Rothman, and J. E. Tropman, eds. *Strategies of Community Organization: Macro Practice,* pp. 3–26. Itasca, IL: Peacock, 1987.

Rubin, H. J., and I. S. Rubin. *Community Organizing and Development,* 2nd ed. New York: MacMillan, (1992).

Sade, P. *A Man Is a Closed Room, His Heart Broken, and Dark Falls Outside* (Ish beheder sagor, libo shabor, ubahotz yoredet affela). Tel Aviv: Schocken, 1993.

Tonnies, F. *Community and Society (Gemeinschaft and Gesellschaft),* C. E. Loomis, trans. East Lansing, MI: Michigan State University Press (original work published in 1912), 1957.

Warren, R.L. *The Community in America,* 3rd ed. Chicago: Rand McNally, 1978.

Yates, D. *Neighborhood Democracy.* Lexington, MA: D. C. Heath, 1973.

York, A. S. "Towards a Conceptual Model of Community Social Work." *British Journal of Social Work* 14 (1984): 241–255.

14.

Sylvia Martí-Costa and Irma Serrano-García

NEEDS ASSESSMENT AND COMMUNITY DEVELOPMENT: AN IDEOLOGICAL PERSPECTIVE

Community development is a process which, through consciousness-raising, promotes and utilizes human resources, leading to the empowerment of individuals and communities so that they can understand and solve their problems and create new circumstances for their livelihood. As part of this process, needs assessment may be utilized as a central method to facilitate the modification of social systems so they become more responsive to human needs.

At the individual level, community development promotes psychological growth and enhancement by channeling energies into self-help projects and through the genuine participation of individuals in those decisions that affect their lives. The basic assumption that underlies this reasoning is that most human beings can solve their problems when they obtain access to resources and create alternatives. The emphasis is on their strengths and their development (Rappaport, 1977).

Awareness of problems and of change possibilities is achieved by raising an individual's consciousness from its current or real level to its possible capacity. Real consciousness is defined as an individual or groups' understanding of reality at a given time. Possible consciousness is the maximum understanding that can be achieved by an individual or group according to its material circumstances at a given historical moment (Goldman, 1970).

Consciousness-raising includes critical judgment of situations, the search for underlying causes of problems and their consequences, and an active role in the transformation of society (Ander-Egg, 1980). It is an awareness of human dignity and is essential in the exploration of the relationship between the social order and human misery and in the discovery of the shortcomings inherent in our society (Freire, 1974). It facilitates individual and collective participation in building a new and less oppressive social order, thus affecting the general well-being of the population by enhancing the relationship between individuals and society. Needs assessment is valuable in the consciousness-raising process, because any social movement should start from and respond to the felt needs of the population, in other words, their real consciousness.

Community development can foster consciousness-raising through the involvement of individuals in change efforts. Community development activities need to be grounded in a specific political commitment that responds to the liberation of the powerless groups of society. This does not ignore the participation of the powerful in the maintenance or change of the present social order. It does, however, require a personal and professional commitment to the oppressed because of the mission of prevention—understanding and relieving human suffering.

Contrary to this view, many social scientists have fostered the value-free, apolitical, and ahistorical character of their disciplines throughout several decades (Moscovici, 1972; Weimer, 1979; Zuñiga, 1975). This position, which may be referred to as "the myth of neutrality," distorts the real value-laden and political nature of theory, methods, and practices and thus serves to alienate us from ourselves and others (Ander-Egg,

1973). It creates divisions and distrust within our ranks and resentment from those that participate as "subjects" or recipients of our work, feeling used, manipulated and misunderstood. Thus, it is necessary to examine this myth which has resulted in the social sciences serving the dominant groups of society.

The "myth of neutrality" has reasons for its existence. In some cases it has been sponsored by individuals who clearly believe in it, but in most cases, it has been accepted inadvertently by social scientists. One of the ways in which this occurs is by considering objectivity and neutrality as synonymous and inseparable concepts which are highly desirable in social scientific endeavors.

Those that hold that neutrality and objectivity must go together state that social scientists should not take political stances toward the object of their studies because this will hamper their research efforts (Myrdal, 1969). To them objectivity is defined as the capacity to study facts as they occur, without adhering to previously formed opinions and judgments and with the willingness to abandon positions that are proven false, inadequate, and unsatisfactory (Ander-Egg, 1977). Neutrality, its inseparable counterpart, is defined as a valueless stance before the objective reality (Martí, Note 1).

It is said that if researchers are not neutral, they cannot be objective (Martí, Note 1). This does not ring true as both concepts are different and clearly distinguishable, and while the pursuit of objectivity is desirable and necessary, the search for neutrality is not only impossible, but unwarranted. Objectivity is desirable because its definition implies the existence of defined values and positions which one is willing to change when an examination of reality requires it. Neutrality is impossible because every activity takes place in a particular political context.

If the political nature of the social sciences is recognized and accepted then an explicit definition of social scientists' values is necessary. It is our position that this value stance must be characterized by a commitment to the disadvantaged and powerless groups within a given society. This commitment is to the abandonment of a spectator role and the activation of a professional's mind and art to the service of a cause (Palau, Note 2). This cause should be the significant transformation of inequities in society which implies activism, risk, initiative, and a willingness to fight for clearly defined points of view.

To summarize, needs assessment is an integral part of community development, the process of consciousness-raising. It implies a political commitment which undermines the traditional view of a neutral science and a firm commitment to the exploited, underprivileged and powerless groups in society.

This paper will show that needs assessment is a political process that can be conceptualized as a tool for the organization, mobilization and consciousness-raising of groups and communities. This implies (1) that the diverse uses of needs assessment methods be placed on a continuum, ranging from the perpetuation of control and the maintenance of the social system to the achievement of radical social change; (2) an emphasis on multiple techniques of needs assessment that facilitate collective activities, leadership development, growth of organizational skills, and participation of community members in interventions within research (Irizarry & Serrano, 1979); and (3) the belief that it is necessary to examine ideologies and values as they influence objectives, the selection of needs assessment techniques, intervention strategies, conceptual frameworks, and the utilization of obtained data.

NEEDS ASSESSMENT

Purpose

Needs assessment is part of a process used to plan social service programs (Pharis, 1976; Siegel, Attkisson, & Cohn, 1977). It is used to determine the problems and goals of the residents of a given community to assure that an intervention will respond to the needs of the population that is being sampled (Warheit, 1976).

The purposes that sustain the use of needs assessment methodology can be placed on a continuum (Table 14.1) according to their political roles. Towards the top of Table 14.1 are purposes that foster system maintenance and control; towards the bottom are ones that promote social change and consciousness-raising. Social system maintenance and control efforts include those activities which are carried out to maintain and/or strengthen the status quo. They also include first order change efforts which alter some of the ways in which the system functions but not the ideology on which it is based (Watzlawick, Weakland, & Fisch, 1974). Radical, or second order, social change efforts imply consciousness-raising and structural and functional alterations.

In consonance with these definitions, the very bottom of the continuum shows needs assessment as a mechanism used by community residents for participation and control in decision making. Needs assessment becomes a technique that facilitates second order social change.

The very top of the continuum lists purposes that foster system maintenance and control, including those that are used to obtain additional funding for already established community programs (Siegel et al., 1977) so as to guarantee their continuation. In the middle of the continuum, but still focusing on maintenance and control efforts,

TABLE 14.1
Continuum of Needs Assessment Purposes

Political Role	Purpose
Control System Maintenance	Guarantee the economic survival of service programs
	Respond to interest group pressures
	Provide services required by communities
	Program evaluation
	Program planning
	Public policy decision making
Social Change	Measure, describe, and understand community life styles
	Assess community resources to lessen external dependency
	Return needs assessment data to facilitate residents' decision making
	Provide skill training, leadership, and organizational skills
	Facilitate collective activities and group mobilization
	Facilitate consciousness-raising

are included purposes such as (a) planning for decision making and program evaluation (Murell, 1976); (b) gaining additional input toward personnel recruitment; (c) describing, measuring and understanding different aspects of community life (Siegel et al., 1977); (d) determining discrepancies between residents' and professionals' points of view (Ronald, Titus, Strasser, & Vess, Note 3; and (e) obtaining knowledge about community resources so as to link these to agency services.

In analyzing this continuum it is important to notice that most needs assessment efforts are directed towards consumer satisfaction and agency survival. These are legitimate and necessary goals; however, if technique development is limited to these goals, it will be incomplete and unsatisfactory. Needs assessment methodology, if it is to respond to a commitment to the powerless and to the fostering of social change,

must (a) emphasize techniques that, singly or in combination, facilitate grouping and mobilizing people; (b) foster collective activities; (c) facilitate leadership development; and (d) involve residents in the entire research process. These characteristics are essential so that the technique can facilitate consciousness-raising.

Categorization and Evaluation of Techniques

At present there is a great diversity of needs assessment techniques. In some instances it is suggested that different techniques be combined focusing on diverse kinds of interventions (Aponte, 1976; Pharis, 1976; Siegel et al., 1977). Others suggest that only one technique be used with one line of intervention preferred (Clifford, Note 4; Evans, Note 5; Zautra, Note 6). In order to respond to the goals of organization, mobilization, and conscious-ness-raising in communities, the multiple technique approach is more desirable since a more precise view of reality is obtained. More data are gathered which will vary quantitatively and qualitatively, thus pro-viding a thorough appraisal of community needs. Another reason for the combined use of techniques is that their limitations and deficiencies can be balanced. Howev-er, it is also important to study how each individual technique contributes to the goal of greater mobilization.

Needs assessment techniques can be grouped in three different categories de-fined by the contact they provide between the researcher and community residents. This contact is extremely important as it may be used to foster collectivization, mo-bilization, leadership development, and resident involvement (Ander-Egg, 1980; Sanguinetti, 1981), characteristics that are essential to a new focus on needs assess-ment goals.

No contact with participants. In this cat-egory, techniques permit no relationship between the intervener and the partici-pants. These techniques are rates or percentages under treatment, social indica-tors, social area analysis and dynamic modeling (Kleemeir, Stephenson, & Isaacs, Note 7; Bell, 1976; Murell, 1976; Pharis, 1976). In general terms, these methods try to determine community needs by utilizing qualitative and quantita-tive data from several sources, such as demographic records and other social indi-cators. They are based on the assumption that community needs and problems that appear in official statistics are representa-tive of community problems. The major limitation of the "non-contact with the par-ticipant" techniques lies in their absolute lack of direct mobilization potential. Since

the residents are not involved in the needs assessment project—in fact, it can even happen without their knowledge—their in-volvement in social action efforts is not to be expected.

Contact with the agency or community. The "contact with the agency or communi-ty" category includes observation (Ander-Egg, 1978), service provider assessment (Kelly, Note 8), key informants (Pharis, 1976), behavioral census (Murell, 1976), surveys (Clifford, Note 4; O'Brien, Note 9), nominal groups (Delbecq, Van de Ven, & Gustoffsen, 1976), and community fo-rums (Kleemeir et al., Note 7) among other techniques. The interaction that these tech-niques allow for takes place basically through three means: observations, inter-views, and group meetings.

Observation facilitates interaction by the observer's mere presence in the setting. In-terviewers interact individually and in groups with community residents, service providers, or other key informants to di-rectly obtain data. This interaction takes place openly, as in community forums, or in a more controlled manner, as in nominal groups.

Key informants, nominal groups, com-munity forums, and surveys respond to the goals of mobilization and consciousness-raising in the community. The first three techniques encourage community input by eliciting residents' discussions and intro-spections about the collective nature of their problems and needs. They serve to strengthen communication networks in the community and they facilitate the process of program planning. Survey techniques share some of these qualities if the survey is constructed, coordinated, and adminis-tered by community members. This process generates great involvement and knowledge and the ready acceptance of

results by the rest of the community (Sanguinetti, 1981).

The nominal group technique has these,
and other, advantages. Because of the
structured nature of its process (Delbecq et
al., 1976), it (1) maximizes the amount,
diversity, and quality of the problems and
alternatives proposed; (2) inhibits the control of the group by a few vocal persons
(Siegel et al., 1977); (3) allows conflicting
opinions to be tolerated; (4) fosters creativity; (5) facilitates attention to the contributions of marginal group members; and (6)
emphasizes the role of needs assessment as
the basis for program creation and planning. These four techniques have the highest mobilization potential.

Combined techniques.   This category includes convergent analysis (Bell, 1976),
community impressions (Siegel et al.,
1977), community meetings/surveys
(Kleemeir et al., Note 7), and others. Convergent analysis techniques include techniques of service utilization, social
indicators, and surveys. Each technique is
used with a specific objective in mind and
it is expected that, overall, the information
offered by the techniques should give an
estimate of those persons whose needs are
not being satisfied.

Community impressions and community
meetings/surveys have several common elements. The former include the techniques of
key informants, data revision, and community forum. The latter includes the first two
steps in addition to a survey, allowing the
data to be validated and permitting additional verbal input from participants. Although
all these techniques require a lot of energy
and effort, they are the best alternative in the
needs assessment process because they
combine high mobilization potential with
the more traditional criteria of representativeness, validity, and reliability.

Criteria to Judge the Adequacy of Techniques

Given the diversity of techniques, it is
necessary to develop specific factors or criteria that should be considered in judging
the adequacy of a technique. Some authors
have examined this issue and have proposed criteria for the selection of techniques. These criteria include: the nature of
the problem, the skills of both the researcher and the participants, available resources (League of California Cities, 1979),
representativeness, the specificity required
of the information (Murell, 1976), and the
amount of political risk that the sponsoring
group desires to tolerate (Aponte, 1976).

Although all these criteria are useful, additional criteria should be considered if the
needs assessment effort is to contribute to
community organization and mobilization.
These criteria are presented in Table 14.2 and
contrasted with more traditional views. The
following dimensions are used as a guideline
for this comparison: the goals, sources, content, and processes of the assessment.

A major distinction between the two sets
of criteria is their goals. One set emphasizes
prevention and promotion and the awareness of the collective nature of needs. The
other works from a remedial perspective
which focuses on the individual and on fostering dependency on external resources.
The impact of these differences is most noticeable in the assessment process since a
collective focus requires a collective intervention and an individual focus does not.

An evaluation of previously mentioned
techniques according to the community
organization and mobilization criteria appears in Table 14.3. As can be seen, key
informants, surveys, nominal groups and
community forums are the most adequate
techniques. It is important to stress, however, that no single technique can be seen

TABLE 14.2
Suggested Criteria to Evaluate the Adequacy of Needs Assessment Techniques

Dimensions of Needs Assessment Process	Criteria	
	Criteria That Foster Mobilization	Traditional Criteria
Goals of Assessment	Prevention and promotion	Treatment
	Awareness of collective nature of needs	Individual focus
	Encourage collective action	Foster dependency on external resources
Source of Input	Community residents Marginal groups	Service providers Total population
Content of Assessment	All perceived needs	Assessment of needed services
	Internal community resources	
Processes of Assessment	Facilitate community involvement and control of process	Assessment carried out by "experts"
	Facilitate face to face interaction between intervener researcher and participants	Lack of community participation
		Interaction highly controlled by scientific standards
	Data belong to participants	Data collection and future planning controlled by agencies
	Planning and collective action carried out by intervener-researcher and participants	

as valid for all times and circumstances; therefore, they should be tailored to the particular situation in which the needs assessment is conducted.

NEEDS ASSESSMENT AND COMMUNITY DEVELOPMENT

Irizarry and Serrano (1979) have developed a model, Intervention within Research, which integrates needs assessment into a community development approach. It uses needs assessment as its methodological foundation and the concept of problematization as its ideological guideline (Freire, 1974). Problematization, our translation for the term *problematización*, refers to the process whereby consciousness-raising takes place. If the latter is seen as the goal, then problematization involves the different strategies whereby it can be achieved.

The model conceptualizes the processes of intervention and research as simultaneous and interdependent. It also assumes that all phases of the model should be permeated with explicit ideological inputs that lead to consciousness-raising.

The objectives suggested for this model include: (1) the creation of collective efforts to solve community problems as defined by community residents; (2) the achievement of individual and group participation in the analysis of social reality; (3) the creation of grass-roots organizations; and (4) the development of political skills among participants, resulting in their increased involvement in public affairs.

The model includes four phases. The first phase, familiarization with the community, includes a review of all written and statistical material regarding the community, and several visits to the same. This approach provides knowledge regarding the community's history, its structures, and the processes which facilitate the intervener's entry into the community. It should emphasize the early identification of key persons in the community through informal communication or through more structured means.

The second phase, which arises from a later revision of the original model (Martí, Note 1), is characterized by the creation of a core group that must be composed of both key community persons and interveners. This core group has planning, coordination, and evaluation responsibilities throughout the entire process of intervention within research.

The creation of this core group has positive psychological and operative repercussions. Since the group is formed with community people, a more effective dialogue can take place. It is also possible to increase their commitment and guarantee the group's continuance in this way. In addition, the key person can acquire skills through modeling or training that will be useful to future community work.

One of the most important tasks of this group is the direction and coordination of the needs assessment. This begins with the core group taking an active role in evaluating the relevance of the different needs assessment techniques to their particular community. The group's next step is the consideration of alternative actions to develop an effective propaganda campaign to inform residents of the needs assessment. In this effort it is essential to obtain the support of other organized groups in the community.

The core group should direct the needs assessment process per se as well as the process of returning the analyzed data to community residents. This can be done through letters, individual visits, group meetings, or community assemblies. The method used will be determined by the needs assessment technique previously used, by the number of participants it entailed, and by the number of human resources available. The data should be returned promptly and should be explained in simple terms.

The third phase, formation of task groups, includes group activities suggested by the needs assessment. In this phase, short- and long-term goals are defined and further action plans developed. To carry out these activities an organizational structure must be created. It is suggested that for this purpose a general community meeting should be held where task groups are formed around the needs assessment priorities. This general meeting should be planned and conducted by all participants with the support and guidance of the core group.

In addition to the task groups, workshops and other social, cultural, educational, and recreational activities must be fostered. Workshops should concentrate on the development of skills so as to help community groups deal effectively with outside forces that rally against their efforts. Some

TABLE 14.3
Evaluation of Needs Assessment Techniques According to Their Potential for Mobilization
Organization and Consciousness-Raising

Criteria	Social Records	Computer Use	Observation	Social Indicators	Dynamic Modelling	Systems Model	Surveys	Key Informants	Forum	Nominal Group	Service Provider Assessments	Behavioral Census	Key Persons
Obtains information from community residents							X		X	X			X
Obtains information from marginal groups	X						X		X	X			X
Achieves change in services provided			X				X	X	X	X	X	X	X
Facilitates identifying a wide range of needs		X	X	X			X		X	X			
Facilitates development of internal resources								X	X	X		X	X
Control of information by residents			X	X			X	X	X	X		X	X
Oriented toward prevention			X						X	X			
Collective view of problems									X	X			
Commitment to residents' participation in general									X	X			
Commitment to residents' participation in research							X		X	X			
a. data collection							X		X	X			
b. instrument construction							X		X	X			X
c. data analysis							X		X	X			X
d. data returns									X	X			X
Fosters relationship between residents and intervener								X	X	X			X
a. more time together							X	X	X	X			X
b. dialogue							X	X	X	X			X
Facilitate collective activities									X	X			X
a. two or more persons									X	X			
b. two or more persons regarding common problems									X	X			
c. adding the discussion of possible solutions									X	X			
d. initiate collective action									X	X			

possible topics for the workshops are leadership, skills to deal with service agencies, interpersonal communication, propaganda, and organizational skills. Particular attention should be given to internal group processes so that the task groups' decision making will improve, their leadership struggles diminish, and their cohesiveness increase. We believe that this last characteristic is particularly important and that both the workshops and group tasks should emphasize cohesiveness.

The last phase in the model, involvement of new groups, is initiated after some of the short- and long-term goals of the task groups are achieved. This involves the development of new goals which should help in bringing together other community groups. The steps described should be repeated in a cyclical manner because needs change throughout the process and the community may develop other goals and interests.

CONCLUSION

This paper has presented an alternative ideological framework to evaluate and direct needs assessment efforts. It has also presented a model for its use for community development. Community residents can and should control intervention within research efforts that directly or indirectly involve them and scientists should facilitate this control. If some of these changes are incorporated into current needs assessment efforts, scientists will be more responsive to the people to whom their major efforts should be directed.

REFERENCE NOTES

1. Martí, S. *Hacia una identificación de necesidades en el sector femenino del Barrio Buen Consejo*. Unpublished M. A. thesis, University of Puerto Rico, 1980.

2. Palau, A. *La investigación con la técnica de observación: ¿Para quién y desde dónde?* Unpublished manuscript, 1977. (Available at Sociology Department, University of Puerto Rico, Rio Piedras, P.R.).

3. Ronald, L., Titus, W., Strasser, G., & Vess, J. *Views of Mental Health: A First Step in Needs Assessment*. Paper presented at the 87th Annual Convention of the American Psychological Association, New York City, 1979.

4. Clifford, D. L. *A Critical View of Needs Assessment in Community Mental Health Planning*. Paper presented at the Second National Conference on Needs Assessment in Health and Human Services, Louisville, Kentucky, 1978.

5. Evans, P. *A Model for Conducting Needs Assessment and a Report on National Ratios*. Paper presented at the 87th Annual Convention of the American Psychological Association, New York City, 1979.

6. Zautra, A. *Quality of Life Determinants: Some Guidelines for Measuring Community Well-Being*. Paper presented at the Second National Conference on Needs Assessment in Health and Human Services, Louisville, Kentucky, March, 1978.

7. Kleemeir, C. P., Stephenson, D. P., & Isaacs, L. D. *Developing a Needs Assessment Approach for Community Consultation and Education*. Paper presented at the 87th Annual Convention of the American Psychological Association, New York City, 1979.

8. Kelly, M. *Halton Region Services for Children: A Needs Assessment*. Unpublished manuscript, 1978. (Available at Faculty of Social Work, Wilfrid Laurier University, Waterloo, Ontario, Canada.)

9. O'Brien, D. *Merging the Technical and Community Catalytic Functions of Citizen Surveys: Toward a Theoretical Framework*. Paper presented at the Second National Conference on Needs Assessment in Health and Human Services, Louisville, Kentucky, 1978.

REFERENCES

Ander-Egg, E. *Hacia una metodología de la militancia y el compromiso*. Buenos Aires: Ecro, 1973.

Ander-Egg, E. *Diccionario del trabajo social.* Barcelona: Nova Terra, 1977.

Ander-Egg, E. *Introducción a las técnicas de investigación social.* Buenos Aires: Humanitas, 1978.

Ander-Egg, E. *Metodología del desarrollo de comunidad.* Madrid: UNIEUROP, 1980.

Aponte, S. F. "Implications for the Future of Needs Assessment." In R. A. Bell, M. Sundel, S. F. Aponte, & S. A. Murell (Eds.). *Needs Assessment in Health and Human Services.* Louisville: University of Louisville, 1976.

Bell, R. A. "The Use of a Convergent Assessment Model in the Determination of Health Status and Assessment of Need." In R. S. Bell, M. Sundel, J. F. Aponte, & S. A. Murell (Eds.). *Needs Assessment in Health and Human Services.* Louisville: University of Louisville, 1976.

Delbecq, A., Van de Ven, A., & Gustoffsen, D. *Group Techniques for Program Planning: A Guide to Nominal Group and Delphi Processes.* Glenview, Illinois: Scott, Foresman, & Company, 1976.

Freire, P. *Pedagogía del oprimido.* México: Siglo 21, 1974.

Goldman, L. Conciencia adecuada, conciencia posible y conciencia falsa. In L. Goldman (Ed.), *Marxismo y ciencias humanas.* Paris: Galiemard, 1970.

Irizarry, A., & Serrano-García, I. Intervención en la investigación: Su aplicación al Barrio Buen Consejo. *Boletín AVEPSO,* 1979, *2,* 6–21.

League of California Cities. "Social Needs Assessment: A Scientific or Political Process." In F. Cox, J. Erlich, J. Rothman, & J. Tropman (Eds.), *Strategies of Community Organization.* Itasca, Illinois: F. E. Peacock, 1979.

Moscovici, S. "Society and Theory in Social Psychology." In J. Israel & H. Tajifel (Eds.), *The Context of Social Psychology.* New York: Academic Press, 1972.

Murell, S. A. "Eight Process Steps for Converting Needs Assessment Data into Program Operations." In S. A. Bell, M. Sundel, J. Aponte, & S. Murell (Eds.), *Needs Assessment in Health and Human Services.* Louisville: University of Louisville, 1976.

Myrdal, G. *Objectivity in Social Research.* New York: Random House, 1969.

Pharis, D. B. "The Use of Needs Assessment Techniques in Mental Health Planning." *Community Mental Health Review,* 1976, *1,* 4–11.

Rappaport, J. *Community Psychology: Values, Research and Action.* New York: Holt, Rinehart, & Winston, 1977.

Sanguinetti, Y. La investigación participativa en los procesos de desarrollo de américa latina. *Revista de ALAPSO,* 1981, *1,* 221–238.

Siegel, L. M., Attkisson, C. C., & Cohn, I. H. "Mental Health Needs Assessment: Strategies and Techniques." In W. A. Hargreaves & C. C. Attkisson (Eds.), *Resource Materials for Community Mental Health Program Evaluation.* Rockville, Maryland: National Institute of Mental Health, 1977.

Warheit, George J. "The Use of Field Surveys to Estimate Health Needs in the General Population." In R. A. Bell, M. Sundel, J. Aponte, & S.A. Murell (Eds.), *Needs Assessment in Health and Human Services.* Louisville: University of Louisville, 1976.

Watzlawick, P., Weakland, J., & Fisch, R. *Change: Principles of Problem Formation and Problem Resolution.* New York: Norton, 1974.

Weimer, W. *Notes on the Methodology of Scientific Research.* New York: Wiley, 1979.

Zuñiga, R. "The Experimenting Society and Radical Social Reform." *American Psychologist,* 1975, *30,* 99–115.

15.

Mohan L. Kaul

SERVING OPPRESSED COMMUNITIES:
THE SELF-HELP APPROACH

INTRODUCTION

The East Akron Community House, a settlement house in Akron, Ohio, invited the author to "develop a program of community development with a view to achieve social justice and equal opportunity through democratic processes and nonviolent methods." This work began in early 1970 in an area that reflected years of general neglect, where residents complained about stray dogs, run-down dilapidated housing, scattered rubbish, congestion, abandoned cars, vacant houses, lack of open spaces, dark and dangerous streets, and a continuous smell of chemicals in the air. However, a closer look revealed that poverty, crime, powerlessness, and, above all, a sense of hopelessness were the deep-rooted problems. In spite of the seemingly insurmountable obstacles, area residents were surprisingly warm and friendly, demonstrated genuine pride in their homes, and unmistakenly indicated a readiness for change. These ingredients pointed to a situation where the existing dormant human resource could be motivated to engage in a self-help process with a definite outcome of a satisfying community life in the foreseeable future.

The author left the East Akron Community House in September, 1971, after eight block clubs and a council of block club presidents were established and their membership was actively engaged in neighborhood improvement projects. Since then, the author's association with block clubs has included membership in one of them, periodical review of the process, occasional consultation, and attendance in selected neighborhood activities.

Akron, often referred to as the "Rubber Capital" of the world, is located in heavily industrialized northeastern Ohio. Its present population is 237,077,[1] a decline of 38,348 persons during the last 10 years, indicating the consequences of rubber and other related industry cutting back or moving out of Akron.

There are approximately 22,000 people in four neighborhoods of East Akron. One neighborhood of approximately 5,000 people is situated in the immediate vicinity of East Akron Community House (the only settlement house in the city of Akron). It is a predominantly black neighborhood where the block clubs are located, and it is referred to as East Akron Neighborhood in this paper.

The East Akron Neighborhood was 20 to 25 years old when East Akron Community House was established in 1915 to aid the assimilation and acculturation of European immigrants. Within one generation, they prospered and moved out of the neighborhood. The second group of people who came to live in this neighborhood were Appalachian whites. They followed the earlier residents' example and left the neighbor-

---

[1]"The Census: Town by Town," Akron Beacon *Journal*, September 6, 1981.

hood within the decade of 1940–1950. Black people are the third population group to find their first homes here[2]; many of them are longtime residents and would like to live in this neighborhood as long as they can.

East Akron Community House determined in 1969, "to muster the resources and skills needed to enable residents to influence and/or control decision making process and neighborhood serving institutions."[3] During the same time period, settlement houses around the country, in response to their constituencies' demands, were in the process of or were working toward neighborhood control. It was also during this time when maximum feasible participation concept propounded by the War on Poverty was being seriously debated and analyzed.[4]

COMMUNITY DEVELOPMENT

In East Akron Neighborhood, a program of community development was seen as a method of motivating people directly affected by neighborhood problems to organize and undertake well-planned action steps as a group, for dealing with such problems. Such a definition may seem to be somewhat narrow, but is realistic and manageable. The term "community" referred to, "an aggregate of families and individuals settled in a fairly compact and contiguous area, with significant elements of common life, as shown by manners, customs, traditions, and modes of speech." The word development implied the element of self-help and citizen participation in a decision-making process for the growth of community spirit and community activities. Citizen participation meant active involvement of individual residents in joint endeavors for better living conditions within the neighborhood.

Community development as a method of solving neighborhood problems is based on the assumption that social change can be brought about more effectively in geographical areas where people live, since the well-being of an individual is directly related to the place he (or she) calls home, the street he lives on, and the neighborhood where he raises his family. Geographic communities, comprised of populations with multiple needs, need assistance in recognizing their common needs, and organizing as a means to achieve common goals assumes pooling of resources, reinforcement of self-confidence, and development of a sense of power to deal effectively with neighborhood problems. Cooperation among residents is somewhat expected. However, cooperation is not seen as an ultimate good; individual efforts are still valid.[5]

ORGANIZING

The idea of neighborhood organizing was not new to the community, since attempts were made in the past by concerned residents to get together with their neighbors. Additionally, some service agencies in the area had taken steps to organize residents around specific issues. Such attempts had invariably been a passing phenomenon.

---

[2]Homer L. Pettengill, a long-time Executive Director of East Akron Community House, provided the information in 1970.

[3]Pettengill.

[4]There was a strong movement for local control of the settlement houses, nationally. EACH decision may have been influenced by that also. For comparative community case studies see Ralph M. Kramer, *Participation of the Poor* (Englewood Cliffs, NJ: Prentice-Hall, Inc., 1969).

[5]Murray G. Ross, *Community Organization* (New York: Harper & Row Publishers, 1967), 77.

The most recent attempt by the Community Action program of the War on Poverty had not materialized. During initial contacts, the resident position to the idea was favorable but had indicated some apprehensiveness about it.[6] Obviously, organizing was a feasible idea. But, maintenance of the groups organized was the challenge.

It was therefore assumed that organized groups are likely to keep up their initial momentum if the local leadership is developed to meet the challenge. In a general way, leaders who could work with people and stimulate them and could help the groups use all the abilities and experiences of its members were not known to the residents.[7] On the basis of a preliminary study it was found that there were not many who had such a specific minimum leadership experience. There were some with church-related experience, others had political experience at the precinct level, and quite a few had a life-long informal problem-solving experience. Their methods of helping included listening and referral. Apparently, there was a need for development of existing leaders.

Since residents were keen to meet with their neighbors on the block to share common concerns and to get to know each other, the strategy to organize, therefore, focused on initial socializing. It was assumed that, once the residents got together, appropriate leadership would develop if appropriate steps were taken. It was also understood that socializing as a means to achieve the goal of initial organizing could become an end in itself unless the organizer skillfully identified rallying points to develop ideological commitment to achieve social change.

Organizing focuses on the location of common problems and joint efforts aimed at their solution. Ecklein and Lauffer's view of organizing "as a means of achieving and guiding local control over problems that originate elsewhere in society"[8] appeared to be in tune with a genuine desire of the residents to exert some local control on those facets of community life that were historically directed from outside—such as education, employment opportunities, housing, social services, and political process of two major political parties. Neighborhood improvement, as an overall noncontroversial and worthwhile initial goal emerged as a top priority and block organization was accepted as a means to achieve it. The idea to hold meetings in a house on the block had a tremendous appeal and was perhaps in line with Kahn's thinking that "block organizing is a highly manageable technique usually an urban technique."[9] The term "block club" was readily agreed upon, as everybody seemed to be familiar with it. It was understood to mean a group of concerned residents who get together to improve their block by working together. In view of the limited resources and the experimental nature of the project, a 25-block area comprised of 4,000 to 5,000 people with census tract 5034 as its core area was determined as the program implementation area; it was chosen for its proximity to the Community House, resident's knowledge of the agency, and readily available demographic information. Streets in the implementation area were designated as blocks on the basis of a face-to-face relationship and identification with the street as one's residence.

---

[6]This is primarily an impressionistic view gathered during initial contacts with local residents.

[7]*Community Action Training, Inc., So, You're on a Committee,* 1975, p. 20.

[8]Joan L. Ecklein, and Armaud A. Lauffer, *Community Organizers and Social Planners* (New York: John Wiley & Sons, 1972), 11.

[9]Si Kahn, *How People Get Power* (New York: McGraw-Hill, 1970), 36.

To create a general sense of accomplishment in the neighborhood, a pilot block was selected. The resident concerns on this block appeared to be resolvable with minimum effort, and the residents were willing to make that effort. However, it was understood that residents would need assistance in: getting together, identifying common problems, building relationships, finding resources, and selecting action steps toward problem resolution. It was also assumed that pilot block accomplishments would generate a positive environment for organizing the neighborhood.

Community organizers have successfully used inclusion of formal leaders in developing community associations[10] since enhancement of social relationships is seen as bringing about greater capacity to deal with common problems. This approach was slightly modified to suit the East Akron Neighborhood. It was assumed that the realistic way to motivate the residents to come forward and participate in a neighborhood organization effort would be through identification of a contact person who may or may not be a formal leader. The contact persons were seen as concerned citizens who are willing to volunteer their time and effort to achieve changes on the block. Often, they are long-time residents and feel a sense of belongingness towards their neighborhood, they are well-known in the area, and they are generally trusted.

The organization was primarily to be neighborhood based and would not be equipped to use conflict and confrontation as deliberate strategies in its formative stage. In that sense the block clubs organization was to be different from five types of contemporary mass organizations;

Alinsky-type programs (1959), the mass organization as part of civil rights movement (1963, 1968), the Mobilization for Youth (1964), the Community Action Program of War on Poverty (1965), and The Welfare Rights Movement (1966).[11] The Community organizer, "a qualified social work practitioner with specialized training in community organization,"[12] was to be a catalyst in the initial stages of organization.

Block Club-Council of Block Club Presidents, a two-level, input and feedback structure, was envisioned as the only grassroots organization accessible to the residents in order to voice their concerns, seek help and support, volunteer for services, and participate in a decision-making process to deal with those concerns. Block clubs would deal with block concerns and the Council of Block Club Presidents would have the responsibility to deal with the problems affecting the entire program implementation area. It was hypothesized that such a viable human resource structure would develop maturity, creativity, flexibility, and confidence as it began to undertake problem-solving activities. Development of such a working structure became the primary objective of the community development effort, and any problem resolution was seen as a by-product during early stages.

---

[10]Murray G. Ross, op. cit., pp. 168–173.

[11]For details, the following references are suggested: Saul D. Alinsky, *Reveille for Radicals* (Chicago: University of Chicago Press, 1946).

Frances Piven, "Participation of Residents in Neighborhood Community Action Programs," *Social Work* (Jan 1966) 4, 74.

OEO, *Community Action Program Guide* (Washington, DC: Government Printing Office (Feb 1965), Vol. 1.

Richard A. Cloward, and Frances Piven, "Birth of a Movement: The War on Poverty," *The Nation* (May 8, 1967).

[12]Arthur Dunham, *The New Community Organization* (New York: Thomas Y. Crowell Company, 1970), 6.

The methodology to organize block clubs developed as a carefully implemented step-by-step process that included: an on-foot survey,[13] a working map, problem observation, informal meetings, house calls, establishing linkages, unit gatherings, finding and getting natural leaders interested,[14] resident involvement in the planning committees, and block formation meetings. The first eight block clubs were organized during 1970–71 and a Council of Block Club Presidents was formed. This concluded the first phase of organization; a neighborhood structure was in place and ready to work for neighborhood improvement. Its first major challenge came sooner than anticipated. The structure successfully mobilized human resources to close a notorious bar in the neighborhood in early 1972.[15] The presence of the bar had created danger to life and property for more than a decade. This single event strengthened and stabilized the block club-council leadership and created an overall environment of neighborhood power and self-confidence in the community. The organizing phase was completed in 1975 when 22 block clubs were organized. As the block clubs got organized, the Council of Block Club Presidents was expanded accordingly to accommodate each new block club.

A summary of their accomplishments[16] is presented to illustrate the wide range of programs and activities of block clubs and the council. This is not a total list.

---

[13]The assumption is that events in the neighborhood can be better understood by walking as compared to riding in a car.

[14]Not necessarily a formal leader: a person who is respected by his or her neighbors and is more likely to be listened to.

[15]For a detailed discussion refer to Mohan L. Kaul, "Block Clubs and Social Action: A Case Study in Community Conflict," in *Journal of Sociology and Social Welfare* (March 1976) 4, 437–450.

[16]Information in this section is based on the data supplied by Grady Appleton, Director, Neighborhood Organization and Development, East Akron.

Recreation and Cultural

Over the years, the block clubs have developed meaningful, locally suited recreational and cultural programs that include an annual Labor Day parade and beauty pageant. A softball league, summer picnic, family night, and Christmas light decoration contest are some of the other regular features.

The sustained efforts of the block clubs have resulted in providing much-needed three parks for the neighborhood: Homestead mini park, Talbot-Whitney mini park, and Joy Park.

Health and Sanitation

Rodent population in the neighborhood is now under control. Trash barrels have been placed on vacant lots and rotten trees have been removed. Stray dogs are no longer a nuisance.

Political Action

A neighborhood elementary school was reopened after remaining closed for one year. Voter registration is a regular activity of the block clubs. Police community relations have improved. Abandoned cars have been removed. High gas billings are protested, and appropriately adjusted. Candidates for political office seek block club leaders for support.

Neighborhood Beautification

Lawncare, flower gardens, street paving sidewalks projects, proper maintenance of home lawns, clean-up and fix-up projects, and planting and trimming trees on devil strips are some of the ongoing activities for beautifying the neighborhood.

Safety

Missing traffic signs and additional street lighting have been secured. A neighborhood citizens alert program to deter house burglaries is in place. Block homes for school children during emergencies are available. Overweight trucks are no longer driving on residential streets.

Housing

The housing task force has secured homestead exemptions, grants, and loans. A number of vacant houses have been rehabilitated.

Miscellaneous

Other activities include a community-sponsored annual family Christmas dinner, telephone and personal contact with shut-ins, Kelly Avenue street extension project, food buckets for Christmas and Thanksgiving, assistance to disaster victims, raising money for children who need shoes, and much-needed help to senior citizens by filling forms, cutting grass, raking leaves, shovelling snow, and providing transportation.

Block Club-Neighborhood Council is primarily a self-help project and is very cost effective. East Akron Community House provides staff services for the Council of Block Club Presidents and assists block clubs as and when necessary. Local universities and colleges place their students for field work experience here and local newspapers have written about the project favorably. Other citizen groups in the city have made inquiries.

The community organization effort initiated in 1970 has stood the test of time during the last 13 years. It is alive and well and will achieve significant objectives in the near future. The success of this project is primarily due to the effective pattern that has developed over the years as a result of an on-the-job training provided by the Block Club-Council of Block Club Presidents structure.

CITIZEN PARTICIPATION AND LEADERSHIP DEVELOPMENT

Each block club has four officers: president, vice president, secretary and treasurer. Generally, at least one additional person gets involved with block club leadership. This person may not be interested in running for office or does not get elected for office. Taking into consideration the entire block clubs organization (20 active block clubs, and a Council of Block Club Presidents), more than 100 persons are involved in leadership roles on a day-to-day basis. Each block club President is also a member of the Council of Block Club Presidents and gets to be nominated to at least one of the eight standing committees of the council. The Block Club-Council of Block Club Presidents provides at least three levels of participation: very active participation for block club presidents; active participation for three officers and one member of each block club; and regular participation for the remaining membership of the clubs. During any one month, 200 to 250 residents of the neighborhood are involved in a decision-making process directly related to neighborhood programs, activities, and problem solving. On a short notice, a group of 100 persons can be mobilized to go to the city hall for a meeting.

Officer's training, orientation workshops, refresher courses, and overnight retreats for planning and policy formulation are regular features of the organization. This has enhanced the personal growth of a large number of residents in addition to the development of effective leadership for block clubs and the council.

To collect the significant data regarding the block club Leadership, a survey was undertaken in 1980 wherein 78 leaders participated. The sample included: 20 presidents; 11 vice presidents, 19 secretaries, 14 treasurers, and 14 regular members of 20 active block clubs serving a population of approximately 5000 people. It was found that 72% of the leaders had less than $10,000 income per year, only 50% had completed high school, 80% were not born in Ohio, 63% were 55 years and over, and 27% were male and 73% were female. The findings substantiate the assumption that local natural leadership can be effectively activated if it is provided an opportunity for true participation. A direct relationship to high education, high income, or younger age was not established.

CONCLUSIONS

The main assumption of the self-help approach—that people can be organized around common concerns in geographical areas where they live and an attainable problem-solving program can be identified, initiated, and accomplished on a self-help basis—is substantiated by the survey. A second assumption that a vigorous neighborhood-based organization can be developed if the accomplished projects are truly community identified and community initiated is also well documented.

The first block clubs organized in the early seventies were seen as vehicles of change on a long-term basis rather than organizations built around specific issues. It was assumed that block clubs would become a part of the neighborhood life and that an effective leadership pattern would emerge. The survey indicates that, prior to the organization of block clubs, only a few individuals had some indirect leadership experience at the neighborhood level.

However, church-related and political-party work were the two most common leadership experiences of the respondents. The block club activities and projects over the years, ranging from achieving a better garbage pick-up service and meaningful advocacy and appropriate political activism to reopening of a closed elementary school, seem to have accomplished the objective of providing a natural setting for training neighborhood leadership.

During initial contacts, residents had indicated their willingness to meet with other neighbors on the block to share common concerns and to get to know each other. It was feared that once the block residents got together, socializing as a means to achieve block organizing could become an end in itself unless other rallying points were skillfully identified to develop ideological commitment to achieve social change. The survey indicated that the local leadership was aware of this possibility, and maintained a well-planned balance between the residents' need to socialize and their commitment to achieve change.

The self-help approach is not intended to be applicable to all communities. It is not appropriate for those areas where the urban decay is apparently insurmountable. In essence, the self-help approach is a practical-realistic approach to serve only those oppressed geographical areas where (1) a community can be identified, (2) the residents indicate a genuine interest in community welfare, and (3) a majority of residents are willing to work with their neighbors for achieving a better community life for all. The self-help approach is also based on the premise that residents need assistance in getting organized and that social workers as catalysts can activate the dormant strength of selected communities by assisting the local natural leadership for initiating the organization process.

16.

Augie J. Fleras

FROM SOCIAL WELFARE TO COMMUNITY
DEVELOPMENT: MAORI POLICY AND THE DEPARTMENT
OF MAORI AFFAIRS IN NEW ZEALAND

INTRODUCTION

The Department of Maori Affairs is one of the oldest departments of state in New Zealand having endured in one form or another since 1840. At one time, the offices associated with native affairs were limited in size and gradually restricted to the administration of Maori land title. But following the creation of the social welfare division in 1944, the department evolved into a bureaucracy of formidable proportions. Of the many functions assigned to it, the department was responsible for solving "the Maori problem" in a fashion consistent with the prevailing ideology of assimilation. As a result of this directive, the social welfare division expanded to the point where it consumed much of the department's commitment and expenditure. But recently, in response to external pressure, the department has undergone a shift in image, style, and philosophy. Community development has replaced social welfare as the underlying philosophy, while a decentralisation in the administration of social services has brought about a significant realignment in the department's relationship with its increasingly assertive clients.

In this paper, I would like to examine recent innovations in Maori policy administration, with particular emphasis on the emergence of a community development philosophy. The paper is divided into three sections. The first part provides the necessary background for contextualising these administrative changes. Events related to the evolution of the department from a minor caretaker body to a large-scale welfare agency of increasingly diminished value are discussed. The second part looks at why the department experienced a dramatic reversal in philosophy, structure, and style after 1977. I shall argue that the eventual emergence of a "Tu Tangata" ("stance of the people") policy, followed by subsequent reforms in departmental organisation, was indicative of a move towards fulfilment of community development principles. The third and final section briefly summarises both the political acceptance of Tu Tangata and, also, Maori reaction to administrative innovations within the department.

THE EMERGENCE OF A SOCIAL WELFARE PHILOSOPHY

A commitment to assimilation has historically characterised the New Zealand Government's policy towards the indigenous Maori. As policy, assimilation sought to eradicate the cultural basis of Maori society and to Europeanise them as quickly as possible into the mainstream. During the 1950s, the concept of integration began to replace assimilation as official policy without, however, making a substantial difference in government treatment of the Maori (see the Hunn Report, 1960; Hunn and Booth, 1962). Notwithstanding surface differences in approach, the collective aim of these policies focused on the creation of an egalitarian society, united under a single government and common set of laws, in which distinctions of class and race were deemed irrelevant (Ward, 1974; Adams, 1977).

To assist in the Europeanisation of the Maori, various offices for managing native affairs were instituted. Ostensibly, their role revolved about the need to protect, civilise, and amalgamate the Maori into the social and political order. In practice, these offices did not take an active role in assisting the Maori since responsibility for Maori welfare was widely regarded as outside the scope of government activity. Instead, most of their energy was expended in matters pertaining to the sale of Maori land to satisfy the demands of land-hungry settlers. This state of indifference and neglect persisted, with minor exceptions, until well into the twentieth century.

In 1935, the first labour government came to power on the platform of universal justice and equality (Orange, 1977). The Maori, in particular, were singled out for treatment because rather than disappearing, as predicted, they had shown a remarkable tenacity for survival. But those who survived were hopelessly behind the pakeha (European) in terms of social and economic standing. Many Maoris lived in rural isolation amidst conditions of poverty, disease, and drunkenness. Worse still, the Depression had undermined the rural foundation of their existence, throwing them off the farms and onto the relief rolls (Love, 1977). Alarmed at the prospect of exacerbating the nation's economic crisis, the labour party acknowledged the need for government intervention in Maori affairs. State resources were plowed into Maori

land development schemes while public funds were set aside for improvements in Maori housing. Of major note, the recently reorganised Department of Maori Affairs assumed responsibility over these programs of rehabilitation. Later, in 1944, the department's social welfare division was established to assist those Maori who had sought employment in war-related industries. From here on in, the rapid growth of social welfare following the Second World War coincided with the massive urban migration of the Maori, many of whom, it appeared, experienced difficulty in coping with the demands of a new environment. The combination of overcrowded housing, juvenile delinquency, and grinding poverty emerged as Maori problems that could not be easily ignored. Accordingly, the department reinforced its welfarist activity in an effort to remove those obstacles which it perceived as interfering with economic progress and cultural absorption of the Maori people.

To sum up, then, it is evident that circumstances arising from events related to the Second World War and the Great Depression contributed to a political awareness of government responsibility to assist the Maori (Hanson, 1980). A new ideology of "more government" arose to replace the earlier philosophy of laissez-faire which had dominated government thinking in the nineteenth century but which was no longer acceptable in the light of Maori indigency. With public acceptance of the need for state intervention in Maori affairs, the impetus was provided to entrench the department's social welfare section and bring about a massive increase in its scope and sophistication. But, unfortunately for the Maori, the enlargement of the department did not lead to a parallel increase in their socioeconomic status. According to all statistics published in the late 1970s, the

Maori were more likely than the general population to end up underemployed, poorly educated, imprisoned, or impoverished (National Party paper on Maori Affairs, 1981). Frustrated and angry over their subordinate status in New Zealand society, the Maori became increasingly militant during the 1970s. The government, in turn, responded to these protests by reappraising the validity of an assimilationist Maori policy and the role of the Maori Affairs Department in servicing Maori needs.

TOWARDS COMMUNITY DEVELOPMENT

In 1977, the Minister of Maori Affairs commissioned a review of his department's material assets and future prospects. The authors of the subsequent report, Mr. I. P. Puketapu and Mr. P. Haber-Thomas, found the department lacking in many respects (The Community Service Report, 1977). The rapid growth of its social welfare division had created a paternalistic, centralised bureaucracy removed from the clients it was expected to serve. Clients were viewed as passive, hapless victims whose primary function related to their role as consumers of services designed for their benefit by faceless experts. Solutions to Maori problems were left in the hands of professionals who stipulated what was best for the Maori, stifling local initiative in the process. Programs were formulated in private boardrooms and imposed upon the population with little consultation over objectives or means (Puketapu, 1982). Under such conditions, the gap between the Maori and Department began to widen as the department drifted along, a law unto itself, with a distinctive logic and rationale often at odds with aspirations of the target group (see Gregory, 1982). Consequently, unless the department could justify

its existence, control expenditures and improve overall effectiveness, the government had little choice but to dismantle the organisation, phase out its operations, and transfer the remaining functions to existing Departments of State. Later that year Puketapu, himself a Maori and career bureaucrat, was appointed Secretary for Maori Affairs to try and restore the department's "image, vitality and accessibility" (Puketapu, 1981) without sacrificing its operational efficiency in the process.

Immediately, he set about to reform the department along the lines of a "people-oriented, people-managed agency." Positive steps were initiated to upgrade its tattered image as "Big Brother" and to dispel any misunderstanding regarding departmental objectives. Puketapu went out to the people and fronted up to them: What did they want? and what could the department do to help? He prodded his senior officials to search for imaginative solutions that concurrently respected Maori cultural values as well as budgetary limitations imposed on the department. In the end, he unveiled a new policy which established a consistent framework for the attainment of Maori self-determination. Tu Tangata, as the policy came to be called, sought to:

promote people in a way that recognises their talents and resources both as individuals and as a group. And in a way that will ensure their fullest development for the advance of Maori communities—and the common good of New Zealand (Tu Tangata Working Paper, 1980).

Tu Tangata focused on the social and economic advancement of the Maori as Maori. It attempted to institute measures whereby the Maori would enjoy the best of both worlds—socioeconomic equality with the pakeha on the one hand, and retention of their cultural identity, language, and land on the other. Maori youth and community development were singled out as priority items under this policy. Shortly thereafter, the department was reformed from top to bottom to logically complete the administrative implications of Tu Tangata.

As part of its new image, the department rejected its former attachment to a welfare ideology with its negative emphasis on crisis intervention, handouts, and Band-Aid solutions. In its place, a community development strategy appeared that emphasised promotion, action-oriented local projects and community involvement in the planning and implementation of policy and programs. The term "welfare" was expunged from departmental vocabulary and replaced with the more affective referent "community." When the social welfare division was closed down, social workers were transferred to other Departments of State or reclassified as community workers. Much of the welfare caseload was placed on the shoulders of Maori voluntary organisations or redirected to the appropriate government agency, a move endorsed by Puketapu in his review of the department in 1977. Finally, to avoid any distortions inherent in focusing on the negative, the Maori were promoted, not as a problem for the government to solve, but as a source of untapped energy, which, if handled properly, enhanced the well-being of all New Zealanders (Department Memo, January 1981).

The concept of community development emerged as the cornerstone of Puketapu's Tu Tangata philosophy. The term itself was not clearly defined (see Constantino-David, 1982; Hayes, 1981 for useful discussions on the uses and abuses of this concept), except in reference to the "development of the Maori people and their resources" (Department Memo, July 1981). By inference, however, this orientation to community development sought to reverse the image of the Maori as passive and incapable of helping themselves to help

themselves. The local community was encouraged to become involved in the planning of priorities and programs on the assumption that local solutions to local problems were more acceptable and more effective than solutions devised through the infusion either of more experts or of more funding. The department's community officers, while providing the backup support for these community-based programs, were instructed to minimise their say in the direction or pace of these projects. This decision lay in the hands of the local community who collaborated with departmental officials to arrive at a common goal, complementing each others' strengths and avoiding unnecessary overlap. Finally, programs were directed at the elimination of the source of the problem, not merely at treating its effects. Prevention, not treatment, became the motto as the department envisaged long-term solutions to recurrent problems through the utilisation of all resources and resourcefulness available to the community. In brief, the department's community development philosophy superseded its earlier "top-down" approach to community services with one that advocated a "bottom-up" participatory strategy, commensurate with the implications of Tu Tangata (see also New Zealand Council of Social Services Report, 1978).

Likewise, in terms of style, the department underwent a number of sweeping changes to accommodate this shift towards a community development philosophy. I indicated earlier that the department was commonly perceived as a pakeha-based institution where the presence of Maori was perceived as irrelevant towards satisfactory completion of the job. But, upon his appointment, Puketapu looked to rectify the situation by imparting a Maori presence to the department. Pakeha welfare officers were taken out of the field and posted elsewhere, preferably outside of the department. For replacements, an effort was made to recruit Maori personnel both from within the public service but also from outside of it. Maori personalities from all walks of life—entertainers, artists, community leaders, former gang members—were seconded into service, not on the basis of their academic credentials, but for their ability to project a Maori image, to relate to the Maori public, and to sell the department's Tu Tangata programs.

In addition to redefining the grounds for employment, Puketapu tried to Maorify the department in other ways. He instructed his senior officers to think and to speak Maori (Indigenous People's International Conference, Wellington 1981) or to use Maori protocol whenever possible. He also exhorted them to search deep inside for that creative energy ("wairua") with which to carry out their assigned mission. Together, their combined spiritual forces would permeate the department with the ethos of Maoritanga (the essence of Maori), and revolutionise its operational style from within.

It was also imperative for the image-conscious Puketapu to devise a new means of interaction between his field officers and the members of the Maori community. In the past, field officers carried out their duties in a manner consistent with the expectations of the social welfare model. They responded to situations which they felt warranted their attention. Members of the community were portrayed as victims who required constant control or supervision. The officers, themselves, were organised on a "line" type of operation consistent with a hierarchical division of labour and bureaucratic rationality. But under Tu Tangata, a novel kind of community administration emerged which, by inverting the bureaucratic pyramid, approached the ideal of community participation in the delivery of social services. These "kokiri" administration units (kokiri = to advance) operated on the principle that Maori community officers were more effective when deployed in daily interaction among their intended clients. Accordingly, each Kokiri team consisted of three community officers permanently stationed in the field and commissioned to respond quickly to the demands of a locally recruited, corporate management committee which itemised monthly priorities for the unit. These officers were expected to use their mobility to focus on concrete problems related mostly to Maori youth at schools, at work, and in courts. Their accessibility and roving style ensured an awareness of Maori sensibilities, for as one kokiri officer said to me in late 1982:

> Kokiri units work in a Maori way. There is no rushing around, fixed to a schedule, but an attempt to get to know the community, talk to the people, let them know community officers are around if needed. We like to think of ourselves as liaison between the department and the people.

It should be evident that kokiri units exemplify the department's preference for community development over social welfare, teamwork over individual casework, and prevention over "patch-up." Maori field officers no longer regard themselves as experts: Instead, they see their role in terms of partners, catalysts, and consultants. As catalyst, kokiri units are in the promotion business. They aim to stimulate the creation of self-help projects by applying those resources available from within the community, the government or the private sector to focus in on problem areas. As partner, kokiri units work alongside members of the community and engage the assistance of the voluntary sector to coproduce local programs. Financial aid (in the form of "seeding money") and moral support are provided to get a project started and to see it through to completion. Finally, kokiri units serve as consultants to advise both government agencies and members of the Maori public on a recommended course of action.

In sum, the Department of Maori Affairs has witnessed a series of far-reaching reforms in its philosophy (community development) and style (decentralisation in planning and delivery of services). Having rejected the "stand-over" tactics of the past, the department now perceives itself as one of the components in the total mix of people's efforts to stand tall (Tu Tangata) and to advance with confidence into the future (Department Memo, January 1981). It hopes to invert the bureaucratic pyramid and replace the traditional approach to Maori affairs with one that emphasises cooperation (kotahitanga), sensitivity (aroha), and Maori self-determination (Mana Maori Motuhake). The inception of a distinctive style of community administration would appear to vindicate the department's desire to redefine its relationship with the Maori as "partner and working mate" (Puketapu, 1981).

REACTION AND RESPONSE TO RECENT DEVELOPMENTS

The Tu Tangata philosophy has been in existence for about five years. To date, response and reaction to the new policy has been positive although sectors of the Maori population have expressed a degree of indifference and, in some cases, scepticism and hostility. On the positive side, numerous programs have appeared under the umbrella of Tu Tangata which reflect the desire of the community to take control over its cultural and economic destiny. Included in this list are homework centres for Maori secondary pupils, vocational and trade training projects for school leavers,

and rural cottage industries. Of these, few have captured the public's imagination to such an extent as the department-inspired "Te Kohanga Reo" program (Maori Language Nests). These Maori preschool centres, based on the principles of "whanau" (Maori extended family values) and conducted entirely in Maori, typify the department's commitment to produce bilingual, bicultural children comfortable both in the Maori and pakeha world.

At the other end of the spectrum, a wide cross-section of Maori, from activists to local leaders, are critical of the Department's motives in coddling up to the Maori. They regard the consultation process as a "sham" which serves to "rubber stamp" decisions already taken in private. Others including the Public Service Commission are upset at the department's intent to eliminate its social welfare division and to service Maoridom "on the cheap," through enlistment of an already overworked voluntary corps. Moreover, not all is well within the department. There, the swiftness of reorganisation has left a number of officials confused over what is expected of them (personal communication). In light of this mix of positive and negative responses, it should be interesting to see whether the promise of community development will result in an authentic devolution of power or, simply, in a redistribution of the workload.

Non-Maori reaction to recent developments has been overwhelmingly positive (Report, Public Service Official Circular, 1982). The Government in power, the National Party (Conservative), has endorsed Tu Tangata and community development as the basis of its Maori policy (Report, National Party's Paper on Maori Affairs, 1981):

The philosophy [of Tu Tangata] is one of growth, independence and cultural identity. This goes to the heart of National Party Philosophy.

Maori people have the resources which are greatly underutilised and the National Party believes that the Tu Tangata philosophy is ensuring that these resources are being used for the greater good of the Maori and for the nation as a whole.

Clearly, the principles underlying Tu Tangata and community development are consistent with the Party's neoconservative philosophy of "less government." This is politically understandable since circumstances ranging from Maori assertiveness to excessive welfare expenditures have inspired party strategies to accept the far-reaching proposals of Tu Tangata as a matter of political expediency and economic survival. After nearly 50 years of uninterrupted expansion in state services, the government has had to acknowledge that the maintenance costs of financing these services have escalated to alarming proportions (Report, New Zealand Planning Council, 1979; Report of the Economic Monitoring Group, 1978). The virtual cessation of economic growth since 1973, combined with high levels of unemployment, ruinous rates of inflation and a massive imbalance of payments have compelled the government to reconsider state spending especially in health and welfare which reputedly consumed nearly one third of the government's budget. Yet, despite the vast sums expended, the high cost of government intervention in the delivery of social services has not had the intended effect of improving Maori performance at school or in the labour force. If anything, the Maori as a group are falling further behind the general population in terms of most economic indicators. To add to injury, the serious decline of Maori cultural heritage, especially among the growing legions of dissaffected urban youth, is viewed with dismay by Maori leaders who point to the failure of government intervention to deliver the goods as promised.

Thus, in an attempt (1) to trim the cost of Government spending on the Maori, (2) to reduce Maori dependency on government services and (3) to pacify Maori pressure for increased self-determination, the National Party has endorsed the department's effort to stimulate local initiative, self-sufficiency and voluntary self-help. Whether or not the government, in conjunction with the Department of Maori Affairs, is successful in transforming the rhetoric of community development into an ongoing reality remains to be seen.

CONCLUSION

This paper has tried to recount the progression of Maori policy administration from one based on the principles of dependency and social welfare to one grounded in the philosophy of self-determination and community development. The impetus for this shift is attributable, in part, to Maori demands for self-determination and, in other part, to the inability of the state to sustain its former levels of social spending. Widespread enthusiasm over Tu Tangata and acceptance of its administrative implications are indicative of the appeal of the community development philosophy in serving the vested interests of the Maori, the government, and the Department of Maori Affairs.

REFERENCE LIST

Adams, P. *Fatal Necessity: British Intervention in New Zealand, 1830–1837.* Auckland: Auckland University Press/Oxford University Press, 1977.

Constantino-David, K. "Issues in Community Organisation." Community Development Journal, 17 (1982) pp. 190–201.

Gregory, R. J. "Understanding Public Bureaucracy." Public Sector 4 (2/3) 1982, pp. 3–12.

Hanson, E. *The Politics of Social Security:* The 1938 Act and Some Later Developments. Auckland: Auckland University Press/Oxford University Press, 1980.

Hayes, S. E. "The Uses and Abuses of Community Development." A General Account, Community Development Journal, 16 (1981), pp. 221-227.

Hunn, J. K. and J. M. Booth. "The Integration of Maori and Pakeha in New Zealand." Study Paper No. 1. Published by the Department of Maori Affairs, 1962.

Love, R. H. N. "Policies of Frustration: The Growth of Maori Politics," The Ratana/Labour Era, Unpublished PhD Thesis, Political Science Department, Victoria University of Wellington, New Zealand, 1977.

Orange, C. "A Kind of Equality: Labour and the Maori People, 1935–1949." Unpublished MA Thesis, History Department, University of Auckland, 1977.

Puketapu, I. P. "The Rogue." Unpublished Paper delivered to the Indigenous Peoples International Conference, December 1981, Wellington, New Zealand.

Ward, A. *A Show of Justice, Racial Amalgamation in Nineteenth Century New Zealand.* Canberra: Oxford University Press/Auckland University Press, 1974.

Reports

1960, Report on the Department of Maori Affairs, Conducted by J. K. Hunn, Wellington, Government Printer.

1970, "Policy Issues Concerning the Future Evolution of Community Development," revised edition prepared by the Regional and Community Development Division, New York.

1977, "The Community Service," Report of the State Service Commission Review on the Department of Maori Affairs, Prepared by I. P. Puketapu and P. Haber-Thomas, Wellington, Government Printer.

1978, "Economic Trends and Policies," Report No. 1 of the Economic Monitoring Group, New Zealand Planning Council, Wellington, Government Printer.

1978, "Sharing Social Responsibility," Report of the New Zealand Council of Social Services on desirable roles and directions in social service development, Wellington, Government Printer.

1979, "The Welfare State? Social Policies in the 1980's," Report No. 12 of the New Zealand Planning Council, Wellington, Government Printer.

1980, "Tu Tangata, Stance of the People," Unpublished Report of the Department of Maori Affairs.

1981, "Maori Affairs," Position Paper, Unpublished Report of the National Party on Maori Affairs, Research Unit Reference 81/39.

1982, Extract from the Report of the State Services Commission, Published in the Public Services Official Circular, No. 41, October 13, Wellington.

1982, "Reform From Within," Unpublished Paper delivered to a Public Service Management Group, January, Wellington, New Zealand.

Miscellaneous

Also consulted were various memoranda, letters, circulars, and unpublished papers housed in the library and archives at the Department of Maori Affairs, Head Office, Wellington, New Zealand.

17.

Jack Rothman and Mayer N. Zald

PLANNING AND POLICY PRACTICE

One characteristic of modern society is the systematic attempt to use tools of rational analysis to lay out pathways to achieving future-oriented goals. As organizations, both private and public, have become larger and developed professional staffs, and as the environments they deal with have become more complex, planning and policy decision-making have become full-blown enterprises. Corporations, governmental agencies, social welfare agencies, community federations, and others have resorted to planning activities to gather information and chart their future courses. Rational, future-oriented decision-making is a hallmark and indeed a widely accepted definition of social planning and policy making. We will use the term *planning* to encompass both concepts.

In this essay we will start by examining planning broadly as a function of the modern state. We will go on to look at particular characteristics of planning in the free-enterprise or capitalist society. We will then focus briefly but more specifically on historical forces that have given rise to planning in the field of social welfare in the United States. We will follow with applications to the field of human services.

THE SOCIETAL CONTEXT OF SOCIAL PLANNING

In this initial section we will nest planning and policy making in the social structure of society. Our questions are sociological and political rather than normative and metatheoretical. When does planning work? Whose goals are served by planning? What are the social and institutional uses of planning? What are the social functions and dysfunctions of planning? Is planning activity in the community and welfare arena different in kind from planning in the economic sector? We do not intend to offer a sociological theory of planning but rather to identify some of the problematics of the planning function in society.

Planning and the State

As a general proposition, the growth of government and the state apparatus in modern times has been accompanied by an increase in planning activities (Shonfield 1965). Yet, modern societies have varied widely in their attitudes toward national planning. Socialist states have attempted comprehensive economic and social planning as techniques for realizing goals of economic growth and national development. These plans not only have established goals for specific industries, but have rationed the allocation of labor and capital. Moreover, these plans have included large social-welfare components such as plans for housing, education, and medical care.

Obviously, the adoption of national planning is related to the ideology of ruling elites and national social structure. Comprehensive five-year plans have been adopted in Communist and Socialist countries. The more fragmented or multilayered the political structure and the more the ruling elites are committed to capitalist laissez-faire ideology, the less likely they are to attempt to adopt national comprehensive planning. Capitalist states with strong central governments are more likely to adopt "indicative planning" where specific industries are singled out for aid and development. And legislation adopted in capitalist countries may plan and allocate resources for the implementation of specific social welfare objectives such as, for instance, the subsidy of thousands of low-income housing units, or plans to establish a nationwide system of community mental health centers.

What have been the results of comprehensive planning on the societal level? It is impossible to review the literature here.[1] But several general conclusions emerge. First, comprehensive planning coupled with a rationing system of resource allocation leads to systematic pathologies of production. The plans emphasize physical unit counts rather than quality criteria, and the production of inferior goods is pandemic. Moreover, there is a tendency to overemphasize the production of goods which meet raw quantity requirements at the expense of differentiated products not measured in the plan. Second, unless goals are constantly updated to record the increments in actual production, goals are rarely fulfilled. Third, comprehensive national plans have endemic problems of work incentives, labor, allocations and stockpiling raw materials to an excessive degree. . . .

Over all, the information shortcomings and incentive shortcomings of national planning have led to either planning as ritual or attempts to mix market pricing systems with indicative planning focusing upon a more limited set of objectives. Yugoslavia

was the prime example of this adaptive response. In spite of the vast increases in information processing capacity provided by modern computer technology and the planning theoretic devices provided by input-output analysis and other programming devices, long-range comprehensive planning eluded achievement. In capitalist societies it is not even attempted.

Social and Economic Planning in the United States

Although the notion of comprehensive societal planning has never been fully accepted in the United States, sectoral, policy-specific, and organizational planning is widely used. There are many examples: State prison systems develop planning models of needed facilities, taking into account projected prison populations, assumptions about crime rates, populations at risk, and sentencing policy. Forest products companies project wood-footage needs and plant seedlings now for harvesting in twenty years. Assuming market goals, large corporations project capital needs for five- and ten-year periods; moreover, large corporations have strategic planning staffs examining new product trends and attempting to project political and economic climates into the future. The Social Security Administration projects revenue needs, given demographic trends, eligibility rules, and benefit formulas. Local councils develop plans for hospital facilities. Universities attempt to develop models of projected enrollments and develop strategies for growth or retrenchment of faculty and facilities.

There is, of course, wide variability among organizations in the extent to which they engage in formal and explicit planning activities. Large organizations with larger professional and administrative

---

[1]For a summary of the problems of comprehensive planning in Socialist societies see Lindblom (1977).

components are more likely to engage in planning than smaller ones. Organizations that have longer time horizons in the procurement of resources, the development of products, or the demand for services are more likely to engage in planning than those with shorter time horizons. (It takes five to seven years to develop a new car model, while dress styles change yearly.)

Organizations with leaders trained in management-by-objectives techniques and other planning-oriented styles are more likely to engage in these techniques. And, finally, organizations that are required by external agencies to develop plans as part of their procurement or legitimation or the receipt of funds are more likely than others to engage in the production of planning documents. For instance, to receive federal grants for law enforcement activities or for community mental health centers, states and committees had to develop planning bodies and plans for services.

Obviously, there is a difference between planning and implementing plans. What kinds of organizations are more likely to implement their plans? Implementation in its simplest form (that is, the translation of plan into action) depends upon the commitment of allocating authorities to the plan. One common problem in private organizations is that the planning group may not be integrally connected to the decision-making authorities. To the extent that planning officers are removed from central authorities, their plans may be pigeonholed. The same problem occurs to an even greater extent in public organizations. Public organizations are to a large extent dependent upon decision-making bodies (legislatures, elected executives) for the establishment of goals and the allocation of resources. These are in turn beholden to constituencies composed of diverse and often conflicting elements.

Since these external interests may have different priorities for the organization and competing demands for resource allocation, we suspect it is more likely that the planning documents of public organizations gather dust or are radically modified than are those of private organizations that engage in long-range planning. Ironically, these same private organizations often express disparagement of planning for public enterprises.

In both public and private organizations the inability to attract resources from outside and the decline of slack resources within organizations inhibit planning implementation. These issues particularly have plagued planning in social welfare. Moreover, as we have indicated, in both private and public organizations, planning is part of a social and political process. It serves ends and purposes apart from its formal or stated functions of gathering information and choosing pathways to goals. Rationalist schools of planning theory have not always been sufficiently sensitive to these realities.

Planning in Social Work and Social Welfare

At some minimal level, planning in social work and social welfare can be said to have occurred when a person or agency, motivated by concerns for clients or beneficiaries, anticipates future needs or programs rather than responding "spontaneously" to demands. Charity is transformed from a spontaneous response to a supplicant in need to a planned system when individuals or organizations anticipate philanthropic demand and set up rules and policies, services and organizations to respond to that anticipated need or demand. The Poor Law is thus an early instance of planning.

A caseworker can be said to engage in planning when he or she conceptualizes a goal of treatment or service delivery and anticipates or shapes alternative courses of treatment or service.

In the last century explicit planning emerged as agencies, both public and private, became aware that their ad hoc and uncoordinated efforts led to inadequate and inefficient provision of services. Sometimes clients would go to several agencies, requesting and receiving financial support from more than one source, without one agency knowing that another had helped. The community council case register movement (Social Service Exchange) began early in the century. Although these agencies may have been more effective at controlling multiple applicants (see Litwak and Hylton 1962) than they were for actually planning and implementing plans for whatever services were to be provided, the community chest and council movements represent an early attempt to assess community needs and to argue for rational decision making in projecting the development and location of community agencies. It is important to note that once a commitment to planning emerged, a methodology was required. The development of the community survey can be seen as an emergent methodology for community planning (Byington 1911; Colcord 1939; Warren 1955).

Another early attempt at planning is found in the efforts of welfare agencies to plan for emergency relief. Whenever a major cataclysm occurs there is large-scale and sudden disruption of the goods and services available to a population. In preplanning periods individual agencies respond in an ad hoc fashion to such needs. The emergence of agencies such as the Red Cross, the development of emergency planning committees, and the legislation of federal and state loan and service provisions are all attempts to plan in advance for unforeseen disasters, to forecast need, and to develop repertoires of response.

This perspective on social welfare planning is consistent with Lauffer's definition: "Social planning refers to the development, expansion and coordination of social services and social policies" (1981:583). Lauffer goes on to state that planning is a method of rational problem solving and that it is conducted at both the societal and the local level.

Both the community council movement and the development of emergency and disaster relief agencies are making plans for the delivery and coordination of service at the local community level. Large-scale planning has also been attempted for specific social welfare programs at the national level. The development of the Social Security system required a projection of the number and size of beneficiary claims and revenues from taxation. The planning system of Social Security has been buffeted by changes in mortality rates, changes in the economy, and political actions that have added claimants and enlarged benefit levels (Derthick 1979; Cates 1981).

Another national example of social welfare relevant planning can be seen in the development of the Comprehensive Community Mental Health Act of 1963. Here we see an effort to use federal incentives (the federal subsidization of local services) to encourage the planning and development of mental health services in a setting close to the patient's home, the provision of outpatient and preventive services, the setting up of provisions for noninstitutional alternatives, community consultation, and local boards.

The tasks of planning in these different cases vary substantially in the complexity of the planning activity: the number of components of the plan; the time horizon of the plan (short term to long term); the locus of the planning (private local agency to national government); and in the representation of interests (client, professional, political). They differ from planning in non–social-welfare arenas not in terms of the difficulty or ease of planning but in that the values to be served by planning are those of the liberal, caring society. It is these values of a humane industrialized society that link these planning efforts to the helping professions.

These humane impulses have led to other forms of organized response to need. Settlement houses, for example, strove to change conditions of life in the neighborhood through social reform or advocacy. They, together with YMCAs and other locally based organizations, also were concerned with citizen participation, public education, and personal development of participants. Planning theory reflects these various empirical crosscurrents of action and practice.

PLANNING THEORY

Planning theory emerged as a response to the need to engage in planning activity. It arose as an answer to questions about how one ought to conduct such activity. It has been a normative exercise. For example, writers have asked what is the best way to plan. What are the limits of different kinds of planning? What alternatives are there to the standard practices? As a normative exercise, scholars have examined planning activity in specific situations as a tool of rationality and choice. They have been concerned with its limits and blind spots. Less often, scholars have raised empirical and descriptive issues: Who plans, in what situations, with what results?

. . .

Rationalistic Decision-Making Theory

The modern era of planning theory was marked initially by a rationalistic model of decision making, crystallized in the writings of Herbert Simon (1957). Planning was viewed as a process whereby through use of proper rules of logic an optimal solution to a problem is determined. Persons are seen as utility-maximizing beings whose relations to others are defined in instrumental terms. Classic decision-making theory involves following a task-oriented set of basic steps, including ordinarily: (1) setting a goal; (2) identifying all the alternative means of attaining the goal; (3) evaluating means in order to arrive at the single best solution; and (4) implementing the decision. Hudson characterizes the approach as examining "problems from a systems viewpoint, using conceptual or mathematical models relating ends (objectives) to means (resources and constraints), with heavy reliance on numbers and quantitative analysis" (1979:389). This may entail use of forecasting and analysis techniques such as multiple regression analysis, Markov chains, econometric modeling, and Bayesian methods. In social work planning literature the work of Kahn (1969), in particular, has been identified with procedures of rational decision making.

Both in social work and in urban planning, the rationalistic approach has been associated with the idea of comprehensiveness. Comprehensive land use planning was the modus operandi in city planning for an extended period of time, and social work planning, according to Lane, was to entail "a progressively effective adjustment between social welfare resources and social welfare needs" (1959:65). Community chests and councils viewed their role to be that of fostering and steering comprehensive social welfare planning at the community level.

Despite, or perhaps because of, its elegance and simplicity, the rationalistic comprehensive concept has been subjected to criticism from various quarters. A variety of limitations has been attributed to the model, including limits to rational cognition, limits to analytic cogency, limits to environmental control, limits to professionalism, and limits of value dissonance.

Limits to rational cognition pertain to the amount of knowledge or information that may be gathered and digested in any decisional situation. In practical terms, far more information was required than could be acquired. The number of alternatives to be identified, documented, and weighted was legion. Technical difficulties in assembling data presented obstacles: the loss or transformation of data through aggregation or mathematical modeling; unavailability of organizational information; delays in data acquisition; faulty or falsified data; computer breakdowns, and so on. Limits to analytic cogency simply mean that what is logical may encounter fierce opposition by those who have not been consulted, or whose narrow "irrational" interests are threatened. Analytic purity is complicated by pluralism of values existing in most urban settings. Rationalism is most applicable when one can assume a unitary set of values (a general public interest), or at least a set of values that are not rancorously contentious. In other words, there are personal and organizational dynamics in formulating or implementing a decision that go beyond its intrinsic analytic features. More recently, this duality in planning has been recognized through conceptualizing "analytic" and "interactional" (Perlman and Gurin 1972) or "technical" and "sociopolitical" (Gilbert and Specht 1977) aspects of planning.

Limits to environmental control relate to the "turbulent" (Emery and Trist 1965), broader social context in which planners operate. The 1960s and 1970s were times of uncertain and shifting social, political, and economic currents, followed by an era

showing signs of similar contextual instability. When the national or community political economy is unpredictable, the more narrow technical area of planning is subjected to unforeseen dislocations. "It is a feature of modern social dynamics that the future does not unroll incrementally but in a disjointed series of crises, breakthroughs and transformations" (Friedman and Hudson 1974:8). This has placed a high burden on the rationalist formulation.

Limits to professionalism suggest that while the planner does not have all the answers, some answers do lie uniquely with other sources. In particular, it is brought out, individuals affected by new services or facilities have a distinctive understanding of their needs and how to fulfill them. Thus families, neighborhood groups, and ethnic and racial communities are viewed as having important contributions to make to decisions concerning delivery of services. The concept of informal helping networks has come to the fore in this connection. Such networks have joined in constructive partnership with planners, both in decision making and in the actual delivery of services at the grass-roots level. The requirement for cost constraints is another factor which has curtailed professionalism and generated increased interest in the idea of self-help networks.

A final limitation deals with value dissonance. Rationalism has been criticized by many for projecting an image of the planner as technocrat. This image is of a policy scientist or systems analyst, surrounded by printouts, engaged in model-building, standing apart from community politics, and devoid of contact with ordinary citizens. The one "best" solution arrived at by the planner in isolation through technical gadgetry is seen as imposed on hapless populations without their input or consent. "Urban renewal as urban removal" conveys the sense of this view. This critique takes rationalism to task for its failure to incorporate an element of citizens' participation into its theoretical structure, which places it in dissonance with basic democratic values.

Rittel and Webber (1973) have pointed to a significant weakness in rationalistic theory. The theory assumes problems that are definable, discrete, and responsive to purposeful manipulation. In the current scene, however, these authors tell us, planning has been obliged to deal with "wicked" problems. These elude bounded definitions, have no clear end point, suggest innumerable potential solutions, are unique and incomparable in each instance, and are enmeshed with other problems of which they are symptoms. Rationalism requires somewhat benign, docile problems. Instead, society spews forth wicked and incorrigible ones. The theory was not up to coping with this discrepancy.

According to Galloway and Mahayni (1977), the evaluation of planning theory can best be understood through application of the work of Kuhn (1970) on the structure of scientific revolutions. A paradigm develops, is articulated, and wins general professional acceptance. Later anomalies appear and a crisis ensues. Alternative competing paradigms appear. In the view of Galloway and Mahayni, the dominant rationalist paradigm broke down in the turbulent 1960s and is being superseded by other approaches.

A useful way to obtain an overview of the main theoretical orientations to planning extant today is through a schema developed by Hudson (1979). Hudson sees rationalistic theory still retaining a foothold on professional thinking, but he suggests that four alternative theoretical positions have also gained currency: incremental planning, transactive planning, advocacy planning and radical planning.[2]

Although planning theory has always acknowledged an implementation aspect or phase, most of the writings have concentrated on decision making. However, in recent years implementation has been given a prominent place as a defined area for theoretical explications (Pressman and Wildavsky 1973; Bardach 1977; Williams and Elmore 1976; Hargrove 1975; Smith 1973). It was as though the struggles and defeats of the Great Society programs, particularly the War on Poverty, brought home to planners and policy analysts the recognition that careful follow-through is essential for the success of the most clearly formulated plan.

Several variables have emerged in implementation studies which are associated with the attainment of planning goals. Conditions identified as facilitating implementation include such variables as commitment of top leaders, organizational capacity, the commitment of implementers, and interest-group support. Variables found to impede implementation include magnitude of change, number of actors involved, alternative preferences of actors, intrinsic complexity of the plan and its timing. Although the label "implementation" may be different, the theoretical issues

---

[2]The Hudson schema has much similarity to the "Three Models" formulation of Rothman (1979). Transactional planning has features in common with Rothman's "locality development." Hudson breaks social planning into rationalistic (which he designates "synoptic") and incremental. He also subdivides social action, arriving at advocacy planning and radical planning. Both authors view the various approaches to

planning not as competing and incompatible initiatives but as available planning strategies providing alternatives that may be used selectively in relation to given planning contexts and objectives. They both also discuss favorably the mixing of different traditions or models for particular planning purposes, taking into account the attributes of the different approaches which permit or impede combining among them.

examined duplicate conceptual work in such theoretical schools as planned change, organizational development, diffusion of innovations, and political science studies of governmental bureaucracies and of interest groups. Nevertheless, the recent impetus by policy science groups may generate fresh ideas and promising reformulations of earlier efforts.

As a starting point in describing the previously mentioned emergent method for generating theory, we draw on Friedmann and Hudson's definition of planning "as an activity centrally concerned with *the linkage between knowledge and organized action.*" (1974:22; emphasis in the original). In keeping with this view, one of the authors has developed a research utilization or social research and development methodology for systematically applying social science research in such a way as to construct social intervention strategies (Rothman 1974; 1980). The approach eschews a "grand theory" approach to planning but starts with more delimited planning issues or problems, such as establishing an innovative program in the community or bringing about a wider level of citizen participation in the planning process. The method proceeds through a series of steps: delineating knowledge areas that contain relevant data; determining appropriate descriptors and key words for retrieving data; evaluating, assembling, and synthesizing data; formulating generalizations concerning the phenomena under consideration; and converting descriptive propositions into prescriptive application guidelines. The methodology proceeds further into field testing and development work so that planning strategies are not only evaluated for workability but are also put into operation to facilitate practice implementation. The objective is to arrive at middle-range theory which is both tested in the user environment and "packaged" for planning practitioners in user-ready form. Since the approach has been detailed elsewhere, it will not be discussed further here.

Social Planning Roles

Planning roles grow out of problems or needs in the society. But the planner does not necessarily define these. The planner is not an autonomous private practitioner, but one of a contemporary breed of professionals who is organizationally based and an employee of a bureaucratic structure. It is the governing bodies of such structures (boards of directors, commissions) that typically establish policy and set the agenda. However, this often takes place in collaboration with planners, who are in a strategic position (formally and informally) to influence decisions about organizational goals.

The character of the employers of planners has shifted over the years. In the early part of the century most of the employers were voluntary philanthropic agencies including community welfare councils, community chests, and specialized agencies in fields such as housing, child welfare, health, and the like. At the same time, settlement houses provided a base for neighborhood organizing and community development. With the advent of the New Deal in the 1930s, the federal government assumed a greater role in social planning. But throughout the 1930s, 1940s, and 1950s voluntary agencies were probably the major arena for planning jobs. This situation shifted drastically in the 1960s and 1970s. Government bodies at the federal, state, and local levels took on heavy responsibility for social programs and vastly overshadowed voluntary planning activity. The political outlook and social philosophy of the New Frontier and Great Society

Democratic administrations provided the impetus for this development.

The Reagan-Bush administrations checked this century-long trend. The expansion of federal activity in planning has been halted. Responsibility is being pushed back on voluntary agencies, private enterprise, and local and state levels of government. At this writing it is too early to predict what balance between governmental and voluntary planning efforts will be reached by the Clinton and subsequent presidencies. One can only note that this is an era in substantial flux.

As planners carry out their roles, a variety of skills is brought to bear. Arthur Dunham (1948) engaged in an early attempt to define this area. In his view, professionals need to exert "creative leadership" around specific tasks, and also facilitate group process in collaborative decision making. In other words, they should be able to expedite both task and process goals. For this reason, according to Dunham, they need, among other qualities, a sound knowledge of the social welfare field as well as interactional capabilities in dealing with people.

A roughly similar twofold schema was developed in a study by Rothman and Jones (1971). It is presented in slightly abridged form below.

Technical or task-oriented skills included the following:

A. Designing
   1. Fact-finding, needs assessment, and social-survey techniques
   2. Policy analysis
   3. Program development
B. Expediting
   4. Decision-making techniques
   5. Political liaison
   6. Legislative drafting and enactment
   7. Administrative procurement

C. Implementing
   8. Administrative role and function
   9. Fund raising and proposal writing
   10. Consultation
   11. Staff development and supervision
   12. Promotional, educational, and public relations techniques
   13. Evaluation

In the interactional domain the following skills areas were identified:

A. Managing Organizational Processes
   14. Initial organizing
   15. Participation
   16. Committee technology
   17. Leadership development and training
B. Exerting Influence
   18. Coalitions and their formation
   19. Bargaining
   20. Advocate role and conflict
   21. Broker role
   22. Identifying and influencing the power structure
C. Conducting Interpersonal Relations
   23. Interviewing
   24. Use of self
   25. Leading group discussion

These are presented as fairly generic skills which should be the equipment of any planner. However, not all planning agencies or situations call for using the full array. The type of agency, its mission, and the model of planning it follows all influence planner role performance. In larger agencies with abundant resources and a multiplicity of projects, staff may be able to specialize. In small agencies the jack-of-all-trades may be required. As new methods develop—nominal group process or computer-aided simulation modeling, for example—they are absorbed into the skill repertoire of planners.

Roles are related to emerging emphases in practice. . . . One of these is community-based services, an outgrowth of deinstitutionalization in fields such as mental health, mental retardation, and corrections. There are also increased activities in rural areas in connection with problems of ecology (water resources, topsoil erosion, and disposal of toxic wastes) and nuclear reactor construction. In addition, planning more and more reflects the interaction of local organizations involved in competition for grant funds.

To these may be added some fields of service that will gain greater attention in the period ahead. With an aging population, gerontology can be identified as a field requiring expanding planning. Health is another, in part in relationship to the aging phenomenon. Work-related services, including industrial social work, will likely expand as efforts to reindustrialize and enhance worker productivity are heightened. Refugee resettlement may also continue to rise in importance as an aspect of political conflict and instability. Areas which will probably decline include mental health and child welfare. The state level will become a more significant arena for social planning as will the locality.

Skills receiving increased emphasis include needs assessment, proposal writing, and research on laws and regulations. In addition, sophisticated use of media—videotapes, recordings, slides, and computer applications—for promotional and other purposes seems to be gaining in importance.

. . .

Social and Political Uses of Planning

Planning theory has largely been a normative exercise in which rationality is viewed as good and planning is advanced as a method or process in the service of rationality. Rational analysis is the medium for reaching desired future states.

Here we turn to uses of planning as an instrument of political and social control and as a ritual of justification. The emphasis is not upon planning as a rational device for the achieving of announced social ends, but as a device for maintaining power, for reaching consensus, and for justifying decisions that may be taken on other grounds.

Any social process can be used for purposes other than its manifest intent. Merton has referred to these as latent functions (1957). Three intrinsic features of planning activities lend themselves to use for other than their manifest purposes. Planning takes time, thus inhibiting current action. Planning requires explicit statement and ordering of objectives into priorities, thus it may become an instrument of conflict resolution and consensus formation. Planning leads to the generation of written documents. These documents may serve to legitimate actions of funders and review agencies, even if the written plans are not carried out.

Planning as Stalling. Any planning activity consumes time. Information must be gathered, alternatives scouted. When groups are pressing for action, yet authorities are unsure what alternative is reasonable (or whether any action ought to be undertaken), a proposal to study action alternatives and plan future steps may be adopted. The proposal to plan gives symbolic reassurance that the group's demands are being met, when in fact authorities are buying time. The results of the planning process may or may not lead to material change, but in the short run authorities buy political acquiescence (see p. 55).

Planning and Consensus Formation. When goals and priorities are clear, planning is transformed into a technical process—the efficient means to achieve ends. But where goals are not clear, where affected parties have different priorities and where authorities are loath to announce goals and priorities *ex cathedra*, the planning process may facilitate debate and the ordering of priorities. It encourages an orderly registering of preferences and a search for compromise solutions.

In a penetrating doctoral dissertation Kenneth McNeil (1973) has examined a number of local community committees and planning boards that operated between politicians, bureaucracies, and citizens in Nashville, Tennessee. These included the local zoning committee responsible for enforcing zoning restrictions, a committee to study the location and design of a new airport, the public health commission, and others. In all these areas there is room for different priorities. Bureaucrats, professionals, and citizens may value ends and means differently. The planning process, which includes the representation of different groups and a procedure for gathering evidence, holding hearings, allows a consensus to emerge. Not only may a compromise consensus emerge, but the process provides the legitimacy of due process. Losers may at least believe that they have had a chance to state their case. In this regard, planning activity takes on a quasi-judicial role in community change. Communication and consensus-building along these lines have been referred to as "process goals" in the social work planning literature (Rothman 1964).

We suspect that planning activities take on this quasi-judicial consensus formation function whenever strong competing interests confront a decision with long-range consequences and central authority is unwilling or unable to override one or another of the competing interests. The planning process in many confederated community organizations, such as local United Way

agencies, resembles the quasi-judicial conflict resolution. Interestingly enough, capital allocation processes in some large corporations and in universities also resemble this process (Pondy 1964).

Documents and the Planning Process. Planning leads to written documents. These documents may be part of the ritual of allocation in grants economies. Kenneth Boulding has drawn our attention to the growth of the grants economy—governmental bodies, international agencies, and philanthropic foundations give grants to countries and organizations for delivery of services or the production of goods, even though the granting agency does not receive or use those goods or services (Boulding, Pfaff, and Pfaff 1973).

To receive the grant, the grantee may have to produce a plan. The plan becomes a justificatory document when the grantor must legitimate his allocation of funds. In the extreme case the grantor does not examine whether the plan is in fact implemented, whether the plan leads to any of the intended results, or whether the money is used for the original purposes. No penalty may be incurred for failure to carry out the plan. When plans are used for justification, without audit of expenditure or sanctions for failure, we can speak of planning documents as rhetorical instruments used as justificatory devices for the transfer of funds (Porter and Warner 1973; Wildavsky 1972).

There are other latent functions of planning activity. The planning process helps solidify networks of agencies and personnel who share information. In a sense, planning serves as a coordinating device, even if the formal plan is not adopted (process goals, again). Thus agencies may learn of each other's intentions and problems. Moreover, planning activity may institutionalize search and scanning activities in organizations, forcing review and reconsideration of established ways. Planning can legitimate a predetermined course of action, or justify moving ahead when there is no rational basis for a particular action path—the opposite of stalling (see Vinter and Tropman, 1970, for an analysis of the uses of community studies). At this point, however, we can only speculate on these by-products of planning, since systematic evaluations of empirical cases are few and far between.

Beyond that, it behooves planning specialists to observe latent functions of planning such as these with a clear eye, both to use them in a deliberative way in practice when considered appropriate, or to defend against them when they are applied to the detriment of one's clients or organization. These functions can be seen as planning tactics that can shape the course of intervention in the service of planning objectives.

SUMMARY

It might be said that the state of the planning art is currently at a metatheoretical level. Much of the theory is highly abstract and anecdotal in character. There is an insufficiency of rigorous literature involving systematic evaluation. There is also lack of attention to mixed models of planning. Theorists generally pursue a single model while ignoring others. Accepting the validity of mixed models, one can examine planning issues with greater refinement. For example, it would be possible to identify certain problems or areas which should be subject to controlled central planning and others which ought to be left to the free play of the market. Similarly, organizations need a mixture of planning and mutual adjustment.

In a socially and ecologically complex world, expert social planning and management by large, rationalistic bureaucracies with specialized professionals and technicians are essential elements of national survival. At the same time, the impulse of such bureaucracies, and their sponsoring governmental regimes, to become heavy-handed, arrogant, rigid, and self-serving is well known. The countervailing influence of local concerns and particular interests helps keep planning fluid and responsive to human requirements. Left alone entirely, however, the perpetual crush of pluralistic adversary pressures can lead to a neo-Darwinian nightmare of chaos and inequity. Both rationalistic-centralized and adversarial grass-roots modes of action have virtues and benefits. Their mix and interplay provide a healthy balance in the real world, at least until more ideal planning theories come into being to guide human affairs.

REFERENCES

Bardach, E. *The Implementation Game*. Cambridge, Mass.: M.I.T. Press, 1977.

Boulding, Kenneth, Martin Pfaff, and Anita Pfaff. *Transfers in an Urbanized Economy: Theories and Effects of the Grants Economy*. Belmont, Calif.: Wadsworth, 1973.

Brager, George A. and Harry Specht. *Community Organizing*. New York: Columbia University Press, 1973.

Branch, Melville. "Critical Unresolved Problems of Urban Planning Analysis." *Journal of the American Institute of Planners* (January 1978), 44(1):47–59.

Burchell, Robert and James Hughes. "Planning Theory in the 1980's—A Search for Future Directions." In Burchell and Sternlieb, eds., *Planning Theory in the 1980's*, 1979, pp. xvii–liii.

Burchell, Robert and George Sternlieb, eds. *Planning Theory in the 1980's*. New Brunswick, N.J.: The Center for Urban Policy Research, 1979.

Byington, Margaret F. *What Social Workers Should Know About Their Own Communities.* New York: Russell Sage Foundation, 1911.

Cates, Jerry. "Social Security: Organization and Policy." Ph.D. dissertation, University of Michigan, 1981.

Colcord, Joanna C. *Your Community: Its Provisions for Health, Education, Safety, and Welfare.* New York: Russell Sage Foundation, 1939.

Cox, Fred M., et al., eds. *Strategies of Community Organization,* 3d ed. Itasca, Ill.: Peacock, 1979.

Davidoff, Paul. "Advocacy and Pluralism in Planning." *Journal of the American Institute of Planners* (November 1965), 31(4):331–38.

Derthick, Martha. *Policy Making for Social Security.* Washington, D.C.: Brookings Institution, 1979.

Dunham, Arthur. *The Job of the Community Organization Worker.* New York: Association for the Study of Community Organization and Community Chests and Councils of America, 1948.

_____. *The New Community Organization.* New York: Crowell, 1970.

Emery, F. E. and E. L. Trist. "The Causal Texture of Organizations and Environments." *Human Relations* (February 1965), 18(1):31–32.

Etzioni, Amitai. *The Active Society: A Theory of Society and Political Processes.* New York: Free Press, 1968.

Friedmann, John. *Retracking America: A Theory of Transactive Planning.* New York: Anchor Press, Doubleday, 1973.

Friedmann, John and Barclay Hudson. "Knowledge and Action: A Guide to Planning Theory." *Journal of the American Institute of Planners* (January 1974), 40(1):2–16.

Galloway, Thomas D. and Riad G. Mahayni. "Planning Theory in Retrospect: The Process of Paradigm Change." *Journal of the American Institute of Planners* (January 1977), 43(1):62–71.

Gilbert, Neil and Harry Specht, eds. "Social Planning and Community Organization Approaches." In *Encyclopedia of Social Work,* pp. 1412–25, 17th ed. Washington, D.C.: NASW, 1977.

_____. *Handbook of the Social Services.* Englewood Cliffs, N.J.: Prentice-Hall, 1981.

Haggstrom, Warren. "Can the Poor Transform the World?" In Kramer and Specht, eds., *Readings in Community Organization Practice,* pp. 301–14. Englewood Cliffs, N.J.: Prentice-Hall, 1969.

Hargrove, Erwin C. *The Missing Link: The Study of the Implementation of Social Policy.* Washington, D.C.: Urban Institute, 1975.

Harper, Ernest B. and Arthur Dunham, eds. *Community Organization in Action: Basic Literature and Critical Comments.* New York: Association Press, 1959.

Hudson, Barclay. "Comparison of Current Planning Theories: Counterparts and Contradictions." *Journal of the American Institute of Planners* (October 1979), 45(4):387–98.

Kahn, Alfred J. *Theory and Practice of Social Planning.* New York: Russell Sage Foundation, 1969.

Kramer, Ralph M. and Harry Specht, eds. *Readings in Community Organization Practice.* Englewood Cliffs, N.J.: Prentice-Hall, 1969.

Kuhn, Thomas. *The Structure of Scientific Revolutions.* 2d ed. Chicago: University of Chicago Press, 1970.

Lane, Robert P. "The Nature and Characteristics of Community Organization—A Preliminary Inquiry." In Harper and Dunham, eds. *Community Organization in Action: Basic Literature and Critical Comments,* 1959, pp. 60–70.

Lauffer, Armand. "The Practice of Social Planning." In Gilbert and Specht, eds., *Handbook of the Social Services,* 1981, pp. 583–97.

Lauffer, Armand and Edward Newman, eds. "Community Organization for the 1980's." *Social Development Issues,* special issue of the journal (Summer and Fall 1981), (5):2–3.

Lindblom, Charles. *The Intelligence of Democracy: Decision Making Through Mutual Adjustment.* New York: Free Press, 1965.

_____. *Politics and Markets: The World's Political-Economic Systems.* New York: Basic Books, 1977.

Litwak, Eugene and Lydia F. Hylton. "Inter-Organizational Analysis: A Hypothesis on Coordinating Agencies." *Administrative Science Quarterly,* 6(4) (1962):395–420.

McNeil, Kenneth Edward. "Citizens as Brokers: Cooptation in an Urban Setting." Ph.D. dissertation, Vanderbilt University, 1973.

March, James Q. and Herbert A. Simon. *Organizations.* New York: Wiley, 1959.

Merton, Robert K. "Manifest and Latent Functions." In Merton, *Social Theory and Social Structure,* pp. 19–84. Glencoe, Ill.: Free Press, 1957.

Morris, Robert and Robert Binstock. *Feasible Planning for Social Change.* New York: Columbia University Press, 1966.

Peattie, Lisa. "Reflections on Advocacy Planning." *Journal of the American Institute of Planners.* 34(2) (1968):80–87.

Perlman, Robert. "Social Planning and Community Organization." In *Encyclopedia of Social Work*, pp. 1404–12. 17th ed. Washington, D.C.: NASW, 1970.

Perlman, Robert and Arnold Gurin. *Community Organization and Social Planning.* New York: Wiley, 1972.

Pondy, Louis. "Budgeting and Inter-Group Conflict in Organizations." *Pittsburgh Business Review* (April 1964), 34(3):1–3.

Porter, David O. and David C. Warner. "How Effective Are Grantor Controls: The Case of Federal Aid to Education." In Boulding, Pfaff, and Pfaff, *Transfers in an Urbanized Economy*, 1973, pp. 276–302.

Pressman, J. and Aaron Wildavsky. *Implementation.* 2d ed. University of California Press, 1973.

Rittel, Horst and Melvin M. Webber. "Dilemmas in a General Theory of Planning." *Political Sciences* (June 1973), 4(2):155–69.

Ross, Murray. *Community Organization: Theory and Principles.* New York: Harper and Row, 1955.

Rothman, Jack. "An Analysis of Goals and Roles in Community Organization Practice." *Social Work* (April 1964), 9(2):24–31.

———. *Planning and Organizing for Social Change: Action Principles from Social Science Research.* New York: Columbia University Press, 1974.

———. "Three Models of Community Organization Practice, Their Mixing and Phasing." In Cox et al., eds., *Strategies of Community Organization*, 1979, pp. 25–45.

———. *Social R & D: Research and Development in the Human Services.* Englewood Cliffs, N.J.: Prentice-Hall, 1980.

Rothman, Jack and Wyatt Jones. *A New Look at Field Instruction.* New York: Association Press in Cooperation with the Council on Social Work Education, 1971.

Shonfield, Andrew. *Modern Capitalism.* London: Oxford University Press, 1965.

Simon, Herbert A. *Administrative Behavior: A Study of Decision-Making Processes in Administrative Organization.* 2d ed. New York: Macmillan, 1957.

Smith, T. B. "The Policy Implementation Process." *Policy Science.* 4(4) (1973): 197–209.

Spiro, Shimon. "The Knowledge Base of Community Organization Practice." In Cox et al., eds., *Strategies of Community Organization*, 1979, pp. 79–84.

Vinter, Robert D. and John E. Tropman. "The Causes and Consequences of Community Studies." In Cox et al., eds., *Strategies of Community Organization*, pp. 315–23. 2d ed., 1970.

Warren, Roland L. *Studying Your Community.* New York: Russell Sage Foundation, 1955.

———. "Application of Social Science Knowledge to the Community Organization Field." *Journal of Education for Social Work* (Spring 1967), 3(1):60–72.

Wildavsky, Aaron. "Why Planning Fails in Nepal." *Administrative Science Quarterly* (December 1972), 17(4):508–28.

Williams, W. and R. F. Elmore. *Social Program Implementation.* New York: Academic Press, 1976.

Wolf, Eric. "They Divide and Sub-Divide, and Call It Anthropology." *New York Times*, November 30, 1980.

18.

Carl V. Patton

BEING ROUGHLY RIGHT RATHER THAN PRECISELY WRONG: TEACHING QUICK ANALYSIS IN PLANNING CURRICULA

INTRODUCTION

Analysts and planners on the front lines say they need quickly applied methods that can be used when they cannot undertake researched analysis. These analysts are often required to conduct studies in incredibly short periods of time, in contrast to university researchers and think tank analysts who have the time in which to undertake intensive research on public issues. Practicing planners and analysts need methods that yield roughly right approximations quickly while the results are still relevant.

Few planners and analysts would take exception with the statement "It's better to be roughly right than precisely wrong,"[1] but do we teach what we believe? Catalogue descriptions for typical planning curricula show a predominance of methods courses in which standard quantitative research techniques are taught. Not that regression analysis, survey research methods, input-output analysis and similar techniques are not useful, important tools, but one has to question the returns to primarily learning these methods when balanced against the planning decisions that are actually based on analyses conducted with them. Although I have only limited evidence to support my contention, I believe that the vast majority of today's planning decisions are based on quick, seat-of-the-pants analyses, rather than on researched analyses.

During the past decade or so, a number of planning programs across the nation incorporated into their curricula courses that focus on methods of quick analysis. While these methods have been taught in a variety of ways, they have often been taught with the use of problem sets and cases based on real experience, with the intent of introducing students to the process of conducting quick analyses like those they will experience in practice. Quick methods have sometimes been taught as a part of methods classes and in other cases as part of studio or laboratory courses. In recent years, their value has been more formally recognized in some planning curricula, with as much as a full course or two devoted to them, and a number of case studies having been published as teaching aids.

This is the situation as David Sawicki and I saw it several years ago when we decided to write a text on quick analysis (1986). At that time, we had been independently teaching quick methods for nearly a decade, had produced course guides and case studies, and had published articles about the quick-analysis approach. Since we were involved in preparing students for

---

Helpful comments on an earlier draft of this version were provided by David Forkenbrock and David Sawicki.

[1]This statement might be attributed to a number of writers. One source is James Coleman (1975), who wrote: "For policy research, results that are with high certainty approximately correct are more valuable than results which are more elegantly derived but possibly grossly incorrect."

policy analyst positions, we decided to write a methods book that incorporated basic, quickly applied methods, exercises and real cases. The basic premise we held in writing the book is that it is better to be roughly right in time to have an impact on decisions than to derive a precise solution but too late for it to be of use. We believe that it is better to identify the critical components of a policy issue and to identify the principal costs and benefits of relevant alternatives than to spend excessive time refining precise estimates.

To suggest that we would teach quick analysis because most planning decisions are made using it is not a defense of sloppy analysis, nor is it an argument that rigorous statistical and quantitative courses should be replaced by ad hoc unscientific methods. Rather, it is meant to raise the question of whether teaching primarily researched analysis that requires substantial data sets and major time commitments is providing our graduates the full range of skills they need to be effective planners and analysts. *In addition to researched methods* that can produce precise answers when ample data, time and money are available, we need to teach methods that can produce roughly right approximations from data that are essentially available—and that produce these results quickly enough to be useful to decision makers who are faced with an immediate decision. The teaching of these quick methods should be accompanied by a standard statistics course and a traditional research methods course.

GOALS OF QUICK ANALYSIS

The goals of quick analysis are quite practical: to give decision makers ball park answers, to provide quick estimates of the pros and cons of relevant alternatives, to help

clients avoid getting caught in major errors, and more idealistically, to inform decision makers well enough so that more enlightened discussions of policy options take place and better policies are adopted as a result. At a very practical level, quick analysis may be all that is justified for a one-time local problem where the cost of a large-scale study would exceed the benefit from the precise solution. One of the more salient goals of basic analysis is to produce clear, honest analyses that the *client and consumers* are able to understand and which in turn lead them to undertake the actions specified. Above all, methods must be selected for their ability to attack the problem in the time available without bewildering the client.

In teaching quick analysis, we attempt to give students an understanding of the key concepts of basic analysis, guidance as to the primary steps in quick analysis, and an appreciation for and experience with its methods.

KEY CONCEPTS

There are a half-dozen or so basic principles that we strive to convey to our students. Among these are such concepts as learning to focus on the central decision criterion, saying it with numbers, checking the facts, avoiding the tool-box approach, and making the analysis simple and clear.

Learn to Focus on the Central Decision Criterion

If the beginning analyst is to survive, then the sea of ambiguities faced at the outset of analysis must be overcome. Getting started is difficult, but focusing on the central decision criterion will help identify needed information. We encourage students to get started and then recycle after several hours of work. Focusing on the central decision criterion is a useful way to begin. To do this, we have students address questions such as the following:

- What factor of the problem is likely to be most important to the client?
- Which actors are likely to be involved in the issue? What are their beliefs and motivations?
- On what criterion is the decision likely to be made (minimizing cost, efficiency, equity)?

Students are guided in identifying the criteria from such sources as legislative intent, political analyses, reports, and of course, the stated and implied objectives of the client. Beginning analysts must learn to focus quickly, or valuable analytical time will be wasted.

Say it with Numbers

Numbers are needed to resolve most policy problems, and most policy problems have an associated data base. Students are guided in using these data to gain insights into the problem through the calculation of such basic statistics as averages, ratios, per unit and per capita costs by mode, by type of system, and so on. These results are then compared with other locales to determine base data and to identify critical, missing data. We spend a great deal of time on exercises that require students to locate data quickly, to learn about typical data sources, and to make estimates about the essential elements of policy issues using several data sources that can be checked against one another.

Check the Facts

In quick analysis we have to use data collected by others, and consequently

students need to develop a healthy skepticism for widely held beliefs and established facts. Such beliefs and facts have a way of becoming baseline information, yet they are not always reliable. Uncovering erroneous or unsubstantiated facts can help the analyst avoid compounding the error. Among the tips we provide for our students are:

- Analyze the source of the facts. (Is the position of the author served by the facts?)
- Use multiple sources.
- Check the facts associated with the central decision criterion for reasonableness and consistency.
- Check the critical definitions for accuracy. Students are usually amazed with the errors and inconsistencies they find and, as a result, become much more careful consumers of the research of others.

Avoid the Tool-box Approach

Since our students come from many disciplines and often are facing an entirely new set of issues and problems, they tend to rely heavily on the standard routines of their disciplines. Because we believe the problem should dictate the method, we work hard to discourage the tool-box approach. We encourage students to use the simplest appropriate method, to use common sense to design an approach if one doesn't already exist, and to use more than one method whenever possible.

Make the Analysis Simple and Clear

For the analysis to inform the client, and for it to be used in making better decisions, it must be *simple*. This doesn't mean simpleminded, but rather, not so complex and involved that a bright, well-informed citizen cannot follow it. If any models or calculating routines are used, the client should be able to see how they work, step-by-step, not merely be given the output. We try to explain these principles to students in the form of cases in which we were involved. For example, I conducted a study of office and hotel potential for a developer in a midwest city who is involved in a controversy over the redevelopment of the 100 percent Central Business District (CBD) block. I use this case to illustrate how one focuses on the central decision criterion (effective office and hotel space demand at the year 1990), says it with numbers (current and future hotel occupancy and office vacancy rates), checks the facts (reconciles differences in the economic estimates and projections by various experts of the city and the metropolitan area), avoids the tool-box approach (uses several methods to estimate space demand by 1990) and makes the analysis simple and clear (writes for the client, city council and interested third parties).

PRIMARY STEPS

We acknowledge that policy analyses can be conducted in a number of ways. However, since most of our students are just beginning their work in planning or policy analysis, we give them a six-step approach we have used, and we ask them to adhere to it quite closely. These steps are:

1. Verify, define and detail the problem.
2. Establish evaluation criterion.
3. Identify alternative policies.
4. Evaluate alternative policies.
5. Display and select among alternative policies.
6. Monitor policy outcomes.

Figure 18.1 depicts this process, showing the steps in the process and the points at which we ask students to loop back and check assumptions, definitions and criteria.

Analysts may take various routes through the process because of differences in education and training, time available, complexity of the problem, resource constraints, organizational affiliation, and so on. The less time available, the more likely that steps in the process will be collapsed or skipped. Compromises of the model have to be made, and we realize students will develop their own versions of the model.

SOME QUICK-ANALYSIS TECHNIQUES

For each step in the policy analysis process, we describe a half dozen or so basic methods that can be applied quickly to derive roughly right approximations (Figure 18.2). Since not all methods can be covered here, I have selected several to illustrate the point, including back-of-the-envelope calculations, quick-decision analysis, and sensitivity analysis.

Back-of-the-Envelope Calculations

The quality of public debate on most issues would be raised considerably by the use of a few simple statistics. As part of the first step in problem definition, we ask students to develop a few simple back-of-the-envelope calculations (BOTECs). BOTECs can answer such policy questions as:

- How many persons or families are affected by the problem?
- How much does a service cost per unit delivered?
- How many clients can be served with a given budget?

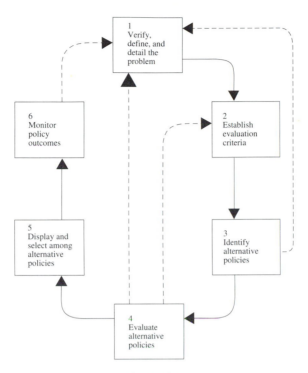

FIGURE 18.1
A Basic Policy Analysis Process (Source: Patton and Sawicki, 1986, p. 26.)

- How many additional households would fall below the poverty line if the income measure were increased $1,000?

This quick-analysis method helps place boundaries around the problem and indicates both the direction and magnitude of the problem. Among the BOTEC methods we teach are:

1. Finding the number in key reference sources.
2. Collecting the number through a quick survey.
3. Guessing the number.
4. Getting experts to estimate the number.

As an example of the value of the BOTEC approach, Max Singer (1971) checked the estimate that New York City heroin addicts stole $2 to $5 billion of private property per year. Singer estimated the number in several ways, checking the consistency of the results, and determined that the total was probably one-tenth of the widely accepted estimate. Singer's approach was to:

- Check the likelihood of there being the number of addicts estimated.
- Multiply the estimated number of addicts by cash required per day.
- Compare this estimate with previous estimates.
- Check what proportion of all stolen property the $2 to $5 billion represented.
- And so on.

STEPS IN THE PROCESS	METHOD
All steps	Identifying and gathering data Library search methods Interviewing for policy data Basic data analysis Communicating the analysis
1. Verifying, defining, and detailing the problem	Back-of-the-envelope calculations Quick-decision analysis Creation of valid operational definitions Political analysis The issue paper/first cut analysis
2. Establishing evaluation criteria	Technical feasibility Economic and financial possibility Political viability Administrative operability
3. Identifying alternatives	Researched analysis No-action analysis Quick surveys Literature review Comparison of real-world experiences Passive collection and classification Development of typologies Analogy, metaphor, and synectics Brainstorming Comparison with an ideal Feasible manipulations Modifying existing solutions
4. Evaluating alternative policies	Extrapolation Theoretical forecasting Intuitive forecasting Discounting Sensitivity analysis Allocation formulas Quick-decision analysis
5. Displaying alternatives and selecting among them	Paired comparisons Satisficing Lexicographic ordering Nondominated-alternatives method Equivalent-alternatives method Standard-alternative method Matrix display systems Political analysis Implementation analysis Scenario writing
6. Monitoring and evaluating policy outcomes	Before-and-after comparisons With-and-without comparisons Actual-versus-planned performance Experimental models Quasi-experimental models Cost-oriented approaches

FIGURE 18.2
Basic Methods by Steps in the Policy Analysis Process (Source: Patton and Sawicki, 1986, p. 37.)

We have students follow the same approach as Singer but applied to other issues. A great amount of commonly accepted baseline data is simply wrong, and as Singer demonstrated, it takes only a few hours to verify standards and avoid an erroneous analysis.

Quick-Decision Analysis

Decision analysis is taught in many planning and policy curricula as an aid to policy making. We teach it as well, but expand its use to include problem definition and political analysis. In this way we can structure the problem so it can be more fully analyzed and reveal questions that need to be investigated. Rather than focus on quick-decision analysis alone, I'll discuss it in the context of political analysis.

In quick analysis, political issues must be considered from the very beginning, if the analysis is to have an impact. Tom Johnson, a former mayor of Cleveland, had a sign on his wall that read: "A good executive always acts quickly and is sometimes right." This bothered a new analyst who went to work for Johnson, but the analyst later wrote: "After a few months of real-world experience. I learned that in government decision making, as in other parts of life, the race usually goes to the swift, and he who hesitates is lost." The analyst went on to say: "When a mayor asks for advice, he's not interested in t-tests or levels of confidence. He wants a quick answer from someone who he suspects knows a little bit more about the issue than he does" (Linner 1979).

What we need, then, is quick analysis grounded in client values, goals and objectives. During problem definition, for example, when the problem is being reduced to a manageable size through back-of-the-envelope calculations, ask questions about the political history of the problem and the political variables that will affect the definition of policy alternatives. We also introduce students to a quick way of defining political problems by looking at the roles of actors in the analytic process and at their motivations, beliefs, resources and the sites at which decisions will be made.

Methods can be combined. Quick-decision analysis can be used in political analysis to help us devise political strategies for resolving policy problems. Figure 18.3 is an example of quick-decision analysis actually used to help decide how to resolve an issue dealing with the submission of a community development budget. The planners involved had to decide whether or not to revise a budget that was opposed by an outspoken council member. The probabilities associated with the alternative decisions and the values of the consequences were estimated as part of the quick-decision analysis, with the result that the planners decided that taking the risky option was worth the risk.

This real example is used to instruct students how to structure a decision analysis, how to estimate the probabilities of events occurring, and how to value consequences using data that are essentially available. Again the point is that a structured analysis can be conducted quickly when time for a research-based analysis is not available.

Sensitivity Analysis

Of all the quick methods we teach, we probably spend the greatest amount of time on sensitivity analysis as a method in itself and as an aspect of other quick methods. Since in quick analysis we usually do not have time to collect very much new data, and existing data are often suspect, we teach students the value of examining alternatives under different assumptions.

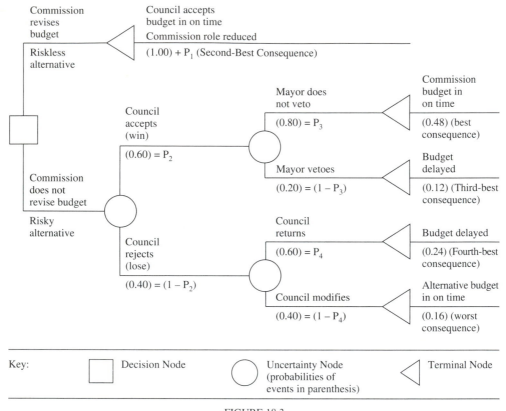

FIGURE 18.3
A Decision Tree: To Revise or Not to Revise the CD Budget (Source: Patton and Sawicki, 1986, p. 127.)

Changing the valuations of decision criteria, perceptions and attitudes about risk and uncertainty, and beliefs in the so-called facts of the case will often produce preferences for different alternatives. Practically any problem, alternative, value, variable or assumption can be subjected to sensitivity analysis. We recommend establishing a reasonable range of values for every variable relevant to a particular problem as well as critical uncertainties and risks. Critical sensitivities are those that, when varied, change the nature of the recommendation. Most policy problems can be reduced to as few as three to five sensitive variables. Then, using a hand calculator or micro-

computer, the analysis can be reestimated under various assumptions. If more time and resources become available, more elaborate researched methods can be used. In our classes we sometimes reassign a problem, providing time for more researched analysis. We are often struck with how little difference there is between the results of the quick and researched analyses.

I personally believe that we do not devote sufficient attention to sensitivity analysis in planning practice as well as in the classroom. Without going into details, I have recently been involved in several projects in which sensitivity analysis revealed major problems with prior analyses and brought into question the basic principles upon which major plans and development decisions were being made.

A research team from the University of Wisconsin–Milwaukee recently completed a project for a state department of transportation that dealt with methods for multi-objective decision making (Alexander 1985). One of the findings of this project related to the outputs of a model used by the state DOT to determine priorities for major highway projects. We discovered, by subjecting the existing model to a sensitivity analysis, that several variables assumed by the state DOT to have an effect were of little or no consequence in determining priorities. Surprisingly, the model had been developed without being subjected to a sensitivity analysis.

Another example of the value of sensitivity analysis can be drawn from my work for a development firm based in the Midwest. Economic and development projections had been made by a national firm as the basis for a CBD development plan. These projections were being used to support city decisions for downtown development and related development incentives. As time passed, some people realized the projections were not being reached. On checking the figures, it was found that the extrapolations did not take into account the realities of the change predicted. For example, had CBD housing been subjected to sensitivity analysis, the planners would have realized their figures called for the CBD to triple the annual amount of housing it had captured in past years and to capture virtually all the housing anticipated for the entire city for the next two decades.

We bring these types of examples into our classrooms and have students conduct quick sensitivity analyses on them. For virtually all problems and cases in our quick-analysis courses we require a sensitivity analysis to be part of the student's analytic approach. In this way, we hope to be able to help our graduates avoid committing major substantive errors.

TEACHING QUICK ANALYSIS: USE OF CASES

In order to teach quick methods as realistically as possible, we use cases drawn from our own experiences. A great deal of effort is put into the cases which begin with problems that can be resolved by an individual student in a day or two using one or two methods to cases that take a couple of weeks to solve using perhaps a half-dozen or more of the quick methods and involving a team of five or six students.

The case-study method has gone in and out of favor over the years, but we believe it can be a very useful way to teach analysis. Our approach is to select cases that illustrate specific policy approaches. Although cases typically do not have one correct solution, we look for cases that have, in fact, been resolved so student solutions can be compared with actual solutions. The cases are assigned with relatively little specific guidance other than a problem statement from the client and a few key data sources. The instructors act as consultants and advisors to the students, and the problems are debriefed as quickly as a day or two after they are completed. Whenever possible, actors involved in the real case are invited to serve as jurors when the cases are debriefed.

Cases that we now use focus on state and local policy issues, including such topics as if the age for obtaining a drivers license should be raised, whether a downtown block should be redeveloped, how to allocate emergency aid for home fuel, and how to select an alternative solid-waste collection method.

THE PLACE OF QUICK ANALYSIS IN THE PLANNING PROCESS

Having taken a strong stand on the value of quick methods and adopting essentially a modification of the rational approach to problem solving, we're faced with the question of whether what we have done is relevant. We tried to indicate how the rational model needs to be adapted to various situations, and how compromises have to be made based on the political situation. We argued that the methods, because they can be applied quickly and produce results when they are needed, could enable planners, analysts and citizens to have an impact on policy decisions. The question may be whether the quick methods can really be applied in today's planning environment. We obviously believe they can, but we would be remiss not to recognize the growing discussion in planning about alternatives to the rational approach.

Writers have been increasingly addressing the issue of whether rationality is a useful model in planning and whether other models might be more appropriate. While this literature is extensive, it consists primarily of criticism of the rational approach, with no widely accepted alternative model having appeared. In the first article in the first issue of the *Journal of Planning Education and Research*, Richard Klosterman wrote that "The critiques of the 'rational' planning ideal continued [through the 1970s] but the models which were proposed for replacing it—Friedmann's . . . 'transactive planning' and Michael's . . . and Schon's . . . 'learning society'—have had little impact on planning practice" (1981). The critique of the rational model has continued into the 1980s, with an overview of the issue provided by such writers as Alexander (1984), Boyer (1983), Breheny and Hooper (1984), Forester (1980) and Mandelbaum (1985), but with no consensus on an alternative to the rational model.

The last word has not been written on this issue, of course, and a widely agreed upon substitute for the rational model has not yet appeared in the literature, much less in practice. Perhaps an alternative paradigm is needed and the challenge before us is to develop that paradigm. But until that alternative is created, I believe that quick methods will not only continue to be used but that the bulk of today's planning decisions will be made using them and we should teach them in our curricula. At the risk of being too practical, I note that planners on the line continue to report they rely upon these methods and employers seek people who have these skills (Forkenbrock 1986; Stern and Patton 1979). There will always be differences in styles of planning practice but it is difficult to believe that any of these approaches will not need to incorporate substantial doses of quick analysis.

CONCLUSION

The teaching of quick analysis must be placed in context. While I believe the ability to conduct analyses quickly is an indispensable skill for planners, it is certainly not the only analytic skill that must be mastered. Just as learning decision analysis alone would be insufficient preparation for planning practice, so would learning only quick analysis be insufficient. Quick analysis is best used when time, money and data are limited, but it also is valuable in a broader sense in that it encourages clearer thinking under time constraints, can increase the likelihood of producing useful analyses, and results in more honest presentations of what we really know about the pros and cons of alternatives.

There is no substitute for experience in

planning practice, although the combination of learning with exercises and actual cases helps prepare students for some of the reality of planning practice. Nonetheless, quick methods will have to be modified, adapted and fine-tuned in practice. Their value depends substantially on the skill of the user to combine these quick quantitative and qualitative methods with sound personal judgment to arrive at a valid policy analysis. Questions of equity, political reality and broader issues in society certainly affect the usefulness or appropriateness of quick analysis. While we try to bring these issues into our courses through discussion, exercises and cases, our emphasis has been primarily on teaching students skills that can be used in a variety of political and social settings, rather than teaching them about the settings themselves—and determining when it is appropriate to use quick rather than researched methods.

Incorporating quick analysis into planning curricula may itself present a problem. Opposition may well come from teachers who see formal researched methods as the only legitimate analytic approach as well as from faculty who see the rational model as an outdated planning approach.

I obviously believe that quick analysis has an important place in the education of planners. To put my comments in perspective, I should note that I have also taught a number of courses on traditional research methods, and I am not rejecting them. My point is that planners must have the answers when decision makers want them—if we are to be useful and effective. When time is short, rather than give merely best guesses, we can produce roughly right answers with some degree of confidence using quick analytic methods. These methods continue to be developed and refined and the challenge is to test their veracity, to share the results with one another, and to make sure they are incorporated into planning curricula.

REFERENCES

Alexander, E. R. "After Rationality, What? A Review of Responses to Paradigm Breakdown." *Journal of the American Planning Association* 50:62–69, 1984.
———. "Rationality and Multi-Objective Decision-Making." Paper presented at the annual meeting of the Association of Collegiate Schools of Planning, 1985.
Boyer, M. C. *Dreaming the Rational City: The Myth of American City Planning*. Cambridge, MA: MIT Press, 1983.
Breheny, M. J., and A. J. Hooper, eds. *Rationality in Planning: Critical Essays on the Role of Rationality in Urban and Regional Planning*. London: Pion, 1984.
Coleman, J. "Problems of Conceptualization and Measurement in Studying Policy Impacts." In *Public Policy Evaluation*, ed. K. E. Dolbeare. Beverly Hills: Sage, 1975.
Forester, J. "Critical Theory and Planning Practice." *Journal of the American Planning Association* 46:275–284, 1980.
Forkenbrock, D. Survey of Methods Used by Planning Practitioners, 1986.
Klosterman, R. E. "Contemporary Planning Theory Education: Results of a Course Survey." *Journal of Planning Education and Research* 1:1–11, 1981.
Linner, J. "Planning and the Political Process: A View from the Trenches." Paper presented at the American Planning Association Conference, 1979.
Mandelbaum, S. "The Institutional Focus of Planning Theory." *Journal of Planning Education and Research* 5:3–9, 1985.
Patton, C. V., and D. S. Sawicki. *Basic Methods of Policy Analysis and Planning*. Englewood Cliffs, NJ: Prentice-Hall, 1986.
Sawicki, D. S. Teaching Policy Analysis in a Graduate Planning Program. *Journal of Planning Education and Research*. 1:78–85, 1982.
Singer, M. "The Vitality of Mythical Numbers." *The Public Interest* 23:3–9, 1971.
Sterk, L., and C. V. Patton. "Hiring the Compleat Planner." *Planning and Public Policy* 4:1–6, 1979.

19.

Janet A. Fuchs

PLANNING FOR COMMUNITY HEALTH PROMOTION:
A RURAL EXAMPLE

Health-care literature seems to indicate a trend toward better organization of health education activities, which is reflected in descriptions of health coalitions, consortia, networks, multi-institutional arrangements, health councils, and clusters. Single-institution, community health-promotion programs should be a "thing of the past" in today's society, yet, often these programs are still conducted in this manner. With limited funds available and growing competition for funding, local health agencies must improve on coordinating and organizing health programming.

In an effort to respond to the need for community organization and planning for health education, the Centers for Disease Control's Division of Health Education developed an intervention effort through which community health promotion programs could be planned on a local level.[1] The program is called PATCH (Planned Approach To Community Health) and it attempts to create a collaboration among federal, state, and local health agencies. PATCH has the standard health-program planning components and includes: agency organization, data collection and analyses, problem identification and priority setting,

intervention planning and implementation, and evaluation.[2]

The PATCH project is currently implemented in 12 states. Ohio was one of the first PATCH states; three pilot sites in the state were selected to conduct the program by the Ohio Department of Health (ODH), Division of Health Education and Promotion. These sites consisted of an urban area, a mid-sized community, and a rural county. This article will describe the rural county's efforts in planning for community health promotion.

PHASE I—COMMUNITY ORGANIZATION

Holmes County is an entirely rural area with a population of 30,000 located in the northeast section of Ohio. Residents are 99.9% white and the eastern portion of the county is the center of one of the largest Amish settlements in the world. Approximately one-third of the county population is Amish, thus only 43% of people aged 25 years and older have completed a high school education. Many of the Amish children attend one of the 96 parochial schools (1st through 8th grades). Total enrollment is 3,029 students and the teachers are mostly Amish.

The county has the usual array of health-related agencies and services. The first task of PATCH was to organize these agencies so that a core group or local advisory group

[1]C. F. Nelson, M. W. Kreuter, and N. B. Watkins, "A Partnership Between the Community, State, and Federal Government: Rhetoric or Reality," *Hygie* 1986: 5(3): 27–31.

[2]C. F. Nelson, R. P. Stoddard, and N. B. Watkins, *Planned Approach to Community Health* (Atlanta, GA: Centers for Disease Control, Division of Health Education, 1985).

could be established. In this rural area, it involved telephoning the agency and asking them to send a representative to an organizational meeting. Of 15 agencies contacted, eight have continued to support and participate in PATCH. These include the health department, park district, hospital, office on aging, cooperative extension, Head Start, counseling center, and county office of education. The health department is the lead or coordinating agency having a doctoral level prepared health educator.

The first meetings involved orienting the agencies to PATCH and seeking a commitment to the project. Many of these agencies had interacted on an informal basis and collaborated on programs as dictated by time, money, and need. These agencies did not have trained health educators or formal health education programs (except the schools), but they did have a "connection to health education" by nature of their activities and clientele.

Phase I included a training session on process activities in conducting a community health needs assessment. During this session, participants identified sources of health data and organized for its collection to include a community opinion survey, mortality and morbidity data compilation, and behavioral risk factor survey.

PHASE II—DATA COLLECTION AND ANALYSES

Key community people were identified for interviews to obtain opinions on the county's leading health problems. Assurances were made that residents from a variety of professions and jobs and from all districts of the county would be interviewed. Forty residents were interviewed and asked open-ended questions, one of which was "What do you think are the most important county health problems?" The top four health problems identified were alcohol/drug abuse, obesity, mental health problems, and teenage pregnancies. A forced-choice survey of health problem areas was also given to the key informants and the highest ranked issues were family/marital problems, overweight/nutritional problems, alcohol abuse, belief in health myths, and smoking.

Mortality and morbidity data were assembled to determine trends and outstanding health problems. Sources for these data were the Ohio Department of Health's vital statistics annual reports for 1979 through 1986. Data are reported in frequencies and rates by county with rates usually expressed per 100,000 people. Using rates, however, was not considered the best way to interpret data, especially when trying to make comparisons with state data. In a rural area with low numbers of death for a disease per year, a difference of four or five deaths can greatly change the rate. For example, in 1984 there were 17 cerebrovascular deaths with a rate of 57.8 per 100,000. In 1985, there were 22 deaths with a rate of 74.8 per 100,000. To better interpret the data, the percentage of the total number of deaths was used for the leading causes of death.

Over this 8-year period, 43.4% of residents died from heart disease, 17.6% from cancer, 8.0% from cerebrovascular disease, 5.5% from accidents, and 3.5% from pneumonia and influenza. A table of the percentage distribution by age group was developed to pinpoint age groups perhaps at higher risk for certain diseases. It was found that 71.1% of those who died from heart disease were 70 years and older; for Ohio it was 67.1% of this age group. One cause of death, nonmotor vehicle accidents, reflected a disparity between Ohio and Holmes County when data were tabulated in this manner. Only 5.7% of the Holmes population over 70 years old died from these accidents, while for Ohio 34% were over 70.

Years of potential life lost (YPLL) data were figured and Ohio's YPLL indices (based on 70 years) ranked cancer, heart disease, and accidents as the leading causes of early deaths. For Holmes County, accidents were the number one YPLL cause of death, followed by cancer and heart disease. There was a greater difference between the county YPLL index for accidents (36.1 years) and cancer (8.4 years).

Two behavioral risk factor surveys (BRFS) were conducted to determine prevalence of 11 risk factors associated to six health areas: obesity, exercise, smoking, seat belt use, alcohol use, and hypertension. A telephone BRFS was administered among non-Amish and a door-to door survey was needed for the large Amish population. A random digit dialing survey technique was used for the telephone survey and multistage cluster sampling procedures were used in the door-to-door interview survey. The CDC's BRFS was used for both surveys and only adults 18 and older were included in the interviews. There were 772 telephone interviews conducted and 400 door-to-door interviews.

Obesity was based on the 1959 Metropolitan height/weight tables and defined as 120% or more of ideal weight. In the telephone survey, 29.4% were obese and among Amish, 34.8% met this criterion. Persons were considered sedentary when reporting less than 20 minutes leisure-time physical activity and less than three times per week. For the non-Amish, 62.4% were sedentary while 92.0% Amish lacked regular physical activity. Data on current cigarette smoking were gathered and only 4.8% Amish smoked while 22.4% in the telephone survey were current smokers.

Seat belt use was determined based on frequency of wearing a seat belt when driving or riding in a car. In the non-Amish survey, 49.5% seldom or never wore a seat belt and 68.9% sometimes, seldom, or never wore a seat belt. Of Amish, 54.0% seldom or never used a seat belt and 73.0% sometimes, seldom, or never wore one.

Three risk factors for alcohol use were measured. Binge drinking was defined as having five or more drinks on at least one occasion in the past month. Only 0.3% of Amish had indicated doing this while 11.1% of non-Amish reported this activity. Drinking and driving was also assessed and 0.3% of the Amish and 2.5% of the non-Amish population reported this behavior. Finally, heavy drinking was defined as totaling 60 or more drinks during the past month. Only 3.7% telephone respondents and no Amish met this criterion.

The last risk factor measured was hypertension. Persons reporting they had ever been told they were hypertensive was one area examined and 21.8% of the non-Amish and 8.8% of the Amish population indicated this was true for them. Another measure was persons indicating they had been told they were hypertensive and that their blood pressure was still high. Very few had uncontrolled hypertension with only 0.8% non-Amish and 0.5% Amish reporting this situation. The final hypertension measure was a combination of persons reporting ever having been told they were hypertensive, being on medication, or the fact that their blood pressure was still high. In the telephone survey, 16.7% reported this while 8.3% Amish indicated this controlled/uncontrolled hypertension status.

These BRFS data were compared to Ohio BRFS figures. For both survey populations, Holmes County had a higher percentage at risk than Ohio for obesity, sedentary lifestyle, and seat belt use. Ohio was higher than Holmes County in smoking, binge drinking, heavy drinking, drinking and driving, uncontrolled hypertension, and controlled/uncontrolled hypertension. Only non-Amish were higher than Ohio in having ever been told they had hypertension.

PHASE III—PROBLEM IDENTIFICATION AND PRIORITIZING

Once data were gathered, tabulated, and analyzed, the local core group and the ODH and CDC representatives were brought together again. During this meeting, data were scrutinized to pinpoint specific health problems and perhaps unique health issues for the county.

Several areas of interest were noted. Heart disease was the leading cause of death; yet, almost three-fourths were living beyond 70 years of age before dying. Of further interest was that obesity and sedentary lifestyle risk-factor behaviors were higher than the state, and that the self-reported hypertension factors were lower than Ohio.

Lack of seat belt use was very high in comparison to Ohio and the nation. This seemed to fit the typical rural characteristics of driving behavior and the higher rate of accidents resulting in injuries and deaths.

It was believed smoking and alcohol use were lower than the state and nation due to the large Amish and related conservative religious groups in the eastern half of the county. These behaviors are discouraged and/or not tolerated among the church groups.

The high rate (92%) of Amish qualifying for the sedentary activity level was surprising at first glance since Amish take pride in their work ethnic. The question, however, deals with leisure activities more suited to the non-Amish population. For example, it requests information on such activities as

jogging, walking, bicycling, gardening, or hiking. Most of the leisure activities listed would not be condoned by the church or not performed enough to fulfill the requirement of greater than 20 minutes for at least three times a week. Although many Amish walk or ride bikes as a means of transportation, very few reported the activities in the survey.

Accidents and injuries were identified as a priority health problem and the core group requested that additional information be gathered to better specify the health problem. Accident data were obtained from two local sources, the hospital emergency room and sheriff's office. The sheriff's office had recently initiated a computer program for tracking motor vehicle accidents and had no data from earlier years. The sheriff was very cooperative in helping obtain information requested and even changed the program format to isolate the project's needed information for future assessment and trend analysis. The hospital emergency room had tabulated visits by location of the accidental injury. That is, it could be determined if injuries/fatalities occurred at home, work, or in a motor vehicle.

The Ohio Department of Highway Safety provided county data through annual reports on the traffic accidents. These reports outline data regarding such areas as alcohol involvement and type of accidents. Also, The Industrial Commission of Ohio provided data on work-related injuries outlining degree of injury, and cause and type of accident.

Finally, death certificates were reviewed to extrapolate the nature of injury deaths. This was done to determine type of motor vehicle accident (auto, buggy, motorcycle, etc.) and nonmotor vehicle accident (drowning, fire, falls, etc.). This was a tedious task since the vast majority of local health departments do not have vital statistics on computer and death certificates were checked by hand.

PHASE IV—INTERVENTION PLANNING AND IMPLEMENTATION

The core group convened again to examine the additional accident data and to plan intervention strategies. A deputy from the sheriff's office was invited to speak on motor vehicle accidents. Holmes County has an exceptionally high traffic-accident rate (highest in the state) per 100 licensed drivers and has 800 to 900 accidents per year. This is due in part to the rural terrain (hills and curves), large deer population, high volume of tourists traveling to the county, and the large number of slow-moving vehicles (tractors, buggies).

It was discovered that the greatest concentration of accidents occur on main state highways and in areas where visibility is good for drivers. Traffic fatalities were more likely to happen on these highways as well, and were attributed to a mix of high rates of speed, sudden stops, slow-moving vehicles, and carelessness resulting from watching Amish and scenery rather than the road and traffic.

Almost 60% of injuries treated at the hospital emergency room were due to accidents at home, 30% were from accidents at work, and the remainder were from automobile accidents. The county averages 6 deaths and 323 injuries per year from motor vehicle accidents. Approximately 10% of all accidents are alcohol-related.

There were three outstanding types of work-related accidents—being struck by falling objects, overexertion, and caught in, on, or between something. Most individuals were men, 20 to 34 years old.

Goals were established and community-level objectives were written that expressed intent to resolve or reduce the accident/injury problem. During the Phase IV meeting, accident risk-factor behavior was reviewed to better understand motivations and characteristics conducive to accidents/injuries. For example, reasons were discussed why people do not wear seat belts. Target groups were also analyzed and those identified were teens, tourists, and local commercial truckers.

Core group members then decided on intervention strategies for reducing injuries/accidents. A community-wide public awareness campaign was considered to be the best means to address the motor vehicle accident issue. A list of activities was developed to conduct the campaign and included slogans and artwork contests, creation and distribution of awareness material (bumper stickers, table tents, road signs), and evaluation of the campaign.

PHASE V—PROGRAM EVALUATION

For each intervention conducted, an evaluation is planned to determine effectiveness of that effort. The overall PATCH program will be evaluated in several ways. First, the behavioral risk-factor surveys have provided a baseline measure of selected health behavior for the two county groups (Amish and non-Amish). The BRFS will be conducted again 5-years postprogram initiation to determine any changes. Also, community opinion will be solicited a second time to see if programs have had an impact on perceptions of county health problems. Mortality and morbidity data will continue to be monitored for change in leading causes of death and illness/disability. Goals for the project's health priority areas are written to reduce incidence of these mortality causes. For example, one project goal is to reduce the mortality rate from injuries in motor vehicle accidents from 22 to 18 per 100,000 in Holmes County by December 1990. The current rate is 20.4 per 100,000.

No assessments have been made at this

writing in Holmes County PATCH. Of course, evaluation is planned as the project continues; the expectation is the program will have an impact on the prioritized health problem.

BENEFITS OF A PLANNED, COORDINATED PROJECT

There are many benefits in taking a planned and coordinated approach to community health promotion. Assembling the local core group has resulted in a more formal network of agencies. Participants have learned more about other agency activities and created avenues for shared programming. Professional material has been exchanged among group members, e.g., articles on learning styles were given to the health department educator from school representatives.

Health problems that were noted as future tasks for PATCH, but not prioritized, have been addressed through select agency efforts. For example, tobacco contract monies were obtained to develop and implement a youth smoking and smokeless tobacco education program which was cooperatively created between the health department and cooperative extension 4-H agent.

Additional program monies have been received primarily due to the PATCH project. Funding agencies are impressed with the baseline data collected and the ability to outline the health problem for proposed programs. The tobacco contract mentioned above also secured money for a worksite smoking policy seminar for area businesses and industries. An Ohio Department of Highway Safety contract has also been awarded for a safety belt education and incentive program.

Other spin-off activities have included the development and implementation of an Amish school health education curriculum. Data from the Amish BRFS were shared with the parochial school superintendent and three Amish teachers. It was decided that health teaching could be done to address the behavioral problems found in the survey.

The public schools are evaluating the school health curriculum and during this assessment PATCH data will be used to make curricular adjustments and revisions. The coordinator of PATCH will serve as a member of the curriculum committee.

Finally, an important benefit is that local residents seem more responsive and interested when county data are presented. A sense of ownership is developed, and concern and support are more readily provided when the presenter can use such terms as "us" and "we." The core group develops a similar attachment and responsiveness to the project when local data are collected and then used for programming. A shared focus and direction are established that many programs cannot create and claim.

SOME THOUGHTS FOR HEALTH PROMOTION

Organizing for community health promotion does not just happen overnight. A great amount of time and support must be committed to the effort. Agencies must be willing to work cooperatively. Rural areas may find this easier than larger communities where programs compete directly for clientele and monies. From the onset of the project, participants should experience a sharing of activities and decision making and old "turf" issues must be set aside. Further, face-to-face interaction may reduce any friction or tension that exists between agencies.

Early in the project, participants must decide on how the group will function, i.e., who will be the key member to organize and do the administrative work for the group. Other activities can then be shared by members, such as coordinating the data collection phase or evaluating programs. In later stages of the planning project, contact with agency members is less frequent and requires special efforts to keep people informed. Memoranda, newsletters, and telephone calls are possible avenues for keeping participants abreast of program activities and additional data or information, and for solicitation of input on problem areas and program direction.

The systematic accumulation of community health data is an important step in community health-promotion organization and planning for several reasons. First, it enables the documentation of local problems, creates need and direction for activities, and provides charting for program progress. Second, local data enhance the relevance of community awareness and programming. Residents develop a sense of ownership for the problems and the responses to them. Third, specificity of data (age, sex, race, etc.) can and should be used by all participating agencies.

It seems apparent that there must be activities to sustain a collaborative project. Evaluating progress and continuing or extending programs are two means to keep the project active and ongoing. Another consideration is finding ways to renew interest, support, and enthusiasm for old and new intervention efforts.

20.

Barry Checkoway

TWO TYPES OF PLANNING IN NEIGHBORHOODS

INTRODUCTION

This paper distinguishes between two types of planning in neighborhoods: "sub-area planning" in which central planning agencies deconcentrate facilities or functions to subareas, and "neighborhood planning" in which community residents develop plans and programs for themselves. This distinction is overdue and not trivial. Little of the growing discussion of neighborhoods draws this distinction or carefully discriminates among alternative meanings and objectives. Yet each type of planning has its own ends, and much of what passes today as neighborhood planning is subarea planning in disguise.

This exercise also has implications for planning research and education. Although many American planners trace their historical roots to the neighborhoods, planning in neighborboods remains a relatively undeveloped area of professional specialization. As a result, there is a tendency to accept either widely varying or singular notions of planning in neighborhoods which embrace all forms of practice. This can be a source of confusion to those who study or teach about planning in neighborhoods. My aim here is to contribute to a greater measure of clarity in conceptualizing domains of practice in the field. I believe that such clarification could help reduce confusion, sharpen the research and action agenda, and make the whole enterprise more purposeful.

SUBAREA PLANNING

Subarea planning is an episode in the history of municipal government reform. This history is not new, although the current episode can be traced to citizen participation movements in the 1960s. This demand originated with the organized actions and protests of minorities and then spread throughout the society. The once-held image of Americans as apathetic gave way under a stampede of civil rights movements, consumer coalitions, neighborhood associations, and other citizen organizations.

Government agencies were frequently the target of these actions. Public confidence in government declined drastically. One study found more than half of those Americans surveyed were "alienated and disenchanted, feeling profoundly impotent to influence the actions of their leaders" (U.S. Senate Subcommittee on Intergovernmental Relations, 1974, p. 17). Most of these people expressed potential to become active in government if the means were available and they could have impact. Without such assurances, however, the growing belief was that independent citizen organizations and local units were more effective than government in solving problems and getting things done. Government itself was perceived as "vast, remote, inaccessible" (Dahl, 1970, p. 98).

Several advisory commissions recommended reforms to narrow the gap between officials and citizens. Some turned toward the neighborhoods. One commission advocated neighborhood subunits with elected councils, another little city halls with decentralized services, and another metropolitan government with neighborhood districts (Advisory Commission on Intergovernmental Relations, 1972; National Advisory Commission on Civil Disorders, 1968; Committee for Economic Development, 1966, 1970). One president advocated "creative federalism" involving neighborhood groups in social planning, another "new partnership" with neighborhoods, government, and business as partners in development.

Government agencies responded with official programs to expand participation in local subareas. Between 1968 and 1976 there were over 25 hearings in Congress focusing on the need for greater participation, and participation became part of most federal domestic programs. For example, the Housing and Community Development Act of 1974 promised to provide residents with "adequate opportunity to participate in the planning, implementation, and assessment of the program," and was interpreted to include subarea programs in addition to traditional public hearings and citizen advisory boards. American city governments developed a wide range of participation structures and methods. Nearly one in three cities adopted some method of decentralization, two in three some type of citizen committee to advise city hall (Advisory Commission on Intergovernmental Relations, 1972, 1979).

City planning agencies shared in this movement for reform. Traditional planning had come under attack from citizens frustrated by unsolved social problems and organized to oppose planning programs perceived as intrusive or unresponsive to local needs (Hartman, 1975; Fellman, 1973; Katznelson, 1981; Mollenkopf, 1975). Planning agencies responded with programs to involve subarea residents in developing plans. For example, San Diego assigned planners to prepare subarea plans for land use, circulation, open space and community facilities. Fort Worth assigned planners to organize subarea councils and propose plans to citywide bodies for approval and use in developing overall programs. Pittsburgh assigned planners to represent districts in community development block grant programs. They operated out of the agency's downtown office, but attended evening meetings in their districts (Hallman, 1976). Needleman and Needleman (1974, p. 25) studied several cities and documented "the opening of city planning to citizen participation on a decentralized basis. Planning departments in a number of major cities have undertaken programs in this innovative type of planning, for the first time encouraging citizens to take a direct and active role in shaping the planned development of their own neighborhoods."

Today, subarea planning operates in agencies across the nation. There has been no systematic study of the scope of the field, but there is an obvious proliferation of programs. For example, Raleigh, North Carolina, planners have formed 18 neighborhood groups to discuss local problems, react to city proposals, and design self-help projects. Baltimore planners have drafted neighborhood social development plans to examine problems, define goals, set priorities, and initiate actions. Portland, Oregon, planners have worked with 63 associations formed to represent 71 neighborhoods through seven district boards. Seattle planners have circulated ballots to neighborhood residents who vote on alternative improvement for their communities.

Subarea planning is usually initiated by municipal officials. The mayor, planning director, or another official proposes the idea; planning commissioners consider and endorse the proposal; city councilors adopt an ordinance and direct the planning agency to implement the program. For example, Atlanta city councilors adopted an ordinance to create 24 subarea planning units. Planners work with citizens to prepare subarea plans for approval and incorporation into the comprehensive plan and city budget. They also assist a citywide advisory board to educate subarea representatives, disseminate information about municipal concerns, and increase communications among residents and officials (Atlanta Department of Planning, 1973; Hallman, 1976; Hutcheson, 1981; Rohe and Gates, 1981).

Subarea planning may follow steps of rational planning. One guide instructs planners to establish a subarea committee, assess community conditions, set goals, and propose plans to higher bodies for implementation (St. Paul Department of Planning and Economic Development, 1981). Another instructs planners to define boundaries, select block representatives, prepare social surveys and land use maps, formulate goals and submit alternative plans for review and implementation as part of the general plan (Boulder Department of Community Development, n.d.). Yet another instructs them to inventory local conditions, set goals and priorities, and submit plans to municipal agencies to assure compatibility with city policies (Baltimore City Planning Commission, n.d.).

Subarea planning may produce written plans. Some plans are comprehensive, as in Seattle and Denver where they include descriptions of history and population; analyses of community assets and problems; elements including population, housing, historic preservation, land use, and transportation; and recommendations for development (Werth and Bryant, 1979). Other plans are problem focused, as in Portland,

Oregon, where they focus on housing rehabilitation and controlled growth (Portland Bureau of Planning, 1975a), or on redevelopment of a single avenue (Portland Bureau of Planning, 1975c), or on land use and zoning in a mixed residential district near the center of the city (Portland Bureau of Planning, 1975b). These are not Master Plans, but are in that tradition.

Subarea plans can help fulfill minimal requirements for citizen participation in federal funding programs, provide information for incorporation into comprehensive plans, or enable review of proposed local changes. In Atlanta they "help blend changes in the neighborhood in the comprehensive planning process" (Atlanta Department of Planning, 1973, n.p.); in St. Paul they "help citizens become involved in the unified capital improvement program and budgeting process" (St. Paul Department of Planning and Economic Development, 1981, p. 1); and in Boulder they "become leverage in requesting neighborhood improvement projects for inclusion in the city's annual program" (Boulder Department of Community Development, n.d., p. 2). Another use is to show municipal concern and provide public relations for city government: "Baltimore is committed to providing necessary improvements, facilities, and services to sustain and strengthen neighborhoods" (Baltimore City Planning Commission, n.d., n.p.). Yet another use is to boost the image of a city as a place of good neighborhoods: "Boston is its neighborhoods" (Boston Office of Program Development, 1978, p. 8).

Subarea planners are municipal employees assigned to local areas. The American Planning Association describes this role in *A Guide to Neighborhood Planning* (hereafter *APA Guide*), which "takes the planner from the point of entry through the completion of the plan" (Werth and Bryant, 1979,

p. 1). It describes the planner as "a resource for both the neighborhood and the city planning agency," who can provide "the directions and skills of a professional planner with specialized training . . . (and) relevant data from the city department files, maps and surveys, and explanations of the city's policies and procedures," and who can "know the personalities of the neighborhood's leaders, how various segments of the neighborhood interact, and the condition or character of the neighborhood. This knowledge can be invaluable to the central planning office in its day-to-day work of reviewing zoning changes and budget proposals, putting together citywide plans, and dealing with citizen complaints" (p. 2). It anticipates conflict between neighborhood and city allegiances, warns against showing partisanship or getting caught between competing interests, and reaffirms responsibility of the planner to city government: "Obviously, as a city employee, the neighborhood planner is accountable to the planning agency in the same way any other employee is" (p. 2).

Subarea planners recognize the importance of citizen participation. But the measure of effectiveness is not that citizens exercise power in planning, but rather that public input is solicited and contributes to a decision that is supported by residents. "After the planner has gathered background information about the neighborhood in the office, the next step is developing citizen interest and participation in the planning process," continues the *APA Guide* (p. 10). It advises the planner to prepare an agenda for a public meeting to introduce the city's program, present an overview of the subarea, and lead discussion of goals for an official plan. It provides practical advice to run meetings: "Make sure all of your department's guidelines or rules are right up front from the beginning," "use examples that are personal to them," "do not come on too strong," "don't hide behind jargon of what you do at the office," "don't try to razzle-dazzle them," and "be careful that your style is not inadvertently insulting or inappropriate for residents" (p. 15). It advises planners to bring citizens "back to the point if they stray blindly from the subject at hand," deflect complaints until they "take care of the planning business first," and listen carefully to all concerns: "Even the most seemingly irrelevant complaint may sometimes point to a fundamental need in the neighborhood. It might take a while to convince people that the plan is *their* plan. As many neighborhood planners reported, although people may be uneducated, it does not mean that they don't know what they want" (p. 15).

Subarea planners also recognize the importance of community organization. In some cities, they work with established groups that meet agency criteria. For example, St. Paul planners recognize groups which demonstrate "that a broadly representative community organization has been developed through an open process" (St. Paul Department of Planning and Economic Development, 1981, p. 4). Salem, Oregon, planners recognize groups which are "firmly established," have "broad based support" and "a regular method of communication with neighborhood residents, businesses, and absentee property owners," and show "basic understanding of key functions in city government, including the structure, role, responsibilities of city council, city departments, citizens advisory bodies, and city policies relating to planning including the area comprehensive plan, growth and transportation study plans, and urban renewal plans" (Salem Department of Community Development, 1975, p. 6f).

In other cities, planners from subarea planning councils that represent citizens "to assure the smooth development of the plan as well as to provide a fair basis for its implementation" (Werth and Bryant, 1979, p. 16). The *APA Guide* advises planners to involve representatives in committees "to assume a leading role in resolving conflicts between the neighborhood and the city's plans, putting pressure on city agencies to fund the plan proposals, and serving as a general lobbying group for the neighborhood" (p. 21). It warns against "members who tend to dominate meetings and seek to channel discussion toward a favorite pet issue or area of expertise. Such problems can best be handled by keeping personal feelings out of the picture and reminding the committee of the broader scope of the planning process" (p. 21).

Subarea councils serve several functions. Hutcheson (1981) finds that they make city councilors more aware of community organizations. Pederson (1974, 1976) finds that they improve communications among citizens and officials. Rohe and Gates (1981) find that they educate citizens about planning issues, develop community cohesion and leadership, and improve neighborhood conditions and services. Elsewhere, Checkoway (1981) analyzes councils that implement plans through project review, education, and advocacy; recruit volunteers and develop leadership skills; and maintain subarea offices which enhance discussion of local concerns.

Subarea councils also can engender community controversy. Some councils are unrepresentative of the area population, frustrate citizens rather than activate them, or antagonize those they are supposed to serve. In New York City, for example, councils and boards were established to increase participation and improve service delivery. But some residents protested elite representation on councils, drafted alternative plans to oppose corporate construction and institutional expansion, and sought guarantees for low-income housing and community control. Planners responded by involving residents in technical planning procedures. Today these councils operate as resource centers and intermediaries between subareas and city hall. They tend to serve administrative ends and residents are largely unaware of them (Baldwin, 1982; Barton et al., 1977, Weber, 1976; Zimmerman, 1979).

Some subarea councils provide an organizing vehicle for community residents. For example, consumers in Illinois organized around a lack of effective participation in a subarea health planning council. They recruited a large number of new members, enlisted candidates to run for the council, and won a majority of seats. Local providers organized in response to these initiatives, elected their own slate by a wide margin, and caused consumers to reconsider their participation. Subarea planning gave consumers an organizational start, although this was an unanticipated consequence and providers recaptured control nonetheless (Checkoway, 1982; Checkoway and Doyle, 1980).

In working with subarea councils, however, planners are not community organizers concerned with political action. On the contrary, the *APA Guide* warns that "this kind of community organization is seldom undertaken by government employees and is frequently viewed with hostility by city agencies. Planners would be unwise to adopt the Alinsky approach. Not only do they jeopardize their jobs by involving their programs and agencies in controversy, but, more important, they jeopardize their nonpartisan role as link between the neighborhood and city agencies" (Werth and Bryant, p. 16). Planners thus involve citizens to facilitate plan development and

implementation, not to build strong local organizations or to transfer power to neighborhood residents.

It is no surprise that this is the case. Planners emphasize administrative values of economy, efficiency, and control, and these may be the antithesis of participation and planning in subareas (Aleshire, 1972; Baum, 1983; Friedmann, 1973; Steckler and Herzog, 1979). They favor reforms that are not disruptive of program management, and oppose measures which would transfer power to local territorial or functional units. They perceive citizen participation to cause delays in action, to expand the number and intensity of conflicts, and to increase the costs of operations (Checkoway and Van Til, 1978). Planners who advocate subarea priorities may experience administrative controls and professional tensions which prove fatal to them in the agency (Baum, 1983; Forester, 1982; Lipsky, 1973; Needleman and Needleman, 1974).

Subarea planning is not neighborhood planning in which community residents plan for themselves, but an approach in which central planning agencies deconcentrate facilities or functions to subareas. It is not decentralization, but a new form of centralization.

NEIGHBORHOOD PLANNING

Neighborhood planning is an episode in the history of community self-determination in large cities. In the 1960s this took the form of citizen protest, often by low income blacks in urban ghetto areas in reaction to federal programs. Some organized around the bulldozers of urban renewal, others the routes of proposed expressways, yet others the intrusion of large institutions into nearby areas. These actions helped individuals to recognize common problems, join together, and build organizations (Hartman, 1975; Fellman, 1973; Lamb, 1975; Lancourt, 1979; Mollenkopf, 1975; Piven and Cloward, 1977).

In the 1970s working class whites in older urban neighborhoods took lessons from their black counterparts and organized around private and public institutions whose practices contributed to decline. Their issues included housing rehabilitation, community revitalization, physical improvement, social services, health and safety, and community empowerment. Some applied high visibility tactics and caused changes in established institutional practices. For example, neighborhood groups pressured Illinois legislators to enact an anti-redlining law to prohibit institutions from denying property loans because of geographic location, and stimulated similar actions in other states (Boyte, 1980; Cassidy, 1980; Goering, 1979; Naparstek and Cincotta, 1976; National Commission on Neighborhoods, 1979; Perlman, 1978; Rosenbloom, 1979).

Neighborhood groups have increased in number and capacity. By 1980, the National Commission of Neighborhoods had identified more than 8,000 neighborhood organizations in the United States; the federal Office of Neighborhoods, Voluntary Associations, and Consumers Affairs had identified nearly 15,000 citizen groups concerned with neighborhood problems; and the U.S. Office of Consumer Affairs had presented case accounts of almost 100 leading local groups working to activate citizens and meet local needs. These groups have diverse origins and encompass a wide range of activities.

These groups also have built coalitions and support networks which help formulate strategies, train leaders, and provide assistance. For example, the Center for Community Change assists poor and minority groups involved in housing rehabilitation and neighborhood reinvestment; the National Center for Urban Ethnic Affairs helps urban ethnic groups involved in community development and commercial revitalization; the National Training and Information Center trains neighborhood workers in enforcing compliance with federal housing programs; and the National Association of Neighborhoods lobbies for legislation and promotes decentralization.

Today, some groups have grown to a stage where they develop plans and programs for themselves. In Chicago, for example, residents formed a temporary organization to protest university expansion, slum landlords and merchants, and segregated schools. They convened a congress of more than 1200 people representing 97 community groups to form The Woodlawn Organization (TWO). They formulated plans in reaction to official city plans for the area; proposed an educational park of four schools on a common campus; worked to eliminate a skid row on a main local thoroughfare; and developed an experimental school project using the neighborhood as an educational research center. Since then TWO has produced low-income housing developments, a comprehensive mental healthcare facility, a supermarket, security patrols, a theater, a management corporation, and a community development corporation to coordinate overall strategy for the neighborhood (Brazier, 1969; Fish, 1973; Lancourt, 1979).

In St. Louis, residents reacted to a federal antipoverty program which misrepresented the community and to a proposed urban renewal project which threatened massive neighborhood demolition. They formed Jeff-Vander-Lou (JVL), an independent organization emphasizing housing, community development, education, social services, and other objectives. They adopted bylaws that provided for community representation, drafted proposals, enlisted support, and began their first project. Since then JVL has built and rehabilitated housing, generated capital development, operated social services, attracted new industry and jobs, and formulated plans to boost the local economy. They have increased awareness of neighborhood issues, developed leadership, and produced results (Checkoway, 1985).

TWO and JVL are exceptional neighborhood planning organizations, but they are not alone in the field. For example, Inquilinos Boricuas en Action in Boston has rehabilitated houses formerly slated for demolition, developed housing for the elderly, and completed a community cultural plaza. Tri City Citizens Union for Progress in Newark has rehabilitated housing, operated adult employment training services, established day care and community health programs, and provided outreach counseling and referral services. Voice of the People in Chicago has bought apartments from absentee landlords, renovated and rented them to low income residents, and helped tenants organize and manage buildings. Communities Organized for Public Services in San Antonio has won a bond issue to fund storm drainage improvements, received federal funds for community projects, and established block clubs which have installed stoplights, removed trash, built pedestrian bridges over railroad tracks, and discouraged junk dealers from locating in poor neighborhoods. Chinatown Neighborhood Improvement in San Francisco has converted a YMCA residence to senior housing, established a nonprofit housing corporation, and made improvements in the business district.

Some neighborhood planning organizations originate in reaction to crises and confrontations. Protest is often a neighborhood's first weapon and source of victories. Over time, however, residents may decide that it is a strategic mistake to react to crises without an independent agenda of their own. This decision can help them to broaden their issues and formulate new plans (Checkoway, 1985; Lancourt, 1979). Other organizations originate when residents decide to redevelop their community. Initial goals may aim "to develop an active, integrated, desirable neighborhood where residents live in harmony and with pride," or "to assure that the community has a capacity to initiate development on as independent a basis as possible," or "to strive for justice and accountability in all areas pertaining to a healthy wholesome environment" (National Commission on Neighborhoods 1979).

Neighborhood planning operates in an imbalanced political arena (Ahlbrandt and Brophy, 1975; Boyer, 1793; Cassidy, 1980; Clay, 1979; Downie, 1974; Gans, 1962; Hartman, 1975; Marciniak, 1977; National Commission on Neighborhoods, 1979; National Training and Information Center, 1976; Stone, 1976). Outside economic interest—including some landlords, real estate agents, financial institutions, and commercial establishments—are more likely to mobilize resources around development and planning than are unorganized neighborhood residents. Individual residents tend to face the neighborhood alone, know little about it as a planning unit, or hesitate to "intrude" in areas that involve concentrated power. In the absence of special circumstances, the key decisions which affect local communities are often made outside them.

Neighborhood planning thus can be viewed as a process of political development. Cohen (1979) describes a five stage model in which neighborhood planning develops countervailing power. First, the

neighborhood is unorganized and fragmented; then primary institutions bring individuals together to share common concerns
and accomplish limited objectives; then citizens organize to deal with housing and other
issues; then the organization recruits members, builds support, and becomes a political
entity of substance and power; and finally
the organization represents the entire neighborhood, widens the range of issues, and de-
livers programs and services affecting all
aspects of social and political life. Organization serves to mobilize individuals, develop
a program, and generate power. It is often
only after individuals organize that they develop programs to meet neighborhood needs
(Schoenburg and Rosenbaum, 1980).

Neighborhood planning can also be
viewed as a process of community development. It may involve steps to identify
neighborhood problems and issues; formulate goals and objectives; collect and analyze data; and develop and implement
plans. But it may also involve efforts to
sweep the streets, knock on doors, pack a
public hearing, and confront the power-
holders. It is not a one-time process to produce a singular plan, but a continuous and
multifaceted process to develop capacity. It
is not a form of mandated participation in
which citizens provide input to plans developed elsewhere, or of advocacy planning in which advocates develop plans to
serve local interests, but of community development in which people strengthen
themselves as well as their communities.

Neighborhood planning organizations
may produce written plans. These plans
generally are not comprehensive but sectoral, not long-range but immediate, not a
series of colored designs describing an
ideal future but a statement of practical
problems and community-based strategy
searching for resources. They may be the
first such statement of strategy, in the
words of those who live there and know it
best. They may proclaim that residents
have taken account of themselves and
know where they want to go, even if they
have little idea of how to get there and how
long it might take.

Neighborhood planning organizations can
benefit from preparing a plan. The process
can help residents articulate goals in systematic fashion, describe problems and causes,
analyze alternatives for revitalization, and
build a foundation for implementation. The
plan can also help legitimate an organization. One Chicago organization was already
well-known and respected outside the
neighborhood when they decided to draft a
plan. The availability of an attractive, technically proficient product helped confirm its
image among constituents and provide
legitimacy among funding sources (Checkoway and Cahill, 1981).

But the process of preparing a neighborhood plan can also have disadvantages. It
can divert residents from direct action,
focus them on narrow issues rather than the
whole social picture, and absorb them in
written drafts when other actions might be
more powerful (Piven, 1970; Piven and
Cloward, 1977). Mayer and Blake (1980)
find that the preparation of plans is among
the least useful activities undertaken by
neighborhood organizations, because such
plans can relate poorly to daily concerns,
create delays, and frustrate supporters.
They find that more useful is a process involving ongoing discussions among key
participants, resourcefulness in moving forward from broad strategy to action, and
ability to recognize opportunities and generate one project from another. Neighborhood planning is not plan preparation alone.

Neighborhood planners combine diverse
roles and skills. Some operate as technical
experts to conduct research on community
problems and complete steps in project

planning and implementation. Others operate as organizers to bring citizens together and generate support programs. Yet others operate as publicists to expand awareness of community issues, or as educators to develop leaders who stand up for the neighborhood. Neighborhood planners often have roving agendas (Henderson and Thomas, 1980; Mayer and Blake, 1980).

Neighborhood planners face problems unfamiliar to traditional planners. When should an organization move from protest to program? Where are the leaders to command a following? What will convince outsiders of local capacity to complete projects? What tactics activate residents without alienating allies and funding sources? How can planners give individuals a sense of the power to participate? These problems are different from those faced by most planners.

There are many obstacles to planning in neighborhoods. It is difficult to plan around neighborhood issues when individuals operate in isolation, or accept the notion of outside control over local development, or show little support for neighborhood public intervention. Several studies document the pattern in which private institutions deinvest from neighborhoods in favor of other locations, and in which public institutions deinvest from an area by reducing service levels. The result is typically a downgrading cycle of inadequate services, deteriorated infrastructure, and withdrawal of people and institutions (Clay, 1979; Cohen, 1979; Naparstek and Cincotta, 1976). Those who remain are often left with poor housing, health care, education, and declining quality of life. It is no surprise that many residents suffer a crisis of confidence and symptoms of alienation from a situation in which they have been displaced.

Despite obstacles, there are neighborhood planning organizations which show exceptional success. Mayer and Blake (1980) analyze such organizations and find common "stages of development" among them. Each has formally incorporated itself, developed competence in specific projects and expanded competence into other areas. Each also has developed effective leadership and staff, attracted involvement and support from community groups and outside actors, and dealt with the economic, social, and political environment.

Yet even exceptional neighborhood planning organizations have difficulties influencing the larger context in which they operate. Such organizations show that citizens can take hold of their surroundings without outside officials telling them what they need; handle local problems without harmful effects of federal intervention; and improve their communities when they determine plans and programs for themselves. But even the most accomplished organizations are unable to reverse citywide decline. Neighborhood problems result from decisions and institutions that operate largely outside the neighborhood, and the consequences flow from that process. To alter the consequences, it would be necessary to alter the process.

TOWARD A SYNTHESIS? IMPLICATIONS FOR RESEARCH AND EDUCATION

Some may think it useful to attempt a synthesis of these two types of planning in neighborhoods, but I believe it more useful to distinguish between them and develop the agenda of each. There is no single notion of planning in neighborhoods which embraces all forms of practice. Subarea planning and neighborhood planning are separate movements, each motivated by its own ends and values, each in its own early stage of development. In the formation of fields such as these, it is more important to develop what is unique to each rather than to attempt a grand embracing conception. Subarea planners are not neighborhood planners, and their roles will likely remain distinct in the future. The two approaches could possibly be used together in mutually reinforcing ways, but at present such an effort is probably not worth the investment.

More research is needed on each type of planning. What do we know about subarea planning? There is need to sort through the fragmented accounts of practice, draw from them general propositions that represent areas of agreement among researchers and practitioners, and indicate unanswered or remaining questions. What is the scope and quality of subarea planning? There is need for a comprehensive, systematic survey of planning agencies on a national scale to inventory the objectives and methods in use, identify major participants and obstacles, and analyze impacts and factors influencing practice. What are the innovative or exemplary methods in use? This study would analyze agencies that employ such methods, and draw lessons for adoption from one area to another.

What do we know about neighborhood planning? There is need for in-depth empirical case studies of neighborhood planning in practice. Recent studies provide brief accounts of individual initiatives, but stop short of systematic analysis (Boyte, 1980; Goering, 1979; National Commission on Neighborhoods, 1979; Perlman, 1978; U.S. Office of Consumer Affairs, 1980). There is also need to use empirical materials to build a conceptual base for further analysis. How do neighborhood planning organizations diagnose local conditions, set goals and priorities, find and make leaders, form and build organizations, formulate strategies and action plans,

and mobilize resources or implementation? There also is need to develop an action theory based on neighborhood practice, although recent work takes steps toward such theory (Henderson and Thomas, 1980). Other work, comprised largely of mimeographed papers by community practitioners, is considerable but restricted in circulation (Booth, 1977; Miller n.d.; Trapp, 1976). Neighborhood planning has reached a point where practitioners require firmer guidance and clarity to extend understanding.

Planning curricula have not emphasized planning in neighborhoods. It is ironic that this is the case, for neighborhoods are important in the history of American planning. But curricula tend to focus on comprehensive urban systems, not community subareas or neighborhoods. Curricula that do include neighborhoods tend to focus on subarea planning, not neighborhood planning. Other professions have a tradition of planning in neighborhoods, but planning educators have largely ignored their work (Cox, et al. 1974; Kramer and Specht, 1969; Lauffer and Newman, 1981). Yet this is a vital area for planning education, surely as vital as urban design, land use, regional development, and transportation planning. No matter how much planners increase knowledge and skills in serving those who dominate downtown skylines and city hall, if there is no parallel concern with planning in neighborhoods, then it is at risk to the people who live there.

REFERENCES

Advisory Commission on Intergovernmental Relations. *Citizen Participation in the American Federal System.* Washington, DC: U.S. Government Printing Office, 1979.

_____. *The New Grass Roots Government?* Washington, DC: U.S. Government Printing Office, 1972.

Ahlbrandt, R. S. and P. C. Brophy. *Neighborhood Revitalization.* Lexington: Lexington Books, 1975.

Aleshire, R. A. "Power to the People: An Assessment of the Community Action Model Cities Experience." *Public Administration Review* 32:428–44, 1972.

Atlanta Department of Planning. "Atlanta's Comprehensive Plan—The Value of Neighborhood Planning." Atlanta: Department of Planning, 1973.

Baldwin, S. "Community Boards in the Buffer Zone." *City Limits* 12:13–16, 1982.

Baltimore City Planning Commission. "The Neighborhood Social Development Plan." Baltimore: Baltimore City Planning Commission, n.d.

Barton, A. H., et al. *Decentralizing City Government: An Evaluation of the New York City District Manager Experiment.* Lexington: Lexington Books, 1977.

Baum, H. S. *Planners and Public Expectations.* Cambridge: Schenkman, 1983.

Booth, H. *Direct Action Organizing.* Chicago: The Midwest Academy, 1977.

Boston Office of Program Development. "Living in Boston: A Guide to Boston and Its Neighborhoods for People Interested in City Living." Boston: Office of Program Development, 1978.

Boulder Department of Community Development. "Guide to Neighborhood Planning." Boulder: Department of Community Development, n.d.

Boyer, B. C. *Cities Destroyed for Cash: The FHA Scandal at HUD.* Chicago: Follet Publishing Company, 1973.

Boyte, H. *The Backyard Revolution: Understanding the New Citizen Movement.* Philadelphia: Temple University Press, 1980.

Brazier, A. M. *Black Self-Determination: The Story of the Woodlawn Organization.* Grand Rapids, MI: William B. Herdman Publishing Co., 1969.

Cassidy, R. *Livable Cities: A Grass-Roots Guide to Rebuilding Urban America.* New York: Holt, Rinehart and Winston, 1980.

Checkoway, B. "The Empire Strikes Back: More Community Organizing Lessons for Health Care Consumers." *Journal of Health Politics, Policy and Law* 7:111–124, 1982.

_____. "Innovative Citizen Participation in Health Planning Agencies." In *Citizens and Health Participation and Planning for Social Change*, ed., B. Checkoway. New York: Pergamon Press, 1981.

_____. "Revitalizing an Urban Neighborhood: A St. Louis Case Study." In *The Metropolitan Midwest: Policy Problems and Prospects for Change*, eds., B. Checkoway and C. V. Patton. Urbana: University of Illinois Press, 1985.

Checkoway, B. and W. D. Cahill. "Student Workshops and Neighborhood Revitalization." *Alternative Higher Education* 6:96–110, 1981.

Checkoway, B. and M. Doyle. "Community Organizing Lessons for Health Care Consumers." *Journal of Health Politics, Policy and Law* 5:213–226, 1980.

Checkoway, B. and J. Van Til. "What Do We Know About Citizen Participation? A Selective Review of Research." In *Citizen Participation in America*, ed., S. Langton. Lexington: D.C. Heath, 1978.

Clay, P. *Neighborhood Renewal.* Lexington: Lexington Books, 1979.

Cohen, R. "Neighborhood Planning and Political Capacity." *Urban Affairs Quarterly* 14:337–362, 1979.

Committee for Economic Development. *Modernizing Local Government.* New York: Committee for Economic Development, 1966.

_____. *Reshaping Government in Metropolitan Areas.* New York: Committee for Economic Development, 1970.

Cox, F. M. *et al.*, eds. *Strategies of Community Organization: A Book of Readings.* Itasca, IL: F.E. Peacock, 1974.

Dahl, R. A. *After the Revolution?* New Haven: Yale University Press, 1970.

Downie, L. *Mortgage on America.* New York: Praeger, 1974.

Fellman, G. with B. Brandt. *The Deceived Majority: Politics and Protest in Middle America.* New Brunswick: Transaction Books, 1973.

Fish, J. H. *Black Power/White Control.* Princeton: Princeton University Press, 1973.

Forester, J. "Planning in the Face of Power." *Journal of the American Planning Association* 48:67–80, 1982.

Friedmann, J. *Retracking America: A Theory of Transactive Planning.* Garden City, NY: Anchor, 1973.

Gans, H. J. *The Urban Villagers: Group and Class in the Life of Italian-Americans.* New York: Free Press, 1962.

Goering, J. M. "The National Neighborhood Movement: A Preliminary Analysis and Critique." *Journal of the American Planning Association* 45:506–514, 1979.

Hallman, H. W. "Neighborhood Planning with Residents: Approaches of Six Local Planning Departments." *Neighborhood Decentralization,* March–April 1976:1–7.

Hartman, C. *Yerba Buena: Land Grab and Community Resistance in San Francisco.* San Francisco: Glide Publications, 1975.

Henderson, P. and D. N. Thomas. *Skills in Neighborhood Work.* Boston: George Allen and Unwin, 1980.

Hutcheson, J. D. "The Neighborhood Planning Ordinance in Atlanta: Implementation and Structural Constraints." Paper delivered at the annual meeting of the American Political Science Association, New York, 1981.

Katznelson, I. *City Trenches: Urban Politics and the Patterning of Class in America.* New York: Pantheon, 1981.

Kramer, R. M. and H. Specht, eds. *Readings in Community Organization Practice.* Englewood Cliffs, NJ: Prentice Hall, 1969.

Lamb, C. *Political Power in Poor Neighborhoods.* Cambridge, MA: Schenkman, 1975.

Lancourt, J. E. *Confront or Concede: The Alinsky Citizen Action Organizations.* Lexington: Lexington Books, 1979.

Lauffer, A. and E. Newman. "Community Organization for the 1980's." *Social Development Issues.* 5, Summer/Fall, 1981.

Lipsky, M. "Street Corner Bureaucracy and the Analysis of Urban Reform." In *Neighborhood Control in the 1970s: Politics, Administration, and Citizen Participation,* ed., G. Frederickson. San Francisco: Chandler Publishing Company, 1973.

Marciniak, E. *Reviving an Inner City Neighborhood.* Chicago: Loyola University, 1977.

Mayer, N. and J. Blake. *Keys to the Growth of Neighborhood Development Organization.* Washington, DC: Urban Institute, 1980.

Miller, N. *Reader in Mass Organization.* San Francisco: Organize, Inc., n.d.

Mollenkopf, J. H. "The Post-War Politics of Urban Development." *Politics and Society* 5:247–495, 1975.

Naparstek, A. J. and G. Cincotta. Urban Disinvestment: New Implications for Community Organization, Research and Public Policy. Washington, DC: National Center for Urban Ethnic Affairs, 1976.

National Advisory Commission on Civil Disorders. Report of the National Advisory Committee on Civil Disorders. Washington, DC: U.S. Government Printing Office, 1968.

National Commission on Neighborhoods. *People, Rebuilding Neighborhoods.* Washington: U.S. Government Printing Office, 1979.

National Training and Information Center, *The American Nightmare.* Chicago: National Training and Information Center, 1976.

Needleman, M. L. and C. E. Needleman. *Guerillas in the Bureaucracy: The Community Planning Experiment in the United States.* New York: John Wiley & Sons, 1974.

Office of Neighborhood Association. Neighborhood Accomplishments in Portland, Oregon 1976–1980. Portland: Office of Neighborhood Associations, 1930.

Pederson, N. C. "Citizen Participation in Portland, Oregon." Paper delivered at the National Conference for Neighborhood Coordinators, 1976.

_____. Neighborhood Organization in Portland, Oregon. Portland: Office of Neighborhood Associations, 1974.

Perlman, J. "Grassroots Participation from Neighborhood to Nation." In *Citizen Participation In America,* ed., S. Langton. Lexington: Lexington Books, 1978.

Piven, F. F. "Whom Does the Advocacy Planner Serve?" *Social Policy.* May/June 1970:32–37.

Piven, F. F. and R. Cloward. *Poor People's Movements: Why They Succeed, How They Fail.* New York: Vintage Books, 1977.

Portland Bureau of Planning. Corbett, Terwilliger, and Lair Hill. Portland: Portland Bureau of Planning, 1975a.

_____. Northwest District Policy Plan. Portland: Portland Bureau of Planning, 1975b.

_____. Union Avenue Redevelopment Plan. Portland: Portland Bureau of Planning, 1975c.

Rohe, W. M. and L. B. Gates. "Neighborhood Planning: Promise and Product." *The Urban and Social Change Review* 14:26–32, 1981.

Rosenbloom, R. "The Politics of the Neighborhood Movement." *South Atlantic Urban Studies* 4:102–120, 1979.

St. Paul Department of Planning and Economic Development. St. Paul Citizen's Guide and Glossary to the Unified Capital Improvement

Program and Bugeting Process. St. Paul: Department of Planning and Economic Development, 1981.

Salem Department of Community Development. *Development of a Neighborhood Plan.* Salem, Oregon: Department of Community Development, 1975.

Schoenburg, S. P. and P. L. Rosenbaum. *Neighborhoods That Work: Sources for the Viability of the Inner City.* New Brunswick: Rutgers University Press, 1980.

Steckler, A. B. and W. D. Herzog. "How to Keep Your Mandated Citizen Board Out of Your Hair and Off Your Back: A Guide for Executive Directors." *American Journal of Public Health* 69:809–812, 1979.

Stone, C. N. *Economic Growth and Neighborhood Discontent: System Bias on the Urban Renewal Program of Atlanta.* Chapel Hill: University of North Carolina Press, 1976.

Trapp, S. *Dynamics of Organizing.* Chicago:

National Training and Information Center, 1976.

U.S. Office of Consumer Affairs. *People Power: What Communities Are Doing to Counter Inflation.* Washington, DC: U.S. Government Printing Office, 1980.

U.S. Senate Subcommittee on Intergovernmental Relations. *Confidence and Concern: Citizens View American Government.* Cleveland: Regal Books, 1974.

Weber, N. "Urban Planning and Community Resistance." Unpublished M.A. Thesis, Goddard College, 1976.

Werth, J. T. and D. Bryant. *A Guide to Neighborhood Planning.* Washington, DC: American Planning Association, 1979.

Zimmerman, J. P. "Community Boards: Neighborhood Planning and Service Delivery in New York City." Paper delivered at the annual meeting of the American Political Science Association, 1979.

SOCIAL ACTION

21.

Robert Fisher

SOCIAL ACTION COMMUNITY ORGANIZATION:

PROLIFERATION, PERSISTENCE, ROOTS, AND PROSPECTS

Social action is a distinctive type of community organization practice (Burghardt, 1987). As articulated by Rothman (1968), in a seminal essay that provides the conceptual framework for this volume, it is different in a number of critical respects from other forms of community intervention, such as community locality development and community social planning. The

"classic" social action effort is grassroots-based, conflict-oriented, with a focus on direct action, and geared to organizing the disadvantaged or aggrieved to take action on their own behalf. It has a long and important history, including, for example, such practitioners and efforts as Saul Alinsky and the numerous Industrial Areas Foundation projects associated with the "Alinsky method" since the late 1930s; Communist Party community organizing in the 1930s and 1940s; civil rights efforts in the 1950s and 1960s; the work of Cesar Chavez and the United Farm Workers;

Parts of this essay appeared earlier in Robert Fisher, "Community Organizing Worldwide," in R. Fisher and J. Kling, eds., *Mobilizing the Community* (Newbury Park, CA: Sage, 1993).

Community Action Programs and the confrontational organizing of SDS, SNCC, the Black Panthers, the Brown Berets, and La Raza Unida in the 1960s; and the wave of community-based social action since the 1970s organized around identity groups based on gender, sexual orientation, ethnicity, race, or neighborhood (Fisher, 1994; Fisher and Kling, 1993). Unlike community development and social planning efforts, social action focuses on power, pursues conflict strategies, and challenges the structures that oppress and disempower constituents. It is the type of community intervention that most lives up to the social justice and social change mission of social work, and yet, because of its oppositional politics, tends to be the least practiced within social work institutions and social service agencies.

Community-based social action, however, is not a static phenomenon. Social action is always changing in response to the conditions and opportunity structures in which it operates. In the 1980s, for example, one hallmark of community-based social action, as practiced by Alinsky groups and many others, was its withdrawal from a singular emphasis on conflict theory and confrontational politics. Involved in developing housing projects, organizing community development projects, and handling job training grants, these efforts, the heirs to classic social action community organization, now look more like a blending of social action with community development and social planning (Fisher, 1994).

This essay seeks to contribute to the expanding knowledge of community-based social action by making four essential points. First, because community-based social action is an evolving and ever-changing phenomenon, we must now view it beyond our national borders, as a global phenomenon. The community development literature

has done this for more than a generation. Moreover, unlike in the past, when social action efforts were said to last no more than six years, current efforts persist much longer and often become important community institutions. Second, these social action community organizations share common characteristics, reflective of what some observers call the new social movements. Third, new social theory and histories of social action efforts have reconceptualized contemporary community-based social action as primarily a product of post-1945 social movement organizing. These movement roots help further distinguish community-based social action from other forms of community organization and help explain why Rothman's model of social action continues to have salience for the study of grassroots oppositional movement efforts. Fourth, like all eras, but perhaps even more so for the current one, our contemporary context poses both significant opportunities and immense barriers to effective community-based social action practice. It is these changing conditions and the responses of organizers and organizations to them that are significantly expanding and altering our knowledge and understanding of social action.

PROLIFERATION AND PERSISTENCE

Two things are certain about contemporary community-based social action organizing. It is both a widespread and a long-term phenomenon. Once thought of as confined to narrow geographic areas (like New York City or Chicago) or to a specific historical era (like the late 1960s and early 1970s), proliferation and persistence, not provincialism and short-term existence, are the hallmarks of contemporary efforts. Without doubt, community-based social action has a long history in both social work practice and social work education (Burghardt, 1987; Fisher, 1994). Most social action, however, occurs outside of social work. That has always been the case. Since the 1960s, when the social work profession first began to take a very strong interest in social action approaches to community organization, grassroots organizing has become the dominant form of popular resistance and social change worldwide. Instead of not "enjoy[ing] the currency it once had," (Rothman with Tropman, 1987, p. 7) these efforts have proliferated widely outside the social work profession, and within as well as outside of the United States.

Jeff Drumtra (1991) recently provided sketches of citizen action in 38 countries. His research emphasized how recent political reform in 25 countries in Asia, Africa, and Latin America now allowed for wide voter participation in free elections with multiple candidates. Durning (1989, p. 5) goes further. In a comparable comparative study he argues that people are coming together "in villages, neighborhoods, and shantytowns around the world," in response to the forces which endanger their communities and planet. Paget (1990) estimates two million grassroots social action groups in the United States alone. Lowe (1986) sees a similar upsurge of activity in the United Kingdom. The same is true for most of Western Europe. Grassroots social action organizing and urban protest have been key elements of politics in the West since the late 1960s. But community-based social action is not limited to Western industrial states. What happened in the West is only part of a widespread escalation of urban resistance throughout the world. The picture shows "an expanding lattice-work covering the globe," Durning (1989, pp. 6–7) continues. "At the local level, particularly among the close to 4 billion

humans in developing lands, it appears that the world's people are better organized in 1989 than they have been since European colonialism disrupted traditional societies centuries ago." Community organizing efforts, with hundreds of millions of members, have proliferated worldwide in the past 20 years, extending from nations in the West to those in the South, and, most recently, with extraordinary results, to those in the East (Frank and Fuentes, 1990, p. 163).

Similarly, the persistence of grassroots social action, as well as their proliferation, is another hallmark of our contemporary era. Many efforts have come and gone in the past decade. But the old rule of thumb that social action community organizing, like that pioneered by Saul Alinsky, lasts no more than six years, is no longer valid. ACORN celebrated its 20th anniversary in 1990, National People's Action (NPA) did so two years later, and COPS soon thereafter. Citizen Action, TMO in Houston, the New Jersey Tenants Union (NJTU), and many others recently passed the ten-year mark, with no signs of declining despite having to organize in very adverse conditions. Grassroots efforts tied to national issues, such as pro-choice, gay rights, and the environmental movement, not only persist but continue to grow.

THE NATURE OF CONTEMPORARY SOCIAL ACTION

But what is the nature of contemporary, community-based, social action organizing? Are these community-based social action efforts all of the same piece? Do prior models (Rothman, 1968; Fisher, 1994) capture the complexity of current efforts? If a global proliferation exists, what are the shared, essential characteristics of contemporary, community-based, social action organizing? Building on the insights from new social movement theory (Epstein, 1990; Melucci, 1989), contemporary social action organizing worldwide shares the following characteristics:

First, the efforts are community-based, that is organized around communities of interest or geography, not at the site of production (the factory) or against the principal owners of capital as was the case of most pre-1960s organizing (Offe, 1987).

Second, the organizations are transclass groupings of constituencies and cultural identities such as blacks, ethnics, women, gay men, neighborhood residents, students, ecologists, and peace activists. Labor becomes one, not *the*, constituency group. Class becomes part of, not *the*, identity (Brecher and Costello, 1990; Fisher, 1992).

Third, the ideological glue is a neopopulist vision of democracy. The groups reject authoritarianism: in the state, leadership, party, organization, and relationships (Amin, 1990). Their organizational form is most often sufficiently small, loose, and open to be able to "tap local knowledge and resources, to respond to problems rapidly and creatively, and to maintain the flexibility needed in changing circumstances" (Durning, 1989, pp. 6–7). Some see contemporary social action as "nonideological," because the organizations dismiss the old ideologies of capitalism, communism, and nationalism and because they tend to be without a clear critique of the dominant system. But others argue that ideological congruence is their essence. Their "neopopulist" principles and beliefs are what make them so important and filled with potential (Dalton and Kuechler, 1990; Offe, 1987; Boyte and Riessman, 1986; Fisher and Kling, 1988; Boyte, Booth, and Max, 1986).

Fourth, struggle over culture and social identity play a greater role in these com-

munity-based efforts, especially when compared to the workplace-based organizing of the past, which focused more on economic and political issues. "After the great working class parties surrendered their remaining sense of radical political purpose with the onset of the cold war," Bronner (1990, p. 161) writes, "new social movements emerged to reformulate the spirit of resistance in broader cultural terms." Feminism. Black Power. Sexual identity. Ethnic nationalism. Victim's rights. Of course, culture and identity—grounded in historical experience, values, social networks, and collective solidarity—have always been central to citizen social action (Gutman, 1977). And, of course, identity and constituency efforts include economic and political issues. But as class becomes increasingly fragmented in the postindustrial city and as the locus of workplace organizing declines in significance, resistances that emerge increasingly do so at the community level around cultural issues and identity bases (Touraine, 1985; Fisher and Kling, 1991).

Fifth, strategies include elements of locality development self-help and empowerment. An aim is building community capacity, especially in an era hostile to social change efforts and unwilling to support them. Some of the more effective efforts go beyond community capacity building to target and make claims against the public sector. They see the future of community-based social action as interdependent with political and economic changes outside their communities. They understand that the state is the entity potentially most responsible and vulnerable to social action claims and constituencies (Piven and Cloward, 1982; Fisher, 1992). But most contemporary community-based organizing seeks independence from the state rather than state power. As Midgley (1986, p. 4) points out, central to the rationale of community participation "is a reaction against the centralization, bureaucratization, rigidity, and remoteness of the state. The ideology of community participation is sustained by the belief that the power of the state has extended too far, diminishing the freedoms of ordinary people and their rights to control their own affairs." Community capacity building becomes a natural focus, reflecting anti-statist strategies and decentralization trends of the postindustrial political economy.[1]

HISTORICAL ANTECEDENTS: THE ROOTS OF IDEOLOGIES AND STRATEGIES

One of the key causes for this common form of social action organization is the common heritage of citizen resistance since the end of World War II. It is this common heritage that continues to struc-

ture and inform contemporary efforts. For our purposes I emphasize five major historical roots: the (1) community-based resistance of Saul Alinsky, (2) liberation struggles of people of color, (3) urban decentralization and citizen participation programs, (4) new left movement, and (5) new social movements. Of course, this is not to suggest that the heritage of community resistance does not include efforts prior to 1945 (Fisher, 1984; Fisher, 1992). Nor is it to suggest that all contemporary community mobilization efforts build on each of these antecedents or that these are the only sources. Admittedly, roots are more numerous and entangled than here suggested, but the following five are essential to contemporary community-based social action.

(1) Community-Based Resistance of Saul Alinsky

While the organizing projects of Saul Alinsky during his lifetime never amounted

---

[1]This argument of a common new social movement form plays out a bit differently in other parts of the world. One key difference is that the old social movements in the Third World (South) and Second World (East) were nationalistic and communistic, respectively, not social democratic as in the West (Wallerstein, 1990). Given their subordinate position in the world economy, the old social movements—in the South, for example—did not have the power to deliver material security or political liberty. They often became arms of Western imperial control. In response, community movements "mushroomed" all over the South. Like counterparts in the West, they are community-based, constituency or identity oriented, neopopulist in ideology, and focused on self-help strategies. But in the South, community movements put greater emphasis on material needs (Frank and Fuentes, 1990). Where old social movements achieved distributional victories only for a few, as in the southern hemisphere, or where such victories did not include significant minority segments, as in the United States, new social movements struggle to achieve a minimal standard of living and get basic services like housing and healthcare. Where material victories have been won, primarily among the more affluent in the United States and Western Europe, the social base tends to be

the educated middle class (Merkl, 1987). But where basic material needs still remain to be won in the South and among the oppressed and disenfranchised in the West, new social movement forms include the poor and powerless and interweave struggle over postmaterial and material objectives.

Of course, basic survival concerns are important even in those groups in the West professing to hold to "postmaterialist" values. Survival is tied to ridding the world of nuclear weapons, toxic wastes, domestic violence, or AIDS, all of which cut across class lines. Relatedly, the politics of identity, concern for personal and political freedom, and the desire to belong to a supportive and habitable community are of concern to new social movement efforts worldwide. Democratic self-help—community empowerment—is their essence. Predictably, new social movements develop easily among the affluent and around postmaterialist issues. But they succeed better as agents of transformative social change when they combine both distributional and postmaterialist objectives. The distributional demands ground identity in a class politics that understands, at least implicitly, the need in a postindustrial global economy to target the public sector and struggle for state power as well as develop democratic alternatives at the grassroots.

to much in terms of material victories and while his projects only took off when the southern civil rights movement shifted to northern cities in the 1960s, the community-based, constituency-oriented, urban populist, confrontational politics developed by Alinsky in the United States provides one of the earliest models of the community-based social action form (Fisher and Kling, 1988). Beginning just before World War II, Alinsky's work in Chicago built on the older, union-based models of social action, such as the Congress of Industrial Organizations and Communist Party United States of America (Horwitt, 1989; Fisher, 1984). From these it drew its labor organizing style, conflict strategies, direct-action politics, and idea of grounding organizing in the everyday lives and traditions of working people. But Alinsky's model added something new: a kind of labor organizing in the social factory (Boyte, 1981). The community organizer was the catalyst for change. The task was to build democratic, community-based organizations. The goal was to empower neighborhood residents by teaching them basic political and organizing skills and getting them or their representatives to the urban bargaining table (Fisher, 1994; Boyte, 1981). Both the site of production (supporting labor demands) and the public sector (making City Hall more accountable) served as the primary targets of Alinsky organizing.

This was an insurgent consciousness of "urban populism," based in neighborhood "people's organizations," oriented to building community power, discovering indigenous leaders, providing training in democratic participation, and proving that ordinary people could challenge and beat City Hall (Boyte, 1986; Booth and Max, 1986; Swanstrom, 1985; Horwitt, 1989). At their weakest, Alinsky efforts sought to replace the political program and ideology of

the old social action efforts with the skills of democratic grassroots participation, the abilities of professionally trained organizers, a faith in the democratic tendencies of working people to guide organizations toward progressive ends, and a reformist vision of grassroots pluralistic politics. At their best, however, Alinsky efforts continue to empower lower- and working-class, black and latino community residents and to demand expanded public sector accountability and public participation in an increasingly privatized political context (Fisher, 1994; Horwitt, 1989; Rogers, 1990; Delgado, 1986; Kahn, 1970). Alinsky may not be the "father of community organizing," but, especially in the United States, his work and the work of his successors has been seminal to social action community organizing (Boyte, 1981).

(2) Liberation Struggles of People of Color

Much more significant in terms of impact are the liberation struggles of people of color throughout the world since the 1950s. The civil rights movement in the United States and the national liberation struggles in the southern hemisphere served as important models for a community-based, ethnic/nationalist politics oriented to self-determination and sharing the political liberties and material affluence of the societies that exploited people of color. As a model for grassroots direct action and insurgent consciousness, the southern civil rights movement spawned most of what was to follow in the United States and established important precedents for others throughout the world (Branch, 1988; Morris, 1984; Reagon, 1979). The liberation struggles in Africa, Asia, Latin America, and the Middle East, as well as specifically early efforts in Ghana, Vietnam, Iran, Guatemala, and Cuba, not only provided models for people worldwide, including activists in the civil rights movement in the United States, but symbolized the mobilization of a worldwide liberation struggle of people of color. The demand for national self-determination for all people (not just those of European descent), the opposition to policies of racism and imperialism, and the plea of the civil rights movement for "beloved community" helped pierce the consensus politics of the 1950s and early 1960s. More recent liberation struggles in Nicaragua, El Salvador, and South Africa, to name but a few, continued to challenge conservative, racist, and imperialist paradigms in the 1980s and 1990s.

The continuous liberation struggles of people of color emphasize three lessons critical to the insurgent consciousness of contemporary community activism. First, citizen insurgency is not a political aberration. It is a legitimate and important, informal part of the political process to which all those without access to power can turn. Second, if oppressed people—often illiterate, rural peasants with few resources—could mobilize, take risks, and make history, then people of other oppressed or threatened constituencies can, with sufficient organization and leadership, do the same. Third, strategy must include both community self-help and constituency empowerment, on the one hand, and the struggle for state power, or at least the targeting of the public sector as the site of grievances and as a potential source of support, on the other. This dual quality of building community capacity and targeting the state, though not always in equal balance and often in tension, as exemplified in struggles between the Southern Christian Leadership Conference (SCLC) and the Student Nonviolent Coordinating Committee (SNCC), was as true for the civil rights movement in the United States as it was for the liberation struggles in the Third World (Carson, 1982).

(3) Urban Decentralization and Citizen Participation

The struggles of people in the southern hemisphere dramatized the exploitative nature of the imperial postwar political economy at the very moment in the 1960s that some progressive capitalists, political leaders, and planners in both the public and voluntary sectors found themselves unable to address mounting urban problems at home. From 1960 onward, as liberal leaders such as presidents Kennedy and Johnson in the United States advocated for modest social reforms and a more democratized public sector, pressure mounted for urban decentralization and citizen participation. The Community Action Program of the 1960s in the United States and the Urban Programme of the late 1960s in Britain were among the most noted of public projects seeking "maximum feasible participation" at the grassroots level. But such programs proliferated widely, making state-sponsored municipal decentralization and community participation an international phenomenon (Kjellberg, 1979; Blair, 1983; Midgley, 1986; Chekki, 1979).

Of course, such postwar programs differ dramatically from Alinsky and liberation movement efforts in their origins and problem analysis. They are initiated largely by reformers in the public and voluntary sectors—professionals such as urban planners and social workers, who either seek modest structural change or find themselves too constrained on the job to do much more in their agencies than deliver needed services at the grassroots level. As such, these initiatives represent a more institutionalized, more formalized wing of the community-based social action phenomenon. They tend, as well, to implement decentralized structure and democratic participation into public agencies without a sense for the contradictions inherent in doing so, but with a knowledge of the importance of linking the state and grassroots activism. The state becomes not the target of democratic insurgency but the employer and supporter of citizen initiatives (Merkl, 1985). At their worst, these measures defuse and coopt insurgency. At their best, contemporary organizing draws from this legacy a commitment to serving the people, to advocacy, and to citizen participation: (a) Deliver services at a grassroots level where people will have better access. (b) Include more people, even lay people, in the decision-making process at a more decentralized level. (c) Make sure they have real power to make decisions and control resources. (d) Struggle from within the state bureaucracies and agencies to achieve economic and participatory democracy for the greatest number of urban dwellers.

(4) The New Left Movement

Despite the efforts noted so far, urban problems and tensions continued to escalate in the 1960s. In response, direct action movements mounted, especially in the United States. Early SDS (Students for a Democratic Society) and SNCC (Student Nonviolent Coordinating Committee) community organizing projects focused on "participatory democracy" and "letting the people decide," seeking not only to pressure local and national policy but to create "prefigurative," that is alternative, social groups (Breines, 1982; Evans, 1979). They also developed a critique of American policy abroad and the liberal consensus at home. They built a movement in opposition to the politics of both corporate capital and the old social movement. After 1965, organizing adopted more nationalist and Marxist perspectives; Black Power efforts, for example, were less concerned with

participatory democracy and more interested in challenging imperialism abroad and at home, winning "community control," and building black identity (Jennings, 1990).

Such efforts in the United States were part of an insurgent trend in the West. Massive peace protests in the United Kingdom registered strong disapproval of Cold War policies, directly challenging social democratic regimes. These early efforts, among others, initiated a widespread "New Left" movement throughout the West, one which was soon to expand beyond university sites and student constituencies to develop, according to Ceccarelli (1982, p. 263), into "an unprecedented outburst of urban movements": Paris and West German cities in the Spring of 1968; Prague, Chicago, and Monterrey, Mexico, during that summer; in Italy the "Hot Autumn" of 1969 and the urban conflicts of the early 1970s; squatters in Portuguese cities after the April Revolution; and urban social movements in Madrid and other Spanish cities after Franco. All testify to a massive grassroots mobilization which developed rapidly, and perhaps even unprecedentedly, throughout Europe, the United States, and parts of the Third World (Ceccarelli, 1982; Teodori, 1969).

Concern for and experimentation with participatory democracy, nonhierarchical decision making, prefigurative cultural politics, linking the personal with the political, direct-action tactics, and constituency based organizing (students, the poor, etc.) characterized new left insurgent consciousness (Jacobs and Landau, 1966; Breines, 1982). Unlike the new social movement resistances to follow, the new left emphasized the formation of coalitions or political parties tied to national revolutionary/emancipatory struggles. There was a sense in the late 1960s, in cities as disparate as Paris, Berlin, Berkeley, and

Monterrey, that "successful and autonomous urban movements are not a real alternative outside the context of a revolutionary national movement" (Walton, 1979, p. 12). The struggle over state power, over who should make public policy, fueled local organizing efforts. Grassroots efforts were for most activists a democratic means to larger objectives which transcended the local community. This strategy persists, in a more reformist form, in certain notable national efforts since then, such as the Green parties in Europe, the Workers Party in Brazil, and the Rainbow Coalition idea in the United States (Spretnak and Capra, 1985; Alvarez, 1993; Collins, 1986).

Community-based social action efforts which followed tended to borrow more heavily from the "newer" side of the New Left. These activists saw community organizing, alternative groupings, and grassroots efforts as at least the primary focus if not the sole end. They emphasized democratic organizational structure, the politics of identity and culture, existential values of personal freedom and authenticity, and the development of "free spaces" where people could learn the theory and practice of political insurgency while engaging in it. So did much of the New Left, but the other, more Marxist segments, closer in style and politics to the old labor-based social action, adhered strongly to older concerns with public policy and winning state power (Evans, 1979; Evans and Boyte, 1986; Carson, 1982).

(5) New Social Movements

Despite a marked backlash worldwide against the radical activism of the late 1960s, the 1970s and 1980s witnessed not the end of community-based activism but the proliferation of grassroots activism and insurgency into highly diversified, single-issue or identity-oriented, community-based efforts. These efforts, the subject of this essay, include women's shelters and feminist organizations, efforts in defense of the rights and the communities of oppressed people of color, struggles around housing, ecology, and peace issues, gay and lesbian rights and identity groups, and thousands of neighborhood and issue-based citizen initiatives, complete with organizer training centers. While these organizing efforts vary from one national and local context to another, they share a common form and movement heritage. Based in geographic communities or communities of interest, decentralized according to constituencies and identity groups, democratic in process and goals, and funded most often by voluntary sources, they serve as the archetype for contemporary social action.

The roots of their insurgent consciousness, while not always direct, can be found in the ideals discussed thus far: (1) that ordinary and previously oppressed people should have a voice and can make history, (2) that citizen and community participation, which gives "voice" to people previously silent in public discourse, is needed to improve decision making, address a wide range of problems, and democratize society, (3) that "by any means necessary" covers the gamut of strategies and tactics from revolutionary to interest-group politics, (4) that culture, whether found in a traditional ethnic neighborhood, battered women's shelter, counterculture collective, or gay men's organization, must be blended with the quest for "empowerment" into an identity- or a constituency-oriented politics, and (5) that "the personal is political," articulated first by radical feminists in the late 1960s, guides people to organize around aspects of daily life most central to them, while keeping in mind that struggles over personal issues and relationships—

personal choice, autonomy, commitment, and fulfillment—are inextricably tied to collective ones of the constituency group and the larger society.

Most commentators tend to see the focus on democracy as the essence of new social-movement insurgent consciousness and the source of its potential. As Frank and Fuentes (1990, p. 142) put it, the new social movements "are the most important agents of social transformation in that their praxis promotes participatory democracy in civil society. Pitkin and Shumer (1982, p. 43) go further, declaring that "of all the dangerous thoughts and explosive ideas abroad in the world today, by far the most subversive is that of democracy. . . . [It] is the cutting edge of radical criticism, the best inspiration for change toward a more humane world, the revolutionary idea of our time." And these democratic projects have had profound impact: empowering participants, teaching democratic skills, transforming notions of political life, expanding political boundaries, returning politics to civic self-activity, strengthening a sense of public activism, raising new social and political issues, struggling against new forms of subordination and oppression, and even advancing agendas of the middle class to which formal, institutional politics remain closed (Roth, 1991; Slater, 1985).

But while the emphasis on democracy unites these efforts, it also helps detach them in the western industrialized nations from the material needs of the poor, and it contributes to their fragmentation into a plethora of diverse, decentralized community organizations. The pursuit of democracy, without sufficient concern for equality, has resulted in the failure of the new social movements to address the material needs of the most disadvantaged. Moreover, the new social movement origins in culturally oriented, identity-based efforts tend to fragment social change efforts in general (Fisher and Kling, 1993). For example, the diversity and flexibility that theorists of postmodernity attribute to contemporary society are nowhere more evident than in the variety of these new social movement efforts. A commitment to diversity embodies their emphasis on democratic politics. It encourages each constituency or identity group to name its own struggles, develop its own voice, and engage in its own empowerment. This may be the future of politics, a "postmodernization of public life," with its "proliferation of multiple publics [and] breaking down of rigid barriers between political and private life" (Kaufmann, 1990, p. 10). But the central challenges to these efforts require more immediate and realistic strategies. How do they encourage diversity *and* counteract fragmentation? How do they influence or get power at levels—the city, state, and nation—beyond their own limited universes *and* at the same time build community capacity? How do we organize grassroots social action efforts *and* at the same time build a larger social change movement or political party, the size of which can only accomplish the needed, large structural changes?

PRACTICE IMPLICATIONS

Without question, the fragmentation of contemporary social action weakens the possibility for coherently imagined challenges to current problems. To address this problem of contemporary organizing, the historical dialectic of domination and resistance must be understood and fashioned in terms of the *interplay* between class, community, and the search for new cultural orientations. In this regard Kling and I have offered elsewhere the following sets of strategies (Fisher and Kling, 1991).

First, mobilization in the fragmented metropolis demands that broad coalitions be sought between various constituency groups, and that community politics be more cohesively integrated with electoral activity. Single community-based efforts are not large enough to challenge the enormous power of corporate capital or centralized government. Because community problems almost always originate beyond local borders, the ability to effect change depends to a great extent upon coalition-building. The success of coalition-building, however, ultimately will be based upon whether specific ways can be found to break down the racial and cultural barriers that are so entrenched in the United States and growing again in Western Europe.

Pressure group politics, even through powerful coalitions, is not enough; movements must also struggle to win and hold power, not simply to influence it. The electoral arena must become a prime target for social movement mobilizing while, at some later point, political parties serve the critical role of formalizing and structuring relationships between loosely formed coalitions and constituency-based groups (Boyte et al., 1986; Delgado, 1986; Spretnak and Capra, 1985). We offer such advice knowing how coalition and electoral efforts draw already scarce resources away from the fundamental task of grassroots organizing. But the local and the global are equally necessary, and numerous models of such dually focused practice have emerged over time. The experience of leading organizing efforts in the United States, such as IAF, ACORN and Citizen Action, and in Western Europe, such as the Green parties, illustrates how, while still focusing on the grassroots, they recognized the importance of coalition-building and electoral activity.

Second, as others argue (Evans et al., 1985) we need to bring the state back in, and use legislative policy to challenge the ideology of privatization and free enterprise that meets so well the needs of international capital. The state, of course, is not inherently an ally of low- and moderate-income people. But in the late 20th century, where private sector targets disappear in the electronic global economy, and where, in a new social movement context, the community replaces the workplace as the locus of organizing, a legitimized and expanded public sector becomes a critical ingredient for continued citizen action. Without it public life cannot even begin to be restored; without it grassroots mobilization devolves into self-help strategies which further fragmentation and perpetuate the use of private, voluntary solutions to massive, public problems (Fisher, 1993).

For example, take the worldwide push for privatization (Barnekov et al., 1989). By undermining government legitimacy and responsibility, it results not only in a declining public life and fewer public services, but also in loss of access to a potentially accountable and responsible public sector, *the* major victory of pre-1945 social movements and a crucial target of some of the earlier antecedents to current social action efforts (Fisher, 1988; Fisher, 1992; Piven and Cloward, 1982). Increasingly, in our current context, as the public sector declines as a source of grievances or solutions, citizen action is undercut. Contemporary resistance focuses its attention on community-based self-help and empowerment partly because the state—one of the primary arenas and targets for antecedents such as Alinsky, the civil rights movement, national liberation efforts, and the new left—has been delegitimized. But contemporary social action community organization requires a public-sector arena and target because, unlike union organizing, which had some power at the site of production, in our current era of high-velocity global capital and declining labor activism, where it is much more difficult for workers and citizens to affect the private sector, community-based social action efforts have the state as the entity most responsible and vulnerable to their constituencies (Fisher, 1992; Piven and Cloward, 1982).

Third, we must move to a more consciously ideological politics. We must seek new, centering narratives, or, at least, more common programs that can draw the decentered narratives of our time toward a focal point. New formations and groupings will make mobilization on local levels more potent, perhaps, but they will not resolve the fundamental divisions that plague the effort to challenge broad, culturally entrenched structures of domination, prejudice, and exploitation.

Organizers must continue to teach the techniques of organization—the knowledge of how to bring people together to identify common grievances; to get them to communicate with each other across differing and even conflicting agendas; to enable them to run effective meetings; and to empower them to recognize what sorts of strategies are most suitable for particular contexts, and identify those points in the political regime most vulnerable to the pressures of collective action. But among the organizer's most valuable skills remains the ability to challenge the accepted vision of things and to develop ideological congruence with other oppositional efforts. Good organizational leadership—and good community practice—lies with understanding what is involved in moving people beyond their received notions of how they are related to other cultural and identity-based groups. An authentic commitment to

"human solidarity, mutual responsibility, and social justice" demands that people engage in a profound reexamination of the values on which their society and way of life are based. Such transformations of consciousness do not emerge without intervention and engagement.

An organizing ideology for our times needs to combine the new postmodern demands for autonomy and identity with older, modernist ones for social justice, production for human needs, rather than profit, and the spirit of connectedness and solidarity among people, rather than competition. Day-to-day organizing, if it is to move beyond fragmented values and cultures, still needs to be informed by this sort of centering, oppositional ideology. To continue to open activists and constituencies to broader conceptions of social action and social change remains the primary responsibility of the organizer in the 1990s.

REFERENCES

Alvarez, S. "Deepening Democracy: Social Movement Networks, Constitutional Reform, and Radical Urban Regimes in Contemporary Brazil," in Fisher and Kling, eds., *Mobilizing the Community*, op. cit., 1993.

Amin, So, et al., *Transforming the Revolution.* (New York: Monthly Review Press, 1990).

Barnekov, T., R. Boyle, and D. Rich. *Privatism and Urban Policy in Britain and the United States.* Oxford: Oxford University Press, 1989.

Blair, H. W. "Comparing Development Programs," In Journal of Community Action I, 1983.

Bonner, A. *Averting the Apocalypse: Social Movements in India Today.* Durham: Duke University Press, 1990.

Boyte, H. *The Backyard Revolution.* Philadelphia: Temple University Press, 1981.

Boyte, H., and F. Riessman. *The New Populism.* Philadelphia: Temple University Press, 1986.

Boyte, H., H. Booth, and S. Max. *Citizen Action and the New American Populism.* Philadelphia: Temple University Press, 1986.

Branch, T. *Parting the Waters: America in the King Years, 1954–1963.* New York: Simon and Schuster, 1988.

Brecher, J., and T. Costello. *Building Bridges: The Emerging Grassroots Coalition of Labor and Community.* New York: Monthly Review Press, 1990.

Breines, W. *Community and Organization in the New Left, 1962–1968: The Great Refusal.* New York: Praeger, 1982.

Bronner, S. E. *Socialism Unbound.* New York: Routledge, 1990.

Burghardt, S. "Community-based Social Action." In *Encyclopedia of Social Work,* 18th ed. New York: NASW, 1987.

Carson, C., Jr. *In Struggle: SNCC and the Black Awakening of the 1960s.* Cambridge: Harvard University Press, 1982.

Ceccarelli, P. "Politics, Parties, and Urban Movements: Western Europe." In N. Fainstein and S. Fainstein, eds., *Urban Policy Under Capitalism.* Beverly Hills: Sage, 1982.

Chekki, D. *Community Development: Theory and Method of Planned Change.* New Delhi: Vikas Publishing House, 1979.

Collins, S. *The Rainbow Challenge.* New York: Monthly Review Press, 1986.

Corbridge, S. "Third World Development." *Progress in Human Geography* 15 (1991): 311–321.

Dalton, R., and M. Kuechler, eds. *Challenging the Political Order: New Social and Political Movements in Western Democracies.* New York: Oxford University Press, 1990.

Delgado, G. *Organizing the Movement: The Roots and Growth of ACORN.* Philadelphia: Temple University Press, 1986.

Drumtra, J. "Power to the People," *World View.* (Winter 1991–92) 4: 8–13.

Durning, A. B. "Action at the Grassroots: Fighting Poverty and Environmental Decline." *Worldwatch Paper* 88. (January 1989): 1–70.

Epstein, B. "Rethinking Social Movement Theory." *Socialist Review* 90. (January–March, 1990).

Evans, P., et al., eds. *Bringing the State Back In.* New York: Cambridge University Press, 1985.

Evans, S. *Personal Politics: The Roots of Women's Liberation in the Civil Rights Movements and the New Left.* New York: Vintage Books, 1979.

Evans, S., and H. Boyte. *Free Spaces: The Sources of Democratic Change in America.* New York: Harper and Row, 1986.

Fisher, R. "Where Seldom Is Heard a Discouraging Word: The Political Economy of Houston, Texas." *Amerika-studien* 33 (Winter, 1988): 73–91.

Fisher, R. "Organizing in the Modern Metropolis." *Journal of Urban History* 18 (1992): 222–237.

Fisher, R. "Grassroots Organizing Worldwide." In Robert Fisher and Joseph Kling, eds. *Mobilizing the Community: Local Politics in a Global Era.* Newbury Park, CA: Sage, 1993.

Fisher, R. *Let the People Decide: Neighborhood Organizing in America,* rev. ed. Boston: Twayne, 1994.

Fisher, R., and J. Kling. "Leading the People: Two Approaches to the Role of Ideology in Community Organizing." *Radical America* 21 (1) (1988): 31–46.

Fisher, R., and J. Kling. "Popular Mobilization in the 1990s: Prospects for the New Social Movements." *New Politics* 3 (1991): 71–84.

Fisher, R., and J. Kling, eds. *Mobilizing the Community: Local Politics in a Global Era.* Newbury Park, CA: Sage, 1993.

Flacks, D. "The Revolution of Citizenship." *Social Policy* 21 (1990): 37–50.

Frank, A. G., and M. Fuentes. "Civil Democracy: Social Movements in Recent World History." In Amin et al., eds., *Transforming the Revolution: Social Movements and the World-System.* New York: Monthly Review Press, 1990.

Gottdiener, M. *The Decline of Urban Politics.* Newbury Park, CA: Sage, 1987.

Gutman, H. G. *Work, Culture, and Society in Industrializing America.* New York: Vintage, 1977.

Horwitt, S. *Let Them Call Me Rebel: Saul Alinsky, His Life and Legacy.* New York: Alfred Knopf, 1989.

Jacobs, P., and S. Landau. *The New Radicals: A Report with Documents.* New York: Vintage Books, 1966.

Jennings, J. "The Politics of Black Empowerment in Urban America: Reflections on Race, Class, and Community." In Kling and Posner, *op. cit.,* 1990.

Kahn, S. *How People Get Power: Organizing Oppressed Communities for Action.* New York: McGraw-Hill, 1970.

Katznelson, I. *City Trenches: Urban Politics and the Patterning of Class in the United States.* Chicago: University of Chicago Press, 1981.

Kaufmann, L. A. "Democracy in a Postmodern World." In *Social Policy*. (Fall 1990): 6–11.

Kjellberg, F. "A Comparative View of Municipal Decentralization: Neighborhood Democracy in Oslo and Bologna." In Sharpe, *op. cit.,* 1979.

Kling, J., and P. Posner, eds. *The Dilemmas of Activism: Class, Community, and the Politics of Local Mobilization*. Philadelphia: Temple University Press, 1990.

Laclau, E., and C. Mouffe. *Hegemony and Socialist Strategy: Towards a Radical Democratic Politics*. London: Verso, 1985.

Lehmann, D. *Democracy and Development in Latin America: Economics, Politics, and Religion in the Postwar Period*. Cambridge: Polity Press, 1990.

Lipsitz, G. *A Life in the Struggle: Ivory Perry and the Culture of Opposition*. Philadelphia: Temple University Press, 1988.

Logan, J., and T. Swanstrom, eds. *Beyond the City Limits*. Philadelphia: Temple University Press, 1990.

Lowe, S. *Urban Social Movements: The City After Castells*. London: Macmillan, 1986.

Mansbridge, J. *Beyond Adversary Democracy*. New York: Basic Books, 1980.

Merkl, P. *New Local Centers in Centralized States*. Berkeley: University Press of America, 1985.

Merkl, P. "How New the Brave New World: New Social Movements in West Germany," *German Studies Review* X. (February 1987): 125–47.

Melucci, A. *Nomads of the Present: Social Movements and Individual Needs in Contemporary Society*. Philadelphia: Temple University Press, 1989.

Midgley, J. *Community Participation, Social Development, and the State*. London: Methuen, 1986.

Molotch, H. "Urban Deals in Comparative Perspective." In Logan and Swanstrom, *op. cit.,* 1990.

Morris, A. *The Origins of the Civil Rights Movement: Black Communities Organizing for Change*. New York: Free Press, 1984.

Offe, C. "Challenging the Boundaries of Institutional Politics: Social Movements Since the 1960s." in C. Maier, ed. *Changing Boundaries of the Political: Essays on the Evolving Balance Between the State and Society, Public and Private in Europe*. Cambridge: Cambridge University Press, 1987.

Paget, K. "Citizen Organizing: Many Movements, No Majority." *American Prospect*. (Summer 1990).

Piven, F., and R. Cloward. *The New Class War: Reagan's Attack on the Welfare State and Its Consequences*. New York: Pantheon, 1982.

Pitkin, H., and S. Shumer. "On Participation." *Democracy* 2. (Fall 1982): 43–54.

Reagon, B. "The Borning Struggle: The Civil Rights Movement." In Dick Cutler, ed. *They Should Have Served That Cup of Coffee*. Boston: South End Press, 1979.

Rogers, M. B. *Cold Anger: A Story of Faith and Power Politics*. Denton, TX: University of North Texas Press, 1990.

Roth, R. "Local Green Politics in West German Cities." In *International Journal of Urban and Regional Research* 15 (1991): 75–89.

Rothman, J. "Three Models of Community Organization Practice." From *National Conference on Social Welfare, Social Work Practice 1968*. New York: Columbia University Press, 1968.

Rothman, J., with J. Tropman "Models of Community Organization and Macro Practice Perspectives: Their Mixing and Phasing." In F. Cox et al., *Strategies of Community Organization,* 4th ed. Itasca, IL: F.E. Peacock Publishers, 1987.

Rude, G. *Ideology and Popular Protest*. New York: Pantheon, 1980.

Sharpe, L. "Decentralist Trends in Western Democracies: A First Appraisal." In L. J. Sharpe, ed., *Decentralist Trends in Western Democracies*. London: Sage Publications, 1979.

Slater, D., ed. *Social Movements and the State in Latin America*. Holland: Foris Publications, 1985.

Spretnak, C., and F. Capra. *Green Politics*. London: Grafton, 1985.

Swanstrom, T. *The Crisis of Growth Politics: Cleveland, Kucinich, and the Challenge of Urban Populism*. Philadelphia: Temple University Press, 1985.

Teodori, M. *The New Left: A Documentary History*. New York: Bobbs-Merrill, 1969.

Touraine, A. "An Introduction to the Study of Social Movements." *Social Research* 52. (Winter 1985): 749–787.

Wallerstein, I. "Antisystemic Movements: History and Dilemmas." In S. Amin et al., *op. cit,* 1990.

Walton, J. "Urban Political Movements and Revolutionary Change in the Third World." *Urban Affairs Quarterly* 15 (September 1979): 3–22.

22.

Warren C. Haggstrom

THE TACTICS OF ORGANIZATION BUILDING

The organizer lives in a world in which everything is called into question, subject to change, where half-perceived and complex structures constantly dissolve and reform before him, a world of possibility in which he [or she] takes a hand to reshape the future. . . .

The organizer cannot afford to believe that he knows his world well because he is engaged in a course of action under barely tractable, constantly changing, and mostly invisible circumstances which contrast sharply with the neat flatland of the sociological theorist.

To build organization in low-income areas is something like playing a long game of blindfold chess in which no player is sure of the rules. The chess pieces move by themselves; skillful players help get this movement channeled into planned patterns, strategies, and tactics. There are standard beginning lines (e.g., house meetings vs. dramatic large public meetings) and some established principles of play ("rub raw the sores of discontent," "the social situation sets the limits for moves"), but much depends on attention to detail, immense energy, and individual brilliance in capitalizing on whatever happens. Finally, these chess pieces can throw an ineffective player right out of the game.

It follows that the question, "How does one build an organization of the poor?" cannot be answered in the same way as the question, "How does one build a house?" or "How does one build a great football team?" One can only relate a history of past organizations of the poor, a description of those currently functioning, and

principles to which some able organizers more or less adhere. The following remarks are directed to the [last-named] task.

THE STARTING POINT

The physical structure and location of a low-income area carry collectively held meanings to the people of the area, meanings which affect the relevance of the physical context to their lives. For example, a hospital may carry the meaning of being a slaughterhouse or of a place in which patients are "treated like dirt." A row of slum houses may mean at once inferiority and deprivation and reassuring familiarity to slum dwellers. Of seven unmarried mothers living in public housing, six may be respectable women and the seventh a scandal—all in accordance with criteria which are not known outside the neighborhood in question. . . .

The social situation in low-income areas, consisting of such collectively held sets of meanings, can vary tremendously around any physical situation. It is a key responsibility of the organizer to come to know the social situation and, further, he must consider as well his own meaning as a stranger in the neighborhood. He starts work where he and the people of the neighborhood are in a social situation which slowly becomes intelligible to him. If people want their windows fixed and the welfare check increased, the organizer helps them to begin to act on these problems even though he may privately believe they would be better

341

off working to open up additional jobs. He is limited by the fact that people consciously and unconsciously misrepresent where they are, and, sometimes, they do not understand how to be relevant to the organizer since he has not clearly defined himself and his purpose in the neighborhood. One can come closest to starting where the people are when one begins in an atmosphere of mutual trust which develops when the organizer places himself clearly on the side of the people with whom he is working and states as plainly as possible his purpose in the neighborhood, but does not presume to define for them their problems or the solutions to their problems.

The people, with the help of the organizer, start to work on problems. Very shortly, their action is contested and the problems are transformed into issues with established institutions opposing the action of people in low-income areas. For example, when a number of people in one city began to seek additional money for school supplies for their children, the Commissioner of Welfare at first acceded to the request. When the number of people making such a request becomes large enough, the commissioner began to deny many of the new requests. At that point, the requests became demands and the resulting struggle drew an increasing number of people into sustained activity of value in building organization. Through a process of struggle around issues perceived in the neighborhood as central the organization develops power which can be used to resolve problems of many varieties.

When an organizer helps people to begin to act on central problems, that is, to make their own decisions about resolving their own problems and to begin to implement those decisions, by that very fact the organizer deliberately creates conflict since the problems of low-income areas cannot be resolved without negative consequences for the self-perceived self-interest and traditional ways of thinking and acting of various advantaged minorities. Until the problems are resolved, so long as the organizer maintains neighborhood action he will by that fact maintain conflict, and requires no artificial strategies leading to artificial confrontations.

THE WAY TO BEGIN

People are usually immersed in private lives centered about work and home. The organizer pulls and jolts them into the public arena.

In the beginning, the organizer is simply another stranger trying to convince people to do something. The organizer is like a salesperson—and is met by the evasive tactics which people use to ward them off. A salesman has only to persuade people to one act, to make one purchase. An organizer has the more complicated job of pulling people into new lives, into long-extended alternative lines of action. . . .

Because people do not yet know him, the organizer has to be credible, creating a convincing picture of what might be, relying on the emotional contagion produced by fire and enthusiasm as well as on the factual account that he gives. Since all this should be appropriate to the people with whom he is talking, he modifies his presentation at first as he talks with different persons and groups until working out an approach which is most effective for him (although not necessarily for other organizers) in the neighborhood in which he is working (although not necessarily in the other neighborhoods).

The organizer starts by persuading people to come to a meeting or begin action. He listens, describing the meeting or action as it is relevant to the situation of those with whom he is talking. He appeals to self-interest, builds anger, works along friendship and relationship networks and other formal and informal social structures. He recruits members without appearing too eager to recruit members; they must see themselves as acting on their own initiative. When people have decided to attend a meeting, join a delegation, etc., then an organizer does his best to make certain that their intention is carried out. People may be reminded again and again of the event, some are provided with transportation, etc.

Once at a meeting an organizer concentrates on moving those attending into decision and action through whatever formal structure may exist. He may make certain that decisions are made to do something concrete about sore points of acute concern: the speeding car that killed Bobby Smith, the lack of police protection for Mrs. Jackson, the slum landlord who runs down the neighborhood, etc. He may ask action-oriented questions, or he may suggest alternatives by describing what other organizations have done in similar situations or on similar problems.

From the point of view of the organizer, the sole point of meetings is to prepare for action just as the sole point of organization is to provide a structure through which action takes place. Thus, he or she helps to clarify alternatives around concrete and immediate courses of action, makes certain that whatever process results in decisions is both legitimate (in accordance with the rules) and efficient (a course of action is undertaken which is likely to attain the objective intended or otherwise to build the effectiveness of the organization).

At first, people defend themselves against accurately seeing their position in the community and against admitting their discontent to themselves and others. An early objective of action is to provide people with experiences which destroy these defenses. A second early objective is to provide people with experience in responsible planning in defining social paths along which they can make actual gains. . . .

The legitimation for action is provided in meetings, but specific action events may develop from the general responsibility of a committee or other group of work in some area, and not directly from meetings. . . .

For example, in one city, people representing a small neighborhood, with the help of the organizers of a large organization, went to a district sanitation inspector to appeal for better street cleaning. During the course of the discussion the supervisor mentioned that there was no point in putting additional equipment into such neighborhoods since the residents didn't care whether their streets were clean or dirty. When the story of this insult was widely reported (the organizer helping the report along), a large number of people wanted to do something to change street-cleaning practices which they had never before clearly understood to be deliberately discriminatory. They planned a series of actions, including sweeping their own streets while newspaper reporters recorded the event, had the implied backing of the large organization, and several times carried the debris to the homes or businesses of politicians who were responsible. They picketed the district sanitation office and protested at the central sanitation office of the city. Since the city had received national beautification awards and the mayor wanted to maintain its reputation and since the various politicians involved feared that their reelection would eventually be jeopardized, the embarrassment was enough to end the discrimination. . . .

During the course of the several actions, people for the first time saw their relationship to one city service with stark clarity;

this alone drove them to action. The insights provided through the experience of people in action are the fuel for a dramatic and broadening rhythm of action. The landlord who denies that blacks are good tenants; the school principal who "confesses" that neighborhood parents do not want their children to get an education—both can become focal points around which a good organizer builds action. As groups of people become drawn into a series of actions, each group working on its own problems but in relation to a common organization, there develops a body of accurate knowledge, enhanced levels of skill, and a larger number of active persons. Together, these enhance to the greatest extent possible the opportunity for each member to resolve his problems through the organizational structure.

ORGANIZER RESPONSIBILITY

An enabler is relatively passive, accepting the prevailing views, and helping people with their problems as defined by current neighborhood perspectives. An organizer is sensitive to current neighborhood perspectives, but may disagree aggressively with people while he remains clearly on their side.

For example, it is common in low-income areas for people to scapegoat their neighbors: "they don't care," "they run down the neighborhood," "people around here will only complain, they never do anything," etc. In this fashion, people repeat the outside stereotypes of low-income areas and develop a rationale for not themselves venturing into organizational efforts. An organizer who agrees with the condemnation not only undercuts neighborhood confidence in the possibility of organizing, but also finds himself rejected as possibly concealing a negative opinion of *everyone* in the neighborhood. Or, the members of an organization may decide on an action that is certain to fail, or which is clearly in violation of the constitution of the organization, or clearly leads to violence, to a collapse of democratic process, etc.

In all these cases, an organizer may find it necessary to disagree aggressively with the members, not to convince people of his own point of view on issues, but rather to make it possible to organize, to build effective organization. The people provide the content of action. The organizer has the responsibility to create and maintain the effective democratic structure of action, that is, a structure through which each neighborhood person has as nearly as possible an equal opportunity effectively to secure self-realization. The organizer, thus, must sometimes assert vigorous, aggressive leadership, even though he is not a member of the organization, and although such leadership should never include projecting his own substantive orientations upon the neighborhood.

On the other hand, the organizer should always refrain from leadership or participation when his intervention is not clearly necessary. For example, when a delegation visits a city official, the preparation ahead of time may not have been enough and the meeting may threaten to dissolve into confusion. An organizer has the responsibility to intervene forcefully to ensure that an effective case is presented. Such intervention should occur rarely, and the organizer should refuse to participate above that minimal level even when urged to do so. To the extent that an organizer has to intervene, to that extent the members will not see the victories as *their* victories, will not maximally acquire knowledge and skills themselves, and will not develop effective organization.

eg: Neighborhood Watch

Thus, the role of the organizer is extremely complex. He or she must stand by the side of the people and see the world from their perspective. But he must also be able to go outside that perspective to analyze and decide accurately what he should do in order to build organization. He should never be a member of the organization and should place the organization in the hands of the membership, but he also should know when and how to intervene to protect the essential characteristics which he is responsible for ensuring in the organization. He must be a passive enabler and an aggressive leader at the time when each is required of him, must use his own judgment to determine when he should do either, and therefore must not *need* to play either role.

In his role of energetic intervener, an organizer does not actually place himself in opposition to the neighborhoods. Instead, he allies himself with the long-term objective self-interest of the people in building organization through which they can act effectively, and he seeks to break up collective distortions and orientations which make impossible the creation of such an organizational structure. With this one exception the organizer stays as close as possible to present neighborhood points of view. By this strategy he makes certain that it will be very difficult for enemies of the organization to isolate him from the neighborhood by attacking him as an outsider, as being on someone else's side, etc. Further, the gradual identification of neighborhood persons with their organization makes it increasingly likely that through, rather than outside of, the organization, they will seek solutions to problems which for the first time become perceived as problems rather than as conditions of existence.

For example, where there is no organization, children playing on busy streets may be injured or killed without any response in the neighborhood. People assume that nothing can be done except, maybe, to watch the children more closely. "Life is like that." The presence of an organization provides a new remedy: "We can get a traffic light." Thus, getting a traffic light becomes a problem which, in the resulting struggle with the relevant city department, is itself transformed into an issue.

The organizer, therefore, not only creates issues and conflict; prior to that he or she creates problems where none were perceived before by creating opportunities where none had been before.

Inexperienced organizers typically fail to understand the necessary self-discipline, the requirement to act (or not) always to build organization and never through needs of the organizer which are irrelevant to or destructive of the building of organization. An organizer who is committed to racial integration cannot organize for racial integration in a community in which people oppose or are indifferent to this stance. . . . An organizer who admires a certain neighborhood leader cannot remain passive while that leader transforms the organization into his own political organization or social club. . . .

The people in a low-income neighborhood may decide not to adopt the kind of organizational structure recommended by an organizer. What then? Should the organizer try to manipulate or coerce the people into accepting what he recommends?

An organizer does not seek to impose himself on a neighborhood; instead he offers his services on the clearly stated basis that he will help build organization with certain characteristics, with the clear understanding that the organizer has responsibility to ensure that the organization meets certain criteria and that the organization belongs and will belong to the members. At first, the members do not yet understand the requirements of organization very clearly; they must be helped to clarity as rapidly as possible and should be made aware that at any time they can discharge the organizer. In short, the organizer must have a legitimated and mutually agreed upon relationship with the organization, a relationship which the organization can cancel whenever it may wish. When the organization achieves permanent status, it may be wise to outline in a written agreement the rights and responsibilities of the organizer and of the organization with respect to each other. . . .

THE STRUCTURE OF SOCIAL ACTION

Any structure through which the poor act on the sources of their problems will be under attack from local governmental and other established institutions. The attack may not be direct; it may consist of subtle attempts to talk organization members out of their concerns, to divert attention to other questions, to ridicule the organization in informal discussions, etc. Attacks by established institutions on an organization of the poor tend to be indirect as much as possible, while it is to the advantage of an organization of the poor to bring these subtle, half-concealed attacks into the arena of open confrontation.

An open attack on the organizational effort in low-income areas usually sharpens the issues and can be used to quicken the pace of organization. Established institutions, realizing this, may choose to attack the sponsors of organization (whoever pays the salary of and supervises organizers) rather than the organizational effort itself. . . .

The sponsor of organization may have any of a wide variety of structures providing only that it is able to refrain from emasculating the work. However, there are fewer alternatives for the structure of the organization being built. It may be a direct membership neighborhood council or an organization of previously existing organizations. In any case, the point is to build a clearly defined structure through which people in low-income areas can act. Thus, although the organization of the poor may carry on social activities, provide services to members, and constitute a forum for militant rhetoric, the basic orientation has always to be the expression of power through the greatest possible number of members acting together to resolve the central problems of their lives.

For people to be able to act through a structure, it must be democratic. Any large number of people can act together democratically in complex activities only when the rules for their participation are clearly stated and equally applied to all members. Complex activities also require specialization of roles (e.g., the spokesperson, the chairperson, the secretary, the committee member, etc.) and a clear definition of the relationships among the roles. Thus, rules must be explicit and generally accepted in accordance with which members of the organization have a formally equal opportunity to participate in decisions and occupy various positions. The organizer is responsible to ensure that such a structure is developed and that formal equality is reflected as far as possible in actual practice. Since many low-income people are learning for the first time to maintain organizational roles, these structural requirements must be communicated and legitimated more vividly than would be necessary with memberships with more organizational experience.

It is common for an inexperienced organizer to attempt to develop movement through the natural relationships among people rather than to create an explicit structured set of interpersonal relationships and decision processes. The movement which results from the former course either is temporary and effective only in carrying out simple activities, or it becomes complex but the instrument of one person rather than of the widest possible portion of the general membership. In either case, the resulting organization is a relatively ineffective structure, relatively unavailable for collective action by the poor. . . .

One way to create [an effective] structure is to hold a series of preliminary unstructured small or large meetings with people in the neighborhoods in which organization is being developed (after organizers have been invited in by neighborhood persons and institutions). In those preliminary meetings issues can be clarified, leadership can become visible in the neighborhood, and a general interpretation can be made by the organizer of the nature of such a proposed organization. Then, an initial general meeting can decide whether to organize, can elect temporary officers, and provide preliminary committees (to develop a constitution, begin action, etc.). A permanent structure (officers, committees, constitution, by-laws, etc.) can be adopted at a later meeting. After such a beginning, there is a legitimated democratic process for replacing persons in various positions, a process which makes it less easy for the organization to become the captive of a single leader, and less likely that the organization will dissolve, turn into a social club, or meet others of the usual disastrous fates of democratic organizations.

THE SOCIAL SITUATIONAL CONTOURS OF CONFLICT

. . . The meaning of a move in a conflict depends on the nature of the move, its context, and may also vary to different audiences. For example, depending upon the context, when a Commissioner of Public Welfare increases clothing allotments this may be understood by everyone as an act of generosity or, alternatively, of weakness. Or, it may be perceived as an act of generosity to members of the welfare establishment *and* as an act of weakness to members of the organization demanding the increase. Further, the divergence of interpretations of the same public act in a conflict situation tends to make the reactions of each side incomprehensible to the other. When the organization renews its pressure, persons in the welfare establishment may believe that the organized welfare clients are simple-minded puppets of organizer manipulation and agitation, and also amoral and naturally parasitic. The organized welfare clients, on the other hand, may believe that the commissioner is trying to deprive them of their rightful allotments, that this is why he is not giving straight answers to their questions.

In a conflict situation the objective consequences of an act by one side or by another, or the intentions behind the act, may be almost irrelevant. The act is one point around which conflict swirls, and a common interpretation may eventually be made as both sides, usually first really brought together by the conflict, begin to know one another better. . . .

SOCIAL ACTION AS MORALITY DRAMA

The organizer conducts the conflict which draws to itself the fascinated attention of a large portion of the entire community. The public conflict creates an audience and actors who play to the audience. The actors invent their own lives in a performance not to be repeated. The organizer ensures that the play is seen as a struggle between the forces of good and the forces of evil (although there will be no consensus concerning which side is which). Through helping keep the initiative with the organization of the poor, through breaking up existing perspectives by unforeseeable improvisations, through drawing the powerful into a conflict in the spotlight of public attention, the organizer enables that organization to begin to control the opponents, thus creating the first interdependency for previously dependent people. From that point, the organizer works with a process which includes the opponents; no longer does he work *only* with the organization of the poor. He conducts the play in which one group of actors (the organization of the poor) creates and controls the conflict, and in which the other mainly responds and attempts to avoid the conflict. The actors write their own lines, but the organizer helps them to improve the performance. There is rehearsal prior to a public event (role-playing) and an analysis afterward. As the play continues, the skills of the poor begin clearly to rival, and then to outstrip, those of the opposition. The public conflict then communicates the ability of the poor to the community which had previously depreciated that ability. . . .

Besides achieving a diminution in dependency and a lesson in equality, the organizer has the task of institutionalizing the new relationships so that, as the audience departs, the poor find themselves with a stable level of power, greater than before, and incorporated into the new community status quo.

The institutionalization of a new social position for the poor is possible because, although the conflict may subside, and the audience may leave, the ability of the organization to create the conflict and draw

the audience has been established. Thus, the actions of the poor now acquire a new meaning. . . .

SYMBOLIC CONCESSIONS

When the organization becomes powerful enough, it will force concessions from opponents. The mayor will appoint a Human Rights Commission, the urban renewal agency will agree to more citizen involvement in relocation of people from the demolition area, the state legislature will pass a resolution setting forth state policy on housing code enforcement, the public education system will announce classes for adult poor, trade unions will state that they no longer exclude anyone from apprenticeship programs on racial grounds, public welfare publicly decides no longer to support slum landlords by paying rent for welfare recipients in slum housing, the police chief assures the organization that there is now a new complaint process to which he pays personal attention, etc.

All these are promissory notes, issued under pressure. It is a responsibility of the organizer to make certain that they are converted into the legal tender of actual changes in practice which benefit the people in low-income areas, that they are not merely used as symbolic substitutes for the actual resolution of problems. When the leaders of an organization of the poor are appointed to this community and that board, the result is usually that they become part of the opponent apparatus by which the lives of the poor are controlled. Until enough experience develops in the organization it is often possible for opponents to take the edge off campaigns against them by making agreements which they intend never to keep. Especially in the early stages of organization, the organizer helps keep attention focused, not on promises and agreements announced with however much fanfare, but on whatever actually occurs in the lives of people in the low-income areas as a consequence of such announcements. When an opponent has agreed to a concession, a new line of action must usually soon be directed to force the opponent to carry out the agreement. Only after a period of time does it become clear to everyone concerned that agreements must be kept or painful sanctions will be imposed by the organization. The organizer repeatedly calls the attention of members, often by Socratic questioning, to what is actually happening within the low-income area, and brings out discrepancies between opponent promises and performances. The organizer agitates; the organization acts; a reluctant opposition is coerced into honesty.

KNOWING OPPOSITION TACTICS

Persons in positions of power have long experience in frustrating opposition to them. An organization of the poor gradually develops equivalent or even superior expertise through its own experience. The organizer helps members, and especially leaders, to think through the strategies and tactics of opponents.

He must, for example, understand the usual initial "cooling out" approach in which someone with a friendly and disarming manner attempts to persuade the neighborhood to accept something other than what is being demanded. He must know that opponents may replace an old and hated injustice with a new injustice about which anger has not yet been developed, as happened, for example, when alienation in public housing was substituted for exploitation by private slum landlords. He must be alert to the use of rules and regulations to

confuse critics. For example, when a delegation went to talk with a welfare commissioner, the members were told that their demands could not be met because everything in welfare is done according to the rules—federal rules, state rules, county rules—and pointed to a huge manual to support his statement. If they had not been prepared, the members would not have been able to describe numerous instances in which public welfare workers used wide discretion in interpreting and applying the rules.

The organizer must know the divide-and-conquer techniques, as, for example, when concessions are offered to leaders or to some portion of an organization in order to create illegitimate advantages and unfair disadvantages within the organization.

Opponents typically portray the organization to the rest of the affluent community as threatening some revered symbol: the nation, the American way of life, law and order, and the appeal for unity against subversion, for harmony rather than disruption, etc. They taunt the people for needing organizers, offer concessions provided the organizers are discarded, praise the people while attacking the organizers as outsiders trying to tell the people what to do. The organizer helps the people to understand the nature of the attack and to turn it back on the attackers in various ways. For example, the organization may publicize the extent to which the opponents violate other symbols: the right to equal opportunity, the value of self-help, the defense of mother and children. . . .

The current action requires development of moves against the vulnerable points of opponents. The organizer jogs members into thinking through what the opponent needs that the organization can provide, interrupt, or otherwise affect. Does a public agency fear public scrutiny? An organization of the poor can draw public attention to it. Does a member of the city council need a thousand additional votes? An organization of the poor can affect many more than that number. Does a department store need a positive image? A margin of profit? A mass organization may be able to affect the one by bringing employment discrimination into the open; the other by a combination of picket lines and boycotts. Does a social agency need to pretend that it is meeting needs? A people's organization can demonstrate unmet needs by helping ten times as many people with legitimate need to apply for help as the agency has openings. Does a school claim that the parents of the neighborhood are not interested in education? The parents can seek public funds to sponsor their own school, picket and boycott the existing school, make it clear that their interest in education is as intense as their opposition to the existing school. Do a variety of people and organizations want to avoid the fray, to stay neutral? The organization can focus public attention on their neutrality, force them to examine the issues, force them to take sides. Since most people with detailed understanding of the issues will agree with the orientation of a mass organization of low-income people, or at least do not want the opposition of such an organization, forcing neutrals to take sides will result in increasing support for it in the affluent community.

Since low-income people lack resources, it is useful to get opponents to work for the organization. If persons in authority are drawn into attack on the low-income people or on the symbols dear to them, the attack itself will build organization more quickly than any number of organizers could do by themselves.

An organization has often to map possible lines of action by opponents in order to make it easiest for them to meet organizational demands. It is not enough only to attack the destruction by urban renewal of low-income neighborhoods; the organization may have to secure competent technical counsel to prepare alternative feasible plans for neighborhood rebuilding, plans which will not violate the professional standards of city planners while having the advantage of support by the people of the neighborhood. . . .

All the moves mentioned above have been tried and found useful in one or another context. No one can say whether they would be useful again in other contexts. One could also consider modifications. Could clients or tenants engage in collective bargaining in order to work out new contractual agreements with a public welfare agency or a public housing authority? Could a low-income area organize to spend the bulk of its entire income in accordance with organizational decisions? What would happen if the poor used cameras and tape recorders to create a record of their treatment compared with that given affluent persons in shops, public offices, banks? Can low-income areas organize a "hiring hall" for jobs of all kinds, the analogue of industrial unionism on a community basis? . . .

THE KNOWLEDGE BASE OF ACTION

In a conflict situation, the organization does what is unexpected, dividing and confusing opponents, keeping them off balance. It seeks out and tackles points of weakness: the fact that bureaucratic organizations depend on clients or customers or constituents, provisions and communication, all of which may be affected at unpredictable times in unpredictable ways; the fact that powerful persons usually need to be jolted before they even begin to take seriously the lives of low-income people; the fact that people and organizations operating on routines cannot tolerate disruption. . . .

The knowledge base of social action must constantly be reformed; the organizer senses changes needed, inspires daily examinations and theoretical reanalyses of the event process. A series of demonstrations which had been projected for weeks may be abandoned without notice; an enemy of years' standing may become a friend; the major issue of one day may have been entirely replaced by another the next day; a drive to force landlords to repair housing may be replaced by a plan for public housing operated by the tenants. Academic observers may be surprised at the apparent lack of a predictable, consistent set of alliances, tactics, orientations, by the organization. However, the organization learns to follow the single principle of building power in the low-income area; it would be disastrous to that ambition if the organization were to become predictable to academic observers. . . .

CAMPAIGNS

The organization grows through actions and activities. Either is carried on by a series of campaigns of strictly limited duration. The actions may include a month of daily picket lines around city hall to protest police brutality, or a two-month period of voter registration and voter education ending in a massive directed vote, or a six-hour sit-in at a public official's office, or a two-hour play-in by children at city hall. The activities may consist of a two-day fund-raising barbecue, a week-long fund-raising carnival, a two-week chest X-ray campaign, a monthly tour of scenic places for elderly persons in the neighborhood, an annual one-day fashion show. Actions are directed toward securing change in the

relationship of the low-income area to the affluent community; activities contribute only indirectly to this outcome: directly they occur within established inside-outside relationships. However, in either case, a large number of people will only become involved for what is known in advance to be a limited period of time after which there will be a time of relative quiescence. It is a responsibility of the organizer to make certain that a series of campaigns is developed, involving the problems and issues and interests and skills of the widest possible number of persons in the area being organized. And, since the organization exists primarily for action, the organizer should ensure that campaign *activities* do not come to occupy the major attention of the membership.

Through such a series of campaigns, the number of persons identified with the organization continues to increase. Provided there is maintained an action emphasis, the pressure on the opponents of the organization will continue to mount. . . .

SERVICES

To some extent, outposts of the affluent community in areas of poverty (welfare, medical care, public housing, private business) are not likely to be responsive enough to organizational demands to supply adequate services sensitively tailored to the self-perceived needs of low-income people. To that extent, the organization can itself sponsor temporary services which will eventually disappear when the area being helped is no longer one of poverty. From the point of view of the affluent community it is prudent to spend a given sum of money (a) more efficiently than it is now spent, and (b) without being open to blame for the inadequacies and inequities involved in the extention of services to a dependent and hostile population. It will therefore become attractive for the affluent community to finance services which will be operated under the direction of organizations of the poor. The organizer will need to acquire some understanding of the pitfalls and advantages of this eventual outcome, and help the organization to secure needed services in such a way that the organization is strengthened and retains its action orientation and in a way that avoids the stigma which attaches to many service programs operated by low-income people. . . .

The organizer should not get so involved in the tough daily struggle of creating organization that he loses sight of the minimum long-range outcomes which will validate the amount of effort by the organization.

WHAT WILL NOT WORK

. . . First, there is no easy or quick way to build powerful organizations in low-income areas. Power only comes to an organization after a large number of people have acquired the skill to work efficiently through the organizational structure. It takes several years to meet these conditions. Building mass demonstrations in a short-lived movement or campaign may leave a residue of change, but they do not provide a structure through which power is exercised. Or, one can pull together existing organizations and groups into an organization of organizations in a convention with mass attendance, but the people who attend such a convention are not yet organized. All that has happened is that groups which previously met separately now meet once together and maintain some subsequent communication. The long, hard work of building a single powerful organization will require additional years. It is important in organizational work that some power be exercised very nearly at the beginning, but the early exercise of power does not mean that a structure has yet been created through which the exercise of power is effective and routine.

Second, an organizer can "look good quick" by organizing at once a mass action effort. However, if he or she does not also concentrate on creation of a structure and decision process through which people themselves can act effectively, his flash flood of action will soon disappear or leave behind an organization run by one person or a clique, not a structure through which the neighborhood can act.

Third, an organizer may have made a brilliant analysis of the need for a revolutionary social transformation, or have a beautiful vision of participatory democracy. But, if he or she projects these perspectives of his upon a low-income population with immediate and concrete problems, even if he also pays attention to these latter problems, he will find that his organization will be small, weak, sectarian, and easily isolated. An organizer must always be directly relevant to present neighborhood perspectives.

Fourth, it is sometimes argued that the appropriate structure for organizational work is that of the storefront church or some other type of organization [of] which low-income people are already members. This argument takes the culture of the poor into account, but not the fact that storefront churches and other organizations in low-income areas do not *do* much, do not perform complex tasks. In addition to the requirement of conforming to neighborhood traditions there is the other requirement of creating a structure adequate to carry on action and activities and operate services simultaneously and efficiently on a wide variety of problems and issues. Over any length of time this requires a

Division of Labor

division of labor, specialization, differentiated explicit role structures. Primitive structures do primitive tasks.

Fifth, existing social welfare institutions usually cannot sponsor organizational work in low-income areas because they cannot tolerate the conflict, because they define the problems of low-income people from outside rather than working with the definitions of low-income people, because they start from a position above the poor and reach down rather than starting with a working respect for low-income people.

Sixth, an organizer cannot follow a political organizational model since such models are developed solely to deliver votes and since they deliver votes by the politician doing things for people rather than by people doing things for themselves. A neighborhood acts through a political organization only in a very limited way. . . .

AWARENESS OF CHANGE

. . . In social action, the power of the poor shifts imperceptibly through their efforts. The public welfare worker is a little more alert to guard their rights, the politician a little more concerned about their opinion, the police officer less inclined to acts of brutality or corruption in the low-income neighborhood and a little more inclined to protect the rights of the people. The neighborhood continues to see the public welfare worker, the politician, the police officer, on the basis of years of experience. It is one task of the organizer to arouse the people from their bad dream which includes an underlying fear of their own weakness and inferiority, to point out and describe the changes which are taking place even outside the areas of concrete actions by the neighborhood organization. It is a task of the organizer to go beyond the creation of

an account of neighborhood action to helping the people in the organization create an alternative and more accurate view of their world and of their position in it. The assumption that blacks and women are excluded from an apprenticeship training program may be generally believed, no longer true, and an important belief for the behavior of young blacks and women. The assumption that the barriers to professional education are fixed and unchangeable may be important and no longer accurate. The organizer points out changes [and] possibilities and helps an appreciation of them to become incorporated in the everyday thinking of most people in the areas of poverty in which he is working.

THE NEW TRADITION

An organizer helps an alternative account of the world to develop in the organization. An organizer may relate the story in detail again and again of how this leader stood right up to the commissioner and told the truth, or how that demonstration led to an increase in police protection or how the voting power of the organization has the council passing ordinances which they never considered before. The action of neighborhood people becomes fixed in a positive account which creates a clear context whereby people can gain self-esteem through action, whether or not individual employment or other opportunities are open to them. . . . A positive collective identity becomes rooted in the past, and no longer subject to the vicissitudes of an uncertain world. This identity is publicly known throughout the neighborhood; it can be revived at any time as it bolsters self-esteem in contemporary actors.

An organizer who recounted traditions would normally be merely a neighborhood bore. But when the account is credible and about what neighborhood people have accomplished in combat on crucial issues against great odds, the account is often quickly grasped and long relished.

Thus, an organizer not only learns to listen carefully when talking with people, but also learns to provide through his words a concrete, vivid, compelling, and credible picture of the situation, a picture that is intended to upset the existing definition, force people to take sides about a proposed course of action, and outline such a course with clarity. This concrete, vivid, compelling and credible picture is often essential for getting movement under way, even though it stereotypes a wide variety of people and events under single labels and thus distorts reality through oversimplification and selection. People learn first to think about action while making only the major distinctions. Later, and through their own experience, people make the exceptions and fill in the details. . . .

The fact that an organizer creates an oversimplified sketch of action space should not be taken to mean that the people of low-income areas think in simple terms. Rather, just as the first knowledge of university students about a new area is stereotypic, for the same reason people who begin collective action must begin on the basis of the major relevant ideas and would be immobilized by a complete and detailed account which would not be easily incorporated in action.

THE LOCUS OF RESPONSIBILITY

The success of action can be undermined in two major ways: (1) it does not attain its objectives and, (2) it attains its objectives, but someone other than members of the organization is seen as responsible for the result. If the enemy is perceived in the neighborhood as having simply decided to give the people what they want, the action may be seen as ending well, but it is a failure as social action. It only becomes a social action success when the outcome is understood in the low-income area to be a direct consequence of organizational activity. Similarly, if the intended outcome is perceived in the low-income area as directly due to the intervention of the organizer, it is a social action failure. The organizer must ensure that the responsibility for securing an intended outcome is always placed squarely on the organization membership. Thus, the organizer typically ensures that meetings are well attended, that the necessary work gets done, that the organization holds such an initiative that an action favorable to the organization by an opponent is perceived as stemming from this initiative. But, the organizer accomplishes these ends as unobtrusively as possible in view of the fact that he may sometimes need conspicuously to intervene and that he must maintain a relationship of candor and responsibility with the people he helps. He interprets his role: "It is your organization, you will call the shots, do the work (and it's hard work)!" . . . Constant attention to placing responsibility with the people of low-income areas not only ensures that action has the most positive outcome for the skills and self-concept of the people involved, but also more people are more likely to become and remain active in an organization structured to increase their self-responsibility.

DEVELOPING THE PERSPECTIVES OF THE PEOPLE

People begin to act for themselves rather than have someone act for them. This requires that people also learn to think for themselves and not merely rely on the organizer's thinking. As much as possible, the organizer helps develop from the action itself a tradition of success; he or she does not only create the tradition and tell it to the people. . . .

Instead of outlining action possibilities for organization members, the organizer will often ask questions which help people to think through action alternatives for themselves and strategies of action by their opponents. Insofar as efficiency is not too greatly reduced, responsibility for thought as well as for action is placed in the neighborhood, not merely with leaders or with organizers.

For example, suppose that an organization is trying to stop the illegal distribution of narcotics by licensed pharmacists in its neighborhood. After learning that state officials will do nothing, the members begin to think of securing legislative remedy. The organizer could simply explain the difficulty of getting legislation, especially in the face of well-financed opposition. But this approach would leave him more vulnerable to the constant attack by opponents: "The idea behind your organization is a fine thing. But aren't you people grown up yet? Do you need an organizer to do your thinking for you?" It would also mean that members may agree, but would not act with much conviction on the basis of ideas that were not their own. An alternative is preferable. The organizer may ask a series of questions about exactly how the organization can use its energy most effectively. Can you put much pressure on the legislature at this stage? Are there any other ways to act? What about direct pressure on druggists in the neighborhood? What has the best chance to succeed? The organization may in any case seek legislation, but the decision will be made after a realistic

examination of alternatives and will clearly be that of the organization itself.

A more complex problem arises when the organizer must respond to attempts (very common in organizational work) to isolate him from the members. For example, suppose that opponents of the organization spread the word that, although the organization itself is basically a good idea, it is hurt by the presence of an organizer who is a "Communist." The line of questioning by the organizer must help the members to an accurate appraisal of the attack: that the allegation is false and that it is an attempt to weaken the organization. . . .

It is not easy to help people to think for themselves in areas outside their usual experience. The organizer can only do it well through self-discipline and great respect for the people (to prevent manipulation in . . . the direction of organizer biases) and through having become perceived in the neighborhood as responsible and trustworthy. People are often afraid to act, uncertain about whom they can depend on, ignorant of the extent to which they are vulnerable to one or another disastrous outcome. The organizer must be the kind of person who can be counted on. He helps them undertake actions on the basis of assumptions which, through their own experience, people discover to have been valid. Even when it would be easier to agitate people by building up unfounded fears, the organizer maintains a relationship of honesty with neighborhood people, helping them to see accurately the possible disasters as well as limitations in the successes before them. Any other approach would lead to initially dazzling demonstrations or other actions followed by a decline in the organization as its members lost confidence in the organizer. For example, suppose people in one area are considering a rent strike to force landlords to fix up slum dwellings. The rent strike would get started very quickly if the organizer stressed only the facts that attorneys will represent the tenants, that money is available for legal expenses, that rent strikes do not appear to be illegal, etc., but did not mention the fact that tenants could probably be evicted after thirty days for nonpayment of rent. After the first few evictions, the reputation of the organizer and of the organization would have been destroyed beyond recovery. Over time, a self-confident critical elaboration of an adequate neighborhood perspective stems from the experience of having acted on a reasonable appraisal of alternatives and possibilities with the help of an organizer who is responsible and honest.

TRANSFORMATION OF RELATIONSHIPS

The relationships in a low-income area are primarily: (a) friendship, familial, or neighbor relationships, all object relationships with persons within the area, and (b) ecological dependency relationships with persons and institutions outside. In the beginning, to some extent people simply shift their dependency from other persons and institutions to organizers. On first appearance, an organizer is interpreted within the context of usual ways of relating. He or she is an outsider on whom people depend for the provision of skills and resources. The organizer is also like a friend. Therefore, at first, he is likely to be loved, at the same time hated, deferred to, and depended on. One task of the organizer is to transform this personal relationship (in which people find it difficult to accept a substitute for him) into a role relationship in a structure with which people identify. He is successful (a) to the extent that members value him as a resource, but in relationships of interdependence in which members make the important decisions and do much of the work; and (b) to the extent to which members want an organizer without needing a specific organizer, and (c) [to the extent to which members] value him for his contribution to the organization rather than for the broad range of his unique personality characteristics. In other words, the relationship of an organizer to the organization becomes gradually depersonalized and egalitarian from a beginning point of personalization and dependency. . . .

SUCCESS

Success occurs when the people in low-income areas can, through organization, solve a wide variety of central problems which they could not solve before, when through organization they can become effective acting persons rather than passive objects of action. Many people are swept into action, not by direct active membership in the organization, but through identification with an acting neighborhood-based mass organization. That organizer has succeeded who has ensured the creation of such a structure which expands the area of freedom for persons in the action area. . . .

As an organization accomplishes a number of things over a period of time, an organizer has to work actively against its decline into a bureaucratic skeleton going through routine motions while major collective problems remain unresolved. Because of the tendency of organizations to fossilize, organizers will very likely be needed to maintain an action emphasis for as long as one can plan ahead. . . .

23.

Megan H. Morrissey

THE DOWNTOWN WELFARE ADVOCATE CENTER: A CASE STUDY OF A WELFARE RIGHTS ORGANIZATION

The National Welfare Rights Organization (NWRO) represented an effort on the part of poor people and concerned third parties to organize a movement of social protest. Through this organization, poor people sought to protect their civil and legal rights and to effect social change on the system of public welfare. When considering the social protest of poor people, it is customary to study the actions of NWRO, which existed from 1966 to 1973.

The story of welfare rights organizations, however, extends beyond 1973. A second wave of welfare rights organizations began to emerge in the mid-1970s. These groups expressed philosophies and goals that differed from those of NWRO. They were much smaller in scale and had a local focus. While the NWRO tried to ignite a poor people's movement, the second wave of welfare rights organizations stressed that welfare is not an issue for poor people, in general, but is more specifically a concern of poor women. Thus, while the first wave of welfare rights groups emerged in response to the civil rights movement, the second wave traced its origins to the women's movement as

well as to the civil rights movement. This article describes a second-generation welfare rights organization, the Downtown Welfare Advocate Center, and its membership arm, the Redistribute America Movement (DWAC/RAM).[1]

HISTORY AND ORIGINS OF DWAC

The early history of DWAC is difficult to piece together because the preserved written records are sporadic and incomplete, but the organization is known to have evolved from a group of welfare mothers who gathered on Sunday afternoons for

Jeffrey Pence's assistance in this work is acknowledged and greatly appreciated, especially in the organization and inventory of the Downtown Welfare Advocate Center/Redistribute America Movement papers at the Social Welfare History Archives. Archivist David Klaassen was also of great assistance in preparing this work.

[1]Data for this article were drawn from the Downtown Welfare Advocate Center/Redistribute America Movement (DWAC/RAM) papers contained at the Social Welfare History Archives (SWHA) at the University of Minnesota at Minneapolis/St. Paul. The director of SWHA is Clarke Chambers. This particular collection was organized by staff member Jeffrey Pence. The collection is 9 linear feet in length and consists of 18 manuscript boxes, two legal-length manuscript boxes, one carton of tapes and other artifacts, and three oversize boxes of banners. Included in the collection are minutes of staff meetings, board meetings, and committee meetings; information regarding chapter organizing; financial records and grant proposals; protest literature for action campaigns; newspaper clippings and press briefings; and correspondence. The papers contain few case advocacy records. Many of these records were stolen from the organization around 1978–79, and afterwards such records were not kept. The activities and many of the members of DWAC/RAM spanned both organizations, the advocacy center and the membership movement. There was no attempt to separate these two groups in the papers, and in this article they are discussed together except where specifically noted.

consciousness-raising discussions.[2] The women sought to inform themselves of laws and regulations related to the awarding of welfare benefits, as well as to share personal experiences. One of the early key members was Anita Hoffman, wife of social activist Abbie Hoffman and mother of a young child, who found herself alone and economically destitute following her husband's retreat underground.[3] Another important member was Theresa Funiciello, who first learned of DWAC from another welfare recipient. Funiciello would eventually become the director of DWAC from 1976 to 1981.

It was during these consciousness-raising experiences of the Sunday meetings that the women became politicized and decided to take action by forming an advocacy organization and staffing a welfare information hotline. They moved into a space they shared with the People's Information Center (PIC), another welfare information resource group. Volunteers originally staffed the phone lines and provided individual advocacy work on a case-by-case basis. The volunteers, primarily welfare recipients themselves, emphasized outreach into the community and gave speeches at public gatherings, held press conferences, and made radio and television appearances to raise public concern about welfare. In public appearances, DWAC challenged the popular myth of the welfare recipient as lazy and dependent and appealed for a grant increase for recipients. They made a conscious effort to reach people at a young age,

making many appearances in grade school classrooms. The early organization also sought to form alliances with other social activist groups and participated at meetings of organizations such as Mobilization for Survival and Advocates for Children.[4]

GOALS OF THE ORGANIZATION

As a self-help organization, empowerment of recipients was a fundamental goal of DWAC. Other goals of the organization were outlined in a brief history of the organization written in 1977. They were (1) to inform and counsel poor people about organizations, services, and entitlements available to them (through government grants, charities, and other sources); (2) to help solve problems of individuals in relation to agencies; (3) to promote a more sane, realistic, and humane approach to dealing with the urban poor in the government, media, and public consciousness; (4) to make information available to poor people and, in that capacity, to act as an information clearinghouse; and (5) to provide crisis intervention services to poor persons.[5]

As a means to reach these goals, DWAC members set up roving welfare clinics in poor neighborhoods in New York City to attract new members and to provide services. They held public meetings to inform recipients of ways to maneuver the channels of the welfare system. In 1977 the organization sponsored the attendance of 20 welfare recipients at economic training sessions held in Massachusetts and New York.[6]

The first two years were particularly

[2]Telephone interviews with one of the key members of DWAC, Theresa Funiciello, on April 12, 1989, and April 26, 1989, provided a great deal of background on the early history of DWAC/RAM. Theresa Funiciello was the director of DWAC from 1976 until 1981.

[3]Theresa Funiciello, telephone interview, April 12, 1989.

[4]DWAC/RAM papers, box 1 (Reports/Meetings), Annual Reports, 1978–83 file.

[5]DWAC/RAM papers, box 1, Constitution and By-Laws.

[6]DWAC/RAM papers, box 1, Annual Reports, 1978–83.

precarious for DWAC. While a major problem was maintaining consistent coverage of the phone lines, a more significant issue was the lack of money. Minutes from an early meeting provide a picture of an office assembled from remnants found in basements and secondhand stores. "The 9 × 5 grey cabinet on top of the desk can be used for client files. We can set up folders for complicated cases. Diane mentioned that she might be able to get a four drawer filing cabinet. Lala added that she might be able to get a car to transport it. . . . Anita went on to say that Diane Rose may get an old typewriter as well as the filing cards. It costs $656 a year to lease a Selectric type writer, but we may be able to use the typewriter in the church office."[7]

THE MEMBERSHIP MOVEMENT: REDISTRIBUTE AMERICA MOVEMENT (RAM)

From 1975 to 1978 DWAC staffed a welfare hotline with volunteers and did individual advocacy work. By 1978, however, members of the DWAC staff realized they could not continue to exist simply on a case-by-case welfare advocacy basis, and they made the decision to begin organizing welfare recipients. To bring welfare recipients together for collective action they added a membership arm, the Redistribute America Movement (RAM), a movement designed to "force the redistribution of this country's wealth, which is now held by the few, to the majority of people—including welfare recipients, elderly persons and low-income wage earners."[8] For DWAC/RAM

this meant the establishment of a just working wage for poor mothers on welfare whom they described as poor working mothers.

The Redistribute America Movement was an organization of poor people whose lives were directly affected by policies touching the poor, particularly those that outlined the awarding of welfare benefits. The first RAM chapters were organized in New York City. Though the movement later expanded to include statewide chapters, most members lived in New York City.

At the state level RAM consisted of a loose affiliation of RAM chapters that were organized at the local level. To form a RAM chapter required three dues-paying members, and by 1981 there were over 5,000 RAM members in 14 different chapters across the state. Members of RAM paid yearly dues of $5.00 to the central chapter, and some local chapters charged dues up to $5.00, in addition. Paying dues and being a member of a RAM chapter allowed a member to vote on decisions, participate in all RAM events, and attend statewide meetings. A support organization, the Friends of RAM, also organized members, but little attention was devoted to this group in the organization papers, and it is felt that it was of marginal influence. Friends of RAM members paid dues and could participate in all open RAM events and meetings, but they were not eligible to vote on RAM decisions.[9]

At the local level the structure of RAM was quite informal. There was a commitment to developing leadership from among the members of RAM, and organizing materials suggested a rotating chair for each meeting. Instructions to groups wanting to

---

[7]DWAC/RAM papers, box 1, DWAC/RAM Meetings to 1978.

[8]DWAC/RAM papers, box 1, RAM Meetings 1979 to 1980; item, Minutes of Meeting, October 22, 1979.

[9]DWAC/RAM papers, box 1, RAM Statewide Planning Meetings, 1981.

begin a RAM chapter emphasized the importance of preparation before actually beginning the chapter. Organizers were urged to become familiar with the geographical area, to know the location of substandard housing, to speak with community leaders including ministers and grocers, and to hold initial meetings in public places. Organizing instructions suggested going door-to-door in poor neighborhoods in order to enlist members in RAM. To sustain membership they noted the need for quick public action and continual evaluation of actions taken by a local chapter. One area of organizing that received a great deal of attention was the need to collect dues and conduct fund-raisers in order to maintain the chapter. "Nobody ensures our survival except ourselves. For our organization to last, the bills have to be paid. We have to be as good at taking in money as we are at spending it. It costs money to maintain local groups and leaders and members of local groups have to realize this. We all must spend a certain amount of time raising money through dues and projects."[10]

Organizing RAM chapters was a difficult task often discussed at the DWAC staff meetings. Minutes of the DWAC staff meetings include accounts of developing strategies to organize recipients. Participants in these meetings observed that welfare recipients needed a clear reason to participate in RAM. Organizers were to stress concrete gains to members from joining a welfare rights organization, such as securing a grant increase and ending brutality at the welfare centers. A popular theme in these discussions was the need to identify "winnable" issues (i.e., issues that would provide immediate benefits to participants) as a way to secure

participation.[11] It is significant to note, however, that while the organization's papers stress "winnable" issues in its organizing literature, the overall goal of RAM—the redistribution of wealth—was not realistically considered "winnable" through available legal channels. This primary goal of RAM was maintained even while smaller short-term goals were stressed in organizing literature.[12]

In addition to active recruitment of members into RAM, DWAC also urged recipients who used the advocacy service to become members. Advocacy assistance was offered to any first-time caller to DWAC. Before advocacy assistance could be used a second time, however, a recipient had to become a member of RAM.[13]

When RAM chapters were formed, DWAC urged them to engage in actions at the local level to raise the issue of welfare in the public consciousness. To accomplish this, DWAC encouraged RAM chapters to borrow from organizing tactics outlined by social activist and organizer Saul Alinsky. Some of the tactics suggested included: "(2) Never go outside the experience of your people. . . . The result is confusion, fear and retreat. . . . (4) Make the enemy live up to their own body of rules. (5) Ridicule is a very important, potent (strong) weapon. It infuriates the opposition who then react to your advantage....(12) Pick the target, freeze it, *personalize it,* and polarize it. The target is always trying to shift responsibility to get out of being the target. PIN THE TARGET DOWN SECURELY. Choose a person as a target, although the reason that person is chosen is because of his/her

[10]DWAC/RAM papers, box 1, RAM Chapter Organizing; item, RAM How will it work?

[11]DWAC/RAM papers, box 2 (Membership/Organizing), RAM Chapter Organizing.

[12]Funiciello, telephone interview, November 27, 1989.

[13]DWAC/RAM papers, box 2, RAM NY City Chapters: Brooklyn, Manhattan, Queens, Latin.

position (center director; etc.). (13) The enemy properly goaded and guided in his reaction will be our major strength.[14]

The Redistribute America Movement enjoyed early success. Despite organizing difficulties and financial hardship, RAM quickly gained new members, and several chapters organized across New York State. By the spring of 1981, however, staff members at DWAC expressed concern about the loss of direction in the leadership of RAM. A memo from staff member Cindy (no last name was indicated) dated April 6, 1981, noted the lack of direction following the development of chapters outside of New York City in 1980. She observed that since March 1980, chapter development had all but ceased in spite of several successful public actions on the part of DWAC/RAM. She further suggested that perhaps chapter development had died out because of the many campaigns undertaken, feeling that energy had been devoted to planning public actions and not maintaining membership. In any case, she felt that RAM had been a much stronger organization at the end of 1980 than it was in the spring of 1981.[15]

THE PHILOSOPHY OF DWAC/RAM

The philosophical and political stance of DWAC/RAM can best be seen in the writings and speeches of Theresa Funiciello, director of DWAC, and through the public demonstrations and statements by members of RAM. As an organization, DWAC/RAM identified welfare as an issue of particular

concern to women and asserted that welfare recipients were poor because they were women.[16] It was dedicated to the empowerment of its members—welfare recipients—whom they consistently identified as women and mothers. They were further dedicated to transforming the social image of welfare mothers. They tried to accomplish this through public actions and demonstrations in which they sought concrete gains for welfare mothers and also to publicly define the work of welfare mothers as the performance of a valuable social role—that of mothering.

The Downtown Welfare Advocate Center/Redistribute America Movement defined itself as a women's organization for several reasons. It was an organization dedicated to improving the life conditions of poor women and was composed primarily of women. The DWAC staff and volunteers were overwhelmingly women, as was the board of directors. Additionally, women accounted for almost 95 percent of the membership in RAM.[17] At the same time, however, DWAC/RAM considered itself to be outside the women's movement as they felt their concerns were ignored by activist women. Specifically, DWAC/RAM felt that concerns of poor women, especially welfare mothers, were overlooked by the National Organization for Women (NOW).

---

[14]DWAC/RAM papers, box 1, DWAC Staff Meetings, 1980. This particular piece contains the title Chapters—Beginning and Maintaining. Handwritten on the top of the document is the following note: "Diane's 'rough' ideas for building chapters."

[15]DWAC/RAM papers, box 1, RAM Statewide Planning Meetings, 1981.

---

[16]This position reflected the organization's stance, but it was not necessarily shared by all members of the DWAC staff or by RAM members. Diana Autin, in particular, in a telephone interview on April 23, 1989, expressed the idea that some on the staff saw poverty as a function of sex, while others saw it as a function of race. Theresa Funiciello, according to Diana Autin, saw poverty as a function of sex. Funiciello, in an interview on April 26, 1989, said that while race and class entered into poverty, the numbers suggest that poverty is more an issue of sex.

[17]DWAC/RAM papers, box 2, RAM Membership Records, 1980, and RAM New York City Chapters: Brooklyn, Manhattan, Queens, Latin (Spanish-speaking).

Conflict with the Women's Movement

While defining itself as a women's organization, DWAC/RAM found itself at odds with the women's movement over the exclusion of the concerns of poor women. Theresa Funiciello, director of DWAC, articulated this position in a speech delivered at a conference on urban women sponsored by the New York chapter of NOW. She challenged NOW members to consider the needs of poor women, and she stated, "We believe it is time the Women's Movement in general and N.O.W. in particular became responsive to the needs of poor women."[18] This tension between DWAC/RAM and the women's movement, in general, and NOW, in particular, is not articulated in the organization's papers. However, it is clearly stated in DWAC's comparison of women in NOW with poor women. Funiciello stated that poor women were less dependent than the members of NOW attending the conference, for poor women had survived outrageous odds without the luxury of someone to support them. Funiciello further accused NOW of overlooking the fact that the majority of welfare recipients were women and, consequently, welfare was an issue about which NOW should be concerned.[19] She urged NOW to adopt the position that poor women deserved an adequate income because they were performing a socially useful role and, further, because they were clever, resourceful, and hardworking.[20]

Though critical of the women's movement, staff members at DWAC knew that supporters of the women's movement represented a possible source of support to DWAC. Staff members were willing to court middle- and upper-class women to get support as well as financial backing for DWAC's goals. An undated memo described a presentation on DWAC to be made at the homes of middle- and upper-class women. It is unclear who wrote the memo, but it provided a detailed set of instructions on how to motivate middle- and upper-class women for political action, provide consciousness raising about welfare as a women's issue, and end an evening by securing a financial commitment from the group.[21]

Actions and Demonstrations

The public actions and demonstrations of DWAC/RAM also expressed their philosophical stance, as well as their analysis of the welfare state. All of the actions were designed to further the long-range goal of RAM, to bring about an equitable redistribution of income, as well as the short-term goals of both DWAC and RAM, to improve the lives of welfare recipients and their children and to transform the public image of the welfare recipient.

Actions generally were one of three kinds. The first called public attention to welfare received by the rich in the form of government subsidies and tax benefits.

---

[18]DWAC/RAM papers, box 12, Speeches/Testimony by DWAC/RAM Members. Speech given by Theresa Funiciello entitled "W.O.W. (Women on Welfare) N.O.W.!" This particular quotation is from p. 7 of the written text. There is no date on the speech.

[19]Funiciello, "W.O.W., N.O.W.!" p. 4 of the written text.

[20]Theresa Funiciello, telephone interview, April 26, 1989.

[21]A footnote at the bottom of these instructions indicates DWAC/RAM's impression of middle- and upper-class feminists. It reads, "Invitations: . . . 'It shouldn't hurt to be born in America' cover. Inside should make the feminist connection very clear, perhaps a quote from Robin Morgan or Gloria Steinem to impress unconvinced feminists." DWAC/RAM papers, box 2, RAM Chapter Organizing; item, Adapting NARAL's House Meeting Concept to One Meeting DWAC's Needs, p. 2.

Actions of this type included demonstrations at Mobil International Headquarters and Saratoga Springs Racetrack. The demonstration at Mobil International Headquarters was held on April Fools' Day in 1981 and was attended by over 500 protesters. It focused on publicly redefining the concept of "welfare." Members of DWAC/RAM pointed out that tax benefits were welfare for the wealthy, and they used the public forum to oppose as well as expose the trickle-down theory. Downtown Welfare Advocate Center director Marcy May noted, "About the only thing that trickles down to the average welfare mother in New York is the leak in the apartment upstairs . . . if her building has running water at all.[22] Part of the demonstration involved street theater that featured guest appearances by "Ronnie and Nancy," who were on hand to present a huge "welfare" check to Mobil.

In the summer of 1981, RAM members protested tax breaks to racehorse owners by demonstrating at the horse auction in Saratoga Springs, New York. About 75 protesters arrived carrying signs proclaiming, "Let Them Eat Oats!" or "Subsidies for Colts and Mares—Welfare for the Millionaires."[23] As part of that demonstration, protesters passed out a fact sheet that listed the names of corporations receiving federal tax incentives and the amount of "welfare" each received. It also pointed out that the "trickle-down" theory meant a diversion of funds from the poor to the wealthy. The distributed flier began: "The billions of dollars of so-called 'tax incentives' offered

to American corporations by an intricate set of federal, state and city programs are traditionally defended in terms of the psuedo-economics of the 'trickle down theory.' The benefits to the public from these programs have historically trickled down no farther than the bank accounts of big business."[24] Among the New York–based corporations named by DWAC/RAM were Tiffany and Company, IBM, New York Hilton, AT&T, and Philip Morris.[25]

A second type of public action was designed to get immediate benefits for women living on AFDC. Examples of this type of action were the Clothe Our Children Campaign and the antibrutality campaign. In 1980, New York State law provided for the replacement of children's clothes when loss was the result of a catastrophe.[26] Members of DWAC/RAM interpreted this law in a new way and used the catastrophic clause to point to the inadequacy of welfare grants. Literature by DWAC/RAM noted that the amount of money welfare had allowed per year for clothing had never been adequate. In 1980, welfare recipients were allowed $48.00 per year for clothing for children from birth to 5 years. Children from 6 to 11 were allowed $73.00 per year, and recipients over 12 were allowed $89.00. The DWAC/RAM pointed out that with such low benefits, welfare mothers could not afford to replace clothes for their children, or prevent them from growing out of their clothes. They further pointed out that

---

[22]DWAC/RAM papers, box 10 (Mobil Action), Mobil Action: Proposal and Support Material.

[23]DWAC/RAM papers, box 11 (COCC [Clothe Our Children Campaign], Saratoga Protests, Donald Trump/Hyatt Hotel action), Saratoga Meetings, Notes. 1981.

[24]DWAC/RAM papers, box 10, Mobil Action: Five-Month Plan and Notes.

[25]Interestingly, this demonstration received very little newspaper coverage except in the sports sections. Sportswriters had come to cover the horse auction, generally a rather unexciting event, and found the proceedings interrupted by the demonstrators (Theresa Funiciello, telephone interview, April 26, 1989).

[26]New York State Department of Social Services Rules and Regulations, Title 18, Section 352.7(d).

welfare grant levels had increased 26 percent in the period from 1972 until 1980. During that same time, inflation increased 120 percent. For recipients of welfare this rate of inflation was truly catastrophic.

The Clothe Our Children Campaign was designed to help recipients apply for catastrophic clothing grants. The campaign included organizing members, assisting them in filling out request forms for a catastrophic clothing allotment, and marching to welfare centers to present the requests.[27] On September 15, 1980, 800 protesters filled out catastrophic clothing allotment requests and marched to the welfare centers. The demonstrators remained at the centers until they received a signed receipt from the welfare worker verifying that the request had been received. It was made very clear by DWAC/RAM that the clothing allotment was not a substitute for a grant increase but simply a means to help tide women over until a grant increase was provided by the legislature. Unfortunately, there is no discussion of the results of the Clothe Our Children Campaign in the organization's papers.

The antibrutality campaign was another example of an attempt by DWAC/RAM to improve the lives of welfare recipients. Newspaper accounts in the organization papers describe different incidents in which women who went to welfare centers to apply for benefits or to see a caseworker were beaten by guards at the center, arrested, and charged with assault.[28] In 1978,

DWAC was receiving up to 10 calls each week reporting violence toward women by the guards at welfare centers. In August 1978, DWAC held a public meeting to call attention to the brutality at the welfare centers. As a result of this meeting, the New York City Council Welfare Committee agreed to begin investigating these reports. In January 1979, the committee announced a new training program for welfare workers and security guards. By September 1979, calls reporting violence in the centers had dramatically declined.[29]

The third type of public action involved large demonstrations at the state legislature in support of an overall AFDC grant increase, DWAC's constant goal despite the attention given to advocacy and organizing. Demonstrations at the legislature began in 1979 and grew bigger each year. The demonstrations generally involved a march of welfare mothers with their children to various symbolic sites, such as the governor's mansion.[30] The planning committee made certain there was a great deal of press coverage at the demonstrations, and weeks prior to the actual demonstration they sent out welfare "fact" sheets to the press. To gain support for their position, DWAC/RAM sought an endorsement for a grant increase from significant individuals and organizations in New York. These groups and individuals conducted letter-writing campaigns to the governor and legislators prior to the vote on an increase. The endorsers included priests, ministers, and New York City council members Mary Codd and Ruth Messinger. Professional organizations, including the Harlem Lawyers Association, the New

---

[27] DWAC/RAM papers, box 11, COCC: Planning/Organizing.

[28] The DWAC/RAM papers contain various newspaper accounts of such actions. These accounts are scattered in various locations in the papers, but many can be found in box 4. An example was the story titled "Brutality in Welfare Centers: Pushing around the Poor," which appeared in the June 25, 1979, edition of the *Village Voice* (DWAC/RAM papers, Box 10, Mobil Action: Press: Correspondence, Planning).

[29] DWAC/RAM papers, box 1, Annual Reports, 1979, 1980.

[30] DWAC/RAM papers, box 12, Albany Demonstrations: Material from First Action, March 14, 1979.

York City Chapter of the NASW, and the Radical Alliance of Social Service Workers, offered their support. In addition, social service agencies such as the Henry Street Settlement endorsed the DWAC position.[31]

The March 1981 demonstration at the state legislature attracted more than 2,000 participants. This demonstration had a 2½-month buildup. Participants followed Governor Carey around the state, demonstrating at many of his public appearances, frequently interrupting public speeches and demanding that welfare grant levels be increased. The press coordinators and demonstration organizers made extensive use of the death of Jessie Smalls, a 47-year-old welfare recipient who froze to death in her apartment after her heat had been turned off. Smalls was the sixth recipient to freeze to death in her apartment in the winter of 1980–81, and the demonstration organizers used the story of her death to indicate the need for a grant increase. Many times they arrived at Carey's public appearances bearing a coffin and carrying signs stating, "Welfare Grants Are Frozen. The Poor and Elderly Are Freezing—to Death."[32]

After three years of demonstrating, a grant increase was won. The New York state legislature passed a 15 percent welfare grant increase in 1981. There was general celebration at DWAC/RAM surrounding the grant increase, but as Funiciello pointed out, it was in some ways a bittersweet victory, and simply an organizer's answer.[33] The increase was a concrete gain DWAC/RAM organizers could claim

to attract new membership, but the increase did not bring grant levels up to the poverty line, nor did it come close to covering 100 percent of need for women on welfare.

The DWAC/RAM adopted an optimistic and triumphant tone in announcing the grant increase. The Ram's Horn, RAM's newsletter, announced in its May 1981 issue, "We Won!"[34] But the attainment of the increase was a mixed blessing. On the one hand, it represented the achievement of a significant short-term goal. On the other hand, the increase did little to contribute to DWAC/RAM's long-term goal of securing a just wage for poor mothers on welfare and, in fact, slowed momentum toward that goal. The optimistic tone adopted by DWAC/RAM in response to the increase was perhaps more indicative of their recognition that it could be used to promote further organization of welfare mothers. Yet, while an important short-term victory, the increase ultimately contributed to the organization's decision to fold.

THE DEMISE OF DWAC/RAM

The written historical record of DWAC/RAM devotes little time or attention to the decision to fold, but a number of factors appeared to have contributed to this decision. A major blow to the organization came with the loss of key DWAC staff persons, most notably Theresa Funiciello and staff member Diana Autin. Funiciello had kept the organization alive almost single-handedly from 1975 through 1976. With her decision to leave as director of the organization in 1981 to work for the Youth Project, it became apparent that many

---

[31]DWAC/RAM papers, box 12, Albany Demonstrations: Material from Second Action, March 27, 1980.

[32]DWAC/RAM papers, box 12, Albany Demonstrations: Material from Third Action, 1981.

[33]Theresa Funiciello, telephone interview, April 26, 1989.

[34]DWAC/RAM papers, box 1, RAM Statewide Conference Participation Material—1981.

funders had supported Funiciello more than the organization.[35] Many of the other DWAC staff members, no longer receiving welfare, moved on to other advocacy organizations.[36]

The organization went into decline from 1981 to 1983, when it became primarily an organization on paper.[37] Diana Autin noted that following the grant increase, the achievement of their short-term goal, there was loss of momentum, and there appeared to be less urgency for a further increase. She herself felt burned out and believed many of the staff of DWAC had similar feelings. She reported that DWAC/RAM made huge demands from the people who worked and volunteered there. While many women and workers were empowered by their involvement with DWAC/RAM, the demands of advocacy, policy analysis, and organizing meant long days for staff workers that finally became too much for them.[38]

CONCLUSION

The Downtown Welfare Advocate Center closed in 1985. It represented a different approach to welfare rights than did earlier organizations, namely, NWRO. First, DWAC insisted that welfare be defined as a women's issue. Women were overrepresented in the welfare roles, and the value of their contribution as mothers was ignored by society. Second, DWAC was run by welfare recipients, not concerned third parties. Third, their goals differed from those of NWRO. The Downtown Welfare Advocate Center did not believe it necessary to eliminate the system of public welfare in order to restructure but believed that it was necessary to socially redefine the role played by welfare mothers.

Though consciously an organization of women, run by women for women, DWAC did not associate itself with the women's movement. Further, they chose not to apply the label "feminist organization," although it was available in their historical context. Instead, they saw the women's movement as indifferent to, even excluding, poor women and not recognizing their contribution to society as mothers. Regardless of this opposition, it cannot be denied that they were bound to the women's movement of the 1970s, if only in the eyes of history. They were, after all, an organization of women concerned with changing the life circumstances of women—today's definition of a feminist organization.[39]

---

[35]Funiciello, telephone interview, April 26, 1989.

[36]The internal forces that contributed to the demise of DWAC/RAM are documented in the archival record. According to Theresa Funiciello, however, there were external forces operating against DWAC/RAM as well. Funiciello stated that there was active pressure from both the state government and various social welfare agencies to silence the political message of DWAC/RAM. Further, DWAC/RAM was subjected to constant infiltration by government agents. Trying to maintain an organization dedicated to social change in the face of such pressures was an overwhelming and exhausting task, and these external pressures contributed significantly to the demise of the organization. This perspective on the demise of the organization is not available in the preserved record. Funiciello, telephone interview, November 27, 1989.

[37]Funiciello, telephone interview, April 26, 1989.

[38]Diana Autin, telephone interview, April 23, 1989.

[39]Several scholars have examined the nature of social service agencies which define themselves as feminist. These scholars have looked most particularly at structure, organizational goals, and decision-making processes. While there are many different characteristics of feminist organizations, some shared characteristics among social services agencies self-defined as feminist are a nonhierarchical structure, shared decision making, and membership composed of women. Other characteristics are funding on an ad hoc basis and having the goal of changing or eliminating social forces which oppress women. (For examples of feminist social service agencies refer to L. Ahrens, "Battered Women's Refuges: Feminist Cooperatives versus Social Service Institutions," *Radical America* 14

Differences existed between DWAC and NWRO in organization and membership. Women on the welfare roles founded and led DWAC, and the power of the organization rested in the hands of those persons most affected by welfare policies—women. The management of NWRO, on the other hand, was dominated by professionals. Guida West wrote of NWRO: "It was a movement of women led by men, a movement of the welfare poor financed by middle-class liberals, a movement of blacks supported primarily by whites."[40]

The Downtown Welfare Advocate Center also differed from NWRO in its goals. While NWRO was intent on disrupting the system in order to bring about its downfall and eventual restructuring at the federal level, DWAC sought a restructuring of the system in a way that would affirm the lives and social contributions of poor women. It sought to redefine the social function of the welfare mother as performing a valuable social role for which she deserved just compensation. Further, DWAC sought public affirmation of welfare recipients in an attempt to transform the social image of the welfare mother.

How is one to evaluate DWAC/RAM? Looking back at its brief history, it might be tempting to dismiss this organization or evaluate it harshly. It was not able to sustain its membership, its one significant "victory" brought about its demise, it was never an organization of national significance, it never achieved its major goals. To evaluate this organization on such terms, however, is to overlook the significance of its contribution.

A different focus is required, and such a perspective presents itself in examining the impact DWAC/RAM had on members and volunteers. Women who came to DWAC/RAM were empowered to act as their own advocates within the welfare system and change the conditions of their own lives, whether that meant getting off welfare or redefining their position as welfare recipients. Autin believed that women who came to DWAC/RAM were empowered to do something about their lives and the lives of their children. Many had their consciousnesses raised about the issue of welfare as a particular concern to women. Funiciello stated that "people who spent time with DWAC/RAM became transformed."[41] She related that women who came to work as volunteers were empowered and gained self-respect and confidence. Often their children, who accompanied them to the center, were impressed by the roles they saw their mothers performing and gained a new respect for them.[42] Women who volunteered at DWAC/RAM were affirmed as mothers and as mothers living on welfare. Further evidence of DWAC/RAM's significance can be found in the many letters written by women who had used the services of DWAC/RAM. One of the most poignant,

[May–June 1980]: 41–47; J. Brenner and N. Holmstrom, "Women's Self-Organization: Theory and Strategy," *Monthly Review* 34 [April 1983]: 34–46; P. Cousineau, "The Support Function and Social Change: A Feminist Case History," *Women's Studies International Forum* 8 [1985]: 137–44; D. Masi, *Organizing for Women* [Lexington, Mass.: Lexington, 1981]; E. O'Sullivan, "What Has Happened to Rape Crisis Centers: A Look at Their Structure, Members, and Funding," *Victimology, An International Journal* 3 [1979]: 45–62; J. T. Pennell, "Ideology at a Canadian Shelter for Battered Women: A Reconstruction," *Women's Studies International Forum* 10 [1987]: 13–123; J. Sealander and D. Smith, "The Rise and Fall of Feminist Organizations in the 1970s: Dayton as a Case Study," *Feminist Studies* 12 [Summer 1986]: 320–41.)

[40]Guida West, *The National Welfare Rights Movement: The Social Protest of Poor Women* (New York: Praeger, 1981), p. 4.

[41]Theresa Funiciello, telephone interview, April 26, 1989.

[42]Ibid.

though not untypical in its tone, was received in 1981. The letter reads:

The people at RAM Jackie, Robin and especially a worker named Sharon Hunt have helped keep me from losing not only my mind but also my infant son when social services closed my case.

When I was being given the run-around by welfare trying to reopen my case they went all out over and above what I believe they usually do to help get to the right people to help me at a time when I didn't know which way to turn. Trying to cope with a newborn, the welfare and a pending eviction was much more than I could handle alone.

Without all their help, and especially their support . . . I would probably have given my son up for adoption as it was impossible to care for myself much less him. I don't know what I would have done without them. I thank God for RAM.[43]

It is perhaps more appropriate to say that, despite DWAC/RAM's failure to achieve its long-term goals, it was a success

---

[43]DWAC/RAM papers, box 5, Correspondence/Other Groups—Democratic Agenda to Environmental Action Fedt.

simply because it existed. Women were empowered to change the circumstances of their lives. Women came together and formed connections of self-help and support. Women engaged in political actions far beyond simply voting or not voting. Through this organization, poor women in New York gained a public voice.

It is important to study and document the histories of such organizations. To end the history of the struggle for welfare rights with the demise of the NWRO is to ignore the continuing struggle of poor persons for economic justice. It is sometimes tempting to conclude that the response to the social activism of the late 1960s and early 1970s was a conservative backswing in the 1980s. The history of DWAC/RAM serves as a reminder that the struggle for economic justice continued into the conservative era. The Downtown Advocate Center/Redistribute America Movement further serves to make the story of poor women a part of the collective consciousness and to make their legacy a part of history.

24.

Dick Flacks

THE REVOLUTION OF CITIZENSHIP

For 100 years, most people who call themselves "Left" throughout the world have shared not only elements of a vision and of an identity, but also a sense of common strategy. The key strategic idea during this century of struggle has been that social transformation depends on the development of the Left as a vehicle of

power, and most particularly on the emergence of a party, capable of winning power and using the machinery of the state to implement a program of change.

This mass party strategy was seen as necessary for several reasons. *First,* it was essential to unify the working class, articulate its shared grievances, and mobilize its collective energy. Ever since the mid-19th century, Left activists and intellectuals have seen the working class as both the moral source and the practical resource for democratic and social transformation. If the working class could be united, its collective power, based in the production process, could eventually achieve revolutionary change; more immediately, the numerical strength of a politically unified working class would be central to the achievement of Left political power.

Second, workers and other subordinated groups needed a vehicle of representation so they could find some means to defend their interests in capitalist society without having to be continuously prepared to strike or engage in other direct action. A working-class party, together with labor unions, would give workers an institutionalized voice, enabling them to be politically defended while they, as individuals, could deal with the demands of personal life.

Third, the party provided the social framework within which an effective professional stratum capable of governing in the name of the working class could be created. The party was to be the institutional arena within which specific policies and programs could be formulated and a leadership cadre groomed and trained. In addition, the party was also to be the primary avenue for political and cultural development of its mass constituency, creating, to this end, all manner of educational, cultural and self-help institutions.

Finally, the party, once assuming government power, would then use the legal, economic and military resources of the state to implement a program of social transformation. Since this program would be mightily resisted by the powers that be, the party in power would not only govern

society in the name of the great majority, but also would be a framework for continuously mobilizing popular energy to sustain the momentum of reform in the face of various kinds of conservative resistance.

Many of the weaknesses of this strategy were clear decades before the dramatic events of 1989. In the European parliamentary states, social democratic mass parties have never been able to win a majority by relying solely on a strategy of uniting the working class: The base of the working class has been too narrow to constitute a majority, and the class itself has been too variegated with respect to skill and sectoral difference to unite around a radical program. Accordingly, all social democratic parties have had to adopt moderate programs or otherwise reduce their ideological clarity and militancy in order to gain majority support.

In the Soviet bloc, the communist parties, exercising a monopoly of power, made bureaucratic, oligarchical party dictatorship synonymous with communism. But some 75 years ago, the German social scientist Robert Michels studied the German Social Democratic Party and observed that the representational character of the party, and the professionalization of its leadership, created an almost inescapable tendency toward "oligarchy." The more party leaders became career politicians, he observed, the more stake they had in maintaining their control of the party and using it as a vehicle for their own well-being. The result: bureaucratic, top-down control, the depoliticizing of the mass membership, the fostering of a privileged elite, corruptions of various kinds, and a growing tendency for the party to abandon its transformative goals. Soviet bloc Communists have effectively discredited the hegemonic party as truly representative of a mass base, but Michels' findings, written before World War I, suggest that hegemonic social democratic parties would not be immune to similar tendencies.[1]

Finally, the experience of seventy years has been that, in parliamentary democracies, party control of government does not equal party control of the state, nor does it provide the power to bring about socialist restructuring. Every move toward radical reform of a capitalist society by a governing socialist party has tended to result in destabilization of the economy by capitalists seeking to protect their investments against the threat of encroachment. The main state functions—the military, the administrative bureaucracy—are not readily controllable by a party just because it happens to win an election. The Leninist solution to this problem was to seize power through military means, use ruthless force to ensure that the state was in fact the vehicle of the party's will, and that the party itself could control the political discourse of the whole society. Such party dictatorship creates the opposite of the socialist ideal; in its absence, however, control of a state by a party has proven difficult if not impossible to maintain.

Indeed, mass hegemonic parties, whether of the Left, the Right or the center, seem everywhere to be disintegrating. I refer here to the collapse of the Eastern European Communist parties, to the decline of such Social Democratic parties as Labor in England and Israel, and also to the weakening of parties as varied in form and ideology as PRI in Mexico, the Liberal Democrats of Japan, Congress of India—and the Democratic Party in the US. All of these have seemed hegemonic, all have contributed to modernizing their societies

and to creating welfare state supports for their mass constituencies. That they were not vehicles of emancipatory aspiration has long been understood. But today they seem obsolete even as vehicles of power, for they seem to have lost their ability to maintain a majority base.

How might we account for the decomposition of the mass party? Here, I think, are some clues:

1. The globalization of the world economy weakens the capacity of mass parties to use the state as an instrument for allocating resources to the benefit of their constituencies. Welfare states face intensifying fiscal crisis, capital flow is beyond state control. Keynesian policies supporting high wages seem to conflict with the need to revitalize national competitiveness. The social democratic/welfare state program no longer seems sustainable, and promises made in its name lose credibility.

2. The very success of the mass parties is part of their undoing. Large numbers of workers now seek to protect relative advantage, resent taxation that supports the welfare state, hope for more opportunity to own things. Many now resist the party's traditional appeals to solidarity; programs promoting equality and social justice now seem threatening to some of those they once helped. Class identity breaks apart into many fragments.

3. All the mass parties established their dominance not only by being a voice for disadvantaged mass constituencies, but also by maintaining the silence of some of these (women, ethnic minorities, the least skilled, for example). One of the primary reasons for the decline of these parties is that previously silent groups are now mobilizing. As a result, the parties find themselves paralyzed, unable to offer a credible, majoritarian program that meets the needs

---

[1]Robert Michels, *Political Parties* (New York: Dover, 1959).

of both the relatively advantaged and the newly emergent groups that constitute their base. Because state-based strategies of social reform—whether called socialist, capitalist, corporatist or something else—appear to be politically and economically unviable; the parties whose programs were based on such strategies seem to have had their day.

DIVIDED WE FAIL

All during this century, Americans of the Left have hoped to see, one day, a party of the European type to represent their hopes and serve as a vehicle for working-class empowerment. For all these years, the fact that no such party formation emerged—the so-called American Exception—has been a source of deep feelings of failure among American Leftists, who have typically measured their efforts against the achievements of various of the European Lefts.

The main reason for the American Exception has been the enormous diversity of the American working class with respect to race and ethnicity. Because ethnic difference and competition became deeply intertwined with differences in life chances, American workers typically found left calls for class solidarity hopelessly impractical. Instead of supporting a left party, American workers joined political machines and unions based on ethnic solidarity and exclusion. Urban machines and craft unions were practical sources of power for the groups they represented. The forms of protection and security they provided reinforced the conception of freedom that was already culturally dominant in the US.

Freedom, in this equation, equals individual autonomy—as opposed to the left's

identification of freedom as the chance to participate directly in decisions about the common future. Moreover, these limited modes of worker empowerment fit well the typically American way of defining rationality as hard-headed practicality based on short-run advantage—as opposed to the Left's appeal to a reason based on the common good. Most Americans have never experienced a multi-ethnic framework of political solidarity. They instead have regarded the good society as one in which they have the opportunity make their own lives, rather than one in which they have the opportunity to shape their common history.

The dominant culture encourages Americans to place their hopes for fulfillment not on collective action in the public sphere, but on the results of their individual efforts within the spheres of work, education and family. Accordingly, rather than endorsing ideological appeals to overthrow the powers that be, Americans in the majority have preferred to live within what amounts to a contract with them—a contract that allows elites to rule in return for continuing provision of the material basis for a "normal" life.[2]

The privatism and accommodation of the American majority is, however, not simply the natural expression of American culture. Periods of mass political apathy and conservatism have always been preceded by mass mobilization and militancy aimed at winning protections, entitlements and rights previously denied. As a result, the specific terms of the American social contract have changed fundamentally from generation to generation, and our

---

[2]For a fuller development of this argument, see Richard Flacks, *Making History: The American Left and the American Mind* (New York: Columbia University Press, 1988).

shared conception of the requirements of "normal life" has greatly expanded. In spite of our failure to create a mass-based European-style Left party in the US, our history has been shaped by the fact that groups disadvantaged by a given contract have, over time, struggled to rewrite the contract so that their rights will be taken into account. The absence of a mass party has not meant the absence of democratic social action.

THE MOVEMENT IS THE MESSAGE

In the United States, the most meaningful progressive political change has consistently come about not through a Left party, but through mass-based social movements. Yet American Leftists for generations have had a contradictory attitude toward their participation in movements. On the one hand, when they ask themselves what they have accomplished in their political lives, overwhelmingly they respond by taking satisfaction from the historic changes wrought by the movements they have helped: the rights that have been won, the entitlements achieved, the ways in which protest has opened up the culture to new voices and expanded the horizons of exploited and oppressed groups. But when conscious Leftists try to interpret the long-term meaning of their activity, they have an overwhelming tendency to view these movements as something less than the Real Thing. The Real Thing, they cannot help but feel, is a unified, class-based movement whose center is a party capable of taking power. The fragmented, nonideological movements of the US—these are at best rehearsals for the revolution, the base from which more "advanced" consciousness and action can be launched.

This attitude toward movements, we can now more clearly see, was delusory. The global decomposition of the Party strategy ought to persuade us of what, in fact, has always been the case: If the Left is understood as a cumulating struggle for the democratization of society, then social movements themselves are the real embodiment of the Left tradition.

Movements rather than parties are more likely to be vehicles of popular voice. Because the party by its nature is set up to represent, it reinforces the passivity of most members (though to be sure it may also serve as a socializing and educative framework for large numbers). Movements, on the other hand, because of their relatively spontaneous, uninstitutionalized character, because they are dependent on high levels of direct participation by large numbers, because they are implemented in manifold activities at a micro level, because they are moments in which previously inarticulate actors find voice and public visibility—for all these sorts of reasons, movements are the closest thing we have, in practice, to authentic popular participation. It is in moments of collective defiance that the possibility for democracy achieves some concrete reality, and lagging democratic faith gets renewed.

After decades in which the American Left looked to Europe for models of advanced action, the tables have turned. If we want to know what can fill the vacuum created by the decline of the popularly based party, we can look to the US experience, where such a vacuum has been a permanent political reality. What we learn from our experience is that social movements, representing a range of distinct interests and identities, constitute the primary vehicle of democratic expression. Indeed, such movement is now taking hold globally as the key to democratic transformation.

INSIDE OR OUTSIDE THE PARTY?

Movements act in the streets, in civil society. They are, by definition, extra-parliamentary, using means of expression and power other than those available within "straight-ahead" politics. But the American experience shows that movements must also interact with the state, not only as a source of pressure on elites from outside, but as a vehicle for achieving goals. Movement demands have to be legislated; rights claimed have to be legitimated. Moreover, the high intensity of mass action is not sustainable indefinitely; movement members need to go home, they want to live in the space their actions helped create. And in order to carry on daily life, they need effective political representation.

As a result, American movements have sought entry into the electoral area. After some decades of experimentation with efforts to create their own parties—of which the Populists, the Socialist Party of Eugene Debs, the LaFollette Progressive Party of the '20s are prime examples on the national level—movements by and large have, especially since the New Deal era, instead sought influence inside the Democratic Party. The movement effort to penetrate the Democratic Party has been going on now for 50 years. It was spearheaded by the labor movement in the '30s and '40s, followed by the civil rights movement in the '60s, by the women's movement in the '70s, by gays, environmentalists, anti-nuclear groups in the years since. Movement strategies have included the following elements:

- the construction of movement-controlled state and local organizations to back candidates especially favorable to movement interests;

- election of delegates to party conventions to directly influence candidate selection and platform planks;
- mobilization to demand change of party rules to reduce power of professional politicians and party machines, and to require representation in party decision making of women, minorities and other under-represented constituencies;
- most recently, formation of national movement–based structures, parallel to the official party structures to influence selection of presidential candidates and party directions.

The Democratic Party has been significantly reshaped by the strategies and claims of diverse movements demanding place. Labor leadership succeeded in gaining access to the New Deal Administration, labor exercised considerable control over a few key state party structures in the '50s, and labor forged some fruitful alliances with key Democratic politicians. In the aftermath of the '60s, the party finally was forced to break the power of white supremacist Dixiecrats and to open its internal procedures so that blacks and other minorities could gain direct access. Machine control over urban party organizations was broken under the pressure of civil rights and Left-liberal mobilizations. By the end of the '70s the party leadership both locally and, to some extent nationally, included sizable contingents drawn from the ranks of civil rights, women's, anti-war and labor movements.

Today, every major movement is both outside and inside the Democratic Party. Movements succeeded in opening sufficient space within the party for many of their distinctive agendas to be voiced, and to be partially endorsed. But the party's leadership remains in the hands of professional party politicians, power brokers and financial supporters. The result is that the party is fundamentally at odds with itself— and is stalemated, paralyzed and stagnating. From the perspective of party professionals and professional politicians, the pressures of the labor, black, women's, environmentalist and other movements threaten the party's organizational efficacy while alienating the support of millions of "moderate" voters (i.e., middle- and working-class voters who are predominantly white, male and middle aged). From the perspective of the movements, the party's professional leadership appears increasingly rudderless, lacking in will and imagination, often cynically using movement symbols to avoid substantive change.

THE "LOCAL LEVEL"

Meanwhile, movement activists have had some success in influencing electoral politics and governmental policy at the level of city and state politics. In the aftermath of the '60s student movement, considerable numbers of New Left activists came to see that the campus constituency as such was a limited vehicle for advancing far-reaching social change. The university, despite its significance in "post-industrial society," remained too isolated from the political and cultural mainstream; the student movement, despite its capacity for dramatic and effective disruption, could not achieve its hopes for basic social change without substantial links to potential majorities. And, from a biographical perspective, student activists quickly learned, as they moved beyond the university, that the styles, issues and perspectives of the wider world were quite different from those appropriate to the campus.

Since the US lacked a national Left party framework that could absorb new Leftists,

many activists embarked on efforts to "organize at the local level"— focusing on issues rooted in the experienced threats and grievances found there. The emergence in the '70s of movements with broader constituencies more firmly located in community life—feminism, environmentalism, gay liberation, and the anti-nuclear movements—had much to do with these organizing efforts.

The localist emphasis of post-'60s activism resulted in part from the limited resources available—most particularly the absence of any central organizational authority that could direct a national strategy. But localism derived also from the ideological perspectives dominating the New Left—the emphasis on participatory democracy, on decentralization, on human scale. The feminist critique of patriarchal leadership encouraged male as well as female activists to work in self-effacing, person-to-person ways—rather than in the self-promoting, top-down manner that "national" politics required.

The various new movements are, accordingly, structured in highly decentralized ways. Although each of them contains national organizational structures, these have relatively little to do with the manifold movement activities that have evolved over the last twenty years—most of which revolve around issues that arise in particular regions, communities, neighborhoods, and workplaces. The "environmental movement" is in fact best understood as constructed out of a host of seemingly disparate local protests and projects: struggles over land use, urban development, population growth, toxic waste disposal, nuclear power, neighborhood preservation, defense of traditional culture, occupational hazards. In each case, members of a local community act in response to a threat—often making use of the resources (language, know-how, material support, etc.) made available by the formal organizations of the national movement.

These local protests have not infrequently succeeded in deflecting the particular threats that initially sparked them, or in achieving various sorts of accommodations and ameliorations. But locally based movement activity rather quickly developed a certain strategic thrust that went beyond the merely reactive. All the new social movements have been struggling for local institutional change that would enable them to exercise direct voice in governmental and institutional policy making.

Beginning in the early '70s, new social movement activists, especially in towns with sizable university populations, embarked on a strategy of competing directly for local office. This effort has widened, and, to some degree, has resulted in local "rainbow" coalition strategies—in which blacks, Hispanics, feminists, environmentalists, gays and peace constituencies have linked forces in electoral contests. Today, progressive coalitions have come to local power in a variety of places rather different from the "progressive" university town. Indeed, there is probably no major city in the country whose local politics has been unaffected by the separate and combined efforts of movement activists to win at least a piece of local power—most especially in the many municipalities in which local elections are nonpartisan.

I will not go into detail about the substantive programmatic reforms that such local efforts have attempted, nor try to evaluate the results. However, it is perhaps a fair generalization to say that the most successful achievements have been those involving symbolic and legal reform rather than material reallocations—more "diversity" and "affirmative action" in governmental staff appointments (so more minorities

and women now occupy administrative and advisory positions), more community recognition of minority identity claims (the Martin Luther King holiday was an early success in this regard; extension of anti-discrimination principles to gays would be another); support for movement-based human service activities (city subsidies for a variety of medical, counselling, legal and educational services—but in the 80s and early 90s, budgetary crunches hit these particularly hard).[3]

Perhaps the most interesting types of reform, however, were those that compelled public accountability and voice with respect to decisions that were previously reserved for specialized or elite arenas. The biggest local gain of the environmental movement in California has been the Environmental Quality Act, which requires that all local development be subject to Environmental Impact Review. The EIR process compels a public weighing of social costs, provides an arena for public testimony, and gives an opportunity for public negotiation of "mitigations" with respect to all changes of land use. This process is a prime example of the way in which governmental procedures such as mandatory public hearings can provide community movements with significant opportunities for mobilization, public education, the development of expertise and the exercise of community leadership. From the perspective of public authority, the process is designed to get movements "off the streets" and into the bureaucratic structure. In

---

[3]The rise of progressive electoral coalitions has been described in Pierre Clavel, *The Progressive City* (New Brunswick, NJ: Rutgers University Press, 1986). Studies of two key cases: Mark Kann, *Middle Class Radicalism in Santa Monica* (Philadelphia: Temple University Press, 1986); W. J. Conroy, *Challenging the Boundaries of Reform: Socialism in Burlington* (Philadelphia: Temple University Press, 1990).

practice, however, it provides a degree of information and opportunity for voice not previously available—especially if those administering the hearing processes were elected with the backing of the movement.

In general, in the last twenty years, a variety of mechanisms embodying principles of public review and participatory planning have emerged in American community and institutional life. In addition to land use and related environmental decisions, similar mechanisms exist in some locales with respect to job hiring and promotion policies, police practices, health service provision, provision of services for the aged, or public education (where such decentralized, participatory mechanisms have a long tradition in the US), for example.

These mechanisms have considerably changed the structure of power at the local level in the US. But the power gained by movements is a limited one; American communities are now places where grassroots groups have some ability to veto or modify unwanted decisions. But the power to veto is purely reactive: We have precious few institutional mechanisms for promoting economic redistribution, for effectively controlling the flow of capital or for effectively determining the planning processes that shape their community's future. The real sources of initiative in American communities are outside the locality—the megacorporation and the national state—and it is these sources that are obviously beyond the reach of locally based mobilization.

THE SEARCH FOR NATIONAL COALITIONS

The national political stalemate, and the limits of local initiative, together define the political situation shared by all of the social movements related to the Left tradition.

Each of the movements—both "new" and "old"—has succeeded in advancing parts of its particular agenda—for certain rights, for certain kinds of political representation and cultural recognition. As a result, a society that earlier denied workers elementary rights to organize, denied blacks and women elementary rights to vote, and whose towns and cities were dominated by tight circles of the economically powerful now more closely approximates the model of a politico-cultural pluralism.

The most evident failure of the movements during the last twenty years, however, has been their inability to meet the material needs of their most disadvantaged constituents. The labor movement presents the most glaring inventory of recent failure, having lost much of its power to protect gains previously won for its members, let alone advancing claims of unorganized workers. The black movement's advances in local power and cultural recognition, and the improved material position of the black middle class, has been accompanied by a frightening deterioration in the life chances of blacks in the "inner city." The gains of the women's movement have not prevented the feminization of poverty. I doubt that many activists, 15–20 years ago, would have expected the degree to which social inequality has deepened and social injustice grown.

In recent years, movement activists have worked toward coalition to find the numbers and leverage necessary to advance a credible program—largely to defend against the conservative efforts to destroy the rights and reverse the gains won in earlier struggles. Today, there is widespread understanding in activist circles of the need to go beyond such reactive and defensive alliances—a recognition that the effects of right-wing political dominance are a burden of unmet needs shared by all of the movement constituencies.

Health care is an example frequently discussed. The American medical system continues to be dominated by a market logic; as a result millions of people remain unable to afford an accepted standard of health care. AIDS has politicized the gay community around health care issues, while it has also exacerbated the crisis in health care provision in all major cities. The nature of the health care system is of obvious relevance to the labor movement, to minority community movements, to the women's movement and to environmentalists—and it is a matter of central concern to millions of relatively unmobilized "middle-class" Americans. Indeed, because the crisis in medical costs deeply worries the corporate sector, there is a good chance that a national coalition, beyond the Clinton initiative, to reform the health system will win some substantive gains.

The same logic is being suggested with respect to several other areas of social crisis—housing, education, and the toxicity of the environment are usually cited. Not only are these areas of evident "national decline," the effects of which are part of the daily, close-up experience of millions—they are also areas of potential movement alliance, since, in each case, already-mobilized constituencies are likely to be particularly impacted. Each of these issues can be defined, not only as general social problems, but as problems having a particular impact on people of color, on workers, on women. It is important to recognize that each of these is an area of budgetary deficiency; but a program of reform would contain more than mere increases in dollars spent. The change needed in each area entails a fundamental restructuring of how funds are allocated and priorities set, and of the authority relations governing these services.

Increasingly, voices within the national Establishment are, in the post-Reagan period, addressing the major social costs that have accrued as a result of "free market" policies. In the last two years, we have heard a lot of talk about the need to make reform in health care, education, housing and the environment. But, despite shifts in elite sentiment concerning social reform, it is evident that little substantive change will result without large-scale popular mobilization.

For all of these reasons, it is now practical to conceive of the development of a political program for domestic reform that could serve as a shared agenda for the major social movement leadership. Such an agenda could be a rallying point for national mobilization, for grassroots organizing, for local political candidacies, and for the mounting of a national electoral drive. . . .

But the promise of a revived climate of state-based social reform is limited. We cannot hope a new movement-based coalition will bring back the New Deal, or the '60s. . . .

The most promising immediate prospect for a way to finance a new social agenda is the peace dividend that ought to accrue with the end of the Cold War. Any coalition for reform must have as its central argument that we now have a chance to meet unmet needs precisely because we are being released from the burden of militarization. But the expected peace dividend seems to be vanishing as a result of the Gulf crisis and the shot in the arm that the "Iraq threat" has provided to the national security apparatus. Meanwhile, the S&L scandal and the looming fear of further banking disaster—as well as the continuing resistance to tax increases in the middle class—represent serious barriers to the enactment of national programs that require a restructuring of budgetary priorities and new public sector investments. Still, we must try to mobilize for a coalition program aimed at domestic reform, in part because of the possibility that some programs that can make a difference will emerge, and in part because such mobilization is the most promising way to forge working coalitions among social movements. Moreover, it would be defeatist to believe that the military industrial complex has already won the struggle for the peace dividend, or that populist anger cannot be directed at genuine social injustice (and away from middle-class resentment of the poor).

We need, however, to think beyond a relatively short-run program of reform. It seems necessary and possible to construct a shared vision of social transformation that is rooted not only in the shared needs of movement constituencies, but in the underlying common logic of grassroots movements. That common logic rests on the democratic axiom. Implicit in the demands and activities of all the great movements, both "new" and "old," has been the demand that society be structured so people can shape the conditions of their lives. The labor movement did not struggle simply for better wages and working conditions—it struggled for workers' voice, for the right to organize and to determine the conditions of their employment. The black movement did not campaign simply for equal treatment—its central demand always has revolved around empowerment. Feminism is not just about gender equality—it aims at the fundamental restructuring of power relations between the sexes. And both the peace and environmental movements are fundamentally efforts to make public decision-making fully accountable to those affected by it, and to give people in their communities the chance to control their own futures.

WHERE TO GO AFTER THE PARTY?

If we can no longer rely on the hope for a party to represent the people, or on a nation state to embody the people's hopes, then we have to make concretely realizable a vision of a society organized so that people have some chance to express themselves directly, and to hold those who speak for them accountable. Perhaps the answer to the domination of megacorporations and the disintegration of the nation-state is to enable people to find power in and through communities.

The logic of social movements suggests that the nature of the state needs to be fundamentally reconceived. If democratization were taken as the guiding principle of political action and the primary standard of political legitimation, the state would be seen not as the center of rule-making and the source of social welfare, but as a vehicle for community empowerment and local control. *We need to think of the national state not as the source of initiative and control, not as the vehicle for solutions of problems, but principally as the potential source of capital and law that would enable people to solve their problems at the level of the community.*

Indeed, such a function may be the only viable one remaining for the national state in a society that is both globalizing and decentering. It may seem absurd to reimagine the central state as a vehicle for decentralization. But the American experience, with its federal constitution and traditions of local control, provides some examples of how such a process could work. Here I will only briefly allude to some of the kinds of federal policies that would support the logic of democratic decentralization:

Legal Recognition of Movement-based Organization

An example in practice is the Wagner Act of 1936, which guaranteed workers' rights to form unions and to strike, and which established machinery requiring collective bargaining between recognized unions and employers. Similar kinds of organizing and bargaining rights have been proposed for public utility consumers, neighborhood organizations, tenant unions. A number of federal programs have required participation in planning service delivery on the part of client groups—such provisions have encouraged the growth of movement organizations among the urban poor, or among senior citizens, for example. The empowerment of "clients" and communities in making policy at the community level will have to be an essential ingredient in any new programs for reform in health care, education, housing and other extensions of the welfare state.

Federal Subsidy for Community Organization

Again, there is precedent, in such programs as VISTA, and the War on Poverty, as well as in a variety of other direct and indirect programs.

Legal and Material Support for Locally Based "Impact Review"

On the model of the Environmental Impact Review, communities could require a wide range of social accounting with respect to a variety of publicly relevant decisions, broadening the concept to include "economic" and "social" as well as "environmental" impacts. Such review could be federally mandated, and federal programs could assist community-based groups by providing technical expertise, research support, and the like.

Federal "Block" Grants

A necessary function of central authority is redistribution; decentralization is bound to result in manifold inequalities. Rather than administer such transfers, subsidies and reallocations through centralized bureaucracies with elaborate rules and programmatic targets, a decentralizing approach is embodied in the idea of block grants (worth considering despite its Nixonian origins)—unencumbered funds provided to communities on the basis of need-based formulas with the use of these funds to be fought out politically at community or regional level.

Federal Allocation of Capital

Community empowerment requires the ability to create community-owned, locally based enterprises where "private," market-based investments do not meet needs defined by the community. Community ownership of public utilities can support local autonomy, provide an infrastructure for "soft" energy alternatives, and generate revenues for local use. Community investment in job-creating enterprises can be a response to the loss of private investment. Community provision of services can offset loss of services from cost-cutting private firms. The national government is a necessary source for capital and expertise for the initiation of such enterprise. A national, public bank could be such a mechanism for social investment.[4]

I do not intend to put forward specific proposals here; my point instead is to illustrate how central government could pro-

---

[4]One of the best sources of ideas and schemes—some derived from other societies—using government as a source of capital for communities is Martin Carnoy & Derek Shearer, *Economic Democracy* (Amonk, NY: M. E. Sharpe, 1980). An important recent statement of a vision of community based economic democracy is Gar Alperovitz, "Building a Living Democracy," *Sojourners*, July 1990, pp. 11–23.

vide the legal, material and technical foundation for various forms of local, participatory democracy.

The outcome of such a process of decentralization would be the institutionalization of social movements as frameworks of everyday popular participation in governance, community planning, and regional resource allocation. Such institutionalization seems to me to be inherent in the logic of the movements. The drive to transform the state in such a direction could be an effective basis for movement alliance. Now that the Party is over, the people themselves are going to have to take responsibility for their collective futures. The movements—as social formations, as repositories of social vision, as training grounds for political competence—seem destined to be the vehicles for such responsibility.

PART THREE
ADMINISTRATION AND MANAGEMENT

Introduction

THE PLACE OF ADMINISTRATION

The administration perspective recognizes that community intervention, as well as the other methods of social work, is practiced overwhelmingly within organizations (Lauffer, 1984; Vinter and Kish, 1984). The functioning of those organizations is a necessary, but not sufficient, condition to effective and efficient intervention by the community practitioner. Administration has, after some uncertainty, come to be recognized as a legitimate method of social work practice in and of itself. The journal, *Administration in Social Work,* publishes a range of relevant articles in this area. Often, community practitioners and administrators are one and the same person, and it is the role, not the person, that shifts. Increasingly, schools of social work offer specialties in administration, and some schools of social work are developing joint ventures with schools of business for these purposes. In addition, some schools of management, such as Yale and UCLA, have trained for the "nonprofit" sector, which includes the gamut of human service agencies.

Organizational structures comprise the *vehicles* through which services and programs are mounted and implemented. The organization provides resources, legitimation, personnel, knowhow, "goodwill," and other instrumentalities through which action is articulated.

Organizations are often the *targets* of professional activity, as well. Frequently the practitioner's goal is the modification of policies or practice of some external organization or institution in the community. Service agencies seek clients and information from other organizations and make reciprocal referrals. Planning agencies coordinate programs among agencies. Locality development agencies bring community agencies into deliberative processes with citizens' groups in order to assess community needs and collaborate in developing ameliorative actions. Social action organizations often pressure organizational entities to drop certain policies and programs that are viewed as detrimental, or to adopt new ones.

Organizations also serve in many instances as the *context* within which practice takes place. An existing pattern of cooperation and communication among organizations may lead a change organization into one mode of action (working on an equal level with all organizations); a climate of distrust and conflict will suggest a different *modus operandi* (working with different factions). Likewise, if agencies generally exhibit high levels of professionalism or have an ample resource base, the form of action by a change agency will be different than when agencies have a low level of expertise or are poor in resources available for programmatic purposes.

If organization is the framework within which action takes place, administration is the practice of running, developing and changing organizations. Administration is the means through which organizations are shaped and directed to pursue particular goals and carry out particular strategies and programs. While administration is viewed as a delineated method of practice, it also cuts across all other methods of practice. Administration provides a basis for steering the work of direct-service organizations. It does the same for all three modes of community intervention, whether social planning and policy, locality development, or social action. Tasks from the rendering of clinical aid to individual clients through to the design of legislation policy at the federal level are typically articulated through organizational processes having a significant administrative component.

Particular elements of administration can be singled out to identify facets of the practice. Parsons (1960) has identified these, respectively, as institutional, managerial, and technical levels of administrative function. First of all, there is the institutional level, the matter of choosing the goals that an organization should pursue and determining the strategies and programs that are consistent with attaining those goals. This requires the ability to assess community needs, design programs, maintain community relationships, and facilitate consensus among organizational constituencies. Next, there is the managerial level, involving the execution of broad strategies in an effective way. The tasks of implementation require the ability to mobilize people, information, and resources so as to make an impact on the needs or problems being addressed. Finally, there are the technical tasks of delivering programs and structuring organizational operations. These tasks focus on the mechanics of delivering services to clients and ensuring that there are enough supplies to run the agency, getting the right staff people to the right place at the right time, acquiring and keeping in good condition the equipment and facilities necessary for program implementation, and so forth.

ADMINISTRATION AND COMMUNITY INTERVENTION

Having described the administrative function, it would be useful to examine it cross-sectionally, employing some of the practice variables that were used to analyze different modes of community intervention. We will do this type of analysis suggestively, selecting out a few practice variables to illustrate the utility of the approach.

Looking first at **characteristic change tactics and techniques,** in *community intervention* different modes lean in the direction of either consensus or conflict. Locality development relies heavily on the former, and social action on the latter. *Administrative practice* often involves the use of formal authority as a mode of influence, and generally favors stability, goodwill, economy, and efficiency of operation. However, this is a preferred rather than an "ordained" tactic.

Examining **practitioner roles** provides interesting insights. *Community intervention practitioners* function in the role of enabler, fact-gatherer, and activist, depending on the given model of action. *Administrative practitioners* tend to rely on their position as an authority figure in a core role, such as executive, associate executive manager, or supervisor.

The **medium of change** shows variations in emphasis. Grassroots *community practitioners* work with many types of groups—block clubs, associations of all kinds, committees and task forces, and the like. Planners also deal with data and formal organizations. For *administrative practitioners* the key medium is the human service agency itself. Changes in structures and programs within the agency are the media through which change typically occurs.

In each perspective there is a somewhat different orientation toward the **power structure.** *Community practitioners* have variable relationships to the power structure, from employees and allies to militant adversaries, depending on the strategic approach. From an *administrative practice* point of view, the chief executive often *is* the power structure as the implementor of programs and services and a key authority figure. It is interesting that sometimes practitioners who become administrators find themselves the targets of the very techniques they had used against their predecessors.

The conception of the **beneficiary role** varies within each perspective. In *community practice,* beneficiary roles are varied, from active to passive, depending on the approach employed. *Administrative practitioners,* particularly in service-providing agencies, tend to view beneficiaries in the same way as planners, that is, as consumers of the agency's product. In this sense, consumer/clients are subordinate participants in the organizational system. In administration, then, often the beneficiary role is passive, entailing recipient forms of participation. The consumer may be active in seeking and reacting to services, but is typically not active in determining the form and availability of services. Progressive agencies vary in this by encouraging the latter form of participation.

Beyond these basic comments about administrative practice, there are four other matters that merit discussion here. These will be treated sequentially and include effectiveness in managing organizations, participation and teamwork among staff, organizational culture, and program development in organizations.

EFFECTIVENESS

If organizational structure is critical to achieving human service objectives, then the effective conduct of management tasks in these structures is a concomitant of optimal outcomes. Effectiveness in the typical dictionary meaning has two aspects. One connotes the producing of the results that are intended, or, in another sense, becoming operative in carrying out the organization's mission. This broadly separates success from failure. The other meaning suggests reaching a level of performance that is striking or impressive—stretching competency to its maximum limits. These two aspects separate success from meritorious achievement, and we will be concerned with both in this discussion, with a leaning toward the optimization notion.

In his contribution to this volume, Patti dissects the organizational effectiveness concept and analyzes its six dimensions. He starts with the task of constructing a value-oriented mission that provides a valid and meaningful purpose for the organization. Infusing these values, symbols, and beliefs is an ongoing role for the effective administrator. With a significant goal in place, it is essential to establish intervention technologies that will meet the needs of clients and constituencies. This involves adapting or designing appropriate strategies and techniques that have a high probability of attaining these service goals.

From the outset, criteria need to be specified for measuring effectiveness outcomes. Where several different goals are being pursued, priorities have to be established. It is important to distinguish between performance outcomes of agency effort (were agency programs actually put in place?) vs. service outcomes that relate to objective benefits that are brought into being for clients and constituents (did clients actually receive better housing accommodations?).

Next, it is important to apply standards that signify a sufficiently high level of outcome attainment. This is the place where tacit success and merit can part ways. What number or percentage of homeless individuals receiving shelter is acceptable? What percentage of decrease in reported cases of child abuse should allow for an agency's sense of accomplishment?

At this point we turn to the nitty-gritty of administrative practices and organizational arrangements. The concern here is with on-the-job performance of workers in the agency and the supervisory and other back-up support that they receive. A final factor that falls under Patti's scheme is the environmental support received for the agency's programs. The acquisition of external support can be an independent factor examined in assessing an agency's program. On the other hand, it might be assumed that if client and constituent outcome are attained at a sufficient level (the central criterion of effectiveness), then adequate external resources must have been acquired.

Effectiveness, leadership, and efficiency have a vital interrelationship. One of the ways that administrators attain merit is through a simultaneous focus on management and leadership. Management entails developing a smoothly running "shop," one that gets things done, motivates workers in an appropriate way, and smoothly executes the scheduling and delegating of work. Being able to accomplish these tasks in an excellent manner is key to management quality.

However, administrators have to be leaders as well. Just keeping the store open is not enough. The administrator has to suggest new directions for the agency, move the thinking of the staff into innovative areas and assist in reconfiguring the agency position as other agencies come into being. Leadership involves visioning and risk-taking.

As one moves to improve the agency, opportunities for change *of* the system and change *in* the system often conflict. Changes in the system relate to managerial acumen—offering the same kinds of services more quickly, in a more focused way, and perhaps in a cheaper way. But effectiveness also links to changes of the system and to managerial creativity. It means adding new subsystems, dropping old ones, or fundamentally reconfiguring the ones in place. This requires leadership.

Efficiency has to be considered as well. It is the element that is often associated with good management. Efficiency means doing things right; effectiveness means doing the right thing. Management tends to work toward improvements along the lines of being more economical and rapid in accomplishing agency tasks. Effectiveness focuses more on choosing *what it is* that the agency should emphasize. Administrators need to be aware of both the demands of efficiency and the requirements of effectiveness. These matters and others that follow are elaborated in a forthcoming volume by John E. Tropman entitled *The Maestro Manager.*

PARTICIPATION AND TEAMWORK

By organizational leadership we do not mean to convey the notion of domination and control of all functions by the executive. Encouraging participation and team performance, instead, is widely recognized as the mark of the enlightened and effective administrator. For example, building an administrative team allows for the utilization of the collective skills and perspectives of various relevant agency members, thus providing balance and scope in the leadership realm. By delegating some leadership tasks, chief administrators are able to concentrate on the roles most requiring their attention, or the ones that they have the greatest competency in performing.

In his contribution, Sager discusses means of fostering participation and improving communication in agency settings, among other administrative roles. He focuses particularly on staff participation in decision making, pointing out that there are a variety of different forms of participation—formal or informal, voluntary or compulsory, and direct or indirect. He also points out that research on participation reveals varied and inconclusive findings regarding the effects on productivity. Therefore, participation needs to be linked consciously to purposes that participation has been found empirically to advance. For example, having a role and stake in decisions is important when involvement by staff is critical for implementation of these decisions. Also, having trained and effective facilitators and group leaders is essential, as is the use of proper group problem-solving techniques.

Regarding communication, Sager points out that people at the top and the bottom of the organization are the richest sources of information, but the types of information they have differs. Operational level staff are in intimate touch with problems of operations and direct service, whereas executives know a great deal about political, legal and financial matters. Information needs to be transmitted in both directions, and programs are available to improve listening and communicating skills of managers and workers. Simply instituting ways for having supervisors learn more about what workers do and the stresses they encounter is a way to enhance necessary communication. Sager addresses other issues beyond participation, including job design and staff training, altering structures, and offering incentives.

ORGANIZATIONAL CULTURE

The culture of the organization provides the social climate in which the executive and the staff operate in carrying out their functions, and it also presents a target for administrative change. It is sometimes necessary to adjust or revamp the climate in order to construct a better atmosphere in which to implement the mission of the agency.

There are many definitions of and approaches to organizational culture. One of the most helpful for community practitioners is developed by Robert Quinn (1989) in his book, *Beyond Rational Management.* Not only is the conceptualization helpful, but Quinn provides materials that allow practitioners to assess their own orientation and that of their agency (available in an easy-to-administer booklet called the PRISM SET).

Quinn identifies two key dimensions—flexibility versus control, and internal versus external focus. These can be organized into four organizational culture types—the clan culture, the hierarchy culture, the market culture, and the adhocracy. The accompanying model illustrates his thinking.

FLEXIBILITY

Clan	**Adhocracy**
Internal Focus	External Focus
Hierarchy	**Market**

CONTROL

The clan style is one that emphasizes membership and connection, but can create an "us" versus "them" mentality. The hierarchy is one that emphasizes rules and procedures, and provides regularity, but can lead to what Quinn calls "trivial rigor" (what Robert Merton has termed the "means ritualism" of the "bureaucratic personality"). The market style emphasizes accomplishment and results, but may also have an excessive focus on short-term results and lack human compassion. And, finally, the adhocracy is a style that emphasizes ideas and creativity, but may result in much chaos.

There are a few key points to stress here. First, organizations, and persons, have dominant "styles." Some aspects of style are positive, but, as just suggested, "too much" of any style can turn a strength into a weakness. Thus, some attention to all styles is needed for an organization to be successful. If a specific administrator does not have all of them, and it is likely that she or he will not, then the administrative team will be especially valuable in providing scope. It is vitally important for administrators to be aware of culture, and to be sure that a balance of cultural components is maintained. Social work agencies tend to fall into the clan and hierarchy cultures, and thus need to take special care to draw upon market (results-oriented) and adhocratic (idea-based) cultural styles.

An interesting portrayal of organizational culture is given in the selection on Shanti, which was an agency established to deal with the AIDS crisis. As an alternative type of service structure, Shanti was serviced heavily by volunteers, carried out its business in an informal atmosphere, and emphasized self-care. It deliberately set out to establish an atmosphere that was different from traditional services.

The value system emphasized collective and equalitarian decision making. Since there were no paid staff, there was an absence of a hierarchical, chain-of-command, authority structure, and other forms and means of functioning had to be invented. All organizational and administrative decisions were made by consensus, with the widest participation of all agency constituencies. There was also a commitment to the fullest personal development of all participants—clients and volunteers—in contrast to more instrumental and delimited service aims. The heavy reliance on volunteers led to an atmosphere in which burnout was common, together with a great deal of turnover among service providers.

In Quinn's framework, this is an organization that can be characterized in large measure in terms of clan and adhocracy cultural attributes. The several problems that were identified in the case study suggest that some elements of hierarchy and market, in measured proportions, might provide necessary balance for the organization.

PROGRAM DEVELOPMENT

Program development is an important aspect of administrative practice within agencies and has a good deal of overlap with the social planning aspects of community intervention. Program development provides a means for systematically designing and structuring organizational interventions to meet the needs of clients. As with problem solving more generally, as discussed in Part One, it starts with assessment of need, specifies objectives, lays out the mechanisms of implementation, and provides for monitoring and evaluation.

A comprehensive approach to program development is presented in the selection by Hasenfeld. He treats the various aspects of problem solving identified above, but in addition focuses on some aspects that are somewhat unique to administrative program planning. For example, specifying the program technology for aiding the elderly may involve choosing between a meals-on-wheels approach, cooperative cooking arrangements, or a hot-lunch program at neighborhood schools. Assuming that the meals-on-wheels concept is selected on the basis of valid criteria (its known success elsewhere, available resources, client receptivity), the necessary tasks of implementation need to be identified. This may mean organizing volunteers with cars, arranging weekly visits by a nutritionist, preparing the meals in the kitchen offered by a neighborhood church, and the like.

To implement the program the personnel factor must be addressed: Appropriate staff must be recruited and trained. For example, it might be necessary to hire a nutritionist to guide or oversee meal preparation in the programs that were suggested above. Next comes the question of developing an appropriate delivery structure. Activities that occur simultaneously or in close proximity might well be grouped together. Those that have different time and space requirements ordinarily should be grouped separately. Routine and nonroutine tasks need to be treated differentially.

There are also certain program-development activities that have an external focus and are similar to those conducted in social planning. Hasenfeld includes among these mobilizing support for the service, acquiring financial resources, and developing interagency relationships.

Clearly, people holding an administrative position can perform community intervention functions in the course of their work. There exists the possibility of role differentiation within the position. As an example, an administrator might decide that the best way to enhance service to clients in a clinically oriented program is to bring them together to see if they wish to form an action group to lobby for legislation geared to improving their situation. This community intervention piece of work could produce material benefits (funds to allow more frequent contact with counselors) as well as psychological benefits (greater feelings of mastery resulting from these empowerment actions). The relationship between administration and community intervention is varied and complex, but can be carried out in a way that is mutually reinforcing and cumulative in impact.

—Jack Rothman
John E. Tropman

REFERENCES

Hasenfeld, Yeheskel. *Human Service Organizations.* Englewood Cliffs, NJ: Prentice-Hall, 1983.

Lauffer, Armand. *Strategies of Marketing.* New York: Basic Books, 1984.

Parsons, Talcott. *Sources and Process in Modern Societies.* New York: Free Press, 1960.

Quinn, Robert. *Beyond Rational Management.* San Francisco: Jossey-Bass, 1989.

Vinter, Robert D., and Rhea Kish. *Budgeting for Non-Profit Organizations.* New York: Free Press, 1984.

25.

Rino J. Patti

MANAGING FOR SERVICE EFFECTIVENESS IN SOCIAL WELFARE ORGANIZATIONS

Although social work administration recently has become more sophisticated technically, little is known about how managers in these settings facilitate the delivery of effective service to clients. In this article, the author discusses a rationale for and an outline of an approach to social welfare administration in optimizing service outcomes for clients. More precisely, this article addresses the relationship between managerial behaviors and the provision of high quality, effective services to clients. The approach is based on the behaviors, attitudes, practices, and strategies exhibited by administrators. These factors significantly, though not singularly, affect the manner in which social services are delivered and the outcome.

DEFINITION OF SERVICE EFFECTIVENESS

What is service effectiveness and how does it differ from other organizational outcomes that concern administrators? *Service effectiveness* is reflected in three not necessarily related aspects of performance. The first aspect of performance relates to the agency's success in generating changes for its client systems. Cases involving individuals and families may require changes in behaviors, cognitions, attitudes, skill levels, alterations in social status, or modifications in undesirable environmental circumstances. On the other

hand, cases that involve organizations as client systems may require measures to improve planning or coordination, to develop new services, or to reallocate resources to new programs or client populations. The second aspect of performance is service quality, or how competently the organization implements those methods and techniques necessary for achieving service objectives. The quality of service can be measured against standards prescribed by the agency, standards advanced in the professional literature, or standards promulgated by regulatory bodies. The timeliness, consistency, accessibility, humanness, or technical proficiency of a service are examples of quality. Client satisfaction, the third aspect of performance, concerns consumers' assessment of the quality and effect of the services. Under some circumstances, client satisfaction also can be inferred from data on attendance rates, premature terminations, reapplications for service, and referrals from former clients.

These outcome variables are distinguishable from the following four other agency performance indicators: (1) output, or the quantity of service provided and whether it is delivered to the appropriate clientele, (2) productivity, or the efficient use of resources to generate the services, (3) resource acquisition, or the agency's success in obtaining resources from the environment, and (4) minimization of budget reductions. Other criteria for assessing performance exist; however, the indicators are most often used to measure an organization's effectiveness.[1]

Output, efficiency, and resource acquisition are important aspects of an agency's performance. Today, it would be naive to suggest that social welfare managers need not be attentive to the aspects of performance. The issue is their priority relative to service. If it is impossible to maximize performance simultaneously in all these areas (as is normally the case), then trade-offs must be made. Effectiveness-oriented management is concerned centrally with how improved performance in output, efficiency, and resource acquisition influences improvements in service effectiveness.

ELEMENTS OF EFFECTIVENESS-ORIENTED MANAGEMENT

What is known about how managers promote or contribute to the delivery of effective services? The development of social welfare administration is a relatively new area of research; it has been pursued seriously for fewer than 20 years, and systematic efforts to link management and service outcomes are even more recent. Much of what is known about management effectiveness is not readily accessible because many accomplishments remain organizational secrets rather than publicized exemplars to study and emulate. Additionally, some administrative practices in social welfare are derived from the for-profit sector where outcome criteria are

different, and the transferability of technique among sectors should not be assumed.

Nevertheless, an approach to managing for service effectiveness is emerging, and so far contains the following six dimensions: (1) infusing the agency with a value-oriented mission that gives meaning to service effectiveness, (2) selecting service technologies, (3) developing service outcome indicators and measurement techniques, (4) assessing the standards to determine whether performance meets expectations, (5) determining the organizational arrangements and management practices needed to motivate and support workers in their efforts to achieve performance goals, and (6) mobilizing constituencies around effectiveness performance criteria to maintain the autonomy necessary to meet the participants' needs.

Infusing Values

Selznick was one of the first students of administrative leadership to describe the link between an agency's mission and its effectiveness, and the critical role managers play in infusing values and shaping the organization's character.[2] For some years, the search for technical proficiency obscured this leadership function.

More recently, Peters and Waterman and some theorists of organizational culture once again sensitized social workers to their role as a major variable in an organization's performance.[3] The theorists suggest that an organization needs not only

[1] R. Patti, "In Search of a Purpose for Social Welfare," *Administration in Social Work,* 9 (Fall 1985), pp. 1–14; and J. Poertner and C. Rapp, "Organizational Learning and Problem Finding," in M. Dinerman, ed., *Social Work in a Turbulent World* (Silver Spring, Md.: National Association of Social Workers, 1983), pp. 76–88.

[2] P. Selznick, *Leadership in Administration* (Berkeley: University of California Press, 1984).

[3] T. Peters and R. Waterman, *In Search of Excellence* (New York: Harper and Row, 1982); and L. Bolman and T. Deal, *Modern Approaches to Understanding and Managing Organizations* (San Francisco: Jossey-Bass, 1984).

clear objectives, structured roles, competent personnel, and adequate resources to perform well, but more importantly, the organization needs values, symbols, and beliefs that attach a social significance to the organization's outcomes and processes, and that help to reconcile ever present ambiguity and uncertainty. The values, symbols, and beliefs are regarded as important sources of direction, motivation, and satisfaction to the organization's participants as well as an essential tool for building support and credibility with external constituencies.

Infusing values is an ongoing process that reflects itself in a manager's daily functions, particularly in allocating resources, rewarding employees, and problem solving. Infusing values is reflected most dramatically, however, in how the chief administrator portrays the agency in the community and in the actions not taken because of an inconsistency with organizational values.

Infusing values is not unilaterally performed by management. The manager interacts with groups internal and external to the agency to understand their values and interests and, when possible, forges a consensus. The essence of this interaction, however, is to maintain a strong and tenacious commitment to the core values, even when confronted with resistance and disfavor.

Effectiveness-oriented administration requires that managers relate service quality and client benefit to a larger statement of purpose—effectiveness for a specific result. Effective service may relate to achieving the least restrictive alternatives for clients, keeping families intact, protecting the rights of women in spousal relations, and ensuring children's rights to stable, long-term familial relations. Hence, without these or similar values, service

effectiveness can become trivialized too easily.

Selecting Service Technologies

A critical requisite of effectiveness-oriented administration is the availability of a service technology that works or appears to work with the clientele of an agency. An agency cannot be effective regardless of its skill and creativity unless it executes program strategy that effectively produces the desired outcomes.

Some observers contend that selecting service technologies is an insurmountable obstacle because not enough information has been accumulated to know how to apply the process to clients: service technologies are "indeterminate"; that is, it is impossible to predict the outcomes of service interventions.[4] One observer asserted that because social agencies cannot verify the effectiveness of their services they should deliberately organize themselves around politically fashionable belief systems, "flitting from political flower to political flower," and engaging in "mystical mesmerizing" to garner the resources necessary to sustain their operations.[5]

Of course, a number of areas exist in which our knowledge and skills are unequal to the problems presented; but the situation is not irrevocable. Rapid strides have been made in establishing the efficacy of some interventions for preventing delinquency, returning foster children to their natural families, preventing out-of-home placement for children who

---

[4]Y. Hasenfeld, *Human Service Organizations* (Englewood Cliffs, N.J.: Prentice-Hall, 1983).

[5]G. Salancik, "The Effectiveness of Ineffective Social Service Systems," in H. Stein, ed., *Organization and the Human Services* (Philadelphia: Temple University Press, 1981), pp. 142–150.

would be institutionalized, and improving the quality of discharge planning in hospitals.[6]

Reid's review of the clinical studies further attests to the progress being made to reduce the indeterminacy of human service technologies.[7] The point is that the indeterminacy of human service technologies is not a fait accompli—that is, a description of what has been should not be confused with a prescription for what will be.

What is the administrator's role in selecting technologies? It is imperative that the manager, especially with direct responsibility for program operations, become knowledgeable about service effectiveness research to select the proper program strategies. The manager should insist that staff assess the available evidence on the efficacy of various service interventions before adopting an approach.

This step sometimes requires that the administrator reject the preferences and interests of staff who favor certain service modes that cannot be documented. In cases in which insufficient empirical information is available for judging the intervention selected, the manager should promote a strategy of search and experimentation in the agency that supports and

rewards workers who systematically evaluate their practice.[8]

Several models for research and development in social work are available to guide an agency in efforts to build its practice-base knowledge.[9] Reserving a small portion of the agency's budget or providing workers release time, technical assistance, and support to attend conferences and workshops are some ways in which the administrator can encourage the search for more effective technologies.[10]

Specifying and Measuring Effectiveness Criteria

Service effectiveness is not a unitary phenomenon nor are its properties easy to identify. Unlike the for-profit field where certain indicators of effective performance are accepted readily, in social welfare administration, the situation is much more complicated. A major dimension of effectiveness, as mentioned previously, is the ability of an agency to change undesirable attitudes, self-perceptions, behaviors, statuses, or social conditions. The dilemma, however, is how to value or prioritize these various outcomes.

Which is most meaningful? It is enough that the young delinquent demonstrates an improved ability to manage his or her aggressive behavior in social situations after a course of treatment, or must we have evidence that he or she participates

---

[6]D. Hawkins and T. Lam, "Teacher Practices, Social Development and Delinquency." Unpublished manuscript, Center for Law and Justice, University of Washingon, Seattle, 1983; T. Stein, E. Gambrill, and K. Wiltse, *Children in Foster Homes: Achieving Continuity in Care* (New York: Praeger Publishers, 1978); E. T. Heck and A. R. Gruber, *Treatment Alternatives Project* (Boston: Children's Service Association, 1976); and N. Bracht, *Social Work in Health Care* (New York: Haworth Press, 1978).

[7]W. Reid and P. Hanrahan, "Recent Evaluations of Social Work: Grounds for Optimism," *Social Work*, 27 (July–August 1982), pp. 328–340.

[8]E. Mutschler, "Evaluating Practice: A Study of Research Utilization by Practitioners," *Social Work*, 29 (July–August 1984), pp. 332–337.

[9]D. Fanshel, ed., *The Future of Social Work Research* (New York: National Association of Social Workers, 1980); and J. Rothman, *Social R & D: Research and Development in the Human Services* (Englewood Cliffs, N.J.: Prentice-Hall, 1980).

[10]S. Briar and B. Blythe, "Agency Support for Evaluating Outcomes of Social Work Services," *Administration in Social Work*, 9 (Summer 1985), pp. 25–36.

in fewer criminal acts? Is it sufficient that an unemployed client acquires job-seeking and work adjustment skills through job training, or is locating and securing employment the real criterion of the program's success? If the client values one kind of outcome, the worker values another, and the funding agency yet another outcome, whose definition of success will be used to determine whether the service has been effective? And what will be the political and organizational consequences of adopting certain criteria and rejecting others?

There are some situations where such criteria are imposed on an agency without the option to adopt the criteria. But when the agency has discretion, choices must be made and the choices relate to whether an agency is effective subsequently. There is no formula for making these judgments. The process is intrinsically political, in which the manager attempts to engineer a consensus among those who support, deliver, and consume services.

It is understandable, therefore, that managers have difficulty specifying desired service outcomes. Unfortunately, they prefer to concentrate on outputs or processes, or worker satisfaction, as surrogates of agency effectiveness. Workers tend to shape their behaviors to fare well on the performance criteria the organization deems important. Indeed, much of the displacement of goals is traceable to agencies pursuing performance outcomes that have little to do with client benefit.[11] Perhaps the agencies can use this same dynamic to promote activities that are directed to client change.

Efforts to specify service outcomes will be successful only if there are ways of validly and reliably measuring results. Some methods, for example, are single subject design,[12] goal attainment scaling,[13] ratio analysis,[14] and Markov modeling.[15] Additionally, currently available are a number of instruments that measure interpersonal and behavioral outcomes in clients,[16] instruments that assess the quality of service environments,[17] and those that tap client satisfaction with the services received.[18] Much work remains for agencies to find and adapt appropriate measures, but administrative leadership and encouragement is critical if middle management and direct service staff are to undertake the task.

Applying Standards

The ability to measure service outcomes is necessary to effectiveness-oriented administration, but it is not sufficient. Unless

---

[11]B. Neugeboren, *Organization, Policy and Practice in the Human Services* (New York: Longman, 1985).

[12]S. Jayaratne and R. Levy, *Empirical Clinical Practice* (New York: Columbia University Press, 1979).

[13]T. Kiresuk and S. Lund, "Program Evaluation and the Management of Organizations," in W. Anderson, B. Frieden, and M. Murphy, eds., *Managing Human Services* (Washington, D.C.: International City Management Association, 1977), pp. 280–320.

[14]R. Elkin and M. Molitor, *Management Indicators in Non-Profit Organizations* (Baltimore: University of Maryland, 1984).

[15]J. Poertner and R. Wintersteen, "Measurement of Client Satisfaction With Social Work Services." Unpublished manuscript, Lawrence, Kans. 1985.

[16]*See, for example*, J. Levitt and W. Reid, "Rapid Assessment Instruments for Practice," *Social Work Research and Abstracts*, 17 (Spring 1981), pp. 13–19; W. Hudson, *The Clinical Measurement Package* (Homewood, Ill.: Dorsey Press, 1982); and T. Tripodi and I. Epstein, *Research Techniques for Clinical Social Workers* (New York: Columbia University Press, 1980).

[17]*See, for example*, R. Moos, *Evaluating Treatment Environments* (New York: John Wiley & Sons, 1974), pp. 278–298; and T. Holland, "Organizational Structure and Institutional Care," *Journal of Health and Social Behavior*, 14 (September 1973), pp. 241–251.

[18]Poertner and Wintersteen, "Measurement of Client Satisfaction With Social Work Services."

the performance data can be compared with some standard or expectation, the outcomes likely are not to have much use as a basis for management intervention. Stated differently, at what point does the manager know whether aggregate performance in a program is at, below, or above expectations? In a program aimed at preventing out-of-home placement for children, how does the manager know whether a 60-percent prevention rate is too much or too little?

Apparently, relatively few agencies, even those capable of measuring outcomes, have established internal standards to assess their performance on service effectiveness.[19] Why not? Herzlinger argues that the failure to establish standards in the human services can be attributed to the ethos of professionalism that stresses autonomy for practitioners, a respect for peers' judgment, and a norm of collegial rather than hierarchical decision making.[20] Rapp has suggested that managers in social agencies generally do not have the skills and training required to make use of performance data in managing their programs.[21] The reluctance to apply standards to performance data might be explained by arguing that unless the manager has reason to believe that achieving performance standards is within the control of the organization, then applying standards to service outcomes is the equivalent of shooting oneself in the organizational foot.

---

[19]R. Herzlinger, "Management Control Systems in Human Service Organizations," in H. Stein, ed., *Organization and the Human Services* (Philadelphia: Temple University Press, 1981), pp. 205–232; C. Rapp, "Information, Performance and the Human Services Manager: Beyond Housekeeping," *Administration in Social Work*, 8 (Summer 1984), pp. 69–80.

[20]Herzlinger, "Management Control Systems in Human Service Organizations," p. 209.

[21]Rapp, "Information, Performance and the Human Services Manager," pp. 71–74.

Nevertheless, managing for service effectiveness rests on a capacity to discern when program performance falls below some level of expectation. In general, performance standards are derived in the following five ways: (1) imposed by some external funding or contracting body, (2) determined intuitively, (3) based on previous performance levels (historical analysis), (4) based on comparative data from agencies providing similar services to similar clientele, or (5) derived from norms established in empirical research. In whatever way these standards were derived, they should be treated as working hypotheses, subject to disproof and modification as experience accumulates or circumstances change, or both. It probably is better to have standards that are flawed than to have none at all.

Determining Management Practices and Organizational Arrangements

Administrative practices and organizational arrangements are thought to have a direct relationship to the delivery of effective services—those actions taken by managers that affect work performance. Here the focus is on practice and arrangements that generally seem conducive to effective service by workers, regardless of setting. Beyond the general practices, it probably is necessary to tailor management practices and working conditions to particular settings.

An especially important practice in effectiveness-oriented management is the provision of feedback regarding service outcomes that is timely, easily understood, and caseload-specific. Workers should be able to link the information they receive back to the clients they see. The information should enable the workers to see the relationship between their actions and outcomes for the client. Within reason, the information should be readily available.[22] The principles of information system design have become almost axiomatic, yet they still are violated in practice. Following the principles provides encouragement for continued cooperation to those practitioners who generated the information inputs. The feedback provided underscores the idea that information about services is intended for the purpose of self-learning and professional development, rather than primarily for managerial oversight and evaluation. Continuous feedback on service outcomes also serves to reinforce continuously the idea that client benefit is the principal concern of the program. Finally, information provided to workers about changes in their clients has been found to affect significantly subsequent performance and appears to reduce vulnerability to burnout.[23]

Supervisory practices are also a key element of the service outcome–oriented work environment. A detailed consideration is beyond the scope of this article, but several key aspects can be noted. Several decades of research have identified two dimensions of leadership that appear to have significant effects on worker performance. One is consideration, or what leaders do to build relationships, support, sympathize, and individualize their subordinates. The other, task, or initiating structure, concerns setting objectives, clarifying tasks, monitoring and evaluating performance, and

providing task-specific feedback. Though few studies have been conducted on the leadership styles of managers and supervisors in social service agencies, those available suggest that leaders, especially supervisors, tend to score low on task-oriented behaviors and high on consideration behaviors.[24]

Friesen, in her study of first-line supervisors in community mental health centers, found that they tended to score much higher on consideration and support than on task-oriented behaviors. The task-oriented behaviors included clarifying roles; specifying rules, procedures, and methods; and assigning specific tasks to subordinates.[25]

The findings would not be remarkable were it not for the growing body of evidence that suggests that many of these task-oriented behaviors are important for supporting and improving worker performance. Four supervisory behaviors that appear to be most consequential in this regard are as follows: (1) clarifying desired performance outcomes, (2) identifying tasks and activities that are instrumental in achieving these outcomes, (3) providing specific feedback to workers regarding what they do well and not so well, recognizing and rewarding successful behaviors

[22]D. Schoech and L. Schkade, "Computers Helping Caseworkers: Decision Support Systems," *Child Welfare*, 59 (November 1980), pp. 566–575.

[23]L. Fredericksen and R. Johnson, "Organizational Behavior Management," *Progress in Behavior Modification* (Vol. 12; New York: Academic Press, 1981), pp. 67–118; and A. Pines, "Changing Organizations: Is a Work Environment Without Burnout Possible?," in W. S. Paine, ed., *Job Stress and Burnout* (Beverly Hills, Calif.: Sage Publications, 1982), pp. 189–212.

[24]S. Olyan, "An Exploratory Study of Supervision in Jewish Community Centers as Compared to Other Welfare Settings." Unpublished Ph.D. dissertation, University of Pittsburgh, School of Social Work, 1972; N. Cohen and G. Rhodes, "Social Work Supervision: A View Toward Leadership Styles and Job Orientation," *Administration in Social Work*, 3 (Spring 1977), pp. 281–291; and D. Granvold, "Supervisory Style and Educational Preparation of Public Welfare Supervisors," *Administration in Social Work*, 1 (Spring 1977), pp. 79–88.

[25]B. Friesen, "Organizational and Leader Behavior Correlates of Line Worker Satisfaction and Role Clarity," pp. 140–144. Unpublished Ph.D. dissertation, University of Washington School of Social Work, 1983.

and outcomes, and identifying competencies that need enhancement, and (4) providing incentives to workers who improve their practice competencies and achieve service objectives with clients.[26] In short, apparently task-related supervisory behavior needs to be emphasized more in an outcome-oriented agency. This emphasis need not mean less consideration and support from supervisors; indeed, it may mean more. Perhaps most critical is an appreciation that these two elements of leadership and supervision are interactive and mutually reinforcing.

Although service effectiveness seems to be facilitated by active administrative and supervisory involvement in the design and assessment of service technologies and the direction and guidance of direct service workers, it would be a mistake to think of this management approach as one in which superiors simply dictate to subordinates. Although a directive style sometimes is appropriate, service effectiveness requires that managers also give attention to promoting involvement in decision making and the use of discretion at the front line. The literature on staff participation in decision making and its relationship to service quality and effectiveness is not large, but in settings as diverse as child care and mental health centers, evidence suggests that the more opportunity workers have to influence administrative decision making, the

more likely they are to perform well on various indices of service quality.[27]

The evidence concerning job discretion is somewhat more substantial. Holland, for example, found that when an institution for the mentally retarded was decentralized and staff were given the responsibility to plan for residents, determine treatment strategies, and devise rules for the living units, that the treatment of residents became more intense and individualized.[28] Similarly, in a study of 31 social service agencies conducted by Olmstead and Christensen, the variable that correlated most highly with worker effectiveness was job discretion and flexibility.[29] Parallel findings have been reported in studies of service quality in halfway houses for alcoholics and other types of social service agencies.[30] Although it is important for the effectiveness-oriented agency to have the structure of specified service outcomes, clearly defined service technologies, rigorous assessment and evaluation procedures,

[26]E. Gambrill and T. Stein, *Supervision: A Decision-Making Approach* (Beverly Hills, Calif.: Sage Publications, 1983); W. Christian and G. Hannah, *Effective Management in the Human Services* (Englewood Cliffs, N.J.: Prentice-Hall, 1983); Gambrill and Stein, *Supervision*; C. Cherniss, *Staff Burnout* (Beverly Hills, Calif.: Sage Publications, 1980); Poertner and Wintersteen, "Measurement of Client Satisfaction with Social Work Services"; and Gambrill and Stein, *Supervision*; Christian and Hannah, *Effective Management in the Human Services*; and Fredericksen and Johnson, "Organizational Behavior Management."

[27]C. Maslach and A. Pines, "The Burnout Syndrome in the Day Care Setting," *Child Care Quarterly*, 6 (Summer 1977), pp. 100–113; M. Vandervelde, "Participative and Influence Based Decision-Making, Performance and Effectiveness: An Analysis of Their Relationship in Human Service Organizations," pp. 76–81. Unpublished Ph.D. dissertation, University of Washington School of Social Work, 1979; J. Steger, R. Woodhouse, and R. Goocey, "The Clinical Manager: Performance and Management Characteristics," *Administration in Mental Health* (Fall 1973), pp. 76–81.

[28]T. Holland, "Organizational Structure and Institutional Care," pp. 241–251.

[29]J. Olmstead and H. Christensen, *Effects of Agency Work Contexts: An Intensive Field Study* (Washington, D.C.: U.S. Department of Health, Education, and Welfare, 1973); and P. Martin and B. Segal, "Bureaucracy, Size and Staff Expectations for Client Independence in Half-Way Houses," *Journal of Health and Social Behavior*, 18 (December 1977), pp. 376–390.

[30]B. Whiddon, "The Effect of Congruence on the Relationship Between Participation/Job Discretion and Staff Performance: The Case of a Social Service Organization." Unpublished Ph.D. Dissertation, University of Florida, School of Social Work, 1980.

it also is important that workers have a role in defining these parameters and the discretion to operate within them as circumstances and judgment require.

Obtaining Environmental Support for Effectiveness-Oriented Programs

Social agencies can mobilize the support of external resource providers around the criterion of service effectiveness. However, pessimism about developing such a management approach is based on the view that because powerful resource providers such as legislative, regulatory, and funding bodies tend to stress performance outcomes like output and efficiency when evaluating agencies, an "organization's capacity to acquire resources depends on its ability to score well on the evaluative criteria used by these groups."[31]

Several strategies are available to administrators seeking to maximize their autonomy and influence vis-a-vis resource providers. The first and most obvious strategy is to demonstrate that the agency or program can be effective on its own terms. The priorities of policymakers and funders can be modified. From time to time an agency's success with a client population enables it to shape the goals of policymakers and funders. For example, the following successful programs have influenced social policy in some states in recent years: permanency planning for children, prevention of out-of-home placement, and support and maintenance of the chronically mentally ill.

A second strategy to increase the autonomy of an agency is to reduce its

dependence by diversifying its sources of support. The intent of this strategy is to increase the agency's ability to pursue the service objectives it defines as desirable without putting itself in financial jeopardy.[32] Recently, many agencies have adopted this strategy to avoid funding cuts.[33]

A third strategy is for the agency to take an active role in the process by which resource controller's demands and expectations are formulated. Lobbying, helping in the campaigns of sympathetic legislators, and participating in hearings where administrative rule changes are being considered, are conduits through which the agency administrator can influence policy priorities.[34] Jansson and Simmons, in their study of hospital social work departments, found that the directors of better staffed, more comprehensive departments were more likely to be involved in high-level decision forums in their hospitals.[35]

This finding suggests that social service directors may be able to influence the allocation priorities of hospital decision makers. A closely related tactic is co-opting resource controllers by involving them on boards, committees, and workshops to expose them to the rationale for, and evidence of, service effectiveness.

---

[31]P. Martin, "Multiple Constituencies, Dominant Societal Values and Human Service Administrators," *Administration in Social Work*, 4 (Summer 1980), pp. 15–27; and Hasenfeld, *Human Service Organizations*, p. 207.

[32]J. Pfeffer and G. Salancik, *The External Control of Organizations: A Resource Dependence Perspective* (New York: Harper and Row, 1978), p. 109; and Elkin and Molitor, *Management Indicators in Non-Profit Organizations*.

[33]R. Petersen, M. Austin, and R. Patti, "Cutback Management Activities in Community Mental Health Centers," *Administration in Mental Health*, 13 (Winter 1985), pp. 112–124.

[34]Pfeffer and Salancik, *The External Control of Organizations*, p. 100.

[35]B. Jansson and J. Simmons, "Building Departmental or Unit Power Within Human Service Organizations: Empirical Findings and Theory Building," *Administration in Social Work*, 8 (Fall 1984), p. 51.

Little systematic information is available on how these strategies are used to effect a greater congruence between resource providers and agencies concerning the importance of service effectiveness as the principal criterion of agency performance. However, clearly the manager who would attempt to make service effectiveness the main performance outcome of an agency must be able to mobilize constituencies around this criteria.

CONCLUSION

Although service effectiveness should be the primary object of social welfare administration, it cannot be the sole concern. To pursue the approach outlined in this article will require careful attention to the interrelationships between effectiveness and other performance criteria. At some point, increments of service effectiveness can be achieved only at unacceptably low levels of output and efficiency. Conversely, it will be important to know when increases in output or efficiency threaten the effects or quality of a service. Analytic models that allow administrators to perform this tradeoff analysis will be needed.[36]

As an effectiveness-oriented model of administration is developed, social workers also will have to be concerned with the ethical parameters of managerial behavior. For example, is it ethically permissible for an agency to select only those clients who can use the agency's services most advantageously? Should programmatic or service strategies that are demonstrably effective be used when they abridge client choice, violate confidentiality, or undermine human dignity? Surely, the answer in both cases would be, no. The search for effectiveness must occur within some ethical boundaries that explicitly define the permissible. Finally, the fundamental question is always, effectiveness in the service of what? If social workers should manage to increase the number of frail, elderly people living at home only to expose them to a mean and undignified existence, what moral purpose has been served? Effectiveness, however it is defined, must be morally defensible.

---

[36] J. Newman and R. Ryder, "Evaluating Administrative Performance," *Public Welfare* (Fall 1978), pp. 45–51.

26.

Jon Simon Sager

CHANGE LEVERS FOR IMPROVING ORGANIZATIONAL PERFORMANCE AND STAFF MORALE

Improving organizational performance and staff morale are important objectives for administrators of human service organizations. Just how to accomplish these ends is especially critical, but difficult, in the current cutback milieu. Although there are numerous approaches said to improve productivity, performance, satisfaction, the quality of working life, and morale, few are successful, especially over time. This reading intends to identify a useful way to conceptualize and organize (as well as critique) approaches, in order to assist administrators in choosing and applying appropriate strategies. The means to accomplish this involves employing the concept of strategic organizational change levers (Cummings and Molloy, 1977; Mohrman and Lawler, 1984; Tichy, 1983; Tichy, Hornstein, and Nisberg, 1977).

Change levers are aspects of organizations that may be directly altered or manipulated in order to change organizational outcomes. Mohrman and Lawler (1984) contend there is a strong theoretical and empirical basis for predicting the impact of changes in these variables (and the contingencies or organizational conditions under which changes in these variables will have a particular impact) on such outcomes as satisfaction and productivity.

According to Mohrman and Lawler (1984), there are seven change levers that have particular relevance. They are: (1) participation in decision making, (2) job and work redesign, (3) job training, (4) altering organizational structure, (5) communication and information management, (6) organizational norms and culture, and (7) rewards. These levers may be used to develop strategies to induce change in organizational and employee performance and outcomes. The change levers are useful also for analyzing existing approaches to improving productivity and satisfaction. In the following discussion the overlap and interdependence among the levers should become apparent. Failure to consider the implications of change in one aspect (lever) of an organizational system for other aspects will compromise change efforts, resulting in little lasting improvement. For example, a person's job may be redesigned, but if this is done without commensurate training to perform the new task, success will be unlikely; employees participating in decision making may contribute little to decision quality, if there is no training in decision-making techniques or group process; and even with such training, the decision-making group's effectiveness would remain compromised if they do not have sufficient information to make high-quality decisions. The interrelationship of the change levers will be addressed again at the end of the reading.

PARTICIPATION IN DECISION MAKING

Allowing subordinates to participate in decision making is a frequently used and much heralded avenue by which to enhance organizational outcomes. Participation can be defined as the opportunity for subordinates to have their input incorporated into managerial decisions at a level above them and have their perspectives accounted for in decisions made (Mohr, 1982, p. 124). Participation in decision making (PDM) has been claimed to reduce everything from absenteeism and turnover to stress, alienation, and helplessness. It has been advocated as a panacea for increasing everything from responsibility, meaningfulness of work, loyalty, commitment, and self-control-esteem-actualization, to performance capability, quality, and productivity; and this is not to mention its positive impact on motivation, satisfaction, and morale.

Despite these lofty claims for the benefits of PDM, the data offer little or modest support at best (Locke and Schweiger, 1979; Miller and Monge, 1986; Mohr, 1982; Sager, 1984; Wagner and Gooding, 1987). Table 26.1 presents my summary of Locke and Schweiger's review of the participation literature.

Little evidence exists for the claims that PDM increases productivity (it is just as likely to decrease it) and, although the majority of the studies indicated some improvement in satisfaction, a substantial number (40 percent) showed no positive changes. Recent reviews continue to find

little support for using participation to make dramatic changes in performance or satisfaction outcomes (Miller and Monge, 1986; Wagner and Gooding, 1987). In response to such discouraging data, some advocates for participation argue an old adage: "A happy worker is a productive worker," but this relationship fares poorly based on empirical evidence. Some happy workers may be lazy workers; in fact some happy workers become unhappy if they are asked to work.

Some of the confusion between what PDM is claimed to accomplish and what it actually does accomplish is due to the variety and forms that participative practices may take and the contexts in which they are used (Locke and Schweiger, 1979; Tannenbaum, 1974). For example, PDM may be formal (e.g., employees participating in a union) or informal (e.g., a supervisor consults an employee); participation may be forced (e.g., collective bargaining) or voluntary (e.g., an organization adopts a quality circle program); participation may be direct (e.g., employees have opportunities to directly assert their views) or indirect (e.g., a representative elected to a decision-making body). PDM may be extensive in scope (e.g., budget and personnel issues) or limited (e.g., to the shop or office floor).

Examining the disappointing PDM results in the light of the forms employed is illuminating. For example, employees

TABLE 26.1
Summary of Studies on the Effects of Participation

	Participation Superior	Participation Inferior	No Difference or Contextual Effect
Productivity	(21.7%)	(21.7%)	(56.6%)
Satisfaction	(60.5%)	(9.3%)	(30.2%)

(From Sager, 1984)

seldom obtain the benefits of PDM when it is indirect, such as through representatives; in such cases the representatives are the ones who benefit, since they experience the direct participation. Often PDM programs do not involve participation in decision making in fact. Rather, they are group suggestion or recommendation programs. For instance, in quality circle (QC) programs, management retains the ultimate authority to accept or reject a circle's decisions. Hence, circles in fact only recommend decisions, which may or may not be adopted or implemented. Thus, QC programs are basically group suggestion programs, and suggestion programs, whether by individuals or by groups, only imply participation to the extent the suggestions are accepted and, once accepted, implemented (Tannenbaum, 1974). Moreover, rejecting decisions (or accepting them but never implementing them) typically demoralizes participants.

Given the inconsistent data on PDM and the numerous pitfalls, observers generally conclude that effectiveness is contextual, and depends on a number of individual, organizational, and situational factors (Lawler, 1986; Locke and Schweiger, 1979; Miller and Monge, 1986; Sager, 1984, 1990). However, it remains difficult to identify the precise contexts and situations under which PDM is effective, and the evidence for the positive effects of participation remains mixed even when situational factors are accounted (Wagner and Gooding, 1987). Nevertheless, some will be suggested here, since the premise of the paper is that a congruent array of change levers enhances performance. So, it makes sense to identify and maximize the factors that make successful participation outcomes more likely.

To begin with, having employees who desire to participate is important, since PDM can be a burden to those who do not desire involvement. Given that most social agencies employ a number of professionals, who may desire autonomy and may not be interested in PDM, it is important that decision areas be of interest to such workers. Another very important factor is using organizational leaders who are committed to shared decision making.

Particular circumstances are typically more suitable for participative practices. When acceptance of the decision by workers is important, then their involvement is critical for effective implementation. When both accuracy and acceptance are important, then leader- or administrator-facilitated participation is necessary. When these factors are not important, administrators can make the decision themselves, or delegate it (perhaps to someone they are developing for leadership roles or to a group that could benefit from practicing PDM). The Vroom-Yetton (1973) model of decision making, with the refinements developed by Vroom and Jago (1988), identifies the kinds of situations (based largely on the variables of decision quality, information availability, and subordinate acceptance) that call for various degrees of PDM. There is considerable support for the effectiveness of using Vroom and his colleagues' approach (Yukl, 1989).

Merely identifying appropriate situations in which to use variations of PDM is a good first step, but other factors are important if groups are to make significant contributions. Having trained and effective group leaders or facilitators is essential. Also, there are numerous problem-solving techniques available, and when leaders and participants are familiar with these problem solving practices (e.g., nominal group techniques), effectiveness is more likely. The effectiveness of group decision making and problem-solving groups in Japan reveals as a distinguishing element that Japanese problem-solving groups approach problems with a set of techniques, methods, and problem-solving tools, whereas groups in the United States are essentially asked to solve problems with minimal and poor training in group process and very little or no systematic problem-solving techniques or approaches (Cole, 1979; Sager, 1984).

It is also important that the organization be committed to PDM over the long term, such that groups can be given sufficient time to develop cohesion and practice group problem-solving skills. Managers threatened by such practices must have their fears allayed and be made to realize the organization's long-term commitment; resistant managers must be convinced that they cannot sabotage participative practices. Given such factors, PDM can be an effective lever by which to improve performance and especially employee satisfaction and morale. Nevertheless, it is also important to keep in mind that other levers need to be invoked concurrently; for example, making information available to problem-solving groups, training leaders and participants in decision-making techniques, and giving rewards, such as recognition to workers for participation and to supervisors for supporting and implementing PDM.

JOB AND WORK REDESIGN

Using the job and work redesign lever involves altering core job dimensions in order to impact psychological states, which leads to changes in personal and work outcomes. Figure 26.1 illustrates this through the job characteristics model developed by Hackman, Oldham, Janson, and Purdy (1975). According to the model, core job dimensions (such as autonomy and variety) produce psychological states (such as meaningfulness and responsibility), which in turn produce personal and work outcomes—motivation, satisfaction, high performance, reduced turnover, and lower absenteeism.

Core job dimensions are related directly to implementing principles or concepts that redesign and enrich jobs. Hackman et al. (1975) label the first implementing principle *Forming Natural Work Units,* which impacts task identity and significance, thereby fostering meaningfulness. Forming natural work units involves the distribution and assignment of natural clusters of work items to workers. This engenders a sense of worker ownership and responsibility for an identifiable grouping or body of work.

The second implementing principle is *Combining Tasks,* which impacts skill variety and task identity, thereby fostering meaningfulness. Combining tasks involves creating larger modules of work from fractionalized tasks (Hackman, 1977; Hackman et al., 1975); for example, Cummings and Molloy (1977) suggest that activities such as communication, checking, and trouble shooting may be "regrafted" onto jobs for individuals or work groups.

The third principle is *Establishing Relationships with Clients.* This impacts: (a) skill variety, fostering meaningfulness, (b) autonomy, fostering responsibility, and (c) feedback, fostering knowledge. Although this appears to be naturally occurring and is sometimes taken for granted in social service and community settings, the concept can be considered in a more comprehensive fashion. For example, support staff, indirectly involved in client services, could benefit from the application of this principle. Moreover, a useful and enriching application would involve viewing "clients" in a more encompassing way;

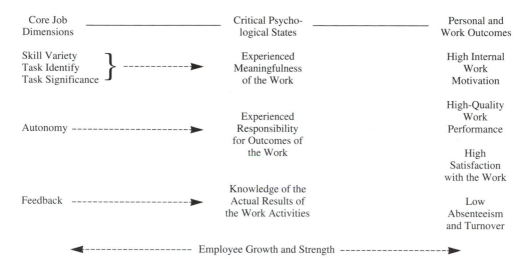

FIGURE 26.1
The Job Characteristic Model of Work Motivation

others within the same organization (e.g., employees in other departments, especially interdependent departments) can be considered internal clients or internal customers. In social service settings, specifically, the term clients is confounded by its limited application to recipients of service. Permitting workers and professional and/or support staff to establish relationships with other providing agencies, funding sources, governing bodies, and the like would significantly impact the job-redesign lever.

The fourth principle is *Vertical Loading,* which impacts autonomy, fostering responsibility. Vertical loading involves transcending from merely "doing" the job to involvement in "planning and controlling" the job. Hackman et al. (1975) suggest that this may be the most crucial of all the job-design principles. Involving workers in more aspects and at different phases of the planning and evaluation of agency services

begins to address how this principle is implemented. Vertical loading can be applied to individuals or groups. When group activities are vertically loaded by substantially delegating responsibility and authority to the group, then the creation of autonomous and self-managing work groups begins to take place; in this way, work redesign impacts the participation lever as well.

The last principle is *Opening Feedback Channels,* which impacts feedback, fostering knowledge. Hackman et al. (1975) use this concept in the sense that a worker learns about performance directly as the job is done, rather than learning only on an occasional basis. Using participation can also increase the amount and accuracy of information that workers have about work practices (knowledge of results) and can increase the degree to which group members "own" their work practices and thereby experience responsibility for work outcomes (Lawler, 1986; Porter, Lawler, and Hackman, 1975). Often there is a tendency to think that feedback in social service provision is readily available from the clients themselves, but this may not be the case; often client outcomes do not accurately represent the quality of worker performance. Moreover, feedback as used here entails a more encompassing view, such as providing feedback on how worker performance impacts overall agency performance; few workers understand such relationships.

According to Hackman and Oldham (1980), redesigning jobs may be limited by: (1) the technology of the organization, which determines the specific tasks performed and how the tasks are arranged and sequenced; (2) the personnel system, which may restrict employees from performing certain aspects of work; and (3) the control system, which may constrain the scope of jobs and the procedures used to perform them. Nevertheless, the creative administrator can find ways to redesign and enrich jobs, especially by viewing the roles of service-providing personnel in a more expanded fashion.

TRAINING

Training impacts employee knowledge, skills, and attitudes (Mohrman and Lawler, 1984). It is most closely related to the job-redesign lever, since training is often necessary to adequately support redesigned jobs. The relationship of training to other levers has already been noted (e.g., decision-making groups are more effective if trained in group process and problem solving, and facilitated by well-trained leaders).

According to Cummings and Molloy (1977), the training lever serves at least three purposes: (1) it prepares organizational members for change programs, (2) it provides employees with knowledge and skills required to perform redesigned jobs, and (3) it enables job rotation. Training is typically broadly defined, but here the emphasis is on specific job-skill training. This emphasis is not meant to minimize the importance of training in human relations, sensitivity, leadership, teamwork, and the like; such training is important and often necessary, but is often conducted at the expense of direct job-skill training. Skill training can directly help employees to perform their jobs more effectively and can teach them to perform new ones. Therefore, in many respects, specific job training may be far more important than human-relations type training, especially the type employees disparagingly call "charm school." Updating and upgrading practitioners' skills, assisting them to perform their jobs better, and teaching them new ones enhances organizational performance. Moreover, it helps keep service practices current, and often enables the organization to augment other programs and implement new ones. Flexible deployment of human resources, job rotation, less dependence on a few employees with specific skills, and numerous other positive outcomes result from skill training. Such training, often viewed as an expense by financial officers, is really an investment in human beings, which increases their value.

Using training to increase organizational and employee effectiveness can be as simple and mundane as showing employees how to fill out forms properly or to manage their time better or as complex as learning to use a computer or identifying and sharing missions and goals. Often training is delegated or left up to individual supervisors, but organizationwide training has the benefit of increasing uniformity, shared perceptions, and understanding; such agreement, particularly with respect to shared goals, usually enhances overall organizational performance.

Although skill training has been emphasized here in response to the accent on and proliferation of human-relations training, the latter should not be neglected, nor should training and education that prepares employees for new programs. For example, among the reasons often cited for the failure of PDM programs are the failure to train leaders to effectively run meetings, the failure to prepare supervisors to accept suggestions from subordinates, and the failure to provide participating subordinates with appropriate skills for effective problem solving and decision making (Lawler, 1986).

Job rotation and cross-training are other areas that can increase organizational performance. Job rotation provides employees with a better sense of integration into the organization and gives them more understanding of the roles of and demands on other employees. Cross-training increases staffing flexibility and coverage when other employees are absent or leave. Both job rotation and cross-training endow employees with additional skills and add variety to their jobs. Training is most likely to be effective if individuals are able to practice what they learn and apply it in environments that support and nurture the newly acquired behaviors. This implies a need to train or sensitize everyone in the environment with whom the trainee is interdependent; such training may involve changes in the behavior of groups, and generally affects group norms and standards (Mohrman and Lawler, 1984)—another instance of the interrelationships among the change levers.

ORGANIZATIONAL STRUCTURE AND DESIGN

Altering and redesigning organizational structure to effectively adapt to and survive in turbulent and uncertain environments is another important change lever. Traditional Weberian bureaucratic forms, often called mechanistic structures, have steep and centralized hierarchies, panoplies of rules and procedures, and workers who specialize in performing specific and circumscribed tasks. Mechanistic structures, effective for routine tasks and predictable environments, are not adaptive or suited for the uncertainty and turbulence characteristic of the environments of today. When uncertainty is high, the environments unstable, and the tasks nonroutine, the more adaptive organizational configuration is the organic form. Organic structures have flatter hierarchies, network forms of control, and decentralized and participative decision making, with decisions made closer to where actual service and work occurs; relationships are personal and there are fewer rules, procedures, and bounding and restricting behaviors; such organizations are staffed by individuals with a variety of skills, who do not perform the same tasks every day in the same way; these workers are able to adapt their skills to numerous and different kinds of tasks and demands (Bennis and Slater, 1968; Burns and Stalker, 1961).

There are numerous ways to use the organizational structure lever. Mohrman and Lawler (1984) identify three that emphasize the decentralization of hierarchy, specifically concerning the way authority is distributed throughout the organization. One technique they identify involves overlapping structures that integrate hierarchical levels. Likert's (1961, 1967) concept of the "linking pin" typifies this approach. Linking pins are members of work groups who share membership in other work groups, which in turn have members who share membership in other groups; this often occurs in a vertical fashion, thereby integrating upper and lower levels of the hierarchy. For example, a staff member from a group of case workers may also belong to an advisory group comprised of various members of the organization; the supervisor of the caseworker group may be part of a supervisory task force; some of the members of the task force may, in turn, belong to a managerial group and so on and so forth up and throughout the hierarchy. Figure 26.2 illustrates the linking pin concept; The small dots represent organizational members and the hashed lines represent the formal hierarchical relationships (a given form of linkage). The encircled dots represent groups and linkages comprised horizontally, vertically, and diagonally within the same organization. The purpose of these overlapping memberships is to establish linkages among different levels of the hierarchy and among individuals who work in different functional groups (e.g., eligibility workers) or programmatic groups (e.g., day care). The network (both communication and authority) emerging from using overlapping memberships is not necessarily

prescribed by the formal organizational chart. Moreover, overlapping networks and groups can include other agency personnel, and in some organizations this is extended to clients. The latter extension empowers clients and increases their access to upper echelons of the hierarchy; such access is not ordinarily available through usual agency channels.

The second approach identified by Mohrman and Lawler (1984) involves eliminating levels of the hierarchy such that decisions are moved "down" closer to where the work is done. For example, self-managing teams and autonomous work groups have been successfully used in industry (Goodman, 1979; Landen and Carlson, 1982), and health care teams are common in medical settings. If coal miners and auto workers can function successfully in self-managing teams, certainly professionals in social service agencies should be able to do this particularly well. The very nature of professionalism creates, to some extent, a form of managerial control: Professionals share norms, values, and a set of skills that make them less dependent on rules or supervisors to carry out complex tasks. In fact, some authorities (e.g., Mintzberg, 1979) consider the defining

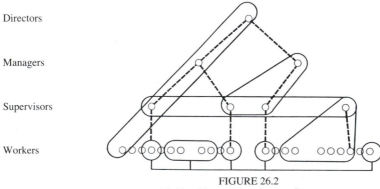

FIGURE 26.2
Linking Pins and Overlapping Structures

feature of professionalism as the self-control and planning of work.

The last approach to altering structure involves collateral or parallel hierarchies. These can be as simple as a special task force or a problem-solving "tiger" team assembled to address problems or perform functions that are ineffectually handled by the primary structure; the collateral structure may also be as complex as a participative management program with its own multilevel structure coexisting outside the primary structure.

Figure 26.3 depicts a parallel hierarchy in a quality circle program. The quality circle hierarchal structure, located in the center of the figure, exists outside the primary organizational structure shown on the left; outside-circle resources and constituencies are identified on the far right. Even though the circle structure contains members from the primary structure, it is essentially a subset of the primary structure (i.e., not all members of the organization participate in the circle program).

The advantage of the parallel hierarchy is decreased constraints from within the primary line function and increased flexibility. For example, circles can request information from different departments and hierarchical levels, whereas employees as part of the line function must go through supervisors or formal protocols to obtain the same information; circles can make presentations to upper management, to whom they would otherwise have little or no access as members of the line function.

In the case of increased flexibility, one of the advantages of the parallel hierarchy is the ease with which it can be dismantled. Since it does not encompass the line function, it is easy to cancel or abolish a program with a parallel hierarchy: Workers simply return to the line full time and refocus energies exclusively back onto the line function. This fragile characteristic, on the other hand, can be a serious disadvantage. With such an inherent vulnerability to dislodging, this weakness can be exploited by adversaries wishing to sabotage programs that embody parallel structures. After all, when a hierarchy is altered, the distribution of authority and power within the organization changes. Those with power typically

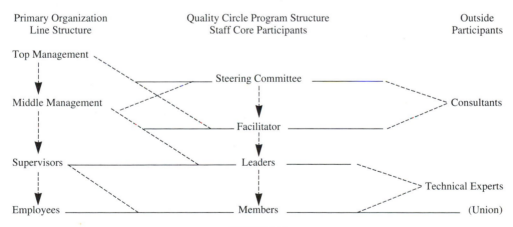

FIGURE 26.3
Parallel Hierarchy in a Quality Circle Program

do not like to give it up and often feel they are already sharing it appropriately; some are simply threatened by power sharing (e.g., a manager threatened by subordinates participating in decision making). On the other hand, parallel hierarchies have the advantage of being essentially adhocracies in which groups or task forces can be convened to solve a particular problem, disbanded when the problem is solved, and even revived if needed again.

Often management and unions create parallel hierarchies or collateral structures; these are often referred to as union-management collaborations and are implemented to improve productivity and the quality of work life (QWL). A "shadow box structure" comprised of members drawn from two separate organizations—the union and the agency for example—is created to oversee and establish policy for the collaborative activities.

Overall, the decentralization of hierarchy and the redistribution of decision-making authority may be the most critical alterations of structural dimensions in order to make organizations more adaptive and effective in uncertain and turbulent environments. Nevertheless, other structural dimensions such as formalization (basically the use of, and emphasis placed on, rules and standard operating procedures) and complexity (in its most basic sense, specialization and the division of labor) impact effectiveness and warrant discussion.

Eliminating or deemphasizing the use of rules and standard operating procedures (SOPs) can be easily implemented; in fact many rules simply fade because of their uselessness or encumbering effects. Less formalization can devolve discretion to workers, freeing them from the restrictiveness of rules and SOPs, and allowing them to become more flexible and adaptive. Less formalization with respect to professionals,

who already share codes of ethics and similar ideologies and values, is a fairly easy transition that is useful and not very risky. The greater skill training enjoyed by and provided to the professional staff facilitates the delegation of authority and responsibility, thereby mitigating the dysfunctional aspects of rules; individuals control their own actions and in some degree are controlled by others with whom they work (see the lever pertaining to norms). The job redesign and training levers are closely related to and directly impact the structural dimension of complexity or specialization. Furthermore, the creation of work groups and teams often alters individual jobs and the division of labor and thus can impact specialization and engender skill variety.

Numerous aprpoaches to the impact of organizational structure and design have been suggested. Typically, the focus has been to create the more adaptive organic structures, rather than to use the rigid bureaucratic-mechanistic forms. The tasks and environments of community organizations and social service agencies at the end of the twentieth century and the beginning of the next are not becoming less turbulent, or more calm and placid. On the contrary, uncertainty is the certainty, and developing adaptive organizational structures will be a primary task of surviving organizations as well as for the creation of settings designed to deal with new and old social problems.

COMMUNICATION AND INFORMATION MANAGEMENT

Managing communication and information involves both the kind and amount of information available to different hierarchical levels of the organization. Generally speaking, those at the top and those at the bottom of the organizational hierarchy are the richest sources of information; they are usually boundary spanners who can access information from outside the organization. However, the type of information available at the respective hierarchical levels is quite different. Executives and upper-level management tend to have information about political exigencies, funding opportunities and constraints, major legal changes, and policy shifts, as well as information about and from comparable hierarchical levels in other organizations. In contrast, lower hierarchical levels and frontline workers interact with clients, link with other agencies, and become the most knowledgeable sources about operations and direct service. Rarely does the top have access to information available at the bottom and rarer still does the bottom have access to information found at the top. Middle managers may be the least informed members of the organization, while at the same time they are the natural "linkage" between upper and lower levels of the hierarchy for exchanging and sharing information; how middle managers filter, gate-keep, distort, change, and pass on information is critical.

Transmitted information changes and becomes more positive as it ascends the hierarchy; the one-hundred-dollar loss at the bottom becomes a thousand-dollar profit by the time it reaches the top. This is because subordinates at each successive level of the hierarchy tend to communicate and pass on to their superiors the "best news," while simultaneously filtering out and minimizing the "bad news." As each subordinate communicates positively filtered information up the hierarchy, these distortions (i.e., minimized bad and accentuated good) leave decision makers with ultimately poor information with which to make decisions. Naturally, misjudgments and misguided decisions become more probable.

Despite this "rose-colored glass" effect, subordinates need to filter and sort some information; if all bits of information were passed up the hierarchy, superiors would quickly become overloaded with information and much of it would be useless. Ideally information should flow freely enough that people are not afraid to pass on important news, whether it is good or bad. Furthermore, subordinates need to be well trained and informed enough to discern the type of information needed at higher levels of the organization. Such openness and judgment highlights the relationship of the communication lever to other levers (e.g., training, norms-culture, and participation) that foster candor, trust and better judgment.

The problem of selective and distorting message transmission is by no means unidirectional. Often those at the top are unwilling to share information with levels below; for example, the failure of participative management programs is often attributed to management's reluctance and sometimes inability to share information with employees (Cole, 1979; Mohrman, 1982; Mohrman and Lawler, 1984; Sager, 1984). The job-redesign model (see Figure 26.1) identifies performance feedback (knowledge of results) as a critical factor for enhancing worker outcomes.

Information is also a source of power (French and Raven, 1959; Raven and Rubin, 1983). People who control information can influence others by withholding it, distorting it, or sending a plethora of useless messages. Therefore, the control of information and channels becomes politicized and a power resource. Effective communication must deemphasize the political aspects of communication, while emphasizing trust and rewarding those who are willing to both part with and impart information. Exchanging useful and unsanitized information is necessary, but it can only exist in a climate that encourages such exchanges. The more the top and the bottom communicate, the more trust will be engendered and a norm established concerning open communication and information sharing. As lower levels become more informed about the organization in general and as middle managers become important conduits for quality information, more effective filtering can occur. As a result, both workers and managers will become better able to identify and distinguish what is important about the information they acquire. Organization intelligence will increase and better decisions can be made.

Programs that improve the listening and communicating skills of managers and workers are one way to tap this lever. Improving communication does not imply instituting weekly staff meetings, although such communication structuring can be important. Improving communication may simply involve supervisors becoming more informed about what workers actually do on their specific jobs and becoming aware of some of the stresses encountered at such levels. Being more available for discussion, providing more information and feedback, and learning about the demands and challenges of employee task accomplishment are important objectives for all levels of the hierarchy.

GROUP NORMS AND ORGANIZATIONAL CULTURE

This lever involves integrating the individual's needs with the goals of the organization (Mohrman and Lawler, 1984). Since individual behavior is supported by sociocultural norms and values, change may be effected by altering normative orientations toward old behavior patterns and by developing commitments to new ones. This involves making changes in the individual's

attitudes, values, knowledge, skills, and relationships (Chin and Benne, 1985).

Organizational development (OD) techniques, such as team building, process consultation, conflict resolution, goal-setting processes, and recently TQM (total quality management) are typically used to effect such change. These OD programs and techniques are basically designed to engender trust among employees, open communication channels, increase cooperation, attain goal sharing, and improve the problem-solving capability of individuals and groups.

Typically OD techniques connotate long-term and encompassing changes in the organizational culture (Blake and Moutin, 1964, 1985; Burke, 1987; Cummings and Huse, 1989; French and Bell, 1990). Although organizational culture is an elusive concept and difficult to operationalize, few would argue that some organizations develop modi operandi that are oppressive and demoralizing and contribute to poor organizational performance, while others create harmonious atmospheres in which conviviality and cooperation characterize organizational and interpersonal relations and efforts. Thus, the operational difficulties of the construct, organizational culture, should not impede the recognition that organizational and managerial practices affect employee attitudes and behaviors.

The success of Japanese corporations is commonly attributed to their use of groups, emphasis on human relations, and their full utilization of human resources (Cole, 1979; Ouchi, 1981). Consequently, attempts to emulate the Japanese have fostered more interest in cultivating the potential capabilities located in the lower hierarchical levels. Japanese management systems, however, are supported by the cultural and economic contexts in which they are embedded (Sager, 1992). Likert's (1961,

1967) work clearly emphasizes the importance of having contexts that support different management practices. Thus, this lever can facilitate or inhibit the effectiveness of all the change levers.

Social service and community organizations have an inherent advantage over other organizations in effectively using this normative lever: Human service organizations are ideologically laden (Hasenfeld and English, 1974). Although ideological bases often create ambiguity in terms of task and goal accomplishment, human service organizations typically attract individuals who share the same values, similar training and client orientations, as well as a commitment to the purpose of the organization. This is extremely important. Shared values and commitment to organizational purposes can energize and enhance esprit de corps and contribute to organizational effectiveness.

REWARD SYSTEM CHANGES AND ENHANCEMENTS

Lawler's (1971, 1981) work on pay and organizational development convincingly demonstrates how rewards, especially pay, can create significant changes in performance and the quality of work life. Unfortunately, the appeal of human-relations approaches, the complexity of using money as a motivator, and its scarcity, have fostered the avoidance and neglect of approaches using money as a reward. Nonetheless, money is a fundamental reason why people work. The fact that other "motivators" such as challenge and altruism are important factors in the human-service worker's performance does not negate or minimize the importance of money as a way to impact performance and morale.

According to Lawler (1981, 1982) gainsharing and bonus plans figure prominently in reward system changes. There are a variety of payout systems and economic formulas whereby workers may share in profits or gains; many of these payout formulas are based on performance-improving suggestions submitted by individuals or groups. Gainsharing and bonus plans have not had widespread use in the nonprofit sector (Herrick, 1983) and may appear to be a contradiction in terms. Nevertheless, there are programs in nonprofits in which managers receive financial rewards for "coming in" under budget and employees receive bonuses for suggestions. Social service organizations, already underfunded, tend to perceive this lever as the least manipulable—and this may be realistic. However, performance tied to rewards, skill-based pay, performance appraisals linked to rewards, and merit increases are ways of tapping this lever within the confines of a budget.

Although it would be ideal to tap this lever by increasing monetary rewards, which are easier to disseminate, funding shortages force administrators to turn to other forms of rewards. Reward system changes are not limited to increased monetary rewards, especially when they involve across-the-board raises. One instance may involve making alterations in the way money is distributed. Equitable and fair rewards are preferable to wholesale incremenetal adjustments in pay. Reward-system changes and plans also work best when employees are involved in their development (Lawler, 1982, 1986).

Rewards system changes also involve promotions, status changes, recognition, and appreciation; these are important rewards that are often and unfortunately neglected by administrators dealing with the exigencies of keeping underfunded agencies afloat. Promotion possibilities in organizations may be increased by creating vacancy chains. If a high-level position becomes open, promoting from within creates another vacancy; promoting to the next position, again from within, creates still another vacancy. One opening at a high-level position can produce numerous opportunities for promotion, thereby increasing the amount and distribution of this scarce reward. In contrast, once a promotion is made from outside, the vacancy chain is plugged. If outside succession occurs frequently, morale is understandably deflated as employees see no opportunity for advancement. Although morale may be boosted by inside succession, there are disadvantages; for example, there is usually less organizational innovation and change initiated from a promoted insider than from an outsider who infuses new blood and fresh ideas into the organization. Promotions in the form of recognition may be created by identifying individuals as lead persons or senior workers; although additional pay may not be forthcoming, the title and recognition can be important motivators. Promotional opportunities can also be increased with the elaboration of organizational structure previously discussed under the structural change lever; for example, workers could assume a position of responsibility and authority in a program with a parallel hierarchy or they could be asked to lead a task force.

Perks are another form of reward. Sending someone to a conference or paying their association dues can be especially meaningful. Recognition is also important, and it is typically free and commonly underutilized. Social service is often considered a "thankless task," and some believe rewards for social work should come from the satisfaction of "helping" others. However, this is limited thinking. Plaques, certificates, photographs of the (social) worker of the month in the lobby, and

getting in touch with the local National Association of Social Workers chapter to recommend someone for social worker of the year honors are all rewards that can be mediated inexpensively and/or freely by the organization. Pats on the back and other forms of "thank yous" should be liberally used when earned.

CONGRUENCE AND CONCLUSION

To maximize effectiveness, change levers should be implemented congruently. Changes in one lever must be supported by changes in interrelated levers. Participation, as pointed out, has implications for job redesign, organizational structure, communication, and norms. Other levers will be impacted by changes in participation and reciprocally affect the intended changes induced by participative practices. Experience indicates that simply changing one lever without making changes in others does not lead to enhanced performance and morale. It is extremely important to tap a consistent array of levers and use them to support one another. In the instance of participative decision making, not only should job redesign, organizational structure, communication, and norms be considered in the development of PDM programs, but training in problem-solving and decision-making techniques for employees and leaders should be provided. Leaders should also be trained in conducting problem-solving meetings and employees trained in effective participation in such meetings. All participants should be given rewards for engaging in the participative practices; education, training, and rewards should also be given to others affected by the program and whose support is vital to its success.

Not only does congruence apply to the design of programs, but it also should be taken into account when evaluating or deciding to adopt a particular program. The core features of programs such as quality circles, management by objectives, and organizational grid development to name only a few, may be examined to see which levers are forcefully impacted, which are moderately impacted, and those ignored or neglected. Through such deliberate and critical consideration, more thoughtful approaches to implementing existing change programs can be developed. Change-lever congruence, then, should be incorporated into the development and implementation of existing and future programs to improve organizational performance and staff morale.

REFERENCES

Bennis, W. G., & P. E. Slater. *The Temporary Society.* New York: Harper & Row, 1968.

Blake, R. R., & J. S. Mouton. *The Managerial Grid.* Houston: Gulf, 1964.

Blake, R. R., & J. S. Mouton. *The Managerial Grid III: The Key to Leadership Excellence.* Houston: Gulf, 1985.

Burke, W. W. *Organizational Development: A Normative View.* Reading, MA: Addison-Wesley, 1987.

Burns, T., & G. M. Stalker. *The Management of Innovations.* London: Tavistock, 1961.

Chin, R., & K. D. Benne. "General Strategies for Effecting Change in Human Systems." In W. G. Bennis, K. D. Benne, & R. Chin, eds., *The Planning of Change,* 4th. ed. New York: Holt, Rinehart and Winston, 1985, pp. 22–45.

Cole, R. E. *Work, Mobility and Participation: A Comparative Study of American and Japanese Industry.* Berkeley: University of California Press, 1979.

Cummings, T. G., & E. F. Huse. *Organizational Development and Change,* 4th. ed. St. Paul: West, 1989.

Cummings, T. G., & E. S. Molloy. *Improving Productivity and the Quality of Work Life.* New York: Praeger, 1977.

French, J. R. P., Jr., & B. Raven. "The Bases of Social Power. In D. Cartwright, ed., *Studies in Social Power.* Ann Arbor: Institute for Social Research, The University of Michigan, 1959, pp. 150–167.

French, W. L., & C. H. Bell, Jr. *Organizational Development: Behavioral Science Interventions for Organization Improvement* 4th ed. Englewood Cliffs, NJ: Prentice-Hall, 1990.

Goodman, P. S. *Assessing Organizational Change: The Rushton Quality of Work Life Experiment.* New York: Wiley-Interscience, 1979.

Hackman, J. R. Designing Work for Individuals and Groups." In J. R. Hackman, E. E. Lawler III, & L. W. Porter, eds. *Perspectives on Behavior in Organizations.* New York: McGraw-Hill, 1977.

Hackman, J. R., & G. R. Oldham. *Work Redesign.* Reading, MA: Addison-Wesley, 1980.

Hackman, J. R., G. R. Oldham, R. Janson, & K. Purdy. "A New Strategy for Job Enrichment." *California Management Review, XVII* (1975), 57–71.

Hasenfeld, Y., & R. A. English, eds. *Human Service Organizations: A Book of Readings.* Ann Arbor: The University of Michigan Press, 1974.

Herrick, N. G., ed. *Improving Government: Experimenting with Quality of Working Life Systems.* New York: Praeger, 1983.

Landen, D. L., & H. C. Carlson. "Strategies for Diffusion, Evolving, and Institutionalizing Quality of Work Life at General Motors." In R. Zager & M. P. Rosow, eds., *The Innovative Organization: Productivity Programs in Action.* New York: Pergamon Press, 1982, pp. 291–333.

Lawler, E. E., III. *Pay and Organizational Effectiveness: A Psychological View.* New York: McGraw-Hill, 1971.

Lawler, E. E., III. *Pay and Organizational Development.* Reading, MA: Addison-Wesley, 1981.

Lawler, E. E., III. "Increasing Worker Involvement to Enhance Organizational Effectiveness." In P. S. Goodman, ed., *Change in Organizations: New Perspectives on Theory, Research and Practice.* San Francisco: Jossey-Bass, 1982, pp. 280–315.

Lawler, E. E., III. *High Involvement Management: Participative Strategies for Improving Organizational Performance.* San Francisco: Jossey-Bass, 1986.

Likert, R. *New Patterns of Management.* New York: McGraw-Hill, 1961.

Likert, R. *The Human Organization.* New York: McGraw-Hill, 1967.

Locke, E. A., & D. M. Schweiger. "Participation in Decision Making: One More Look." In B. M. Staw, ed., *Research in Organizational Behavior,* Vol. 1. Greenwich, CT: Jai Press, 1979, pp. 265–339.

Miller, K. I., & P. R. Monge. "Participation, Satisfaction, and Productivity: A Meta-Analytic Review." *Academy of Management Journal, 29* (1986), 727–753.

Mintzberg, H. *The Structuring of Organizations: A Systhesis of the Research.* Englewood Cliffs: Prentice-Hall, 1979.

Mohr, L. B. *Explaining Organizational Behavior: The Limits and Possibilities of Theory and Research.* San Francisco: Jossey-Bass, 1982.

Mohrman, S. A. *The Impact of Quality Circles: A Conceptual View.* Paper prepared for the Bureau of National Affairs Conference on "Current Directions in Productivity—Evolving Japanese and American Practices." Houston, Texas, May 13, 1982.

Mohrman, S. A., & E. E. Lawler, III. *Quality of Work Life* (Tech. Rep. No. G 83-14 [45]). Los Angeles: University of Southern California, Center for Effective Organizations, 1984.

Ouchi, W. G. *Theory Z: How American Business Can Meet the Japanese Challenge.* Menlo Park, CA: Addison-Wesley, 1981.

Porter, L. W., E. E. Lawler, III, & J. R. Hackman. *Behavior in Organizations.* New York: McGraw-Hill, 1975.

Raven, B. H., & J. Z. Rubin. *Social Psychology,* 2nd. ed. New York: John Wiley and Sons, 1983.

Sager, J. S. *Quality Circles, Group Decision Making, Participation and Organizational Change.* Ann Arbor: The University of Michigan, School of Social Work, 1984.

Sager, J. S. *The Emergency Organizational Model.* (Working Papers No. 1990-91-05).

Ann Arbor: School of Social Work, The University of Michigan, 1990.

Sager, J. S. *Japanese Management: Dispelling the American Myths About Japanese Management.* Paper presented at the meeting of Industrial Relations Research Association, Ontario, CA, June 1992.

Tannenbaum, A. S. *Social Psychology of the Work Organization.* Belmont, CA: Brooks/Cole, 1966.

Tannenbaum, A. S. "Systems of Formal Participation." In G. Strauss, R. E. Miles, C. C. Snow, & A. S. Tannenbaum, eds., *Organizational Behavior: Research and Issues.* Madison, WI: Industrial Relations Research Association, 1974.

Tichy, N. M. *Managing Strategic Change.* New York: John Wiley & Sons, 1983.

Tichy, N., H. Hornstein, & J. Nisberg. *Organizational Diagnosis and Intervention Strategies: Developing Emergent Pragmatic Theories of Change.* In W. W. Burke, ed., *Current Issues and Strategies in Organizational Development.* New York: Human Science Press, 1977.

Vroom, V. H., & A. G. Jago. *The New Leadership.* Englewood Cliffs, NJ: Prentice-Hall, 1988.

Vroom, V. H., & P. W. Yetton. *Leadership and Decision Making.* Pittsburg: University of Pittsburg Press, 1973.

Wagner, J. A., III, & R. Z. Gooding. "Shared Influence and Organizational Behavior: A Meta-Analysis of Situational Variables Expected to Moderate Participation-Outcome Relationships. *Academy of Management Journal, 30* (1987), 524–541.

Yukl, G. A. *Leadership in Organizations,* 2nd ed. Englewood Cliffs, NJ: Prentice-Hall, 1989.

27.

Nancy R. Hooyman, Karen I. Fredriksen, and Barbara Perlmutter

SHANTI: AN ALTERNATIVE RESPONSE TO THE AIDS CRISIS

Social and health service professionals' general insensitivity to and lack of information about issues faced by gays and lesbians have long been problematic (Messing, Schoenberg, & Stephens, 1984; Dulaney & Kelly, 1982). Such insensitivity and misinformation have been highlighted by the helping professions' inadequate response to the specific psychosocial needs of people with AIDS (acquired immune deficiency syndrome), the majority of whom thus far are gay men and intravenous drug abusers (Lopez & Getzel, 1984). The occurrence of AIDS has engendered widespread anxiety in the public mind, diverting attention from the enormous problems facing people with AIDS. Such anxiety undoubtedly underlies instances where people with AIDS have been socially isolated, dismissed from their jobs, evicted from their homes, received inadequate health care, or even been denied social and health services (NASW, 1984; Cecchi, 1986). Health and social service professionals have gradually begun to become more aware of the needs of people with AIDS. Nevertheless, both those with AIDS, as well as populations at high risk of contracting AIDS, often still face social ostracism and direct abuse of their rights as citizens (Lopez & Getzel, 1984).

Although AIDS was first recognized as a perplexing and tragic medical phenomenon, the intrinsic psychosocial dimensions of AIDS—the shattering emotional reactions of those who have the illness, those who are at risk and those who are a family member, friend, or lover of a person with AIDS—must also be attended to by health and social service professionals. Because of the prognosis associated with AIDS, the initial diagnosis, in and of itself, can be emotionally devastating. Typical psychological responses that accompany the diagnosis include fears of death and the dying process; guilt, isolation and stigmatization, confusion and concern over options for medical treatment; and an overriding sense of despair, helplessness, social rejection, and the loss of esteem typically associated with terminal illness and, often for gay men, the exposure of sexual orientation. Because the fear of AIDS tends to be compounded by homophobia (an irrational fear of homosexuals), persons with AIDS may also find themselves without the support of families, friends, and coworkers.

Traditional health and social service systems, preoccupied with the provision of medical care, reimbursement constraints, and cost-containment, may be unable to respond adequately to the "roller coaster" ride of emotional reactions experienced by persons with AIDS (Lopez & Getzel, 1984). For example, interviews with people with AIDS have shown that although their medical needs were generally addressed adequately, their psychological needs were not given sufficient attention (Morin, Charles, & Malyon, 1984). Human service professionals who work with persons with AIDS are caught in a powerful dilemma: They need to support the person in overcoming immediate crises through problem solving and the provision of concrete services while simultaneously enabling the person to explore the wide range of feelings associated with his/her remaining life, dying process, and death. A crisis intervention model of social practice, for example, fails to capture the special qualities of intervention required with people with AIDS (Golan, 1978).

In an effort to respond to this dual dilemma, Shanti, a Seattle-based alternative agency, focuses on meeting the emotional needs of persons with life-threatening illnesses and those grieving another's death. Although Shanti was formed to address psychosocial needs associated with all types of life-threatening illnesses, it now primarily serves people with AIDS or AIDS-related conditions, and those grieving the loss of a person from AIDS. In addition to providing emotional support to individuals, Shanti serves the larger community through public speaking and education, information and referral, and providing training and technical assistance to community organizations.

This article (1) reviews Shanti's mission and objectives and how these have changed over time in response to the growing AIDS crisis; (2) describes the decision-making structure that has evolved from these objectives to meet the changing needs of clients and volunteers; (3) identifies the major strengths and limitations of this structure for serving the unique needs of people with AIDS and other life-threatening illnesses; and (4) suggests implications for those presently engaged in designing and delivering services for persons with AIDS. One of the more striking characteristics of Shanti is how its objectives, the clients served, and the characteristics of volunteers have shifted over a relatively short time period in response to the rapidly changing social context created by the growing AIDS epidemic. These rapid internal and external changes, which have

placed extraordinary demands on people's energies, are also discussed.

LITERATURE REVIEW

The development of Shanti as an alternative service is consistent with Grossman and Morgenbesser's (1980) definition of alternative agencies which view themselves as departing significantly in terms of goals, modes of operation, philosophy, and structure from the traditional social service network. According to Grossman and Morgenbesser, the founders of alternative organizations are usually motivated by the desire to meet the needs of an unserved, underserved, or inappropriately served group; the initial funding is outside of traditional agency, community, or governmental sources; staff may have some professional training, but their primary characteristic is direct identification with the client group to be served. Collaborative, equalitarian structures are emphasized. Similarly, Rothschild-Whitt (1979) characterized alternative organizations by their small size, economic marginality, internal support base, diffusion of knowledge for task performance among staff positions, and mutual and self-criticism of the members or volunteers. According to Kanter and Zurcher (1973), alternative organizations value small size for allowing more interaction and attention to individual needs. Organizational stability is less important than the potential for growth and change, with the process as product. The concept of wholeness translates into efforts to integrate personal and professional aspects of member's lives, to assert the importance of relationships, and to value the person as a whole.

According to Parsons and Hodne (1982), founders of alternative organizations choose to develop an alternative services structure rather than directly challenging and trying to change the larger social and health care system. In the process of establishing an alternative structure, founders must continually assess who they want to reach, the resources available, and whether their strategy of a separate agency is politically feasible. Careful assessment of these questions is necessary for both the immediate objectives of providing direct services and the long-term objectives of organizational growth.

Although research on alternative organizations is limited compared to that on traditional bureaucracies, there appear to be characteristic dilemmas that arise in the development of alternative service agencies. These dilemmas contrast with the life-cycle stages of self-interest, professionalism, and social interest typical of traditional social agencies (Perlmutter, 1969). One dilemma faced by most alternative organizations is achieving a balance between process and product (Crow, 1978; Riddle, 1978). For example, in the development of alternative health services for women, Parsons and Hodne (1982) noted the failure of one organization to delegate responsibility and share ownership of the project with all workers, while another rotated jobs too quickly. In one health clinic, insufficient attention was paid to reaching consensus, while in another, the time spent on processing group decisions inhibited the ability to carry out tasks essential to the clinic's operation. Although the original members of alternative organizations generally share a value commitment to the importance of process, time pressures, increased size, or the demands of outside funders may result in a move toward greater task specialization in an effort to "get the job done." When knowledge needed to perform the organization's tasks be-

comes unevenly distributed, the alternative structure tends to be undermined, pushing it in the direction of power inequities (Rothschild-Whitt, 1979). Yet it is unlikely that all members will be equally skilled and interested in performing all administrative and direct service tasks, a factor that over time works against shared responsibilities.

Staff turnover generally has a negative impact on the maintenance of alternative structures. New staff may not share the founder's commitment to collective goals and structure, and therefore may not value diffusion of knowledge among staff nor more informal processes of decision making. Rapid changes in staff composition may also disrupt the personal relationships that are conducive to collective decision making. Without such strong personal ties and shared commitment to the collective structure, new staff may be more comfortable with specialization and formal structure than were the founders (Morgenbesser et al., 1981).

External funding, more than any other factor, generally alters the structure of alternative organizations (Morgenbesser et al., 1981). This is because external funding often carries other requirements, such as a board of directors, a designated division of labor, or changes in the types of clients served. When funding is readily available, the temptation to accept such funding, despite the "strings" attached, becomes strong. In addition, linkages to traditional agencies through in-service education, referral networks, and community boards can intensify the pressure to accept outside resources. According to Rothschild-Whitt (1979), organizational dependence on an external base of support tends to increase the likelihood of goal displacement and to decrease the level of internal participation by members, staff, or clients. Internal participation declines largely because as staff devote time to writing grant proposals and cultivating funding agencies, they simply have less time to attend to volunteers and clients.

As the following case study illustrates, Shanti has faced similar dilemmas in its development: conflicts between process and product, staff burnout from administrative responsibilities to which they were less committed than to direct-service tasks, resultant staff turnover, and increasing pressures from the larger environment as the AIDS epidemic has escalated and the funding for services to people with AIDS has grown.

ORIGINS OF SHANTI

The Seattle-based Shanti was started in 1983 by four volunteers, three women and one man, each cognizant of the need for such a service from their own personal experiences of loss. They were trained by the fifteen-year-old Shanti Project in San Francisco. Although not formally related, Shanti Project served as a model for the organizers of Shanti in Seattle. In 1983, social and health professionals were just becoming aware of the AIDS epidemic. Even though the founders defined Shanti as serving the full spectrum of those who were dying or grieving, they also recognized the lack of support services for those with AIDS or AIDS-related illnesses. The founders of Shanti therefore viewed themselves as developing an alternative structure to meet a growing and critical need in the community. Similar to the health clinics studied by Parsons and Hodne (1982), the founders deliberately chose to develop separate services to meet the growing need rather than to try to change existing agencies, such as hospice, which did not share

their commitment to AIDS and gay-sensitivity, nor Shanti's other goals and objectives.

Mission and Objectives

Shanti, a volunteer psychosocial support organization, serves individuals facing a life-threatening illness or grieving the loss of a loved one. A primary objective of Shanti is to provide free, confidential emotional support to individuals, both from the gay/lesbian community and from the community at large. Equally important is a focus on the personal growth, development, and support of volunteers. Shanti's philosophy emphasizes volunteers' learning to care for themselves in the process of caring for others.

In meeting these objectives, Shanti explicitly chose to be different from traditional services in a number of ways. Although hospice programs exist in local hospitals and home care agencies, eligibility for their volunteer services tends to be linked to receiving professionally provided skilled nursing services, which are expensive, or to those who are Medicare or insurance-eligible. Shanti provides services without charge regardless of a person's income, age, sex, race, religion, marital status, or sexual preference. Social-emotional needs are emphasized rather than primarily providing respite care or assisting with the practical activities of daily living and medical concerns. Clients are served during all phases of a life-threatening illness, in contrast to hospice services which are generally limited to those in their last few months of life. Shanti also differs from most hospice-related agencies in its commitment to serving the dying person's family and loved ones as primary clients with or without the dying person's involvement. By defining family to include nonrelated persons, Shanti reaches those who might not be recognized and supported by more traditional agencies. At the most basic level, Shanti's founders did not want to create another hospice; instead they intended to provide those facing a life-threatening illness and their loved ones, including gays, lesbians, and people with AIDS, with a deliberately structured alternative that would primarily address their emotional needs. The impetus for Shanti is thus similar to that of most alternative organizations: to meet the needs of an unserved, underserved, or inappropriately served group and to work with others who share similar philosophical beliefs and values (Grossman & Morgenbesser, 1980).

Decision-Making Structure

An emphasis on collective and equalitarian structure tends to be part of the shared beliefs and values. During Shanti's first two years, the four founders were largely responsible for planning and administering the organization—setting policy; program development; screening, training, and supervising volunteers; providing information and referral services; day-to-day administration, public relations, and marketing; and working with other service organizations. Simultaneously, all staff provided clinical services. For the founders, Shanti was a way of life, a full-time commitment, for which they received no financial compensation.

Although Shanti has designated staff who coordinate services, there are no paid staff. All persons, including staff, volunteer to work with Shanti. Volunteers, including the staff coordinators, are therefore both service providers and policy makers. The underlying philosophy that all volunteers

should have the opportunity to learn all tasks was reflected in the low level of specialization at this stage of organizational development. As a result, personal development of volunteers was often emphasized at the expense of long-range organizational development. In other words, priority was placed upon involving volunteers in both service and administrative responsibilities, rather than assigning tasks according to individuals' abilities or preferences.

Organizational and administrative decisions were made by consensus. If consensus could not be reached, policies were not changed. This emphasis on consensus reflects the founders' commitment to collaboration and shared decision making. Frequent feedback from volunteers and clients was also encouraged by staff. For example, staff meetings were open to all volunteers. Clients were systematically contacted for their feedback approximately six to eight weeks after being matched with a Shanti volunteer. These efforts at generating feedback and shared decision making have generally resulted in decisions that reflected the needs of all three constituencies—clients, volunteers, and staff.

When consensus could not be reached, staff and volunteers agreed upon the following principles for resolving conflicts. Each person was committed to giving and receiving feedback and to assuming responsibility for resolving issues, whether or not he or she was personally involved in the issue. As much time as needed was taken to deal with the conflict. If the conflict was not resolved, an outside person was brought in to assist in problem-resolution.

Since its founding, Shanti's structure has changed as a result of the growing numbers of new staff and volunteers. This growth resulted primarily from the escalating AIDS epidemic and with it, both the demand for Shanti to provide services to more people with AIDS and the increased need to obtain outside funding. The newcomers who replaced the original staff were frequently pressured by the need to respond to the growing community problem of AIDS. In addition, Shanti was called upon to participate in intra-agency planning meetings and task forces regarding the development of AIDS services—external demands that vied for the limited amount of time and energy available for responding to intra-agency needs.

Along with the growing number of volunteers and clients served, work demands intensified, new staff were added, and the level of specialization increased. Consistent with the effects of staff turnover and increased size noted by Morgenbesser et al. (1981), a departure from the original staff-directed structure emerged. Five task-oriented committees were established. These committees, composed of volunteers, are: office support, public relations, volunteer and client services, fund-raising, and long-range planning. All committees include a staff person, who serves as coordinator and sits on a committee of coordinators. This coordinating committee (e.g., the staff) receives input from each of the five committees, providing the overall structure for decision making and policy direction. All committees operate according to a consensus model of decision making. Major decisions are brought before the entire membership for feedback and occasionally for a vote. However, the current organization is also planning to implement a board composed of volunteers, clients, and outside representatives, a move which appears to be a shift away from an emphasis upon shared decision making solely by staff and volunteers.

The Central Role of Volunteers

The extent to which Shanti relies upon volunteers and emphasizes their emotional growth as part of its overall mission and objectives also differentiates it from other agencies. As noted above, all persons volunteer to work with Shanti. Shanti has demonstrated major strengths in the area of providing its volunteers with a wide range of opportunities for personal and professional development as service providers, administrators, policy makers, and trainers.

Shanti has also been effective in recruiting a diverse pool of volunteers. As the AIDS epidemic has escalated, and with it Shanti's response, the range of individuals who make the service commitment to Shanti reflect the growing recognition of AIDS as a community concern, not only a gay concern. Volunteers of both sexes, diverse ages, lifestyles, educational levels, and backgrounds are actively involved in all phases of the organization. Such a varied group of volunteers has permitted a valuable exchange of information and experiences among volunteers, as well as assisted in meeting the individual needs of each client.

The process of volunteering, which in itself builds support for volunteers, begins with the completion of an in-depth application, followed by a careful personal screening interview. These measures are intended to serve both the potential volunteer and the trainers in determining the suitability of volunteering at Shanti. If both parties agree, the next step is participation in the 40-hour intensive training. This is both experiential and educational, and covers two consecutive weekends. Throughout the training, support and feedback are provided to volunteers. If the trainee successfully completes the training, an invitation to join Shanti is extended. At that time, volunteers are asked to commit to one year of service and to volunteer a minimum of five hours a week; this encompasses working with clients, attending a weekly supervision and support group, and participating in optional committee work. The two-hour supervision and support group is the primary mechanism of support and is specifically structured to promote emotional growth and prevent burnout by providing volunteers with opportunities to process the feelings which arise in relation to their work with clients. It is also the place where volunteers receive feedback about their own development and their work with clients.

Another method that supports the volunteers' growth is the encouragement to participate in subsequent volunteer training sessions, to act as support/supervision group coleaders, and to assume new administrative and organizational tasks both within Shanti and within the larger social service community. Thus, the volunteer chooses whether to develop administrative skills while acquiring peer counseling skills.

Preventing Burnout

The risk of burnout exists in most service work. When working with people with AIDS, the risk of burnout is even greater, largely because of working primarily with young people for whom death is now inevitable, the debilitating physical and mental progression of the disease, and the societal isolation and rejection surrounding people with AIDS. Many volunteers have chosen to work with Shanti because of their own experiences with grief and, increasingly, with AIDS. Many of them have lost a friend or loved one to AIDS. A Shanti volunteer was recently diagnosed with Kaposi's sarcoma, one of AIDS' lethal opportunistic illnesses. Volunteers are being

increasingly called upon to support each other as AIDS claims the lives of clients, friends, and coworkers.

Although the sensitivity and skill of volunteers are undoubtedly enhanced by such experiences, their emotional vulnerability may be heightened. Regardless of past experiences, the work performed by volunteers is extremely demanding emotionally. There is often a waiting list of clients needing services. Given these pressures, volunteers could easily slip into a "helper" role, where there is always more to do and one has never done enough.

Shanti staff have deliberately aimed to minimize burnout by requiring that volunteers participate in training, support groups, and retreats. A strong support system is created by frequent telephoning, "checking in," and socializing among volunteers. The training program and support groups emphasize taking care of oneself, not solely caretaking others. Volunteers focus on cultivating self-forgiveness and self-acceptance as a way to acknowledge their own needs and recognize their own limits. The hope of developing caring and compassion for themselves in order to provide caring and compassionate service to others is a cornerstone of Shanti's philosophy. Shanti staff also believe that burnout occurs when people do not allow themselves to face their own emotions. Providing opportunities for volunteers to confront their own feelings is viewed as essential to renewing their energy in order to provide sustained support to dying and grieving individuals. In addition, volunteers are deliberately affirmed for their ability to have responded to 150 persons who would otherwise have been inadequately served in the community during the past three years. Shanti therefore represents a model of self-caretaking as well as for providing services to the dying and grieving.

However, burnout from administrative tasks tends to be higher than from the emotionally demanding work with clients. As policy makers, administrators, and direct-service workers, volunteers are involved in all aspects of administering the organization. Yet most volunteers choose to be involved in Shanti because of the chance to work directly with clients and to confront their own issues of loss, not because of organizational opportunities. As Shanti has grown, volunteers increasingly find themselves devoting more time to administrative and organizational development tasks. These time demands can be especially constraining for the majority of volunteers who are employed full-time, many of them in other service capacities.

Funding Base

Funding has always been a critical issue for Shanti. The reliance on volunteers as both policy makers and direct-service providers stems largely from an ideological position. Another primary force behind the use of volunteers is a more practical one—the limited funding available for alternative services, such as Shanti. To compound this situation, most persons with AIDS are minorities, historically disfavored by mainstream American society. The funds available for AIDS services were, until recently, extremely limited. Even as the demand for AIDS services increased and partial funding became available, resources for social services for persons with AIDS have had lower priority than research, prevention, and education. Shanti has lacked the volunteer resources to devote full-time to fund-raising efforts, and for the first 2½ years relied primarily upon donations and small-scale fund-raising efforts. Priority was initially placed on the type and quality of services which were provided

rather than on rapid growth or obtaining external funding for long-range development. However, with the increased availability of funds for direct services to persons with AIDS, current Shanti staff has placed priority on obtaining external funding. What is unknown is the extent that these fund-raising efforts will, over time, result in less attention to the personal development needs of volunteers (Rothschild-Whitt, 1979).

Shanti . . . received operating expenses and office space from the local AIDS fund-raising organization. This physical move from one of the founder's homes to their office in itself is a reflection of the staff's increased priority on serving people with AIDS. Having set this priority, staff are faced with the reality that resources for people with AIDS are gradually increasing, but that little funding exists for services to those who are dying and grieving as a result of other types of illnesses. As another step in the process of obtaining funding, Shanti is planning on establishing a board of directors, thereby moving away from having only staff and volunteers as policy makers. Shanti has also been included in recent grant-writing efforts for services to people with AIDS, which, if funded, will create paid positions for a full-time volunteer coordinator and part-time clerical support. If granted, Shanti would be obligated to serve more people than previously, as well as to increase the number of volunteers dramatically—all changes which may alter Shanti's alternative structure.

Implications

In sum, Shanti has undergone significant changes since its inception. During its development, it has faced a dilemma common to most alternative organizations: how to achieve a balance between process and task performance (Crow, 1978). Shanti has also experienced the additional tension of how to provide sufficient time for conflict resolution and the personal growth of volunteers while needing to devote tremendous energies to organizational demands.

Although reliance on highly committed volunteers is central to Shanti as an alternative service agency and, in fact, has been one of its major strengths, it has also presented organizational problems. Due to volunteer burnout from administrative and organizational demands, staff turnover has been fairly high. Morgenbesser et al. (1981) found that staff and volunteers who join an alternative organization after its creation are often less involved in viewing the agency as a primary reference group and are less uncomfortable with specialization and formal structure. Rapid changes in staff composition can also disrupt the personal relationships that seem to facilitate collective management. As original Shanti staff have been replaced by newcomers, increased priority has been placed on serving people with AIDS, expanding in size, establishing a board, and obtaining outside funding.

In addition, the administrative tasks that have consumed considerable staff time have tended to be those required for daily operation. As a result, issues of long-range planning, program development and fundraising have been inadequately addressed. Also compounding this situation has been the changing nature of the organization's larger social context: the growing AIDS epidemic, the lack of services to meet such needs, and the increased availability of external funds for services to people with AIDS, all of which have resulted in increasing service specialization. Although Shanti continues to maintain a structure that contrasts with more hierarchical agencies, factors such as these make it vulnerable

to goal displacement and movement toward a more traditional structure (Rothschild-Whitt, 1979; Morgenbesser et al., 1981; Parsons & Hodne, 1982).

These findings raise several implications for other alternative organizations. Early in Shanti's development, it would have been useful to have devoted additional time to defining collective goals; for example, to what extent should Shanti serve only persons with AIDS and their families, or the larger population of individuals who are dying or grieving? The periodic reevaluation of such goals and appropriate strategies for meeting them would also have been helpful.

Through both Shanti's philosophy and integrated service elements, a high priority has been to prevent burnout from performance of direct service tasks. The potential for burnout from administrative tasks, however, has not been as clearly recognized nor addressed. More efforts to meet the administrators' needs, through frequent staff retreats and other structured support activities, might have served to reduce staff burnout and turnover. Such structures might also have served to clarify and resolve individual differences among staff.

An additional problem facing Shanti throughout its development has been that major organizational needs, such as long-range planning, program development and fund-raising, have not been met adequately, due largely to the volunteers' time constraints and areas of interest. This problem might have been reduced if more volunteers with administrative interest and skills had been specifically recruited to participate in Shanti. Another option would have been to recognize the necessity of delegating responsibility for specialized tasks without sacrificing the benefits of exchanging skills and information through some job rotation (Parsons & Hodne, 1982). A more traditional approach might have been to seek funds in order to hire a staff person to assist with ongoing fund-raising and long-range development, or to utilize an outside consultant specializing in organizational development. Although options such as these might have reduced administrative burnout and met long-range organizational goals—and may actually become a reality as Shanti increases in size and staff—the extent to which they jeopardize Shanti's alternative structure is as yet unknown.

REFERENCES

Cecchi, R. "Living with AIDS: When the System Fails." *American Journal of Nursing,* 1986, *86*(1), 45–47.

Crow, G. "The Process/Product Split." *Quest,* 1978, *4*(4), 15–23.

Dulaney, D., & J. Kelly. "Improving Services to Gay and Lesbian Clients." *Journal of Social Work,* 1982, *27*(2), 178–183.

Furstenberg, A., & M. M. Olson. "Social Work and AIDS." *Social Work in Health Care,* 1984, *9*(4), 45–60.

Golan, N. *Treatment in Crisis Situations.* New York: Free Press, 1978.

Grossman, B., & M. Morgenbesser. "Alternative Social Service Settings: Opportunities for Social Work Education." *Journal of Humanics,* 1980, *8,* 59–76.

Kanter, R. M., & L. Zurcher. "Concluding Statement: Evaluating Alternatives and Alternative Valuing." *The Journal of Applied Behavioral Science,* 1973, *9*(2/3), 381–397.

Lopez, D., & G. Getzel. "Helping Gay AIDS Patients in Crisis." *Social Casework,* 1984, *65*(7), 387–394.

Messing, A., R. Schoenberg, & R. Stephens. "Confronting Homophobia in Health Care Settings: Guidelines for Social Work Practice." Special issue on homosexuality and social work. *Journal of Social Work and Human Sexuality,* 1984, *2*(2/3), 65–74.

Morgenbesser, M., et al. "The Evolution of Three Alternative Social Service Agencies." *Catalyst,* 1981, *11,* 71–83.

Morin, S., et al. "The Psychological Impact of AIDS on Gay Men." *American Psychologist,* 1984, *39*(11), 1288–1293.

National Association of Social Workers. *Acquired Immune Deficiency Syndrome, Public Social Policy Statement.* Silver Spring, MD: NASW, September 1984.

Parsons, P., & C. Hodne. "A Collective Experiment in Women's Health." *Science for the People,* July/August 1982, 9–13.

Perlmutter, F. D. "A Theoretical Model for Social Agency Development." *Social Casework,* October 1969, *50*(8), 467–473.

Riddle, D. "Integrating Process and Product." *Quest,* 1978, *4*(4), 15–23.

Rothschild-Whitt, J. "Conditions for Democracy: Making Participatory Organizations Work." In J. Case & R. Taylor, eds., *Co-ops, Communes and Collectives.* New York: Pantheon Books, 1979.

28.

Yeheskel Hasenfeld

PROGRAM DEVELOPMENT

INTRODUCTION

Program development and implementation is a common and crucial task of community intervention practitioners, yet it has not received adequate attention in practice theory. There seems to be an implicit assumption that, once the community practitioner has successfully mobilized action groups or planning task forces to grapple with important community issues, the function is essentially completed. Yet, the most critical element in any community organization activity is the emergence of some idea and design for a *program,* be it a direct service delivery, a training program, a coordination council, a fund-raising program, or the like.

The implementation of such a program, which in almost all instances requires the development of some organizational framework, is in the last analysis the true test of successful community organization, since the program provides in very concrete terms the outputs or services desired and needed by the community. Thus, the overall thesis of this paper is that the community intervention practitioner has the dual role of action mobilizer and planner, and of organizer and program implementer. In this paper, then, I discuss some of the major tasks and skills that the practitioner needs to know and fulfill in order to successfully implement a community-generated program. The term planner-organizer is used to designate the complexity of such a role.

Most frequently, the planner-organizer is asked to develop a program for direct-service delivery. Social action groups often develop service programs in order to serve people ignored by existing services, or as a means of gaining community support, or as a device to stimulate existing service providers to change their own programs. Examples include unions instituting information and referral services and recreation programs for retired workers, and the Black Panthers setting up a breakfast meal service and elementary school education program for neighborhood children. Thus, the discussion that follows will focus on program development for direct services. Nevertheless, the tasks and skills involved are clearly applicable to other types of programs.

Development of a new program is by no means an easy undertaking. It often requires a prolonged process of negotiation and planning. Launching a new service inevitably results in some disruption of the delicate balance that exists among various service providers. Some agency representatives may feel they were excluded from participation. Others may see the new program as a challenge to their own domain. While the planner-organizer may find it necessary to disagree with certain groups who oppose the program, he or she must have enough support and sufficient resources to withstand countervailing pressures.

Every new program requires resources—in particular, money and manpower. Without a fair chance of obtaining these, no effort to develop a new program is likely to succeed. The key to the success of a new venture could be the extent to which the planner-organizer is in a position to control at least some of the funds allocable to the relevant social service programs. Yet money without capable or trainable assistance is of little avail. And without facilities, legitimacy, or some other needed resource, both money and assistance may be expended without benefit to consumers. The planner-organizer must be willing to invest a significant proportion of time to mobilize needed resources and to influence this allocation.

THE SYSTEMS PERSPECTIVE

In considering the establishment of a new program or agency, the planner-organizer may find a "systems" perspective to be particularly useful. Each agency can be viewed as an open "system," composed of a set of interrelated units designed to achieve a common objective or complex of objectives. The activities of these units are aimed at (1) recruiting such *inputs* into the agency as money and credit, manpower, and clients; (2) transforming these inputs into actual services such as medical care, counseling, or community planning; (3) producing *output* in such forms as improved social services coordination, reduction in the incidence of need for protective services, etc.[1]

Service and Maintenance Functions

A second assumption underlying the systems perspective is that the activities of the agency staff are guided by two basic motivations. The first can be termed the goal-seeking motive leading to "service" objectives

and the second the self-maintenance motive leading to "survival" objectives. The first motive informs those staff activities designed to achieve the *output* goals of the agency. The self-maintenance motive informs those efforts by staff to maintain the agency through enhancing its access to resources, expanding its services, building a positive climate of public support, etc. Clearly, no agency can achieve its service objectives without consideration of its maintenance needs or survival objectives. Yet if the agency invests all its energies in self-maintenance it will be accused of not accomplishing, indeed of subverting, its service objectives.[2] Both sets of activities are often in tension, causing intraorganizational competition for scarce resources. Improper allocation of these resources reduces the effectiveness of any service provider.

The interplay between the goalseeking or service function of an agency and its survival needs or maintenance function can be observed in its internal structure. From a systems perspective, five subsystems within an organization are identifiable, each fulfilling an important function without which the agency is likely to experience strain and possible disintegration. Each subsystem is characterized by the function it fulfills in the agency and by a common motivation of those participating in it. The subsystems may be characterized as: (1) the technical, (2) the environmental support, (3) the institutional, (4) the intelligence, and (5) the managerial subsystems.[3]

Subsystems and Their Functions

1. The function of the *technical subsystem* is to provide a service. In a social

---

[1] See for example, D. Katz and R. Kahn, *The Social Psychology of Organizations* (New York: Wiley, 1966); F. Baker, ed., *Organizational Systems* (Homewood, IL: Richard D. Irwin, 1973).

[2] R. A. Scott, "The Factory as a Social Service Organization," *Social Problems* 15 (Fall, 1967): 160–75.

[3] D. Katz and R. Kahn, op. cit., Chapter 4.

service agency, it is generally designed to improve or maintain the well-being of a client or client population. The primary motivation of the agency staff providing these services is to achieve proficiency in these assigned tasks. The range of tasks they perform may include assessment of the client's needs; evaluation of the client's resources; counseling or treatment; and referrals to other service providers. The manner in which these tasks are performed is called the agency's service technology.

2. The *environmental support subsystem's* function is to manage or recruit those resources from the environment necessary to the performance of the tasks of the technical subsystems. At least five categories of resources must be brought into the agency: (1) money and credit to cover the costs involved in providing the services and performing other functions; (2) personnel such as administrators, social workers, counselors, clerical staff, and other support staff; (3) clients whose needs or interests can be served by the agency; (4) knowledge and expertise necessary for the successful implementation of the services; and (5) complementary services of other agencies necessary to ensure that the agency's services are effective.

Procurement and management of these resources requires a variety of transactions or exchanges with those external units in the environment (other systems) that control these resources. This requires that certain agency employees perform what systems theorists call "boundary roles": roles that are necessary to develop and facilitate transactions between the organization and its environment. Boundary relationships are generally managed by agency staff with special responsibility for these tasks. For example, when budget staff negotiates with state and national officials for the allocation of fiscal resources, it manages boundary relationships leading to input of fiscal resources. When personnel workers interview or recruit potential staff, intake workers screen potential clients, and various staff members develop relations with other social service agencies, each also performs a boundary role or assumes a boundary function. In most smaller agencies, many of these boundary relationships are likely to be fulfilled by the same person or persons. These activities enable the agency to achieve some mastery over its environment, leading to procurement of needed resources with some degree of certainty or stability.[4]

3. Staff performing *institutional subsystem* functions seeks to obtain social support and legitimation for the agency from the environment. Without such support, the agency cannot hope to obtain the resources necessary for other functions. Sometimes, legitimation is in the form of a legal mandate, such as the Housing Act, Medicare, the Social Security Act, or other legislation.

Without understanding the importance of these legislative acts, one should not ignore the importance of obtaining social support in the very community in which the program operates. This includes support from potential clients, various civic organizations, governmental agencies, and other social service agencies. Staff activities involve the development of ties with key community influentials, contribution of resources to important community functions, public exposition of the agency's services, etc. Such activities are oriented toward "institutionalizing" the agency in the community, assuring it will be perceived as integral and indispensable to the community's interests.[5]

[4]H. Aldrich, "Organizational Boundaries and Interorganizational Conflict," *Human Relations* 24 (1971): 279–293.

[5]C. Perrow, *Organizational Analysis* (Belmont, CA: Wadsworth, 1970): 92–132.

4. The ability of the agency to develop effective linkages with its external environment as well as an effective service delivery system is dependent on the operation of the agency's *intelligence and feedback mechanisms.* The functions of the intelligence subsystem are: (1) to gather and interpret vital information about the conditions of the target population for which the service is developed and about other potential client populations, about new service opportunities, about the needs and attributes of the clients served, etc.; and (2) to provide feedback to the staff of the agency on the outcomes of their efforts. This may include information about the results of client referrals to various services, evaluation of staff activities in the counseling and treatment of clients, or assessment of the "progress" being made by those clients.

Intelligence activities can help the agency to reduce uncertainty about its efforts and can be used to plan on a more rational basis. Without adequate intelligence, any agency is in danger of finding itself off target or out of the mainstream of client needs.

5. Activities of the *managerial subsystem* cut across all the other subsystems in the agency. Management is in charge of making the key decisions regarding what services get delivered, by whom, and how; relations with the environment; and the use of intelligence. The major tasks of management are: (1) to coordinate the activities of the various subsystems in the agency; (2) to resolve conflicts between the various hierarchical levels, and to elicit the compliance of staff to its work requirements; and (3) to effect coordination between the external demands on the agency and its own resources and needs. Management acts to achieve control and stability within the agency and to mediate and achieve a compromise between the various needs and demands of the subsystems of which it is composed.

From this rather brief overview, it should be apparent that each subsystem is dependent on inputs from the others in order to fulfill its function. The quality of the performance of each subsystem profoundly affects the quality of work done in other parts of the agency. A change in one subsystem is likely to affect the performance of the others. For example, increased intelligence activities may result in increased capacity to enlist new services for the target population, which in turn influences the ability of those performing the service technology of the agency to help those clients.

Starting a New Service or Program

An understanding of these systemic functions is necessary in any effort to establish a new service or program or to modify and expand an existing one. In choosing whether to work through an existing agency or to establish a new agency, the planner-organizer must consider the costs and advantages of building from what already exists as against building something entirely new.

Developing a new agency to serve certain needs has the clear advantage of freeing the planner from the constraints of existing arrangements. These may include competing objectives of ongoing community agencies as well as tradition, and the custom of following established procedures. Overcoming such obstacles is by no means easy. Consider, for example, the difficulties that might be anticipated in attempting to shift the program focus of a medical clinic serving primarily young mothers and their children, to a medical checkup program for the aging, or of getting a citywide planning agency to develop neighborhood planning "outposts."

Adding a new program to an existing agency may result in serious coordination problems between functional units, may lead to conflict with other agency activities, and may ultimately lead to its "benign neglect."

On the other hand, establishing a new agency is often costlier than expanding the services of an existing organization. An established agency is often well recognized and supported in the community. Its staff has the training and experience to run the agency and knows how to handle all its administrative details. Moreover, the agency may have all the basic equipment necessary for the new service or program. New agencies often flounder because of the lack of experience and expertise.

PROCEDURES IN ORGANIZING A NEW SERVICE OR PROGRAM

Identifying the Need for Service

No new agency or program should be initiated unless it is propelled by the existence of a concrete and viable need. Self-evident as this may seem, attempts are too often made to develop new services without a clear definition and articulation of the needs to be met. Lack of clarity and specificity of needs is likely to result in two undesirable consequences. First, it makes it far more difficult to mobilize community support for the new program. Second, the actual design of the program may be haphazard, ad hoc, often leading to ineffectiveness and inefficiency. A cardinal principle in program design is that the greater the clarity of the program's objectives, the better its chances for success.

Identifying unmet needs in the community is a complex task that necessitates sev-

eral steps. The concept of "need" itself often defies adequate definition. What is perceived as a need by one group may not be so considered by another. Nevertheless, there are a number of ways in which planners can get a quick orientation to needs. The following are illustrative strategies:

1. Planners might start by examining available statistical reports such as census data, local Social Security office data, county government surveys, health surveys. While information on the number of potential clients in a given area, their distribution in various neighborhoods, their level of income, housing patterns, health conditions and the like might not indicate what they "need," such information is often suggestive.

2. The planner-organizer might then take a second step: identifying the various agencies in the area that serve the community. This involves finding out whom these agencies serve and what types of services they offer. Statistical reports issued by relevant agencies, the local welfare council and the public social service agencies may be of particular importance. Some communities may have developed information systems for a network of agencies that could provide invaluable data to the planner-organizer.[6]

3. A third step is to explore with the staff of the agencies that are current or potential providers of services to the target population the concerns and problems it has identified regarding gaps or inequities in services.

4. Very early in the process, planners should meet with community groups to discuss their wants, preferences, and interests.

---

[6]See for example, CHILDATA. Council for Community Services in Metropolitan Chicago.

5. A more systematic data-gathering procedure might be developed through a "needs survey" of the neighborhoods in which potential clients are most likely to reside. The facilities of a college or university or a local mental health center, as well as civic groups and volunteers, can be mobilized to conduct the survey. Questions should be designed to elicit information about the problems and unmet needs of those interviewed. A social-indicators–type survey is one of the most useful of the new devices to get at such information.[7]

An important concomitant of the planner's information-gathering activities is his or her effort to increase the community's awareness of the needs of the target population. Involvement of community leaders and representatives of agencies in determination of these needs sensitizes them to existing problems and lays the groundwork for mobilizing them into action. Awareness on the part of key groups and agencies in the community is often fundamental to the initiation of new programs.

Mobilizing Support for the Service

It is extremely difficult to develop a new program without the existence and active support of a group in the community that is highly committed to its development. The planner-organizer must often initiate and organize such an action group. The action group then gathers resources and influence, actively representing the new program's objectives, and fights for its support in the community. In short, it assumes an advocate function. Sometimes this group will be the planner's advisory council. At other times it will be a specially organized task force on transportation or protective services or some other need. Again, it may be a purely ad hoc coalition of interested parties.

What persons should the planner-organizer mobilize into such a group? Perhaps more than anything else, participants should share a keen interest in and concern for the welfare of the target population. To be truly responsive, it must include representatives of the clients themselves. Potential for influence is another criterion for inclusion. The greater the individual prestige of the members, the greater their potential for collective influence. Influential members may include representatives of civic organizations, financial institutions, church organizations, and the like.

The higher the level of understanding about the problems of the target population among members of this group and the greater their expertise in the delivery of services to them, the more realistic will be the group's efforts and the greater the credibility of its suggestions to the community. Planners often enlist members of professional associations, physicians, social workers, etc., to assure this expertise. Having representatives of community agencies in the group increases the chances that their support for a new program will be forthcoming.

The function of such a group might be: to formulate the overall objectives of the new program; to identify the target population to be served; to identify sources of financial support for the new program; to present the program objectives to important institutions in the community (such as city council, county government, mental health board, United Fund); or all of these.

This group might also examine in detail the information and ideas developed by the planner-organizer. Although the group

[7]D. Fruin, "Analysis of Need," in M. J. Brown, ed., *Social Issues and the Social Services* (London: Charles Knight, 1974): 27–56.

itself need not develop a detailed plan for action, consensus regarding the type of program to be developed is helpful. Sometimes, of course, consensus is difficult to reach. Participants must be aware that differences in opinion or in conclusion are possible, and that these experiences can be healthy. An action group should provide the arena where ideas can be exchanged, proposals explored, and creative thinking encouraged. Ultimately, the group should formulate a basic plan for a new program by identifying and agreeing upon its major objectives and the population it should serve.

It is from this action group that a body in charge of defining or reviewing the policies for the new program may ultimately be drawn. This may be formalized as a board of directors, as an advisory council, or as an internal task force within an existing agency. The importance of an action group of this kind cannot be overemphasized. In the founding stages of the new program, the planner-organizer will need to rely heavily on its support, energy, and creativity, and most importantly, on its ability to mobilize necessary resources for the program.[8] The existence of an advocate group is no less crucial when the planner decides to launch the program within an existing agency, than when an entirely new structure is to be developed.

Assigning Responsibilities to a Board or Advisory Council

When the interest group has developed an adequate level of cohesion and formulated a basic statement regarding the mandate of the new program, it may be reconstituted as a formal board or council. It might then be given any of the following charges:

1. Development of a specific plan for the implementation of the new program
2. Responsibility for obtaining the basic resources to get the program started
3. Authority to hire or approve the director of the new program
4. Accountability for the activities of the program director and the disbursement of fiscal resources

The board or council must be helped to develop some internal division of labor to ensure that the necessary tasks will be fulfilled. This may involve designating members as president or chairman, secretary, treasurer, program planning subcommittee and the like. In addition, clear procedures for decision making must be formulated. These steps are of particular importance since the board's decisions are bound to have critical impact on the character and direction of the program.

Defining the Mission of the New Agency or Program

Establishment of a new program requires a carefully planned blueprint that specifies both mission and operational objectives. It requires a thoughtful assessment of the feasibility of achieving each objective and identification of the essential means for implementing it. Identified needs coupled with available resources and means must be translated into a series of program objectives aimed at meeting these needs.

The planner-organizer plays a crucial role at this stage. Possessing critical information regarding needs, as well as knowledge about potential resources, he or she

---

[8]M. Zald, "The Power and Function of Boards of Directors: A Theoretical Synthesis," *American Journal of Sociology* 75 (July 1969): 97–111.

must help the board, advisory council, or task force to reach consensus on what the organization's mission will be.

This mission is defined in terms of needs to be met, populations to be served, and services to be given. This mission, however, must be translated into operational terms. This requires first of all, *specification of the needs to be addressed*. These *needs are prioritized* (step no. 1), and *objectives specified* (step no. 2). It is not necessary that the most crucial need be acted on first. Sometimes what is most easily accomplished takes precedence on the planner's timetable. But the ultimate mission must always be kept in mind.

Specifying the Objectives

Specifying the objectives of the program is a process of moving from the general to the specific through careful assessment of alternatives. Assume, for example, that there is a consensus to focus on the needs and problems of aged persons living alone. In the process of identifying the needs of such a population there arises a growing awareness that they are most likely to experience problems in personal management. Such consensus does not lead directly to programs or services. Are these problems expressed in poor household management, in inadequate diet, in poor personal care, in social isolation? Which of these problems are of the greatest urgency? If agreement on the urgency of these problems can be reached, they may be ordered on a chart. In Figure 28.1, four specific problems are identified and ordered in terms of importance.

The next task (step no. 3) is to *specify* the "target" population to determine more exactly what older persons are to be helped by the new or expanded services. A similar process is followed to identify those who manifest the problems most acutely. These may be found in a minority population with low income, residing in a specific neighborhood. Agreements must be reached concerning this target population, as its characteristics will determine the feasibility of various alternatives for responding to the needs.

The choice of the target population should also reflect contingencies regarding the attainment of needed resources. Grants

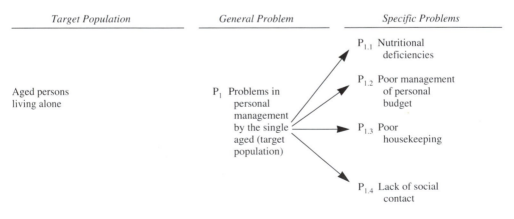

Target Population	*General Problem*	*Specific Problems*

$P_{1.1}$ Nutritional deficiencies

$P_{1.2}$ Poor management of personal budget

Aged persons living alone — P_1 Problems in personal management by the single aged (target population) — $P_{1.3}$ Poor housekeeping

$P_{1.4}$ Lack of social contact

FIGURE 28.1

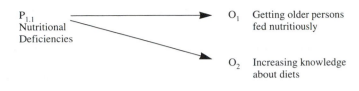

FIGURE 28.2

may be earmarked for certain categories of older persons. Certain agencies may be able to provide certain services only to older persons living in their geographical jurisdiction. Also, if it will take two years and $200,000 to develop a service for persons living in neighborhood X, while a similar level of service to persons in neighborhood Y is possible for far less and in only nine months, the choice of initial target population may be clear.

Next comes *exploring alternative program approaches* to dealing with specific problems of the target population (step no. 4). For example, in addressing the problem of nutritional deficiencies the objective may be to provide meals to a given population. Alternatively, the service might be an educational one, in which older persons are taught about proper diet (see Figure 28.2).

Similarly, in response to financial management problems, program objectives may include helping older persons to use their financial resources more efficiently, increasing access and use of banking services, and the like (see Figure 28.3).

Through this process a list of potential agency or program objectives can be developed.

Doing a Feasibility Study

After an inventory of alternative objectives has been formulated, a feasibility study of each (step no. 5) is necessary.

Some of the criteria to be used are as follows:

1. What would be the fiscal cost?
2. What would be the manpower requirements?
3. What facilities and equipment would be needed?
4. How receptive to the objective could the community be expected to be?
5. What would be the anticipated support of the objective by other community agencies?

With such information on each objective, the planning task force must now shift its focus to the other side of the coin,

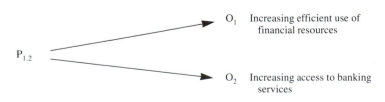

FIGURE 28.3

namely *assessing the potential money and credit* the new program could hope to obtain (step no. 6). Some of the elements in such considerations are:

1. The availability of federal and/or state grants
2. Potential contributions by local government
3. Donations and contributions by local private organizations such as United Fund
4. In-kind contributions by social service agencies and social clubs
5. Availability of volunteers to offset or reduce staffing costs

In considering various sources of support, it is often necessary that the new program be affiliated with, or an integral component of, an existing agency. The auspice-giving or sponsoring agency may be able to allocate a certain portion of its budget for the new program, cut the administrative or overhead costs, or provide the organizational auspices required as qualification for grants.

Following the feasibility study, the board, council, or task force must then, on the basis of all the information on options and constraints, determine which services the new program will provide. This process culminates in a comprehensive policy statement specifying the consented objectives of the new program, the rationale for their adoption, the kinds of services to be provided, the clients to be served, and the individuals and groups who have assumed responsibility for the program and will be accountable for it to the public. Such a statement may serve as a charter, which may be required if the program is to become incorporated. In any event, it is a claim for domain and a statement of intent.

Obtaining Seed Money for Start-Up

Some planner-organizers assume that no project should commence unless all the resources needed to ensure its success are secured. This view fails to recognize that the most effective way to obtain needed resources may be to start the project and count on its visibility, demonstrated utility, and receptivity by clients to attract new resources. A program once started often generates its own momentum, attracting supporters unknown prior to the project's initiation and quickly developing spokesmen for itself in the community. This, of course, is not always the case. Many programs have foundered on inadequate funding, regardless of the need for the services. Every beginning necessitates some risk taking. The constraint of inadequate financial resources is a limiting factor, but it need not be an inhibiting one.

Nevertheless, basic "seed" or "start-up" money is often necessary. The planner-organizer, with a knowledge of federal and state funds and grants, and through contacts with local agencies, plays a crucial role in locating and obtaining funds. Together with the sponsoring agency or members of the board, task force, or advisory council, the planner-organizer may initiate or provide technical assistance toward: (1) the submission of grant proposals to federal or state governmental agencies or to private foundations; (2) fund-raising campaigns with the help of local civic associations, fraternal clubs, or churches; (3) solicitation of donations from industrial and commercial organizations; (4) competition for local or revenue-sharing funds; (5) presentations before the United Fund; (6) development of contracts with established community agencies, such as a community mental health board, for the provision of funds for the new program; (7) locating in-kind resources (such as facilities and equipment) through enlistment of the aid of social clubs and the news media; (8) mobilizing volunteers to provide the initial manpower needed to start the program.

The initial resources gathered for the new program must be allocated for two basic purposes: to set up the actual service or program, and to promote the program in the community, attracting additional resources. Often, because of inadequate financing, there is a tendency to ignore the second purpose. Yet if those resources are not allocated to promotion, the program may quickly reach a dead end. While it may be difficult to divert limited dollars from needed services, failure to do so may be shortsighted, ignoring the fact that organizations must survive to be successful. Promotion requires more than money, however. It usually requires the assignment of staff to carry it out.

Specifying the Program Technology

The program objectives formulated in the new program's policy statement do not necessarily define the means to achieve them. The "set of means" by which the objectives are to be accomplished is called the *program technology* of the organization.

As the technology becomes articulated, it provides a series of guidelines for the type of staff and skills needed and the daily tasks to be performed in serving clients.[9]

The components of a program technology can be derived from the program objectives discussed earlier. In the previous example, the problem of nutritional deficiencies led to identification of two objectives—getting older persons fed nutritiously, and increasing their knowledge about diets. In attempting to implement the first of these objectives, the planner-organizer should explore every possible type of service that relates to providing adequate meals for the aging. Schematically, the process can be presented as shown in Figure 28.4.

Thus S_1 may be a meals-on-wheels service, S_2 may represent a cooperative cooking program for small groups of older persons in a given neighborhood, and S_3 might be a hot lunch program at the neighborhood schools. The choice of the specific service may be based on such criteria as: (1) known success of similar programs elsewhere, (2) availability of expertise to implement it, (3) availability of other

---

[9]On the concept of human service technology see Y. Hasenfeld and R. English, eds., *Human Service Organizations* (Ann Arbor: University of Michigan Press, 1974): 12–14.

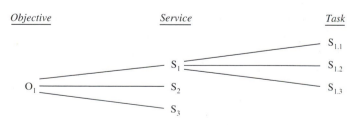

FIGURE 28.4

necessary resources, (4) receptivity by the aged to be served.

Assuming that the meals-on-wheels program has been adopted, the next series of specifications identifies the major tasks required to provide the service. For example, $S_{1.1}$ stands for organizing volunteers with cars; $S_{1.2}$, preparation of weekly visits by a nutritionist; $S_{1.3}$, preparing the meals at the kitchen of the local church, etc.

In short, this process provides a blueprint of all major tasks necessary to make the program operative.

Implementing the Program Technology

Once the choice of technology is made and its components identified, the new program can proceed to obtain the needed personnel. The program technology itself can be used to provide guidelines for the type of personnel required, and to specify the skills required of staff. It can, in fact, be used as the basis for writing job descriptions—although these should not be overly prescriptive or rigid.

Any program, in its initial phase, will require a great deal of flexibility from its staff. Staff may be called upon to switch roles and assume various tasks as the need arises, even though tasks calling for particular skills must be performed by qualified personnel.

The success of the meals-on-wheels program, for example, may hinge on the skills of a nutritionist needed to plan well-balanced meals. A program in which volunteers cook and deliver meals may only seem to be successful but in fact be missing the objective of getting older people fed nutritiously.

Once personnel are hired they must be given the responsibility to perform those tasks for which they are qualified. A nutritionist, for example, may not be the right person to supervise or organize drivers for the "wheels" part of the meals program. There is often a tendency to assume that a higher level of credentials implies proficiencies in many areas. Yet a nutritionist with an academic degree may know little about counseling or working with volunteers. Often a volunteer is much better qualified.

Developing an Appropriate Delivery Structure

Division of labor, then, is all-important. Effective division of labor requires three critical organizational decisions: Who does what? In what order must various tasks be performed? Who is accountable for what is done? The first decision requires identification of the tasks to be performed and the persons to perform them. The second decision is related to sequence and coordination. Some tasks must be performed before others can be begun. Those that are performed sequentially may be separated among several work units. Other tasks must be performed together and belong to the same work unit.

In every organization there are certain sets of activities for which a supervisory person may be held accountable. The following principles may prove useful in guiding the development of an appropriate set of structural relationships.[10]

1. Those activities which need to be done simultaneously or in close proximity to each other are generally best grouped together. In the example given, the menu planning and the cooking activities should be in the hands of certain

---

[10]P. R. Lawrence and J. W. Lorsch, *Organizations and Environment* (Cambridge, MA: Harvard University Press, 1967).

staff, while the handling of the delivery of the meals can be in the hands of another group. A set of activities which must be closely coordinated should be conducted or supervised by a single unit supervisor.

2. Activities that have different time and space schedules and contingencies should generally be grouped separately. For example, the meals-on-wheels program should be separated from a group counseling program.

3. Tasks which can be performed through explicit routines should be separated from tasks that are nonroutine. For example, determination of membership, registration, and fee assessment are routine tasks. They should not be performed by those who provide consultation to community groups, a highly nonroutine activity.

4. Activities which require different ways of relating to the clients should be separated. For example, recreational activities for older people should not ordinarily be provided by the staff who give intensive individual counseling. While the same staff could conceivably do both, there ought to be a clear distinction between their two functions.

5. Staff should not be subjected to multiple supervision if at all possible. If it is necessary for more than one supervisor to relate to a particular staff person because of multiple roles that staff person performs, clear distinction must be made regarding the areas of jurisdiction of each supervisor.

The period of initial implementation of program technology is a period of trial and error. It requires a great deal of flexibility and no little tolerance for failure and for ambiguity. Open-mindedness and willingness to explore alternative routes are essential ingredients. During the early stages of program development, lines of communication with staff and clients must be kept as open as possible. Feedback is essential if the program is to adjust to unexpected exigencies. Staff who work directly with the community can provide invaluable information on the operationalization of the technology and its problems, its failures, and its successes.

It is probably desirable to have a "dry run" of the technology to test its organization and to acquaint the staff with its roles and duties. This can be accomplished through simulation techniques prior to putting the program into the field. Another approach is to select clients who are willing to volunteer for the service, even though the "bugs" in it may not have been fully shaken out.

Developing Inter-Agency Relationships

Concurrent with development of the technology of an agency or program is the development of a "support structure." This structure refers to the organization's patterned relationships to those elements in its environment that provide it with the resources necessary to attain its service and maintenance objectives. These elements include:

1. Clients or *consumers* of its service
2. Fiscal, manpower, technical, and other *resources* essential to the goal-oriented performance
3. *Complementary or supportive services* without which an agency's services would be unattainable, inadequate, or ineffective
4. Support or recognition from regulatory and auspice-providing bodies which give the program its *authority or mandate*

Managing the flow of these elements to and from the program requires establishment of a variety of exchange relationships with other organizations in the environment. This environment is described as an agency's "task environment." It is composed of all those groups and organizations whose actions directly affect the agency's goal attainment. Exchange activities leading to receiving elements from the task environment may take the form of: (1) competition, (2) contractual agreements, (3) cooptation, or (4) coalition formation.[11]

Agencies and programs are frequently in *competition* with each other for needed resources. One agency may compete with another for a federal grant by offering to serve more clients per dollar; it may compete to obtain better-trained staff by offering better benefits.

Human services agencies often make *contractual arrangements,* in which one organization agrees to do something for another (often in return for something). Without such arrangements, many services would be poorly performed or left undone. Examples abound. Agencies may exchange staff with complementary competencies on a temporary basis. One agency may do the mailing and publicity for another. A community group may contract with the Welfare Council to assess the service needs of a particular neighborhood. A county department of social services may purchase services from other agencies for its clients, including recreation, mental health, or protective services it does not have the staff to provide directly.

A new program or agency may also attempt to *coopt* key persons from other agencies whose services it seeks. Cooptation is accomplished through involving others in the design of a service or delivery of a service program. Cooptation strategies are employed when involvement and its rewards are likely to give those who might otherwise oppose a program a greater appreciation for why it is needed and what it is intended to accomplish. Their involvement may not only nullify potential opposition, but may actually increase support.

When agencies pool their resources in a joint venture, they form a coalition. Coalitions differ from contracts in that the latter require explicit agreements about what one party will do for the other. Coalitions, on the other hand, are binding only insofar as working together leads to some mutual goal attainment.

It is not essential for parties in an exchange relationship to benefit equally from the exchange, or to have fully complementary goals. It is only necessary that each part perceive the relationship as being of some benefit to itself.

The choice of each of these strategies depends on numerous conditions, particularly those pertaining to the perceived status and desirability of the new program in the community. The more secure and the greater the importance attached to the agency's services, for example, the more likely it is to employ competitive and contractual strategies.

Enlisting Needed Elements from the Environment

In the discussion that follows, attention will be given to how agencies recruit resources or manage the flow of needed elements from the environment itself.

Clients. Clients can be recruited through referrals by other agencies informed about the new program. Clients may also be

[11]K. Benson, "The Interorganizational Network as a Political Economy," *Administrative Science Quarterly* 20 (June 1975): 229–46.

informed of a service through the news media. To reach some isolated clients, it is often necessary to launch a door-to-door campaign using volunteers.

Inadequate interpretation of an agency's services or intake policy may result in inappropriate referrals. An agency that turns away many ineligible clients causes a serious and unnecessary hardship to those clients and to its staff as well. It does harm to its own image, often damaging its relationships to other agencies. Thus it is critical for the new program to disseminate accurate and specific information about eligibility, both to the public and to other social agencies. Changes in eligibility criteria should be promptly communicated to all referral sources.

Permanent Sources of Funding. Often a new program must expend some of its initial and temporary resources on activities aimed at securing additional, more permanent sources of funding. Examples of such activities include: (1) entering into negotiations with the United Fund or United Way; (2) preparing grant applications to federal and state governmental agencies; (3) organizing a group of community influentials willing to sponsor an annual fund drive; (4) negotiating with local governmental bodies such as community mental health boards or county commissioners to incorporate the program under its sponsorship.

These and other activities require that certain staff members spend considerable time and energy meeting with potential funding sources, exchanging ideas, and presenting the agency's case.

It is often desirable to designate a specific staff position for such activities and hire a person with considerable experience in mobilization of resources.

Knowledge and Expertise. No new program can function without adequate access to at least the minimal amount of necessary knowledge and expertise. In the long run, the success of an agency may hinge on the quality of services it offers, and that quality may be in direct proportion to the knowledge and expertise of its staff. Inadequate and erroneous information could be disastrous.

The planner-organizer can mobilize expertise through: (1) enlisting the services of experts in the field from nearby institutes and universities; (2) consulting with and visiting programs of similar nature in other communities; (3) arranging information exchanges between the staff of the new agency and that of an established one in another area; (4) exploring the available literature on the problems or needs the program attempts to deal with; (5) obtaining consultation and relevant publications from appropriate state and federal agencies; (6) arranging for training and continuing education seminars.

Complementary Services. The effectiveness of any program is dependent in no small measure on the availability of complementary services for its clients. It is not enough to give one's own service well. No matter how highly specialized a service, the organization providing that service must still assume some responsibility for the general welfare of its clients. It cannot shy away from its obligation to make sure that clients receive other needed services.

This is particularly true when the effectiveness of the very services provided by the agency is dependent on the complementary services of other agencies. For example, if an agency develops a child-care program, it cannot in good conscience ignore the health needs of the children, and it may contract for periodic medical examinations with the local "well baby" clinic. A nutrition program for the aged might not be successful unless it also enlisted cooperation from the outreach staff of the Information and Referral Service, the Visiting Nurses Association, or the Mental Health Crisis Center.

A new program must identify the crucial services it will need to enlist from other agencies and programs in order to meet its own objectives. It is within the planner-organizer's responsibility to see to it that such services are or will be made available. Without them, the new program may fail.

These complementary services can be arranged through several means: (1) actual purchase of such services from another agency; (2) contract of exchange of services between the two agencies; (3) a unilateral decision by the other agency to provide the needed services as a gesture of goodwill; (4) a coalition of several agencies with different services all committed to serve the same clients.

Monitoring and Evaluation. Every program is subject to the monitoring and evaluation of some overseeing agencies. These may be state licensing organizations, other governmental units, local administrative boards, professional associations, citizens' groups, or other interested parties. Often these regulatory agencies exert considerable influence. They may impose very specific requirements for the agency to meet.

A state agency, for example, may annually audit the financial transactions of the program, or it may check the extent to which the facilities conform to state regulations. A professional organization may be responsible for accreditation without which outside grants cannot be received.

The planner-organizer must see to it that the program has developed the appropriate mechanisms by which it can meet the requirements of these regulatory agencies. This is not a mere bureaucratic formality.

Accrediting bodies and standard-setting organizations are often the key sources of legitimation and support of a new program. For example, an agency approved for internship of urban planners will gain considerable prestige and recognition in the professional community and could, therefore, attract good staff. Similarly, an agency that receives a favorable evaluation by a state agency is more likely to obtain future state grants.

Maintaining appropriate relations with the various agencies and organizations necessitates the establishment of "boundary roles" for program staff. Persons in these roles develop and maintain linkages between the new program and relevant organizations in its environment.[12] A staff person may be designated as the liaison with the state social service agency, county government, local hospital, etc. The duties of boundary personnel include: (1) establishment of the necessary relations with outside groups and organizations; (2) resolution of whatever difficulties may arise in the course of a relationship; (3) obtaining relevant up-to-date information about the activities of the partner to the relationship; (4) establishment of contacts with key staff in that organization or group who may be favorable toward the agency; (5) alerting the agency to new developments that may alter the relations between the two.

The ability of an agency to seize on new opportunities in the environment, to adapt to new changes, and to be prepared for new constraints depends on the effective job performed by the occupants of these boundary roles. They serve as the ears and eyes of the agency, without which its ability to adapt, grow, and develop would be seriously hampered.

---

[12]H. Aldrich and D. Herker, "Boundary Spanning Roles and Organization Structure," mimeographed paper (Ithaca, NY: Cornell University, 1974).

Legitimation and Social Support. Underlying all the inter-agency relations described above is a pervasive need of the program to obtain legitimation and social support. The success of the program in achieving viability is dependent on its ability to become a recognized "institution" in the community. Once the program is perceived by key elements in the community as desirable, indispensable, and an important contributor to the general welfare of the community, it has been "legitimated." Legitimacy implies that the community is willing to accept it as a viable and necessary component of the service structure.[13]

Support and legitimacy do not come easily; neither are they cheap. Concerted efforts to achieve them must be made by program staff. Support generally requires at the very least a satisfied community group or gratified clients. This is the core of an agency's constituent base. This constituency should also include other social service agencies that benefit in some direct way from the services offered by the new program. The constituent base should also include community influentials and professionals who are committed to the well-being of the target population.

Other mechanisms to promote support for the program include: lectures and presentations by staff to various community groups; establishment of an influential board of directors; public visits to the agency's facilities; reports by the news media of the activities of the agency; etc. But necessary as these are, none is sufficient without solid constituent support.

Getting Staff to Perform Adequately

Persons choose to work in organizations and agencies for a variety of reasons. They often join an agency staff with personal expectations and aspirations. The agency, on the other hand, expects them to perform in accordance with its needs, demands, and schedules. There may be many points of incongruity between personal aspirations of staff and organizational expectations. The larger the discrepancies, the greater the strains and the less likelihood that staff will perform adequately.[14]

Planner-organizers can help a new program determine adequate criteria for staff selection and realistic expectations for performance. Individuals who become employees of an agency make a contractual agreement whereby they accept the role requirements assigned to them in exchange for the various inducements provided by the agency (salary, work satisfactions, good working conditions).

A great deal of misunderstanding can be avoided if the agency specifies its requirements at the point of recruitment. Clearly written requirements can guide the agency to hire staff who have the needed skills, aptitudes, and attributes. Recruitment, however, is only a limited mechanism to ensure that staff will perform adequately. Socialization is a critical organizational process through which staff internalizes agency norms and values and learns specific role obligations. Two important socialization mechanisms are training and staff development.

In the final analysis, however, effective and efficient role performance by staff is predicated on the design of a work unit that is congruent with the tasks it has to perform.[15] Tasks can be categorized by two major variables: (1) *Task difficulty,* which

---

[13]P. Selznick, *Leadership in Administration* (New York: Harper, 1957).

[14]L. W. Porter, E. E. Lawler, and J. R. Hackman, *Behavior in Organizations* (New York: McGraw-Hill, 1975).

[15]C. Perrow, op. cit., Chapter 3.

refers to the degree of complexity, amount of knowledge needed, and reliance on non-routine decision making. For example, determination of service eligibility may be a very simple task based on few explicit decision rules, while planning community services necessitates consideration of many factors, reliance on extensive knowledge, and complex decision making. (2) *Task variability,* which refers to the degree of uniformity and predictability of the work to be done. For example, preparation of monthly statistical reports is a relatively uniform and predictable task, while developing ties with various agencies calls for a variety of procedures.

Tasks which are low in complexity and variability call for a work unit structure which is essentially bureaucratic in the classical sense of the word. Tasks which are high in complexity and variability necessitate a work unit structure which is "human relational." In a bureacratic structure line staff has very limited discretion; there is a clear hierarchy of authority; and coordination of staff is based on an extensive set of rules and operating procedures. In a human relation structure, the discretion of line staff is high; relations with supervisory staff are collegial; and coordination is based on feedback from the other staff.

When the task has both complex and noncomplex components or variable and nonvariable elements which cannot be separated, a "mixed" structure will be most appropriate.[16] Based on the nature of the "mix" such a structure may provide line staff with high discretion in some specific areas and none in others. For example, the task of intake may be of such type. Workers may have high discretion in defining

the problem of the client, but none concerning determination of fees, scheduling, and the like.

It can be readily shown that each structure is most efficient if appropriately matched with the characteristics of the tasks to be performed. This is so because the work unit structure is designed to elicit the behavioral and role prescriptions that each task requires.

When conflict arises between two units or among several staff members because of overlapping jurisdictions, lack of coordination, or lack of mutual understanding, an ad hoc task force to deal with the conflict may prove helpful. In a multi-service center, for example, a conflict could arise between the outreach staff and the counseling staff. The former may feel that they do not get any help in scheduling appointments and in coping with problems they encounter in the field. The counseling staff, on the other hand, may feel that it is asked to do the work of the outreach staff and that the outreach staff fails to understand what the counselors are trying to accomplish. To resolve the conflict, an ad hoc task force might be established with representatives of both parties to arrive at an acceptable solution, or an integrator position might be created.

The integrator role requires that a third party become the mediator between parties in the dispute. The integrator is generally a person with adequate knowledge of the activities of the units of persons he or she attempts to bring together, and may be in an authority position in relation to both. In the example above, the integrator might be a person who has expertise in both outreach and counseling, so that his directive to both units will be respected. His function is to identify areas where coordination needs to be established and procedures that can be developed to minimize conflict. He also

---

[16]Eugene Litwak, "Models of Organization Which Permit Conflict," *American Journal of Sociology* 67 (Sept. 1961), pp. 177–84.

serves as a mediator, interpreting to each unit the issues and problems the other unit needs to solve.[17]

A further word: Conflict is not necessarily dysfunctional to an organization. To the contrary. It can help to effectively identify operational problems, philosophical differences, or staff deficiencies. Properly managed, conflict situations assure a changing and responsive pattern of agency operations. Conflict is often a symptom of healthy adaptation to changing needs and expectations.

Developing an Intelligence and Feedback System

There is a strong correlation between the extent to which an organization can adapt to changes in its environment and the effectiveness of its "intelligence" system. An effective system enables the organization to evaluate its own activities in relation to changes and developments in its environment. Without such a system, the organization may find that its services and modes of operation are rapidly becoming obsolete. An effective and efficient intelligence system can provide the program with the new information and knowledge required to adjust to changes from both within and without.

In general, an intelligence system fulfills three interrelated functions: monitoring the external task environment of the agency, internal auditing of staff and client activities, and evaluation of the agency's outputs.

The *monitoring of the agency's external environment* is intended to alert the agency to important changes and developments in the various units upon which it is dependent.

These include federal and state programs, the programs of local social service agencies, new legislation, etc. Monitoring activities can also be directed at identifying new developments in service techniques. Finally, external monitoring is required to inform the agency of changes in the character of the population it seeks to serve.

The main purpose of *internal auditing* is to inform the agency of the activities of the staff vis-à-vis the clients. Information generated by internal auditing enables staff to assess the progress of the clients and to determine future courses of action, and enables the agency management to evaluate the operation of the service technology. Without such evaluation, the agency has no way of determining whether it is achieving its service goals at some reasonable level.

Evaluation of agency *outputs* occurs after clients have been served by the agency. The emphasis is on what happened to clients and how many were served.

Fulfillment of each of these intelligence functions requires several steps: (1) collection of the necessary data; (2) analysis of those data so that they are useful and used; (3) transmission of relevant information to appropriate decision makers; and (4) interpretation of the information in order to generate additional knowledge. Since the final step of the intelligence process is the generation of knowledge, malfunction in any of the previous steps is likely to adversely affect the capability of the intelligence system to develop that knowledge.

Effective external monitoring systems are dependent on the performance of boundary personnel who maintain close ties with external units and who actively scan the environment for new resources. Staff members assuming boundary roles may develop specialized working relations with a given set of organizations. The contact person gathers essential information about

---

[17]P. R. Lawrence and J. W. Lorsch, op. cit., Chapter 9.

the availability of given resources and the conditions of their use, and transmits this information to staff members who can use it. This is a necessary function if the agency is to remain up-to-date on changes and developments in its environment.

Personnel who perform boundary roles must develop expert knowledge about the characteristics of the resources in their areas of specialization. They must also be able to develop cooperative and informative relationships with the major suppliers of these resources, and must develop analytic skills necessary to assess and evaluate developments and changes in the nature of the environment. Perhaps most important, they must acquire effective and efficient communication channels to decision makers within their own organization.

Internal auditing enables staff to carry out its activities on an informed and rational basis. Internal auditing is directed at (1) the case or client level, and (2) the operational or departmental level. The function of internal auditing at the case or client level is to provide staff with all the necessary information for decision making at every juncture of the client's career in the agency.

This often requires the use of a client "case record." Each client served by the agency should have a record which includes basic information about him, his own perception of his needs, and the service objectives for him. Actions taken by staff and periodic evaluations of the client's performance in the agency should be systematically recorded and the impact of those services noted. A client record could be organized around topics such as background information, health status, income, housing, nutrition needs, and interpersonal problems. Each action or referral should be recorded in the appropriate topic section.

A scheme must also be developed for the uniform classification and codification of the information items to be used; and procedures for information gathering, update, and retrieval must be planned. This process requires that the basic information the agency plans to collect and use be classified and coded in a system of categories that are explicitly defined, unambiguous, and uniformly applied throughout the entire agency. This process can be used to enable staff to develop an orderly and rational sequence of services aimed at assisting the client to achieve his service goals. It can also be used to monitor the actions taken and to signal staff when new or different decisions need to be made.

Auditing procedures at the "operations" level attempt to answer basic managerial questions about the modes of operation of the agency or units thereof. These could include the analysis of all activities done for clients suffering from visual handicaps; the success of various treatment technologies; analysis of the type of referrals used by the agency; or the responses of staff to clients who drop out. The findings of such auditing enable the agency to evaluate its operating procedures and make necessary adjustments or changes.

Findings may specify such information as (1) the type of clients arriving at the agency, the range of problems they present, and the services they request; (2) assessment of the services given to different cohorts of clients, the consequences of those services, or whether adequate follow-up is done by staff; (3) the performance of various staff regarding size of case load; average number of contacts with clients; (4) type of resources or intervention techniques used.

Perhaps the most important function of an intelligence system is to enable the agency to evaluate its service outcomes. In the final analysis, an agency can justify its existence only if it can show competence in attaining its service objectives. To do so, it must develop reliable procedures to evaluate the use of its services. The problems involved in attempts to measure are extremely complex. They stem from the fact that there is no consensus regarding a norm of "success," nor are there valid and reliable methods to measure success.

There is, however, some risk of developing inappropriate *output measures*. This can be observed when the number of clients seen by staff becomes the measure of success. When this criterion is adopted by staff, it may gear its efforts to obtaining a high ratio of clients per worker while reducing the amount of time spent with each. There is also a tendency of organizations to adopt "symbolic" criteria when faced with the difficulties of developing substantive criteria. Symbolic criteria are testimonies by staff or clients, display of the "successful" client, self-evaluation, and other approaches that may be highly misleading and in fact could cover up serious failures by the organization.

Any evaluation of an agency may be painful in that it is likely to expose serious gaps between expectations and accomplishments. Such an exposure may undermine the legitimacy of the agency. Yet an agency cannot improve its services if it lacks adequate outcome measures or fears the consequences of such measures. In the long run, lack of adequate outcome measures may lead toward the deterioration of the organization.

An agency's service goals are often multidimensional, with various subgoals and tasks. The design of valid and reliable outcome measures requires recognition of this fact. In general, outcome measures should relate to the goals of each subsystem in the agency. Outcome measures differentiate between the initial state of the client at the point of entry and the terminal state of that client at point of exit from the agency.

In a complex service program, the new client goes through a series of assessments, which are often updated and corrected with the collection of additional information. These assessments may cover a range of attributes and problems, such as personal care, motivation to participate, health status, financial problems, etc. These include the gamut of areas in which the agency activity plans to intervene in order to improve the status of the client. At point of exit, these same attributes are reassessed and the amount of progress shown by the client through actual performance or his own evaluation is recorded. Because an agency may have succeeded more in some areas than in others, one measure cannot summarize the range of activities undertaken by the agency, nor can it reflect the complexity of attributes and problems presented by the client.

Multiple measures are necessary. Each of these should include concrete and precise descriptions of client attributes and behaviors. These measures must become an integral part of the service technology itself. They may serve as assessment devices for the client's progress in every stage of his association with the agency. In fact, they should logically follow the activities that have been specified in the service technology. They should be embedded in the daily work of the staff and not external measures imposed on the agency without direct reference to what it actually does. Needless to say, such measures must be constantly reexamined, updated and refined.[18]

Successful use of measures for service outcome necessitates a comprehensive and effective *follow-up* system. Without one, the information necessary for evaluation

---

[18]C. Weiss, *Evaluation Research* (Englewood Cliffs, NJ: Prentice-Hall, 1972).

could not be obtained. The basic function of follow-up is to gather the necessary information regarding the consequences for the client of services given. It is the basic mechanism by which the agency can find out what has happened to its clients. Unfortunately, few service agencies have established such sophisticated measures. In a number of cases, in fact, output measures of the type described could be overly costly in relation to the sophistication of the services provided.

CONCLUDING NOTE

The process of establishing a new program is highly complex and requires considerations of many inter- and intra-organizational factors. It is not surprising, therefore, to find that while community workers and action groups may conceive of imaginative and innovative service programs, their ability and success in implementing them are at best modest. As was shown in the above discussion, each step in the process of implementation requires a particular set of skills, expertise, and resources. Inability to enlist them at crucial points in the program development may lead to failure or to detrimental consequences in the ability of the program to fulfill its objectives.

Thus, the systems approach used here alerts the planner-organizer to the intricate interrelations among the various building blocks of the program. It identifies the points at which the establishment of certain subsystems must assume priority over other organizing activities. Nevertheless, it should not be concluded that the model presented here is deterministic, in that each of the steps identified must be so followed. It should not be assumed a priori that an organization is a tightly coupled system in which each component must be closely articulated with all others. There is evidence to suggest that many programs may function quite adequately even if some components or subsystems are not fully developed or are not closely inter-linked. The systems approach advocated here enables the planner-organizer to assess at each point in the program development process the need for the establishment of certain organizational components. For example, the planner-organizer may find that a feasibility study is unnecessary since resources have already been earmarked for certain types of programs, or that whatever service technology will be developed, support of key groups in the environment is assured.

Moreover, it has been stressed throughout that agency or program development involves a great deal of trial and error in the face of many unknown parameters. The approach developed here merely attempts to identify the critical parameters the planner-organizer must consider and thus reduce some of the risks that are inherent in any program implementation.

Name Index

Subject Index

STRATEGIES OF COMMUNITY INTERVENTION
Editing and production supervision by John Beasley
Cover design by Lesiak/Crampton Design, Park Ridge, Illinois
Composition by Point West, Inc., Carol Stream, Illinois
Printed and bound by Quebecor, Kingsport, Tennessee